THE ORGANIZATION AND PERSONNEL
OF THE SHAKESPEAREAN COMPANY

THE
ORGANIZATION
AND
PERSONNEL
OF THE
SHAKESPEAREAN
COMPANY

By THOMAS WHITFIELD BALDWIN, PH.D.

Assistant Professor of English in the University of Illinois

New York

RUSSELL & RUSSELL

1961

PREFACE

MY ultimate objective is to write on "The Evolution of William Shakespeare," in the sense of how under the existing circumstances he worked himself out. But before this can be done with any accuracy, we must establish (1) the chronology, and (2) the canon of Shakespeare's work. It was upon the canon that I first began work. After a year of intensive study of the Beaumont-Fletcher-Massinger collaboration under Professor Parrott of Princeton, I centered my attention for some years on the problem of really scientific verse tests, with the Shakespeare canon as an objective. That work I outlined, and of it have written several chapters in rough form; but the evidence I found seemed to indicate that authors regularly wrote for the same company, and that consequently a knowledge of what authors were writing for a company at a given time would presumably limit the field in the case of a doubtful or disputed play. Thus a knowledge of the organization and personnel of a company should prove a powerful ally in settling such questions of authorship. After following several clues that seemed to lead nowhere, I finally noticed the simple fact that the patents and official documents for the Shakespearean company named regularly the same number of actors. This fact suggested the clue to the general principles of organization and personnel. With these principles known, the accumulated mass of disconnected and frequently trivial facts concerning these matters took on significance, making it possible to reconstruct with a fair degree of accuracy many things that had seemed hopelessly lost, the result being the present volume.

This particular study has been slow in taking form—it was outlined by the summer of 1918, and the first draft completed by the spring of 1920—because of certain difficulties, inherent and accidental, that were hard to overcome. To begin with, materials in print for the first-hand study of the gild system are scarce. Hitherto the system seems to have attracted the attention chiefly of those who had some business or social axe to grind, and were more interested in a glowing picture, or at least in generalities, than in presenting prosaic facts. By good fortune, I was at once directed to Dunlop's work on apprenticeship, the most concrete thing that has yet been done in this field. This reference I owe to my friend and former teacher, Professor L. C. Galloway of Erskine College. So far as I can find, the present work is the first to show in any detail a business organization working on gild principles. By the irony of fate, it is chiefly the impractical researches of a long succession of Shakespearean scholars, in recent years much added to by Professor Charles W. Wallace, that have finally made accessible the chief of these principles as they affected the acting companies. It is hoped that the use made of Professor Wallace's discoveries in this work will give some idea of how fundamentally valuable they really are. Because the principles here established have not previously been generally known or accessible, I have not deemed it either necessary, practicable, or even fair ordinarily to catalog the errors of predecessors concerning them.

The work has also insisted on spreading into most departments of Shakespearean research. Particularly, it demanded an examination of the chronology of the plays supplied by the chief dramatists of the Shakespearean company, and has in turn given many important clues to the chronology. This series of studies I hope soon to publish. In the meantime, I use the chronology there arrived at, submitting the dates merely as opinion till I can bring forward the evidence on which they rest.

To give my work as broad basis as possible, I have also worked out the general facts of organization and personnel for the other chief Elizabethan companies, but for lack of space cannot include the material in the present volume. This examination clears up to a considerable extent most of the remaining company entanglements. All these items I hope to publish as soon as circumstances permit. Because they are all closely related and have grown up together, I have found it necessary to refer to these unpublished articles more frequently than I like, but they are ready to be presented on sufficient demand.

Following up these ramifications has been all the more difficult for me because I have had neither surcease from the business of

making a living nor regular access, while this work was being written, to adequate library facilities. The rescued evenings and holi-
days of more than seven years have gone to the work, and the
kindness of many libraries in loaning books has made it possible.
I owe special thanks to the libraries of Princeton University, Ohio
State University, Chicago University, University of Wisconsin,
University of Minnesota, University of Nebraska, Stanford University, and University of California for the loan of books either
directly or through the libraries of South Dakota State and Reed
colleges. I am also indebted for library privilege of nearly a week
in passing at Princeton, several Christmas and spring vacations at
Ohio State University, nearly a month snatched between summer
and regular session at the University of Chicago, and every privilege for the years 1923-25 at the Goucher, Hopkins, Peabody, and
Pratt libraries in Baltimore. From broad experience, therefore, I feel
it my duty to record that librarians are a very kindly race. I owe
especial thanks to Professor W. H. Powers, Chief Librarian of
South Dakota State College, and to Miss Ruth Compton, now Mrs.
Osborne, formerly Chief Librarian of Reed College, for diligence
in borrowing for me when I no longer had even the courage to ask.
Without the present generous system of inter-library loans, and
library courtesies, this work would have been impossible for me.

Perhaps the method of recording references and bibliographical
information calls for brief explanation. I had planned originally
to give a critical bibliography, modelled upon the admirable one
of Professor J. Q. Adams in his *Shakespearean Playhouses*. But I
found that I had no bibliography, and consequently could only
have given a classification of sources. Faced with a similar dilemma,
Dr. E. K. Chambers in his *Elizabethan Stage* (Vol. I, pp. xviii *ff.*)
frankly gives a "list of books . . . mainly intended to elucidate the
references in the foot-notes." Since I had no bibliography, I saw no
reason to retain the semblance of one. Instead, I have given the full
title of a work the first time it occurs, and have referred to it thereafter in as abbreviated a form as possible. I have aimed to give
definite reference for every specific fact, and in this respect have
intended to err on the side of inclusion rather than that of exclu-
sion. Since it has been necessary, however, because of considerations

PREFACE

of space to pare these references down as much as possible, I am not sure that I have been able always to observe my ideal.

For aid and comfort in this undertaking I owe especial thanks to two people. My wife was my co-worker in analyzing the Shakespearean, Jonsonian, and Beaumont and Fletcher plays into "lines," the lines themselves usually representing our joint opinion. Besides, she has done much of the typing. No inconsiderable share is hers. Professor Parrott of Princeton has still further added to my already large debt of obligation to him, not only by words of encouragement, but also by reading the manuscript in its various stages, and giving me much valuable criticism. How much that has meant to me and the work only those who have similarly received can know. Mr. Robert H. Ball of the Princeton Graduate College has also read the manuscript, and made many excellent suggestions, especially upon presentation.

With these apologies and acknowledgments, I send the work forth in the hope that it will at least open another avenue of approach to a fuller understanding of Elizabethan drama and the society in which it grew.

CONTENTS

CONTENTS

CHAPTER I

THE LAWS AND CUSTOMS
GOVERNING THE ORGANIZATION OF AN
ELIZABETHAN COMPANY

WE are coming more and more fully to realize that genius, even the most consummate, is conditioned in greater or less degree by the circumstances of its environment. Some would contend that it is not merely so conditioned but even so determined. Whatever the truth, this attitude of searching for possible influences upon careers of genius has led us to make minute studies of every phase of the life and age that might have had its bearing upon a given subject. This is particularly true of the genius of William Shakespeare. We have treasured every point, however trivial, that has any connection with his life and work. We ransack every possible and impossible corner for one word more concerning the master, and count ourselves fortunate if by chance we find. From it all has been emerging not a god but a very human man, so human that many have denied this man the power to produce so mighty works.

It has become evident that while Shakespeare was not for his age merely, yet he was very truly of it. Perhaps blunt Ben Jonson never said a truer thing than when he denominated him "Soul of the age." Volumes have been written upon how Shakespeare portrayed his age, and now other volumes are being written upon how the age portrays him. "Of making many books there is no end." We have tried to reconstruct the England and London of his time, and repeople them with his friends and acquaintance that we may estimate their influence in the making of the man and his work. We have treasured the chronicles of his company chiefly for his sake that we may gather something of his fortunes. We have striven to reconstruct the physical conditions of the playhouses for which he wrote that we may find why he did certain things and to that extent read his mind. We have made special studies of him as dramatist, husband, father, man, etc., etc. But little has yet been said concerning Shakespeare the actor, and that little has been admittedly based on too meager a knowledge of the acting conditions of the time to be of much value. Professor Thorndike records that on actors and acting for this period "there is no general work of authority."[1] It seems therefore highly desirable to study the organization and personnel of the Shakespearean company that we may get a fuller idea of the conditions under which Shakespeare worked, and of the influence those conditions must have had upon both plays and playmakers of his time. To that end this work is addressed.

It is evident that as a business organization the Shakespearean company must have conformed to the laws, and would probably have conformed to the customs governing its particular type of industry. It is necessary, therefore, for us first of all to consider the chief of these laws and customs.

In considering this matter of business organization, we must remember that, whatever the ideals, the social structure of Elizabethan England was theoretically and in reality still essentially medieval. We must thus examine this organization from the medieval point of view, and not from the modern. Each age has its characteristic way of looking at life, and all its institutions are shaped in general conformity to that view. The Middle Ages saw, not the individual, but the class. In the state, this point of view was expressed by the feudal system, with its carefully graded classes, each fitting as a cog into a machine, the motive power of which came, not from the people below, but from the king above. The same attitude is found in the church, with its classes, ranks, and orders, theoretically all directed by the pope under God. This idea naturally looms large in literature, a typical example being Chaucer's *Canterbury Tales*, in which the author has tried to give a sample of every class to be found in contemporary life, labelling each specimen with his class name, and giving one or two personal names only by accident. Amusingly enough, Chaucer seems to have forgotten a few classes in his original catalog and to have amended matters by making representatives ride furiously to catch the procession that they too might be passed to posterity.

[1] Thorndike, A. H., *Shakespeare's Theater*, p. 459.

We may be perfectly certain then that business in the Middle Ages was organized on the same fundamental idea.[2] The idea expressed itself in business as the gild system. In this system, there were at first two large divisions; masters, and apprentices. When the apprentice had received sufficient education and had attained sufficient maturity, he too was admitted a master. But as the potential supply of masters became larger than the demand, the conditions for attaining mastership became more stringent. As a result, an intermediate class of journeymen or hired men grew up, men who had completed their education but who could not or would not qualify as masters in the full sense of the term. Even in the aristocracy of masters there came to be different ranks, just as was true in state and church, each rank being subservient to the higher rank as there. In the association of these gilds for city government, as in London, the pinnacle of the system was the mayor, chosen only from the highest rank of the federating gilds. It is evident then that medieval business, church, and state were all built on the same ideal of graduated class. It is also evident that the gild was a political as well as a business organization.

It is necessary then first of all to find into what cogs of the medieval system the acting company fitted both in the political and business worlds. We must know who controlled and was responsible for it, and whom it controlled and was responsible for. Its position in the political scheme was in great part determined by its evolution. When Queen Elizabeth was striving desperately to refurbish the old machinery of state, the problem of "masterless" men—rogues, vagabonds, and wandering actors included—demanded vigorous and continuous attention. Miss Gildersleeve has shown[3] how the privilege of retaining actors was gradually restricted to a constantly higher rank of nobleman and magistrate till finally, at the accession of King James, it was practically limited to the crown itself, for the administering of which privilege there had evolved specially delegated officers. The person under whom the actors se-

---

[2] I find this fundamental idea clearly presented, but with different emphasis and illustration, in Gardiner, S. R., *History of England* 1603-1642, Vol. I, pp. 7-9.

[3] Gildersleeve, V. C., *Government Regulation of the Elizabethan Drama,* pp. 21-42.

cured their licence was theoretically responsible for them, and the
privileges granted by the licence extended only over the jurisdiction of the grantor. Hence it was to the advantage of a travelling
company to secure a patron of as wide jurisdiction and as powerful
an influence with other executives as possible, in order that he might
not only give permission for his own jurisdiction, but also obtain
the same permission for his company in other jurisdictions. As an
example of how the system worked, we have a letter[4] from the
Earl of Leicester in June 1559, to the Earl of Shrewsbury, asking
the latter to give Leicester's men licence to play in Yorkshire as
others had done for the shires under their authority. A similar
document, this time addressed to a foreigner, is referred to by Heywood when he writes: "the King of Denmarke, father to him that
now reigneth, entertained into his service a company of English
comedians, commended unto him by the honourable the Earle of
Leicester."[5] A surviving illustration of such a request to foreign
authority is that of Charles Howard, Lord Admiral, dated February 10, 1592, in favor of four of his men[6] who wished to travel
abroad, asking the various foreign authorities "to shew and afford
them every favour in your countries and jurisdictions, and to grant
them in my favour your full passport under the seal of the states,
to the end that the Burgomasters of the towns being under your
jurisdiction, do not hinder them in passing from practising their
said profession everywhere."[7] Such permission, however, at home
or abroad, was only by courtesy and not by compulsion.[8]

Theoretically, the evolution of the system forced the vouching

---

[4] Murray, J. T., *English Dramatic Companies*, 1558-1642, Vol. II, p. 119.
[5] Heywood, T., *An Apology for Actors* (Shakespeare Society Reprint,
p. 40).
[6] See below, p. 325.
[7] Murray, Vol. II, pp. 120-1; Greg, W. W., *Henslowe's Diary*, Vol. II,
p. 84.
[8] This political arrangement caused travelling players to resort to various
subterfuges, the chief of which is recorded in *Ratseis Ghost* (Stationers'
Registers, May 31, 1605; quoted in Halliwell-Phillipps, J. O., *Outlines of
the Life of Shakespeare* [1887], Vol. I, p. 325). "For being far off, for their
more countenance they would pretend to be protected by such an honourable man, denying their lord and maister, and comming within ten or
twenty miles of him againe, they would shrowd themselves under their
owne lords favour." This pretence varied all the way from mere pretence
to flat forgery.

patron and the actors into very close relationship. The proclamation against retainers, issued January 3, 1572, to take effect the following February 20, determined this relation at least to the closing of the theaters in 1642. We have an instance of how this edict worked, in the case of Leicester's men, who petitioned their patron to retain them as his "houshold Servaunts and daylie wayters" without fee further than their liveries, and to give them licence certifying the same.[9] This statute was but one of a long series, extending back at least to the first year of Richard II.[10] The laws were originally directed against the giving of livery to retainers who swore to support the giver in all his undertakings, and who in return were to receive his full protection. In this way a nobleman might build up a great army whose first allegiance was only to himself. Consequently, the laws limited the giving and wearing of livery in times of peace to the actual household servants of each nobleman. The Act of 1572 was aimed at a stricter enforcement of this limitation, though with a slightly different end in view. Hence the actors asked that they might become technically members of Leicester's own household, with all the privileges but without the pay.[11] This remained the relation between actors and patron till the closing of the theaters. Consequently, when the actors passed

[9] The Malone Society's *Collections*, Vol. I, pp. 348-53. For another case, this time of a musician, see Historical Manuscripts Commission, Tenth Report, Appendix, Part IV, p. 474.
[10] A possibly incomplete list of such statutes from Richard II to Elizabeth is subjoined.

1 Rich. 2. c. 7.	Against giving liveries for maintenance.
16 Rich. 2. c. 4.	Who may wear another's livery.
20 Rich. 2. c. 2.	Concerning liveries. (Same as preceding.)
1 Henry 4. c. 7.	Against giving liveries.
2 Henry 4. c. 21.	Concerning liveries.
7 Henry 4. c. 14.	Concerning liveries and retainers.
13 Henry 4. c. 3.	Confirmation of the statutes against liveries and retainers.
8 Henry 6. c. 4.	Against giving liveries and retainers.
8 Edw. 4. c. 2.	Concerning liveries of companies.
12 Edw. 4. c. 4.	Concerning liveries to be given by the prince of Wales.
3 Hen. 7. c. 12.	The King's officers shall not be retained by liveries, &c. with others.
19 Hen. 7. c. 14.	Penalties for unlawful retainers and giving of liveries.

[11] Of course, this is merely the final step in the evolution of the companies that had long been kept by noblemen purely for their own amusement (Gildersleeve, *Regulation*, pp. 22-3).

under royal patronage at the accession of James, they became sworn servants to their particular royal patron, ranking as grooms of the chamber, with the livery and particular privileges thereto attached, but without pay.[12]

[12] The surviving warrants are explicit that these grooms of the chamber were "without fee" (Stopes, Mrs. C. C., *The Shakespeare Jahrbuch*, Vol. XLVI, pp. 94, 95, 96, 98, 103). But Miss Mary Sullivan (*Court Masques of James I*, pp. 252-3) argues that "without fee" may mean that the actors paid no fee for their position. While offices of various kinds were in effect bought, yet Miss Sullivan gives no instance where an office not so purchased was said to have been acquired "without fee." Nor does she quote a single instance where these player-grooms received the annual fee, even though all references throughout her work are carefully made to the original documents. She alleges a document to be published by Professor Wallace, but if her statement of the contents of that document be accurate, it is hard to see how it does anything more than add another instance of the phrase "without fee." The only definite evidence we yet have is the record of payment to the King's and Queen's companies for acting as grooms at the entertainment of the Spanish ambassador in August 1604. They received the pay of grooms for the exact time of their service only (Law, E., *Shakespeare as a Groom of the Chamber*, p. 42). Had they been entitled to the annual fee, they would hardly have been so paid.

Professor Adams (*A Life of William Shakespeare*, p. 358, note 1) would give these players still another fee, quoting an entry of 1608: "Players of Enterludes," "The fee to every of them £3.6.8." But we have trace of such players at the specified fee long before any of these commercial companies were taken into royal patronage. So far as I can find, there is no record that any member of a commercial company ever received this fee. Since these companies were paid by the play, even the need for an annual fee to them is not apparent.

We have the very best of evidence that at least Queen Elizabeth's men did not receive this fee. In a report on lay subsidies, the commissioners of the royal household report under date of June 30, 1588, that eight of the players had been assessed viij s iiij d each and a ninth v s on a fee they did not have (Malone Soc. *Coll.*, Vol. I, pp. 354-6). Since the assessment was two fifteenths, the eight players were assessed on £3 2s 6d, which doubtless represents the regular fee of £3 6s 8d, with some slight necessary reduction made which I cannot explain. Possibly too the ninth man is supposedly retired on half pay. Evidently the tax authorities had inferred that the appointment as actors carried with it the old fee for players, but found that it did not. In view of the wrong inference of these officials, I am disposed to believe that a statement in Stow, *Annals* (1615), p. 197, that the members of this company also received pay as grooms arose in the same way. The full assessment for the household would probably settle this matter definitely also.

There is also direct evidence that each of the five companies for men in King James's reign became "sworn servants" to its particular patron (Law, *Groom*; Murray, Vol. II, p. 400; Vol. I, p. 209; Malone Soc. *Coll.*, Vol. I, pp. 273, 274). There is also direct evidence that the companies of the King, Queen, and Prince Henry were sworn as grooms of the chamber, each to his particular patron (Law, *Groom;* Murray, Vol. II, p. 400; Vol. I, p. 209; The New Shakspere Society's *Transactions*, 1877-79, pp. 15*-19*). We have no

This arrangement was not without considerable value, particularly to the Shakespearean company, which from 1603 more especially belonged to the King's own protection and household. Its members were thus, as grooms of the chamber, entitled to all privileges of the King's own servants. One of the most important of these privileges is illustrated in the case of Philip Henslowe, who was not the man to overlook its practical value. Richard Topping petitioned the Lord Chamberlain in 1595: "May it therefore please yor ho: in that the sayd Inclowe (as he saith) is her ma^{ts} servant, to graunt wth yor hono^{r}s favor leaue to yor suppli either to arrest him" or to force a proper adjustment in some other way.[13] In the words of Mr. Greg, "as servant to her Majesty, he could only be ar-

direct evidence for the company of Prince Charles before 1625 (N.S.S. *Transactions*, 1877-79, p. 19*). Nor do we have direct statement that the managers of Princess Elizabeth's company when sworn became grooms of her chamber. But these missing details are unimportant, since we have sufficient evidence to establish the rule that members were regularly sworn as grooms of the chamber.

In the period of readjustment following the death of James, it seems to have been the policy of Charles to retain for the previously protected companies all the privileges that had been theirs under his father; but not having family enough to go round, he himself had to undertake a proportionately greater individual sponsorship. Princess Elizabeth, as Queen of Bohemia, no longer maintained an establishment in England. The fragments of Queen Anne's household were taken over by Queen Henrietta (*H.M.C.*, Twelfth Report, Appendix, Part I, pp. 195, 198). King Charles had no children to assume the place of sponsor till Charles, second of the name, was born in 1630, whereupon he was immediately pressed into service as a patron, each member of his company becoming "a groom of the chamber of the Prince in quality of Player" (Stopes, *Jahrbuch*, Vol. XLVI, pp. 96, 98, 103). It seems clear then that when Charles came to the throne, in the dearth of establishments, there being only his and the Queen's, he permitted the members of the formerly protected companies to become grooms of his own chamber till other establishments were provided (Stopes, *Jahrbuch*, Vol. XLVI, pp. 94, 95). This solution would naturally have been suggested by the fact that Charles was already patron of one company and heir to the patronage of his father's famous organization. In fact, these two companies shared approximately the same fate as the households to which they belonged. Charles took over his father's household, dismissing his own (Cary, R., *Memoirs of Robert Cary* [1808], p. 159; *H.M.C.*, Twelfth Report, Appendix, Part I, pp. 194-5, 198-9), but making readjustments. In the case of the companies, this readjustment consisted of replacing three of the King James company by three of his own. In all cases, since the King's chamberlain was the superior of the chamberlains of other members of the royal family, the companies were in effect placed directly under his regulation (*Encyclopedia Britannica*, article Lord Chamberlain; Malone Soc. *Coll.*, Vol. I, pp. 391-2).

[13] Greg, W. W., *Henslowe Papers*, p. 44.

rested on the Lord Chamberlain's warrant."[14] So frequently was the privilege used after Henslowe's manner that parliament about July 1610 included as one of six requests to the King for redress of grievances "that it might be lawfull to arrest the King's Servants without leave," which James refused, though adding, "nor should my Lord Chamberlaine deny the arresting of any of his Majesty's Servants if just Cause were shewed."[15] The ability to extend this privilege temporarily to those in the service of the Revels so long as they were in royal service had been granted to Tilney as Master of the Revels in 1581, and regularly to his successors thereafter.[16] The original proviso reads: "And also if any person or persons beinge taken into our said workes of the said office of our Revells beinge arrested comminge or goinge to or from our saide workes of our said office of our Revells at the sute of any person or persons then the said Edmunde Tilney by vertue and aucthoritie hereof to enlarge him or them as by our speciall proteccion duringe the tyme of our said workes."[17] Under this proviso, then, the actors could secure from the Master of the Revels a protection against arrest so long as they were performing at court. When at the accession of James, the sanctioned actors were taken under royal patronage, becoming thereby grooms of the chamber through their connection with the different royal personages, this protection was automatically made permanent. Doubtless it was with this purpose in view that royal patronage was extended.

We have a few surviving records of the formal process whereby an actor became a groom of the chamber. We have a "Warrant to swear the Queen of Bohemia's players groomes of his Majesties chamber without fee," given June 30, 1628, for ten men; and another warrant for three more of the same July 2, 1629.[18] There is a warrant

[14] Greg, *Diary*, Vol. II, p. 12; Stubbs, William, *The Constitutional History of England* (1880), Vol. I, pp. 384-5; Nicolas, Sir Harris, *Proceedings and Ordinances of the Privy Council of England*, Vol. VI, Preface CCXXVI, note 1; Wright, Thomas, *Queen Elizabeth and her Times*, Vol. II, pp. 231, 242.

[15] Winwood, Sir Ralph, *Memorials of Affairs of State in the Reigns of Q. Elizabeth and K. James I.* (1725), Vol. III, p. 193.

[16] Adams, J. Q., *The Dramatic Records of Sir Henry Herbert*, p. 74, note 2.

[17] Feuillerat, A., *Documents Relating to the Office of the Revels in the Time of Queen Elizabeth*, p. 52.

[18] Stopes, *Jahrbuch*, Vol. XLVI, pp. 94-5.

of the same tenor to eleven players for the young Prince Charles, though these, of course, became grooms of the Prince's chamber, May 10, 1632; again four more December 12, 1635; and one more December 17, 1640.[19] But the fullest illustration of the process is a warrant of January 22, 1641, to swear six persons "as grooms of his Majestie's chamber in ordinary without fee to attend his Majesty in the quality of players, and to be of the company of his Majesties servants at ye Blackfriars, viz. Michael Bowyere, William Robins, William Allen, Hugh Clarke, Theophilus Bird, Steven Hamerton." On the same date, a warrant of protection was drawn for them: "Whereof I advise all such as it may concern to take notice, and to be very cautious how they do any act to the prejudice of the said Theophilus Bird," etc.[20] The actors thus formally came under the jurisdiction of the Lord Chamberlain. This removed them from the jurisdiction of any court that might have prejudices against them, puritanic or otherwise. The crown became directly and absolutely responsible for them and all their works, and they in turn were answerable directly to the crown. As a visible sign of this relation, they were given the livery of the royal household.[21] It is thus

[19] Stopes, *Jahrbuch*, Vol. XLVI, pp. 96, 98, 103.

[20] *ibid.*, pp. 103-4.

[21] The character and frequency of this livery is shown by the allowance to the Shakespearean company May 6, 1629, "to each the several allowance of 4 yards of Bastard Scarlet for a cloak, and a quarter of a yard of crimson Velvet for a cap, the usual allowance every second year," "and due at Easter last past." (Stopes, *Jahrbuch*, Vol. XLVI, p. 95; Malone, E., *The Plays and Poems of William Shakspeare* [1821], Vol. III, p. 61, note.) Many other similar livery warrants for the various companies are extant. We have even the details of cost for this livery in one instance. "To George Johnson, draper, for 3 yardes of bastard scarlett cloth for a livery for Richard Perkins, one of his Ma[ts] Players, at 26s. 8d. per yard—£4." "To Richard Miller for ¼ of a yard of crimson velvett for a cape, at 26s. 8d.—6s. 8d." (Law, *Groom*, p. 40, note.)

It is to be noticed that one transcriber bestows a cap on each actor, the other a cape. These are only variant spellings to denote two derivatives from the same thing, both of which retained the original name. They both come from LL. *Cappa*, meaning hood or cape. When the hood got cut off from the rest of the garment, it celebrated its independence by cutting off the *e* from the cape it had been and became cap. More accurately, one came through the Anglo-Saxon, the other through the French, being affected accordingly, both in name and use. Stow's account of fashions in Headgear (Stow, John, *A Survey of London*, Oxford reprint, 1908, of ed. 1603, Vol. II, pp. 194-5), as well as the amount of cloth allowed, would indicate, I think, that in this case the article was a cap. For illustrations of caps and capes, see Hatcher, O. L., *A Book for Shakespeare Plays and Pageants*,

apparent that the actors were very decidedly given the stamp of official approval, as well as full protection in their profession.

This protection, however, extended only to the members of the company, and did not extend originally to the hired men or apprentices. Consequently, the companies still shielded themselves from injury through the arrest of their hired men by means of a "protection" from the Master of the Revels. We have such a protection granted by Herbert December 27, 1624, to twenty-one "Musitions and other necessary attendantes" of the Shakespearean company, to extend "(dureinge the tyme of the Revells) In Which tyme they nor any of them are to bee arested, or deteyned vnder arest, imprisoned, Press'd for Souldiers, or any other molestation Whereby they may bee hindered from doeing his Maiesties service, Without leaue firste had and obteyned of the Lord Chamberlyne of his Maiesties most honourable houshold, or of the Maister of his Maiesties Revells. And if any shall presume to interrupt or deteyne them or any of them after notice hereof given by this my Certificate, hee is to aunswere itt att his vtmost perill."[22] A protection was also granted to eleven employees of the Shakespearean company January 12, 1637, but whether by Herbert or by the Lord Chamberlain himself does not appear from Mrs. Stopes's abstract of the record.[23] Neither does its extent appear. If it is from the Lord Chamberlain, it may be during pleasure, thus representing full protection for the hired men also. A similar protection was granted to four of the Prince Charles hired men April 25, 1640.[24] We have too a note by Herbert in 1624 concerning a couple of protections he had granted to individuals "dureing the tyme of the Revells."[25] Thus it is evident that the London actors had built up their legal fortifications till under the Stuarts they became fairly impregnable from malicious assault. These actors, at least, were rogues and vagabonds only in the mouths of their enemies.

When these companies passed into royal patronage at the acces-

---

p. 283, and references there cited. Mr. Law gives a verbal picture of this uniform in his little book, *Shakespeare as a Groom of the Chamber*, p. 19.
[22] Adams, *Herbert*, pp. 74-5.
[23] Stopes, *Jahrbuch*, Vol. XLVI, p. 99.
[24] *ibid.*, p. 103.
[25] Adams, *Herbert*, p. 75.

sion of James, the nobleman's licence became a royal patent. Even before this time, however, Queen Elizabeth's players had been sworn her servants as grooms of the chamber (1583),[26] and the Earl of Leicester's servants had been granted, so far as we now know, the first royal patent (1574). Thus neither of these expedients was an innovation introduced by James. It is characteristic of the two rulers and their methods that though Elizabeth found these expedients, she used them cautiously, in order to arouse as little opposition as possible; but James extended them freely, regardless of what any might think. Elizabeth ruled by the grace of the people; but James commanded by the grace of God.

We have just traced the bearing of the first of these expedients, and may now consider more in detail the expedient of a royal patent. As we have seen, the patron's licence naturally takes the form of a royal patent when that patron is royal. The first royal patent to players, however, was not granted to a company under royal patronage; but to players of the Earl of Leicester, a nobleman who at one time was generally supposed to be a rather promising candidate for royal honors. Leaving the then existent personal relation between Leicester and Elizabeth out of the question, we do not find it hard to see why such a method should have been used for giving support to a famous company of players. Patents were the mania of the time, and royalty sought by their means to establish and foster all manner of industries. It is not our purpose to discuss the merits or demerits of this commercial panacea but simply to record its predominance. The promoter of innumerable subjects for patents was so ever-present a nuisance as to have been a stock character in the drama of the time. Rare Ben Jonson was not the only dramatist to "take his humor."[27] A prevalent and characteristic form of the patent in this age was that of monopoly, the

26 ". . . there were xii of the best chosen, and at the request of *Sir Francis Walsingham*, they were sworne the Queenes seruants, & were allowed wages, and liueries, as groomes of the chamber" (Stow, *Annals* [1615], p. 697). The only difference between this arrangement and the regular one under James is that this company was to receive wages, but so far as we know did not receive a patent. Still the records should be checked to see if Stow is in error on either of these points. See above, p. 6, note 12.

27 For a partial list of satires on monopolies, see Andrews, C. E., *Richard Brome*, p. 132, and his references.

theoretic justification for which seems to have been that by this means a new or superior industry might be established or fostered for the good of the whole nation. History records the working of the system and the contentions of Elizabeth, but especially those of James and later of Charles, therefrom arising. It is but natural that a royalty which considered it both its mere pleasure and its solemn duty to aid by its royal patent in establishing any in its opinion deserving but handicapped industry should extend that protection and encouragement to those who were its especial favorites. It needed only opposition to those favorites to call forth the aid of the patent.[28]

The royal patent under the regulations existing in 1574 was just as much more valuable to the acting company than the nobleman's licence as the royal authority was greater than the nobleman's. When licensing was later limited practically to the crown, the patent was used for permanent organizations, and the licence of the Master of the Revels for the temporary organizations. So far as we know, Leicester's men were the first to secure the written sanction of the crown itself, as expressed in the fostering patent of 1574, which permitted them to act in London or anywhere else in England, legal authorities or previous regulations notwithstanding. Thus the patent form was evolved for the acting companies out of their need of protection and the sovereign's desire to control but willingness to foster them.

The playing patent was of course subject to the rules and regulations governing all other patents, granting protection to the extent specified in the instrument itself. These, like other legal documents, follow a regular formula, with only the necessary modifications. All patents for men's companies,[29] from that of Leicester on, follow the same general formula even to wording, with only the necessary variations in the names of sovereigns, companies, patrons, and houses, such as are provided for in modern printed legal instru-

[28] It has been pointed out that this device was probably but one of the moves of the court in the contest between court and city, a move that was at once checkmated by the city (Adams, J. Q., *Shakespearean Playhouses*, pp. 21-5).

[29] For a full collection of these patents see Malone Soc. *Coll.*, Vol. I, pp. 260 *ff.*

ments by blank spaces to be filled in. The patent of 1574 may be taken as the progenitor of them all. After the preamble, it (1) names the patentees, (2) states their patron, (3) names privilege granted, (4) gives its extent in time and place, (5) states qualifying conditions. The first two sections, of course, vary with each patent; but the other three are nearly always essentially the same. The privilege is uniformly "to vse, ex'cise and occupie the arte and facultye of playenge Comedies Tragedies Enterludes stage playes and such other like." The privilege is granted during pleasure to extend "aswell within oure Citie of london and li^{berti}es of the same as also within the li^{berti}es and fredomes of anye oure Cities townes Bouroughes &c.' whatsoeu' as without the same thoroughte oure Realme of England." The patents of James and Charles, when the companies had come to have regular playing places, named those places and then proceeded to grant the same powers for the rest of the kingdom as before. The qualifying conditions are that (1) their plays must be subject to the licence of the Master of the Revels, and (2) they must not be performed in time of common-prayer or during a plague. The licensing clause is in all surviving patents for men's companies, except the three for the Shakespearean company and the draft for a patent to the Queen's players about 1604. On the other hand, the plague provision occurs only in the patents of the Shakespearean company, in the draft for the Queen's players about 1604, and in the patent to Leicester's men in 1574. The common-prayer provision does not occur in any other patent than that of Leicester's men. Leicester's men were granted the special privilege "also to vse and occupie all such Instrumentes as they haue alredie practised or hereafter shall practise." It was doubtless under this special clause that Leicester's musicians performed.[30] Thus the patented powers granted to a company remained practically the same, though the specific interpretation of them was from time to time modified through the proper channels by the crown, as exigencies demanded. Hence an office had grown up for the specific control and direction of these companies and of acting in general.

[30] These inclusions and omissions show that the drafting officers had two variant forms for patents, both based on the patent of 1574. I doubt, therefore, that the inclusions or omissions in any patent after that of 1574 have any further significance (Gildersleeve, *Regulation*, p. 64).

THE SHAKESPEAREAN COMPANY

Theoretically then, these patented companies might act anything, anywhere, at any time, subject only to the provisions made directly by the crown through the patent itself and through its specially delegated officers. But practically, the power granted was exactly commensurate with the absolute authority of the crown, which was more absolute in claim than in fact. Consequently, there were many practical restrictions. The struggle in London is so well known that it need not be rehearsed here.[31] In general, the playhouses were in the liberties of the city and not under the jurisdiction of the city authorities, who were so consistently opposed to plays and playing that the actors were early practically excluded from the city proper, after which the main fight of the city was to exclude them from the liberties as well. Various other cities also objected more or less successfully. A typical instance is that of Norwich, which based its objection on the hindrance caused by actors in drawing the workmen away from their manufactures,[32] a strong appeal to a crown whose pet project was to foster industries of all kinds, and probably also a strong reason, as well as supposed puritanic ideas, for the opposition in London.[33] The Norwich authorities received permission May 27, 1623, and again March 15, 1640, to suppress all playing; the first during the pleasure of the Privy Council, the second without term.[34] Before this provision was made, the best they could do was to bribe the players not to perform. They record May 29, 1616, that Thomas Swinnerton had been permitted to play four days at Easter but now was returned again and demanded permission to play, which was refused him, he being told "yf you will play yoᵂ must doe yt at yoʳ pᵉrill wᵗʰout oʳ leaue his answer was wee will adventure the pᵉrill & we meane on monday next to play in the

---

[31] For a summary, see Thorndike, *Theater*, pp. 221 *ff.*

[32] Murray, Vol. II, pp. 347, 355, 359. Cf. Chester in Murray, Vol. II, p. 235.

[33] As Nashe informs us in *Pierce Penilesse* (1592; McKerrow, R. B., *The Works of Thomas Nashe*, Vol. I, pp. 213-14): "some Petitioners of the Counsaile against them [plays] obiect, they corrupt the youth of the Cittie, and withdrawe Prentises from theyr worke." In an order of June 22, 1600, the Lords of the Privy Council claim that plays have been too frequent "not servinge for recreation but invitinge and callinge the people dayly from their trade and worke to myspend their tyme" (Halliwell, *Outlines*, Vol. I, pp. 307-8).

[34] Murray, Vol. II, pp. 359-60.

Cytty, yet afterward this howse offered him a gratuitie to desist he was content to accept the same & pmised desitance accordyngly."[35] The provincial records as given by Murray have many instances of such "gratuities," which the players usually considered it the wisest policy to accept. It is thus evident that in spite of their almost unlimited bestowal of privileges, the royal patents for players were subject to many practical limitations, to as many in fact as any other royal command in that time of theoretically harmonized but practically divided and conflicting authorities.

It is to be noted further that the patents confer their privilege on all the patentees equally; it is a cooperative body that receives sanction. This seems to have been both the letter and the spirit of the law for patented companies. Each patentee bore his share of the labor and expense, and received his share of the reward. I know of no instance where the patentee-actors did not bear and share equally, and the terms are sometimes explicitly given as "equall ffellowshippe."[36] Any attempt to increase one's own gain at the expense of one's fellows was naturally viewed with great disfavor. It is recorded of James Burbage, "And many tymes [he] wold thrust some of the money Devident betwene him & his said ffellowes in his bosome or other where about his bodye Disceyving his fellowes of ther due Devydent wch was equally to haue bene devyded betwene them."[37] Later, Christopher Beeston was accused by Queen Anne's men of having exhibited a similar spirit. But while the patents conferred equality, yet merit was recognized by the granting of some special concession to the best actors of the company. In the Shakespearean company, membership in the housekeeping group came to be the valuable concession by which special merit was supposed to be rewarded. But within a given class all members shared equally.[38]

---

[35] Murray, Vol. II, p. 341.

[36] *Jahrbuch*, Vol. XLVI, p. 240.

[37] Wallace, C. W., *The First London Theatre* (U. of Nebraska *Studies*, Vol. XIII, pp. 1 *ff*.), p. 142.

[38] For instance, it would not be characteristic of the time to attach Shakespeare to the company by giving him an exceptionally good price for his plays; that would be making him an exception to his class. The same end was attained by making him successively a member of the company and of the special housekeeping group, in both of which groups he was on an equal basis with all others of his particular class. He was permitted for merit to rise from class to class, but within his given class was on an

This "class" attitude of the Elizabethan is radically different from that of the individualistic modern, and must be constantly borne in mind if we are to understand Elizabethan organizations.

So much for the place occupied by the actors in the body politic. In much the same way, they fitted into their cog of the medieval business world. Having obtained a patent, the patentees invoked whatever of the common laws of the realm were necessary to enable them to organize successfully for carrying out its provisions. The minor details of organization would of course vary according to the need of the company, but certain customs soon came to be established. In general, the acting company, patented or unpatented, had two main needs; a theater, and theatrical furnishings, the latter term including plays. By the time the Shakespearean company was established, certain well defined customs governed the method of securing both of these. The company secured the theater by giving the owner half of the gallery receipts, itself retaining the other half and the full receipts from the outer door. No other custom is recorded, and this custom is definitely known to have been followed at nearly every one of the theaters, at some period of its existence.[39]

exactly even footing with his fellows. He really received a greater reward for his work, though not directly but through concessions open to any for special merit.

[39] This was the custom for the Shakespearean company at the Globe and Blackfriars in 1635 (Halliwell, *Outlines*, Vol. I, pp. 312, 313, 317). The fact that John Witter in his suits claims a share in the "play howse galleries" (Wallace, C. W., *Shakespeare and his London Associates* [U. of Nebraska *Studies*, Vol. X, pp. 261 *ff.*], pp. 64, 68), shows that the custom was in force during his connection with the company 1606-13. We are given to understand by Cuthbert Burbadge in 1635 that this had always been the custom with the company and in the Burbadge houses, except in the early days at the Theater, when the actors received only the receipts from the doors. It is certain that at the Theater the profits to the owners did not come from the doors but from the galleries, since these profits are frequently specified as so arising (Wallace, *First London Theatre*, pp. 105, 114, 152, etc.). Also Cuthbert Burbadge stated in 1635 that the actors received the door receipts (Halliwell, *Outlines*, Vol. I, p. 317). Since the owners did not share in the receipts from the doors, John Alleyn's statement that he demanded certain money of James Burbage, "wch he deteyned from this depot and his fellowes of some of the Dyvydent money betwene him & them growing also by the vse of the said Theater" (Wallace, *First London Theatre*, p. 101) can only mean that the actors shared in the gallery receipts. Thus the evidence shows that by 1590, and probably from the beginning, the Theater had observed the regular custom. It is true that Cuthbert Burbadge seems at first sight distinctly to state that the actors received only the receipts from the outer doors. But this statement probably means merely that James

The origin of this custom is not hard to find; it must have been the regular custom in the inn-yard days of the drama. The inn-keeper would not be especially entitled to a share in the receipts at

Burbage in the first days of the Theater received the actors' half of the gallery receipts for furnishing them, leaving them in reality only the receipts at the doors. In all other cases where the theater building was controlled by a capitalist—Henslowe, Langley, Beeston,—the owner sought and usually held the privilege of furnishing the company, receiving therefor the actors' half of gallery receipts. It is therefore inherently probable that this was in the earliest days the arrangement at the Theater, especially since at that time Burbage was certainly manager of his company, acting at his own theater. Since in 1590 the Curtain and Theater had for some years been in a merger; we may infer that the same custom applied to the Curtain. Henslowe followed this custom at the Hope (Greg, *Papers*, pp. 24, 87, 124). Beeston followed this same custom with Queen Anne's men, certainly at the Red Bull for some years after 1612, and almost as certainly at the Phoenix 1617-19 (Wallace, C. W., *Three London Theatres* [U. of Nebraska *Studies*, Vol. IX, pp. 287 *ff.*], pp. 30, 35, 36, 38, 48). Langley followed it at the Swan 1597-98 with Pembroke's men (Wallace, C. W., "The Swan Theatre and the Earl of Pembroke's Servants," *Englische Studien*, Vol. XLIII, p. 352). Of all the theaters, this leaves unaccounted for only the Rose, the Fortune, and Salisbury Court. Mr. Greg has shown that this custom must have existed at the Rose (Greg, *Diary*, Vol. II, pp. 133-4). Since Henslowe was connected with the Rose, the Fortune, and the Hope, and since this custom was used at the Rose and the Hope, we may be certain that it was the custom at the Fortune also, especially since this theater is really the continuation of the Rose, with the same company and practically the same ownership. There is also conclusive evidence that the same general custom prevailed at Salisbury Court in 1639 (see below, p. 43). In view of this evidence, we must regard it as the universal custom for a company of men to hire its house by giving the owner or owners one-half of the receipts of the galleries as rent. The company received the other half of the receipts from the galleries and all the receipts at the outer door or doors. The tiring-house door, however, was not considered an outer door, since the receipts therefrom went with the galleries, of which apportionment we have definite instances at the Globe (Halliwell, *Outlines*, Vol. I, p. 313) and at the Hope (Greg, *Papers*, p. 124). But the stage seats, also reached through this door, were the perquisites of the actors, since the housekeepers agreed in 1639 at Salisbury Court that the actors should have "one dayes p'ffitt wholly to themselves every yeare in consideration of their want of stooles on the stage, wch were taken away by his M^ts comand" (The Shakespeare Society's *Papers*, Vol. IV, p. 100). It seems certain that in the Shakespearean company these stools were regarded as the perquisites of the actors. For instance, at the Globe in 1604 it was the tireman, an employee of the actors, who refused to permit sitting on the stage (see opening lines of the Induction to *The Malcontent*). Another allusion shows that the actors controlled the stools at Blackfriars:

> let players know,
> They cannot recompence your labour, though
> They grace you with a chayre upon the stage,
> And take no money of you nor your page.

(*Notes from Black-fryers*, 1617; quoted in Malone, *Variorum*, Vol. III, p. 165, note 5.)

the entrance for those who used the public yard to see the play. But if any one used a place in a gallery of his inn for the same purpose, then the innkeeper was entitled to a share in the fee. The system of division adopted for the galleries between innkeeper and company was the natural one of half and half. This system made a divided admission charge necessary. The would-be spectator paid his fee at the gate and entered the yard. If he wanted better accommodations, he paid a further fee for a place in the galleries. Naturally, this second fee would vary with the advantage and accommodations of the place chosen. It was thus to the advantage of the innkeeper to make his galleries as attractive to the audience as possible, and in the early days of the Shakespearean company some of these inns rivalled the theaters themselves. When the first playhouse was built, it merely adapted more closely to acting needs the quadrangle and triple galleries of the typical inn, and hence the old customs naturally survived. Even the division of the receipts at the tiring-house door between actors and owners is probably a survival of the method used in disposing of fees from those who were putting up at the inn and not subject to the admission at the outer gate.

But this arrangement was made with the controller or controllers of the theater, who were not necessarily nor even usually the owners of it.[40] Thus it becomes evident that the owner of the building might sublease his interests arising therefrom to whomever he saw fit. Housekeeping theatrical shares were salable commodities, governed by exactly the same laws as other such pieces of property. It follows as a necessary corollary that those who controlled the building naturally became responsible for all expenses connected with its repair and upkeep.

Since the owners or controllers of these buildings could not get

[40] Henslowe owned the Rose building only, but leased the land upon which it stood (Adams, *Playhouses*, pp. 143-4) ; Langley owned both house and land at the Swan (*ibid.*, pp. 161-2) ; Burbage had titles to the house but leased the land at the Theater (*ibid.*, pp. 37-40), as was also true of Lanman at the Curtain (*ibid.*, pp. 78-80). When the Globe was built on leased land, a special company was formed to own and control the buildings erected. In 1618, the whole company at the Fortune leased that property from Alleyn directly ; but when this building was burned in 1621, various people acquired shares in the new building (Greg, *Papers*, pp. 27-30), only a few being actors. This building was also on leased land.

anything like the same returns from the use of them as anything else than playhouses,[41] they were naturally anxious to secure a steady occupancy. This they did regularly by requiring the company to give bond in a sufficient amount that it would remain for a certain length of time. Attempts to collect or to prevent collection on alleged forfeited bonds have given us much of our information concerning the business affairs of the various companies. The company of Princess Elizabeth gave Henslowe bond in the sum of £500 August 29, 1611, in connection with transactions with him;[42] the amalgamated Rossiter-Princess Elizabeth company gave Henslowe and Mead bond about March 1614,[43] like transactions regularly occurring. The Shakespearean company seems to have been the first to try a different method for attaining the same end, a method that seems to have been successful only with them and but partially so even there. When the Burbadge brothers were forced to move to the Bankside, they found it expedient to become partners in the lease with the chief actors of the company, their probable purpose being to attach them to the place. This system was also extended by the company to the Blackfriars when it opened that house, with what success we shall later see.

When the companies were not able to furnish capital for their own supplies, they had a regular custom for obtaining these also. They made arrangements with some person or persons to furnish their supplies, paying for them out of their half of the gallery receipts. The most obvious person to do this furnishing was the owner of the theater, since in various ways he would have accumulated such furnishings. Henslowe supplied furnishings at the Hope and part of the time at the Rose;[44] James Burbage did it at the Theater and possibly at the Curtain;[45] Langley did it at the Swan;[46] and Beeston practised the custom certainly at the Red Bull and probably at the Phoenix.[47] This was the natural solution of the matter. So

[41] Fleay, F. G., *A Chronicle History of the London Stage*, pp. 221, 234.
[42] Greg, *Papers*, p. 111.
[43] *ibid.*, pp. 88, 89.
[44] *ibid.*, pp. 24, 87, 124; Greg, *Diary*, Vol. II, p. 134.
[45] See above, p. 16, note 39.
[46] Wallace, *Englische Studien*, Vol. XLIII, p. 352.
[47] Wallace, *Three London Theatres*, pp. 30, 48.

long as a company wandered from place to place it would be obliged to carry its theatrical furnishings with it, but it would be under rather different conditions in a permanent theater. It was not only natural but inevitable that the owner of a theater should acquire theatrical furnishings. If a company broke in his theater, with or without his help, he might be obliged to take its property for his debt. Since these furnishings were costly and the average company impecunious, the company would naturally be obliged, especially at the beginning, to rent these furnishings or to get some one to advance the amount necessary to buy them. Who should do this more naturally than the financier who owned the building and had necessarily already acquired some furnishings?

The mode of repayment was also naturally determined by circumstances. Half the receipts of the galleries, under the origin of the custom naturally collected by the owner, belonged to the actors. Consequently, the owner could be certain of getting his pay from this half, or of retaining the goods for which the expenditure had been made. But he protected himself still further against depreciation and trickery by requiring the personal bond of each actor to the effect that he would pay for his share of the furnishings and would not illegally make away with any of them. As the actors in 1615 say of Henslowe, he required both: "bond^s for his stocke; and our securitie for playing wth: him."[48] Henslowe's bond for individual players in 1614 was about £40;[49] in 1597, it had been either £40 or 100 marks.[50] Evidently the custom would have originated with or immediately after the origin of this system of securing furnishings, though the amount of the bond would differ with different managers. For instance, the amount was £100 each when Langley bound eight of Pembroke's men to play at the Swan from February 20, 1597, to February 20, 1598.[51] If the owner bought theatrical furnishings for the company and was repaid out of its half of the galleries, the furnishings then legally belonged to the company. But the shrewd owner would use every device to have these furnishings

---

[48] Greg, *Papers*, p. 89.
[49] *ibid.*, pp. 123-5.
[50] Greg, *Diary*, Vol. I, pp. 201-3.
[51] Wallace, *Englische Studien*, Vol. XLIII, pp. 345 *ff*.

declared forfeit that he might not only reap the profit of selling his goods but might also retain the goods themselves to be again sold at a profit. Langley did this with Pembroke's men in 1597-98; Beeston did it with Queen Anne's men in 1618;[52] and Henslowe seems to have reduced the practice to a regular system at the Hope.

It also appears that the company might be financially able to furnish itself, as was the Shakespearean company at the Globe; or it might be furnished by an outside, non-acting, financier—a Langley or a Henslowe; by one of its members who was more wealthy than the others, as Beeston and probably James Burbage; or by an inner group of members, as was true of the Admiral's men, who numbered eight actors but whose theatrical supplies were in the possession of only four of these January 3, 1589, and at that date passed into the hands of three, eventually becoming the property of one man, Edward Alleyn, who thus became a regular financier.[53]

Of course, just as the actors were forced to give bonds both as a company and as individuals for the performance of their part of the contract, in the same way the owners of the building and the furnishers of supplies should have given bonds for the performance of their part. Henslowe and Mead promised to do this for the company about March 1614, but managed to avoid it.[54] Probably most other theatrical dealers were usually just as successful in avoiding the giving of bonds, since it is always they and never the actors who sue on them. Inasmuch as the owners under the limited number of theaters had a commodity vital to the actors, the former could dictate their own terms.

In all these undertakings, the actors would need to be assured of a permanent organization before they took the various financial risks. We find them invoking certain legal devices among themselves to secure this end. Where both house and theatrical furnishings were provided by financiers, not much financial risk was incurred by the company as an organization except from the possible loss of an important member at some crucial time. But since this contingency was sufficiently guarded against by the securing bonds

[52] Wallace, *Three London Theatres*, p. 48.
[53] Murray, Vol. I, p. 45; Vol. II, pp. 121-2; below, pp. 327ff.
[54] Greg, *Papers*, p. 88.

of the financier, there would be little need for further legal means on their part to bind themselves together. If, however, they furnished either house or supplies for themselves, they would naturally have recourse to legal means of security. The Duke of York's men agreed March 15, 1609, to hold together for three years; and if any one withdrew without the written consent of the others within that period, he was to forfeit all his holdings in the company.[55] In the case of the special housekeeping company to control the Globe, practically the same principle was invoked, since each agreed not to dispose of his part without the consent of the others, such part to return to them unless they willed otherwise.[56] Prince Henry's company aimed at practically the same end by giving a certain sum to a member at withdrawal, provided he left with the consent of the other members. Thus Charles Massy writes Edward Alleyn shortly before August, 1613, "th[at ther] is [the] composisions betwene ovre compenye that if [any] one gi[ve] over w[th] consent of his fellowes, he is to r[ece]ve thr[ee] score and ten povnd[s]."[57] If he died, his legatees were to receive £50. This custom had seemingly existed in the company as early as its connection as Admiral's men with Henslowe, since two of its number, Jones and Shaa, received £50 together upon leaving the company February 7-23, 1602.[58] Susan Baskerville claimed in June 1623, that the amount to be paid in this company for such a share in 1612 was £80.[59] The same custom existed in the Shakespearean company, since Alexander Cooke on January 3, 1614, willed "the some of fiftye pounds allso, which is in the hand of my fellowes, as my share of the stock."[60] We have direct evidence then that in all four of the regular companies for men 1609-14 it was the custom to pay a member who withdrew with the consent of the other members for his share of the theatrical furnishings, or if he died to pay his heirs. If he withdrew without consent, he forfeited his holdings. We have already seen that the

[55] *Jahrbuch*, Vol. XLVI, pp. 239-40.
[56] Wallace, C. W., "Shakspere's Money Interest in the Globe Theater," *The Century Magazine*, Vol. LXXX, pp. 508-9.
[57] Greg, *Papers*, p. 64.
[58] Greg, *Diary*, Vol. I, p. 164.
[59] Fleay, *Stage*, p. 280.
[60] Collier, J. P., *Memoirs of the Principal Actors in the Plays of Shakespeare*, p. 187.

custom was as early as 1602 in the Admiral's company. The custom existed in this group of actors as early as January 3, 1589, when Edward Alleyn bought Richard Jones's share of theatrical property for £37 10s.[61] Indeed, because of the very nature of the custom there can hardly be doubt that it had existed among the companies from the beginning as the only logical and fair action under such circumstances.

The converse of this principle requires that each actor on entrance to the company, at formation or later, should contribute his proportional share to the stock, which usually means that the successor bought out his predecessor or his predecessor's heirs and legatees. If the company was to be furnished by a financier, this adjustment amounted chiefly to the actor's agreeing to the arrangement. Our principal direct evidence on this matter comes from *Henslowe's Diary*, and the lawsuits concerning Blackfriars. Francis Henslowe received a loan of £15 May 3, 1594, "for his share to the Quenes players,"[62] and of £9 June 1, 1595, "for his hallfe share"[63] with some company. The same principle would apply to the housekeepers in the private companies. Edward Kirkham claimed November, 1612, that he and his partners, William Rastell and Thomas Kendall, spent £200 on apparel after they were admitted to Blackfriars in 1602.[64] About July 26, 1608, when the partnership was being dissolved, the accumulated goods were appraised and proportionately divided.[65] George Andrews claimed that in 1608 he paid £70 for a sixth share in Whitefriars.[66] Certainly this would be the only fair business arrangement, and was probably always observed in principle.

The larger steps just outlined in the formation of a company are satirically but realistically portrayed in *Histrio-Mastix*. Belch the beardmaker, Gut the fiddle-string maker, Incle the peddler, and Posthaste the poet, decide to form a company of "Politician players," "For we can all sing and say." They then call in a scrivener

---

[61] Murray, Vol. II, pp. 121-2.
[62] Greg, *Diary*, Vol. I, p. 4; Vol. II, p. 80.
[63] *ibid.*, Vol. I, p. 6.
[64] Fleay, *Stage*, p. 248.
[65] *ibid.*, pp. 221-2, 246.
[66] N.S.S. *Transactions*, 1887-92, p. 273.

so as to "be bound for running away." Next, they consider a patron, and decide to be Sir Oliver Owlet's men. Finally, they bargain with Master Bougle to secure proper theatrical apparel. Since they are to be a travelling company, they do not trouble about a theater; but use the town houses, etc. This is a realistic picture, even to the fact that the players were frequently tradesmen.

In the case of the patented companies, we have no instance of the formalities that took place when one member for any cause dropped out and was succeeded by another, but the same rules would apply to these patents as to others. By 3 & 4 Edw. VI, c. 4 (A.D. 1549) it is provided that grants and gifts made by patentees out of letters patent shall be as good at law as the original grants themselves, and by 13 Eliz. c. 6 (A.D. 1570) it is provided "that the Exemplification[67] or Constat of the Letters-patent shall be as good and available as the Letters-patent themselves." While these particular acts were occasioned by the royal land patents, still they establish the rule. Consequently, we find in Murray various instances of a company's acting in the provinces under an exemplification of the patent under which its parent company was acting at London. This had become so much a custom that the Earl of Pembroke, then Lord Chamberlain, issued an order July 16, 1616, against it. "The order states that there were at the time of issue two such Queen's companies, one Prince's company, one Children of His Majesty's Revels company, and one Prince Palatine's company."[68] Not long before this, Princess Elizabeth's men also had a provincial company.[69] Thus every one of the patented companies is known to have followed the practice except the Shakespearean.[70] The practice of dividing into a London and a provincial company by means of an

[67] "A certified copy, under seal, as of a record."
[68] Murray, Vol. I, p. 251.
[69] *ibid.*, p. 252.
[70] I have a suspicion, but no proof whatever, that the relation of Laurence Fletcher to the Shakespearean company may have been precisely this, and that it is for this reason that he is not mentioned in any of the actor lists, and is the only patented member omitted from the list of principal actors in the folio of 1623. Before 1603, he is traceable with a provincial company; but not definitely so after the patent (Murray, Vol. I, pp. 104, note 3, 146, 183; Vol. II, pp. 195, 268). There is nothing in the entries themselves, however, to show that the company acting in the provinces was the London company rather than a provincial one under Fletcher with exemplification.

exemplification may have existed as early as 1588, when we find
the Queen's men so divided.[71] We do not have a patent for this
company, however, though it may have had one. If not, it was acting under some form of royal licence which could be as readily ex-
emplified. One of Leicester's two organizations, 1585-88, quite
likely worked under an exemplification of their patent of 1574.[72]
The practice of exemplification, then, was an old and well established one.

Presumably, also, the right of one member in a patent was at
his death or withdrawal transferred by proper legal means, established in the first mentioned statute above, to his successor, though
as far as I can find we have no surviving example of this. At any
rate, it is for this reason that the patented companies tend to keep
the same number of members under each patent, a new member
being admitted usually only at the death or withdrawal of an old.[73]
Thus the patent served as a stabilizing influence in the organization
of the company. Of course, the patentees as a whole could take in any
new member or members they wished by regular process of law;[74]
but the actual tendency was only to replace missing members. We
may be sure that the patentees would not admit to their number
more than were absolutely necessary for carrying on their work,
since every admission above the necessary number meant that much
less profit for each. The ordinary licence would have the same tendency to stabilize, but in a less degree, since it was less formal, of
shorter duration, and could be more readily manipulated.

The members of the company, however, patented or unpatented,
could not unaided carry on completely the work they proposed.
Therefore, they secured necessary labor regularly from two other
sources; hired men, and apprentices. In this, they were but follow-

[71] Murray, Vol. I, pp. 11 *ff*. This country company was simply Strange's
former company of boys under Simonds, transferred shortly after Leicester's death in September 1588 to the Queen's patronage to permit the transfer of Leicester's men to Strange (see below, p. 79). The company may have
worked under an exemplification but more probably had its own special
licence.

[72] See below, p. 76.

[73] See Chap. II.

[74] It was, however, a deterringly difficult process, since it involved gain-
ing the favor of and liberally feeing a goodly proportion of the King's
officers.

ing the gild organization of the time, which called for the regular gradation of apprentice, freeman or journeyman, and master. This threefold division every business undertaking of the time would naturally show. But in the Shakespearean company at least, in its patent days, promotion was from apprentice to master and rarely if ever through the intermediate stage of hired man as such.[75] The reason is not far to seek; if a man had not shown great ability as an actor in his apprentice days, he would not likely show it in manhood. Since the number of members was limited and vacancies not very frequent, the patentees could choose the best for their recruits.

In securing their hired labor, the patentees would follow the law of the time, which is rather minutely laid down in the Act of 1562 (5 Eliz. c. 4). We get the fullest information on actual practice in these matters from Henslowe, whose dealings in this respect are typical of all employers of labor, since he was merely acting in accord with the law laid down for all. From the *Diary* we learn that in the Henslowe organization, 1597-1600, it was the custom to hire a man for a two-year period, with a graduated scale of wages to meet theatrical conditions.[76] The lowest wage was four shillings a

[75] Of course, a graduated apprentice might serve technically as a hired man till an opening occurred for him in the membership.

[76] Thomas Hearne bound himself to Henslowe July 27, 1597, for two years to play with the Admiral's men at five shillings a week the first year and six shillings, eight pence the second (Greg, *Diary*, Vol. II, p. 272). William Kendall bound himself December 8, 1597, for two years at ten shillings a week in London and five shillings in the country (Greg, *Diary*, Vol. II, p. 291). Thomas Downton hired a man whose name is not given January 25, 1600, for two years from the following Shrove Tuesday, to whom he was to pay eight shillings a week while the company was playing, but only half as much when the company had been idle as much as a fortnight. The six shillings, eight pence, paid to Thomas Hunt by Alleyn for the company October 14-29, 1596, was quite likely his weekly wage. An allusion in Stephen Gosson's *School of Abuse* indicates six shillings as the weekly wage of a hired man in 1579. He says: "the very hyerlings of some of our plaiers, which stand at reversion of VI s by the weeke, jet under gentlemens noses in sutes of silke." Richard Jones was evidently a hired man on the regular scale when early in 1592 he wrote "sometimes I have a shillinge a day, and some tymes nothinge" (Murray, Vol. I, p. 50; see below for date, p. 325, note 24). Thus six shillings a week represent the normal wage of a hired man in the latter part of the sixteenth century. This would be £15 12s. per annum. The price seems to have remained approximately the same throughout the period. Even Henry Evans agreed April 20, 1602, to act as manager of the children at Blackfriars for eight shillings a week (Fleay, *Stage*, pp. 224-5; 243-4; Wallace, C. W., *The Children of the Chapel at Blackfriars*, 1597-1603 [U. of Nebraska *Studies*, Vol. VIII, pp. 103

week and the highest ten shillings, the normal wage being six shillings. This would give an annual income of from £10 8s. to £26, the normal income being £15 12s. It is evident, then, that the amount given váried slightly with the individual in spite of the fact that, for industries at least, the Act of 1562 makes elaborate provisions for standardizing wages.

Neither are these rates to be sneered at; they really represent top market price for skilled journeymen, as is evident when we compare them with those in other trades. "In the year of the Armada the wages of the 'best and most skillful' journeymen of the London crafts were assessed at rates varying from £3 6s. 8d. to £6 13s. 4d. by the year, or from sixpence to ninepence by the day with meat and drink. For those who provided their own meat and drink the rates were from tenpence to fourteenpence per day; and the highest of these rates was about double that of the highest paid to a country weaver or farm labourer at the same period."[77] Journeymen actors received the wages of journeymen, whether those journeymen were mariners, bakers, or what not. Yet around this standard slight differences were permitted in order to distinguish individual worth.

Probably we should consider in this connection the arrangements by which a dramatist might be retained. Since everybody else was bonded, it is not to be expected that so important an individual as the dramatist would escape. Thus we find Henslowe recording March 25, 1602, as a loan to Henry Chettle on the authority of Downton and Alleyn of the Admiral's men "at the sealleynge of h Chettells band to writte for them the some of iij[ll]."[78] Unfortunately, the bond has not survived to give us its conditions. Henry Porter also gave Henslowe "his faythfulle promysse" February 28,

---

ff.], p. 88). Henslowe hired a man to look after the theatrical clothes, 1613-15, at six shillings a week (Greg, *Papers*, p. 89). The price seems to have been approximately the same with Queen Anne's men in 1616-17, since they owed William Brown £16 9s. 9d. as wages, presumably for that year. His wage was thus probably six shillings, sixpence a week. John Melton in his *Astrologaster, or the Figure Caster* (1620) speaks of "the twelve penny hirelings" who made the lightning at the Fortune (Lawrence, W. J., *The Elizabethan Playhouse*, 2nd ser., p. 18). This would be six shillings for the six day week. Thus the normal weekly wage for a hired man throughout the period under consideration was six shillings.

[77] *Shakespeare's England*, Vol. I, p. 331; cf. Vol. I, pp. 167, 318.
[78] Greg, *Diary*, Vol. I, p. 165.

1599, that the latter should have all his plays.[79] Later, Robert Daborne was usually bound for each play; £20 April 17, 1613; £40 December 10, 1613,[80] it being probably a similar bond that Henslowe returned on his death bed.[81] In these cases, Henslowe seemed chiefly to aim at binding his hacks more securely to him so that he would not be forced to face a competitive market on every play. It seems likely from what we know of production under him that his general bonds simply bound the playwright to turn over to Henslowe all his product in the specified period. The bonds for individual plays then designated the price and day of delivery.

But fortunately most poets did not find such driving taskmasters as Henslowe. It seems that a company usually had its chief poet or poets under bond to supply some reasonable number of plays each year, frequently two, sometimes three. Professor Wallace has discovered that Richard Brome signed a contract July 20, 1635, with Salisbury Court Theatre "to write three plays a year for three years at a salary of 15 s. a week, plus the first day's profits from each new play as a benefit."[82] It was proposed in August 1638 to renew the contract for seven years at twenty shillings a week for Brome's exclusive services, it being stipulated that Brome should not publish any play without consent of the company; but the new contract was not signed, Brome having been lured with a better offer to the Cockpit. That this company at Salisbury Court had but one poet, and that he was to receive twenty shillings a week is also shown by Heton's jottings September 14, 1639, of proposed changes in company matters, mentioning the poet's wages in this amount.[83] While Brome's contract called for three plays a year, the proviso was probably intended only to cover his total output, since he actually supplied but two plays each year. It is significant, however, that he also supplied "numerous songs, epilogues, and revisions of scenes in revived plays." He was thus expected to supply one new play for each of the two seasons annually and to refurbish for the company all revived plays. Since actually he wrote but two plays a year, and

[79] Greg, *Diary*, Vol. I, p. 103.
[80] Greg, *Papers*, pp. 68, 80.
[81] Greg, *Diary*, Vol. II, p. 20.
[82] Wallace, *Century Magazine*, Vol. LXXX, p. 751.
[83] Shak. Soc. *Papers*, Vol. IV, p. 100.

since his benefit is given as about £5, he received under the first contract about £49 per annum, somewhat less than £25 per play; and should have received under the second contract about £62 per annum, or £31 a play. The *Actors' Remonstrance* (1643) refers to an arrangement similar to that at Salisbury Court when it reports "some of our ablest ordinarie Poets, instead of their annuall stipends and beneficiall second-dayes, being for meere necessitie compelled to get a living by writing contemptible penny-pamphlets."[84] At the break-up of the Revels company about July 26, 1608, Kirkham is reported to have "discharged divers of the partners & Poetts,"[85] indicating that a similar system of retaining poets existed there.

We have no surviving bond for the Shakespearean company, but we are told on good authority that Shakespeare was expected to supply two plays each year.[86] During the last days of his syndicate, Fletcher regularly participated in three plays per annum.[87] His successor, Massinger, usually supplied two plays a year,[88] and so did his successor Shirley, though he had sometimes written three a year before coming to this company.[89] It would seem then that two plays a year was a normal number to be expected of a regular dramatist. It is significant that after the Restoration when Dryden was under contract for three plays a year, he actually supplied "not one in a yeare."[90] The document which gives us this information shows also that poets were regularly bound. The custom for the Restoration is given in 1676 by Shadwell, who at least partially deviates into sense when he says:

> Now Drudges of the Stage must oft appear,
> They must be bound to scribble twice a Year.[91]

[84] Ashbee, E. W., *Facsimile Reprints*, p. 7.
[85] Fleay, *Stage*, p. 222.
[86] Munro, John, *The Shakspere Allusion Book*, Vol. II, p. 111.
[87] Malone, *Variorum*, Vol. III, pp. 226-7.
[88] Baldwin, T. W., *An Edition of Philip Massinger's Duke of Milan*, p. 6; Malone, *Variorum*, Vol. III, pp. 230-1. Since Herbert did not always name the author of a play, and since Malone did not have a complete list of Massinger's plays, he doubtless does not record all that were licensed.
[89] Malone, *Variorum*, Vol. III, p. 232.
[90] Malone, E., *Supplement to the Edition of Shakspeare's Plays Published in 1778* (1780), Vol. I, p. 395.
[91] Adams, J. Q., and J. F. Bradley, *The Jonson Allusion Book*, p. 385.

It is significant that references to a specified salary for poets are for children's companies and private theaters, since this particular system probably arose out of the evolution of the former. At first, the masters of these companies usually supplied their own entertainments;[92] but by the eighties of the sixteenth century some such "Vicemaster" as John Lyly needed to be employed, among whose duties was that of furnishing the Christmas play. When these companies later became fully commercialized, the old custom of paying the poet a regular stipend would then still survive.

While it seems clear that the poets of the children's companies received a regular wage, it seems equally clear that the poets for men were usually not so paid. For instance, Henslowe's accounts make it certain that Chettle did not receive a salary; but was paid principally by the play or part of a play, as was true of all poets for this organization, or, so far as the records at present go, for any organization of men[93] at a public theater. It seems, however, finally to have been the custom not only to pay the author a fixed lump sum but in addition to give him a benefit performance of his play. In two or three instances, Henslowe records at the Rose a small gratuity given to authors for especially successful plays, as a kind of thank offering; but there is no indication of a regular benefit. Also, later under date of August 23, 1613, Daborne states, "we will hav but twelv pownds and the overplus of the second day."[94] Daborne is probably referring to the same custom and indeed the same play in an undated letter when he says "J pay y^u half my earnings in the play,"[95] since in all other cases he bargained for a lump sum payable in instalments. But what he means by "the overplus of the second day" is still to be settled. Since at this very time the company was under contract with Henslowe to repay any lump sum he might advance in payment for a play, out of the earnings of the second or third day,[96] it does not seem that "the overplus of the second day" could refer in this case to a benefit per-

---

[92] Wallace, C. W., *The Evolution of the English Drama*, chap. V.
[93] Details of arrangements and prices paid will be discussed from time to time in the succeeding chapters, especially in chap. VI.
[94] Greg, *Papers*, p. 75.
[95] *ibid.*, p. 71.
[96] *ibid.*, p. 24.

formance. Since payment of the lump sum advanced by Henslowe would take most of the actors' returns for the second day anyway, it may have been the actors' custom in some instances to give "the overplus" to the author by way of gratuity. If so, this would be in effect giving the author the benefit of the second day for his play, but guaranteeing him a certain amount by means of a lump sum paid down.

Just a few years before this, we have the earliest allusion,[97] as yet recorded, to the author's benefit. Dekker in the prologue to his play *If it be not good the Devil is in it*, about August 1612,[98] for "the Quenes Maiesties Seruants: At the Red Bull" says that the usual poet does not care:

[97] Davenant's reference to the tradition that in the days of Faustus, Tamburlaine, and the Beauchamps bold the poet received the second day is too general—even if it could be shown that Davenant was so minutely informed—to be of value (Malone, *Variorum*, Vol. III, p. 157, note 6).

[98] There are numerous allusions in the play, of which that to Ravaillac is later than May 14, 1610. The play itself is supposed to take place August 14. Fleay (*A Biographical Chronicle of the English Drama*, Vol. I, p. 133), supposing the day indicated was Tuesday, would thus date the play in 1610, when August 14 was Tuesday. But the days are so huddled together in the passage alluded to that it is impossible to say what day is intended. Besides, we hear "theile send me of a voiage to the yland of Hogs and Diuels, (the *Barmudas*)" (*The Dramatic Works of Thomas Dekker* [1873], Vol. III, p. 340), an echo certainly either of *A Discovery of the Barmudas, Otherwise called the Ile of Divels* . . . 1610, in which the plentifulness of hogs in the Bermudas is an outstanding point, or of some similar later pamphlet. Since the author dates this, the first publication on the subject, October 13, 1610, Dekker's echo is certainly an appreciable time later, and the August is not earlier than that of 1611. Further, it seems now a question of colonizing the Bermudas. February 12, 1612, we hear that there is "an under-companie erecting for the trade of the Bermudes," and June 18, 1612, we hear that it is determined to establish a post of three hundred men and sixty women in Bermuda, the expedition to sail in July 1612 (Brown, A., *The Genesis of the United States*, Vol. II, pp. 537, 560; *Calendar of State Papers, Domestic Series*, 1611-18, p. 120). Thus it seems clear that the August of Dekker's play is 1612. There are other confirmations of this date. For instance, the famous pirate Danziger is said to be dead, though Ward is still alive (Dekker, Vol. III, p. 352). Ward lived till about the latter part of August 1623 (Grosart, A. B., *The Lismore Papers*, 2nd ser., Vol. III, p. 68). Since Danziger was still alive January 3, 1611, though in trouble (Winwood's *Memorials*, Vol. III, p. 248), the play is later. There is also allusion to Moll Frith's difficulties (Dekker, Vol. III, pp. 352-3), amusingly described for us in a letter of February 12, 1612 (Birch, Thomas, *The Court and Times of James the First*, Vol. I, p. 161; cf. S. R. February 18, 1612; for a similar experience of Moll in 1605, see *Review of English Studies*, Vol. I, pp. 77-8), again indicating that the August of the play is 1612.

so hee Gaines,
A Cramd *Third-Day*, what *Filth* drops from his *Braines*.

More definite information is furnished by Herbert's office book. Malone says, "I have learned from Sir Henry Herbert's office-book, that between the year 1625 and 1641, [authors'] benefits were on the second day of representation."[99] Thus when Herbert demanded the second day of a revived play, 1628-33, he was merely taking the author's place, a peculiarly characteristic, egoistic, and patronizing touch, as well as a shrewd, grasping trick. For this benefit he was given all proceeds except enough to cover the actual daily expense. Probably therefore this is the sense in which benefit is used for the Shakespearean company. Since the price of admission was usually greater for a new play than for an old, the author would probably receive somewhat more than Herbert did from the actors. However, the author could not logically expect any share from the house-keepers, since they had nothing to do with furnishing plays. Herbert received an average of £8 19s. 4d.; and due allowances being made as indicated above, the author's benefit for the second day of an exceptionally popular new play in the same period might have been somewhat greater. The evidence seems to indicate this benefit was in addition to the lump sum advanced, being merely a device for putting the author partially on a share basis. Since so many of the other payments were on the share basis, this would have been a natural solution of the matter.

It seems clear then that in all companies the poet was usually under contract to supply a play or a certain number of plays within the time limited in his bond. In the latter part of the sixteeenth century the poets for the children's companies received a certain salary, but those for men received a specified sum for each play. Then gradually in both types of company grew up the custom of giving the poet a benefit on the first, second, or third day of his new play.

Besides hired men, an acting company also needed a considerable number of apprentices, who would be taken under the provision of the apprentice law. According to this law (5 Eliz. c. 4), the appren-

---

[99] Malone, *Variorum*, Vol. III, p. 158, note; Adams, *Herbert*, p. 67. This statement is confirmed by various allusions. See for instance the Epilogue to Shirley's *Cardinal, Parson's Wedding*, etc.

tice must serve a minimum of seven years and must be at least twenty-four at the end of his apprenticeship. The enforcing of these provisions, however, was left principally to the gilds themselves. "Whatever the length of a lad's apprenticeship, he would, when he came to take up his freedom, have reached manhood. According to the Statute of Artificers he must not be less than twenty-four years old at the end of his apprenticeship. Probably this clause had not always been observed, for many companies found it necessary to make bye-laws to enforce it, while others made a new rule of their own, fixing the minimum age at twenty-one. We can at least be sure that no well-regulated company would admit an apprentice under this age."[100] "The probability is that the age and householders' qualifications were fairly well observed in the seventeenth century."[101] "Where there are no rules, we can gather incidentally, from indentures and enrolments, that fourteen was a very usual age at which to bind apprentices. But rules forbidding the apprenticeship of married men suggest that others than mere boys were sometimes apprenticed; while boys under fourteen were undoubtedly taken; in Sheffield the minimum age for Cutlers' apprentices was twelve years."[102] The minimum or usual age would be determined by the particular purpose for which the apprentice was to be used, and hence would vary. Consequently, we must consider it for the acting companies.

We happen to know this minimum age pretty closely in a few cases. The stock example is Salathiel Pavy, of whom Jonson says:

> Years he number'd scarce thirteen
> When fates turn'd cruel,
> Yet three fill'd zodiacs had he been
> The stage's jewel.

Thus he began acting about ten and had acted three years, dying when he was barely thirteen. His fellow-actor, Nathan Field, could have been but little older when he began. He heads the lists of his company in 1600 and 1601. Henry Clifton tells us[103] in the

[100] Dunlop, O. J., *English Apprenticeship and Child Labour* (1912), p. 167.
[101] *ibid.*, p. 159.
[102] *ibid.*, p. 135.
[103] Fleay, *Stage*, pp. 127-8.

latter part of 1601 that Field had been kidnapped by Evans, Gyles, and Robinson. Since the power to take up children, under which these men acted, was granted to Gyles July 15, 1597, Field must have been taken between that date and 1600, when he appears in the first list of the company as a principal actor. Presumably then he was taken near the former date, when they were making up their company.[104] Since he was baptized October 17, 1587,[105] he was taken by Evans, Gyles, and Robinson probably about the latter part of 1597 when he was ten, and was a prominent actor by 1600, in October of which year he was thirteen. Since Field and Pavy were about of an age, and since Pavy was apprenticed at ten, it seems indicated that Evans, Gyles, and Robinson proceeded at once about July 1597 to take up a company of ten-year-old boys. It is likely, therefore, that Thomas Day,[106] Robert Baxter, John Frost, John Underwood, William Ostler, and Thomas Martin were all about the same age as their companions. Probably then Thomas Martin, son of Anthony Martin, goldsmith, baptized at Allhallows, Honey Lane, June 10, 1589, is the actor, who could thus not have been above twelve when he appeared in *The Poetaster*, 1601. Underwood and Ostler must have been at least as old as Field and Pavy, since they could not have been under twenty-one at entrance to the Shakespearean company the autumn of 1608.[107] Thus when Evans was so ill-advised as to impress young Clifton, he was simply matching his company. Thomas Clifton was thirteen either at the time of the complaint (the latter part of 1601), or of being impressed (about December 13, 1600), or of being sent to school, probably the first, in which case he was about twelve when impressed.[108]

[104] Brinkley, E. Florence. "Nathan and Nathaniel Field," *Modern Language Notes*, Vol. XLII, pp. 10-15, shows conclusively from documentary evidence that the actor was Nathan Field, and the stationer his brother Nathaniel.

[105] Collier, *Memoirs*, p. 206.

[106] A Thomas Day was buried June 28, 1604, at St. Martin in the Fields; but this was hardly the actor, who is pretty certainly the Thomas Day of Prince Henry's musicians May 9, 1610 (*A Collection of Ordinances and Regulations for the Government of the Royal Household* [1790], p. 329).

[107] See Chap. II.

[108] Fleay, *Stage*, pp. 127-8.

The only fairly definite cases known to me for any other company are those of John Honyman, Alexander Goffe, Stephen Hammerton, and Nicholas Birch of the Shakespearean. John Honyman was baptized February 7, 1612,[109] and was first mentioned as a principal actor in *The Maid in the Mill*, licensed August 29, 1623, when he was not yet twelve. Thus he must have been with the company at least a year or two previously. Goffe was baptized August 7, 1614,[110] and had his first recorded part as Caenis in Massinger's *Roman Actor*, licensed October 11, 1626, when he was only twelve. However, Goffe had evidently already had previous training; and since certain apprentices became free about the latter part of 1624,[111] he must have entered about that time, when he was only ten. Hammerton became an apprentice about 1629, and a member by January 1641, when just budding into manhood.[112] It appears then he had served about eleven years and must have been taken about ten. Nicholas Birch was born not before the autumn of 1619 but was with the company by the summer 1631.[113] Thus of eight fairly definite cases, one apprentice entered at ten, and five others almost certainly did; all were certainly taken before they were thirteen.[114] It would seem then that ten was probably the usual age for a boy to begin his training as an actor.[115]

Unfortunately, we haven't a single direct instance, so far as I can find, of the age at which such an apprentice might take up his freedom and become a member of the organization. However, Ezekiel Fenn and Theophilus Bird were with Christopher Beeston at the Cockpit by the latter part of 1621, and remained till after May 1637, more than fifteen years at least.[116] Of course, they may have

109 See below, p. 222.
110 Collier, *Memoirs*, p. 266.
111 See below, p. 223.
112 See below, pp. 192-4.
113 See below, p. 58, note 63.
114 If the Thomas Grimes, son of Nicholas Grimes, tailor, baptized at St. Mary Woolnoth September 14, 1589, is the actor who was taken for the Chapel about 1600 (Murray, Vol. I, p. 333), he must also have begun acting about ten.
115 The indirect evidence of the Shakespearean company, later to be adduced, chaps. V-VII and Appendix VII, confirms this conclusion.
116 Murray, Vol. I, pp. 236, note 3; 367. Since William Mago was with the Shakespearean company by December 27, 1624 (Adams, *Herbert*, p. 74), and as late as 1631, while Rowland Dowle was with them at least 1631-37

remained with Beeston of their own accord and not from legal necessity. They were still playing the parts of women in 1635,[117] which would indicate that they were probably still apprentices at that time. At some time before 1641, Bird had become a freeman and had joined the Shakespearean company.[118] The length of their connection with Beeston would indicate that they began by ten at least and were apprenticed probably till twenty-four, the full legal age. As has just been pointed out, however, Underwood, Ostler, and Hammerton must have entered the Shakespearean company when they were about twenty-one, and every definite piece of evidence points to twenty-one as the usual age of graduation in the Shakespearean company. In the companies for men, where these apprentices acted only the parts of women, there would be no point in keeping them till the full legal age of twenty-four, since they would ordinarily have lost their feminine charm some years before. In the children's companies, however, where most of the apprentices acted the parts of men, it would probably be to the master's advantage to retain the apprentices as long as possible.

These apprentices seem to have been taken by individual members, who then received a certain wage for them from the company. Our most detailed account is again from Henslowe's *Diary*. Henslowe records: "bowght my boye Jeames brystow of william agusten player the 18 of desemb3 1597 for viij^{ll}."[119] He then hired him to the Admiral's company "after the Ratte of iij^s a wecke."[120] As we have seen, hired men about the same time were receiving four to ten shillings a week, the normal wage being six. It seems, therefore, that children went half price even then.[121] John Shank says in 1635 that he paid £40 for John Thompson and had paid his share of

(Murray, Vol. I, opp. p. 172; Stopes, *Jahrbuch*, Vol. XLVI, p. 99), their appearance together in *The Witch of Edmonton* is before December 27, 1624, hence presumably for the production in 1621, in which Fenn and Bird appeared with them.

[117] Murray, Vol. I, opp. p. 266.

[118] See below, p. 59.

[119] Greg, *Diary*, Vol. I, p. 203.

[120] *ibid.*, p. 134.

[121] We cannot, of course, draw any conclusion for a higher rate from the satiric allusion in *May Day* (III, 3.232) to three crowns a week as a possible wage for an apprentice actor.

£200 for other boys since he came to the company,[122] which was about 1615. We know to whom several apprentices belonged in the Shakespearean company, and in every case it was to some individual member of the company, not to the company itself.[123] The same is true of the Admiral's company under Henslowe.[124] Even in the case of a company of children, all seem to have been apprenticed to the master, as is shown by Martin Slaughter's company in 1608.[125] Shank, therefore, must mean that he had paid his share of the specified sum as wages, the "wages to hired men and boyes" being one source of expense enumerated by his fellows in answer to his assertions.[126] In fact, it follows from the theory and nature of the apprentice system that the apprentice should be articled to an individual master for training in his trade, and not to a corporation.[127]

[122] Halliwell, *Outlines*, Vol. I, p. 316.

[123] See below, p. 226.

[124] See Greg, *Diary*, Vol. I, pp. 71, 73; *Papers*, pp. 137, 138, 142, 147.

[125] N.S.S. *Transactions*, 1887-92, p. 276.

[126] Halliwell, *Outlines*, Vol. I, p. 313.

[127] Perhaps the situation will be clearer if we remember that Parliament determined the law (5 Eliz. c. 4) for the whole kingdom, under which within the stated limits, any one might be apprenticed to anything the proper law officers would recognize. Not only so, but the candidate must serve a formal apprenticeship to a given "Arte Misterye or Manuell Occupacôn" before he could exercise it, unless his father had exercised it. Then the crown incorporated the larger trades in the various cities, as gilds, giving them within specified limits the power of self regulation. While the actors did not have a gild, each patented company was incorporated by the crown as a brotherhood, a temporary method of attaining the same thing. As Stephens puts it in 1615, "Hee is politick also to perceive the common-wealth doubts of his licence, and therefore in spight of Parliaments or Statutes hee incorporates himselfe by the title of a brotherhood" (Halliwell, J. O., *Books of Characters*, pp. 199-200). It was out of a brotherhood of printers, etc., that the Stationers' Company grew (Arber, *Transcript*, Vol. I, p. xix); and it is significant that by 1619, the patented companies for men were cooperating in matters of common interest as "the four companys" (Adams, *Herbert*, pp. 48, 62, 63, 65, 121). Under licence or as a corporation then the actors could secure boy labor only through the apprentice law, and they could admit as "masters" in their legal corporation only those who had conformed to that law. They might have apprenticed their boys directly to acting, if the law officers did not object; but they seem not regularly to have done so. Perhaps this is due to the fact that most of these actors had been tradesmen, etc., and as such, already members of gilds. They might thus formally apprentice these boys to their own trades, probably with the added advantage in London of giving them civic status as gild members, which otherwise they would not have. There was also the possibility that the boys might not succeed in acting, and thus would find a trade a desirable refuge. For the statement of the actors

I have found no proof that the latter was even a legal possibility. If so, it was certainly the exception and not the rule. Further, as shown by the examples quoted: "The services of an apprentice were a piece of property which a man had a right to dispose of, and masters occasionally sold some years of an apprentice's service to another freeman."[128] The foregoing are the essential features of the apprentice system as it affected the actors.

Necessarily, for a company containing twenty to thirty-five or more individuals—members, hired men, apprentices—and earning thousands of pounds yearly, some system of accounting would be indispensable. Much of the accounting, however, was frequently obviated by the share basis. Since the owner of the theater collected the receipts from the galleries and turned half over to the actors, the item of rent did not need to be checked, unless the owner, as did Henslowe, needed or wished for some reason to keep track of receipts. If some financier was furnishing the company, as Alleyn, Langley, Henslowe, etc., he would keep account of the receipts for the other half of the galleries, as also of his disbursements from those receipts. A company so financed would need only sufficient accounts to keep disbursements for apprentices and hired men, in order that the members might share net proceeds. Where this division was daily or weekly, as was frequently the custom, very little accounting would be necessary. If, however, the company furnished itself, more accounting would be necessary on its part; and if a select group of its membership also controlled the theater, as was the case from 1599 in the Shakespearean company, a still more elaborate system would be necessary. The companies that were not under the thumb of some financier seem usually to have designated some member of their own company as manager. This person figures prominently in the payments at court and in the lawsuits for and against the company. Christopher Beeston was manager of Queen Anne's company for several years; but, according to several

themselves on this point in December 1581 and Gosson's acknowledgment in 1582, see below, p. 286.

[128] Dunlop, *Apprenticeship*, p. 57. Thus the manager of Whitefriars children was required in 1608 to give £40 bond not to dispose of any of the boys without consent of his fellow housekeepers (N.S.S. *Transactions*, 1887-92, p. 276).

members of the organization, was as grasping as the financiers, finally becoming a financier himself. These derogatory statements, however, were made after these members had fallen out with him. For many years, according to their own statements, they placed exceptional trust in him.[129]

The members of the Shakespearean company were more fortunate in having their fellow John Heminges as manager for more than a quarter of a century. Heminges received the pay for all court performances from December 21, 1596, till his death in 1630.[130] Up to 1601, one other member was usually associated with him, regularly Pope, but Bryane once and Cowley once. In 1595, Heminges had not appeared at all, but Kemp, Shakespeare, and Burbadge had received the reward.[131] After 1601, Heminges received the reward alone till 1628, when Lowin and Taylor were associated with him. After the death of Heminges, Lowin alone received the first payment, 1631, and Lowin, Taylor, and Swanston regularly received the payments thereafter till the closing of the theaters. The various lawsuits and the surviving fragments of Sir Henry Herbert's accounts also show that Heminges was business manager for the company. The good management of the financial affairs of the company is to be credited chiefly, if not entirely, to him. There is no surviving complaint of any actor against him. We have no fragment of his accounts surviving, but the nature of his duties follows naturally from the organization of the company and need not be summed up here.

These then are the main features of organization in an Elizabethan company for men. It is apparent that there were four classes concerned in such an acting company. First, is the patented or licensed company proper. This is the controlling element in the whole organization. This patented or licensed company rented a theater

[129] Wallace, *Three London Theatres*, p. 30; Fleay, *Stage*, pp. 273-97.

[130] Murray, Vol. I, pp. 106-7, 177-83; Stopes, *Jahrbuch*, Vol. XLVI, pp. 94-5; *Burbage and Shakespeare's Stage*, pp. 252-8; Chambers, E. K., *Modern Language Review*, Vol. II, pp. 11-13; *The Elizabethan Stage*, Vol. IV, pp. 165 ff.

[131] Incidentally, this warrant of 1595 is frequently interpreted as showing that Burbadge, Shakespeare, and Kemp had been chief actors in the play. It merely shows that these three were the members deputed to receive the pay for the company. They may or may not themselves have acted in the play.

from, second, its owners or controllers, who were in the Shakespearean company called housekeepers. These housekeepers simply stood in the relation of landlord to the companies. It is the exception, perhaps, rather than the rule when the housekeeper is also a member of the company, though it would be to the advantage of a company to control its own building. Further, the patented or licensed company regularly furnished, third, the hired men of all descriptions, who were used directly or indirectly to carry on the acting, and fourth, the necessary apprentices as well, though officially these belonged to the individual members. In succeeding chapters we shall consider in detail each of these four classes in the Shakespearean company in order to derive the particular customs in each and to evaluate the influences of these customs upon the plays and playwrights.

We have now to see how the companies for children fitted into this scheme of things. At first these companies were composed simply of the choir boys of chapels, who acted occasionally, as did other students. We need consider only the children of the Queen's Chapel, since they are both typical and of chief importance among children's companies. The Chapel Royal had been in existence almost from the time of the Norman conquest.[132] "The constitution of this most ancient choral body of England ranged with time from 24 to 38 men, and from 8 to 12 children."[133] Both men and children acted occasionally at court till the reign of Queen Mary (1553), after which the gentlemen appear as actors no more. The children did not have a separate master till about the middle of the reign of Henry VI,[134] the first royally appointed master having been John Plummer, who began his duties September 29, 1444. The master was also head of the gentlemen of the choir, receiving a salary of £30 per annum for that office, besides other perquisites. The first masters received forty marks per annum, raised to £40 in 1523, for the expenses of the children.[135] In addition, various allowances were made from time to time. By November 1583 "hir Matie alloweth for the dyett of xij children of hir sayd Chappell daylie vj^{d} a peece by

[132] Wallace, *Evolution*, pp. 11-13.
[133] *loc. cit.*
[134] Wallace, *Evolution*, p. 21.
[135] *ibid.*, pp. 22, 61.

the daye, and xl[li] by the yeare for theyre aparrell and all other furneture."[136] This would be £149 10s. for all expenses of the children, a sum that the master considered insufficient.[137] Since then the motive, the demand, and the supply had all met together, it is not surprising that the master should have the children perform to paying audiences, especially since this might readily be done under the guise of practice. And thus the children's company entered the commercial field.

At his appointment, the master received a patent under which he might press singing boys practically wherever he found them. Thus the master did not pay anything for his apprentice labor, which was even at least partially supported for him by the crown. Further, he could still use the boys for acting when their voices had broken, thus solving another problem. All the master would need to provide at his own expense would be a theater and theatrical furnishings. If he did this alone, total expenses and total profits would both be his. As these expenses were usually great, it was the common practice for the master to establish some kind of a partnership, each member contributing his proportionate share of the expenses and receiving his share of the profits. Since the company was subsidized to the extent of having labor supplied practically free by the crown, membership in the sharers was rather a good bargain. Hence we find various tradesmen holding shares. In establishing such a partnership, the members would use the same legal devices as did the housekeepers of the companies for men. Incidentally, a share or part-share in one of these children's companies necessarily means a housekeeping share and not an acting share.[138] This was the general principle of organization for the children's companies, whatever the authority under which they were formed.[139] Of course, when the later children's companies under royal patronage were

[136] Wallace, *Evolution*, p. 156, note 3.

[137] Chambers, *Eliz. Stage*, Vol. II, pp. 47-8 adds "possibly the breakfast allowance of £16 a year and the largess of £9 13s. 4d. for high feasts."

[138] Dr. Thaler's references (*Publications of the Modern Language Association*, Vol. XXXV, pp. 144-9) to fractional shares, wherever they can be localized, are to these housekeeping shares or to shares in the more or less irregular country companies.

[139] cf. the company formed at Whitefriars in March, 1608 (N.S.S. *Transactions*, 1887-92, pp. 269 ff.).

severed from the chapel, they lost their subsidy. This subject of the organization of children's companies is worthy of more detailed consideration when Professor Wallace shall have completed his publications concerning these companies. The subject is especially important because it was from these companies and their private theaters that the Restoration drew managers, organization, and part personnel, not from the men's companies, though the actors themselves naturally wanted the old independent organization for men.

It should be noted here that at least one company for men represented a kind of hybrid between the ordinary organization for men and that for children. The managers of Princess Elizabeth's company received a patent, as did the master of the children or the actor-members themselves in the men's companies. They then hired members to do the acting, as the master had pressed children. They simply substituted the hired labor of men for the articled labor of boys. In other respects they would follow the laws and customs governing theatrical affairs. What details we have show that these actors were hired usually on a share basis. It is evident that the hired actors of this organization when they were with Henslowe followed the usual custom for men's companies of paying half the receipts of the galleries for a theater and applying the other half to the debt incurred to a corporation or capitalist for furnishings. The evidence also indicates that the managers of the company became housekeepers with and under Henslowe. Thus they made their profit from furnishing or helping to furnish the company, for which their corporation received half the receipts of the galleries in a regular playhouse or inn, but a proportion as yet unknown when the company received a reward in travelling, or acted at the town house.

The children's type of company naturally appealed to the financiers, since it took completely away all independence from the actors, and reduced them simply to hired servants. The controversy would be especially aggravated where a company of men succeeded a company of children, since the financier would want to continue his former control. This was the root of the difficulty at Salisbury Court in 1639. Heton's directions for his desired patent here show that three factions were concerned: the actors, Heton, and the housekeepers. Heton's statements date after March 26, 1639. Heton informs us that the company had been at Salisbury Court "for a yeare and halfe last past."[140] Thus he is referring to the amalgamated organization supervised by Herbert about October 1637,[141] and by "first articles" is alluding to the original agreement for this period. Heton at first proposed that the company should "enter into Articles wth me to continew there for 7 yeares, upon the same condicons they haue had for a yeare and halfe last past, and such as refuse[,] to be removed, and others placed in their roomes."[142] Seemingly the first articles were not accepted and Heton submitted a note of the proposed change, dated September 14, 1639. Under this proposal, no change was to be made in favor of the housekeepers, who had paid under the first articles all repairs, half of the wages to gatherers, sweepers, stagekeepers, half of the poor rate, and half for carrying away the soil. Under the new articles, the housekeepers agreed also to pay half of the poet's wages, or ten shillings a week, half the licence fee for each play or twenty shillings, to allow the actors one day's profit in lieu of the stools that the King had ordered from the stage, and also an added room or two. They further agreed to pay for half the lights, about five shillings per diem, half "for coles to all the Roomes," half for rushes, flowers, and strowings on the stage, and half for the boys' gloves at a new or a revived play. It is evident from this summary that the company and housekeepers were on the regular half and half basis. There seems, however, to have been some adjustment by which the actors received either more or less than merely the fee at the outer door, since under the proposed adjustment they were to be allowed one or two more rooms than previously. It appears then that in some way Heton had secured the rights of Blagrove and Gunnell to Salisbury Court and had then formed or continued a joint arrangement with others, whom he terms the housekeepers, with whose faction he identifies himself by his use of "we." It would seem too from Heton's claim of considerable expense on behalf of the company that he and the housekeepers had been

[140] Shak. Soc. *Papers*, Vol. IV, p. 96.
[141] Adams, *Playhouses*, pp. 379-80.
[142] Shak. Soc. *Papers*, Vol. IV, pp. 95-6.

supplying the furnishings for the company. We have then the salient characteristics of the regular arrangement.

It appears from this dispute of 1639 that both actors and house-keepers were seeking adjustment, each faction in its own favor. The actors now have forced the housekepeers to bear half the expense of practically everything except dressing the play, having secured many "new imposicons upon the housekeepers," so irritating to Heton. Whereas before, the actors had paid for the plays and their licensing, after which the housekeepers regularly managed to retain the plays as their own under the guise of forfeiture, etc., now the housekeepers were to pay half for, as well as eventually to own, the plays. The housekeepers were also to pay half for light and heat, at least the first of which items had at Blackfriars been supplied by the actors, though they protested at the expense.[143] Lights had not been necessary, and heat had not been possible at the public theaters. Hence at the Globe the housekeepers had paid only rent and repairs. Because of the interlocking directorate of house-keepers and actors, the housekeepers at Blackfriars managed to retain the same conditions there as at the Globe and to pass the added expense wholly to the actors. But where there were no such complications, as at Salisbury Court, the actors would naturally be forced to demand some mode of sharing the extra expense. Possibly these details had already been worked out at the Cockpit, and were now being forced into Salisbury Court by the four Queen's men who had transferred from the Cockpit in 1637. Probably too the actors would find it easier to persuade the housekeepers at Salisbury Court because the latter had been accustomed to furnish everything for the children's companies.

But at the same time the housekeepers were trying to get the same control over the men as they had over the children. In trying to curb what he regarded as pernicious independence, Heton proposed that the company be put in the same situation as had been the Princess Elizabeth's under Henslowe. Heton was to be made governor of the company, with autocratic power to retain or dismiss whatever members he saw fit. The title "Queen's Servants" was to be vested in him rather than in the company, as had been

143 Halliwell, *Outlines*, Vol. I, p. 313.

true for the managers of the Princess Elizabeth company. Thus Heton was trying to remove all independence on the part of the actors, as was so successfully done at the Restoration, simply by subjecting them to the rules for children's companies. The actors' unsuccessful fight for independence at the Restoration was but the last of a long series of struggles, extending well back into the reign of King James. They were gradually brought into subjection by being forced under the rules for children.

It is evident, however, from this discussion that each type of company founded itself upon and adapted itself to the general custom, this custom having originated in the inn-yard days of travelling companies. Since the companies formed for travelling were usually more or less temporary, they were more irregular and had more of makeshift in their organizations than the London companies.[144] They seem to have had the common peculiarity of only a few sharers, either of the actor or housekeeper type, these sharer-managers usually ranging from three to five. Because of their makeshift organization, it is probable that every permutation and combination of the general custom might be found in these travelling companies, but it is practically certain, nevertheless, that each company was organized around that custom.

It is evident from the foregoing facts that a company, especially a London company for men, at the time the drama flourished was no merely haphazard aggregation of actors, but an established business organization, working under definitely established laws, and in accord with well-defined customs. Our study of the Shakespearean company will show that this definite organization extended even to the most minute details. In fact, the ordinary Elizabethan London company was fully as well organized and established, according to the laws and customs of its day, as any modern company; and its social position was in many respects more honorable.

[144] For a collection of references to these country companies, see Thaler, *Modern Philology*, Vol. XVII, pp. 489 ff.

CHAPTER II

MEMBERSHIP OF THE
SHAKESPEAREAN COMPANY 1588-1642

A S we have seen, the controlling element in an acting company was the patented or licensed actual company. Its members made and controlled all necessary arrangements for the carrying on of their quality. Consequently, we must consider this element of the Shakespearean company first.

We can trace the membership of the Shakespearean company with almost absolute certainty from 1603 to 1635; and with practical certainty from 1588 preceding, and to 1642 succeeding this period.[1] There were nine members of the company May 19, 1603, as is shown by the patent from King James of that date.[2] This number was increased to twelve before August 9, 1604,[3] since Augustine Phillips,[4] John Heminges, "and tenne of their fellowes" received

---

[1] Most of the lists of actors will be found conveniently tabulated in Murray, Vol. I, opp. p. 172. I have checked all these lists to the originals or authentic facsimiles, and use these corrected forms in some ten instances where Murray is in error, chiefly from accepting Fleay without checking originals. These lists, of course, need rearranging in chronological order. There are now available still further lists in Wallace, C. W., "Gervase Markham, Dramatist," Shakespeare *Jahrbuch*, Vol. XLVI, pp. 346-50; Adams, *Herbert*, pp. 74-5; Stopes, *Jahrbuch*, Vol. XLVI, pp. 99, 103.

[2] Malone Soc. *Coll.*, Vol. I, pp. 264-5.

[3] Law, *Groom*, p. 21.

[4] In adopting a spelling for names, I have assumed that a man was his own best authority, using the spelling of autograph signatures wherever available. From Greg, *Papers*, we get Duke, Eccleston, Field, Hobbs, Pallant, Penn, Rice, Rowley, Smith, also Smyth, and Taylor. Field's given name was Nathan, not Nathaniel, he himself always writing "Nat." Others used the two forms indifferently. For instance, in the lists of actors made up for the second Beaumont and Fletcher folio by one who must have known Field well, he is called Nathan in four cases and Nathaniel in the other two, though the actual distinction may be due to the different compositors on the work. From Cohn, A., *Shakespeare in Germany*, pl. I, we get the autographs of Kinge, Stevenes, Bryane, Pope, and Persey. The wills of actors (Collier, *Memoirs*) furnish us the spelling for Cooke (p. 188), Cundall (p. 149), Goffe (p. 88), Phillips (p. 88), Pope (p. 128), Robinson (p. 45), Tooley or Wilkinson (pp. 45, 242, 244), and Underwood (p. 231). The wills also give us Cuthbert Burbadge (p. 45). Cuthbert spells the

payment for waiting on the Spanish ambassador August 9-27, 1604.[5] The patent of March 27, 1619,[6] also names twelve. The patent from King Charles of June 24, 1625,[7] lists thirteen, though, as will appear later,[8] the number was really twelve. There were twelve members October-November 1633. At this date a committee of the Privy Council reported that there were sixteen housekeepers and actor-sharers at Blackfriars.[9] Since four of the housekeepers were not actor-sharers,[10] there were then twelve members. There were still twelve members in 1635. The petitioners in the complaint of that date represent that there were six housekeepers and nine actors at the Globe, a total of fifteen.[11] Three of the housekeepers were not actors, leaving twelve as the number of members. Thus from 1604 to 1635 there were twelve members in the Shakespearean

family name Burbadge in two surviving signatures, but his father James spells it Burbage (Wallace, *First London Theatre*, pp. 61, 63, 252). I know of no autograph of Richard, the one given by Malone (*An Inquiry into the Authenticity of Certain Miscellaneous Papers and Legal Instruments*, opp. p. 136, pl. II, No. 14. See p. 87 of the same) being probably a fabrication, though not of Malone's concoction. Malone, *Inquiry*, p. 417, gives John Heminges as autograph February 10, 1618, and publishes facsimile, opp. p. 136, pl. II, No. 6. Eyllaerdt Swanston signed a bill for the Shakespearean company in 1636-37 (Law, E., *More about Shakespeare "Forgeries,"* Appendix). A facsimile signature of Theophilus Bird is given in Shak. Soc. *Papers*, Vol. IV, p. 101. Robart Armin so signed his indenture of apprenticeship as a goldsmith October 13, 1581 (Denkinger, Emma Marshall, "Actors' Names in the Registers of St. Bodolph Aldgate," *Publications of the Modern Language Association*, Vol. XLI, p. 96). The signatures of the dramatist seem to indicate that he preferred to write himself Shakspere, though in one signature he may have varied (Tannenbaum, S. A., "Reclaiming one of Shakspere's Signatures," *Studies in Philology*, Vol. XXII, pp. 396 ff.). Therefore I shall myself regularly use that form; but in the present work I conform to the standard of The Princeton University Press. In all other cases, I have regularly followed the form given by Fleay, *Stage*, pp. 370-7, varying usually only for a simpler form.

[5] Possibly the players were pressed into this service because King James came up in post to London from a progress, bringing "but part of his company and carriages" (*H.M.C.*, Tenth Report, Appendix II, p. 94).

[6] Malone Soc. *Coll.*, Vol. I, pp. 280-2.

[7] *ibid.*, pp. 282-3; Fleay, *Stage*, p. 323, says twelve, omitting Pollard.

[8] See below, pp. 52-7.

[9] Murray, Vol. I, p. 166; Collier, J. P., *The History of English Dramatic Poetry to the Time of Shakespeare; and Annals of the Stage to the Restoration* (1879), Vol. I, p. 478.

[10] Murray, Vol. II, pp. 156-8.

[11] Halliwell, *Outlines*, Vol. I, p. 313; Murray, Vol. II, p. 161; Fleay, *Stage*, p. 327.

company. That the number was a fixed one is also shown by the fact that when King Charles brought in three of his former company in 1625,[12] they replaced three members of the Shakespearean company, leaving the number the same. We have no evidence of a change in the number of membership between 1635 and 1642.[13] On the contrary, as we shall see later, there is rather strong evidence that the number was still twelve in 1641.

It thus appears that the number of members at any time during this period was fixed, and consequently that a new member was admitted only to replace a loss through death or withdrawal. It further appears that the company had in 1603-04 increased the regular number of members from nine to twelve, presumably under powers similar to those granted to patentees by the act of 3 & 4 Edw. VI. c. 4 (A.D. 1548), certainly with the approval of the proper crown officers. This number the company then retained as the norm for the remainder of its existence. The same number had been chosen for the first royal company under Elizabeth, a circumstance that probably had its due weight when this second royal company prepared for its new honors.[14]

For the same period, we know with almost complete certainty not only the number of members but also their names and the order and time of their successions. In 1603, the nine members were Laurence Fletcher, William Shakespeare, Richard Burbadge, Augustine Phillips, John Heminges, Henry Cundall, William Sly, Robert Armin, and Richard Cowley.[15] Our next complete list of members is given by Phillips's will, May 4, 1605.[16] As we have already seen, the number was now twelve. Phillips made John Heminges, Richard Burbadge, and William Sly executors and conditional overseers of his will, each receiving bequests of a £5 bowl of silver. He also made bequests to his "fellows," William Shakespeare and Henry Cundall, of thirty shillings in gold; to Laurence Fletcher, Robert

---

[12] See below, pp. 54-6.

[13] The players' pass of May 17, 1636, probably indicates twelve members at that date, since it includes but two members, yet mentions that there are ten other actors (Stopes, *Jahrbuch*, Vol. XLVI, pp. 98-9).

[14] There were also twelve of the chapel children under royal patronage (Wallace, *Children*, p. 59, note 3).

[15] Malone Soc. *Coll.*, Vol. I, pp. 264-5.

[16] Collier, *Memoirs*, pp. 86-7.

Armin, Richard Cowley, Alexander Cooke, and Nicholas Tooley, twenty shillings in gold by the same title. Thus he leaves bequests to ten of his "fellows," both those already known and those here for the first time specifically so designated, noticeably grading his gifts according to intimacy and length of service. Only one of the twelve, then, is not named and designated in Phillips's will. This is John Lowin who, as we know from other sources, came to the company in 1603[17] from the Worcester organization. The omission is hardly a slight, since Phillips probably had little acquaintance with Lowin, having retired to Mortlake because of illness shortly after the latter entered the company. Thus the three new members added in 1603-04 were Lowin, Cooke, and Tooley. Also, Lowin's entrance in 1603 shows that the reorganization must have been in that year, but after the issuance of the new patent about May; and hence was probably to take effect on Whitsun Monday, June 13, 1603, the beginning of the company's financial year. The list in May 1605, then, was Laurence Fletcher, William Shakespeare, Richard Burbadge, Augustine Phillips, John Heminges, Henry Cundall, William Sly, Robert Armin, Richard Cowley, John Lowin, Alexander Cooke, and Nicholas Tooley. As we have seen, this had been the list at least as early as August 8, 1604, and probably as early as June 1603.

We have no direct statement as to who succeeded Phillips in 1605, but we shall see presently that it was his brother-in-law, Robert Goffe. The next break in the ranks after the death of Phillips in 1605 was in 1608, when Sly died and was buried August 16, and Fletcher September 12.[18] Their places were filled by William Ostler and John Underwood of the newly "broken" Revels company, as we learn from the following evidence. Cuthbert Burbadge tells us in 1635 that these two entered as members.[19] The lists of 1610-11[20] show us that they were already in the company at that time. The list of *Epicoene* shows that they had left the children's company before the end of 1609. Their only opportunity to join had been about the autumn of 1608, at which time their former company was

[17] Actor list of Jonson's *Sejanus*, 1603.
[18] Collier, *Memoirs*, p. 156, Introduction, p. x.
[19] Halliwell, *Outlines*, Vol. I, p. 317.
[20] Murray, Vol. I, opp. p. 172.

in process of dissolution, their lease on Blackfriars having been given up in August of that year.[21] Thus the list in 1610 was, and had been since the latter part of 1608, William Shakespeare, Richard Burbadge, John Heminges, Henry Cundall, Robert Armin, Richard Cowley, John Lowin, Alexander Cooke, Nicholas Tooley, William Ostler, John Underwood, and the successor, or his successor, of Augustine Phillips.

Comparing this list with that in the patent of 1619, we see that five of the members had died or dropped out before the latter date— Cooke, Ostler, Shakespeare, Cowley, and Armin—and that six new members are given, the additional name being that of the successor of Phillips. The new names in the order of the 1619 patent are Nathan Field, Robert Benfield, Robert Goffe, William Eccleston, Richard Robinson, and John Shank. Cooke was buried February 25, 1614.[22] Since he is the only member to drop out at this time, he must have been succeeded by Eccleston, who had been an apprentice in the Shakespearean company, had gone after graduation to Princess Elizabeth's, and was now returning to the company as a member, between March 1613 and March 1614, evidently then near the latter date.[23] Since Henslowe, under whom Eccleston had been, formed a new company March 1614, the transfer almost certainly took place at that date.[24] Shank is evidently the successor of Armin as chief clown of the company, succeeding Armin as the latter had succeeded Kemp. Armin was still alive and active in the latter part of 1610, since he is mentioned by John Davies in his *Scourge of Folly*[25] as continuing wisely to play the fool. The 1611 edition of *Tarlton's Jests* still says men may see Armin at the Globe.[26] Since Shank was with another company so late as 1613, but was almost certainly in the Shakespearean company by 1617, he must have succeeded Armin 1613-17. Thus Shank doubtless came to the company about the time of Armin's burial November 30, 1615.[27] It is true that Armin does not appear in a play list after 1610, but neither

[21] Fleay, *Stage*, p. 235.
[22] Collier, *Memoirs*, p. 185.
[23] Murray, Vol. I, pp. 245, 248; Greg, *Papers*, pp. 86-7.
[24] Greg, *Papers*, p. 87.
[25] S. R., October 8, 1610.
[26] Grosart, A. B., *The Works of Robert Armin* (1880), p. vii.
[27] *Publications of the Modern Language Association*, Vol. XLI, p. 95.

had he before, the reason being that the clown is seldom mentioned in such lists, as is true of Shank himself. Since all other members of the 1619 patent were in the company by 1617 at latest, Robinson is the only one left to succeed Cowley, March 1619,[28] the only other missing member after Shakespeare's death in 1616. Since Shakespeare is the only other member who drops out after 1615, and Field is the only other member who comes in after that date, Field must have succeeded Shakespeare. Thus Field came into the company about the middle of 1616. He had been with the amalgamated Princess Elizabeth's as late as June 11, 1615.[29] Thus of all the entrants 1614-19, only Benfield is left for successor to Ostler, confirmed by the fact that Ostler's part in *The Duchess of Malfi* fell to Benfield at the revival of the play.[30] We now have remaining only Goffe for successor to his brother-in-law Phillips in 1605. That he appears in none of the play lists before 1619 does not argue against his membership, since he appears in none of the formal lists

[28] Collier, *Memoirs*, p. 163; Fleay misinterprets this date as 1618.

[29] Murray, Vol. I, p. 262. The statement of Cuthbert Burbadge in 1635 (Halliwell, *Outlines*, Vol. I, p. 317) that Ostler, Underwood, and Field were taken from the Revels to strengthen the King's company has been interpreted to mean that all three entered at the same time before 1610 (Murray, Vol. I, pp. 154-5), and that Field then immediately withdrew. As we have seen, there were only two vacancies at the period. Besides, the actor list of *Epicoene* (1609) shows that Field had remained with the reorganized company of 1609 (Murray, Vol. I, p. 155), from which the other two had gone. It is also to be remembered that Burbadge does not mention dates at all in his statement but merely gives a complete list of those not bred as King's men who had been admitted practically at entrance, to the housekeeping group at Blackfriars. Thus the evidence is that Field was not a member of the company before 1616.

Probably we should note here that a paralleling career as stationer formerly attributed to Nathan Field is now shown conclusively by documentary evidence to belong to his elder brother Nathaniel (See above, p. 34, note 104), this clearing up the traditional confusion which had fused the two into one. Nathaniel now becomes the staid family man, and Nathan remains a gay bachelor till death, which accords better perhaps with certain surviving allusions. Jonson tells us in 1614 that "he is extremely beloved of the womenkind, they do so affect his action," there are various surviving hints about his Lady May, and he was the subject of a scandal just before his death (See below, pp. 204 ff., and E. J. L. Scott, *Athenaeum*, 1882, Part I, p. 103).

[30] Murray, Vol. II, p. 147. Daborne's letter, countersigned by Thomas Foster, stating "for m^r Benfeeld we hav made an absolute end wth him to y^r content" (Greg, *Papers*, p. 126) thus probably dates early in 1615, instead of August 1613(?) as Mr. Greg gives it.

thereafter, his only assigned parts being in the folio edition of *All's Well*, and in the manuscripts of *The Second Maiden's Tragedy*, and *Barnavelt*.[31] Though a member, he was not a principal actor. Thus we have been able to establish the full succession from 1603 to 1619. Probably the most interesting point here is that Shakespeare remained formally a member till his death.

The members in the patent of 1619 were John Heminges, Richard Burbadge, Henry Cundall, John Lowin, Nicholas Tooley, John Underwood, Nathan Field, Robert Benfield, Robert Goffe, William Eccleston, Richard Robinson, and John Shank. But before the livery list of April 7, 1621, Burbadge and Field had been replaced by Joseph Taylor and John Rice. Burbadge died March 13, 1619,[32] being replaced by Taylor between the patent of March 27, and the livery list of May 19, 1619.[33] Thus Rice had replaced Field. Since Rice first appears in *Barnavelt*, August 14-27, 1619,[34] Field probably left the company between May 19, when he is mentioned in the livery list, and that date.[35] The 1623 folio list of members indicates that there had been no further change by the time it was made.[36]

Our next fully official list is in the patent of June 24, 1625, supported by the company's submission of December 20, 1624, for having played *The Spanish Viceroy*, and by the livery list of March 27, 1625.[37] These lists show that there were now thirteen recognized members, whereas both before and after there were only twelve. But besides members there were still others entitled to livery. A comparison of the livery list for the funeral of King James with the list of the patent of 1625 shows that three non-members—Richard Perkins, George Vernon, and James Horn—were then entitled to

---

[31] Greg's reprint of *The Second Maiden's Tragedy*, ll. 1723-24; Bullen, A. H., *A Collection of Old English Plays*, Vol. II, p. 236, note 2.
[32] Collier, *Memoirs*, pp. 44-5.
[33] Murray, Vol. I, opp. p. 172.
[34] *C.S.P.D.*, 1619-23, pp. 71, 73.
[35] Field was dead before August 2, 1620, when letters of administration for his goods were granted to his sister Dorcas, then the wife of Edward Rice (Brinkley, *Modern Language Notes*, Vol. XLII, pp. 12-13). Presumably then his leaving the company by August of the previous year was caused by death at that time.
[36] See below, p. 68.
[37] Murray, Vol. I, opp. p. 172.

livery. Vernon and Horn again received livery in 1629, though there were at the time but twelve members. Now Miss Sullivan[38] has discovered the record of payment for the materials of this livery—"six and fiftie y^{ds} of bastard skarlet cloth for Play:^{rs} Liueries." Since the livery list informs us that each player was to receive four yards, it follows that fourteen received livery, as we already know from the list itself. At the next preceding distribution, about Easter 1627, the amount of cloth was the same, showing that the number receiving livery was also fourteen. In the year 1627, there is besides, an entry of three and one-half yards "of Crimson velvett," which was used for the caps. Since each cap required a quarter of a yard, provision was thus made for only fourteen in this year. It appears then that between 1625 and 1627 one man, Perkins, had dropped out, and that by Easter 1627 the number of members was twelve. Since Perkins was with Queen Henrietta's men before May 1626,[39] he had probably changed companies in the readjustments of 1625. The payments for 1625 are not given, but in 1623 we again have some clue. The caps and a couple of suits for Archy Armstrong got on the same item, but the total amount has a tell-tale half yard attached. Had the number of actors been twelve, the number of yards should probably have been even. This conclusion as to numbers is confirmed by the next entry for liveries. Either the liveries of 1623 are entered for 1624 or there was an extra distribution in the latter year. That it was an extra distribution at some time between Michaelmas 1623 and the same day, 1624, seems clearly indicated by the fact that caps were also ordered, whereas we already have the cap record for 1623. This year 1623-24 the livery required thirty-nine yards, being now but three yards to the livery, as we learn from the separate issue to Richard Perkins. Thus thirteen liveries were provided in this batch, and another was provided by special order for Richard Perkins. It is evident then that there were fourteen livery servants in 1623-24.[40] The separate issue to Perkins between Michaelmas

[38] Sullivan, *Masques of James I*, p. 251.
[39] Murray, Vol. I, opp. p. 266.
[40] The only event I can think of within these dates to occasion such furbishing was the expected arrival of the Spanish Infanta as the bride of Charles. Such expectations could not date long after Michaelmas 1623.

1623 and Michaelmas 1624 probably indicates that he had just come to the company. This leaves only thirteen entitled to livery, whereas there had been fourteen at Easter 1623. The clue is found in the fact that Herbert issued a protection to Richard Sharp individually December 29, 1624,[41] although Sharp was then certainly a member. Evidently he had not yet been sworn, and thus received no livery and needed a protection. It is practically certain then that Vernon and Horn had come to the company between Easter 1621, when only twelve received livery, and 1623, when fourteen received it; and that Perkins came between Michaelmas 1623 and Michaelmas 1624. Horn had come to the company in time to take part in *The Pilgrim*, performed at court January 1, 1622.[42] Thus Horn came to the company between Easter and Christmas 1621, and *The Pilgrim* must have been put on between those dates. Presumably, though not certainly, Vernon came with Horn. It also follows from these facts that Sharp was not a member at Easter 1623, since all twelve received livery at that time; but he was a member at the time of the extra issue, certainly before Michaelmas 1624.

This summary makes it evident that there were officially thirteen members for but a short time around 1625. The reason for the number at this time can also be ascertained. The livery list of May 6, 1629,[43] gives the twelve members as John Heminges, John Lowin, Joseph Taylor, Richard Robinson, John Shank, Robert Benfield, Richard Sharp, Eyllaerdt Swanston, Thomas Pollard, Anthony Smith, Thomas Hobbs, and William Penn. Comparing the patent of 1625 with this livery list, we see that one member had died—Cundall, December 1627,[44]—and three others had for some reason left the company—Birch, Rowley,[45] and Rice,—a total loss of four. The accessions were three—Anthony Smith, Thomas Hobbs, and William Penn—all from the former company of Prince Charles.

The surviving records seem to indicate in some detail what happened. As has been stated above, in general Charles retained his father's household but made adjustments. On May 12, 1625, Sir

[41] Adams, *Herbert*, p. 75.
[42] *ibid.*, p. 49; Murray, Vol. II, p. 193.
[43] Murray, Vol. I, opp. p. 172.
[44] Collier, *Memoirs*, p. 144.
[45] See below, p. 56.

MEMBERSHIP

J. Coke, Master of Requests, notes: "His Majesty's Comedians to be sworn again in ordinary."[46] About the same time their patent must have been started wending its weary way to the final form of June 24, 1625. Seemingly the players were immediately sworn, for Sir J. Coke notes under May 23, 1625: "Thomas Hobbs, comedian, now left out of the number new sworn, being engaged for the stock debt of their company in 500*l.* desireth to be sworn as the rest are or to be disengaged."[47] The entry occurs under the heading "King Charles his servants," where the Shakespearean company now belonged, and could hardly refer to the Prince Charles organization, concerning which no order for swearing had been given. I take it then that Hobbs, and presumably his fellows Smith and Penn, had been taken into the Shakespearean company by May 23, 1625, though many of the legal details were not yet completed.

Seemingly the old Prince Charles company, as such, was now broken. The list for funeral liveries March 27, 1625, names Robert Hamlett, Antony Smith, William Rowley, William Carpenter, William Penn, John Newton, Gilbert Reason, and Thomas Hobbs.[48] Of these, Rowley had already gone to the Shakespearean company, though he was still attached to Prince Charles's household. Reason had long been leading a provincial company and still continued to do so. As we have seen, Hobbs transferred to the Shakespearean company about May 1625. Smith appears in the first record for the Shakespearean company after the patent of 1625, the actor list of *The Roman Actor*, licensed October 11, 1626.[49] Smith and Penn both appear as actors in *The Lover's Melancholy*, licensed November 24, 1628.[50] Of the remaining three, there is no further record, indicating that the company as such was now disbanded, the three best remaining actors going to the Shakespearean company to replace three of their number.

This supposition finds further confirmation in the fact that

[46] *H.M.C.*, Twelfth Report, Appendix, Part I, p. 194.
[47] *ibid.*, p. 198. The index of the second volume has also wrongfully bestowed parliamentary honors upon Hobbs.
[48] Murray, Vol. I, p. 237.
[49] Adams, *Herbert*, p. 31.
[50] *ibid.*, p. 32; Bang, W., *John Fordes Dramatische Werke*, Vol. I (Materialien zur Kunde, No. 23).

[55]

neither Rowley, Rice, Birch, nor Cundall appears in any list of the Shakespearean company after the patent of June 24, 1625, while Cundall had been superannuated as an actor since 1619. The fact that we find Cundall at his "country house" at Fulham in the summer of 1625, where his will was made December 13, 1627,[51] would also indicate that he had withdrawn from all active connection with the company by 1625, though none of these facts necessarily indicates loss of membership. When Heminges made his will October 9, 1630, Rice was "clerk, of St. Saviour's, in Southwark."[52] It is significant too that Rowley's fat clown does not appear in the very last plays of Fletcher, which pretty certainly means that Rowley had withdrawn at some time before August 25, 1625. It is fairly certain then that there was a reorganization of the Shakespearean company about May 1625, soon after Charles came to the throne, three former members dropping out in favor of three of the Prince Charles men.

If these three men came to the company in 1625, then certainly Cundall had ceased to be a member by Easter 1627, since as we have seen, there were then but twelve members, who are named for us in 1629, all of whom had been members since the reorganization of 1625. These facts would indicate that by 1625 Cundall was only an honorary member, and that the number of members in 1625 was really but twelve as before and after. Since all members of the 1625 patent who had entered after 1621 signed the submission of December 1624, this honorary arrangement was in force by that date. This arrangement, I take it, is the reason that in his will October 4, 1624, Underwood calls Heminges and Lowin "my fellowes," but does not so distinguish Cundall, even though the latter was made an executor and the other two but overseers.[53] Thus the twelve members in December 1624 were John Heminges, a member both before and after but being no longer active not required to sign the submission of that date, Joseph Taylor, John Lowin, Richard Robinson, John Shank, Eyllaerdt Swanston, John Rice, Thomas Pollard, William Rowley, Robert Benfield, Richard

51 Collier, *Memoirs*, pp. 142-4.
52 *ibid.*, p. 76.
53 *ibid.*, p. 231.

MEMBERSHIP

Sharp, and George Birch. This list indicates that Robert Goffe, who died in February 1625,[54] had also withdrawn from membership before death, an indication that may be confirmed by the fact that Robert Goffe, messenger, received warrant from the Privy Council August 30, 1624, to bring in Middleton's son.[55]

It appears then that between Easter 1621 and December 1624 two members had died—Tooley, June 1623;[56] and Underwood, October 1624[57]—and three had left the company—Eccleston, last mentioned as a principal actor in *The Spanish Curate* (licensed October 24, 1622) ;[58] and Cundall and Goffe, whose successors are not mentioned in the folio list of 1623,—a total of five losses. To counterbalance these losses, there were, of course, five accessions. These were William Rowley, Eyllaerdt Swanston, Richard Sharp, Thomas Pollard, and George Birch. Three of these—Sharp, Pollard, and Birch—were promoted from the company. We have seen above that Sharp had become a member before Michaelmas 1624, though even in December of that year he had not yet been sworn. Since Pollard and Birch needed no protections, though Sharp did, they had evidently been sworn and were elder members than Sharp. Thus no one of the three could have succeeded Underwood, who died October 1624. Since Rowley was in the company by 1623, Swanston alone is left for Underwood's successor. Malone, drawing on Herbert's office book,[59] tells us that Swanston joined the company at Blackfriars in 1624. Since he joined at Blackfriars, he came either early or late in the year. He was certainly with the company in time to act in, and sign the submission for having acted in, *The Spanish Viceroy*.[60] Thus he could have succeeded only Underwood, who died in October 1624. Either Pollard or Birch succeeded Eccleston about the spring of 1623. Eccleston's last mention in the records of the company is as an actor in *The Spanish Curate*, licensed October 24, 1622. He does not appear in the revival of *The*

---

[54] Collier, *Memoirs*, p. 267.
[55] Malone Soc. *Coll.*, Vol. I, p. 381.
[56] Collier, *Memoirs*, pp. 238-9.
[57] *ibid.*, p. 229.
[58] Second Beaumont and Fletcher folio ; Adams, *Herbert*, p. 24.
[59] Adams, *Herbert*, p. 63 ; Malone, *Variorum*, Vol. III, pp. 59-60, note 2.
[60] *ibid.*, p. 21.

Duchess of Malfi, in which Tooley did appear. Thus the revival was later than the winter of 1622-23, when Eccleston was still acting, but earlier than June 3, 1623, when Tooley made his will just before death.[61] Pretty certainly then Eccleston ceased acting about the spring 1623, just before the revival of *The Duchess of Malfi* for that summer. That Eccleston did not die but merely withdrew is shown by the bequest to him in Tooley's will. It is likely then that the date of his withdrawal was quarter day, March 24, 1623. Since Rowley did not take part in the revival of *The Duchess of Malfi*, he pretty certainly did not succeed Eccleston. Thus since Sharp was the junior of Birch and Pollard, still acting the woman in *The Duchess of Malfi*, one of the latter two must have succeeded Eccleston about the spring of 1623. Tooley died in June 1623, and was evidently succeeded either by the other of these two or by Rowley, who first appears with the company in *The Maid in the Mill*, licensed August 29, 1623.[62] Thus Sharp succeeded either Cundall or Goffe late in 1623 or early in 1624. Cundall's work on the folio of 1623 probably indicates that by that time he was otherwise unoccupied. The succession then is probably as follows, though not quite certainly in some cases. Cundall and Eccleston withdrew about the spring of 1623 to be succeeded by Birch[63] and Pollard. Then Tooley died in June, to be succeeded by Rowley; not many months after which Goffe withdrew, to be succeeded by Sharp.

---

[61] Collier, *Memoirs*, pp. 239-44.

[62] Fleay, *Stage*, p. 302, gives August 27 incorrectly; Adams, *Herbert*, p. 25.

[63] George Birch doutbless owed his position, at least in part, to his marriage. He married Elizabeth Cowley at St. Saviour's, Southwark, January 28, 1619 (*Genealogist*, N.S., Vol. VIII, p. 120). That this was Elizabeth, daughter of Richard Cowley, we learn from the latter's will, made in favor of Elizabeth Cowley January 13, 1618, and proved in the parish of St. Leonard's, Shoreditch, April 6, 1619, by "Elizabeth Birch, *als* Cowley" (*Notes and Queries*, 10 S VI, p. 369). The young couple settled in St. Leonard's, doubtless in Richard's house, as we learn from Gervase Markham, who claimed about May 16, 1623, that he was creditor "to George Burgh att the vpper end of Shoreditch" in the sum of 5s. on a wager performed by October 4, 1622 (Wallace, *Jahrbuch*, Vol. XLVI, p. 347). Under the circumstances, it is fairly certain that the Nicholas Birch who appears in 1631 as an apprentice of John Shank was the eldest son of George and Elizabeth. Doubtless the record of his christening is to be found at St. Leonard's the latter part of 1619, or in 1620. Quite likely too George was carried off by the plague of 1625, and record of his burial should also be found at St. Leonard's. I know of no record for George before 1619.

After 1629, our next complete list of the company dates January 22, 1641, when a warrant was issued for swearing six persons "as grooms of his Majestie's chamber in ordinary without fee to attend his Majesty in the quality of players, and to be of the company of his Majesties servants at ye Blackfriars, viz. Michael Bowyere, William Robins, William Allen, Hugh Clarke, Theophilus Bird, Steven Hamerton."[64] This is the only such warrant for the Shakespearean company that has yet been discovered in the Chamberlain's records from 1628 to 1642.[65] If these records are complete and the search accurate, these six were the only members to be sworn as grooms in this period. As we have already seen, a few were entitled to wear the livery as grooms who were not members; but the evidence seems conclusive that these six men were members, as the words of the warrant imply. The Beaumont and Fletcher folio early in 1647 was signed by ten actors,[66] presumably the survivors of the old company as it had been before the closing of the theaters. All of the 1641 warrant-list appear here except Robins and Bowyer. Robins had been killed at Basing House October 14, 1645.[67] Concerning the fate of Bowyer, we know nothing further; but it had presumably overtaken him before 1647. Thus it appears that six members had been replaced about 1641, leaving but six of the former members, who were still alive in 1647. The company then, in January 1641, was Joseph Taylor, John Lowin, Richard Robinson, Robert Benfield, Eyllaerdt Swanston, Thomas Pollard, Hugh Clark, William Allen, Stephen Hammerton, Theophilus Bird, Michael Bowyer, and Williams Robins.

Thus between 1629 and 1641 six members disappeared from the company—Heminges, Shank, Sharp, Smith, Hobbs, Penn—and were replaced either directly or indirectly by the six of the 1641 warrant. Heminges was buried October 12, 1630;[68] Sharp January 25, 1632;[69] and Shank January 27, 1636.[70] Of Smith we have no further record after 1629; but Hobbs and Penn had been with the com-

---

[64] Stopes, *Jahrbuch*, Vol. XLVI, p. 103.
[65] *ibid.*, pp. 92-105.
[66] Murray, Vol. I, p. 172.
[67] Collier, *Memoirs*, pp. 271-3.
[68] *ibid.*, p. 71.
[69] Malcolm, J. P., *Londinium Redivivum* (1802-3), Vol. II, p. 376.
[70] Collier, *Memoirs*, p. 278.

pany as late at May 17, 1636.[71] Of the six entrants in 1641, all but Hammerton had been with Queen Henrietta's company before and seemingly up to 1636,[72] and Hammerton had been an apprentice in the Shakespearean company. Thus no one of the six entrants in 1641 could have succeeded either Heminges or Sharp. This means that the successors of these two had themselves disappeared from the company by 1641.

One of these successors was pretty certainly John Honyman. His part in the revival of *The Wild Goose Chase*, autumn of 1632, is that of juvenile lead. The actor list of this play as published in 1652 distinguishes those who had become members before publication from non-members by "Mr.," even in the cases of those who were at the revival of 1632 playing the parts of women. The only one designated "Mr." and not known from other sources eventually to have been a member is Honyman. It is implied, therefore, that he was at some time before 1652 also a member. Sir Aston Cokain wrote some very flattering verses in praise of Honyman, even comparing him to Shakespeare himself.[73] Thomas Jordan's epitaph on Honyman, published 1637 in his *Poeticall Varieties*,[74] also seems to indicate that at his death in April 1637 Honyman was an actor of some importance. Almost certainly he was a member at the time of his death. Too, by March 11, 1631, necessity had forced some youthful actor to "write him man/Before his time," by taking the leading rôle in Massinger's *Emperor of the East*. By 1631 Honyman was writing himself man before his time, taking minor parts as a man, though he was hardly twenty-one before 1633. Now the person who should have taken the part of the juvenile Emperor in 1631 was John Thompson, who had been the regal lady for some years, and should have graduated about 1629.[75] But Thompson died about 1630.[76] It seems indicated then that the play had been

---

[71] Stopes, *Jahrbuch*, Vol. XLVI, pp. 98-9.
[72] Murray, Vol. I, opp. p. 266.
[73] Munro, J., *The Shakspere Allusion Book*, Vol. II, p. 72.
[74] Collier, J. P., *A Bibliographical and Critical Account of the Rarest Books in the English Language* (1866), Vol. II, p. 185, and note.
[75] See below, p. 221.
[76] Halliwell, *Outlines*, Vol. I, p. 316; Malcolm, *Londinium Redivivum* (1802-03), Vol. III, p. 304. Unfortunately, Malcolm is indefinite both as to the date and the nature of his entry.

planned for Thompson, who had died before presentation, forcing the company to use the younger Honyman. Now *The Emperor* was one of Massinger's plays for 1630, probably for the winter, deferred in licence and presentation by the plague till March 20, 1631. It appears then that Thompson was carried away by the plague of 1630, leaving Honyman as the juvenile lead and next in succession for promotion. It is thus practically certain that Honyman was a member before his death. Pretty certainly then he succeeded Sharp in 1632, since he completed apprenticeship just at this time.[77]

Who had succeeded Heminges in October 1630? One possible clue is furnished by the manuscript of *Believe As Ye List*, licensed May 6, 1631, in its mention of "Mr. Balls."[78] The rule is that this title "Mr." is bestowed only on members. I take it that the person involved is probably mentioned in the following entry by Edward Alleyn: "5 [April 1620] I dind w^t Mr Hewitt and ther wase ye princes musitions Mr Ball and Mr Drewe."[79] John Drew is named among the king's musicians both in the list of December 20, 1625, and that of April 17, 1641,[80] but Ball appears in neither. Probably he had come to the Shakespearean company after their list of December 1624, in which he is not named, but before the list of king's musicians December 20, 1625, in which also he is not named. Then he may have succeeded Heminges in October 1630. But then his title of "Mr.," our sole indication of membership, may be due to his having been the Prince's servant.

Another possibility is that William Rowley, displaced in 1625, but in 1632 described on the title page of *A New Wonder, A Woman Never Vext*[81] as "one of his Maiesties Servants," had returned to the company at the first opening. If so, Rowley had probably returned before November 24, 1631, when his play was entered S.R. and could have succeeded only Heminges, the first missing member

[77] cf. below, p. 222.
[78] *Believe As Ye List*, facsimile, p. 15r.
[79] Warner, G. F., *Catalogue of the Manuscripts and Muniments of Alleyn's College of God's Gift at Dulwich*, p. 183.
[80] Collier, *Annals* (1879), Vol. I, p. 441, note 1; Vol. II, p. 34, note 1.
[81] Greg, W. W., *A List of English Plays*, p. 90.

after 1625. But again Rowley's title in 1632 may be the result merely of his past membership.

A third suggestion, by Fleay, has no value. He states that Thomas Heywood had come to the Shakespearean company from the Queen's by 1634.[82] Probably his reason for the supposition is that about that time Heywood's *Challenge for Beauty* was acted, according to its title page, "By the King's Majesties Servants." This statement, of course, signifies nothing as to Heywood's membership, since with the exception of Shakespeare regularly and Field temporarily the dramatists of the company were not members, and there is no further evidence that Heywood even became one of their regular dramatists. Nor is there any indication that Heywood ever acted after 1619.[83] We may thus safely omit Heywood.

The known candidates then for successor to Heminges are William Rowley and Ball. The successor, as we have seen, had evidently died or withdrawn before 1641. Unless he or Smith had previously dropped out, the next break was caused by Shank's death January 1636, followed by that of Honyman in April 1637. These two could not have been succeeded by Bird—with Beeston's boys as late as May 1637—nor by Hammerton, an apprentice in the Shakespearean company till about 1640. Thus we have four Queen's men succeeding 1636-40, two of whom must have succeeded Shank and Honyman 1636-37.

The history of the Queen's company at this period makes it certain that the other two also came to the Shakespearean company at this time to replace losses, either by death or withdrawal. The old company broke up 1636-37, because it had lost its theater. The owner of the Cockpit, Christopher Beeston, was sworn as governor of a new company, the King's and Queen's boys, February 21, 1637.[84] This turned the former company adrift, without a theater. a serious predicament in that time when playing places were strictly limited. There had been ten of the company, including Beeston, entitled to livery in December 1634.[85] Of the other nine, Herbert

[82] Fleay, *Stage*, p. 372.
[83] Murray, Vol. I, p. 256, note 1.
[84] Stopes, *Jahrbuch*, Vol. XLVI, p. 99.
[85] *ibid.*, p. 97.

disposed of four—Richard Perkins, John Sumner, William Sherlock, and Anthony Turner—to Salisbury Court at some time in
1637.[86] Of the remaining five Queen's men, certainly three, almost
certainly four, reappear as members of the Shakespearean company
in the warrant of January 1641. Bird had not been a member but
an apprentice, and Clark had probably, though not certainly, been
a member. This leaves only one, possibly two, of the company unaccounted for. Two who had been apprentice actors of women's
parts, Ezekiel Fenn and Theophilus Bird, appear with Beeston's
boys in May 1637.[87] This was to be expected, since the owner of
the theater usually controlled a majority of the hired men and
boys. Besides these, George Estoteville also appears, seemingly as
a manager, with Beeston's boys in May 1640.[88] He had been with
the Queen's men in 1635, coming to that company from 4 King's
Revels after March 10, 1635.[89] It seems that he had been a manager
of the King's Revels[90] and was thus probably the tenth member of
Queen Henrietta's company. Consequently, by way of summary, it
appears that the Queen's company broke late in 1636, or early in
1637, because of the loss of its theater.[91] Beeston became manager
of the new company of boys, and Estoteville remained with him in
some capacity, these two retaining the majority of the boys and
hired men of the old organization. Perkins, Sumner, Sherlock, and
Turner went to Salisbury Court, giving their name to the new organization with the consent of Herbert. The other four—Bowyer,

[86] Murray, Vol. I, pp. 267-8; Adams, *Herbert*, p. 66; Malone, *Variorum*,
Vol. III, p. 240. This amalgamated company was known as the Queen's
men; and Perkins and Turner seem to have been its managers, appearing
regularly in the official records. There were fourteen of this latter company
entitled to livery in January 1641 (Stopes, *Jahrbuch*, Vol. XLVI, p. 103),
indicating that the four Queen's men had been joined to ten Salisbury
Court players to form the new company.

[87] Murray, Vol. I, p. 367.

[88] *ibid.*, p. 369.

[89] *ibid.*, p. 279, opp. p. 266.

[90] *ibid.*, Vol. II, p. 356.

[91] This situation explains why *The Hollander or Love's Trial* was licensed
for the Queen's men March 12, 1636, but later printed as acted by "their
Majesties Servants" or Beeston's boys (Lawrence, W. J., London *Times*,
Literary Supplement, November 29, 1923). Since the Easter prohibition
would extend to April 18, and the companies were closed by the plague
May 12 (Murray, Vol. I, p. 167), the play was probably not acted in 1636.
Beeston simply retained it, as he attempted to do with all Queen's plays,
and had it performed by the new company of boys.

Allen, Robins, and Clark—reappear in the Shakespearean company in January 1641.

When did these latter four enter the Shakespearean company? Not before 1635, the logical time being the breakup of 1636-37. As we have seen, the Shakespearean company would need at least one of them to replace the loss of Shank, January 1636, and another to replace Honyman in April 1637. Hobbs and Penn also disappear from the Shakespearean organization between May 17, 1636, and January 1641. Smith is mentioned no more after 1629. We have, however, only three records for members between that date and 1641; the players' pass of May 1636 and the actor lists of *Believe As Ye List* (1631), and *The Wild Goose Chase* (1632). The pass mentions only two members, and the actor list of *Believe As Ye List* is made up from the prompter's incomplete notes on the manuscript, the major actors being named only by lucky accident. The list of *The Wild Goose Chase* gives only principal actors, among whom Smith does not regularly appear, except in very full lists. Consequently, the lists do not give any indication as to whether Smith was or was not with the company after 1629.[92]

The fact that all six of the successors to these men were sworn grooms of the chamber at the same time in January 1641, does not necessarily mean that they all had entered at the same time just previous to that date. There is pretty clear evidence that at least Bowyer was with the Shakespearean company before 1639. In that year Robert Davenport dedicated *A Crowne for a Conquerour, and Too Late to Call Backe Yesterday. Two Poems, the one Divine, the other Morall* "To my noble friends; Mr. Richard Robinson, and Mr. Michael Bowyer,"[93] indicating that Bowyer was by that time with the Shakespearean company. Also, what records we have indicate that the companies did not usually go to the trouble and expense of having a single member sworn. Of four warrants for recruits, only one is for an individual; one is for three, one is for four, and one for six. The warrant for four can be shown to cover replacements over a period of at least two years. The company

---

[92] An Anthony Smith, silkman, was buried June 19, 1634, at Allhallows, Honey Lane (see printed *Registers*, edited by Bannerman, W. B.); but there is nothing to indicate that he was the actor.
[93] Bullen, A. H., *Old English Plays*, n.s., Vol. III, p. 311.

could take care of the new members at crucial times by means of the Master's "protection." Thus Richard Sharp had probably been a member for some time when in 1624, December 29, he secured such a protection from Herbert "dureing the tyme of the Revells."[94] It would seem then to have been the custom of the companies to wait till there were several new members before they proceeded to have them sworn. There was probably no real need for hurry in this case, since the former members of the Queen's men were already grooms. There would thus be no real occasion for such procedure till the former apprentices, Bird and Hammerton, became members. The company would then take the opportunity of setting the record straight in the case of the others, who had been sworn as the Queen's servants. If so, one or both of these apprentices became members probably about 1640. It thus appears that in 1636-37 four of the Queen's men succeeded Shank, Honyman, and two others of the Shakespearean company; the other two missing ones probably died or dropped out about 1640, to be succeeded by Bird and Hammerton. The heavy casualty list 1636-37 may have been due to the readjustment of companies consequent on the ravages of the plague, which between May 12, 1636, and August 17, 1637, took 13,153 in London.[95] At least among the housekeepers the mortality from the plague had been heavy at this time.[96]

Besides these actors, one of the former dramatists of the Queen's company, James Shirley, also came to the Shakespearean company before June 1, 1640, evidently to supply the place of chief dramatist, made vacant by the death of Philip Massinger in March of that year. Shirley wrote regularly for the company till the closing of the theaters, his chief productions being printed in 1653 as "Six New Plays."[97]

---

[94] Adams, *Herbert*, p. 75.

[95] Fleay, *Stage*, p. 162; Murray, Vol. II, p. 188.

[96] See below, p. 111, and note 63.

[97] There is also some evidence which at first sight might seem to indicate that Timothy Read was connected with the Shakespearean company. In 1647 he was arrested at Salisbury Court while playing in *A King and No King*, a play which had belonged to the Shakespearean company (Collier, *Annals* [1879], Vol. II, pp. 37-8; Rollins, H. E., "A Contribution to the History of the English Commonwealth Drama," *Studies in Philology*, Vol. XVIII, pp. 283-4). He was of the "Friars" in 1641. This information is given by *The Stage-Players' Complaint*, printed in that year, and dating itself

It seems that the old company gradually disintegrated after the closing of the theaters. As we have seen, there were ten survivors in 1647, Robins having been killed in 1645 and Bowyer having died or withdrawn, the signatures of the 1647 folio thus representing the surviving members of the old company. They still gave surreptitious performances occasionally, our last record being *Rollo or the Bloody Brother*, 1648.[98] Robinson died March 1648;[99] Lowin August 1653;[100] and Taylor in November, 1652.[101] Pollard was still alive in 1648, taking the part of the Cook in *Rollo or the Bloody Brother*. Of the other six, we have no record after the signing of the folio in 1647. Thus, as was to be expected, the company seems to have been no longer recruited after the closing of the theaters. It was probably permitted to die out with its then members.

Many of the company's personnel, however, appeared with Killigrew's company after the Restoration. Michael Mohun, Robert Shatterell, Charles Hart, Nich. Burt, Wm. Cartwright, Walter Clun, and William Wintersell of that company state in a petition October 13, 1660, that Killigrew had suppressed them till they agreed to act with women, in a new theater and with stage scenery. They also state that "according to your Majesties approbation,

by its allusions to suppression of the High Commission Court and Star Chamber later than July 5, 1641, when these were abolished (Gardiner, S. R., *The Constitutional Documents of the Puritan Revolution*, 1625-1660, pp. 179, 186). Read had been connected with the Queen's company (Murray, Vol. I, opp. p. 266) ; but had gone to the 4 King's Revels before March 10, 1635 (Murray, Vol. I, p. 280) ; presumably becoming a Queen's man again when the companies amalgamated at Salisbury Court 1636-37. That he did not become officially a member of the Shakespearean company is shown by the list of 1641 and by the folio list of 1647. It is practically certain then that Read had remained at Salisbury Court, and that the reference to "Friars" in 1641 is to that theater, sometimes so called (Adams, *Playhouses*, p. 368, note 1). Fleay (*Stage*, p. 359) thinks Read was of Whitefriars, but Professor Adams (*Playhouses*, p. 323) ends that house in 1614. There is some kind of record concerning Read in the registers of St. Giles, Cripplegate 1643-50. See Malcolm, *Londinium Redivivum* (1802-03), Vol. III, p. 304.

[98] Wright, J., *Historia Histrionica*, selection in *Social England Illustrated*, p. 427.

[99] Collier, *Memoirs*, p. 273.

[100] Collier, *Bibliographical Account* (1866), Vol. II, p. 285. Collier had given March 16, 1669, as the probable date of Lowin's burial in his *Memoirs*, p. 179; and does not correct this date in the 1879 edition of his *Annals*, for a reason.

[101] Dyce, A., *The Works of Beaumont and Fletcher*, Vol. VIII, p. 106, note d ; Cunningham, P., *Revels at Court*, p. l.

from all the companies we made election of one company."[102] Since the list of "the King and Queens Company of Players" in the agreement of June 4, 1662, between Herbert and Killigrew mentions the same seven actors in slightly different order,[103] they are evidently the complete membership of the company. Wright not only gives us the same list but also sums up the past history of each member in the following paragraph:

"Hart and Clun were bred up boys at the 'Blackfriars,' and acted women's parts. Hart was Robinson's boy or apprentice. He acted the *Duchess* in the tragedy of the *Cardinal*; which was the first part that gave him reputation. Cartwright and Wintershal belonged to the 'Private House' in Salisbury Court. Burt was a boy, first under Shank at the 'Blackfriars,' then under Beeston at the 'Cockpit': and Mohun and Shatterel were in the same condition with him, at the last place. There Burt used to play the principal women's parts, in particular Clariana in *Love's Cruelty*: and, at the same time, Mohun acted Bellamente, which part he retained after the Restoration."[104] The same authority informs us:

"Mohun was a Captain; and, after the Wars were ended here, served in Flanders, where he received pay as a Major.

"Hart was a Lieutenant of horse under Sir Thomas Dallison, in Prince Rupert's Regiment. Burt was Cornet in the same troop; and Shatterel, Quarter Master."[105]

In several instances we have confirmation of these statements. Hart and Burt were captured by soldiers while acting *Rollo* with the Shakespearean company at the Cockpit.[106] We have official record that Mohun had been with Beeston's boys in May 1637.[107] "Willm. Cartwright, Jun." had been a member of the 4 King's Revels as early as March 10, 1635.[108] The meaning of the actors thus becomes evident when they said, as quoted above, that they had been assembled "from all the companies." It is also evident

[102] Adams, *Herbert*, pp. 94-5.
[103] *ibid.*, p. 113; there were, however, several others entitled to livery (Thaler, A., *Shakspere to Sheridan*, p. 287).
[104] Wright, *Historia*, p. 423.
[105] *ibid.*, p. 426.
[106] *ibid.*, p. 427.
[107] Murray, Vol. I, p. 367.
[108] *ibid.*, p. 279.

that the old Shakespearean company had supplied some excellent material to this collected company. Besides these who appear among the members, Theophilus Bird and Richard Baxter were also connected with the company in some way.[109] Also, John Rhodes, a former bookkeeper at Blackfriars, was for a time manager of another Restoration company (see below, p. 128). So far as I can find, no other person who had been in any capacity with the Shakespearean company was connected with any of the Restoration companies.

Knowing the organization of the Shakespearean company from 1603 to its disbanding, we are now in position to trace its history previous to 1603. Our best point of departure is the folio of 1623, which lists "The Names of the Principall Actors in all these Playes" as follows:

William Shakespeare	Samuel Gilburne
Richard Burbadge	Robert Armin
John Hemmings	William Ostler
Augustine Phillips	Nathan Field
William Kempt	John Vnderwood
Thomas Poope	Nicholas Tooley
George Bryan	William Ecclestone
Henry Condell	Joseph Taylor
William Slye	Robert Benfield
Richard Cowly	Robert Goughe
John Lowine	Richard Robinson
Samuell Crosse	Iohn Shancke
Alexander Cooke	Iohn Rice

The list thus purports to give all the principal actors since Shakespeare began writing for the company. What is meant by "Principall Actors?" We shall see[110] that in the Beaumont and Fletcher folio of 1679 the term always meant members and the apprentice actors of the chief women's parts. In the 1623 folio the term evidently includes all active members, since all members from 1603 to 1623 are included except Laurence Fletcher. We have absolutely no record of Fletcher's ever having taken active part in the company. He

---

[109] Downes, J., *Roscius Anglicanus* (1708; copy belonging to the Library of the Peabody Institute), p. 2; Thaler, *Shakspere*, 287; at his death Bird was possessed of some kind of share in the company (Chalmers, G., *An Apology for the Believers in the Shakspeare Papers*, p. 529, note g).

[110] See below, p. 175.

seems to have been a purely honorary member thrust upon the company by the King's royal favor, but possibly also the leader of a provincial King's company.[111] In either case, he would have been a kind of outsider, and would have taken no part. Only Kemp, Pope, Bryane, Crosse, and Gilburne do not appear on the list of members after 1603. That the first three are members we know from official record in May 1593.[112] Only Crosse and Gilburne are thus left doubtful. According to Phillips's will,[113] Gilburne was his "late apprentice" in May 1605. Thus he could hardly have been a member at any time, since our record of membership is almost certainly complete for this period. There is, of course, the possibility that the folio list refers, not to the apprentice but to an older Gilburne, possibly his father. Still we have no record of such a person.

Concerning Crosse we have no direct evidence beyond the folio list. It has been supposed that Heywood was referring to this Crosse in the following passage from his *Apology for Actors* (1612):

"To omit all the doctors, zawnyes, pantaloones, harlakeenes, in which the French, but especially the Italians, have beene excellent, and according to the occasion offered to do some right to our English actors, as Knell, Bentley, Mils, Wilson, Crosse, Lanam, and others, these, since I never saw them, as being before my time, I cannot (as an eye-witnesse of their desert) give them that applause, which no doubt they worthily merit; yet by the report of many juditiall auditors their performances of many parts have been so absolute, that it were a kinde of sinne to drowne their worths in Lethe, and not commit their (almost forgotten) names to eternity. Here I must needs remember Tarleton, in his time gratious with the queene, his soveraigne, and in the people's generall applause, whom succeeded Wil. Kemp, as wel in the favour of her majesty, as in the opinion and good thoughts of the generall audience. Gabriel, Singer, Pope, Phillips, Sly, all the right I can do them is but this, that, though they be dead, their deserts yet live in the remembrance of many."[114]

Thus Heywood divides his lists of dead actors into those "before

[111] See above, p. 24, note 70.
[112] Murray, Vol. I, p. 88.
[113] Collier, *Memoirs*, p. 87.
[114] Heywood, *Apology*, p. 43.

my time" and those whose "deserts yet live in the remembrance of many," making the transition on Tarleton, whom he "must needs remember." Since Tarleton died in September 1588,[115] the earlier list would probably belong before that time. Of the s x mentioned in that list, all but Knell and Crosse had belonged to the Queen's men November 28, 1583.[116] An allusion connects Knell also with the same organization. It is related in *Tarlton's Jests*[117] how Knell as Henry V (presumably in *The Famous Victories*, which belonged to this organization) gave Tarleton, who was substituting as the Judge, a box on the ear. In two other references Knell is coupled with Bentley, a Queen's man. In an undated letter,[118] one of Edward Alleyn's early admirers urges him to win fame by surpassing "either Bentley or Knell" in parts these actors had played. Such a letter could hardly have been sent to Alleyn after he created the famous rôle of Tamburlaine in 1587, indicating that Bentley and Knell had by that time passed from the stage. That Bentley belonged to an earlier day is also indicated by Dekker's statement in 1607 that he was "molded out of" the pens of Watson, Kyd, and Atchlow.[119] In another reference, Nashe says[120] he intends in a future work to appraise the work of "Tarlton, Ned Allen, Knell, Bentlie," and to give the parts in which they surpassed, as also how they dressed the parts. It is practically certain then that Knell was also connected with the Queen's company. This leaves only Crosse of the first list not known so to have belonged.

It also appears from this summary that of the six mentioned in this first list before Tarleton, who died in September 1588, the majority had pretty certainly died by 1587. The will of John Bentley, All Saints, Lombardstreet, London, "servaunt to the Queene," was recorded March 24, 1585-March 23, 1586,[121] and John Bentley

---

[115] Collier, *Memoirs*, p. 191.

[116] Wallace, *First London Theatre*, p. 11.

[117] Halliwell, J. O., *Tarlton's Jests* (Shak. Soc. Reprint, 1844), pp. 24-5.

[118] Greg, *Papers*, p. 32.

[119] McKerrow, *Nashe*, Vol. V, p. 152. Since Bentley was dead by August 19, 1585, Kyd on this evidence would have written several plays, presumably for the Queen's men, by that date.

[120] *Pierce Penilesse*, S. R., August 8, 1592; McKerrow, *Nashe*, Vol. I, p. 215.

[121] *Index of Wills proved in the Prerogative Court of Canterbury*, 1584-1604, Vol. IV, p. 39.

"one of ye Queens players," aged thirty-two, was buried at St. Peter's, Cornhill, August 19, 1585.[122] If it was the actor's widow that John Heminges married, as Chalmers has suggested, then Knell died between January 30, 1586, when he married Rebecca Edwards, and March 10, 1588, when Heminges married his widow, though at his parish church there is no record of his death.[123] Mills was buried July 11, 1585.[124] Since Wilson does not appear in the certificate of lay subsidies June 30, 1588,[125] the last mention of him being the court payment of March 14, 1585,[126] it is certain that he too had died or withdrawn from the Queen's men before Tarleton's death.[127] If he withdrew, pretty certainly he ceased acting, since he could hardly have considered any other company better. Only John Laneham of this first list is known to have survived Tarleton, his last recorded appearance being March 7, 1591.[128] Thus it appears that Heywood is roughly classifying his actors as those before Tarleton's death and those after, the presumption being that Crosse also flourished in Tarleton's time.

It is further to be noticed that Heywood is grouping not only by actors before his time and after but also by the companies to which they belonged. After the list of five Queen's men and Crosse, who had been before his time, he "remembers" Tarleton and mentions Kemp as his successor; he then mentions Gabriel Spencer, and Singer of the Admiral's, and finally Pope, Phillips, and Sly of the King's company. This grouping then would also indicate that

---

[122] Printed Registers.
[123] Chalmers, *Apology*, pp. 432-5; Collier, *Memoirs*, p. 63. The Bishop of London's record of licence (Chester, J. L., and Armytage, G. J., *Allegations for Marriage Licences issued by the Bishop of London 1520 to 1610*, p. 168) contains further information concerning Heminges. 1588 "Mar. 5 John Hemminge, of St Michael, Cornhill, Gent., & Rebecca Knell, Widow, relict of William Knell, late of St Mary, Aldermanbury, Gent.; at St Mary Aldermanbury." Heminges already in 1588 claimed the title gentleman. What his connection with St. Michael, Cornhill, was does not appear. There are no other Heminges records here at the period except the marriage of "Lettyce Hemynge." Possibly Heminges's master was of this parish.
[124] Chambers, *Eliz. Stage*, Vol. II, p. 330.
[125] Malone Soc. *Coll.*, Vol. I, pp. 354-5.
[126] Chambers, *Eliz. Stage*, Vol. IV, p. 160.
[127] The fact that *Three Lords and Three Ladies of London* refers to Tarleton's death does not necessarily indicate that Wilson was then still alive as Fleay argues (*Drama*, Vol. II, p. 280), since this may be an insertion.
[128] Cunningham, *Revels*, p. xxxii.

Crosse, as well as the five others, was a Queen's man, probably before 1588. The evidence is thus fairly conclusive, as circumstantial evidence goes, that Samuel Crosse of the Shakespearean company is a different actor. The position of Samuel in the 1623 list would indicate that he was with the company about the same time as Gilburne. Thus the 1623 list gives all known members but one, whose omission is accounted for, and includes only two not otherwise known to have been members. Since many of the apprentice actors of the chief parts for women became members,[129] the list was probably intended to contain all members and the famous apprentice actors, its definition of "Principall Actors" being the same as that of the second Beaumont and Fletcher folio, later to be given.

We are therefore to conclude that the 1623 folio purports to give a complete list of all members who belonged to the company after Shakespeare began writing for it. How far back then does this roster of members date? Our first official record connecting Shakespeare himself with the company is dated March 15, 1595;[130] but there is fairly conclusive evidence that he was with the company several years earlier, though not as a member. His name does not appear in the official licence for the company May 6, 1593,[131] which from its nature should give the complete membership. This licence names six men, "being al one companie, servantes to our verie good the [sic] lord the Lord Strainge," though the list is headed by Edward Alleyn, "servaunt to the right honorable the L. Highe Admiral." Then follows the list of five Strange's men: William Kemp, Thomas Pope, John Heminges, Augustine Phillips, and George Bryane. The plot of The Seven Deadly Sins, March 1592, furnishes curious confirmation that this is a complete list of the membership of the Shakespearean company at that time. Of the five members mentioned in the licence of May 1593, only three took part in the play; but each of the three always receives his official title of "Mr." or Master, "which is the title that men give to esquiers and gentlemen,"[132] a

---

[129] The folio list seems to contain all principal actors who had graduated before Shakespeare ceased writing except three, probably Ned, Jack Wilson, and John Edmans. (See below, p. 432.)

[130] Murray, Vol. I, p. 106.

[131] ibid., p. 88; Greg, Diary, Vol. II, pp. 74-5.

[132] Shakespeare's England, Vol. II, p. 76, quoting from Harrison's Description of England.

[72]

distinction no one else in this list is given. Among the there un-
adorned later members are plain "Rich. Burbage, Rich. Cowley,
Will Sly, and Harry [Cundall]," besides a few others who were
then but apprentices, as is shown by the fact that they took the parts
of women. Since the list just quoted gives us all members who entered from the company itself between 1592 and 1603, except
Shakespeare, who is not mentioned in the plot, and since these
are distinguished as non-members in the plot of 1592, we may be
sure that the licence of May 1593 gives the complete roll of members for Strange's men at that date, as indeed it purports to do.[133]
Further, all these members except Heminges and Phillips are known
to have come from Leicester's men.[134]

It is necessary then for us to consider briefly what we know of
the organization and personnel of Leicester's men. This company
had been granted the first known patent to players May 10, 1574.[135]
The patentees were five: "Iames Burbage Iohn Perkyn Iohn lanham
wi[ll]m Iohnson and Ro[bt]e wilson." This patent seems to be based
on a petition which must date early in 1572, signed by the same
men, with the addition of "Thomas Clarke" at the end, the names
occurring in exactly the same order.[136] We know nothing further
concerning Clark who, since he signs last, may have been only
their chief apprentice. It is also barely possible, however, that his
name being last might have been dropped at some one of the many
stages through which a patent went.[137] However this may be, the
company had a patented membership of five. This membership remained intact probably till the formation of the Queen's company
in 1583. Into the membership of the Queen's company of twelve
went Wilson, Lanham, and Johnson.[138] Early in June 1584 "the
owner of the Theater" had declared himself very pronouncedly as
"my Lo of hunsdons man."[139] Since James Burbage was the only

[133] Hence all arguments based on this licence to prove that Shakespeare
was not on this tour of 1593 are unfounded. It simply licenses members, to
which rank Shakespeare had not then attained, and gives no indication concerning non-members.
[134] Murray, Vol. I, p. 73.
[135] Malone. Soc. Coll., Vol. I, pp. 262-3.
[136] Murray, Vol. II, pp. 119-20; Malone Soc. Coll., Vol. I, p. 349.
[137] Malone Soc. Coll., Vol. I, pp. 260-1.
[138] Wallace, The First London Theatre, p. 11.
[139] Malone Soc. Coll., Vol. I, p. 166.

actor ever connected with the ownership of the Theater, he is the only owner to whom the statement could possibly apply, as Professor Wallace has shown in the mass of lawsuits and other evidence he has marshalled around the Theater. I see no reasonable way then to deny that James Burbage was a member of Hunsdon's company at the Theater by June 1584.[140] We have no further record of Perkins, unless he is "Iohn Perkins Trompeter" of the certificate of Lay Subsidies June 30, 1588, who was reported as "dead before the Seasment."[141] It is thus evident that the personnel of the old Leicester company was completely scattered by or about 1583. It also seems evident that the actual scattering of the former personnel was occasioned by the formation of the Queen's company in 1583, which absorbed probably all members except James Burbage, who would naturally remain with his theater and be of whatever company occupied it, as was later true of Christopher Beeston also.

But a company of Leicester's men still continued to act in the provinces regularly from 1585 to September 1588.[142] It was also acting in London;[143] but appeared at court only once, December 27, 1586.[144] This latter entry settles the fact that the Leicester company abroad was a separate organization, since precisely at this time it was in the service of Christian I of Saxony. For this organization abroad we have more details than for the one which remained in England.[145] William Kemp, "instrumentist," received pay in Denmark for himself and his boy Daniel Jones on account of two months' service from June 17, 1586, and in addition a month's pay as a parting gift. Then in a separate account Thomas Kinge, Thomas Stevenes, George Bryane, Thomas Pope, and Robert Persey, "instrumentister och springere," were paid for three months' and three days' service from June 17 to September 18, 1586, receiving the same rate

---

[140] Professor Adams, *Playhouses*, p. 70, is also convinced that the reference is to James Burbage.

[141] Malone Soc. *Coll.*, Vol. I, pp. 354-5.

[142] Murray, Vol. I, pp. 41-2.

[143] Collier, *Annals* (1879), Vol. I, p. 257.

[144] Chambers, E. K., *Modern Language Review*, Vol. II, p. 9.

[145] Herz, E., *Englische Schauspieler*, pp. 1-6; Riis, Jacob A., *Hamlet's Castle* (*Century*, n.s., Vol. XXXIX, pp. 391-2); Bolte, Johannes, *Englische Komödianten* (*Jahrbuch*, Vol. XXIII, pp. 99-106).

as Kemp and his boy but without a parting gift in money.[145a] The fact that Kemp was with the organization in 1586 makes it probable that the company of English whom the crowd broke a fence to see at Elsinore in 1585, and that which appeared at Leipzig July 19, 1585,[146] is this same company, since on November 12, 1585, Kemp was at Dunkirk, away from his master, the Earl of Leicester, who arrived in Flushing December 19, 1585[147] (new style, December 9 old style), having left England early in the same month. Probably Kemp and the company had been on the Continent in 1585, and Kemp was in November working into the Low Countries to meet his master.

After Kemp's departure in 1586, the other five members were sent September 25, 1586, in charge of an interpreter, because of their ignorance of the language, to Christian I of Saxony, arriving October 16 at Waidenhain. It had taken considerable correspondence to persuade them to go so far into a country whose language they did not know. In all the correspondence they are spoken of as "instrumentister," sometimes with the further limitations of English and five. Christian himself tells how they entertained him with instrumental music and acrobatic performances. They remained with him till July 17, 1587. The Dresden account of that date again informs us that they were "Funf Instrumentisten und Springern aus England." This account is also especially important because each member signed his name to it instead of permitting Stevenes, evidently the manager, to sign for all as at Elsinore.[148]

It is evident then that this foreign organization was a company of five musicians and tumblers, to which Kemp and his boy did not

[145a] Mr. J. L. E. Dreyer, in the Literary Supplement of the London *Times* for January 21, 1926, p. 44, refers to C. Thrane, *Fra Hofviolonernes Tid*, as authority for his statement about "the English band of musicians engaged for King Frederic II by his envoy Henrik Ramel in 1586, among whom were William Kemp and Thomas Pope. They did not stay long at the Danish court, as one of them (Thomas Bull) murdered another of the band, and the King was glad to get rid of them, after which they entered the service of the elector of Saxony." But Thrane seems clear that neither Bull nor his victim was a member of the imported group.

[146] Witkowski, G., *Englische Komödianten in Leipzig (Euphorion*, Vol. XV, p. 441).

[147] *The Cambridge Modern History*, Vol. III, p. 619.

[148] Murray, Vol. I, p. 34, note 2; Cohn, *Shakespeare*, pl. I. It is supposed that the company returned to England by way of Danzig.

belong, as is shown by the separate account for them and by Kemp's leaving; but with which for a short time they were associated. Incidentally, Kemp, "the Lord of Leicester's jesting player," was probably returning to the English branch of the company, which had been acting in the provinces at least since early in 1585.[149] The members of this foreign branch did not know the language; they were only five; they are always called either or both musicians and tumblers; and there is never a word, so far as I can find, in the numerous records that can be fairly interpreted as meaning that they really acted. Under the conditions stated, it is hard to see how they could have been an acting organization in any fair sense of the term. Some have interpreted the words of Thomas Heywood, writing in 1612, some twenty-five years later, as meaning that this was a company of actors. Heywood uses the general term "comedians," but implies that they were actors in that others "of the same quality" were then in Germany. But in all the descriptive terms applied, Heywood has uppermost in his mind the members from his own organization. Thus the evidence seems clear that this former organization was that of Leicester's musicians and tumblers. This need not be surprising, for as we have seen, his players were in England. The supposition is made still stronger by the fact that in England we hear more than once before this time of the Earl of Leicester's musicians. That they were a distinct organization is implied by the fact that Leicester's players accompanied by Leicester's musicians appeared at Coventry in 1582-83.[150] Still, it will be observed that even though they were abroad and but musicians and tumblers, they nevertheless retained the talismanic five of the 1574 patent. Indeed, they probably worked under an exemplification of the original patent of 1574, which

[149] Murray, Vol. I, pp. 35, 41-2.

[150] *ibid.*, p. 41; Vol. II, p. 238, etc. Murray notes in each instance that he has quoted only a few entries concerning musicians but that the entries were fairly numerous. The selected records name about a dozen organizations of musicians. In several instances the patron had both musicians and players under his patronage, who travelled both separately and together. Cf. Murray, Vol. II, pp. 198; 223, note 2; 229; 236; 237; 238; 239, also note 2; 240, note 1; 242, note 1; 245; 246, note 2; 249; 256; 337; 375; 391; 399, note 4; 413.

MEMBERSHIP

specifically provides for plays but "to gether with their musicke."[151]

The Shakespearean company then had not only the majority of its members but also its organization of five from the Leicester organizations. Nor is any other company of the time known to have had this number. The Queen's had twelve; Worcester's, later the Admiral's, had eight; Strange's earlier company was of tumbling boys with an almost totally different type of organization; there is no trace of a Pembroke company for sixteen years before 1592, but it can be shown that the number in the later company was eight. Thus of what Murray calls Greater Men's Companies, Strange's later company agrees in organization with Leicester's, and with Leicester's alone. On the organization of the lesser companies, there is practically no information; but there is no reason to suspect that the Shakespearean company sprang from one of these.

Further, the two members of the Shakespearean company not known directly to have come from Leicester's, Heminges and Phillips, probably did not come from either of the other two companies with which the Shakespearean had, or is supposed to have had, connection 1588-94. These organizations were two: the company of Strange, and that of the Admiral. The connection of the Shakespearean company with the Admiral's is discussed elsewhere,[152] the evidence appearing conclusive that the Admiral's men did not lose a single member to the Shakespearean company. Since the contact was not formed between the companies till 1590, there was indeed no probability that the Admiral's company would contribute to the membership of the original company in 1588. We may therefore leave the Admiral's men out of further consideration.

We reach much the same conclusion from a study of the connection between the earlier and the later Strange organizations. The records of court performances[153] show that the earlier company performed "feats of activity" and tumbling, under the manage-

[151] Malone Soc. *Coll.*, Vol. I, p. 263; Murray, Vol. I, p. 28. We need too to remember that musician and actor were by no means exclusive terms (*Acts of the Privy Council*, December 3, 1581; Chalmers, *Apology*, p. 381, note v; Chambers, *Eliz. Stage*, Vol. IV, p. 218).
[152] cf. below, pp. 326 *ff.*
[153] Wallace, *Evolution*, pp. 221 *ff.*; Chambers, *Modern Language Review*, Vol. II, pp. 7-10.

ment of John Simons, who himself took part.[154] The first such recorded performance of "lorde Straunge his Tumblers" is January
15, 1580. Then the "Servauntes of the lorde Straunge" receive pay
"for certen feates of Activitie shewed" December 28, 1581. The next
reward is to John Simons for "certen ffeates of Actiuitye and Tom-
blinge" on January 1, 1583. From the Revels Accounts of November 1, 1582-October 31, 1583,[155] we learn that "Sundrey feates of
Tumbling and Activitie were shewed before her maiestie on Newe
yeares daie at night by the Lord Straunge his servauntes." This
double entry establishes the fact that Simons was the leader of
Strange's Tumblers, as is more directly done by a later entry. For
"feates of Activitye and Vawtinge" on January 1, 1585, John
Simons and his fellows received reward.[156] Reward was given to
"John Symonds and Mr. Standleyes Boyes . . . for Tumblinge
and shewing other feates of activitye" performed January 9, 1586.
Again John Simons received reward for "feats of activitie" per-
formed December 28, 1587. The organization missed but three
Christmas seasons at court between that of 1579 and that of 1587.
All other companies during this period had been rewarded for plays,
as is distinctly stated, and never, so far as I can find, for tumbling.
Strange's players also appear in the provinces from about 1577.[157]
Strange's early company is thus to be traced over a period of about
eleven years, extending from about 1577 to the Christmas of 1587.
Further, it appears to have been a company of boys trained for
tumbling, under the leadership and management of John Simons,
who is the only definitely known member of the organization.

But by 1588-89 Simons was in the provinces with the "Quenes

[154] Feuillerat, *Documents, Elizabeth*, p. 390.
[155] *ibid.*, p. 349.
[156] The Declared Accounts read, "To John Simons and other his fellowes
servantes to Therle of Oxforde vppon the Counselles warrant dated at
Grenewᶜʰ xiiijᵗᵒ marcij 1584 for presentinge before her maᵗⁱᵉ vppon New-
yeres daye at nighte last feates of Actiuitye and vawtinge bye waye of her
maᵗᵉˢ rewarde. Xˡⁱ" (Wallace, *Evolution*, p. 255). This must be a mistaken
attribution, since Simons was with Strange's boys before and after this
entry and since no other company but Strange's is recorded at this period as
giving feats of activity and vaulting. Besides, Henry Evans received reward for Oxford's organization April 7, 1585, on a performance December
27, 1584. If this play had belonged to that organization, pay would have
been given for both in one warrant as in the preceding year.
[157] Murray, Vol. I, pp. 107-8.

players."[158] He had been with Strange's boys certainly January 9, 1586, and almost certainly December 28, 1587. In a children's company, the leader and manager was "the whole show" so far as control of the apprenticed boys was concerned. It is thus significant that a second Queen's company appears in the provinces at exactly this time, led by Simons and sometimes designated "tumblers."[159] Evidently the company had transferred about 1588 from Strange's patronage to that of the Queen. Why? The answer is found in the fact that at Leicester's death in September 1588 several of his men, as we have seen, retaining the Leicester organization, went under the patronage of Lord Strange, the new Strange organization getting its organization and all its members, with the possible exception of two, from the Leicester organizations. It is thus clear that at Leicester's death in September 1588 his company passed to the patronage of Lord Strange, the latter's former company of tumbling boys under Simons passing to the patronage of the Queen.[160] Since these were both specially favored companies, the arrangements were probably made by the crown officials.

While Simons's company doubtless transferred its patronage in 1588, and seemingly did not combine with the Shakespearean company, still this fact does not preclude the possibility that some of its graduated apprentices may have become attached to the company, as was later true in the combination of Rossiter's Revels, Princess Elizabeth's, and Prince Charles's men. It is thus necessary to see if any members of Strange's company of 1588 could have come from this organization. Since Pope, Bryane, and Kemp are known to have belonged to Leicester's organizations till the death of this patron in 1588, only Heminges and Phillips of the 1593 list of Strange's men could have come from Strange's early company of tumblers. Now as Heminges was old enough to be married March 10, 1588,[161] it is hardly probable that he had been one of Strange's tumbling boys. Phillips may have been young enough to have belonged to this early company, since he took the part of the

[158] Murray, Vol. I, p. 12, note 1; Vol. II, p. 375.
[159] *ibid.*, Vol. I, pp. 11, 12, note 1; Vol. II, p. 202.
[160] Simons cooperated with the Admiral's at Court 1588-89 (Chambers, *Eliz. Stage*, Vol. II, p. 119).
[161] Collier, *Memoirs*, p. 63.

effeminate young Sardanapalus in 1592, appearing in woman's dress.[162] Also, Mrs. Phillips shows all the marks of a "gay young widow" after her husband's death in 1605.[163] Thus in his case alone we have no fair indication that he had or had not been a member of Strange's tumblers. Those who may have come from any of these companies as hired men we have no means at all of checking. By way of summary then, we may say that in view of the negative facts that the Shakespearean company received none of its members from the Admiral's organization, and could have received but one, if any, from Strange's tumblers, also that it could have received its organization from neither of these companies; and in view of the positive facts that the majority of the members came from Leicester's patronage and that they retained the patented and traditional Leicester organization, we may be as sure as indirect evidence can assure us that the source of Shakespeare's company was the Leicester organizations. The Shakespearean company is really then only the continuation of Leicester's famous organizations, inheriting the fulness of their customs and traditions, as well as part of their personnel.

We may now connect up the Leicester organizations and see what happened at the reorganization in 1588. As we have seen, the musicians and tumblers started homeward in July 1587. The players have regular record in the provinces till September 14, 1588. Leicester died September 4, 1588, necessarily leaving both his organizations patronless. The two organizations of five members each then formed one organization of five members under the patronage of Lord Strange. What became of the other five, which included the manager of the musicians and tumblers, Thomas Stevenes, as well as Thomas Kinge and Robert Persey, we do not know. Possibly these three, together with the rejected two of the players, continued under the patronage of someone else. Thus presumably all the members of the Shakespearean company of 1588 came from one or the other branch of the old Leicester's men. Certainly Bryane and Pope were from the musicians and tumblers and

[162] Murray, Vol. I, p. 79.
[163] Wallace, *Associates*, pp. 48 *ff*.

Kemp from the players.[164] Also, Heminges and Phillips probably
did not come from any of the other organizations with which
Strange's company had been associated 1588-93. Neither had they
been with Leicester's musicians abroad. Thus they, together with
Kemp, had probably belonged to the playing branch of the organization.

It is finally evident from all this that the folio list of 1623 was
intended to contain all members from the time the company passed
under the patronage of Lord Strange in 1588 to its own date, and
does contain all such licensed members except Laurence Fletcher.
The only possibility of error here is that Heminges or Phillips may
have replaced some other member or members between 1588 and
1593. The later statistics of the company show that this is improbable. From 1603 to 1629, a period of twenty-six years, there were
eighteen losses from the company, or an approximate average of
one each year and a half. Only once in that period did the company
go five years without loss, the latter part of 1608-February 1614.
The next longest period is four years, 1619-23. Both of these
periods are just after heavy mortality in the company, which had
caused important reorganization. In those years, the number of
members was twelve, whereas in 1588-93 it was only five, less than
half. This ought at least to double the average length of time between losses, and should probably at least double the length of extreme periods between losses. This would give an average of at
least three years between losses, and an extreme of at least ten years.
As a matter of fact, Bryane was the first of the original organization to drop out, about 1597, unless indeed as already stated some
one had dropped out before 1593. This confirms our theoretic ten
years. The less than five years between the latter part of 1588 and
May 1593 would not make it probable, then, that any member had
dropped out during the period, especially since the interval followed directly upon organization out of companies that from their
very natures were probably composed of comparatively young men.
Heywood's list in 1612 of the honorable dead from this company
further confirms our conclusion, since he mentions every missing

[164] Murray, Vol. I, p. 35.

member except Bryane, who was still alive,[165] and the interloper Laurence Fletcher. The folio list then seems certainly to contain all members, except Laurence Fletcher, from 1588 to 1623. But it does not date earlier than 1588, since several known members of Leicester's organizations just before that date do not appear in the list. If then these were the principal actors "in all these Playes," no one of the plays in the folio dates before 1588.[166] From the same statement it follows that our list can not begin later than the reorganization of 1588, if, as I hope in later publication to show, Shakespeare began writing for the company at that time. Our list then would appear to go back to the reorganization of 1588, but seems certainly not to go further back. Both the list of actors in the plays and the chronology of those plays would thus indicate that Shakespeare was with the company by the reorganization of 1588.

Now that we have established the origin and earlier connections of the company, we may summarize its membership from 1588 to 1603. As we have seen, the original membership was almost certainly William Kemp, Thomas Pope, John Heminges, Augustine Phillips, and George Bryane. We have also seen that this was certainly the membership in May 1593, as is shown by the licence of that date, whose significant order of naming I have followed. There were at least seven members by 1595, since Burbadge and Shakespeare are mentioned in a warrant dated March 15 of that year,[167] while the five of the 1593 list were still surviving. As we have seen, there were nine members by 1603. It is thus almost certain that the number of members was changed to nine when the company became the Chamberlain's men in 1594, after April 16, probably after May 16, certainly before June 3.[168] This reorganization then pretty

---

[165] Chambers, *Eliz. Stage*, Vol. II, p. 304.

[166] Unless indeed Samuel Crosse should prove to be the Crosse who was before Heywood's time, and Samuel Gilburne should prove to be the father of Phillips's apprentice. In that case, the folio list would include only members; and Crosse, and presumably Gilburne, would antedate the reorganization of 1588, being the two other members of Leicester's actors, who were replaced by Pope and Phillips of Leicester's musicians and tumblers. We should then have evidence that Shakespeare had begun writing for the company before the reorganization of 1588. Thus further information on these two men, especially Crosse, is highly desirable.

[167] Murray, Vol. I, p. 106.

[168] *ibid.*, pp. 91-2; Greg, *Diary*, Vol. I, p. 17.

certainly was effected on Whitsun Monday, May 20, 1594, the beginning of the company's financial year.

However, there is some indication that the number may have been only seven when the company took up the Globe project in 1598-99. All seven of the known members of 1594-95 took part in the venture except Bryane, who seems to have left the company during the inhibition of 1597.[169] This situation might seem to indicate that the number was increased to seven in 1594 and remained at that number till 1597, when Bryane dropped out to be replaced by a younger actor. All the other members would then have entered the scheme, though Kemp soon withdrew. At the same time, the number would have been increased from seven to nine, leaving three junior members of the company unrepresented among the housekeepers. Still, the lines for actors in the Shakespearean plays are practically conclusive that two other actors must have entered in 1594,[170] making nine, the number that had certainly been established by 1603. Also, the fact that companies were very tenacious of their traditional numbers would argue for the one change instead of two.

If there were nine members by 1595, who were the added two members? As we have seen, they could have come only from three— Cowley, Sly, Cundall,—all of whom were members in 1603.[171] Two pieces of evidence seem to point to Sly and Cundall as the added members. They both appear among the six principal actors of *Every Man out of his Humour* (1599), while Cowley does not, and both were given sixth shares as housekeepers at the same time between November 1606 and August 1608,[172] a distinction that Cowley never attained. Thus the members by 1595 were William Kemp, Thomas Pope, John Heminges, Augustine Phillips, George Bryane, William Shakespeare, and Richard Burbadge certainly; William Sly, and Henry Cundall probably.[173]

---

[169] See below, p. 257; Bryane was an ordinary groom of the chamber at the time of Queen Elizabeth's funeral in 1603, and still held the same office under King James, 1611-13 (Chambers, *Eliz. Stage*, Vol. II, p. 304).
[170] See below, Chapter IX.
[171] See above, p. 48.
[172] Wallace, *Associates*, p. 57.
[173] The fact that the lines of Sly and Cundall are major ones by 1594, as we shall see below, also indicates that these actors became members at that time instead of 1598-99. Certainly the actors drew a distinct line of

Comparing this list of 1595 with that of 1603, we find that three have dropped out—Bryane, Kemp, and Pope—and three others have entered—Richard Cowley, Robert Armin, and Laurence Fletcher. Kemp dropped out by or before the middle of 1599,[174] and was succeeded by Armin about March or April 1600.[175] Fletcher could hardly have succeeded Bryane, since our last record of Bryane is December 21, 1596,[176] and he must have dropped out about the end of the summer of 1597, while our first record of Fletcher in the company is the patent of 1603. Fletcher had been a favorite of King James in Scotland as early as 1595, probably as early as 1594, and can be traced there as late as 1601, when he is designated "comediane to his Majestie," leading "The Kingis servandis."[177] Fletcher then doubtless owed his position in the Shakespearean company to the royal favor, and would thus have been admitted in 1603. He almost certainly never acted in the company, this being the reason that he alone of all members is omitted from the 1623 folio list. Thus Fletcher must have succeeded Pope, whose last official record with the company is dated October 2, 1599, but who did not die till shortly after July 22, 1603.[178] He was thus probably ill at the reorganization and withdrew. This leaves Cowley, certainly a member before March 31, 1601, when he received

cleavage between the older group, ending with Sly and Cundall, and the younger group, beginning with Cowley. As we have seen above, admission to the housekeepers did not come to Cowley or his younger associates. Phillips draws the same line in his will in 1605 when he appoints Heminges, Burbadge, and Sly as executors, with a £5 gift, and leaves Shakespeare and Cundall thirty shillings each; but gives all others of his younger fellows but twenty shillings each. Shakespeare is drawing the same line in 1616 when he leaves bequests only to Heminges, Cundall, and Burbadge, they being the only survivors of this the first company of which he was a member. Then Burbadge died in 1619 and only Heminges and Cundall were left to preserve the memory of their fellow Shakespeare in the folio of 1623. Thus the folio is a monument to that early association.

[174] Wallace, *Associates*, p. 54.

[175] Murray, Vol. I, p. 146; Vol. II, p. 31; Baldwin, T. W., "Shakespeare's Jester," *Modern Language Notes*, Vol. XXXIX, pp. 451-2.

[176] Murray, Vol. I, pp. 106-7.

[177] *ibid.*, Vol. II, pp. 195, 268-9.

[178] In Pope's will of July 22, 1603, he provides that since most of his money was out on bonds, settlement should be deferred for six months. Since the will was proved February 13, 1604, it appears that Pope was dead by August 13, 1603, his death thus occurring July 22-August 13, 1603 (Collier, *Memoirs*, pp. 125-8).

pay for the court performances, as the successor of Bryane, who dropped out about the end of the summer of 1597. It is thus significant that Cowley's line in the Shakespearean comedies comes to considerable prominence at this very time.[179]

It may be noted here that the company changed its number to twelve on becoming the King's company, probably following the precedent of Queen Elizabeth's company, which originally contained that number of members.[180] No other company for men had so many members at this time, and probably no other regularly had so many before. Only one other organization had approached this number; the Worcester company when it became the Queen's before March 1604 had ten members.[181] It would doubtless seem proper that the King's company should have a greater number of members, for appearance sake if for nothing else. This possibly furnished one motive and Queen Elizabeth's company the precedent for the number chosen.

Now that we have established the membership of the Shakespearean company, it will be well to see from what sources the members came and, so far as we can, how the members were chosen. It will be best to limit the inquiry to the period 1603-29, since there is practically no doubt concerning the roster of members during that period. In that period, there were thirty members all told connected with the company. Subtracting the nine members of the 1603 patent, we have twenty-one additions within this period of twenty-six years, an average of slightly less than one accession each year. Since, however, the membership was changed from nine to twelve shortly after the 1603 patent, three of the accessions were not to replace losses, the total number of losses thus amounting to eighteen, a rough average of one loss each year and a half. Of the twenty-one gross total accessions, fourteen came from other companies, all becoming members at entrance. It is true that Eccleston and Rice had been apprentices in the Shakespearean company,[182] going to Princess Elizabeth's and later returning to membership in the Shakespearean

179 See below, pp. 254-5.
180 Murray, Vol. I, p. 6.
181 Malone Soc. *Coll.*, Vol. I, pp. 265-7.
182 See below, pp. 417-18, 422-3.

company; but they should probably be included in the above classification. The remaining seven, or one-third of the gross total accessions, had been apprentices in the company. The chance of an apprentice to become directly a member was thus one in three. Since the average accession of members was slightly less than one each year, this means that approximately every three years on the average one apprentice became directly a member.

The Shakespearean company thus drew two-thirds of its members from other companies. During most of this time, the number of rival men's companies was three or four. Of the fourteen members who came from other companies, only Lowin came from the Worcester-Queen-1 Red Bull-Children of the Revels organization.[183] Only Shank came from the Admiral-Prince Henry-1 Palsgrave-3 Prince Charles's company. Except the three who were transferred in 1625 when Charles shifted patronage, only Taylor and Rowley came from the Prince Charles-2 Red Bull company. Thus most of the entrants had come through the Princess Elizabeth organization and its amalgamations. Eccleston and Rice, who had been apprentices in the Shakespearean company, passed through this organization on their way to final membership in the parent organization. Benfield and Field on their way from 2 Queen's Revels to membership in the Shakespearean company had been connected with the company in the Rossiter amalgamation of 1613-17. Taylor had also at one time been with the organization. The large number from the Princess Elizabeth organization is to be accounted for by the fact that it was a kind of reservoir for young actors, being a hybrid in organization between the companies for children and those for men.[184] The Shakespearean company also recruited two of its members, Ostler and Underwood, directly from the Children of the Chapel-1 Queen's Revels-Whitefriars-2 Queen's Revels company. Thus half of its outside recruits came from or through the Revels and Princess Elizabeth companies; one came from each of the two old established companies, two came from Prince Charles's company before he took over the Shakespearean company in 1625, and three

<hr>

[183] The terminology is from Adams, *Playhouses*, Index.
[184] See above, p. 42.

more from the same organization at that date. It may be noted in this connection that no member came from the "hired men."

On the other hand, the losses of the Shakespearean company were due to death, or to permanent withdrawal from acting. For this full period, 1603-29, we have no record that even one member withdrew to enter another company, though our information on this point is not absolutely complete. These facts taken together show that there was very little changing of actors between the four patented men's companies. The idea that the Shakespearean company could snap up any good actor it had a mind to is not borne out by the facts. There are several probable reasons for this state of affairs. Probably they couldn't, and probably they wouldn't have if they could. The definitely limited number of actors would make it possible for them to recruit only at the death or withdrawal of former members. This same condition would limit their choice to the best which happened to be available at such a time of death or withdrawal. Therefore most of their recruits, as we have seen, came from apprentices just completing their terms or from men who were under short contracts, as in the Princess Elizabeth company. Besides, their whole theory of organization would favor this method of recruiting. They worked together as an organization, not as an aggregation of individuals. Each of the other principal organizations for men probably attempted to do the same. Since these organizations were not machine made, their parts were not readily interchangeable. It was necessary by a long process of preparation to fit the material for a particular place. Hence they would naturally prefer to take the likeliest young candidates they could get and shape them to the needs of the company. Still, if they could get better material from another company, they would naturally do so.

It may be noticed in this connection that only a few of the hired men of the Shakespearean company are traceable to other organizations. From the final breakup of the Worcester-Queen, etc., organization in 1623 had come Richard Perkins.[185] From the Children of the Revels to the late Queen Anne had come Richard Baxter after

[185] Stopes, *Jahrbuch*, Vol. XLVI, p. 93.

April 9, 1624,[186] almost certainly after December 1624,[187] but by 1628.[188] James Horn had entered from some other company between Easter and Christmas 1621, and George Vernon between Easter 1621 and Easter 1623, probably with Horn. Since they were entitled to livery, they would seemingly have come from some branch of the other patent companies, though we have no record of their membership elsewhere. William Mago and Rowland Dowle had been hired men with the Prince Charles organization at the Cockpit 1621-22, and appeared in the Shakespearean company, Mago December 27, 1624, Dowle October 11, 1626.[189] Edward Knight witnessed an agreement of the Princess Elizabeth-Prince Charles amalgamation for Edward Alleyn and Jacob Mead at the Hope March 20, 1616,[190] was still with the Prince Charles men in 1623, dwelling "att the George Alley in Gouldinge Lane,"[191] but appears with the Shakespearean company December 27, 1624. Curtis Greville had come in by 1626,[192] probably after December 1624, seemingly by way of the Admiral, etc., organization. Richard Hanly and William Hart became hired men in the company before May 17, 1636, Hanly coming probably from the company of Ellis Guest, and Hart from Daniel's 6 King's Revels, when the two amalgamated in 1635.[193] While the record for these non-members is far from complete, still it further confirms the principles established above.

It becomes evident from the preceding discussion that the Shakespearean company had not merely a definite but even a rigid organization in the matter of membership. The number of members was definitely fixed, and no member was ordinarily admitted except as a successor to a former member. The company secured its recruits from the best of its own long-trained apprentices, or failing that, from the graduating apprentices of other organizations; but rarely

---

186 *H.M.C.*, *Report on the Records of the City of Exeter*, pp. 171-2.
187 Adams, *Herbert*, p. 74.
188 Murray, Vol. I, opp. p. 172.
189 *ibid.*, p. 236, note 3; see above, p. 35, note 116; Adams, *Herbert*, p. 74; *The Roman Actor*.
190 Greg, *Papers*, p. 91; Adams, *Herbert*, p. 74.
191 Wallace, *Jahrbuch*, Vol. XLVI, p. 347.
192 Murray, Vol. I, opp. p. 172.
193 Vol. II, pp. 8-9, 103-5.

received members of rival organizations. As a result, the majority of the members were bound together by long years of association, in many cases extending back to earliest apprentice days. The organization was principally but not rigidly self-perpetuating. It seems to have given the preference to the best of its own training, but to have taken the best available wherever found. Its graduated apprentices left only when they were leaving the "quality" or found no suitable opening in the parent organization, in which latter case they seem to have returned at the first opportunity. Most of these traditions of the organization had probably been already established in the Leicester companies, giving the Shakespearean company finally a tradition and practice that was the outgrowth of the greater part of a century. It has by far the longest pedigree of any of the Elizabethan companies. Its principles and practice, therefore, stood the supreme test of time and, conversely, were the reasons that it might stand such a test. Surely William Shakespeare could have taken his degree as an actor and playwright in no better school, even though he had been *Utriusque Academiae in Artibus magister.*

CHAPTER III

HISTORY OF THE
HOUSEKEEPERS IN THE SHAKESPEAREAN
COMPANY

BEFORE the Globe project was undertaken, the Shakespearean company seems to have rented its theater on exactly the same terms as other companies. It had played at the "Crosse Keys" in November 1589,[1] and seems to have been at the Curtain about February 1590.[2] It seems then to have gone to the Theater with the remnant of the Admiral's men by the autumn of 1590.[3] Our next information places the company at the Rose by March 1592,[4] where it remained, but with forced intermissions of acting in the provinces and at Newington Butts, till June 13, 1594.[5] Probably on the preceding Whitsun Monday, the Shakespearean company passed under the patronage of Lord Hunsdon, who was then Chamberlain.[6]

We find Lord Hunsdon asking permission October 8, 1594, of the Mayor for his company to play "this winter time within the Citye at the Crosse Kayes in Gratious Street,"[7] where they "have byn accustomed." Professor Murray thinks this means that they had already been playing at the Cross Keys that autumn till a dispute arose between them and the Mayor, which their patron was attempting to settle. In view of the fact that the company had been playing at the same place in November 1589, it is also possible that the company had been regularly accustomed to play here within the city whenever it could secure the necessary permission. We do not have direct statement that Hunsdon's request in 1594 was granted, but the circumstantial evidence seems to indicate so. In 1596, at Huns-

[1] Murray, Vol. I, p. 75; Adams, *Playhouses*, p. 14.
[2] See below, p. 327.
[3] See below, p. 327.
[4] Murray, Vol. I, p. 76.
[5] *ibid.*, p. 92.
[6] *ibid.*, pp. 91-2; see above, pp. 82-3.
[7] *ibid.*, p. 93.

don's death Nashe informs us that this company: "as if they had writt another Christs tears, ar piteously p^{er}secuted by the L. Maior & the aldermen, & howeuer in there old Lords tyme they thought there state setled, it is now so vncertayne they cannot build vpon it."[8] Had the company been already at the Theater or Curtain, it would have been safe from the Mayor's special persecutions, whether its patron lived or died, as was demonstrated for instance just the previous September 13, 1595, when the Mayor had tried in vain to have the Privy Council suppress all these public theaters.[9] Seemingly then at Hunsdon's death in July 1596, the Shakespearean company was being maintained by his authority within the Mayor's jurisdiction, thus presumably at the Cross Keys.

One other point also indicates that the company was playing in the city at this period. We are now fairly certain that *Richard II* was produced the autumn 1595.[10] It will be remembered that Queen Elizabeth protested vehemently in 1601 that this play had been acted "forty times in open streets and houses" within London. Since the play was not acted at all in London in 1601, the Queen must have referred to its original run in 1595-96, which would thus presumably have been at the Cross Keys.[11] Probably then the company remained at the Cross Keys till July 1596.

By November 15, 1596, however, the company was at the Theater,[12] whence James Burbage's dispute with Allen concerning the

---

[8] McKerrow, *Nashe*, Vol. V, p. 194.

[9] *Halliwell, Outlines*, Vol. I, pp. 355-6.

[10] Smith, R. M., *Froissart and the English Chronicle Play*, pp. 143-54; Chambers, *Eliz. Stage*, Vol. II, p. 194, note 4; *Rev. of Eng. Studies*, Vol. I, pp. 75-6.

[11] Since we can trace the occupancy of the company in such detail from the autumn 1596 as to make it certain that the company did not thereafter have a theater in London, Shakespeare's first version of *Hamlet*, acted in the city of London, would date before the autumn 1596.

[12] Adams, *Playhouses*, pp. 73-4. Professor Adams thinks this connection with the Theater dates from 1594. The Theater and Cross Keys have a curious number of double mentions. June 23, 1579, James Burbage, owner of the Theater, was arrested for debt as he was on his way to the Cross Keys, presumably as an actor in the performance or he would not so readily have paid up (Wallace, *First London Theatre*, p. 9). The Shakespearean company was playing at the Cross Keys November 6, 1589 (Malone Soc. *Coll.*, Vol. I, p. 181), and was at the Theater in 1590. Finally, October 8, 1594, the Shakespearean company had "byn accustomed" to play in the winter time at the Cross Keys, whence it had gone by the

lease seems to have driven the organization to the Curtain alone about 1597, where it probably remained till the materials of the Theater were transported across the Thames to reappear in the Globe, which was complete by May 16, 1599.[13] Since both the Theater and the Curtain had previously been under one management,[14] the arrangement may have been still in existence, this accounting for the company's shuttling from one theater to the other.

Throughout this period, the company would have observed the general custom, known to have been practised at the Theater and the Rose,[15] of renting a theater from the owner, paying him half the receipts from the galleries, and in case he supplied the theatrical furnishings paying him for these out of or with the other half of the galleries. But at the formation of the Globe project, 1598-99, the custom received a slightly different application. The Burbadge brothers, to whom both the property and problems of James Burbage descended, were to own one-half of the lease, and five of the older actors were to own the other half.[16] This arrangement simply substituted a syndicate for an individual as owner of the lease. It was novel in that it was the largest syndicate, so far as we know, that had ever been formed for the purpose, and in that the actors of the company that was to occupy the house were heavily represented. However, James Burbage and John Brayne had really formed such a syndicate to build and control the first of all theaters;[17] and Henslowe and Cholmley formed such a syndicate for the Rose in 1587.[18] Such organizations must have been quite common in other fields of the business world at the time. Neither was it

end of 1596 to the Theater. It seems likely therefore that there was some as yet undiscovered connection between the two places.

[13] Wallace, C. W., "Shakespeare and the Globe," London *Times*, May 1, 1914; Adams, *Playhouses*, p. 249; Baldwin, *Modern Language Notes*, Vol. XXXIX, p. 451, note 26.

[14] Wallace, *First London Theatre*, p. 12.

[15] See above, p. 17, note 39.

[16] Professor J. Q. Adams has an admirably clear article in *Modern Philology*, Vol. XVII, 1 ff., on "The Housekeepers of the Globe," a clarity that because of my purpose of giving a complete history I fear I cannot approach. This chapter was completed before his article appeared and I have not made any alterations of fact.

[17] Wallace, *First London Theatre*, p. 5.

[18] Greg, *Diary*, Vol. II, p. 44.

probably an absolute innovation for actors to have shares in the theaters. Thomas Pope left by will such a share in the Curtain.[19] He would presumably have acquired this share while the company was at the Curtain about 1597-99. Indeed, so far as we know in the present state of the evidence, the Globe arrangement may have been only a continuation of the arrangement at the Curtain, or even just possibly at the Theater itself. Of the other members, Phillips does not mention his theatrical shares specifically in his will; neither does Shakespeare. Heminges did not die till 1630, many years after the last record of acting at the Curtain; and of Kemp's possessions we have no record. Since then Pope is the only one of the five Globe sharers for whom we have detailed record and since he had a share in the Curtain, it is altogether possible, though not very probable, that the arrangement had its beginning there. Later, both actors and non-actors frequently bought such shares. The second Fortune, owned by Edward Alleyn, furnishes an exaggerated illustration of the principle.[20] The owner of the building might sublease any part of it to anyone he chose. That such a one might be an actor was only accidental, except in so far as an actor might be supposed to have more interest in such property than others. If an actor had the money and the inclination, there would be no discrimination against him as a lessee. By the law of chances, it was inevitable that some actor should soon become a lessee.

The novelty of this transaction then, so far as is yet apparent, was chiefly in its large scale. This association may too have been the first to invoke a joint-tenancy to insure proper successors in the actors' half; though even this device did not affect the Burbadge half, which might have been sub-let to whomever the Burbadges pleased. Indeed, the success of the whole undertaking is probably to be found in the comradeship built up by the company's traditions and customs of membership rather than in any legal devices. It was always those "new men, that were never bred from children in the Kings service" with whom trouble arose. Neither is it necessary to suppose altruistic motives on the part of the Burbadges to account for such an arrangement. It was not a case of giving the actors, free

[19] Collier, *Memoirs*, p. 127.
[20] Greg, *Papers*, pp. 28-30.

THE SHAKESPEAREAN COMPANY

of charge, shares in a theater already established. The whole thing
was a transaction to be made and not one made. In the projected
arrangement, the Burbadges had nothing whatever more than the
actors. All were on an equal footing except in the amount each one
might be able to invest. The Burbadges probably had more property
than any of the others, and consequently could invest more heavily
than the five actors. For this particular undertaking, the Burbadges were also better supplied than their companions in that they
had the old Theater, if they could only get it moved. It may be significant that the various legal papers were not drawn up till the
association had successfully transported the materials across the
river to the site selected for the new undertaking. But the actors had
their contribution to make, and Cuthbert Burbadge furnishes a very
good reason for admitting "those deserveing men" to the ownership
when he records that the Globe was built with "summes of money
taken up at interest."[21] So far as we know, in neither the Globe
nor the Blackfriars did the Burbadges ever give "those deserveing
men" a penny or a privilege the said men didn't pay as well for as
others would have done. The only privilege they gave was that of
being associated with themselves in the business transactions. I give
this matter so much attention and such strong statement because
Cuthbert Burbadge in the deposition above referred to plainly implies otherwise, especially in the case of Blackfriars.[22] In plain
terms, the Burbadge brothers and five others of their friends, who
happened to be fellow actors of Richard Burbadge in the Shakespearean company, formed a business agreement under the laws of
the time for securing a desirable commodity, from which each
profited in proportion to the financial risks he incurred. We know
from other sources that the closest comradeship existed among these
men, but it had no traceable influence upon the legal form of their
organization. Even the joint-tenancy entered into by the five actors

21 Halliwell, *Outlines*, Vol. I, p. 317.
22 It is to be remembered that at the time Burbadge made this statement
in 1635 a share in Blackfriars had sold for as much as £180. But the Burbadges received just as much rent under the agreement of 1608 from the
Shakespearean company as they had previously from Evans. Consequently,
they gave the company nothing; they merely rented a building to the
housekeepers at the same rent they had been receiving, and the company
made values soar.

was not the outgrowth of sentiment, but an application of the regular forfeiture clause existing among actors, to apply when a member left without the consent of the others.[23] It would have proved more sentiment and less business if they had made no legal agreement at all.

I have not found any other instance of joint-tenancy in other companies of the time. It has been suggested that some such device was contemplated at the Fortune in 1608, when Thomas Downton bargained for an eighth of a fourth share;[24] since there were eight members of the company at that time, and since it was stipulated that he must act at that particular theater so long as he held his share. The coincidence of eighths is probably accidental, however, since the eighth of a fourth was a regular unit in the second Fortune, where there was certainly no joint-tenancy among the actors.[25] Of course the acting stipulation is itself a natural one. At any rate, the scheme if contemplated was not put into effect.

Professor Wallace thinks that such a joint-tenancy existed at the Red Bull,[26] seemingly basing his conclusion on the fact that Thomas Swinnerton had leased a one-seventh share from Aaron Holland in 1605.[27] But this share passed to the non-actor Philip Stone in February 1608, and from him to the non-actor Thomas Woodford in 1612. If, therefore, there was such a joint-tenancy, it did not long survive. In fact, this very evidence indicates that there was no such joint-tenancy. Of course, the fact that an actor held a share is no indication of such an arrangement, since the most natural interpretation is that he had secured the share as an individual and not as a member of his company. It appears then that the arrangement in the Shakespearean company was also peculiar in that the company owned shares as members of a corporation and not merely as disconnected individuals. So far as we know, it was the only company to follow this method, though the Palsgrave's company doubtless was aiming at somewhat the same thing when it rented the Fortune

[23] cf. above, p. 22.
[24] Greg, *Papers*, pp. 13-14.
[25] *ibid.*, p. 30.
[26] *Century*, Vol. LXXX, p. 510.
[27] Wallace, *Three London Theatres*, pp. 8-9.

in October 1618. How the device worked in the Shakespearean company the sequel will show.

Having determined the origin of this system, we may now trace its history, first at the Globe and later at Blackfriars. In the Witter-Heminges case,[28] Heminges gives a detailed history of the Globe shares from the beginning to April 28, 1619, the date of his answer to Witter; and this account is supplemented by information given in the suit of Thomasina Ostler, 1615-16.[29] In an instrument of February 21, 1599, the Globe property was leased from Nicholas Brend for thirty-one years, to begin from the "ffeast or the birth of our Lord god Last past" (December 25, 1598). The lease would thus regularly expire December 25, 1629. Under this lease, Cuthbert Burbadge and Richard Burbadge were to bear half the expenses of the housekeepers, and to receive half of the profits accruing. William Shakespeare, Augustine Phillips, Thomas Pope, John Heminges, and William Kemp were to bear the other half of the housekeeping expenses, and to receive the other half of the profits accruing, bearing and sharing equally. These five actors then had recourse to the legal device of granting their half to William Levison and Thomas Savage, who regranted a fifth share of it to each of them in joint-tenancy.

Professor Wallace explains the meaning and purpose of this arrangement as follows: "While the first purpose of a joint-tenancy was to prevent the breaking up and scattering of an estate into fractions by keeping the property always in the hands of the members, or the longest survivors or survivor, of them all, thus not allowing it to descend to heirs, one of the commonest uses was to prevent dower and other inheritance through will or legal process."[30] It was thus in full accord with the original agreement that the shares in the Globe should finally rest principally in the hands of Heminges, the sole survivor of the original pact, and in those of his chosen partner Cundall.

Under the terms of the original agreement, Cuthbert and Richard

[28] Wallace, *Associates*, pp. 47 *ff*.
[29] Wallace, C. W., "Shakespeare in London," London *Times*, October 2 and 4, 1909. All future statements of fact in this section are based on this and the preceding article unless other reference is given.
[30] *Century*, Vol. LXXX, pp. 508-9.

Burbadge held one-half of the Globe shares, and the five actors before mentioned held the other half. All divisions and sub-divisions of the actors' half under the original lease had no effect upon this relative division between the two sections. Whatever the number of shares, the brothers or their assigns held half of them, and the actors or their assigns held the other half. The history of the Burbadge half of these holdings is soon told. At the death of Richard Burbadge, his shares became the property of his wife, who afterward became Mrs. Richard Robinson.[31] We learn from the contention of 1635,[32] that there was no further change in the Burbadge shares till after John Heminges had died in 1630, which was after the first lease had expired December 25, 1629. But by that time a new generation of actors had arisen, who could see little justice in continuing such an arrangement, now that this formerly controlling element no longer had a single representative in the acting class. Consequently, as a beginning, a half share each was taken from Cuthbert Burbadge and Mrs. Robinson, to be given to Lowin and Taylor. Again, in 1635, the younger actors succeeded in getting another share from each, so that instead of having eight out of the sixteen shares into which the property was then divided as would have been true under the original agreement, the Burbadge family now had but five. They had finally come to have but two and a half shares each, which was but half a share more than several of the acting section then held. Whatever the details of arrangement under the new lease, the spirit under it was to bring the members of this formerly privileged class to an equality with the members of the acting class. Since we have no record at all concerning the ownership of shares after 1635, we do not know whether this levelling movement was continued, or whether it stopped where it was.

In the actors' half, under the terms of the original agreement, each of the five actors had an equal share, or one-tenth of the whole. This arrangement in effect made ten shares, of which the Burbadge brothers jointly held five and the five actors one each. But "about the time of the building of the said Playhowse & galleryes or short-

[31] Stopes, *Stage*, p. 140.
[32] Halliwell, *Outlines*, Vol. I, pp. 312-19.

lie after"[33] William Kemp withdrew. He assigned his fifth to Shakespeare, Phillips, and Heminges in equal thirds. They assigned the share to Thomas Cressey, who reassigned it to the same three, together with Pope, in a joint-tenancy of equal fourths. The effect of this step was to make the number of shares eight, of which the Burbadge brothers held four and the four actors one each. Technically and legally, however, as Heminges shows in the lawsuit, much to Witter's confusion, each of the actors held one-fifth of the actors' half under one joint-tenancy, and one-fourth of a fifth of the actors' half under another joint-tenancy. As has been pointed out by Professor Wallace,[34] this division of Kemp's share was in accord with both the spirit and the law of the joint-tenancy.

Then Pope died, leaving by will of July 22, 1603,[35] all his rights in the Globe to "Marie Clark, alias Wood, and to the said Thomas Bromley." The joint-tenancy was evidently not interpreted in this case as cutting off inheritance, since we find these heirs and their legal representatives still possessing Pope's share as late as 1612. Neither did the device prevent Phillips's widow from controlling her deceased husband's share and passing it on to a second husband, John Witter. If the joint-tenancy was of any avail in this direction, surely the company would have been justified in using it to get rid of Witter. Phillips by his will[36] of May 4, 1605, left his property in the hands of his wife Anne as executrix, but with the proviso that she should lose that power in case of her remarriage. In such event, John Heminges, Richard Burbadge, William Sly, and Timothy Whithorne were to become executors. Anne married John Witter secretly between July and November of 1606, thus bringing in the chief source of trouble to the housekeepers for the next fourteen years. Witter's particular breed of cat was not long in coming out of the bag. He needed money, as usual, to pay off some debts; and offered, in November 1606, to have Anne mortgage her share to Heminges for £50 at 50s interest for six months. Heminges, sus-

---

[33] In the London *Times* for May 1, 1914, Professor Wallace gives very good grounds for his statement that "The Globe was begun in January and finished before May 16, 1599."

[34] *Century*, Vol. LXXX, pp. 508-9.

[35] Collier, *Memoirs*, pp. 126-7.

[36] *ibid.*, pp. 85-8.

pecting that Anne was already secretly married to Witter and consequently her single signature worthless, stipulated that both sign
the mortgage, whereupon they confessed their secret marriage. The
loan was duly repaid with the interest while Witter according to
his own testimony was in King's Bench prison, Southwark. But
Heminges did not return the original lease from Brend, since it
concerned all four of the actor-housekeepers, for whose papers as
business manager Heminges was official custodian; neither did he
return Phillips's will. Instead, "wth the consent and intreatie" of
Anne he became the executor of Phillips's will May 16, 1607, in
order to protect the Phillips children against the squanderings of
Witter. Witter joined with the rest of the actors after his marriage
in taking into their half Henry Cundall and William Sly.[37] This
must have been after the discovery of the marriage in November
1606, but before the death of Sly, August 1608. The effect of this
arrangement was to make the number of shares twelve instead of
eight, of which the Burbadge brothers held six, and each of the
six actor-housekeepers or his assigns held one. But Sly soon died
(August 1608), leaving his part of the Globe to Robert Brown by
a nuncupative will of August 4, 1608.[38]

In the meantime, Witter had been causing Heminges, the business manager, considerable trouble, till finally February 10, 1611
(eighth year of James I) Witter and Anne signed a "dede pole,"

[37] Wallace, *Associates*, p. 57. Professor Wallace says in The London
Times for October 2, 1909, that the division into fifths continued till 1610,
when the actors divided their half into sixths to take in Cundall, and
refers as proof to documents to be published in *New Documents on
Shakespeare, the Globe and Blackfriars.* Heminges's statement seems to
mean that Cundall was admitted before August 1608, at the same time with
Sly, when "two sixth partes" were granted. The exact words of Heminges
are: "And this def^t saith that after the said intermariage of the said
Complainant wth the said Anne he the said complainant did ioyne in the
graunting of two sixth partes of the said Moitie of & in the said Playhowse
galleryes gardens and groundes wth this def^t & the rest then interessed
therein vnto William Slye and the said other def^t Henry Condell." Since
the shares had been really fourths before the admission of Sly, they would
become sixths only by the admission of two, as the words of Heminges
imply. Early in 1612, Cundall owned a share and a half, the half share
coming from the division of Sly's share between him and Heminges, between August 1608, and February 1612. I suspect therefore, that if Professor
Wallace is not simply in error, he is referring to this latter transaction,
which thus presumably took place in 1610.
[38] Collier, *Memoirs*, p. 157.

releasing all their rights in the Globe property to Heminges, where-upon Heminges gave Witter and Anne a lease by indenture February 14, 1611, for a sixth part to run eighteen years "from the birth of our Lord god then last past" (December 25, 1610),[39] at a rent of 24s. 2d. per annum, payable quarterly. If Witter did not pay the stipulated rent at the proper times, and if he did not pay two legacies of £10 each and one of £5 from Phillips's will, then the lease was to become void. After this arrangement and before the burning of the Globe (June 29, 1613), Witter joined the other members of the actor-housekeeping group in admitting William Ostler to a share (February 21, 1612). The effect of this arrangement was to make the shares fourteen instead of twelve, of which the Burbadge brothers held seven and each of the seven actor-housekeepers or his assigns held one. According to Thomasina Ostler, the signers and their shares concerned in this lease to her husband were Basil Nichol ½, William Shakespeare 1, John Witter 1, John Heminges 1½, Henry Cundall 1½, John Edmans and his wife Mary ½, six shares in all.

Basil Nichol held half of Pope's share as executor in the right of Thomas Bromley; and John Edmans and his wife Mary held the other half.[40] The contract also shows that Sly's share had been

[39] Shouldn't the date be December 25, 1611, or the term nineteen years, since this paper was seemingly intended to cover the remaining years of the lease, which expired December 25, 1629? The rent charged was the regular amount on a one-sixth share. I suspect the contract was dated in 1612, to run from December 1611, since this would make the expiration of the contract the same as that of the lease and since the housekeepers were readjusting their affairs just about this time by the admission of Ostler as a sharer February 21, 1612. Witter was a party to this agreement. If his contract had been made in February 1611, he would already have been out before this transaction in 1612, since Heminges claimed that Witter failed in his first two payments, thus forfeiting his contract. February 10 and 14, 1612, would be logical dates for this transaction, at the reorganization in preparation for admitting Ostler February 21, 1612.

[40] As we have seen, Pope had left his rights in the Globe to Thomas Bromley and Marie Clark, alias Wood. He appointed "Bazell Nicholl and John Wrench, to be the executors." Since Bromley was baptized August 28, 1602 (Chalmers, *Apology*, p. 388, note), he was still in 1612 a mere child, and Nichol, the executor, is representing him. It was probably this Thomas Bromley who married Mary Dunning at St. Saviour's, his parish church, June 26, 1625 (*The Genealogist*, n.s., Vol. IX, p. 237). Mary or Marie Clark, alias Wood, had evidently married John Edmans, who was Pope's apprentice, and it is as her husband that he signs. I do not find this marriage recorded at St. Saviour's; but a John Edmonds married Elizabeth

divided equally between Heminges and Cundall. As we have seen, Sly had left his share by nuncupative will of August 4, 1608, to Robert Brown. Probably Robert had turned the share over to Heminges and Cundall, just as Robert's wife had turned the Blackfriar's share over to Richard Burbadge. Professor Wallace may refer to this transaction when he says Cundall was admitted in 1610, whereas Heminges tells us it was much earlier.[41] How the Browns came to give these shares up we do not know. Collier[42] considers the circumstances of the will itself very suspicious, and expresses surprise that it was permitted to stand. Possibly Heminges and Cundall used these suspicious circumstances as a lever to pry the share out of the hands of Robert Brown; but more probably they used the joint-tenancy, which according to Professor Wallace might prevent inheritance. If so, it means that it was the policy of the actor-housekeepers to permit the direct dependents of one of their number to inherit his share as a kind of rightful pension, but that they drew the line at permitting a share to go to non-dependent strangers. Such a policy would be at least a just one.

The next important event in the history of the housekeepers was the burning of the Globe June 29, 1613. It was at once decided to rebuild, a decision that yet again raised the problem of what to do with Witter. Heminges wrote him asking that he make initial payment of £50 or £60 as his share toward the new enterprise, but received no answer. Since Witter had failed in all the conditions of his last contract, Heminges took over the forfeited share and gave half of it to Cundall, each of the two now having two shares. This was not done, however, till after Heminges had awaited payment of rent for two quarter days, which would be not before January 4, 1614. Also, the lease from young Matthew Brend for thirty-one years from December 25, 1613, shows that all these transactions took place shortly after December 25, 1613. Still, even after the forfeiture Heminges continued to give Anne sums of

Dowton December 4, 1614 (*Genealogist*, n.s., Vol. VII, p. 98), and John Edmundes married Katherine Seaman November 17, 1625 (*Genealogist*, n.s., Vol. IX, p. 239).
   41 See above, p. 99, note 37. It is probable that Sly's share is the one-sixth share which Heminges says sold for less than £60.
   42 Collier, *Memoirs*, p. 157.

money, and paid her funeral expenses when she died. Business was not merely business with him, and he had observed the spirit of Phillips's will under most trying circumstances.

The rebuilding of the Globe probably forced Pope's heirs out also. As we have seen, Pope had a share in the Globe and one in the Curtain as well. By his will of October 4, 1624, Underwood left a share in the Globe and one in the Curtain also.[43] It is thus evident that it was Pope's share that Underwood had secured between February 20, 1612, and October 4, 1624. The expense consequent on rebuilding the Globe would furnish Pope's heirs a very good reason for turning their shares over to someone who would want to bear the burden. If this transfer took place at this time, the shares belonged at the rebuilding of the Globe early in 1614 as follows: Burbadge brothers 7, Shakespeare 1, Heminges 2, Cundall 2, Ostler 1, Underwood 1.

In the meantime another source of trouble had arisen. After the death of Nicholas Brend, October 12, 1601,[44] his half-brother, Sir John Bodley, was to look after the interests of the young heir, Matthew Brend. Bodley in 1608 caused the Globe property to be deeded to himself absolutely, and in 1609 made the housekeepers pay him £20 to recognize the lease they had from Nicholas Brend. When the Globe burned, Bodley granted the company a new lease, embodying practically the same terms as the old, dated October 26, 1613, and extending to December 25, 1635. But the housekeepers, not intending to leave any weak points in their claim, about the same time also secured the signature of young Matthew to the old lease, with extension to December 25, 1644. This extension gave them thirty-one years from December 25, 1613, thus placing them in the same position as at the original building in 1598-99. So armed against all eventualities, they proceeded to build.[45]

The building was being used by June 30, 1614, and was then reported "to be the fairest that ever was in England."[46] Further, the company evidently did not start to build before Heminges and

[43] Collier, *Memoirs*, p. 230.
[44] Actual possession of the Globe lease had passed to Sir Matthew Brown and John Collett in trust as part security for a debt.
[45] Wallace, London *Times*, May 1, 1914.
[46] Wallace, *Children*, p. 35, note 1; Halliwell, *Outlines*, Vol. I, p. 246.

Cundall took over Witter's share, after January 4, 1614. It was pretty certainly this continued uncertainty on the part of the company which caused the watermen in the person of John Taylor, the water poet, to petition "In the month of *Ianuary* last 1613"; i.e., 1614 as is clearly shown by the fact that Bacon was "then the Kings Atturny generall," to the effect that all playhouses be prohibited on the London side of the river, so that they would be forced to the Bankside.[47] But while the petition was ostensibly aimed at bringing all players to the Bankside, where only the King's men were, yet it was these very King's men who answered that it was unjust "to confine them," whereupon they appealed to their official head, the Lord Chamberlain. Seemingly the watermen were trying specifically to prevent the King's men from leaving also, but at the same time wished to bring all others back for their commodity. The suit is an illuminating example of the business thinking of the day, and especially well illustrates the political thinking of Francis Bacon, whose pithy style projects itself through the verbosity of Taylor. Howes is thus doubtless correct when he tells us that the Globe was rebuilt in the spring of 1614.[48] Evidently then the company simply transferred to Blackfriars for the remainder of the summer of 1613, and rebuilt the Globe only in time for the summer of 1614, as was the practical thing to do. Also, the second Globe took no longer in building than did the first, even though it was "farre fairer."[49]

The next adjustment was after Ostler's death, December 16, 1614, soon after which we find his widow Thomasina, as administratrix, suing her father Heminges, as manager of the company, for her husband's share.[50] She claims that she had become executrix December 22, 1614, and on the same day had for safe keeping turned over Ostler's leases on his shares in both the Globe and Blackfriars to her father, John Heminges, who, she alleges, now refuses to return the papers or give her the profits on the shares. We haven't a record of how the dispute was settled, but our next

[47] *Works of John Taylor the Water-Poet comprised in the Folio Edition of* 1630 (Spenser Society, 1869, pp. 333 ff.).
[48] Wallace, *Children*, p. 34, note 5.
[49] *ibid.*, p. 34, notes 5, 7.
[50] Wallace, London *Times*, October 2 and 4, 1909.

information shows that Heminges had the Globe share. Probably Heminges felt justified in invoking the joint-tenancy to prevent his daughter from inheriting, to which Thomasina must refer when she says Heminges claims a "grant and assignment" from Ostler, under which he retains the shares.[51]

Once more the shares were increased after Shakespeare's death to admit Nathan Field. The effect of this increase was to make the shares now sixteen instead of fourteen, of which the Burbadge brothers held eight. The other eight were held by the actor-housekeepers as follows: Shakespeare's assigns 1, Heminges owned or controlled 3, Cundall 2, ?Underwood 1, Field 1. The housekeepers had also granted two small parcels of ground to John Atkins in trust for John Heminges, upon part of which the latter had built a house, paying but twenty shillings a year for rent as Witter declares. For privilege of building this house, Heminges had to pay Sir John Bodley forty shillings in 1615,[52] this fact establishing the approximate date of building. Witter now caused his last spasm of trouble. On April 20, 1619, he sued Heminges and Cundall for a one-sixth share that had, as he alleged, belonged to Phillips, claiming that Anne had assigned it to him July 1606, before their marriage. Heminges and Cundall appeared April 23, 1619, and were assigned April 28, 1619, for reply, when they summed up the facts pertinent to the case as above given, to which Witter replied May 10, 1619. Heminges was ordered May 28, 1619, to bring in the lease and deed of mortgage and show cause why they should not be left in custody of the court as Witter had demanded. Another now mutilated order was given in the case June 5, 1619. Thomas Woodford and James Knasborough were examined for Witter February

---

[51] Wallace, London *Times*, October 4, 1909. That Heminges probably had good reasons for trying as a father to curb the twenty-one year old widow we may infer from the fact that she had occasion about the same time to sue young Walter Raleigh for insult and slander. She won a verdict of £250 against him it is true; but it was by default, since Raleigh was at the time in hiding with Prince Maurice in the Low Countries for having wounded one Robert Finet in a duel (Wallace, London *Times*, October 2, 1909). One fancies also that Heminges as business manager didn't want any more gay young widows to get the affairs of the company into a snarl, now that he had just been able finally to correct the mess Phillips's widow had caused. The share would remain in the family anyway.

[52] Wallace, London *Times*, May 1, 1914; see below, p. 159.

1620. The case was dismissed from court forever November 29, 1620, Witter having failed to proceed; and he was ordered to pay the defendants twenty shillings costs. So ended the controversy that gives us our principal information concerning the distribution of Globe shares.

When Matthew Brend came of age, he sued for the Globe property, which was awarded him by the Court of Wards in 1622, the property being transferred February 21, 1622. Matthew was knighted in April 1622, and married Frances Smith in 1623, to whom he gave the Globe property March 12, 1624, as part of her jointure, it remaining in her possession till her death in 1673. Sir Matthew, about 1633, tried to cancel his extension to the original lease but as we shall see, did not fully succeed.[53]

Fortunately for us, there was another controversy in 1635, which practically fills the gap for the housekeepers between 1619 and 1635. Robert Benfield, Eyllaerdt Swanston, and Thomas Pollard presented their grievances to the Lord Chamberlain May 18-July 12, 1635.[54] They say: "That the house of the Globe was formerly divided into sixteen partes, wherof Mr. Cutbert Burbidge and his sisters [sic] had eight, Mrs. Condall four, and Mr. Hemings four. —That Mr. Tailor and Mr. Lowen were long since admitted to purchase four partes betwixt them for the rest, vizt., one part from Mr. Hemings, two partes from Mrs. Condall, and halfe a part a peece from Mr. Burbidge and his sister.—That the three partes remaining to Mr. Hemings were afterwardes by Mr. Shankes surreptitiously purchased from him, contrary to the petitioners expectation, who hoped that, when any partes had beene to bee sold, they should have beene admitted to have bought and divided the same amongst themselves for their better livelyhood."[55] Since Mrs. Cundall is mentioned, the time referred to is after Cundall's death in December 1627. It is further to be noticed that the Mr. Heminges of the three successive sentences is evidently one person. The third sen-

---

[53] Wallace, London *Times*, May 1, 1914.
[54] Lord Chamberlain's Books, Class V, Vol. XCIV, p. 45. Printed first by Halliwell, *Illustrations of the Life of Shakespeare*, pp. 86 ff., then in *Outlines*, Vol. I, pp. 312-19, and again by Stopes, Mrs. C. C., *Burbage and Shakespeare's Stage*, pp. 230-40.
[55] Halliwell, *Outlines*, Vol. I, p. 312.

tence shows conclusively that this Mr. Heminges is William Heminges, the son of John Heminges. Consequently, the list given in the first sentence must date after the death of John Heminges in October 1630, and before Shank's alleged surreptitious purchase of shares about the middle of 1633. We may thus date it 1631-32. Further, Taylor and Lowin became the managers of the company at the death of John Heminges. It was doubtless at this time that they were given shares as represented in the second quoted sentence above. The list then would represent the ownership directly after the death of John Heminges in October 1630. In the consequent readjustment, Lowin and Taylor were admitted to shares as recorded in the quotation. Thus about 1631 the shares stood Cuthbert Burbadge 3½, Mrs. Robinson 3½, William Heminges 3, Mrs. Cundall 2, Taylor 2, Lowin 2. The most significant fact about this adjustment is that the Burbadge half of the Globe is for the first time invaded by the actors. True, the invasion was light, but it established the precedent; it could be done. This indicates that the original joint-tenancy had been permitted to expire with the original lease in December 1629. Since it had brought all the actors' shares into the hands of two, there was no longer much need for its renewal. At the death of Heminges, the actors were without representation in the Globe, the ownership having reverted to the ordinary capitalistic type. But the tradition of actor-participation had been too strongly established for this condition long to last, and the process of adjustment began at once. This process we shall treat a little more in detail later.[56]

Before proceeding further, we may notice what changes had taken place 1619-30. The shares had not been increased in the period, and Cuthbert Burbadge and Mrs. Richard Burbadge Robinson still held at the end of it half the shares between them. But the shares of the actor-housekeepers by the end of the period were equally divided in the Heminges-Cundall firm. This means that the shares of

---

[56] It may be noted also that in the readjustment Mrs. Cundall gave up the most shares. She may have been the more willing to sell half her shares because under the terms of Henry Cundall's will his son William was to receive a stock of £300 at the end of his apprenticeship, which would have been about May 1632, if he became a freeman at twenty-one, about May 1635, if at twenty-four.

Shakespeare, Underwood, and Field, as well as that of Ostler, had finally passed into their hands and had been divided equally. We saw that the process had started before 1612. Probably the principle of the joint-tenancy was strictly applied after the trouble caused by Phillips's share. If so, the shares of Shakespeare and Field probably passed into the hands of the firm at the death of the former and the withdrawal of the latter, as pretty evidently Ostler's share had passed in 1614.

Only in the case of Underwood's share do we have further record. Underwood by his will of October 4, 1624,[57] left his share in the Globe to his children. The will provides that all Underwood's property be divided equally among his five children after each has been educated and placed in life. "Provided always, and my true intent and meaning is, that my said executors shall not alienate, change, or alter, by sale or otherwise, directly or indirectly, any my part or share which I now have, or ought to hold, have, possess, and enjoy, in the said playhouses called the Blackfryars, the Globe on the Banckeside, and Curtaine aforementioned, or any of them," profits to be paid to the executors for his children as now they are to him. It is further provided that if the profits are not sufficient both to educate and place his children, then, "when the eldest of my said children shall attaine to the age of one and twenty years, my said executors shall pay, or cause to be paid, unto him or her so surviving or attaining, his or her equal share of my estate so remaining undisbursed or undisposed for the uses aforesaid in their or either of their hands; and so for every or any of my said children attaining to the age aforesaid." The executors, however, might pay each child at majority his or her estimated share without selling the property, if they judged it for the best interests of the minors. It is thus evident that under the terms of the will, the share in the Globe could not be sold before the majority of the oldest child. Now

---

[57] Collier, *Memoirs*, p. 230. Underwood appointed Cundall, Thomas Sanford, and Thomas Smith as his executors; and Heminges and Lowin as his overseers. The will was proved by Cundall February 1625, the authorities reserving power to give a like commission to Sanford and Smith when they should apply for it. Cundall seems to have administered the will alone, since in his own will of December 13, 1627, he charges his wife to see certain conditions of the trust fulfilled.

the oldest child was John, baptized December 27, 1610,[58] who would thus attain his majority in December 1631. If the terms of the will were permitted to hold against the joint-tenancy, the list quoted above must have dated after December 1631, since in it a share in the Globe is no longer attributed to Underwood. It is not likely that the share has merely been entered under the name of the executrix instead of the owner, since the Blackfriars share is entered to Underwood, not to Mrs. Cundall. This situation leads one to suspect that the joint-tenancy was invoked to overrule the will in the case of the Globe share, as we have seen reason to believe it had been in previous cases from about 1608. The Black-friars share would remain to the heirs under the terms of the will, since so far as we know there was no joint-tenancy to frustrate the provision in its case. All these facts taken together seem to indicate that the principle of joint-tenancy was invoked in the case of Underwood's share in 1625, giving John Heminges four shares and Cundall four, this arrangement remaining till after the death of John Heminges in 1630, when a new business manager had to be selected and consequent readjustment made.

After this adjustment of 1630, we are on fairly firm ground till 1635. The process of disintegration and decentralization now sets in. Sir Matthew Brend was founding a family estate by 1633, and was needing every penny he could come by for the purpose. Consequently, he attempted to abrogate the old lease and secure a more advantageous one. He was evidently trying to enforce the terms of the lease given by Bodley to end December 25, 1635, since when John Shank bought his shares from William Heminges in 1633 there were "about two yeeres to come."[59] Professor Wallace promises to publish the documents in the suit,[60] but in the meantime we get some of its echoes from the controversy of 1635. By 1635 the housekeepers had won their case and a new lease was drawn. The lease drawn up in 1635, but not yet confirmed at the time of the complaint, was for nine years from March 25, 1635. It would thus expire March 25, 1644. It evidently was confirmed and did expire

[58] Collier, *Memoirs*, p. 227.
[59] Halliwell, *Outlines*, Vol. I, p. 314.
[60] London *Times*, May 1, 1914.

at the time given, since the building was pulled to the ground April 15, 1644.[61] The owner wasn't going to take any more chances with this previously favored company, even though the theaters were officially closed. The time of this lease was slightly changed from that of the extension, which called for December 25, 1644. Now March 25, 1644, counting from the burning of the Globe, lacks but one quarter of being thirty-one years, the length of the original lease. Shank tells us that the housekeepers made their plea for the extended lease "in consideration that they and their predecessors had formerly beene at the charge of 1400 *li.* in building of the sayd house upon the burning downe of the former."[62] Brend had tried to oust the company; but, failing in that effort, probably took advantage of the plea of the housekeepers to get half a year cut off the extension, making the very best he could of a bad matter. As we shall see later, the compromise recognized his ownership of the building and consequent right to charge a much increased rent.

This suit gave the actors a club to hold over the heads of the housekeepers, as the three belligerents intimate in their petition. In these years of litigatory uncertainty, various compromises were necessary among the actors themselves. The actors as a group would naturally not be very anxious to pull chestnuts out of the fire for a few housekeepers, the majority of whom were not actors. Of course it would be to the advantage of the actors to hold the old playing place, advertised by many successful years; but their goodwill was also of supreme importance to the housekeepers. Consequently, the decentralizing counter movement received impetus. The first move, as we have seen, had been the admission of Lowin and Taylor as housekeepers. Shank then secured the three Globe shares of W. Heminges, "surreptitiously" according to the belligerents. Shank bought one of these shares in 1633 and the other two in 1634. Thus the list given in the lease of 1635 is the same as it was about 1631, except that Shank now had the three shares formerly belonging to Heminges. Then the other three principal actors—Benfield, Swan-

---

[61] Collier, J. P., *The Life of William Shakespeare* (1844), p. ccxlii, note; Wallace, London *Times*, April 30-May 1, 1914.
[62] Halliwell, *Outlines*, Vol. I, p. 316.

ston, and Pollard—claimed they should be admitted also. They did not claim equality with the older three principal actors, but asked that the older three should have two shares each and that they themselves should have but one each. To this end, they asked that Shank's shares be reduced by one; and that the original Burbadge shares be again reduced by two, one from each branch. The Burbadge clan were naturally very much offended because their once sacred shares were again about to be invaded. They began to feel that "it is onely wee that suffer continually." They fell back on the plea of distinguished former service of long duration in comparison with these "men soe soone shott up," one of whom had been a principal actor but slightly over ten years and the other two but slightly over twenty. Evidently "antiquity and desert" were likely to suffer if such a thing should be permitted. Shank claimed that this transaction was purely and simply a matter of driving a bargain, and that the complainants had just as good an opportunity to buy the shares as he himself had, but had wanted them for nothing. The Chamberlain decided in favor of the complainants.

This decision marks a radical difference of attitude from the one that had been prevalent at the time the housekeeping association was formed. At that time, a theater was considered merely as a building for rent, and was usually erected by some capitalist purely as a business venture. The Burbadges and the five chief actors of the Shakespearean organization had entered such a venture in 1598-99. The actors had made use of their part of the enterprise to bind their best actors by admitting them to an equal share in their part. With these transactions, at the Globe, the Burbadges had nothing to do. None of these transactions had any effect at all on their half of that venture. To save the whole in time of stress, the Burbadge interests had granted about 1631 half a share from each branch to Lowin and Taylor. But the thing they had offered as a concession was by this decision of 1635 recognized as a right. The main object was, of course, to keep his Majesty's best actors well enough paid to stay with the organization, and there was no scruple about dipping into what some people regarded as their private property in order to do so. After the decision in 1635, the shares stood: Cuth-

	1598	1599–1603	1603–1605	1605–1606	1606–1608	1608–1612	1612–1613	1613–1614	1614–1616	1616–1619	1619–1624	1624–1627	1627–1631	1631–1633	1633–1634	1634–1635	1635–
Cuthbert Burbadge, Richard Burbadge and wife	5	5	5	5	6	6	7	7	7	8	8	8	8	7	7	7	5
William Kemp	1																
William Sly					1												
Augustine Phillips	1	1¼	1¼														
Anne Phillips Witter				1¼	1	1	1										
William Ostler							1	1									
William Shakespeare	1	1¼	1¼	1¼	1	1	1	1	1								
Nathaniel Field										1							
Thomas Pope	1	1¼															
Marie Edmans			5/8	5/8	½	½	½										
Thomas Bromley			5/8	5/8	½	½	½										
John Underwood								1	1	1	1						
Henry Cundall					1	1½	1½	2	2½	3	3½	4					
Mrs. Cundall													4	2	2	2	2
John Heminges	1	1¼	1¼	1¼	1	1½	1½	2	2½	3	3½	4	4				
William Heminges														3	2		
John Shank															1	3	2
Joseph Taylor														2	2	2	2
John Lowin														2	2	2	2
Robert Benfield																	1
Thomas Pollard																	1
Eyllaerdt Swanston																	1
Total	10	10	10	10	12	12	14	14	14	16	16	16	16	16	16	16	16

bert Burbadge 2½, Mrs. Robinson 2½, Mrs. Cundall 2, Shank 2, Taylor 2, Lowin 2, Benfield 1, Swanston 1, Pollard 1.

These very involved transactions through 1635 I have tried to make clearer by means of the tabulation to be found facing this page.

We have no further record of the housekeepers at the Globe after 1635. Mrs. Cundall died in October 1635; Shank died in January 1636; both Cuthbert Burbadge and his wife died in 1636;[63] Mrs. Robinson died in 1642, just before the closing of the theaters. What readjustments were made because of these deaths we have no means at present of knowing, though the suit brought by some of James Burbage's grandchildren may throw light on these points when Professor Wallace publishes it.[64]

In the case of Blackfriars, Richard Burbadge had inherited the theater from his father, who owned it. It had been leased September 2, 1600, to Henry Evans for the Children of the Chapel at a yearly rental of £40, for a term of twenty-one years, from September 29, 1600.[65] But Evans and his company got into difficulties which ~meant~ necessitated the giving up of the lease in August 1608.[66] Richard Burbadge then proceeded to form a housekeeping organization somewhat similar to that at the Globe. August 9, 1608, Richard Burbadge, Cuthbert Burbadge, William Shakespeare, John Heminges, Henry Cundall, William Sly, and Henry Evans formed an equal partnership in a lease, each having a one-seventh share, term to begin June 24, 1608, for a period of twenty-one years, each to pay a yearly rental of £5 14s. 4d., or £40 altogether, the same amount Evans had paid. The term of twenty-one years is a regular one, being the term of Evans's lease; but there was probably the added reason in this case that the lease would in this way expire in the same year as that at the Globe. Cuthbert Burbadge *et al* asserted in 1635 that Heminges and Cundall "had theirs of the

---

[63] Some sentimentalist viewing the casualty list of the first fifteen months after the fateful decision of 1635 might lament the broken hearts that had sent their owners in sorrow to the grave. But more probably the cause of demise was a combination of the plague and old age.

[64] Wallace, *First London Theatre*, p. 24.

[65] Wallace, The London *Times*, October 2 and 4, 1909; Fleay, *Stage*, pp. 211, 233-4, 239-40.

[66] Fleay, *Stage*, pp. 235, 245.

Blackfriars of us for nothing,"[67] which merely means that they did not pay any premium for admission. Since the Burbadges received exactly the same rent as from Evans, they lost nothing by their "gift," which was thus merely the privilege of entrance to the company. These men were all housekeepers in the Globe[68] except Evans, who probably received his share for having given up his lease, though Keysar claimed this concession was made to keep Evans from forming another company with him.[69] All the housekeepers at the Globe at this time are here represented except the heirs of Pope and Phillips, who in part at least had become common nuisances. Sly was buried August 16, 1608, leaving his share by nuncupative will, dated August 4, 1608, proved August 24, 1608, to Cicely Brown, executrix,[70] who, according to Thomasina Ostler, returned it to Richard Burbadge to be cancelled.[71] Richard Burbadge had then distributed the share equally among all the housekeepers at Blackfriars. The remaining six cancelled their parts of this share, and leased the full seventh share to William Ostler, May 20, 1611, for eighteen and a quarter years from the preceding March 25, at an annual rent of £5 14s. 4d., payable quarterly.[72] The amount was simply his seventh of the full rent, and the term was made to coincide with the expiration of the lease.

But before this, the housekeepers, except Evans and Shakespeare, had been sued by Robert Keysar, February 8, 1610.[73] Since, however, the suit arose from affairs connected with the previous organization at Blackfriars and throws no further light on the organization under consideration, we need not review the case. Thomasina Ostler also sued Heminges[74] in 1615-16 for her husband's share, at the same time she sued for the Globe share; but we do not know with what results. It is from her statement that we get most of our information concerning the early housekeeping affairs at Blackfriars.

[67] Halliwell, *Outlines*, Vol. I, p. 319.
[68] See above, pp. 98-101.
[69] Wallace, *Associates*, pp. 89-90.
[70] Collier, *Memoirs*, p. 157.
[71] Wallace, The London *Times*, October 2 and 4, 1909.
[72] *ibid.*
[73] Wallace, *Associates*, pp. 80-100.
[74] Wallace, The London *Times*, October 2 and 4, 1909.

Our next full record of housekeepers at Blackfriars is in 1635, when Benfield, Swanston, and Pollard inform us that there were then eight shares, owned as follows: Shank 2, C. Burbadge 1, Mrs. Robinson 1, Taylor 1, Lowin 1, Mrs. Cundall 1, Underwood (heirs) 1.[75] On the same authority, we learn that Shank had secured his shares from William Heminges, one in 1633, and one in 1634. The shares had come into the hands of William Heminges at the death of his father, John Heminges, in 1630. One of these shares belonged to John Heminges originally, and the other may well have been the one Thomasina Ostler sued for in 1615-16. Heminges probably won his case as was his usual habit. Cuthbert Burbadge had been among the original housekeepers; Mrs. Robinson held the share of her first husband, Richard Burbadge; Mrs. Cundall controlled the share of her deceased husband. The eighth share had been almost certainly created for Field when he entered the company in 1616, for the actor-housekeepers in both companies were in every recorded case the same. All actor-housekeepers of the Globe had been taken into Blackfriars when the original lease was made; Ostler was taken into both in 1611-12, and Underwood held membership in both at his death.[76] The actor-housekeepers were the same in both houses in 1635, and the three petitioners were asking admission to both in the contention of 1635,[77] their plea being granted. We may be certain then that when Field was admitted to the Globe he was also admitted to Blackfriars, and it is practically certain that the eighth share was created for him at this time in Blackfriars, just as an eighth part of the actors' half had been created for him in the Globe. In our list then, Taylor, Lowin, and Underwood had come into the shares that had originally belonged to Field, Evans, and Shakespeare. If Underwood was admitted to the Globe about 1613, as we saw reason to suppose, he would almost certainly have been admitted to Blackfriars at the same time. In such a case, he could have received only Evans's share; but of course this particular succession is built wholly on plausible suppositions, not on facts. If the general procedure of admitting to both houses held good in

75 Halliwell, *Outlines*, Vol. I, p. 313.
76 Collier, *Memoirs*, p. 230.
77 Halliwell, *Outlines*, Vol. I, pp. 312-13.

every case, as we have shown it certainly did in the majority of cases, and in all recorded cases, Taylor and Lowin did not receive their shares in Blackfriars till they received those in the Globe, probably about 1631. The shares of Shakespeare and Field would probably have come directly or through heirs into the hands of some of the original members, probably into the Heminges and Cundall firm, where they would have remained till the readjustment that admitted Taylor and Lowin. They could not have gone to other actors, since Taylor and Lowin were the most prominent of those not in the housekeeping class and would thus have been admitted first, as they finally were. This same statement also applies to the Globe shares, as we can now see, after having established the custom of admission. Cuthbert Burbadge confirms this conclusion in the case of Blackfriars by giving as a reason for admitting Ostler, Underwood, and Field the fact that they had been bred in royal service, whereas these "new men" had not been.[78] Burbadge is indirectly trying to justify the inclusion of all previous shareholders on some principle or prejudice that would exclude the petitioners. Incidentally his words have been taken to mean that Field, Ostler, and Underwood all came to the company at the same time in 1608. As we have already seen, this was not true. The statement considered alone should not be so interpreted, since Cuthbert Burbadge was evidently naming all shareholders who had been admitted to Blackfriars, and not merely actors admitted to the company at a particular date.

We learn from the same contention of 1635 that since Shank had purchased a share in 1633 with six years to run, the original lease had been renewed or a new lease made for ten years from the expiration of the first lease June 24, 1629. This supposition is confirmed by the fact that the lease had four years to run in 1635.[79] Cuthbert Burbadge gives the reason for this new length of term when he says in 1635, "makeing the leases for twenty-one yeeres hath beene the destruction of ourselves and others, for they dyeing at the expiration of three or four yeeres of their lease, the subsequent

[78] Halliwell, *Outlines*, Vol. I, p. 317.
[79] *ibid.*, pp. 313, 314.

yeeres became dissolved to strangers, as by marrying with their widdowes and the like by their children."[80]

The rent had also been raised, since Shank was to pay £6 5s. yearly for one share, which would make a total rental of £50 for Blackfriars, instead of the original £40.[81] This rental is confirmed by the report of the committee of 1631, which mentions an item of £50 rent yearly. The fourteen years purchase mentioned in this same report does not purport to be the length of the lease but "an indifferent recompense to the said Burbidges"[82] in case the lease was abrogated.

Benfield, Pollard, and Swanston asked in 1635 that one of Shank's shares be divided in thirds among them. This request was granted at the same time and on the same grounds as the Globe shares. The shares then after the readjustment of 1635 were held as follows: Shank 1, Burbadge 1, Mrs. Robinson 1, Mrs. Cundall 1, Underwood (heirs) 1, Taylor 1, Lowin 1, Benfield 1/3, Swanston 1/3, Pollard 1/3. This is our last record of shares in Blackfriars.

It becomes apparent that the chief actors of the Shakespearean company had become housekeepers, first at the Globe and then at Blackfriars, by way of investment, the process having been mediated by their common membership with Richard Burbadge, who with his brother was at the time of inception newly become an owner of theatrical property. Richard and Cuthbert Burbadge were not opposed to the arrangement, since its natural effect would be to attach permanently an excellent company to the theater in which they held chief shares. These chief actors first invoked a joint-tenancy to guarantee the permanence of their part of the enterprise. They next fell upon the device of admitting specially promising members to their body in order to attach them to the company, both

---

[80] Halliwell, *Outlines*, Vol. I, p. 317.

[81] *ibid.*, p. 314.

[82] Collier, *Annals* (1879), Vol. I, p. 478; this fourteen years purchase was the standard value of landed property at the time (Lodge, E., *Illustrations of British History*, Vol. II, p. 454 and note). Shakespeare refers to this standard in *Twelfth Night*, IV. 1. 23-5. "These wise men that give fools money get themselves a good report after fourteen years' purchase," which means, I take it, that if a wise man wants a fool's good report, he simply buys it. See Variorium edition, and the criticism there assembled.

by making their salary better than they could obtain elsewhere, and also by giving them a further personal interest in the enterprise. Personal interest would prevent this device from being overworked, since every admission lessened profits for the individual house-keepers. Thus the ordinary members would try to force member-ship, and the housekeeping members would refuse until forced. The actors would first look on admission to the housekeeping group as a privilege, and then by tradition as a rightful reward.

This attitude, however, never applied under the original lease and joint-tenancy, to the Burbadge half of the Globe. But when Blackfriars was taken over in 1608, it was taken over equally by each of the seven participants, all the former actor-housekeepers at the Globe forming part of the membership, the Burbadges being here on the same footing as the others. This established the custom of admitting an actor to an equal share in Blackfriars at the same time he was admitted an equal sharer in the actors' half of the Globe. Consequently, by 1635 when the prestige of Richard Bur-badge's name no longer cast such a spell, the younger actors could not see why the non-producing Burbadge clan should have any more privileges in the Globe under the new lease than in Blackfriars. Therefore, they asked that the levelling process be applied, as it was. The Burbadges created and lost the suit of 1635 when they entered the Blackfriars arrangement on an equal footing with the others, and permitted the same customs to become the rule for them-selves there as for the actor-housekeepers in the Globe. It was no part of their plan to sow such seed, and they were properly pained and surprised at their harvest. Neither had the actor-housekeepers intended that matters should take such a turn. It was from their own mere pleasure that they had originally conferred membership in their body for merit, such merit to be recognized and determined by themselves. Thus the survivors of the old régime of actors were equally surprised at these new men so soon shot up, who demanded as a right what they had been accustomed to confer as a privilege. The housekeepers had adopted an expedient and it had come to be a principle. To the younger generation of actors, the housekeeping shares had become merely a device belonging to them of right, whereby they might "reape some better fruit of their labours then hitherto they have done."[83]

It is now finally evident that the Shakespearean company had a regular gradation of classes, the housekeeping class being the highest and the goal of every man's ambition. The apprentice looked forward to becoming a member of the company, and the member strove by merit or otherwise to belong to the inner circle of actor-housekeepers, finally regarding it as his right after fitting service to be so admitted. This was one great advantage of the Shakespearean company over others; but even this scheme was very roughly worked out and had many weaknesses. The apprentice could not become a member directly at the end of his apprentice-ship, unless some former member obligingly died or withdrew at the opportune time, for the number of members was fixed. He could of course remain as a hired man, perhaps with some concessions; or join a short-term company, as did Eccleston and Rice, until a vacancy occurred; but the most pronounced merit could not be absolutely sure of preferment at the end of apprenticeship, unless the fates were kind. This same limitation also prevented the free recruiting of desirable actors from other companies. The desirable actor would have to be both in the position and in the notion to accept when the opportunity came. But even once a member, there was no regular rule of procedure whereby one could become an actor-housekeeper, an honor and emolument that few attained. He might marry the privilege as did Richard Robinson, and be barely mentioned by inference as somebody's husband, possibly buy it as Shank wished to do, or have it conferred for merit when the actor might be tempted to seek a new theater, as seems true of Taylor and Lowin. Admission depended chiefly therefore upon the "pull" an individual candidate could exert. But on the whole the system worked, and we have no record that under it the company ever lost a single member to another company.

[83] Halliwell, *Outlines*, Vol. I, p. 312.

CHAPTER IV

THE HIRED MEN OF THE SHAKESPEAREAN COMPANY. THE BOOKKEEPER AND SHAKESPEARE'S MANUSCRIPTS

T HE actual patented company could not carry on its work without help. This help it regularly secured by taking apprentices, or by hiring free men. The hired men are pretty well classed in the protection of December 1624 as "Musitions and other necessary attendantes."[1] But about the same time there grew up a kind of intermediate class, who were hired by the company like regular hired men, yet were entitled to the livery like members. Richard Perkins gives the clue to this class. He had been an original member of the company of Queen Anne in 1603, and had remained with the organization after her death till it finally went to pieces about May 1623.[2] He had received livery May 13, 1619, for the funeral of Queen Anne.[3] When he went to the Shakespearean company at the breakup of his own organization, it is not surprising to find that at some time in the year between Michaelmas 1623 and Michaelmas 1624 he received the regular livery.[4] Perkins was also granted livery with the company March 27, 1625, for the funeral of King James,[5] though he was not a member. The explanation is evident. As a member of the Queen Anne organization, Perkins had been a groom of the chamber entitled to the livery, and in consequence retained that right when he became a hired man of the Shakespearean company. So far as the records go, there had been no case of this kind in the company before 1621. The lists of 1619 and 1621 call for twelve liveries to be delivered to the twelve, named, actor-members only. I know of no other case of a livery ser-

---

[1] Adams, *Herbert*, pp. 74-5.
[2] Murray, Vol. I, pp. 185, 199.
[3] *ibid.*, p. 196.
[4] Stopes, *Jahrbuch*, Vol. XLVI, p. 93; Sullivan, *Court Masques of James I*, pp. 250-1.
[5] Murray, Vol. I, opp. p. 172.

vant before 1621, but in the later shifts in companies the Shakespearean company picked up several such, having six in March
1641.[6] The livery list for the funeral of King James shows two
other such livery servants in 1625. These are James Horn and
George Vernon. Where and how they acquired the right we do not
know. This is the first mention of Vernon with any company; but
Horn had been a principal actor in *The Pilgrim*, acted at court
January 1 and December 29, 1622.[7] He is not mentioned in the
livery list of 1621. He probably came to the Shakespearean company then in the readjustments of 1621-22, and doubtless is named
in the not yet discovered livery list of 1623. Presumably Vernon
came with him at the same time and from the same source, but the
source we do not know.[8]

As we have seen, there were three of these livery servants in 1625.
Perkins soon dropped out, going to Queen Henrietta's men before
May 1626.[9] Horn and Vernon were still on the livery list of 1629,
but there were no additional livery servants. After this list of
1629, we haven't the names of the actors given in the livery lists,
but only the number of actors to whom livery is due. Two was still
the number of livery servants in 1631,[10] but there were three in
1633 and in 1635.[11] This number had jumped to six by 1641,[12] indicating that the Shakespearean company probably acquired several
livery servants in the general breakup and readjustment consequent
upon the plague of 1636-37. We have practically no clue as to who
any of these later livery servants were.

Presumably, these men who had been members of other companies would be a better class of actors than ordinary hired men,
but the scanty records concerning Perkins, Vernon, and Horn in
the Shakespearean company do not show it. Perkins is not connected
with any rôle in the Shakespearean company; Vernon has only two

[6] Stopes, *Jahrbuch*, Vol. XLVI, p. 104.
[7] The dates are as given in Fleay, *Stage*, errata on p. 424, which Murray
overlooked; Murray, Vol. I, pp. 176, 180, except as noted in Adams,
Herbert, p. 49, note 4.
[8] See above, p. 88.
[9] Murray, Vol. I, opp. p. 266.
[10] Stopes, *Jahrbuch*, Vol. XLVI, p. 95.
[11] *ibid.*, pp. 97, 98.
[12] *ibid.*, p. 104.

unimportant mentions; and Horn three, though his part in *The Pilgrim* was sufficiently well done to give him mention among the principal actors. They seem then to have been on a par with the other chief hired men, except in their privileges.

As we have seen, the protection of December 1624 divides the hired men into "Musitions and other necessary attendantes." Their names are given as: "Edward Knight, William Pattrick, William Chambers, Ambrose Byland, Henry Wilson, Jeffery Collins, William Sanders, Nicholas Underhill, Henry Clay, George Vernon, Roberte Pallant, Thomas Tuckfeild, Roberte Clarke, John Rhodes, William Mago, Anthony Knight, and Edward Ashborne, William Carver, Allexander Buklank, William Toyer, William Gascoyne."[13] Of these men, we know that "Harry: Willson" was a musician in *Believe As Ye List* (1631), William Toyer had been a trumpeter in *A Midsummer Night's Dream* (summer 1594), and Robert Pallant, probably the father of this Robert, had been a musician in *The Seven Deadly Sins* (1592). Concerning the others, so far as I know, there is no record as musicians. But Pallant, Patrick, Underhill, Vernon, Tuckfeild, Mago, Ashborne, Rhodes, and Gascoyne were also minor actors. One of the Knights seems to have been book-keeper[14] for the company as well as musician or necessary attendant. It is thus evident that the musicians filled in as actors and other assistants. Hence the protection groups them with the "necessary attendantes" of the company.

There is some evidence, however, to indicate that it was the custom shortly after this for the musicians also to pay the "Master of the Revels an annual fee for a licence to play in the theatre."[15] Herbert is referring to such a document when under date of April 9, 1627, he enters: "For a warrant to the Musitions of the king's company . . . £1."[16] Unfortunately, we have no list of these musicians attached. Whether this licence had also the effect of a protection does not certainly appear. Another protection for eleven men "employed" by the company "and of special use to them" was

[13] Adams, *Herbert*, pp. 74, 75.
[14] Duties of this official will be explained below.
[15] Malone, *Variorum*, Vol. III, p. 112.
[16] Gildersleeve, *Regulation*, p. 70.

granted January 12, 1637.[17] This list names only Patrick of the earlier list, and probably includes him as an actor rather than as a musician. It is thus probable that the company secured protection for the musicians alone, for the attendants alone, or for both together, according to the particular need.

These musicians were a famous organization. Whitelocke in describing the Inns of Court Masque of February 1634, mentions "the Blackefryars Musicke, who were then esteemed the best of common musitians in London."[18] He had some reason, however, to be prejudiced in favor of these musicians because of their flattering use of his Coranto. We know very little more concerning these or other musicians for players. They were paid by the actors;[19] but whether they were paid as an organization or as individuals we do not know, though their varied functions would suggest the latter. *The Actors' Remonstrance*, January 24, 1644, says: "Our Musike that was held so delectable and precious, that they scorned to come to a Taverne under twentie shillings salary for two houres, now wander with their Instruments under their cloaks, I meane such as have any, into all houses of good fellowship, saluting every roome where there is company, with *Will you have any musike Gentlemen*?"[20] The same work speaks of "the very musique betweene each Act"[21] as being worth more than the puppet plays, which were still permitted. We do not know directly to what particular company these statements were supposed to apply; but Blackfriars, Salisbury Court, and the Cockpit are mentioned in the work. The mention of the poets' "annuall stipends and beneficiall second-dayes"[22] would rule out Blackfriars, where the poet did not receive a stipend, and Salisbury Court, where he received the first[23] day as a benefit, so that we have the Cockpit left as the probable

[17] Stopes, *Jahrbuch*, Vol. XLVI, p. 99; Chalmers, *Apology*, p. 512, note, records that in Sir Henry Herbert's Office Book "there are many *tickets* of privilege to the players, and *the dependants on the players*."
[18] Malone, *Variorum*, Vol. III, p. 113.
[19] Halliwell, *Outlines*, Vol. I, p. 313; since musicians are not mentioned in the expenses to the housekeepers at Salisbury Court 1639, it is to be inferred that there also the actors were to pay them.
[20] Ashbee's facsimile, pp. 6-7.
[21] *ibid.*, p. 5.
[22] *ibid.*, p. 7.
[23] See Chap. I.

theater. The fact that the cracking of the boys' voices is enumerated as a main grievance also indicates that the writer was thinking chiefly of Beeston's boys at the Cockpit, where too music would be a chief feature. If the musicians of the Shakespearean company formed a considerable proportion of the twenty-one persons named in the list of 1624, as seems probable, and if they received only the average wage of six shillings each per week, they would very nearly average "twentie shillings salary for two houres" each day. For the Shakespearean company, however, the musicians would seemingly play "betweene each Act," occasionally sing or accompany songs within the act, and probably play, at least at times, before the performance itself began.[24] Besides, many if not most of these musicians also filled unimportant parts as actors in the play itself.[25] Further than this, our present information does not seem to extend.

One of these hired men, however, exercised an extra function that is of considerable importance from our point of view in studying the Shakespearean company. Herbert directs a note October 21, 1633, "to Knight, their book-keeper."[26] Knight had also paid Herbert £2 October 12, 1633, to license Jonson's *Magnetick Lady*.[27] I do not know whether this was Edward or Anthony Knight or even some other Knight. It was evidently Knight's business as bookkeeper to get the plays licensed. Herbert's letter concerning *The Tamer Tamed* gives the clue to Knight's further duties in this connection. "In many things you have saved mee labour; yet wher your judgment or penn fayld you, I have made boulde to use mine. Purge ther parts, as I have the booke. And I hope every hearer and player will thinke that I have done God good servise, and the quality no wronge; who hath no greater enemies than oaths, prophaness, and publique ribaldry, wh[ch] for the future I doe absolutely forbid to bee presented unto mee in any playbooke, as you will answer it at your perill." It thus appears that Knight was accustomed to "correct" the author's manuscript before he carried it to Herbert to be licensed. Herbert then proceeded to "correct" the

---

[24] See Graves, T. S., "The 'Act Time' in Elizabethan Theatres," *Studies in Philology*, Vol. XII, pp. 117-24.
[25] It is to be remembered that one root of players was the minstrels.
[26] Adams, *Herbert*, p. 21.
[27] *ibid.*, p. 34; *Jonson Allusion Book*, p. 177.

manuscript according to his own notions, placing his signature and the date at the end to signify that he had done so.[28] He returned the corrected and licensed manuscript to Knight with instructions to "Purge ther parts"[29] and henceforth to amend both his judgment and his pen. We have no such part written out for any actor in the Shakespearean company, but we have one surviving in the Alleyn Papers.[30] This part is "Written on slips, originally pasted together so as to form a long roll, six inches wide." It has inserted corrections, Mr. Greg thinks by Alleyn, but probably in the light of the above by the bookkeeper, who may, however, have been Alleyn himself. It was thus Knight's business to see that these corrections were made in the parts of the actors. Whether it was also his business to copy those parts for the actors we do not know from direct evidence; but after the Restoration it was the duty of at least one bookkeeper, John Downes, to write out these parts for the actors.[31]

But his duties were not yet done, for the players were "still poring in their papers, and never perfect,"[32] so that the bookkeeper must "Be sure that you hold not your book at too much distance. The actors, poor lapwings, are but pen-feathered; and once out, out for ever."[33] It was the bookkeeper's duty also to prepare the original manuscript for the prompter, who was himself. We know that at the Restoration John Downes for more than forty years was both "Book-keeper and Prompter"[34] at the theater in Lincoln's Inn

---

[28] For another illustration of the system, see Herbert's note to *The Seaman's Honest Wife*, June 27, 1633: "I commande your Bookeper to present me with a fairer Copy hereafter and to leaue out all oathes, prophaness & publick Ribaldry, as he will answer it at his perill" (Boas, F. S., *Shakespeare & the Universities*, pp. 99, 184; Adams, *Herbert*, pp. 34-5; Bullen, *Old English Plays*, Vol. II, p. 432).

[29] This instruction and Herbert's specific statement: "The players ought not to study their parts till I have allowed of the booke" may indicate that the parts had already been copied before the manuscript was sent to the master for licence, but it doesn't seem likely that the players would take so much risk of extra work in embodying the master's corrections.

[30] Greg, *Papers*, p. 155. This part is minutely examined and described by Greg, W. W., *Two Elizabethan Stage Abridgements*. pp. 135 ff. Reference in the plays of the period to these parts is so frequent as to make quotation unnecessary.

[31] *Roscius Anglicanus* (1708 and Knight's reprint, A₂).

[32] *Wily Beguiled*, Prologue.

[33] *Lady Alimony*, Dodsley, Vol. XIV, p. 279.

[34] *Roscius Anglicanus* (1708 and Knights' reprint, A₂).

THE SHAKESPEAREAN COMPANY

Fields. For the Shakespearean company, John Taylor tells us[35] "I my selfe did know one *Thomas Vincent* that was a Book-keeper or prompter at the Globe play-house neere the Banck-end in Maidlane." Thus Vincent was holding the double office at some time after the Globe was built in 1599. Since Taylor's hoary joke itself, to which the sentence above is prologue, involves both Vincent and Singer, the latter of whom disappears from the records in 1603, a literal interpretation would date Taylor's record 1599-1603. At least we may infer by the coupling with Singer that Vincent belonged to early days, and by the time of Taylor's record in 1638 was retired or dead. Our only other record of Vincent is as a musician in *The Seven Deadly Sins*, about March 1592, just as Knight appeared in 1624 in the list of musicians and necessary attendants. It is thus to be inferred that Vincent was probably already bookkeeper by 1592. If Shakespeare did begin as prompter's attendant, then Vincent was doubtless that prompter.[36]

Summer's Last Will affords an amusing illustration of what the practice was elsewhere. Says Summer to the bookkeeper-prompter:

---

[35] *Taylor's Feast*, Spenser Society, 3rd Coll., pp. 70-1.
[36] If Vincent actually "could not endure the sight or scent of a hot Loyne of Veale" as Taylor says, then Shakespeare had a constant example before him of those natural antipathies to which he refers. Certain references in the plays also indicate that for the Shakespearean company the bookkeeper was the prompter as well. A reference in *The Spanish Tragedy* to the bookkeeper may belong to this organization:

> Heere, brother, you shall be the booke-keeper:
> This is the argument of that they shew.
>
> *He giueth him a booke* (IV. 4).

Up to the time of putting on the play, Jeronimo had been the bookkeeper, giving the actors "seuerall abstracts," with instructions how to dress their parts (IV. 1), and taking general oversight of preparations for the performance. Shakespeare alludes to this official as prompter, in *Romeo and Juliet*, I. 4. 7-8.

> Nor no without-book prologue, faintly spoke
> After the prompter, for our entrance.

Again in *Othello*, I. 2. 83-4.

> Were it my cue to fight, I should have known it
> Without a prompter.

The following allusion from *The Maid in the Mill* (Darley's edition, Vol. II, p. 589 a) certainly represents the practice of the Shakespearean company in 1623:

> they are out of their parts sure:
> It may be 'tis the book-holder's fault; I'll go see.

"You might haue writ in the margent of your play-booke, Let there be a fewe rushes laide in the place where *Back-winter* shall tumble, for feare of raying his cloathes: or set downe, Enter *Back-winter*, with his boy bringing a brush after him, to take off the dust if need require. But you will ne're haue any ward-robe wit while you liue. I pray you holde the booke well, we be not *non plus* in the latter end of the play."[37] It is also made evident in the induction to *Cynthia's Revels* that this custom existed for the children at Blackfriars. We hear that the author is not "in the tiring-house, to prompt us aloud, stamp at the book-holder, swear for our properties, curse the poor tireman, rail the music out of tune, and sweat for every venial trespass we commit, as some author would, if he had such fine enghles as we." Such exhibitions of temperament were even then associated with:

> poetry, a kind a' fury,
> A disease runs among scholars.
>
> . . .   .
>
> 'Twill make some stamp and stare, make a strange noise,
> Curse, swear, beat tire-men, and kick players' boys."[38]

That the bookkeeper himself was accustomed on occasion to use strong language is indicated by the following passage: "he would swear like an Elephant, and stamp and stare, (God blesse us,) like a play-house book-keeper when the actors misse their entrance."[39] It seems fairly certain then from these instances that the book-keeper was regularly the prompter,[40] and took his place in the tiring-house along with the sweating poet[41] and the long-suffering tireman.

---

[37] McKerrow, *Nashe*, Vol. III, p. 290.
[38] *Your Five Gallants* (Bullen, A. H., *The Works of Thomas Middleton*, Vol. III, p. 154).
[39] *Every Woman in her Humour*, IV. 1. (Bullen, *Old Plays*, Vol. IV, p. 354).
[40] Even as early as the miracle plays some one was regularly paid for "beryng of the boke" (Chambers, E. K., *The Mediaeval Stage*, Vol. II, p. 140).
[41] cf. "The poet sits within," Epilogue to *The Lover's Progress*. Also: "There is no poet acquainted with more shakings and quakings, towards the latter end of his new play, (when he's in that case that he stands peeping betwixt the curtains, so fearfully that a bottle of ale cannot be open'd, but he thinks somebody hisses) than I am at this instant" (*The Woman Hater*, II. 1.; Darley, Vol. II, p. 434 a).

All the stages in the preparation of a manuscript are most clearly shown in that of *Believe As Ye List* (1631). Here the prompter's notes are not at all intended to give the part taken by each actor. They are simply jottings to aid the prompter's memory. Thus he makes notes concerning properties needed and who is responsible for putting them in place. We find "Ent: Rowland wth the Records" (13r), "Ent: R: Baxt: wth swords" (26r), "Ent: Rowland wth swords" (26r). On the verso of page 29, the prompter has entered the various small properties, such as letters, coins, etc., that would be needed by the principal actors at certain places, these items being arranged by act and scene. It is these properties which identify most of the major actors in the play, since the prompter almost never makes any note concerning their entrance unless it is necessary to have someone prepare for it, as "Gascoine: & Hubert below: ready to open the Trap doore for Mr Taylor" (18v). If he makes a reference to an actor, it is likely to be to the character rather than to the performer, as "Antiochus ready; vnder the stage" (19r). Under ordinary circumstances the major actor would take care of his own entrances and exits. If he bungled, the prompter knew what part he was taking, without having to jot his name on the manuscript. But for the host of minor characters he could not trust his memory. Consequently, wherever Massinger has called for attendants, the prompter has sometimes stricken out the indefinite word and inserted the names of those who are to take the parts. At other times, he merely inserts the name under the part to be taken. Thus besides the principal performers of II. 2. Massinger called for "others." The prompter struck this word out so heavily that it is barely decipherable and added "Rowland: Wm Mago: Nick:" (10r). Not understanding what took place, previous compilers of the list of actors for this play have supposed that Rowland took the part of Amilcar, Mago that of Hanno or Asdrubal, and Nick that of Asdrubal or Carthalo.[42] The prompter did not always need to make note of these attendants, since some principal actor might be responsible for his particular satellites. Thus we hear only of three merchants until Berecinthius enters IV. 3. with only one mer-

[42] Murray, Vol. I, opp. p. 172; Fleay, *Stage*, p. 324.

chant, where the prompter inserts "& J: Hony:" (21v). When the second and third merchants enter in V. 1., the prompter inserts "Wm Pen: Curt:" (23r), and again he does the same thing later (27r). The latter entries show that Pen and Greville were the second and third merchants, but are worth very little as showing which was which. The prompter sometimes changed the author's instructions in order to distribute his attendants more expediently. Thus Massinger in III. 2. (15v) originally brought in Demetrius with Flaminius and Titus in order to send him directly out on an errand; but the prompter brings him in with the previous group (15r) and leaves him at their exit to perform the errand of the entering two. The prompter was also responsible for getting music at its proper place as is shown by the entry "Harry: Willson: & Boy ready for the song at ye Arras:" (20r). There are several other entries, but these illustrate the typical classes. It appears, therefore, that the prompter was responsible for about everything, but made jottings on the manuscript only to help his memory when there might be occasion. These jottings he made in a very heavy ink, and sometimes heavily retraced Massinger's lighter writing in order to make it clearer, as in the heading of V. 1. (23r). It follows from the nature of them that these jottings give us a clue to major actors only by lucky accident.

This fact is well illustrated by *Barnavelt* (1619), where no principal actor is named. But since in this play a different prompter is at work, as is shown by the handwriting,[43] we had better sum up what we know of the succession of these officials. The prompter of *Believe As Ye List* had also prepared a copy of *The Honest Man's Fortune* which was relicensed by Herbert "8 Februa. 1624," for the Shakespearean company.[44] We also have a presentation copy of *Bonduca* in his handwriting. To *The Honest Man's Fortune*, he signs himself "John."[45] Thus we are certain that "John" wrote the prompter's jottings from February 8, 1625, to May 7, 1631.

Who then was "John"? Since we have very full lists of actors and attendants in this period 1625-31, it is highly probable that he

[43] Greg, W. W., *The Library*, series 4, Vol. VI, p. 154.
[44] Chambers, *Eliz. Stage*, Vol. III, p. 227.
[45] Sisson, C. J., *The Review of English Studies*, Vol. I, p. 422.

is to be found among them. Of the patented members, John Heminges died before 1631, and John Rice withdrew, leaving only John Lowin and John Shank. But since both of these were active as actors, and were alive and still active with the company after Knight appears to succeed "John" by 1633, we may be certain that neither is bookkeeper John. John Thompson and John Honyman were both active apprentices, and consequently to be ruled out. Job or John Bacon appears in *Love's Pilgrimage* which can be shown to have been printed from the copy relicensed by Herbert September 16, 1635.[46] Bacon is also mentioned in the protection of January 12, 1637,[47] but not in that of December 1624. Thus Bacon also is ruled out. The only remaining candidate is John Rhodes, who appears along with the Knights in the protection of December 1624. Now we are told that Thomas Betterton had been bound "Apprentice to one Mr. *Rhodes* a Bookseller, at the Bible at *Charing-Cross*," this "*Rhodes* having formerly been *Wardrobe* Keeper to the King's Company of *Comedians* in the *Black-Fryars*."[48] Since, as we have seen and shall see, it was the business of the prompter also to look after the wardrobe, this Rhodes had evidently been prompter. The Rhodes in question was John Rhodes,[49] an important figure in the reestablishment of the stage. Now John Rhodes was a bookseller in London in 1628, and 1641.[50] It seems clear then that John Rhodes of Restoration fame is John Rhodes of the Shakespearean company 1625-31. But, as we have seen, Knight appears as prompter October 12, 1633, indicating, it seems, that between May 7, 1631, and October 12, 1633, Rhodes had been replaced by Knight. Probably Knight's newness at the task was in part the reason Herbert lays the law down so minutely to him in October 1633.

---

[46] Adams, *Herbert*, p. 36.
[47] Stopes, *Jahrbuch*, Vol. XLVI, p. 99; Adams, *Herbert*, pp. 74-5.
[48] Gildon, C., *The Life of Mr. Thomas Betterton*, p. 5.
[49] *The Life and Times of that Excellent and Renowned Actor Thomas Betterton* (1888), pp. 7, 8, 10, 18, 19, 32. This author, Lowe, says that Rhodes "was at one time wardrobe-keeper and prompter to the theatre in Blackfriars"; but I have failed to find any early writer who describes him as a prompter.
[50] McKerrow, *Dictionary*, p. 227; Johnson, A. H., *The History of the Worshipful Company of Drapers*, Vol. IV, p. 155. Rhodes had a total of seven apprentices, two of whom presumably were Betterton and Kynaston, on whom these records should also throw considerable light.

It should be noted in passing that this situation clears up for us the channel through which some Shakespearean stage traditions may have passed to Thomas Betterton. Since Rhodes was not closely connected with the company during Shakespeare's lifetime, nor for several years after, his information is not so direct as that of William Beeston; but both men should be good authorities.

As we have seen, a different writer made the prompter's jottings upon *Barnavelt*, about August 1619. We do not know directly who this was, nor when he was succeeded by Rhodes, though a certain amount of suspicion attaches to Ralph Crane, who recorded in 1621:

> And some imployment hath my vsefull *Pen*,
> Had 'mongst those ciuill *well-deseruing Men*,
> That grace the *Stage* with *honour* and *delight*,
> Of whose true *honesties* I much could write
> But will compris't (as in a Caske of Gold)
> Vnder the *Kingly-seruice* they doe hold.[51]

The fact that Crane had used his pen for the company does not mean necessarily, however, that he had been bookkeeper or prompter. A comparison of *Barnavelt* with the known surviving specimens of Crane's work would probably settle the question. If he was not the prompter, then we have a case of a professional scribe called in on occasion as copyist. The fact that Crane made a transcript November 27, 1625, in Rhodes's régime, of the company's play of *The Humorous Lieutenant* for Sir Kenelm Digby would probably indicate that Crane was occasional scribe rather than regular prompter.

I do not know whether the bookkeeper of *Barnavelt* had come to office as early as the time of *The Second Maiden's Tragedy*, licensed October 31, 1611,[52] since Miss Frijlinck in her edition of the former play does not give a facsimile of the bookkeeper's notes. The next and earliest bookkeeper of whom we have trace in the company is Thomas Vincent, who was with the company by 1592,

[51] Graves, T. S., "Ralph Crane and the King's Players," *Studies in Philology*, Vol. XXI, p. 364. Wilson, F. P., "Ralph Crane, 'Scrivener to the King's Players,'" *The Library*, n. s., Vol. VII, pp. 203-5, 212, has now shown that Crane was only a copyist, not a bookkeeper.

[52] Greg, W. W., Malone Soc. *Reprints*, p. v.

and if John Taylor is accurate in his statement, remained at least till after the Globe was built in 1599.

If this reconstruction of successions is correct, then we have no known manuscript of Knight's writing or annotating, though we have three for John Rhodes, whose habits have been described in the case of *Believe As Ye List*. Since *The Honest Man's Fortune* has not been reproduced or minutely described, I must omit consideration of it.

In *Barnavelt* the bookkeeper attends to exactly the same classes of chores as in *Believe As Ye List*, but his habits differ slightly. The bookkeeper of *Believe As Ye List* insisted on getting most of his annotations on the left margin of the page, while the bookkeeper of *Barnavelt* prefers the right margin for his jottings. The bookkeeper of *Believe As Ye List* usually strikes out the indefinite directions for attendants when he substitutes names of actors, while the book-keeper of *Barnavelt* lets them stand. These and other characteristic small habits also indicate that the bookkeeper of *Believe As Ye List* was not in office in 1619, when *Barnavelt* was prepared for acting. This bookkeeper of the time of *Barnavelt* is not quite such a marti-net as Rhodes. Thus his annotations are not quite so copious and precise; nor does he make at the end of his manuscript a catalog of the needed properties, etc. Still he makes his notes for the same purposes as did Rhodes. He too annotates for properties; "Table: Bell" (1184, 1216), "Taper: pen & inke Table" (1610-11), "Son abed" (1656), etc.; jots the names of minor actors under the host of small parts, as

> "—Enter 2 Captaines"
> "Io: R: migh."

(146-7); and sees that the music and other incidentals chime in at the proper time, as "Hornes" (1727), "Daunce" (2156). There are also a few reassignments in *Barnavelt*, Miss Frijlinck thinks by the original scribe (XIV), though she is not positive. In a few cases, however, she seems positive that the change is due to the book-keeper, as at lines 395, 905, 3,000. Surely too the cutting out of the two ministers Taurinas and Utenbogart, and reassigning their lines to Hogerbeets, thereby causing a snarl in the play,[53] is not due to

[53] Frijlinck, *Barnavelt*, pp. 7-8, 85.

the author, but to the bookkeeper, who is trying to economize on minor actors. At any rate, it is evident that the bookkeeper also makes minor reassignments in *Barnavelt* as he had done in *Believe As Ye List*. Thus the bookkeeper in *Barnavelt* follows the same principles as did Rhodes.

The manuscript of *The Second Maiden's Tragedy* (1611) required practically no such annotation,[54] since its characters are few and easily kept track of, so that the prompter needed only to make notes of the various flourishes, to put Goffe's name to an inserted speech (1723-24), and to indicate that Richard Robinson was to be the ghost of the character he had represented alive, while somebody or something else was to be her dead body (1928-9).

Still another of these surviving official prompt copies may have belonged to the Shakespearean company in its early days, that of *Sir Thomas More*. In this play, opposite the entry of a messenger there is a jotting of the performer's name, T. Goodal. Evidently here is the work of the bookkeeper preparing the manuscript for presentation. Now Mr. Greg has shown[55] that this entry is probably written by what he calls hand C, which corrects the work of all other hands except the few lines of hand A, and the still fewer lines of hand E. Mr. Greg also shows that C is pretty certainly a copyist and not an original author. "He revises the stage directions throughout, both in the original text and in the additions, and seems responsible (as is most clearly shown in the case of [addition] VI) for fitting the latter into their places. As B seems to have had the literary, so C appears to have had the dramatic, side of the revision under his charge. He can patch up a line or two when needed, and edits D, a careless writer, freely, but I do not think that there is anything to suggest that he was an independent author."[56] Certainly this is the bookkeeper, and certainly Mr. Greg is right in his surmise that this man is no author.

But this play is an extremely interesting illustration of what might happen at any time. For in view of the routine through

[54] Greg, W. W., *The Second Maiden's Tragedy* (The Malone Soc. Reprints).

[55] Greg, W. W., *The Book of Sir Thomas More* (The Malone Soc. Reprints), p. 89.

[56] *ibid.*, p. XVIII.

which a manuscript went, we can pretty well reconstruct the history of this one. The bookkeeper sent the fair form, in handwriting S, to Tilney for his approval; but Tilney disapproved highly of so much that the poets had to be set to work preparing patches, hastily inserted. It then became the duty of the unfortunate bookkeeper to edit the whole hashed manuscript for performance, which he did. After editing it sufficiently to be able to make head and tail of it, he would then proceed to copy out the actors' parts, omitting the things Tilney had condemned, and inserting the additions by the poets, all in their proper places.[57] Thus the fact that the parts Tilney objects to have not been cut from the present surviving manuscript is in itself no sign either that these parts were performed contrary to order or that the whole play was dropped without presentation. The known routine shows that the play had passed through Tilney's hands before the bookkeeper proceeded to cast it. With Tilney's objections before him, certainly the bookkeeper would not have gone to the trouble of casting the play unless it was still the intention to perform it. There is thus every reason to believe that the play was performed.

This unravelling of the case also has some bearing on the date of the manuscript. It seems not to have been written before 1588, being based on a work of that year,[58] which would also give some slight probability that it does not date long after that year. Since Goodal is mentioned in a section written by C, who edits the whole manuscript, certainly he was cast to take part in the present form of the play. Now we have only three other records of Goodal as an actor. The first connects him with Lord Berkeley's players July 11, 1581.[59] The second is in the plot of *The Seven Deadly Sins*, March 1592, where Goodal was Lucius, Phronesius, Messenger, and a Lord.[60] The third is a record of his signing a bond with John Alleyn and Robert Lee, May 18, 1593.[61] But Goodal was still alive,

[57] It is just possible that the bookkeeper may have had the manuscript recopied, and submitted the corrected form to Tilney for approval, as was later done with Massinger's *Believe As Ye List*.
[58] *The Library*, series 4, Vol. IV, pp. 48-9.
[59] Greg, *Sir Thomas More*, pp. XIX-XX; Chambers, *Eliz. Stage*, Vol. IV, p. 282.
[60] Murray, Vol. I, p. 79.
[61] Warner, *Catalogue*, p. 127. Since, as this record shows, Goodal was

and still "a Player" so late as November 23, 1599.[62] It is impossible for him at this period to have been attached to the Admiral's Men, since so important a handy man as *The Seven Deadly Sins* and *More* show him to have been would certainly have been mentioned frequently in the numerous surviving plots for that company. Thus *More* could not have belonged to the Admiral's in the late nineties of the sixteenth century, nor the first years of the seventeenth. Since all other actors in *The Seven Deadly Sins* whose affiliation is known were attached to the Shakespearean company, we may be certain that Goodal was so attached at least from March 1592, probably through November 1599, and certainly not to the Admiral's. But since the bookkeeper who prepared *More* belonged, at least by 1598, to the Admiral's organization,[63] the play must either have been prepared in the period of cooperation, 1590-94, or for the Shakespearean company alone before 1598. In either case, Shakespeare's connection with the play becomes almost a certainty, since it is hardly conceivable that such a hasty muster of the available dramatists of the company or companies could have omitted the chief dramatist of the dominant company, unless he happened to be absent or incapacitated. It is highly probable that the play belongs to the period of cooperation 1590-94. If it was acted, as we have reason to believe it was, it probably belongs before Henslowe's accounts begin in February 1592, or it should have appeared in them. We would thus date it 1590-92. Possibly then this play of *More*

a mercer, a search of the excellently preserved records of the Drapers' Company should yield further information concerning him. I do not find any reference to him in Johnson, A. H., *The History of the Worshipful Company of Drapers*. But in a list of August 1641 appears "Goodale John in Woodstreete" as a "Musitioner," among the yeomanry of the company who were judged not able to pay £3 poll tax (*op. cit.*, Vol. IV, p. 150). Pretty certainly this is the son of Thomas, who is following in father's footsteps. Since Wood Street was the home of Heminges, the natural inference would be that Thomas Goodal was a musician with the Shakespearean company, through the Heminges influence. Thomas Goodal, the player, had been in the parish of St. Botolph, Aldgate, 1594-99, where two of his children were born and buried (*Publications of the Modern Language Association*, Vol. XLI, p. 100). Perhaps, then, his later records are to be found near Wood Street. At any rate, the company and parish records should clear up Goodal's life.

[62] *Publications of the Modern Language Association*, Vol. XLI, p. 100.

[63] Pollard, A. W., and others. *Shakespeare's Hand in The Play of Sir Thomas More*, pp. 19, 55-6.

gives us a bookkeeper's practice in the early days of the Shakespearean company. This bookkeeper, however, as has been said, belonged, at least eventually, to Alleyn's organization, and probably never to the Shakespearean company.[64] It is not likely then that he is Thomas Vincent.

In all these manuscripts, the notes are made on the copy which was licensed or refused licence by the Master of the Revels. Since this copy would presumably remain in the hands of the bookkeeper, the inference is that he was also the prompter and was responsible as we have seen above. This piece of evidence, fortified with the allusions quoted, and coupled with the fact that in the only known instances, those of Vincent and Downes, the bookkeeper was also the prompter, makes it certain that the two functions were regularly combined, as we also saw reason to infer in the case of Rhodes.

The evidence just adduced and a contemporary allusion show that at least in some cases the bookkeeper-prompter was also "Stagekeeper." In the induction to the second part of *The Return from*

---

[64] Pollard, A. W., and others. *Shakespeare's Hand in The Play of Sir Thomas More*, pp. 19, 55-6. There are, however, various other inconclusive indications of a later date for *More*, to which we may add yet another. In the play (1. 1151), there is a puzzling reference to "Mason among the Kings players." Chambers (*Eliz. Stage*, Vol. IV, p. 33) considers that this reference "does not prove a Jacobean date, as Henry VIII had players. No actor of the name in either reign is known, although an Alexander Mason was marshal of the royal minstrels in 1494." But so too was a Thomas Mason one of King James's musicians January 1, 1606, presenting as a New Year's gift "one payre of perfumed playne gloves," and receiving in return five ounces of gilt plate (Nichols, *Progresses of James* I [1828], Vol. I, p. 598). Mason is not named in any of the lists given by Nichols for Queen Elizabeth, the last of which is for January 1, 1600 (*Progresses of Elizabeth* [1823], Vol. III, pp. 457-8, 465-6). He is mentioned, however, December 20, 1625, among King Charles's "Musicians for the Hautboys and Sackbuts," and probably again in a list April 17, 1641, under "Musicians for wind-instruments," though the name is there given as John Mason (Collier, *History*, [1879], Vol. I, p. 441, note 1; Vol. II, p. 35, note). If the allusion is to this Mason, Munday's draft of *More*, in which the allusion occurs, dates after the accession of King James in 1603. Since the play was censored by Tilney, it hardly dates after 1607. We would then be safe in dating the allusion and Munday's draft 1603-07. Since Mason joined the musicians between January 1, 1600, and January 1, 1606, accurate determination of the time of his coming might further limit the date.

The chief objection to the identification is that the reference occurs in a speech comparing Sir Thomas More's impromptu acting with the valuable services of Mason, implying that Mason was the King's player-actor and not his player-musician. On the whole, it appears more likely that Mason was some still remembered performer of the time of Henry VIII.

Parnassus the boy-prologue forgets his part, whereupon the stage-keeper says "A pox on't this booke hath it not in it," and picks up the youngster under his arm, with whom he goes quarrelling off.[65] In this case at least, the bookkeeper-prompter is represented as stage-keeper also. It is in this double or triple capacity that the stage-keeper is represented as entirely suppressing the prologue to the first part of *The Return from Parnassus.* The induction to the second part of *The Return* further defines the duty of the stage-keeper when it records that "The Pilgrimage to *Pernassus,* and the returne from *Pernassus* haue stood the honest *Stagekeepers* in many a Crownes expence for linckes and vizards."[66] As we have already seen from our study of the manuscript jottings, it was the business of the bookkeeper-prompter to see that these various stage properties were in place. Another of his duties is given when in *Lady Alimony,* Siparius, "book-holder to my revels," is questioned in his own dialect "Be your stage-curtains artificially drawn, and so covertly shrouded as the squint-eyed groundling[s] may not peep into your discovery?"[67] It seems then that this person was a kind of *Johannes factotum,* whose business it was to see that everything was ready and in place for the play. It was certainly not an unimportant position.

The functions of this ubiquitous official, as well as a few of his typical trials and tribulations, may be found humorously set forth in the person and problems of Quince in *A Midsummer Night's Dream.* When the farce opens, Quince has presumably attended to all the preliminaries of licence, etc.; and is ready to "fit" his play. "First, good Peter Quince, say what the play treats on; then read the names of the actors, and so grow to a point." Accordingly, Quince proceeds to give a general idea of the play, names the assignment of parts to actors—not of course without considerable absurd objection and suggestion on the part of the said actors,—gives out the written parts at once for the benefit of the "slow of study," makes appointment for rehearsal, and then proceeds to "draw a bill of properties, such as our play wants," embodying we

[65] Macray, W. D., *The Pilgrimage to Parnassus,* etc., p. 77.
[66] *ibid.,* p. 78.
[67] Hazlitt, W. C., *A Select Collection of Old English Plays* (1875), Vol. XIV, p. 278.

may presume the numerous suggestions the various members of his company have made as to their choice of beards, masks, etc. At the rehearsal, Quince receives a shower of suggestions from the actors, such as how to prevent the ladies from being frightened at Pyramus's death, or at that fearful wild-fowl your lion, the favored solution being to put the explanation in a prologue, to be procured by Quince. Quince is also puzzled as to how to represent moonshine and wall, but Bottom of the fertile suggestion solves those problems; and the rehearsal is ready to begin, with Quince holding the book, directing entrances and exits, attempting to correct ludicrous errors on the part of his actors—errors that creep out in the finished product nevertheless,—and wearing his honest patience out till Bottom breaks up the show by getting translated. It is the incorrigible Bottom who gives the actors final instructions for Quince. "Get your apparel together, good strings to your beards, new ribbons to your pumps; meet presently at the palace; every man look o'er his part; for the short and long is, our play is preferred. In any case, let Thisby have clean linen; and let not him that plays the lion pare his nails, for they shall hang out for the lion's claws. And, most dear actors, eat no onions nor garlic, for we are to utter sweet breath." And so they come to the performance of their play, where "The best in this kind are but shadows, and the worst are no worse, if imagination amend them." In this farce, Quince's triple duty as bookkeeper, prompter, and stage-keeper is clearly indicated. The skit becomes even more significant when we remember that, if tradition is correct, Shakespeare's first connection with the company had been as prompter's boy[68] or attendant. Quite

[68] We have seen that Thomas Vincent, a hireling musician, was the early prompter. He would thus receive his orders from some member. Daborne's request: "I pray Sr let yr boy giv order this night to the stage-keepr, to set up bills agst munday for Eastward hoe, & one wenasday, the New play" (Malone, *Variorum*, Vol. XXI, p. 401) shows that at the Hope it was the bookkeeper's duty to schedule the play. The induction to *Lady Alimony* also indicates that it was the bookkeeper's duty to have the bills posted, but is not clear as to whether he scheduled the plays. Now in the Shakespearean company the ill-advised performance of *Richard II* in 1601, shows that it was at that time the duty of Augustine Phillips to schedule plays. Since Phillips was an original member, while only two former members had dropped out before this time, it is probable that Phillips had held this function from the beginning. Phillips was thus probably Shakespeare's chief's chief.

likely this is the point to Greene's gibe at Shakespeare as an absolute *Johannes factotum*. Doubtless then in this skit Shakespeare knew whereof he spoke.[69]

These customs of this triune official explain why so many of the old printed plays have the names of minor actors inserted with, or instead of, the names of the parts they were to take. For the first folio of Shakespeare's plays, in *3 Henry VI*, instead of the Keepers of the old *True Tragedy* we have "Enter Sinklo, and Humfrey." Also "Gabriel" was a messenger in the same play. When the rustic players in *A Midsummer Night's Dream* were to present their play before their sovereign, they were preceded by Toyer with a trumpet.[70] Kemp, a major actor in a minor rôle, was Peter in *Romeo and Juliet*.[71] He was also Dogberry in *Much Ado*, in which play Cowley was Verges, Jack Wilson as Balthasar sang "Sigh no more, Ladies,"[72] and "Andrew" appeared as a member of the watch. Sinklo or Sinkler appears as "A Player" in the induction to *The Taming of the Shrew*,[73] in which "Andrew" again appears. "Nicke" also appears as a messenger in this play. Harvey and Russel took part in *1 Henry IV*.[74] Russel's name is also substituted for Bardolph in the quarto of *2 Henry IV*; Sinklo appears in the same play. G. and E., Goffe and Eccleston, also appear in *All's Well*. At least these eight plays then in the first folio derive from the official licensed copies.[75]

It follows that these marked editions certainly furnish the authentic texts, the amount of error depending only on the printer's accuracy. None of the manuscripts or customs as analyzed above gives support to the idea that these playhouse copies "often embodied the ill-conditioned interpolations and alterations of actors

[69] Since Shakespeare became a member of the company about the time this play was put on, it may be regarded as his graduating exercise, in which with gentle satire he pays his respects to his former position.

[70] This actor does not appear in the quartos of the play.

[71] Kemp had also appeared in the second quarto.

[72] Since Wilson does not appear in the quarto, while the others do, evidently both the quarto and the folio used the official manuscript.

[73] The "San." of the induction of the old *Taming of a Shrew* is clearly Sander or Sanders, Ferando's man; and there is nothing to suggest that this is an actor's name (Chambers, *Eliz. Stage*, Vol. II, p. 311).

[74] Harvey and Russel had also appeared in the quartos.

[75] Fleay (*Drama*, Vol. II, p. 194) points out that *Midsummer Night's Dream* and *2 Henry IV* are also shown by their court references to be from the official manuscripts.

and theatrical managers."[76] The evidence for the official manuscripts seems to be that only the authors or the Master of the Revels, with occasional help from the bookkeeper beforehand, made such corrections. If cutting or alteration was made by others, it was probably on the parts supplied to actors but not on the official manuscript itself.[77] It has been supposed that some of the manuscripts used for the folio of 1623 were not the official manuscripts —some of which may have perished with the first Globe,—but more or less imperfect copies and restorations. That all these original manuscripts did not perish is shown by the fact that at least *3 Henry VI*, *Midsummer Night's Dream*, *Taming of the Shrew*, *Much Ado*, and *All's Well* survived. In fact, I know of no positive evidence to show that a single original copy perished with the Globe. It is merely a probable but not a necessary supposition that these official copies were kept in the playhouse itself.[78] If they were, there is no more evidence that they were kept at the Globe than at Blackfriars. In fact, the latter would be far the better and safer place of storage. Even if they were in the Globe, the tiring-house door was handy, and it is not necessary to suppose that the man

[76] Craig, W. J., Preface to *The Oxford Shakespeare*. So far as I can find, this theory was started by Pope and still survives. That it was purely an ignorant assumption on Pope's part without real basis in fact anyone may see by checking Pope's knowledge, not only of Elizabethan acting conditions but even of those of his own times.

[77] Moseley says plainly that the official manuscripts of Beaumont and Fletcher were not cut, though the actors did in their acting cut and change scenes. Jonson implies the same when he publishes *Every Man Out of his Humor*, "As it was first composed by the author B. I. Containing more than hath been Publickely Spoken or Acted." See below, pp. 142-3.

[78] The companies seem usually to have kept their theatrical supplies, including plays, in the tiring house. The Palsgrave company did in December 1621, and lost them at the burning of the Fortune (Birch, *Court of James First*, Vol. II, p. 280). The apprentices destroyed apparel and playbooks belonging to the Queen's men at the Cockpit in March 1617 (Birch. *Court of James First*, Vol. I, p. 464; Vol. II, p. 3). Incidentally, had the actors at the Globe lost their playbooks, it would surely have been mentioned as in these other cases. Henslowe's inventories show that plays and apparel were kept in the tiring house at the Rose (Greg, *Papers*, p. 116). But it is to be noticed that at the Fortune the fire occurred at night; at the Cockpit the damage was done by a mob. In the two hours it took the building to burn, a well disciplined company of some thirty-odd men, as was that at the Globe, should have been able to remove most of their possessions through their private door to safety.

who saved his trousers "by the benefit of a provident wit" and bottled ale was the only man there who kept at least a cool head. The building seems to have taken its time about burning down, and it stands to reason that when Burbadge, and stuttering Heminges, and the Fool, and Henry Cundall ran out, they probably took along a few manuscripts and other theatrical supplies. Until there is positive evidence that some manuscript perished, we are not justified in making Heminges and Cundall liars or even over-zealous press agents when they profess to give the plays "absolutely in their parts as he conceived them," they having "scarse received from him a blot in his papers." Certainly in the five plays already mentioned their profession is vindicated, whatever the truth may be about the blots. At least one other manuscript probably survived, that of *Titus Andronicus*, since a scene is added in the folio that does not occur in any of its quartos. Also in the case of *1 Henry IV*, *2 Henry IV*, and *Romeo and Juliet*, the editors either followed the official manuscript or used a quarto which they knew had done so.

We happen to know that one manuscript was "missinge" about the time the folio was published. Herbert records "For the king's players. An olde playe called *Winter's Tale*, formerly allowed of by Sir George Bucke, and likewyse by mee on Mr. Hemmings his worde that there was nothing profane added or reformed, thogh the allowed booke was missinge; and therefore I returned it without a fee, this 19 of August, 1623."[79] Almost certainly the printers of the 1623 folio were the cause for the "missinge" official manuscript August 19, 1623,[80] and the assumption that it had been burned in 1613 is wholly gratuitous, with not a single bit of evidence, so far as I can find, to support it. Probably then this entry concerning *The Winter's Tale* really shows that this play too was published from the official manuscript.

Indeed we have now almost readmitted Heminges and Cundall to honest society. Says a recent summary of Mr. Pollard's work: "The twenty plays which appeared in print for the first time in the

---

[79] Malone, *Variorum*, Vol. III, p. 229; Adams, *Herbert*, p. 25, also note 2: *Shakespere All. Book*, Vol. I, p. 321.
[80] Lee, *Shakespeare*, p. 556.

First Folio[81] were taken in all probability directly from copies in the possession of Shakespeare's company. Their texts are, upon the whole, excellent. In the case of the sixteen other plays the editors substituted for eight of the plays already in print in quartos [*Richard III, Henry V, 2 Henry IV, Merry Wives, Hamlet, Lear, Troilus and Cressida, Othello*],[82] independent texts from better manuscripts. This act must have involved considerable expense and difficulty [I don't see how], and deserves the highest praise. Five of the printed quartos [*Titus Andronicus, Richard II, 1 Henry IV, Much Ado, Midsummer Night's Dream*] were used with additions and corrections. In the case of *Titus Andronicus* a whole scene was added. In three cases only [*Romeo and Juliet, Love's Labor's Lost, Merchant of Venice*] of the sixteen plays already printed did the editors follow a quarto text without correcting it from a later theatrical copy."[83]

In effect then we admit that in all cases but three Heminges and Cundall used some manuscript for each play in the folio, though we still claim that in five other cases they really based their text on a previous quarto, checking it by some manuscript. If so, they made their task just as hard as was possible. The easiest and most natural way for them would have been simply to turn this more authentic manuscript over to the printer and have done with it. Thus this supposition does great credit to their zeal but little to their ingenuity. In view of the fact that *Much Ado* uses directly the official version both in quarto and folio, I have not yet been able to find any certain evidence that the folio also made use of the quarto, establishing some presumption that the same situation exists in at least some of the remaining cases. A thorough study of these plays in the light of existing practice when they were composed would probably vindicate Heminges and Cundall completely. Certainly

---

[81] If, as I hope to show in later publication, the First and Second *Contentions* are only *2* and *3 Henry VI* printed from damaged manuscript, these plays should also be included here, giving us eighteen of the thirty-six plays in the first folio printed for the first time. Then it would follow that of the previously published eighteen, the folio prints ten from independent manuscripts, five with corrections from manuscript, and three without change.

[82] Pollard, A. W., *Shakespeare Folios and Quartos*, pp. 14-63, 109-10, 121.

[83] Mac Cracken, H. N., Pierce, F. E., and W. H. Durham, *An Introduction to Shakespeare*, pp. 123-4.

a minute study of all corrections on surviving manuscripts of the company should be made to ascertain their source, extent, and kind, in order that we may know the state in which Shakespeare's manuscripts went to the printer.[84]

For it is highly probable that these manuscripts were Shakespeare's own final form. The preface to the folio practically says so. Professor Boas shows that there are about thirty manuscript plays surviving from before the closing of the theaters, having in general the usual characteristics of being the autograph, licensed, prompt copies.[85] The only play surviving in manuscript on which Shakespeare is supposed to have collaborated, *Sir Thomas More*, is said by some experts to contain Shakespeare's own writing in the part he is supposed to have revised.[86] The hack-writers of Henslowe were also accustomed to hand in their plays only in fair form, presumably of their own writing. Judging from some surviving samples of the writing of several chief playwrights, I am willing to admit that the Master of the Revels sometimes earned his fee for reading their productions. Indeed, it may at times have been necessary to call in the professional scribe before submitting the author's work. Robert Greene's printer averred that he was obliged to have Greene's manuscript transcribed before offering it for licence: "it was il written, as sometimes Greenes hand was none of the best; licensd it must be ere it could bee printed, which could never be if it might not be read."[87] But if Shakespeare's official manuscripts suffered no more at the hands of the correctors, including Shakespeare himself, than most of the surviving manuscripts of others, Heminges and Cundall are reasonably correct in saying that they "scarse received from him a blot in his papers." This state-

---

[84] It is thus desirable to get as accurate information as possible on the personalities and practices of Tilney and Vincent, some touches from whose pens certainly survive in Shakespeare's plays. It may also be noted that there is no evidence whatever for three playhouse copies of each play as postulated by Fleay, F. G., *A Chronicle History of the Life and Work of William Shakespeare*, pp. 192-3.

[85] Boas, F. S., *Shakespeare & the Universities*, pp. 10 ff ; also *The Library*, series 3, Vol. VIII, pp. 225-39.

[86] Brooke, C. F. T., *The Shakespeare Apochrypha*, pp. xlviii-xlix; Thompson, E. M., *Shakespeare's Handwriting;* Pollard, *Shakespeare's Hand*.

[87] Halliwell, *Outlines*, Vol. I, p. 329.

ment does not mean, however, that he may not have blotted those papers many a time before they reached their final official form.

But to return to the prompter's custom of jotting the names of minor actors next their parts on the official manuscript of the play, we have several instances of the same custom in the Beaumont and Fletcher folio of 1647. Thus Ashton, John Bacon, and Rowland Dowle took part in *Love's Pilgrimage*. Rowland is also mentioned in *The Chances*. Curtis Greville and Thomas Tuckfield took part in *The Two Noble Kinsmen*; William Adkinson in *A King and No King*, and R. Baxter in *The Mad Lover*. Also, Hugh Clarke spoke the prologue to a revival of *The Custom of the Country*. It follows that the manuscripts used for these five plays and a prologue were the official manuscripts of the company, as is claimed for them. It does not necessarily follow, however, that any one of these manuscripts is the original one of the author, since many of the Beaumont and Fletcher plays are known to have been revived with alterations. A sixth play, *The Maid in the Mill*, by its inclusion of the prompter's characteristic jotting at the end of Act II, "Six Chaires placed at the Arras" shows certainly that it too is from the official manuscript.[88]

These six plays from the official manuscripts justify Moseley's claim that he "had the originals from such as received them from the authors themselves; by those, and none other, I publish this edition." In advertising for the missing *Wild Goose Chase*, Moseley implies that he had the plays from the actors, a claim that is further confirmed by their signatures to the folio. Too, there was but one copy of *The Wild Goose Chase*, which was later recovered and published. There was also but the one manuscript of *The Mad Lover*—as we have just seen, the official one,—recovered by the printers from Sir Aston Cokaine, who had procured it through his near kinsman and Fletcher's close friend, Sir Robert Cotton.[89] Thus

---

[88] Davenant's *Cruel Brother*, licensed January 12, 1627 (Adams, *Herbert*, p. 31), for Blackfriars, by a similar direction, "A Chair at the Arras," V. 1., shows that it is also from the official manuscript.
[89] Cokaine, A., *Small Poems of Divers Sorts* (1658), Author's Apology. For another illustration of how play manuscripts circulated among gentlemen see *H.M.C.*, Fourteenth Report, Appendix, Part II; *The Manuscripts of His Grace the Duke of Portland*, Vol. III, pp. 46, 47.

Moseley is doubtless only telling the truth when he says these originals had been dispersed into many hands. It is also important to notice that Moseley claims these were the full originals, not merely what was acted, showing that the cuts were not made on these official manuscripts but upon the parts of the actors, as we saw reason to infer above in connection with Shakespeare's work. These facts show then that the Shakespearean company had employed this system of official manuscripts at least from 1591 or 1592 (*3 Henry VI*) to the closing of the theaters in 1642. Presumably it had used the same plan 1588-91.

Nor was this custom confined to the Shakespearean company. Several plays of Prince Charles's company show that this company used the same custom in the early thirties.[90] By its mention of Edward May, *Wit Without Money* shows that this same custom was used by the amalgamated Queen's company after 1637. Also, *The Witch of Edmonton*, which was performed by Prince Charles's men at the Cockpit and at Court 1621-22, was printed in 1658, in a quarto that names "Phen or Fenn, Bird or Bourne, W. Mago, W. Hamlen, Rowland, and Jack."[91] Daborne's *Poor Man's Comfort* by its "senseless addition" of "Enter 2. Lords, Sands, Ellis"[92] shows that Queen Anne's company followed the practice about 1617. At least four other early plays show the custom. These are *Summer's Last Will and Testament*, possibly for Paul's boys, *Antonio and Mellida* for Paul's, and *The Blind Beggar of Bethnal Green* and *The Honest Whore* for the Admiral's. The custom certainly existed then in practically all the Elizabethan companies from early days.[93]

The annotated manuscript, however, was, and could have been, only for the prompter's own use. How were the actors to learn and keep up with their entrances, exits, etc., without bedevilling the life out of the poor prompter? Marston gives us the clue in the second

---

[90] Boas, *Shakespeare & the Universities*, pp. 96 ff.
[91] Murray, Vol. I, p. 236, note 3.
[92] *Anglia*, Vol. XXI, p. 382.
[93] How important these facts concerning the prompter and his official manuscripts are any one may see by checking up the elaborate structure Mr. J. Dover Wilson is rearing in his edition of Shakespeare on very ingenious theories, which, in view of the facts here given, I must regard as needing at least a thorough modification.

part of *Antonio and Mellida*, IV. 1. 226-7, when Antonio says in stage terms:

> quick observation, scud
> To cote the plot, or else the path is lost.

There was thus a plot which the actors were themselves to consult in case of doubt. Several of these plots for the consultation of actors have been preserved for us in Alleyn's papers.[94] They are mounted, and their mountings have each a hole at the top so that they might be hung on a peg, where they might be seen and "coted" of all men, much to the relief we trust of the overburdened prompter. These plots go usually into considerable detail. The typical plot assembles all entrances and exits of characters, together with all performers of the parts, so that the actors needed only their lines and the plot to keep moving. At least one of the seven plots given by Mr. Greg, however, names only unimportant attendants in much the same fashion followed in the manuscripts. This is the plot of the *Dead Man's Fortune*, in which "Burbage a messenger" appears.[95] As I shall show later,[96] this plot must have belonged to the Admiral's men before 1590, considerably earlier than Mr. Greg places it.[97] In this plot then, the prompter seems to have followed the same method as with his manuscript, only making his jotting on the plot instead of the manuscript. But by 1592, we have a full-fledged actor's plot. This plot of *The Seven Deadly Sins* names not only the unimportant attendants as do the manuscripts, but also almost all of the chief performers. But our prompter went only so far as he was absolutely obliged. Henry VI and Lidgate were to remain on the stage throughout the four subdivisions. Consequently, the prompter did not make any entry of the actors for these parts, thereby possibly robbing us of a first reference to Shakespeare[98] as an actor, and to Heminges. On the

---

[94] Not quite all the surviving plots can be proved absolutely to have belonged to Alleyn, but it is practically certain that they all did.

[95] Malone, *Variorum*, Vol. III, opp. p. 356.

[96] See below, p. 429.

[97] Greg, *Papers*, p. 133.

[98] If, however, Shakespeare was the prompter's attendant, he would surely have been needed behind the scenes in this unusually complicated play.

other hand, at least three of the six plots for the Admiral's men name practically all actors for characters, and two others probably did so. That the plot of *The Seven Deadly Sins* belonged to Alleyn is shown by the fact that it remained in his possession. Also, this plot was written by the prompter of Alleyn's organization, not by the prompter of the Shakespearean company.[99] It can be shown, I think, that the play itself belonged to him. Thus this plot represents the practice of the Admiral's prompter, but not necessarily that of the Shakespearean official. Still, the advantages of such a device are so obvious that one would expect it to have been generally used. Such plots for Shakespeare's plays would be a priceless find.

But if these plots were generally used, it is strange that, so far as I can find, there is only the one literary reference, quoted above, to such a plot. General references of the period are not to the actors' plot, but to one of a different type. We have surviving the printed "Plot of England's Joy,"[100] which is only an advertising summary of the projected "play," and seemingly served both as program and advertising poster or "bill," just as the title pages of books were similarly contrived a double debt to pay. Similar plot summaries, however, were frequently written out and mounted on pasteboard.[101] These then are the programs for the information of the audience.

Now that we have considered the bookkeeper-prompter and his ways, we may return to the other less important hired men of the company. But since their duties will appear in our later discussions of acting customs, we need only sum up a few general points here. Many or all of these hired men were unimportant actors and supers in the company. They simply filled in wherever needed. Many of them probably were responsible for menial tasks regularly, and filled out processions, etc., whenever needed. Thus in the plot of *Frederick and Basilea* for the Admiral's men,[102] we learn that the gatherers were "guard, confederates, jailors." The prompter's jottings on the various manuscripts of the Shakespearean company show that these hired men brought in various properties, opened

---

[99] Pollard, *Shakespeare's Hand*, pp. 19, 55-6.
[100] *The Harleian Miscellany* (1813), Vol. X, pp. 198-9.
[101] Bullen, *Middleton*, Vol. IV, pp. 393-4; Vol. VI, pp. 362, 363, etc.
[102] Greg, *Papers*, p. 153.

trap doors, etc. Some of the musicians also took part in the acting, as we have seen. It seems then that whatever one's principal and special function might be, he would also help in the actual acting wherever he could.[103] This of course is only an obvious arrangement for making the fullest use of material at hand.

One other class, the gatherers, calls for some special mention. It was the business of the gatherers to collect the admissions. There would thus be at least one at the outer door and one at the entrance to each section of the galleries. This would probably call for a considerable number, but so far as I know we have no record of either the number or names of gatherers at any time in the Shakespearean company. But it required nineteen gatherers for the galleries and tiring house door at the Hope 1613-15.[104] In addition, there must have been one or more[105] at the outer door. Since all public theaters were of the same general arrangement, it is probable that the Shakespearean and other companies required not less than twenty gatherers. The wage paid to a gatherer at the Hope is also interesting, being one penny for each performance. Thomas Woodford in a suit beginning in 1613, and extending nine years, may indicate that at the Red Bull there were approximately twenty-one gatherers, each receiving a penny a performance.[106] There are several allusions to show that there was a disposition on the part of the actual gatherers to increase their wages surreptitiously. One of the most picturesque runs: "Nay, our very Doore-keepers, men and women, most grievously complaine, that by this cessation they are robbed of the priviledge of stealing from us with licence: they cannot now, as in King *Agamemnons* dayes, seem to scratch their heads where they itch not, and drop shillings and half Crowne-

---

[103] From an amusing story of Jo. Haynes and Hart, it appears that after the Restoration all actors who received less than 50s per week might be called on for such duties (Malone, *Variorum*, Vol. III, p. 289, note). Some such rule was then necessary, since all actors had in effect become hired men.

[104] Greg, *Papers*, 89, 110.

[105] The number at Blackfriars seems certainly to have been but one (*Jonson Allusion Book*, p. 301).

[106] Wallace, *Three London Theatres*, p. 10. For detailed discussion of the number and fees of gatherers, see an article "Posting Henslowe's Accounts," to be published in *The Journal of English and Germanic Philology*, Vol. XXVI, pp. 42-90.

pieces in at their collars."[107] There is no absolutely conclusive evidence, however, that the Shakespearean company followed either the system of the Hope or that of the Bull for securing gatherers.[108] Cundall's bequest to "my old servant, Elizabeth Wheaton" of "that place or priviledge which she now exerciseth and enjoyeth in the houses of the Blackfryers, London, and the Globe on the Bankside" pretty certainly means that she was a gatherer.[109] But gathering may also have been, and probably was, but one of the duties of some of their full-time hired men.

Since we have had and shall have occasion in other sections to give practically all the important facts known concerning the individual hired men, we need not consider them further in this connection.

Here then in the hired men we find the transient labor of the Shakespearean company. This labor was almost purely on a wage basis, and had practically no prospects of belonging to the class of masters. But in the Shakespearean company even this labor was stable. Many of the hired men, as William Toyer, spent their lives with the company. Indeed there was little incentive for change. They could not expect anywhere to be masters, and the wage of journeymen or hired men in all trades was fixed by law and custom at the same approximate level of six shillings a week. Their chief choice lay in getting the most congenial working conditions. Presumably those conditions in the Shakespearean company were no worse than elsewhere. Thus these men regularly renewed their contracts every two or three years, and were content as necessary cogs in the machine to share the reflected glory if not the increased emoluments of their masters. At least in theory they accepted Menenius's orthodox parable of the belly, and were not ill content.

[107] *Actors Remonstrance,* Ashbee's facsimile, p. 6.
[108] cf. above, p. 120.
[109] Collier, *Memoirs,* p. 148.

CHAPTER V

THE SHAKESPEAREAN CLAN

NOW that we have considered the various classes of people concerned in the Shakespearean company, it becomes evident that this was not merely a business organization but a self-propagating society as well, still retaining much of the original social purposes of the gild. The masters were not only joint owners in the enterprise but intimate friends as well. Thus at death the members, especially the earlier ones, made some of their fellows overseers or executors of their wills, still placing their all in the protection of their society. The apprentices were not merely menials, hired for so much cash on an efficiency basis; but pupils and prospective successors of their masters. Indeed, the model apprentice of story was supposed to marry his master's daughter or widow, whichever fate made first available, and to carry on the business. Neither was this expectation a romantic, Cophetua-Beggar Maid affair as we moderns are prone to suppose; but a natural mating of equals. It is apparent then that we have here to do with a clan, devoted to the carrying on of a particular enterprise by which it earned its daily bread.

Naturally, the lives of the clan clustered in community fashion around the clan centers, in this case the theaters at which the company might be acting. It is thus a significant fact that the members of the Shakespearean company from 1588 to 1642 lived in three groups or centers of London. Of the five original members of 1588-94, three lived on the Bankside, one probably in St. Andrews, Blackfriars, and one in Aldermanbury.[1] The probable reason for the residence of John Heminges in Aldermanbury away from his fellows on the Bankside is to be found in the record of his marriage on March 10, 1588, at St. Mary's, Aldermanbury, to Rebecca Knell,

---

[1] Collier, *Memoirs*, is authority for all information unless otherwise noted.

possibly the youthful widow of the famous actor Knell, whose name in that case was William. The circumstance probably indicates that the young widow was richly left with property in that neighborhood. It may even be that John Heminges, grocer, had married his master's widow. At any rate, Heminges lived in this section till about 1618, when he moved to the neighborhood of his work on the Bankside, there to remain till death. Even so, he and his wife were both buried at St. Mary's in Aldermanbury, which was evidently home to them.

Here in Aldermanbury Heminges's apprentices, Cooke and Rice, would have spent their youthful days, though afterward they married and settled down near their work on the Bankside.[2] When William Ostler married Heminges's daughter Thomasina in 1611, he too settled in the Aldermanbury neighborhood. We also find Ostler's companion of the Revels, John Underwood, in the adjoining parish of St. Bartholomew the Less as early as December 27, 1610, where he remained till his death in 1624.

Heminges's partner Cundall is also found in Aldermanbury by 1599, where he remained till after his retirement from acting; but moved a few years before his death to his country house at Fulham, where he died. Whether Cundall had been Heminges's apprentice, whether his friendship with Heminges carried him to this neighborhood, or whether his residence in the neighborhood occasioned the friendship we do not definitely know; but certainly the famous partners lived and planned here together.

Professor Wallace has shown that Shakespeare also lived in this neighborhood for a time.[3] We are certain that he was living in 1604 with Christopher Montjoy at the corner of Muggle and Silver Streets in the parish of St. Olave, only a short distance from the residences of Heminges and Cundall. A literal interpretation of Shakespeare's words would make his residence with Montjoy date from 1598, since he says that Montjoy showed goodwill and affection to his apprentice Bellott "all the tyme" of the latter's apprenticeship,

---

[2] Rice was "of the Bancksyde" 1622-23 (Wallace, *Jahrbuch*, Vol. XLVI, p. 348). He had married Mable Hayward at St. Saviour's, May 1, 1616 (*Genealogist*, n.s., Vol. VII, p. 168), and with his wife was living "near the playhouse" in 1619 (Collier, *Memoirs*, p. 282).

[3] Wallace, *Associates*, pp. 3-44.

which began in 1598.[4] This statement need not be taken too literally, since Professor Wallace has shown that several witnesses are a few years off in their approximate statements of time; but it certainly must mean that Shakespeare knew Bellott, presumably as his fellow lodger, for the approximate length of the latter's apprenticeship. Shakespeare also says that he had known the family ten years or thereabouts in 1612; but as the face of it shows, the time given was not intended to be exact. Bellott in this same approximate way states that he had been married five years, when really the time was seven and one-half years. This statement of Shakespeare's taken literally would date his residence from early in 1602. He thus took up his residence at Montjoy's sometime between 1598 and 1602. There is seemingly no evidence that Shakespeare did not go to Montjoy's about 1598 when his unfinished tax in Southwark, last recorded payment 1598, indicates a move. All things considered, the evidence seems to be for 1598 as the beginning of his residence in St. Olave;[5] but we are certain only of 1602-04. Nor do we know how long he remained here after 1604. His deposition may be interpreted as implying knowledge of later happenings in the family. Also, another apprentice of Montjoy, William Eaton, who had known his master "about ffoure yeares and A halfe" preceding June 19, 1612, or since the beginning of 1608, claims to have heard Shakespeare make statements concerning the case at issue. This would indicate, but not prove, that Shakespeare had been a resident with the family as late as 1608. It is probable then that Shakespeare had resided here from 1598 till his long vacation at Stratford beginning about 1608. Indeed he may still have resided with Montjoy after his return to London in 1610, this being one reason for his reticence in testifying against him in 1612. It would seem then that Shakespeare too had been drawn to this neighborhood by the Heminges-Cundall group of the clan, and spent his greatest days there.[6]

[4] Wallace, *Associates*, p. 22.
[5] Since the Herald Montjoy of *Henry V* is taken from the source, we cannot infer that he is named for the wigmaker, and that in consequence Shakespeare had come to know him by 1599.
[6] Professor Adams (*Shakespeare*, p. 378) points out that Shakespeare's fellow Stratfordian, the printer Field, moved to Wood Street by 1600,

John Shank is found in the adjoining parish of St. Giles, Cripple-gate, by December 10, 1610, being at that time a member of Prince Henry's company at the nearby Fortune in Golding Lane. Probably it was his connection here with the Heminges-Cundall group that later gave him membership in the Shakespearean company. In this neighborhood Shank remained till his death in 1636. His home would have been the home of his apprentices Thomas Pollard, Thomas Holcomb, John Thompson, and Nicholas Birch. Both John Lowin and Nathan Field had been baptized at St. Giles, the former December 9, 1576, the latter October 17, 1587, possibly con-necting with the Shakespearean company in this way. In later days, Robert Benfield is found in the parish of St. Bartholomew the Great, October 15, 1617; but still later at St. Giles, though I do not know just how he became connected with the neighborhood. William Penn was living in 1623 at the George Alley in Golding Lane near the Fortune, where most of the Palsgrave's men were to be found clustered around their work,[7] though Penn himself was at that time a member of Prince Charles's men at the Red Bull not far away. On June 30, 1616, Penn had married Sibilla West of St. Botolph's, Aldgate, at which time he is described as being of St. Leonard's, Shoreditch; but the family records continue in St. Bo-tolph's through March 31, 1619.[8] Between 1619 and 1623 he had moved to the Red Bull-Fortune neighborhood, where he seems to have remained many years, for in 1636 he is recorded as of St. Giles, Cripplegate.[9]

One other of the Shakespearean company is also connected with this neighborhood, Eyllaerdt Swanston, who according to Wright, after the closing of the theaters "professed himself a Presbyterian,

presumably that his French wife might be nearer her church. Possibly this fact had some influence on Shakespeare as Professor Adams thinks. Field seems to have continued his connection with the Shakespearean group till death, since Hum. Dyson and his servant Ro. Dickens, who made his will November 24, 1624 (Plomer, H. R., *Wills of English Printers and Stationers*, pp. 50-1), had also performed the same service for Tooley June 3, 1623, and later for Cundall December 13, 1627 (Collier, *Memoirs*, pp. 149, 243, 244).

[7] Wallace, *Jahrbuch*, Vol. XLVI, pp. 347-8.

[8] *Publications of the Modern Language Association*, Vol. XLI, p. 104.

[9] Chambers, *Eliz. Stage*, Vol. II, p. 332; Malcolm, *Londinium Redivivum* (1802-03), Vol. III, p. 304.

took up the trade of a jeweller, and lived in Aldermanbury."[10] He had seemingly lived in this section for a long time before, since Collier tells us that the records of the parish contain many entries of the births of his children from 1622 to 1638; but no records at all of him after the latter date. He was with the Princess Elizabeth company in 1622 at the Phoenix or Cockpit in Drury Lane; but joined the Shakespearean company in 1624, remaining with this company to the end. He was thus at all times quite distant from his work, and must have had some other reason for his residence in this neighborhood, though what, I do not know. It may have been associations formed here that enabled him in 1624 to succeed his neighbor Underwood in the Shakespearean company.

George Bryane probably lived in the nearby parish of St. Andrews, Blackfriars, where Collier found the entry "George, sonne to George Bryan," baptized February 17, 1600. It was in St. Anne's, Blackfriars, that Richard Sharp was buried January 25, 1632.[11]

Some of the minor actors in the earlier company had also lived in the Aldermanbury neighborhood. Humphrey Jeffes was buried at

---

[10] Wright, *Historia*, p. 427. Swanston must thus in his youth have been a jeweller's apprentice, as Armin also had been. Miss Emma Marshall Denkinger has located the record of Armin's apprenticeship, which he signed October 13, 1581, for eleven years, to "John Lowyson." (*Publications of the Modern Language Association*, Vol. XLI, p. 96.) He would thus have taken up his freedom late in 1592. Since the legal age for becoming a master was twenty-four, Armin was born probably about 1567-68, and the record is doubtless to be found at Lynn in Norfolk, where his father, John Armin, was a tailor.

John Lowin was also a goldsmith. Lowin was chosen by the company in 1611 to perform in its Lord Mayor's Pageant. He had been apprenticed to Nicholas Rudyard for eight years from "Cirstmas in Anno 1593," or till Christmas, 1601. (*Publications of the Modern Language Association*, Vol. XLI, pp. 96-7.) Two facts indicate clearly that this John Lowin was the actor. In the first place, the actor was the son of Richard Lowin, carpenter, of London, as this apprentice was, though the "carpenter" seems illegible in the apprentice entry. In the second place, the law at this time was that an apprentice might not become a master before he was twenty-four, though enforcement was left with the individual gild, so that practice varied slightly, and needs to be determined for each organization. Now John Lowin the actor was christened December 9, 1576, and would have been twenty-five at Christmas, 1601, when the goldsmith apprentice should have graduated. It is highly improbable that we should have two John Lowins of the same approximate age, each the son of Richard Lowin of London.

[11] Malcolm, *Londinium Redivivum* (1802-03), Vol. II, p. 376.

[152]

St. Giles August 21, 1618, probably having moved to that neighborhood when the company to which he belonged opened the Fortune. According to Collier, "Jack" Wilson the musician was born in this neighborhood, and was baptized April 24, 1585, either at St. Giles or St. Bartholomew the Less, Collier doesn't make clear which. There are several records of the Wilson family in this neighborhood. In this section Ben. Jonson, Thomas Dekker, Anthony Munday, James Shirley, and possibly the actor Robert Wilson all lived at some time. Thus it appears that in Aldermanbury a group of the Shakespearean company had grown up around John Heminges, and that this group had in process of time formed connections with the neighboring clan which centered around the Fortune in Golding Lane, this connection probably resulting eventually in the acquisition of some of these members for the Shakespearean company.

With the exception of Heminges and probably Bryane, who both lived in the Aldermanbury neighborhood, all other original members lived on the Bankside, where the company is known to have acted at the Rose 1592-94. Here in Southwark at the church of St. Mary Overies, now St. Saviour's, in the Liberty of the Clink, close by London Bridge, are to be found most of the records concerning actors in the company.

Augustine Phillips and his probable former apprentice William Sly were living in Horseshoe Court in 1593, where R. Jones, and T. Downton of the Admiral's organization were living at the same time. Sly is traceable in this neighborhood 1588-96, after which he followed his work to the Theater in Shoreditch, only to have that work play hide-and-seek with him shortly afterward by returning to the Bank. Phillips remained on the Bank till 1604;[12] but just before his death in 1605 moved to Mortlake in Surrey, probably for his health. It is a characteristic fact that Phillips's probable former apprentice Sly was dwelling in Horseshoe Court—probably with the family of his former master—in 1593, was made an overseer of Phillips's will in 1605, and at his own death in 1608 had

[12] Phillips had a daughter buried at St. Botolph's, Aldgate, September 7, 1597, but this does not necessarily denote change of residence (*Publications of the Modern Language Association*, Vol. XLI, p. 105).

control of Phillips's orphaned apprentice, James Sands. Being master and apprentice was not so different from being father and son.[13] Sands's predecessor and Sly's successor as Phillips's apprentice, Samuel Gilburne, would also have dwelt here with his master.

Thomas Pope is also traceable at St. Saviour's from 1593 till his death. His apprentice, Robert Goffe, married Phillips's sister Elizabeth February 13, 1603, and at Phillips's death in 1605 succeeded to his membership in the company. Indeed, it is possible that Pope and Phillips were already closely related. In his will, Pope calls his mother Agnes Webb, showing that she had married again. Now Phillips speaks of his "brothers" William and James Webb. He also mentions "Agnes Bennett, my loveing mother." These likenesses of names, the fact that the men were close neighbors, and that Pope's apprentice had married Phillips's sister would seem to indicate some close connection between Pope and Phillips. Perhaps Phillips's wife Anne was a Webb, sister of James and William, younger children of Agnes Pope, widow, later married to Webb. Thus Pope would be a half-brother of Anne Phillips. This would imply that Agnes Webb of July 1603 married yet again, becoming the Agnes Bennett of May 1605. This theory would account for all the facts and probably doesn't misrepresent the good lady; her daughter Anne was remarried almost within a year. If this is the situation, then Goffe did the best he could for his bachelor master by taking the master's half-sister's sister-in-law to wife. Pope's younger apprentice, John Edmans, solved the problem of his duty by marrying Pope's young ward and chief legatee, Mary Clark.

Pope's fellow comedian, William Kemp, also lived on the Bank, certainly from 1595 till his death and burial at St. Saviour's November 2, 1603.[14] In 1602 he and Pope had both lived in Langley's New Rents, this Langley being probably the owner of the Swan, so that we may suppose his rents were near that theater. Richard

---

[13] A shrewd but strongly prejudiced observer about a century earlier attributed the whole apprentice system in England to selfishness and want of affection in fathers, intimating that the apprentice's master or mistress did more for him than would his father or mother (*A Relation, or Rather a True Account, of the Island of England*, Camden Soc., 1847, pp. 24 ff., 75).

[14] Collier, *Memoirs*, p. 116.

Cowley had probably been Kemp's apprentice, spending his early days here on the Bank; but after graduation, he married, and settled down in Shoreditch while the company was playing in that neighborhood. Here then in Southwark the members of the early company had formed a group around their work.

But when the company left the Rose in Southwark for the Cross Keys in Gracious Street and the Theater and Curtain in Shoreditch, it was natural for the younger members to settle around the Burbadges in the latter community, though the older members remained where they had already settled. The Burbadges, owners of the Theater, resided in Halliwell or Holywell Street, Shoreditch, in the parish of St. Leonard's, where the registers give us considerable information concerning the marriages, births, deaths, and places of residence of several of the actors. James Burbage, the father of Richard and Cuthbert, had built the Theater in Shoreditch, 1576, the first record of the family there dating in the spring of 1576, when we find recorded in the registers of St. Leonard's, "Alice Burbage, d. of Jeames Burbage, bap. March xith, 1575. Halliwell Street." Here in Holywell Street after 1576 were born, and thence were buried, the children of James Burbage and of his sons Cuthbert (born about 1566-67) and Richard (born about the summer 1573) after him.

With Richard Burbadge, his apprentices would also have resided during apprenticeship. Indeed, we find two of his former apprentices, Nicholas Tooley and Richard Robinson, still residing with their master at his death. To an apprentice his master's house was home. Tooley, the bachelor, then took up his residence with Cuthbert Burbadge till death severed his relations with the Burbadge family, to whom chiefly he left his worldly all, taking special pains to remember the children of the family. But Richard Robinson, model apprentice that he was, married his master's widow and carried on the business. It is for this reason that in 1622-23 Robinson is said to reside "att the vpper end of Shoreditch."[15]

Naturally, many members of the company when it was performing in this neighborhood during the last years of the century would

[15] Wallace, *Jahrbuch*, Vol. XLVI, p. 347.

also become attached permanently to this locality as home. During this period, Richard Cowley married, and settled in Holywell Street, there to remain till death. William Sly also settled in the Shoreditch neighborhood, probably with the family of Robert Brown, to whose members at his death he left his all.[16] John Duke, one of the hired men in the company certainly 1592-98, is also found dwelling in Holywell Street, certainly 1604-09, and prob- ably for several years preceding, his residence probably dating from the time of his connection with the Shakespearean company there.

It also seems probable that the chief poet of the organization, Shakespeare himself, lived close by in the parish of St. Helen's, Bishopsgate Street, from before 1593 till some time before October 1596.[17] If he did live there, he was only a short distance from his work at the Cross Keys and later at the Theater, belonging to the group of actors clustering around the latter building.

Of course there would also be in this neighborhood members of other companies that had played at the Theater and Curtain. Christopher Beeston, who had been Phillips's "servant," certainly 1592-98, had a son baptized Augustine November 16, 1604, at St. Leonard's in honor of his master or in memory of Phillips's two-year old son, who was buried July 1, 1604. He had doubtless come to the neighborhood while his company, at that time the Queen's men, was acting at the Curtain 1604-05. Between 1607 and 1611 he seems to have followed his company to Clerkenwell near the Red Bull;[18] but since burials are still at St. Leonard's, and since his son William is found residing in Shoreditch 1680, it seems that this famous family of actors came to regard Shoreditch as home.

Joseph Taylor had also been in this neighborhood "in Bishopps-

---

[16] This Robert Brown is not the actor who had before 1590 belonged to the Admiral's men, since he was probably still abroad at this time (Herz, *Englische Schauspieler*, pp. 20-1, 26-7), and at least in April 1612 was living in Clerkenwell, not Shoreditch (Greg, *Papers*, p. 63). Besides, this Robert Brown of Sly's will and Cicely his wife must have been much younger, since they had twin sons baptized at St. James, Clerkenwell, as late as August 1620. At this same period, the other Robert seems to have been in Germany. There are records of several Robert Browns at St. James, Clerkenwell.

[17] Lee, *Shakespeare*, pp. 274-5.

[18] Stopes, *Burbage*, pp. 139-41; Registers of St. James, Clerkenwell.

gate neare the Spittle" in 1622-23.[19] It is possible that here he formed the associations that made him Richard Burbadge's successor in 1619. His coming to the community, as well as that of Thomas Hobbs, later a member of the Shakespearean company, who was living 1622-23 "att the vpper end of Shoreditch," is probably to be connected with the fact that their company, Prince Charles's men, was playing at the Curtain, certainly in 1622-23. The poet John Webster had a daughter baptized from Holywell Street May 9, 1606; and another poet, George Wilkins, was buried from the same street August 19, 1603. Gabriel Spencer, then an Admiral's man but formerly Pembroke's, was buried at St. Leonard's from Hog Lane September 23, 1598, having had the distinction of "being slayne" by Ben Jonson. Too, he is the Spencer who is mentioned as having been a minor actor in *3 Henry VI*. It is also worthy of note that Richard Tarleton had lived in Holywell Street, and was buried at St. Leonard's September 3, 1588.

Here then in Holywell Street was the powerful Burbadge group, settled around its theater. Since it had been connected with other companies than the Shakespearean, members of these companies are found to have connections with the group. Also, the actors at the nearby Curtain are found in the neighborhood. It was doubtless to associations thus formed with the Burbadge group that some of these actors owed their entrance later to the Shakespearean company.

After the Shakespearean company built the Globe and returned to the Bankside in 1599, the actors who did not have some special connection with either the Heminges or the Burbadge groups regularly settled on the Bank. When Alexander Cooke, John Heminges's apprentice, completed apprenticeship, he married and settled on the Bank, where he remained till his death. Joseph Taylor is traceable here 1607-16, but for some reason removed to Allhallows in the Wall, where he and his wife Elizabeth had a daughter Hester baptized April 12, 1618, a daughter Anne August 8, 1619; and a son Samuel, March 18, 1621. He was in the Shoreditch neighborhood about 1622-23. After he became a member of the Shakespearean company in 1619, he soon returned to the Bankside, about 1623, where he continued to live many years, probably at least till the

[19] Wallace, *Jahrbuch*, Vol. XLVI, p. 347.

closing of the theaters in 1642. John Lowin married Joan Hall, widow, at St. Botolph's,[20] Bishopsgate, October 29, 1607, and took up residence on the Bankside, where he is traceable till 1623,[21] and after 1627, at least till the closing of the theaters. In the interim, 1623-26, he had probably been at Lambeth, where he was certainly living in 1623.[22] Lowin was evidently a man of some local importance, since he was one of the overseers in charge of the poor rates of the Liberty of Paris Garden 1618, 1627, 1629, 1630, 1631, and finally 1634. He had probably become closely acquainted with Taylor when they both were living "near the playhouse" 1608-16, and this acquaintance as well as that of the Burbadge family may have helped Taylor into the company in 1619.

Nathan Field also may have lived in the parish for a time, our only evidence to connect him with St. Saviour's being a letter supposed to be his to Mr. Sutton, preacher at St. Mary Overies (St. Saviour's) 1616, in which he defends himself and players in general. He complains that Sutton had preached, not merely against the profession in general, but had in particular stated that Field and others, calling them by name, were damned. One wonders if the "others" includes the long list we have just been considering. Sutton had tried to hinder Field from receiving the sacrament and to banish him from his own parish church.[23] But on August 2, 1620, Field is described as "late of the parish of Saint Giles in the county of Middlesex bachelor deceased," which may mean, as Miss Brinkley suggests, that Field had finally been forced out of St. Saviour's by Sutton. The situation may just as well, however, raise decided suspicions as to the authenticity of the letter.

John Heminges moved from Aldermanbury to a plot of ground on the Globe property, where Heminges himself tells us he had a house, which Witter says was "new" in April 1619. We hear in

---

[20] Since Robert Armin had been a resident of St. Botolph's, Aldgate, from as early as October 11, 1600, till his death in 1615 (*Publications of the Modern Language Association*, Vol. XLI, p. 95), possibly it was through him that Lowin met widow Hall. Armin and Lowin were not only fellow actors, but also fellow goldsmiths.

[21] Ordish, T. F., *Early London Theatres*, p. 276, note.

[22] Wallace, *Jahrbuch*, Vol. XLVI, p. 348.

[23] Collier, *Memoirs*, pp. xxxvii-xxxviii. Brinkley, *Modern Language Notes*, Vol. XLII, p. 13.

1634 of two houses adjoining the Globe, one of which is specifically stated to be a dwelling which was built about the time of the second Globe.[24] Since Heminges had to pay Sir John Bodley a fine of forty shillings in 1615 for permission to build his house, and since he mentions the leasing of the ground in connection with taking Field into the company, which was shortly after Shakespeare's death in 1616, it appears that Heminges was then preparing to move.[25] The fact, however, that about Christmas 1617-18, a messenger was sent "to wodstrete to heminges the player"[26] would seem to indicate that Heminges had not yet moved. Since Heminges was business manager, whose function it was to keep all accounts, documents, etc., this move was necessary, as he was now at least entering his sixties. He seems to have lived in this house on the Globe property and in this parish till his death in 1630, since he speaks in his will of Aldermanbury, "where I long lived, and whither I have bequeathed my body for burial." It is probable then that the work of Heminges on the 1623 folio of Shakespeare was done here on the Globe property. Heminges also leaves a legacy to "John Rice, clerk, of St. Saviour's, in Southwark," seemingly his fellow actor and former apprentice, who had dropped from the company in 1625. One wonders if Mr. Sutton, preacher, of 1616, still presided at St. Saviour's. Rice had lived in this section at least from 1616 through 1630, and probably for some time before and after. Heminges in his will speaks of this former apprentice as "my loving friend," and makes him, together with Cuthbert Burbadge, an overseer of that will, another illustration of the close relation usually existing between master and apprentice.

There were a number of other theatrical residents on the Bank. Here lived Henslowe and Alleyn in proximity to their theatrical interests.[27] Humphrey Jeffes, mentioned in *3 Henry VI*, had a daugh-

[24] *Harrison's Description of England* (New Shak. Soc.), Part II, Appendix I, p. xvii.
[25] Wallace, London *Times*, May 1, 1914; Wallace, *Associates*, pp. 63, 72.
[26] Sullivan, *Masques of James First*, p. 181, note 2.
[27] Cooke and his wife seem to have had some close connection with Henslowe and Alleyn, since Mrs. Alleyn on October 21, 1603, notes in a letter to her husband that they wish to be remembered (Warner, *Catalogue*, p. 25; Young, W., *The History of Dulwich College*, Vol. II, p. 19), and since in 1606, Henslowe, Alleyn, and Cooke had six sacrament tokens between them (*Harrison*, Part II, Appendix I, p. xxvi).

ter baptized at the parish church January 25, 1601. Laurence
Fletcher was living in Hunt's Rents, Maid Lane, in 1605, 1606 and
1607,[28] being buried at St. Saviour's in 1608. It is also recorded
that Edmund Shakespeare, "player" brother of William, was buried
in St. Saviour's December 31, 1607. The poets of the Shakespearean
company, Beaumont, Fletcher, and Massinger, lived here; and the
latter two were buried at St. Saviour's, the former in Westminster
itself.

It is believed that William Shakespeare also lived in this neighborhood for a time. The William Shakespeare who had lived in
St. Helen's, and left by the autumn of 1596, was located for taxa-
tion in October of that year in the Liberty of the Clink, Southwark.
He paid two instalments on his debt, the first in 1597, the second
in 1598. Malone quotes a missing memorandum of Alleyn to the
effect that Shakespeare's residence was "near the Bear-Garden" in
1596.[29] Sir Sidney Lee thinks there is no doubt that the reference
is to our Shakespeare.[30] Professor Wallace thinks the reference may
be to him, but that it applies to him "not because he was a resident in
Southwark, but because of his ownership of property there, at the
Globe theatre."[31] But Shakespeare had no business interests in
Southwark, as Professor Wallace has himself shown, in theatrical
affairs at least, till early in 1599, after the above transactions. Professor Wallace thus thinks it probable that Shakespeare moved
directly to Montjoy's in St. Olave's from St. Helen's. In view of
Alleyn's confirmatory note quoted by Malone, it would seem that
the Shakespeare concerned was the actor-dramatist, though it is
hard to see why he should move to this neighborhood at this time,
and then later move away about the time the Globe was erected in
the same neighborhood. He was in St. Olave's in 1604, and from his
own testimony had evidently been there for some time, probably
from about 1598. Thus Shakespeare probably moved[32] from the
Bankside about the time the Globe was erected there. Malone had

---

[28] *Harrison*, Part II, Appendix I, p. xxvii.
[29] Malone, *Inquiry*, pp. 215-16.
[30] Lee, *Shakespeare*, pp. 274-5.
[31] *The Nation*, Vol. XC, p. 260.
[32] Is his moving the reason Shakespeare's payments on his subsidy are
not recorded after 1598, though eventually the tax was paid in full?

some curious document which he thought offered strong presumptive evidence that Shakespeare remained on the Bank "to the year 1608."[33] Possibly he is referring to the record of Edmund Shakespeare's burial at St. Saviour's, though his description of the evidence seems hardly appropriate to this entry. Shakespeare may have returned to the Bank by 1607, but the present evidence is far from conclusive.

Evidently then the actors of the Shakespearean company tended to congregate in this section in order to be together near their work, unless they had formed some special connection with the Heminges group in Aldermanbury or the Burbadge family in Shoreditch. Of the Shakespearean actors not known to have been connected with either of these three groups, the residence of Robert Armin was in St. Botolph's, Aldgate, 1600-15,[34] but that of William Rowley, and Anthony Smith, together with that of the six entrants in 1641, is so far as I can find unknown, though Bird was living near the Fortune playhouse May 20, 1622,[35] and Michael Bowyer was in St. Botolph's, Aldgate, 1621-22.[36] These members were probably affiliated, however, with one or the other of the three groups.

It was of course the natural thing for these actors to be thus closely connected with each other. The gild system emphasized and fostered the clan spirit, each gild tending to center in some particular region. In the case of a company of actors the natural center would be its theater. This principle accounts in the Shakespearean company for the centers in Shoreditch and Southwark; but not that in Aldermanbury, the key to this latter center lying in Heminges's attachment there. It is interesting to note that Shakespeare was connected with all three of these centers, being thus a kind of connecting link. This business was founded, especially in Shakespeare's day, both in theory and in practice on a closely knit, self-propagating society of friends, whose whole aim in life was to make their mystery a success. From youth they were educated for it, and in death their last thoughts were of it.

[33] Malone, *Inquiry*, pp. 215-16.
[34] *Publications of the Modern Language Association*, Vol. XLI, p. 95.
[35] Warner, *Catalogue*, p. 243.
[36] *Publications of the Modern Language Association*, Vol. XLI, p. 98.

CHAPTER VI

COMPANY FINANCE

NOW that we have established the various customs and classes in the Shakespearean company, we can make a fair approximation of the various phases of their financial outlay and reward. It seems advisable, however, to relegate details to an appendix[1] and here summarize only general results.

Our most definite information concerning the income of the Shakespearean company is to be found at the Rose in 1592-93, and at the Globe and Blackfriars 1634-35. Unfortunately, the company was able to act at the Rose only about two-fifths of the year February 1592 to February 1593. The remainder of the time it was inactive or travelling in the country, where it claimed it could not make expenses. The net gain of the company was certainly not greater than £225 per annum, some £45 for each of its five sharers, and probably was considerably less, possibly even a loss. In an average year before 1594, the company might have cleared about £40 to £50 for each of its five members at a regular theater; but probably cleared much less because it was forced to travel. For the period at the Cross Keys, 1594-96, we have no estimate. At the Curtain and Theater, 1596, the company probably received about £235 net per annum, which would be £26 for each of nine, or £33 for each of seven members. At the Globe 1599-1608, average net returns were probably £300, about £33 for each of the nine members before 1603, £25 for each of the twelve thereafter. We may thus estimate the average net receipt of an actor from 1594 to 1608 in the Shakespearean company as from £25 to £35 per annum, the number of members being regularly increased to keep pace with increased earnings. To this amount, rewards at court added about £3 per member at the beginning of the period, but about £8 toward the end, making a total net average of £28 to £42 per annum. Re-

[1] Appendix II.

ceipts remained much the same at the Globe till the closing of the theaters, but the total income of the company was much increased by the acquisition of Blackfriars in the latter part of 1608 as a winter house. About 1608-12, the actors were clearing from the two houses around £35 each, divided about equally between the two. By 1635 this amount had increased to £50, of which approximately £12 10s. came from the Globe and £37 10s. from Blackfriars. It is thus evident that the added revenue came chiefly from Blackfriars, and not chiefly nor necessarily from a general rise in prices or increased attendance. The rewards at court added each year about £10 per member, 1608-25; from 1625 to 1641 the reward averaged £16 per member. Thus the total average net income per member 1608-12 was around £45, but by 1635 was about £66. Total net incomes had thus increased from about £28 in 1594 to £66 by 1635. They had considerably more than doubled.

Another source of income for an inner group of actors in the Shakespearean company was housekeeping, first at the Globe and then at the Blackfriars. All the older members of the company formed a joint-tenancy in 1598-99 to build the Globe. Presumably each in some form contributed his share to the enterprise, which was valued at £600, or £60 for each of the ten original shares. When an actor was later admitted, he simply contributed his pro rata share of the original cost. When there were twelve shares, about 1606-12, each would thus have cost £50. When there were fourteen, 1612-13, each would have been valued at £42 11s. 2d. The second Globe was built in the spring of 1614 at an estimated cost of £1400, or £100 per share. When there were sixteen shares, about 1616-35, each share would be valued at £87 10s. Besides the cost of the building, each share was responsible for its part of repairs and of the annual rent for the leased ground. Rent at the Globe was £14 10s. from 1598 to 1635. At the end of this period, the building seems to have been awarded to Brend, and consequently the rent raised to the same amount as at Blackfriars. When the company took over Blackfriars in 1608, the same inner group of actors, together with the owners of the building, Richard and Cuthbert Burbadge, and the previous lessee, Henry Evans, took over the housekeeping. Since in this case the building was already erected, the only cost of a share was the proportional cost of rent and repairs; but the rent was of course much higher. It had been £40, 1608-29; but was then raised to £50, this same amount being charged for the Globe also after 1635. Repairs to both buildings probably did not average above £10 per annum.

As a return on the investment, from 1599 to 1608, the house-keepers at the Globe received in an average year about £500 gross. This would be about £50 for each of the ten original shares; about £62 10s. when the shares were eight; £42 when there were twelve. It is to be remembered, however, that returns had been gradually increasing throughout the period, so that our estimate per share is probably too large at the beginning and too small at the end of the period. It seems likely that the shares remained about £50 each throughout the period, extra shares absorbing the surplus as cre-ated. The expense of rent and repairs probably did not amount to more than £5 per share. Thus net returns on a share at the Globe 1599-1608 were about £45 per annum. After 1608, the returns at the Globe were cut about in half, since the house was then used but half the year. Blackfriars 1608-12, returned about £360 per annum, a net return of about £45 for each seventh share. This had in-creased by 1635 to about £600, a net return of about £75 for each eighth share. Thus a housekeeper in both buildings, 1608-12, would clear about £67; by 1635, nearly £100.[2] It is evident then that housekeeping shares in the company had also more than doubled in value 1599-1635.

We have these details of expense and income for all groups with considerable accuracy for the year 1634-35. In this year each actor received a gross sum of £180, which would be £2160 for all twelve actors. About half of this sum went for expenses, the net receipt of each actor thus being about £90. Of this £90, he received about £22 10s. at the Globe and £67 10s. at Blackfriars. His receipts came from two houses and two sources in each house. Of the actors' £2160 gross receipt, about £795 came from the Globe, about £400 of it from their half of the galleries and £395 from the total receipts

[2] Thus it was not unreasonable to expect that a sixth share of both housekeeping and acting at Whitefriars in 1608 should net £100 per annum (N.S.S. Transactions, 1887-92, pp. 269 ff.).

at the doors. About £1365 came from Blackfriars, about £816 of it
from their half of the galleries and £549 from the doors.

The housekeepers received about £1205 during the same year.
Their source of income was half the galleries in both houses, about
£400 from the Globe and £816 from Blackfriars. Each housekeeping share thus produced about £25 at the Globe and £102 at
Blackfriars. As between the two theaters, the Globe produced about
£1195 and Blackfriars about £2170 of the gross yearly income of
£3365. Of the £1195 at the Globe, about £800 came from the galleries and £395 from the doors, a ratio of about two to one. Of the
£2170 at Blackfriars, about £1632 came from the galleries and
£538 from the door, a ratio of about three to one. From these facts
it becomes apparent that a housekeeping share at Blackfriars was
worth about four times as much as one at the Globe, and an acting
share was worth about three times as much. It is easy to see why the
company always fought so hard to save Blackfriars.

Besides these returns, however, the actors received £250 for
twenty plays at Court this year,[3] this being practically clear profit.
This would add about £20 to the net gains of each actor, giving
him for the year a net receipt of about £110.

However, our previous figures are for an uninterrupted acting
year of three hundred days, whereas the actual average acting year
in the latter nineties at the Rose was only about three-fourths of an
uninterrupted year. Consequently, for an average year, total annual
receipts would be only three-fourths of those given above. This
means that in an average year of this period each actor of the Shakespearean company would receive a gross sum of about £135, which
would total £1620 for the company. About £1000 of this sum would
go for expenses, the net receipt of each actor thus being about £50.
Of this £50, he received about £12 10s. at the Globe, and £37 10s.
at Blackfriars. Of the actors' £1620 gross receipt, about £600 came
from the Globe, about £300 of it from their half of the galleries,
and £300 from the total receipts at the doors. About £1000 came
from Blackfriars, £600 from the galleries, and £400 from the doors.
The housekeepers received about £900 for an average year. Their
source of income was half the galleries in both houses, about £300

[3] Stopes, *Jahrbuch*, Vol. XLVI, p. 98.

from the Globe and £600 at Blackfriars. Each housekeeping share thus produced about £19 at the Globe and £75 at Blackfriars. As between the two theaters, the Globe produced about £900 and Blackfriars £1600 of the gross yearly income of £2500. Of the £900 at the Globe, about £600 came from the galleries and £300 from the door, a ratio of two to one. Of the £1600 at Blackfriars, about £1200 came from the galleries and £400 from the door, a ratio of three to one.

It seems too that at any given time returns were not startlingly different for any of the established companies at any of the regular houses. Thus the returns at the Theater and Curtain 1587-92 were approximately the same as at the Rose 1592-1600; and the same approximate returns prevailed at the Fortune 1600-08, and at the Hope 1614-15. Further, the Swan must have returned approximately the same amount in 1597 as the other theaters. Five of Pembroke's men alleged that for this period, February 20 to July 25, 1597, approximately five months, each half of the galleries returned at least £100.[4] Half of the galleries at the Rose for the same period returned £132 6s.[5] The returns at the Globe, 1599-1608, could not have been startlingly different from those at the Fortune for the same period. The Red Bull seems to have had receipts at least as large as the others. It seems then that returns were much the same at all of these public theaters.

The fact of approximate equality in receipts implies, but does not prove, approximate equality in size, because income depends directly on the size of the regular audience and only indirectly on the size of the building. The Swan is said to have been larger than the Theater, Curtain, or Rose,[6] and the Hope was modelled upon it. The larger size of the Swan and the Hope was due to the fact that these theaters were to be used also for bear and bull baitings. The Globe was fashioned from the material of the Theater, and the Fortune was modelled on the Globe except in shape. Wright[7] tells us that "The 'Globe,' 'Fortune,' and 'Bull' were large houses." These relations and the matter of incomes seem to indicate that all

[4] Wallace, *Englische Studien*, Vol. XLIII, p. 352.
[5] *ibid.*, p. 363.
[6] Adams, *Playhouses*, pp. 164, 167-8.
[7] Wright, *Historia*, p. 426.

the public theaters were about the same size, except the Swan and Hope, which were larger. It seems likely then that the Theater was in a very real sense the progenitor of them all.

It follows that the financial success of a company was not thrust upon it chiefly by the lucky accident of its having procured some especially favored house. It lay rather in the good organization and business management of the company itself, an organization and management whose success did not depend, at least in the case of the most successful, on its mechanics; but on the personalities bound by goodwill behind it. This success finally traces back to men, not materials nor methods.

We are now in position to figure Shakespeare's average income from the theater. His receipts came from three sources; acting, housekeeping, and writing plays. Up to 1594, he was either an ordinary hired man or an apprentice, and as such would not likely receive more than the normal wage of six shillings a week, or £15 12s. per annum. To this amount must be added his earnings as a playwright. We do not know precisely on what system the Shakespearean company bought its plays, but there is no reason to suppose that it would be very different from that practised in the few cases concerning which we have definite information. Mr. Greg has shown that in Henslowe's records plays were normally £6 each 1597-1602, but a decade later they sold at from £10 to £20, and Daborne "constantly" asserts he can get £25 elsewhere.[8] Nor was there any startling or even notable difference between prices paid to different authors. Even Jonson in 1618 declared that "of all his Playes he never gained two hundreth pounds."[9] Jonson had published ten plays in his folio of 1616, and had written before 1618 two other plays not then published, a total of twelve acknowledged plays. Besides these plays, we know that Jonson wrote at least parts of several others. It is evident then that Jonson received no greater remuneration than did other authors under Henslowe, and hence that Henslowe's prices represent the market price of the time. Since prices rose from £6, 1597-1602, to from £10 to £20 in a

[8] Greg, *Diary*, Vol. II, pp. 126-7.
[9] Conversations with Drummond, quoted in *Shakespeare's England*, Vol. II, p. 210.

decade, it is suggested that the price had been even less than £6 before 1597. Thus the tradition recorded by Oldys[10] that Shakespeare received only £5 for *Hamlet* is doubtless correct, referring to the first version, which I think can now be placed in 1593. Under these market prices, Shakespeare would probably have considered £10 exceptionally good pay for his two plays per annum before 1594, and he may not have received so much for some of his numerous revisions. Thus his total income from theatrical affairs up to 1594 was probably not more than £25 per annum, and may have been some pounds less.

When we consider, however, that the Stratford schoolmasters, and vicars, always able and well educated men, received but £20 per annum,[11] we may suppose that Shakespeare with his £25 considered himself a rising man. Nor were the Stratford scholars receiving less than the regular wage for such services. Edward Alleyn paid his schoolmaster at Dulwich £20 per annum.[12] In 1631 John Williams, Bishop of Lincoln, was sentenced to "erect a free schoole at Eaton or else at Greate Staughton, and endowe the same with 20*l.* per ann. for the maintenance of the schoolmaster for ever."[13] That schoolmaster has probably found his stipend a bit scanty long ere this, even though so late as Goldsmith's *Deserted Village* (1770) the parson was considered "passing rich with forty pounds a year." Further, the salary mentioned in Stowe for a schoolmaster is with one exception always £20.[14] Still another illustration of the scholar's stipend is the £20 per annum salary of Edmund Spenser in 1580-81 as secretary to Lord Grey.[15] Thus the

[10] Malone, *Variorum*, Vol. III, p. 162, note 8. It is to be remembered, however, that even so early as the late eighties Greene is said to have sold a play for twenty nobles or £6 13s 4d (Collier, *Annals* [1879], Vol. II, p. 529, note 1).

[11] Rolfe, W. J., *Shakespeare the Boy*, pp. 98-9; Stopes, Mrs. C. C., *Shakespeare's Warwickshire Contemporaries*, pp. 234-49.

[12] Collier, J. P., *Memoirs of Edward Alleyn*, p. 147.

[13] Murray, Vol. II, pp. 148-9.

[14] Stowe, *Survey* (1603), Vol. I, pp. 111, 113, 114-15, 116.

[15] Carpenter, F. I., "Spenser in Ireland," *Modern Philology*, Vol. XIX, p. 416. Shirley was a bit more fortunate as schoolmaster. As Master of St. Alban's Grammar School, he was entitled to £24 13s 4d per annum, and allowed in addition 4d per quarter for each resident scholar and 12d per quarter for each non-resident (Baugh, A. C., "Some New Facts About Shirley," *Modern Language Review*, Vol. XVII, p. 228). Even when Bacon was fixing the ideal salary for a university professor, he asked no more

Cambridge Students were but representing the facts when in the second part of *The Return from Parnassus* they declared:

"*Rec.* . . . Well it were to be wished that neuer a scholler in England might haue aboue fortie pound a yeare.

"*S. Rad.* Faith maister Recorder, if it went by wishing, there should neuer a one of them all haue aboue twentie a yeare: a good stipend, a good stipend, maister Recorder."[16]

From 1594 to 1599, we have not very accurate information as to probable receipts; but we have some reason to guess about £29 to £36 per annum to each member, and Shakespeare's plays probably returned but little more than before 1594.[17] It is likely, therefore, that he did not average more than £45 to £50 net per annum 1594 to 1599. From 1599 to 1608, he received about £35 to £40 net per annum as an actor. His plays might now net him £25 or £30 per annum. He had also an added income of about £45 per annum as a housekeeper at the Globe. It is probable therefore that his net annual income, 1599-1608, was £105 to £115. For at least two years, summer 1608 through summer 1610, Shakespeare, it seems, neither acted nor wrote; and the theaters were for the greater part of the time closed by the plague. It is thus probable that Shakespeare received practically no return from theatrical affairs these two years. For 1610-11, if he still received a share as an actor, which is uncertain,[18] he would probably get £35 to £50 net, to which is to be

than £100 (Spedding, J., *An Account of the Life and Times of Francis Bacon*, Vol. I, p. 653). For the preachers, the Commons had thought in 1604 that £20 per annum should be the minimum salary (Gardiner, *History*, Vol. I, p. 179). In 1617, it was decided that the Scotch preachers were to receive a minimum of £27 15s 6¾d, a maximum of £44 9s od (Gardiner, *History*, Vol. III, p. 226, note 2). A few years later a preacher was content to preach "the next parish once a week / Asleep for thirty pounds a year" (*The City Match*, Dodsley, Vol. XIII, p. 276.).

[16] Macray, *Parnassus*, p. 119.

[17] We would naturally reason that as Shakespeare became more popular he would receive a much better price for his plays; but, as we have just seen, Henslowe's records show little notable distinction in prices paid to different authors. I have shown above (cf. above, p. 15, and note 38) that this situation is the result of a fundamental attitude of the age, and have attempted to show how the company reached the same end in the case of Shakespeare by a different method.

[18] If for good cause an actor missed a single performance, it seems to have been the custom for him to receive his share. "There's better law amongst the players yet, for a fellow shall have his share, though he do

added about £10 for rewards at court. His plays may now have netted him some £40. As a housekeeper at the Globe, he probably received about £15 to £25 per annum net, and at Blackfriars about £45. His total net income would thus be about £145 to £170 per annum. If he did not receive a share as an actor, his total annual income would be £100 to £110. When he stopped writing entirely in 1613 and retired to Stratford, his income would probably be confined to returns for housekeeping, which would likely be some £60 to £70 per annum.

We are to remember, however, that this income is figured on the basis of the average year, which was three-fourths of the uninterrupted year. Consequently, after Shakespeare became a member of the company and a housekeeper he might have received in a particularly good year considerably more than the average amount. But he might just as easily have lost money in a bad year. For instance, after the company took over Blackfriars in 1608, we have seen reason to believe that Shakespeare might possibly have received some £145 to £170 in a good average year, £100 to £130 from other sources than his plays. This £130 might be £175 in a good uninterrupted year, which, plus £40 for plays, would give a maximum income of possibly £215 for a particularly good year. It is exceedingly doubtful, however, as indicated above, that Shakespeare ever reaped much benefit from the increased income ensuing upon the acquisition of Blackfriars. He seems to have dropped all connections that brought financial returns, except housekeeping, about 1613, though he remained a member till his death. He had ceased acting probably as early as 1608. It is likely therefore that Shakespeare's best income came from the Globe just before 1608. It is quite a liberal guess under the circumstances to suppose that Shakespeare ever received in the very best years as much as £250 net from all his sources of income connected with the theater. More probably he never received over £175.

Nevertheless, his income was not beggarly, nor even to be sneered at. It has been supposed that money was worth about eight

not play that day" (*A Cure for a Cuckold*, II, 3; Hazlitt's *Webster*, Vol. IV, p. 36). But we have no direct evidence that an actor emeritus was pensioned with his share.

times as much in Shakespeare's time as it was just before 1914, but Professor Wallace says money would purchase then only "3½ to 4 times the same value of necessities as now" [1913].[19] Sir Sidney Lee uses five as the ratio in his estimates. Since at best we are only getting approximate values, we may use both the 4 and 5 ratios. Thus Shakespeare's income before 1594 was probably not over £25 per annum, which would be £100 or £125 in modern money, some $500 or $625. Between 1594 and 1599, his income was probably not over £50 per annum, which would be £200 or £250 in modern money, some $1,000 or $1,250. From 1599 to 1608 his income was probably around £110 per annum, which would be £440 or £550 in modern money, some $2,200 to $2,750. For 1610-11, his income may have been about £155 per annum, which would be £620 or £775 in modern money, some $3,100 to $3,875. After 1611 his income probably dropped back to about £65, which would be £260 to £325 in modern money, some $1,300 to $1,625. He probably never received in any particular year more than £250, which would be £1,000 or £1,250 in modern money, some $5,000 or $6,250. It is more likely that he never received more than £175, which would be £700 or £875 in modern money, some $3,500 to $4,375. It is probable, therefore, that Shakespeare received about the same income in his own day as the literary professional man receives in the present day.[20]

Our knowledge of receipts in some of the theaters throws light upon the further question of size for the dramatic audience in the Elizabethan times. If we know average receipts at the outer doors

[19] Wallace, *First London Theatre*, p. 21; Lee, *Shakespeare*, p. 296, note 1.
[20] We may notice here some of Thomasina Ostler's statements concerning shares in 1615-16. She claims damages on a seventh share in Blackfriars, and a fourteenth share in the Globe. The damages include not only the value of the shares but the income on them for one year. Thus her total bill of £600 should cover both these items, though it has been interpreted as covering only the income for a year (Wallace, London *Times*, October 2 and 4, 1909). As we have seen, the share at the Globe was probably estimated as worth about £100. Since the share at Blackfriars seemingly required no initial payment, we cannot place a valuation on it, the principle of bargain being denied by the company. The net income from the two shares for a year was probably £60 to £75 for an average year, but might be about £100. Actual damage therefore from the sources enumerated would be probably between £200 and £300. Consequently, a £600 damage claim is quite modest as damage claims go.

and the price of admission, we get the average audience, since all paid this admission except those on the free list, and probably a very few who entered through the tiring-house door. We know that the average daily receipts from the outer doors at the Rose were £1 17s. 9d. in 1597. We do not know directly what fee was charged at the outer door of the Rose; but it was the almost universal custom in public theaters to charge one penny, certainly so on ordinary occasions. This would mean an average daily attendance at the door of four hundred and fifty-three people. But this estimate of entrants at the door must be rather liberal, since our average receipts include new plays when two and three times the ordinary fee was charged. However, this excess is probably balanced by the select entrants at the tiring-house door. We may thus fairly estimate that the average daily audience at the Rose in 1597 numbered between four and five hundred. Since the receipts from the galleries remained much the same throughout the existence of the Rose, as also later at the Fortune, this estimate may serve as a fair indication of the average audience at both places. It will be noticed that the comparative size of the Rose and Fortune has little to do with the problem, since the size merely indicates the maximum audience that might be accommodated in either building, but does not show the size of the audience that actually was accommodated.

We happen also to know something of the size of the audience at the Globe. During Herbert's benefits the Globe returned an average of £7 1s. 8d. daily. We have seen too that the galleries returned about twice as much as the doors. Therefore, the average receipts from the door would be about £2 7s. 3d. The price of admission here seems also to have been a penny. This would mean an average daily attendance through the outer doors of five hundred and sixty-seven individuals. The daily attendance was thus probably five to six hundred at the Globe.

Blackfriars had returned a daily average of £16 5s. during Herbert's benefits. Here the ratio of galleries to doors was about three to one, so that the average daily return from the door was £4 1s. 3d. The ordinary price of admission is usually guessed as half a shilling. If this was the price, the average audience would number one hundred and sixty-three persons. Professor Wallace has shown that the maximum seating capacity of the building could hardly have been more than six hundred.[21] Certainly Professor Wallace has stated a maximum, and I suspect the actual capacity was considerably less.

Financial returns at the Red Bull would indicate that it had at least as good an audience as the Globe. We may thus allow it also five or six hundred.[22]

We may now form some idea of the number of theatergoers 1599-1608. According to our estimates, there were five to six hundred for the Shakespearean company at the Globe, and probably three to six hundred for the Queen's at the Rose, Curtain, and Red Bull. There were four to five hundred for Prince Henry's at the Rose and Fortune. There were probably two to three hundred for the children at Blackfriars. On any particular afternoon, therefore, 1599-1608, one might have found some fourteen hundred to two thousand people at the various theaters in London. Even the watermen in January 1614, when trying to make out a most touching case of their woes claimed only: "the Players haue all (except the Kings men) left their vsuall residency on the Banke-side, and doe play in Middlesex farre remote from the Thames, so that euery day in the weeke they doe draw vnto them three or foure thousand people, that were vsed to spend their monies by water."[23] Since the watermen would naturally under the circumstances take peak figures and even stretch those all they dared, our average estimate of but slightly less than half of theirs is reasonable enough. Considering the fact that London was a city of at least 100,000 inhabitants and at this period probably almost twice as large,[24] we must admit that the situation of the playhouses outside the walls is but symbolical of the position occupied by the drama in London. The heart of London was puritan.

It seems therefore that the London populace was hardly more theater mad in Shakespeare's time than is that of most modern cities of the size of London. Certainly, its enthusiasm cannot compare with the "movie" craze of present-day America.[25] Neverthe-

---

21 Wallace, *Children*, p. 52.
22 See Appendix II.
23 *Works of John Taylor* (Spenser Soc., 1869), p. 334.
24 Lee, *Shakespeare*, p. 40.
25 For instance, in Portland, Oregon, a city of slightly over 250,000,

less, that audience was large enough to put its especial favorites in comfortable financial circumstances, provided those favorites had sufficient business acumen to make use of their opportunities. Water is not held in a sieve, and there were financial sieves among the actors then, just as there are in the same class today. It is not surprising therefore that some of the most successful actors, including William Shakespeare, could retire from active business before they died of old age. Neither is it surprising that none of them became exceedingly wealthy from the theater alone, though some of them did become substantial citizens. Sir Sidney Lee has shown that Shakespeare in his will made bequests in money of £350, and had real estate for which he had paid £1,200, besides his personal property. Excluding personal property, his fortune would thus be £1,550, which would be £6,200 or £7,750 in modern money, some $31,000 or $38,750. He could hardly then have been worth more than £2,000 in money of his own time, some £8,000 or £10,000 in modern money, $40,000 or $50,000. While, then, we may give Shakespeare credit for commendable industry and a moderate degree of business ability, yet we can hardly class him among great financiers.[26]

there was in 1921 an average daily attendance at both "movies" and legitimate performances, of 50,000 paid admissions, or roughly an average attendance of one in five. For the legitimate performances alone, the average was well above the one in fifty which is the highest that could have obtained in London during Shakespeare's lifetime (Statistics taken from *The Oregon Daily Journal* for March 1, 1921, and checked through the courtesy of Mr. Marshall N. Dana of the *Journal* staff). It is apparent then that at least in Portland even the legitimate theater is probably as well supported now as it was in London at Shakespeare's time, and that the "movies" surpass the Elizabethan London theaters in drawing power.

[26] It is of course to be remembered that Shakespeare's financial ability is demonstrated only in his own private affairs. He had no more to do with the financial affairs of his company than any other member. His chief contribution to the success of the company was his plays, that of Burbadge his acting, etc.; but it was the special business of John Heminges to keep the finances of the company in order, and to him the credit for success in this field is chiefly due (See above, p. 39).

PLAYS WITH ASSIGNED LISTS, 1626–1632

ACTORS	Roman Actor	Lover's Melancholy	Picture	Deserving Favorite	Believe As Ye List	Wild Goose Chase
	5+2	7+4	7+3	5+2	4+0	5+3
Joseph Taylor	2 Paris 443	3 Palador 252	1 Mathias 590	2 Duke 559	1 Antiochus 780	1 Mirabel 753
John Lowin	1 Caesar 702	2 Corax 254	4 Eubulus 329	6 Jacomo 222	2 Flaminius 633	2 Belleur 366
Robert Benfield	Rusticus 69	1 Meleander 308	8 Ladislaus 183	5 King 323	4 Marcellus 191	6 De Gard 174
Eyllaerdt Swanston	5 Aretinus 148	Menaphon 234	6 Ricardo 263	Utrante 64	Chrysalus 49	8 Lugier 170
Thomas Pollard	Lamia {64 6 Stephanos 63} 127	6 Rhetias 224	5 Ubaldo 278	1 Lysander 626	3 Berecinthius 295	5 Pinac 221
Richard Sharp	3 Parthenius 278	8 Amethus 200	Ferdinand 60	7 Orsinio 175	Lentulus 40	
Richard Robinson	Aesopus 43					
John Shank		9 Cuculus 171	7 Hilario 210		{?2nd Merchant 80 Jailor 35	La Castre 86 Petella 0
William Penn	Philargus 53	Sophronos 73	10 Baptista 107	Gerard 16		
Anthony Smith		Aretus 52			Calistus 26	Nantolet 65
Thomas Hobbs						
Curtis Greville	{? Tribune Latinus 60				?3rd Merchant 77 Captain	
William Patrick	Sura 25					
George Vernon	{? Tribune {? Lictor					
James Horn	{? Tribune {? Lictor	Grilla 52				
John Thompson	4 Domitia 258	4 Thamasta 245	3 Honoria 414	4 Cleonarda 488	1st Merchant 78	Factor 83
John Honyman	7 Domitilla 106	7 Eroclea 210	2 Sophia 484	3 Clarinda 501		3 Bianca 359
Alexander Goffe	Caenis 43	10 Cleophila 118	Acanthe 25			4 Rosalura 254
William Trigg	Julia 46	11 Kala 101	9 Corisca 115			7 Oriana 172
Stephen Hammerton						
Edward Horton				Mariana 98		

NOTE: The numbers at the top of the columns give the number of characters in the play having one hundred lines and over, men at the left, women and boys at the right. To the left of each character of one hundred lines or more is placed its relative rank according to number of lines; to the right of all characters the number of lines. In this reckoning, part lines of either verse or prose have been counted as whole lines. The count has been carefully made but not checked, since absolute accuracy is not demanded by the purpose of the table.

The Lover's Melancholy is included among the assigned lists for mere mechanical convenience. Parts are not assigned in the play, but a complete list of actors is given, in accordance with which the above assignment is made.

CHAPTER VII

DIVISION OF LABOR
IN THE SHAKESPEAREAN COMPANY

NOW that we have established the membership of the Shakespearean company and worked out most of its business arrangements, we may next see what part the members bore in the performances themselves. Since the company had definite organization and customs of procedure in business matters, we shall expect also to find a regular division of labor in the actual production of plays. A study of the assigned play lists of the company will give us this information, as also knowledge concerning the duties performed by the hired men and apprentices of the company, for whom we have very few other sources of information.

We have five plays of this company that have fairly complete assignment of parts, four of them dating 1626-32, the fifth a few years earlier. These five plays are *The Duchess of Malfi*, principal list dating 1623, minor list 1613; *The Roman Actor*, 1626; *The Deserving Favorite*, published 1629; *The Picture*, 1629; and *The Wild Goose Chase*, revival autumn of 1632. The lists of *Barnavelt*, August 1619, and *Believe as Ye List*, 1631, are fragmentary; but supply additional information.[1] There are also several occasional references to parts taken by the more famous actors.

From the analysis of these five plays, representing four authors and covering some twenty years of time, several things are evident. First, the typical play seems to have been constructed for eight principal characters, six men and two women, or five men and three women. This is the reason the typical list of principal actors in the second Beaumont and Fletcher folio contains eight names, six members and two apprentices, or five members and three apprentices. The sixth man, however, often has no more lines than some

---

[1] For convenience, a tabulation of parts taken is given opposite and the detailed mechanical analysis of the plays is relegated to Appendix III.

of the minor characters. Second, members took the parts of men, almost never those of women. We have only one certain recorded instance of a member taking the part of a woman; Shank takes a silent part in *The Wild Goose Chase*, seemingly for the purpose of coaching the two apprentices upon whom he attends. The parts of women are practically always taken by apprentices, who may occasionally have been permitted minor men's parts toward the end of their apprenticeships. Third, seven or eight members always took name parts. Concerning these seven or eight, further conclusions can be drawn. Taking *The Roman Actor*, *The Picture*, *The Deserving Favorite*, and *The Wild Goose Chase*, we find that Lowin, Taylor, Benfield, and Swanston played in all four; Pollard, Sharp, and Robinson played in three each; and Shank, Penn, and Smith in two each. This means that all members took part in these plays except Heminges, who had ceased acting about 1611, and Hobbs, who appears, however, both in *The Lover's Melancholy*, licensed November 24, 1628,[2] and in *Believe As Ye List*, 1631. Thus all active members of the company took part as actors. Exactly in accordance with this, we find between 1619 and 1622 that four members appear on every one of the Beaumont and Fletcher lists, and that two miss only a few, their places being supplied by other members.[3] Fourth, there are usually four women's parts, two major and two minor. Fifth, hired men are never given major parts; but are used simply to supply more or less unimportant places. Briefly, members took the major men's parts, apprentices took the women's parts, and the hired men supplied the unimportant places for men.

---

[2] Fleay, *Stage*, p. 334; Adams, *Herbert*, p. 32.

[3] Thus the fact that *The Custom of the Country*, *The Little French Lawyer*, and *Women Pleased* have the same list of actors does not mean that these plays came in immediate succession as Mr. Cyril Brett (*The Works of Francis Beaumont and John Fletcher*, Variorum Edition, Vol. IV, p. 94), following Mr. Oliphant (*Englische Studien*, Vol. XVI, p. 185), has supposed. Because of this very fact, it is highly improbable that these plays are successive. The identity simply means that the plays were performed in the same general period, when all these actors were in the company. The limits in this case would be set by Taylor, who entered in 1619, and Tooley and Eccleston, who dropped out in 1623. The actor lists, therefore, merely show that these three plays date 1619-23; but show nothing of their relative order, or of their order as compared with other plays of the same general period.

As we shall see, this division of labor was naturally evolved from the organization of the company.[4]

How were the parts assigned? In the period 1626-32, there are seven members who supply these six major parts for men. These seven members are Lowin, Taylor, Benfield, Swanston, always appearing; and Pollard, Sharp, and Robinson supplying the other two places. In case there is a major clown part, it is of course taken by Shank. But this part is usually supplied by the clown himself, and is not written into the play.

An analysis of the known parts in the preceding and all other plays of the Shakespearean company shows that each of the major actors had his particular "business." In every instance but one, Taylor takes the part of the hero of the story. As the beloved Paris, jealous Mathias, the love-sick Duke in *The Deserving Favorite*, long-suffering Antiochus, and wild-goose Mirabel, he is the leading man. As Rollo in *The Bloody Brother*,[5] he is still the leading man; but one who degenerates into an open villain. As "leading man," he would inherit the parts of Richard Burbadge. Thus we find the names of both Burbadge and Taylor attached to Ferdinand in *The Duchess of Malfi*. Of the Shakespearean and Jonsonian parts, Wright tells us that Taylor took Hamlet, Iago, Truewit, and Face.[6] To these Flecknoe[7] adds Mosca. We know that Hamlet was a Burbadge part, and may be fairly certain that the Jonsonian parts were also his. Edmund Gayton gives us still another of Taylor's characters:[8] "He was instantly metamorphosed into the stateliest, gravest, and commanding soul that eye ever beheld: Taylor acting Arbaces, or Swanston D'Amboys, were shadows to him." Although

[4] See below, pp. 306 ff.
[5] Wright, *Historia*, p. 427.
[6] *ibid.*, p. 424. Downes, *Roscius Anglicanus* (1708 and Knight's reprint), p. 21, also tells us that Taylor acted Hamlet; but is evidently wrong in saying that Shakespeare taught him how, since Taylor did not enter the company till after Shakespeare's death. Since Lowin was the original Henry VIII, we may be sure Burbadge was Wolsey and bequeathed the part to Taylor. The Comedy *Knavery in All Trades*, 1664, says Taylor and Pollard acted with Lowin in Henry VIII, but seems not to assign parts (Halliwell, *Outlines*, Vol. II, p. 295).
[7] Collier, *Memoirs*, p. 261.
[8] *Festivous Notes on Don Quixote*, 1654. Quoted by Collier, *Annals* (1879), Vol. I, p. 488, note 1.

Taylor could not have been the original Arbaces, yet the character is thoroughly in his line, and commanding dignity is evidently one of this actor's characteristics.

It is then only necessary to find the "leading" rôle to know what part Taylor took. In five of the six known characters created by him, he plays the lover. Of course, in the time of romantic comedy, he must be a lover if he would pretend to be a leading man. Still, his often taking the part must mean that he was adapted to it. We are told that Paris:

> would perform
> A lover's part much better[9]

than he did the orator's, and that Domitia is much taken with his shape. Mathias too is considered a desirable commodity by waiting maids and ladies. The Duke in *The Deserving Favorite* is a perfect chivalrous knight and lover, though more emphasis is here put on his mental or moral than on his physical qualifications. Mirabel is also "A young and handsome man."[10] This part was written for Taylor when he first came to the company; though he could still qualify for it in 1632, at the age of forty-seven. But at the same time, he could represent Antiochus, who before the end of the play had been four and twenty years wandering over the world. He could then represent both youth and age when he himself was an old man. Besides handsomeness and grace, he must also have had a noble dignity. Paris, the Duke, and Antiochus all have this quality, and Mathias also to a less degree. Still, upon occasion he must have the devil-may-care dash of a Mirabel, or the petulant bloodthirstiness of a Rollo; he must even be honest Iago. In short, Taylor seems to have been characterised by versatility and polished grace rather than by blunt force. He must have been naturally a gentleman in the best sense of the term.

John Lowin is an exact complement to Taylor. His is the bluntly humorous, bluff character. To him falls the impolite villain, the gruff counsellor, the plain-spoken friend. He is the cruel tyrant

---

[9] *Roman Actor*, II, 1. 415-16. The lining for Massinger's plays is my own, counted on Cunningham's edition.
[10] All quotations from the Beaumont-Fletcher plays may be located through the table at the beginning of this chapter, and Appendix IV.

Caesar, revelling in blood even from his youth; the honest Jacomo, who is an exceedingly lame Iago and could have given Lowin but little joy; the equally honest Flaminius, relentless devil incarnate, hounding the hero for love of evil, of brusk, imperious manner, haughty and overbearing; the wise old counsellor Eubulus, who mistakes blunt impudence for plainness of speech, humorous withal; the equally humorous and blustering Belleur, the brave but bashful lover, who wins by main strength and awkwardness, or rather is caught because of it; and the "huffing" lord Aubrey, who in his own imagination is "A wise man and a valiant man, a just man"; but to his enemies a "swash buckler" nevertheless.

Lowin had certainly been taking this line as early as 1612-13. The quarto of 1623 indicates that Lowin was the original Bosola in *The Duchess of Malfi*, 1613.[11] Also, Downes[12] says that Lowin was Henry the Eighth and "had his Instructions from Mr. *Shakespear* himself." Since "Bluff Harry" is a characteristic rôle for Lowin's line, we may accept the statement as true, and be sure that Lowin created the part about 1612. Thus when Wright[13] informs us that Lowin was Volpone (1605), Mammon (1610), and Melantius (1610), we may be fairly certain that he created these parts also. In the case of Mammon, who is the "fat knight" and only the third part in the play instead of the second as was later Lowin's right, we have added indication in the physical characteristics that the part must have been written originally for Lowin and retained by him to the end. Wright is also authority for the statement that Lowin was Morose, after *Epicoene* came into the Shakespearean company. Lowin then is the heavy lead or villain of the company, a line he had taken certainly since about 1612, and almost certainly from his entrance to the company in 1603.[14]

Indeed, we have fair evidence that Lowin was the original Iago.

[11] For date, see below, p. 250, note 59.
[12] Downes, *Roscius Anglicanus*, (1708 and Knight's reprint), p. 24.
[13] Wright, *Historia*, p. 424.
[14] Thus Roberts the actor states the case fairly well in 1729: "I am apt to think, he (Lowin) did not rise to his perfection and most exalted state in the theatre till after Burbage, tho' he play'd what we call second and third characters in his time, and particularly Henry the Eighth originally" (Halliwell, *Outlines*, Vol. I, p. 243).

Gildon tells us in 1694:[15] "I'm assur'd, from very good hands, that the person that acted Iago was in much esteem of a comedian which made Shakespear put several words and expressions into his part, perhaps not agreeable to his character, to make the audience laugh."[16] Now Iago belongs to the "honest" soldier type so much affected by Lowin. Further, Iago is "four times seven years" old in this play, which was composed no long time before its presentation at court November 1, 1604. This is approximately Lowin's age at the time of presentation, since he was baptized December 9, 1576,[17] and would be twenty-eight about December 9, 1604. Besides, there is no other part of Lowin's type in the play. It is thus fairly certain that Lowin was the original Iago.[18]

These parts furnish us an excellent personal description of Lowin. Bosola was of an "excellent shape."[19] Belleur (1621-32) was a "tall fat fellow," "a maypole, a great dry pudding," "a mighty dairy maid in man's clothes." Aubrey was "somewhat high of stature," "And fat," "somewhat corpulent," "about seven-and-fifty," and "His head and beard inclining to be grey." Mammon was the "fat knight." Lowin was, then, a large man, seemingly fat even before he was forty, though of course his flesh could have been assumed.

Still, Lowin's size and later corpulency are confirmed by a portrait "1640, Aetat. 64," printed by Malone[20] as "Engraved by T. Holloway, from an original Picture in the Ashmole Museum, Oxford." The engraving shows a very large man with long, curling hair, small mustache, and tufted under lip. The eyes are not very

---

[15] Furness, *Variorum, Othello*, p. 397.

[16] We need to remember, however, that some years before this Clun was performing Bessus, Falstaff, and Iago (Collier, *Annals* [1879], Vol. III, p. 187, note 2). This situation may represent the original casting, or it may have suggested the inference concerning the original casting, which then came to Gildon as a fact.

[17] Collier, *Memoirs*, p. 165.

[18] By the thirties Lowin was being tamed by age, so that an adjustment was made, by which Swanston took Othello and Taylor Iago. See below, p. 182.

[19] *Duchess of Malfi*, V. 2. 126.

[20] Malone, *Plays and Poems*, 1790, Vol. I, Part II, opp. p. 205. For other reproductions, see Lane, W. C., and Brown, N. E., *A.L.A. Portrait Index*, under Lowin.

dark, probably grey. The nose is heavy and straight, mouth comparatively small, hands large but in proportion to stature. It is a picture full of aggressive character, and shows a man well suited by nature for the rôles Lowin represented.[21] It was doubtless this exceptional physique and aggressive personality, as well as the £200 he paid for the place, that made Lowin King James's porter, and retained him in office under Charles.[22] With these characteristics in mind, it need not surprise us that according to Wright[23] Lowin in later days took the part of the blustering fat knight, Falstaff. Indeed, when the *Merry Wives* Falstaff was revamped in 1604, it must have been for Lowin, this being in part the reason that he is not the same man as the Falstaff of *Henry IV*.

Swanston is supporting villain of the smooth, scheming type. As Aretinus, Caesar's spy, he is an ardent supporter and bootlicker of Caesar (Lowin), a good "bloodhound," a conscienceless smooth villain, taking pleasure in his sneaking work. As Ricardo, he is older and more experienced in villainy than Ubaldo (Pollard), taking the lead in planning and carrying out their various courtierly plots, though after they are into the comic situation, Ubaldo leads. Since there is but one full villain in *The Deserving Favorite*, the best part Swanston could get was that of the father Utrante, who to save himself would persuade his unwilling daughter to marry the Duke. As Chrysalus, Swanston is frankly the villain again, robbing, taunting and betraying the man who for years had been a good master to him.[24] As Lugier, he is the scheming tutor of the young ladies, plotting to get them married to his will. Since Swanston found a character suited to his turn in each of the plays listed, he was evidently also a utility man, taking whatever important part was best suited to his ability, when no fully characteristic representative of his own line was in the play. His chief rôle, however, was

---

[21] The portrait is reproduced in an article by Alexander Cargill. "Shakespeare as an actor," *Scribner's*, Vol. IX, p. 634; but the reproducer has given Lowin a shave, and has otherwise smoothed much of the aggressiveness from the face, unless indeed it is Malone's engraver who has given Lowin a beard by courtesy.

[22] *H.M.C.*, *Twelfth Report*, Appendix, Part I, Vol. I, p. 194.

[23] Wright, *Historia*, p. 424.

[24] Unfortunately, most of this part is on the leaf that was torn out of the *Believe As Ye List* manuscript.

the schemer, preferably the villain plotter, in which he was thus a support and understudy to Lowin.

Because of the smoother quality of his villainy and also of his greater youth, Swanston fell heir to some of the old parts, which had been fitted to a certain quality in Burbadge that Taylor had little of and Lowin had not at all. Besides, by the thirties Lowin was growing old. The prologue to *Bussy d'Ambois* opens up the clue to the necessary adjustment when it informs us concerning the play that Field "first did give it name," and that:

> one
> Who came the nearest to him, is denied
> By his gray beard to show the height and pride
> Of D'Ambois' youth and bravery;

but that another actor takes the part, of whom we hear "As Richard he was liked." Edmund Gayton[25] gives us the clue to this actor when he tells us that Swanston as D'Ambois was "the stateliest, gravest, and commanding soul that eye ever beheld." Professor Parrott[26] shows that the prologue is pretty certainly for a revival at the Cockpit April 7, 1634.[27] The fact that *Richard III* precedes Bussy in this same court season, November 16, 1633,[28] clinches Professor Parrott's arguments to make it certain that Swanston personated Richard III for the performance at court November 16, 1633, and D'Ambois April 7, 1634. Thus by 1633 Swanston was beginning to divide the headlines with Taylor, now nearing fifty, and Lowin, now nearing sixty. One such divided reference throws a flood of light on Swanston's mode of acting. In *The Virtuoso*, Snarl, whose humor it is to praise the olden time before 1640, says that he has "seen Joseph Taylor, and Lowen, and Swanstead: Oh, a brave roaring Fellow would make the House shake again." Thus when Lowin found it necessary because of age to ease up on his work, it was altogether fitting that Swanston should fall heir to the jealous Othello,[29] leaving Iago to the quieter Taylor. It is

[25] Quoted by Collier, *Annals* (1879), Vol. I, p. 488, note 1.
[26] Chapman, *Tragedies*, p. 547.
[27] Adams, *Herbert*, p. 55.
[28] *ibid.*, p. 53. For a suggestion that Bond may have been this actor, see *Modern Philology*, Vol. XXIII, pp. 3-5.
[29] Wright, *Historia*, p. 424. Collier, *Memoirs*, p. 220 would give Field as another actor of Othello, but I am suspicious of his evidence. Winter,

apparent then that Swanston under the excuse of greater youthful fire and vigor was by 1633 supplying the more juvenile and smoothly villainous parts of the old plays. Evidently Swanston became an actor of considerable versatility and reputation. We have no clue to his theatrical age and appearance further than that as Ricardo he was supposed to be older and more experienced than Ubaldo (Pollard).

The business of Robert Benfield is also well established. He always takes dignified parts, such as kings, senators, and old men, regularly ranking third or fourth in number of lines taken. As the senator Junius Rusticus, he leads the opposition to Caesar, exhibiting some oratory but little hard acting. As Ladislaus, he is a henpecked husband and a king, never showing suspicion or jealousy, though strongly provoked. As the King in *The Deserving Favorite*, he is chiefly a dignified and important part of the machinery, delivering his edicts in right royal style. As Marcellus, he is a noble Roman governor, who stands for the right and disciplines the fiendish Flaminius. As De Gard, he is a wholly serious father striving to untangle the nets of Cupid. None of his parts calls for the delineation of any passion stronger than royal anger of an oratorical turn. He seems to have inherited his line from Ostler, whom he succeeded in the company about the beginning of 1615. Their names are jointly attached to the part of Antonio in *The Duchess of Malfi*. Beyond this, we have no record of old parts taken by Benfield. Neither are there any references to his physical characteristics; but to represent his parts he must have been of good appearance and stately bearing.

It is interesting to find Taylor, Lowin, Swanston, and Benfield playing their accustomed parts in a drama of real life. Herbert records "The 24 Octob. 1633, Lowins and Swanston were sorry for their ill manners, and craved my pardon, which I gave them in presence of Mr. Taylor and Mr. Benfeilde."[30] The occasion was Herbert's attempt to do "God good servise, and the quality no wronge," by purging *The Tamer Tamed* of "oaths, prophaness, and

Century, LXXXII, p. 503, says Underwood also acted the part before the death of Burbadge, but gives no authority.

[30] Adams, *Herbert*, p. 21.

publique ribaldry, wh^{ch} for the future I doe absolutely forbid to bee presented unto mee in any playbooke, as you will answer it at your perill. 21 Octob. 1633."[31] Evidently some of the quality did not agree that Herbert was doing them no wrong. It is probable that the villains suffered most from Herbert's method of purgation, this arousing their strong protest. Hence we have the peppery Lowin, and his understudy in villainy Swanston, eating humble pie for their faults in the presence of the gentlemanly Taylor, and the dignified Benfield, who were both probably as much exasperated by the "fussy" Herbert as were Lowin and Swanston, but knew better how to treat one in authority. Indeed, Taylor succeeded so well as to be appointed Yeoman of the Revels under Herbert a few years later. This incident taken in connection with the evidence already, and still to be, adduced shows that there is probably as much truth as aphorism in the statement that these men did not act; they were themselves. In that fact lies the key to much of the company's success.

Like Lowin, Taylor also had an understudy. This was the "juvenile lead" Richard Sharp. He takes prominent part in all these plays before 1630. He is Parthenius, in the beginning of *The Roman Actor* Caesar's chief handyman; but later, alienated by Caesar's treatment of his father, the leader of the plot against Caesar. He is easily the third man character in this play, only Lowin and Taylor surpassing him. He is Ferdinand, the blunt, frank soldier of good presence, contrasting strongly with the courtiers, Ricardo and Ubaldo. He is Lysander, a fine looking young lover, who has the greatest number of lines in the play and is the chivalric antagonist of the only more chivalric Deserving Favorite, Taylor himself. Sharp was thus quite a capable actor. As an apprentice, he had been leading lady of the regal type till about 1623, playing, among other characters, the noble Duchess of Malfi. We have no personal allusions to him as a member, further than that in two of his three assigned parts he is a young man, and in the third probably was not represented as old. Thus his acting age corresponds with his actual. As we shall see, while still an apprentice, he came to be a giantess and:

[31] Adams, *Herbert*, p. 21.

[184]

three foote
Too high for a Woman.[32]

He was thus probably of fine physique, and rather a handsome young fellow.

Pollard regularly did light comedy. He is Ubaldo, the typical courtier of Massinger, full of leering lechery till he is disciplined by Sophia with comic results. He is the "corpulent Flamen" Berecinthius, jesting at his own ungainliness and at death itself. He is Pinac, the running mate of Belleur and a comic figure. He is the Cook in *Rollo*, very much in the Berecinthius humor. As Ubaldo and Berecinthius, he clashes in comic battle with Lowin. As Stephanos in *The Roman Actor*, he is still a comic figure, though not so heavily marked as in the preceding characters. Only as Aelius Lamia, the wronged husband in *The Roman Actor*, is he not openly comic. It is difficult for a modern to imagine the desirability of comic treatment for this character, yet cuckoldry was often a comic subject with the Elizabethans. Pollard has no part in *The Deserving Favorite*, because there is no light comedy figure there. Wright tells us that Pollard was a comedian,[33] and a contemporary pamphlet tells us he was a humorist, causing much laughter in *The Humorous Lieutenant*, being named with the famed comedians Cane and Robins,[34] as we would naturally expect of Shank's former apprentice. In earlier time, he took the unimportant part of Silvio in *The Duchess of Malfi* (1623), a supposedly humorous character as the author is at some pains to tell us.[35] He also took the part of Holderus in *Barnavelt* (1619), again a humorous character. Since the light comedy is not always important, Pollard will not always appear among the principal actors;[36] but if he does appear, we know what kind of part he will take. He was originally Shank's apprentice, and probably came with him to the company about the winter of 1615. He appears five times in the sixteen actor lists of

---

[32] Baldwin, *Duke of Milan*, II, I. 189-90; and note, p. 156.
[33] Wright, *Historia*, p. 424.
[34] *A Key to the Cabinet of the Parliament*, 1648. Quoted by Collier, *Annals* (1879), Vol. II, p. 38, note.
[35] *Duchess of Malfi*, I, 1. 136-8.
[36] Pollard is thrust stumbling in to speak the epilogue to Shirley's first tragedy for the company, *The Cardinal*, licensed November 25, 1641 (Adams, *Herbert*, p. 39), giving us another of his ways of amusing.

1616-22, and in nearly every list thereafter. We have no very satis-
fying description of Pollard's physical appearance. As Berecinthius,
he was of Falstaffian proportions, but his fat may not have been
permanent. As the Cook in *Rollo*, his speech:

> Oh, what a goodly swing
> I shall give the gallows

appears also to intimate that he was somewhat weighty, at least in
makeup. The Cook and his crew seem all to be young, and each
sings the ballad of his own death. Yet the fat Cook was originally
a Rowley part, which accounts for his weight. As Pinac in 1632,
Pollard is a "young man" and sings; but there is a possibility that
this character was created for Eccleston. Thus Pollard's picture is
indefinite, though he was probably but not certainly corpulent.

It is now easy to define the general relations of the six principal
actors. Taylor was hero "lead" and Lowin gruff, "honest" soldier
or domineering villain, the "heavy lead."[37] Akin to Lowin on his
comic side was Pollard for "light comedy," and on his villainous
was Swanston for "scheming villain," either serious or comic. Benfield was nearest Taylor in dignified parts, being the major "old
man,"[38] and Sharp was "juvenile lead." Thus Taylor, Benfield,
and Sharp are usually opposed as heroes to Lowin, Swanston, and
Pollard as villains and comedians. If a play is full of villains and
comic characters, that branch is prominent, and vice versa. Since
there is nearly always an important "old man," two of the three
hero lines will practically always be among the six principal actors;
but the third, the "juvenile lead," may either star or not appear
among the principal actors at all. The same is true of the villain-
comedy lines, except that only one is absolutely certain to appear,

---

[37] It is to be noticed that the fundamental characteristic of Lowin is a
certain bluff gruffness, which may be of the "honest" soldier type, or that
of the rather domineering villain. Hence he is both comedian and villain.
We shall later see that this same combination of types, though with different emphasis, had been the custom in the Shakespearean company
from the beginning. Probably this combination is the direct descendant of
the Vice or Devil in the older plays. It is in the sense just defined that the
term "heavy lead" is here used for Lowin.

[38] The term "old man" is used only in its technical sense as indicating
dignified characters, and neither states nor implies anything concerning
the actual age of the actor.

though at least one of the other two usually does. Our difficulties then in assigning parts will not be in general principles but in specific applications.

Besides these six principal actors, Richard Robinson also usually has a place in each play, rarely, however, in a part that places him among the six leading male actors. He seems usually to have played important minor parts, and as a result to have been occasionally thrust into the lowest rank of the six most important actors. Usually, eight members take part in a play, and Robinson is nearly always one of the minor two, below the principal six. As Aesopus, he is a young man, a companion of Paris and a kind of minor satellite. He can hardly be said to have a character. As Orsinio, he is in point of lines the fifth man character in the play. He is, however, more an expositor than an actor. Most of his work is done in telling of the past, which itself unravels the present, requiring merely a certain oratorical theatricalness. As Lentulus, he is only a messenger to Flaminius, having but thirty-three lines, and being unmarked as to character. As LaCastre, the father of Mirabel, he is sixth man character in the play, yet has only eighty-six lines, being little more than a lay figure. If he has any character, it is that of a good old man who wishes his son to settle down. Thus Robinson ranks as about first dignified handyman, of good presence and oratorical ability.

William Penn and Anthony Smith about tie for the second handyman, with Thomas Hobbs trailing closely behind. Penn is Baptista, the magician-friend and companion of Mathias (Taylor). Dignity in appearance, and probably cleverness in make-up would be the chief requisites for this character. Seemingly he is rather up in years, though no specific reference is made to his age. As Nantolet, father of the girls, Penn is an unimportant old man, much like the preceding. As the Jailor in *Believe As Ye List*, he seems to be both sympathetic and a bit whimsically humorous, though not broadly comic. Smith, as well as Penn, seems also to take the parts of necessary old men. He is Philargus, an old man, father of Parthenius, the cunning avaricious old miser, and from general hints probably with something of Cassius's "lean and hungry look." He is also the deer-keeper Gerard; but since this person has but sixteen lines,

we know little of his characteristics. He is simply the keeper of
Gerard's lodge, around which much of the later action revolves.
There seems to be little distinction between Penn and Smith, yet if
Philargus is a typical part, Smith probably was stronger in intense
or comic characters, and Penn in those requiring dignity. It is to be
noticed that they are not both named in any one of the plays, though
they are both mentioned in the unassigned list of *The Lover's
Melancholy*. Thus they played the parts of unimportant old men,
either alternating, or, more probably, Smith taking comic and Penn
more serious parts. For Hobbs, we have but one character, Calistus
in *Believe As Ye List*, a freedman of Flaminius, and as such his
obedient messenger and informer. He has but twenty-one lines, and
two appearances. It is thus evident that Hobbs is unimportant as
an actor.

The only other active member at this period was Shank, the chief
clown. He is rarely mentioned, for the simple reason that most of
his work was done outside the play, bearing about the same relation to it as music does now, simply to amuse in the breaks. If the
clown part was written, however, Shank was named. The only
illustration we have in this period is Hilario. Shank is also mentioned as Petella, a waiting-maid who hasn't a single line. His part
was probably impromptu, the assignment being only to get him on
the stage, almost certainly that he might coach the merry actors of
Rosalura and Lilia-Bianca. From the description in *The Picture*,[39]
and other direct statements in the play, it appears that Hilario was
very thin. It follows that Shank could not have been a fleshy man,
and was probably quite thin. Wright tells us that Shank was Sir
Roger in *The Scornful Lady*,[40] a clownish Curate to the lady; but
since the play, according to the quarto of 1616, was originally acted
by the Children of the Revels in Blackfriars, Shank could not have
been the creator of the part. If there is a pure major clown part
written, we may be sure that it belongs to Shank. If not, he may
not appear at all among the characters, or he may take the part
of one who has little to say but is often on the stage in such situa-
tions as would permit clownery.

[39] *The Picture*, III. 1. 1-21.
[40] Wright, *Historia*, p. 424.

Besides members, there were a few other men for odd jobs. Thus Curtis Greville was Latinus, an old man, rather of the clown, burlesque type, and also one of the Merchants in *Believe As Ye List* who is somewhat after the same humor. William Patrick was Palphurius Sura, a senator with little to say, and also a captain with little to do, both parts suggesting that he was probably of good appearance. George Vernon and Richard Baxter were also with the company at this period, serving as various minor officers and attendants. Vernon seems to have been a tribune and a lictor in *The Roman Actor*; and Baxter was Titus, chief spy to Flaminius, in *Believe As Ye List*. James Horn, as well as George Vernon, was entitled to the livery at this period, though he is not mentioned in any of the playlists except in the unassigned *Lover's Melancholy*, and probably as a tribune and lictor in *The Roman Actor*. For various petty odd jobs, there were also several more servants, whose number we shall attempt to determine when we have established the number and parts of the apprentices.

At this period, there were in the company several apprentice actors of women's parts. The "leading ladies" were John Honyman, and John Thompson. Thompson was evidently the larger in 1626, calling Domitilla (Honyman) dwarf.[41] He took the part always of the proud independent beauty or the haughty queen, the regal line. He is the haughty, proud, disdainful Domitia, the siren villainess. Since Domitia is more than once called on to sing, Thompson evidently had a good voice in 1626. He is the haughty, self-opinionated, and overbearing Honoria, ambitious to be considered the greatest and most beautiful of her sex. We are given to understand too that Honoria sings. Thompson is also the athletic huntress, the Princess Cleonarda, who will not be tamed of man. In his earliest days with the company, he had taken the part of Julia, the Cardinal's mistress, in *The Duchess of Malfi* (1623), Sharp playing the Duchess. Thompson, then, is the forceful regal lady.

Contrasting with and complementing Thompson was John Honyman, who in 1626 was a dwarf as compared with Thompson. Since he was but fourteen,[42] while Thompson was some four years

[41] *Roman Actor*, IV. 1. 16.
[42] See below, p. 222.

[189]

older, the comparison was based on actual physical difference. As
Domitilla, Honyman is the small, rather pert spitfire; but as
Sophia he is the modest wife, contrasting most favorably with
Honoria; yet Sophia too knows her own value, and still has the
sarcastic tongue of Domitilla. As Clarinda, Honyman is of the
delicate feminine type, contrasting strongly with masculine Cleonarda. But by 1631 he has become a man, and as the "starveling"
First Merchant in *Believe As Ye List* is attached for comic effect
to the corpulent Flamen, Berecinthius.[43] He was also in the autumn
of 1632 the Factor in *The Wild Goose Chase*, another unimportant
male character. It is easy then to distinguish between the characters
of these two leading ladies.

If we may believe the epitaph upon Honyman by Thomas Jordan:[44]

> he was a man
> So sweetly good, that he who wisely can
> Describe at large must such another be,
> Or court no Muses but Divinitie.

His stage part as an apprentice was thus thoroughly in accord with
his natural character. Some lines of Sir Aston Cokain pay Honyman
high praise not only as an actor but also as an author. He says:

> *To Mr.* John Honyman
> On hopefull youth, and let thy happy strain
> Redeem the Glory of the Stage again:
> Lessen the Loss of *Shakespeare's* death by thy
> Successful Pen, and fortunate phantasie.
> He did not onely write but Act; And so
> Thou dost not onely act, but writest too
> Between you there no difference appears
> But what may be made up with equal years
> This is my Suffrage, and I scorn my Pen
> Should crown the heads of undeserving men.[45]

We must of course remember that this latter is the enthusiastic
praise of one young man for another of about his own age. Still

[43] *Believe As Ye List*, III. 2. 30-1; III. 2. 83-4; IV. 3. 22.
[44] *Poeticall Varieties*, quoted by Collier, *Bibliographical Catalogue*, Vol.
II, p. 185, note 1.
[45] *Small Poems of Divers Sorts*, 1658. Epigrams, Book I, Epigram 10, pp.
140, 141. Quoted *Shakspere All. Bk.*, Vol. II, p. 72.

DIVISION OF LABOR

the tributes of Jordan and Cokain show that Honyman was regarded as an extraordinarily capable young man.

Besides these two leading ladies, we also have Alexander Goffe, aged twelve at his first mention in 1626;[46] and his running-mate, William Trigg, probably about the same age. Goffe's part is described in *The Wild Goose Chase* (1632), when he was eighteen, as of a small body. Yet since this allusion belongs probably to the original production, it does not necessarily show us anything about Goffe. He is Caenis in 1626, and Acanthe in 1629, both mere pieces of necessary machinery; but by 1632 he has become a leading lady, and as Lilia Bianca is a demure "starched piece of austerity" in public; but a merry wench in private, a typical Fletcher girl. Trigg is the female comedian. As Julia, he is a mere piece of necessary machinery, but as Corisca he is of the humorous turn, the rather pert and somewhat erotic waiting-maid. Corisca is not large, since she has to "stand a-tip-toe" to kiss Mathias (Taylor), and in turn Ricardo (Swanston) has to "descend" to take a kiss.[47] But by 1632 Trigg too is a leading lady with Goffe, playing Rosalura, "a merry wench" in public but modest in private. He is still small enough and pert enough to be "that grass-hopper," though here again the allusion is probably to the original performer. Thus Goffe is the "modest" lady, and Trigg the pert, madcap waiting-maid, the female comedian. They are both mentioned in the players' pass of May 17, 1636, the last record for Trigg as an actor.[48] Goffe was then nearing twenty-two, and Trigg was seemingly somewhat older. Since Goffe had formed the acquaintance of the gentry, he was the messenger of the company in Oliver's time whenever a sur-

[46] Collier, *Memoirs*, p. 266.

[47] *The Picture*, I. 1. 98; III. 2. 27.

[48] Trigg became a captain in the wars; but if the following refers to him, as it seems to do, he must eventually have changed his opinions as did Swanston.

On Trigg
Trigg having turn'd his sute he struts in state,
And tells the world he's now regenerate.

This is quoted in *Wits Recreations*, first published in 1640, though this particular skit must belong to a later version. Possibly, too, the William Trigg who married Elizabeth Morton at St. Botolphs, Bishopsgate, June 6, 1641, was the actor.

reptitious performance was to be put on, but there is no record that he ever became a member of the company.[49]

Thus in 1626 there were four apprentice actors of female parts. Thompson, about eighteen, was then the chief apprentice, sufficiently large and forceful to take regal rôles. Honyman was some years younger, thus being adapted to the modest, virtuous lady. Still younger than both these were Goffe and Trigg, but newly entered the company and taking as yet only very small rôles. Besides these four, Edward Horton was also an apprentice in the company by 1629. In the revised *Mad Lover* (folio 1647) we read, "Enter Stremon and his Boy Ed. Hor.," which shows that Horton was an apprentice. Since Stremon is "a soldier that can sing," we seem to have the same situation and probably the same actors as in *Believe As Ye List* (1631), dating about the same period, where we read "Harry: Willson: & Boy ready for the song at ye arras:." Horton's first and only rôle was that of Mariana in the *Deserving Favorite*, about 1629. Since Horton does not appear in later plays as one of the leading ladies, he was probably used rather as a musician than as an actor.

Another occasional actor of female parts was James Horn, a livery servant from about 1621. He almost certainly took the part of Grilla in *The Lover's Melancholy*,[50] a boy disguised as a girl for comic effect. Thus he appears to have been a comedian, who might on occasion disguise as a girl. Thompson seems to have graduated about 1629, and to have died about 1630. At graduation he should presumably have become a juvenile lead, leaving to Honyman the leading lady. It seems, however, that Thompson perished in the plague of 1630, which forced Honyman into service as a juvenile lead.[51] Thus Goffe and Trigg were left as the leading ladies.

In the meantime, other apprentices had entered to be put in training. One of these was Stephen Hammerton, who in the autumn

[49] Wright, *Historia*, p. 427. Wright's statement of Goffe's position is substantiated by, or based upon, the publication in 1653 of *The Queen or the Excellency of her Sex*, "Found out by a Person of Honour, and given to the Publisher, Alexander Goughe" (*Modern Language Review*, Vol. III, p. 292).
[50] See below, p. 368.
[51] See Chap. II.

of 1632 was cast for so important a rôle as Oriana in *The Wild Goose Chase*, showing that he must already have had a few years of training. This conjecture is now confirmed by a recently reported petition of Blagrove and Beeston, asking under date of November 12, 1632, "that his Lo^p would restore vnto them a boy named Stephen Hamerton inveigled from them by one Christopher Babham & by him imployed at the Blackfryars playhouse."[52] The original Oriana was "a tall woman," of "a fair size," "eighteen." These references are likely to Sharp, who seems to have been this age at the original performance in 1621,[53] also of this build; and probably do not apply to Hammerton. That Hammerton at entrance in 1632 was still quite young is indicated by the fact that he did not enter the membership till about January 1641, being probably just out of his apprenticeship at that time. Indicative of this situation is the fact that he was the very youthful "juvenile lead" of the company by the winter of 1640-41, seemingly a quite famous one. In the epilogue to *The Goblins*, the winter 1640-41,[54] after the wishes of various classes have been mentioned, Suckling gives as the opinion of:

> The women—O, if Stephen should be kill'd
> Or miss the lady, how the plot is spill'd.

This allusion shows that Stephen Hammerton must have been

---

[52] Allardyce Nicoll, "Some Notes on William Beeston," London *Times*, Lit. Sup., November 22, 1923. The order on this petition was that Herbert after examination should "make such an accomodation of the difference therein mentioned as may bee best for his Ma^tes service & the satisfaccon of the pet^rs." The King's men kept Hammerton. No only so, but they secured a "Warrant. Whereas the late decease, infirmity, and sickness of divers principal Actors of his Majesty's company of players, hath much decayed and weakened them, so that they are disabled to do his Majesty's service in their quality, unless there be some speedy order to furnish them with new Actors, his Majesty having signified his royal pleasure . . . to you to choose, take, and receive into your company any actor belonging to the licensed companies in or about London as you shall think fit or able to do his Majesty service &c. To John Lowen and Joseph Taylor. May 6th 1633" (Stopes, *Jahrbuch*, Vol. XLVI, p. 97). Thus the King's men became empowered to take any acting apprentice or hired man they had a mind to. Further comment is unnecessary.

[53] This means that the text is that for the original performance, while the cast is for the revival of 1632. Thus the play was not rewritten, any necessary minor alterations being made only on the parts of the actors and not in the manuscript.

[54] See Preface.

Orsabrin, who stands every possible chance of being killed till the last few lines of the fifth act, when he gets the lady. From this part, we get a good description of Hammerton. "He's something tall" (I. 4. 1.), and has just enough beard "to speak him drawing towards a man" (I. 4. 4.). "His hair curls naturally: a handsome youth" (III. 2. 1.). Again, in Killigrew's *Parson's Wedding*, acted this same winter 1640-41 at Blackfriars, we hear "Stephen is as handsome, when the play is done, as Master Wild was in the scene."[55] And Wild was "a new young thing, that has the vogue of the town for handsomest."[56] Also: "The match, you see, is made. If you refuse, Stephen misses the wench, and then you cannot justly blame the poet; for, you know, they say that alone is enough to spoil the play."[57] It is interesting to note the similar parts played by Hammerton in these contemporary plays and especially the similar expressions about his missing the lady. Since Hammerton became a member about January 1641, he must have become an apprentice before January 1630. This conjecture is confirmed by the fact that Hammerton belonged originally to the Children of the King's Revels, formed in 1629. Evidently Hammerton became an apprentice about the age of ten in the King's Revels company, 1629, was transferred to the King's company in 1632, and was graduated at twenty-one, about 1640. Wright tells us Hammerton played Amintor to Lowin's Melantius. This would probably have been 1640-42, about the time he became a member. His line is very well summed up by Wright, who says he "was, at first, a most noted and beautiful Woman-Actor; but afterwards he acted, with equal grace and applause, a young lover's part."[58] Our last record of Hammerton is his signing the 1647 Beaumont and Fletcher folio.

About the time Hammerton entered, or shortly after, Nicholas Birch or Burt was brought to the company as Shank's apprentice, passing after Shank's death in 1636 to Beeston at the Cockpit.[59] Nicholas was pretty certainly the son of George Birch, who was with the company 1619-24, and had married Richard Cowley's

---

[55] Dodsley (1875), Vol. XIV, p. 534; Fleay, *Drama*, Vol. II, p. 25.
[56] *ibid.*, p. 412.
[57] *ibid.*, p. 535.
[58] Wright, *Historia*, p. 424.
[59] *ibid.*, p. 423.

daughter Elizabeth January 28, 1619. Thus Nicholas was born hardly before 1620, and could not have been much above eleven when he appeared with the company in 1631. We have no known part for Birch as an apprentice, though he took some part in *Believe As Ye List* (1631). In 1648, he was the villainous Latorch in *The Bloody Brother*, and afterward became famous on the Restoration stage.

When Hammerton became a man, he was seemingly succeeded in fame as a woman actor by Charles Hart, the grandson of Shakespeare's own sister, concerning whom Wright[60] tells us: "Hart was Robinson's boy or apprentice. He acted the *Duchess* in the tragedy of the *Cardinal*; which was the first part that gave him reputation." As the Duchess (1641), Hart was "One of so slight a making and so thin" (IV. 2), and his hand was "too weak, I fear, alone" (IV. 2). We do not know exactly when Hart entered the company; but we shall see later that it was about 1634, as the fact that he was a leading lady by 1641 would imply. He was almost certainly with the company by 1636, when his father William Hart is mentioned with the organization. This would give him about the usual six or seven years of training before he finally became the chief leading lady. Malone informs us that William Hart was the eldest son of Shakespeare's sister Joan, and conjectures that Charles was born about 1626.[61] Since an apprentice entered about ten and became a leading lady in about five to seven years, and since Charles succeeds to that rôle in 1641, when still small, Malone's date cannot be much more than a year or so wrong either way. Nevertheless, when the wars broke, Hart was able to be "Lieutenant of horse under Sir Thomas Dallison, in Prince Rupert's Regiment,"[62] though he could hardly have been out of his teens. After the wars, he continued to act with surreptitious companies;[63] and finally became a noted Restoration actor.

Another possible apprentice actor of the period was Andrew Pennycuicke, as we learn from the quarto of *The City Madam*, 1658, which was published for him as "one of the actors," with his

60 Wright, *Historia*, p. 423.
61 Malone, *Variorum*, Vol. III, p. 167, note 6.
62 Wright, *Historia*, p. 426.
63 *ibid.*, p. 427.

name to the dedication. If he took part in the original performance, licensed May 25, 1632, it was probably as an apprentice, since he is not mentioned in our fairly complete lists of hired men. A further clue is furnished by the fact that Pennycuicke also took part in Davenport's *King John and Matilda*, "my selfe being the last that Acted *Matilda*."[64] Now this play had belonged originally to Queen Henrietta's company at the Cockpit, and was claimed August 10, 1639, by Beeston.[65] Since we have so many actor lists for Queen Henrietta's men about the period this play must originally have been produced,[66] in none of which does Pennycuicke appear, it is practically certain that he did not personate Matilda for the Queen's men, but did so with Beeston's boys, being, as he says, the last to perform the part. It is thus significant that a third publication of his, *The Sun's Darling*, was first performed at the Cockpit in 1638-39.[67] It appears then that Pennycuicke had been with the Shakespearean company as an apprentice in 1632, but passed while still a boy to Beeston. Doubtless he too, like Nicholas Birch, had been one of Shank's three apprentices, and had passed after Shank's death in 1636 to Beeston at the Cockpit. From his taking Matilda, it would appear that Pennycuicke was finally a regal lead, but we have no part assigned to him in the Shakespearean company.

It appears then that each apprentice also had his distinct line, to which he had been specially trained. At the graduation of one apprentice, a second was already trained to take his place, and a third was articled to begin his training. This system made it necessary to keep several apprentices.

Besides those members, hired men, and apprentices already mentioned, there were several other "servants." In a "protection" of January 12, 1637,[68] eleven "servants" were named, of whom two are well known handymen but not members, the other nine being simply "of special use" at Blackfriars. In a similar protection of

[64] Bullen, *Old Plays*, n.s. Vol. III, p. 4.
[65] Stopes, *Jahrbuch*, Vol. XLVI, p. 101.
[66] Murray, Vol. I, opp. p. 266.
[67] Lawrence, W. J., "The Problem of Lyly's Songs," London *Times*, Lit. Sup., December 20, 1923.
[68] Stopes, *Jahrbuch*, Vol. XLVI, p. 99.

December 27, 1624, twenty-one "Musitions and other necessary attendantes" are named.[69]

It appears then that in the period 1625-32 there were eleven active members, and one or two superannuated, at least five important servants, four or more important apprentices, and several other "servants." We can name about forty persons who were actively connected with the organization in December 1624. We can name at least twenty-three who were with the company in March 1592; and there must have been more. That some such number was available can be seen from the fact that one scene of *Cataline* (1611; V. 4) calls for a minimum of twenty on the stage at once, and urgently requires several more for proper presentation. We are certainly justified in calling this a large organization. But even though it was large, yet it was well organized, each person having his duty definitely assigned.

Thus an examination of these plays with assigned parts has shown us that each actor had a definite line, that there were five or six principal men actors and two or three apprentices, that each play was so written as to contain a representative of the line of each principal actor, thus typically containing eight major "lines," five or six for men, and two or three for apprentices. There was very evident understanding as to the duties of each class in the organization, the major parts for men being supplied by members, the parts for women being supplied by apprentices, and the minor parts by hired men. It is evident then that the division of labor was very definitely established, and that the play was regularly fitted to the company, not the company to the play. It ought therefore to be possible to trace these established "lines" backward, in the plays with unassigned lists, and so to trace out the "line" of each actor, together with the majority of characters in each "line."

[69] Adams, *Herbert*, pp. 74-5.

CHAPTER VIII

THE BEAUMONT AND
FLETCHER ACTOR LISTS

WITH the key given in the preceding chapter, we may now proceed at least partially to unlock the riddle of the unassigned lists of principal actors in the second Beaumont and Fletcher folio. Taylor had been the leading man from the time he succeeded Burbadge in 1619, appearing on every list. His line is readily evident. He is usually the handsome, heroic young lover, who worships some paragon of perfection and performs wonders in her name.[1] We know that this is his line, not only because it is the backward projection of his later line, but also because he was Mirabel, "A young and handsome man," in *The Wild Goose Chase*, a characteristic specimen of the type, written in the midst of this period. These gallant young lovers have little to distinguish them but different names as labels, and new settings for their deeds. Demetrius, Dinant, Arnoldo, Pedro, Armusia, Silvio, Albert, Antonio, Lisander, Valerio, Cesario differ chiefly in the differing proportions of lover and warrior required by the plot. At times the warrior may predominate over the lover as in Antinous, Virolet, and Perez, or the lover may be entirely suppressed as in Orange or Jamie; but regularly we have the dashing young hero. Occasionally, however, Taylor may be the equally handsome and dashing near-villain, as in his known part of Rollo, or in the very similar Maximinius. To this phase of the type doubtless belongs also the uncharacteristic, plotting eunuch Photinus.[2]

---

[1] See tables, to which the text of this chapter is really an extended note.
[2] The construction of *The False One* is especially interesting. In its structure, it does not fit in fully with the other plays of this period, the reason being that the authors are modelling upon its analogue, *Antony and Cleopatra*. Caesar = Caesar, technically an old man in both. Septimius = Enobarbus, both betrayers. The plot itself demands a predominant place for Photinus. Thus we account for three of the chief places. Caesar would go to the "old man" Benfield, just as Shakespeare's Caesar had gone

From these parts collectively we learn that Taylor was a "sweet young man," and "a handsome young fellow."[3] As Albert he was "A middle stature, and of brown complexion," and had known the seas "these twenty years." As Pedro, his brown complexion is again referred to. He is:

> Both young and handsome;
> Only the sun has been too saucy with him,

is "strongly built," and "has a manly face yet,/A goodly shape." Antinous is under twenty-five; Silvio has been "twenty years" a friend of Claudio; Arnoldo finds that he has been poor "these thirty years" but is finally rich; and Cesario, though young, has seen "thirty and odd winters." Thus we may characterize Taylor at this period as a handsome young man of middle stature and, on the stage at least, of brown complexion; also a "curl'd-hair gentleman," "A handsome timber'd man," and a "mighty Mars," his age not being definitely stated but being once under twenty-five and once "thirty and odd," his memory being fixed at twenty, and once at thirty years. As a matter of fact, he was just thirty-four when he came to the company in 1619. Thus he was probably represented on the stage as being not much under his actual age.

to the "old man." Caesar is also actually old, as is true of most of Benfield's parts. Since Septimius takes the life of royalty, he must be a sneaking villain unrelieved. Hence he is more darkly colored than Enobarbus. Septimius would thus naturally go to Underwood's line of princely rascals. Photinus because of his importance must go to either Lowin or to Taylor, but is typical of neither. Lowin is the antithesis both of the eunuch and of the politician. Therefore Taylor must make the best of Photinus, and Sceva is created for Lowin. In reality Enobarbus has been split in two to make Septimius and Sceva. Underwood got the villain function, and Lowin got the gruffness of character. Achoreus, "an old, blind Counsellor, Priest of Isis," was then fitted out for Tooley, and Ptolemy for Eccleston. Since a prominent Captain of the guard was needed, Achillas was fitted out for George Birch, now the regular performer of such parts. The minor parts were then filled in as needed. But the imitative aim caused the play to be in structure neither fish nor flesh nor good red herring, and the execution of the plan was still further injured by collaboration.

[3] All quotations and personal allusions from the Beaumont and Fletcher plays may be located through the tables for this chapter, and Appendix IV. Perhaps in our interpretation of the general terms of age which are to follow, Howell's definitions in his *Dictionary* of 1660 might help us (Section XXI). He defines infancy as being to the fourth year, childhood from four to fourteen, adolescence from fourteen to twenty-two, youth from twenty-two to forty-one, manhood or virility from forty-two to fifty-six, old age from fifty-six to sixty-eight, and decrepitness or doting old age from sixty-eight till death.

In all the plays 1619-25, Taylor's part is in point of lines the first or second for male characters. The other male line sharing this prominence is regularly the gruff soldier of John Lowin, represented by Belleur in 1621, a rôle he had taken from the beginning of these Beaumont and Fletcher plays in 1610, as we know from the fact that he created Melantius and Henry VIII, as also that in this period he created Bosola and Mammon.[4] The description of Leontius in the dramatis personae of *The Humorous Lieutenant* as "a brave old merry Souldier"[5] may well serve as a placard for this type. To gruff old general Melantius, a "sturdy fellow," "stout and able"; bluff Henry; and Belleur, "of a stout blunt humour," the tables of dramatis personae add "merry Souldier" Fabritio, "A merry Captain, but somewhat wanton" Petilius, "old merry Souldier" Chilax, "valiant merry Dane" Norandine, "valorous but impatient" Theodore, "merry Gentleman" Cleremont, "free Speaker" Captain Sceva, "merry Gentleman" Rutilio, "old angry Gentleman" Alphonso, "merry Captain" Piniero, "merry Gentleman" Tibalt, and "merry old man" Dorilaus. Incidentally, the stereotyped formula used by the compiler of these tables, probably Eccleston,[6] indicates that he knew these characters belonged to the line of one actor. To the same gruff soldier type belong "old and rough" Mardonius; "crazed" old Duke Messina; "old stout Gentleman" Antonio; "old lame angry Soldier" Sanchio;[7] old general Cassilane; rough, old Duke of Sesse; the equally rough old sea-dog Alberto; loutish Leon; and lecherous, "old," "Captain" Bartello. Compounded of the lecherous soldier and the bluff sovereign is the "unnatural and libidinous" usurper Frederick. To Melantius and Mardonius we may with Professor Thorndike[8] also add those other "blunt counsellors, brave soldiers, and devoted friends," Dion and

---

[4] See preceding chapter.
[5] Professor Parrott's definition of merry, "i.e., foul mouthed," is of course the proper one (Chapman, *Tragedies*, p. 726).
[6] See Appendix V.
[7] It is curious that as Sanchio the active Lowin should have had so small a part, and should have been constantly carried around in a chair. Possibly he was temporarily injured, say by the gout, and this device was hit upon to solve the difficulty.
[8] Thorndike, A. H., *The Influence of Beaumont and Fletcher on Shakspere*, p. 123.

Martell, all of whom "possess a rough humor, an impatience of deceit, and an eagerness for action," having "scarcely an individual peculiarity among" them. With these gruff "faithful friends," we may also place Conon and the faithful-false Martine. It was doubtless because of this needed gruffness in the crucial scenes that Bartolus was fitted out for Lowin.[9] As soldier-potentate, Lowin appears in Diocles, Barnavelt, and Valentinian. Finally, Palamon is this same soldier, with the accustomed realistic excrescences of the type prevented by the strength of the knightly tradition.

There are rather frequent references to those physical characteristics of Lowin which, as we have seen, peculiarly fitted him to play this rôle. Melantius is "stout and able," a "sturdy fellow." Palamon is a "tall young man," "swarth and meager,"[10] with a heavy eye, still temper, "bold gravity," "brown manly face," and "menacing aspect," this being as decidedly Lowin's description as that of Arcite is Burbadge's. Chilax in disguise is "a tall stallion-nun." Norandine has "too much flesh" to be a knight of Malta. Rutilio is "A wondrous able" man, "of a goodly person," "A goodly gentleman,/Of a more manly set I never look'd on," "Strong and goodly." Sceva is:

> a porter
> A strong one too.

Alphonso "has flesh and hide enough." Belleur is "a great fellow," "The tall fat fellow", "a maypole! A great dry pudding," a "mighty dairy-maid in man's clothes," "has weight enough," is a "great thing." Bartello is "fat," a "dry neat's tongue." Sesse is "A goodly personage." Bartolus is a "churl," and has "that fat of thine." Dioclesian is "cut with an axe out." Aubrey is "somewhat high of stature," "fat," "somewhat corpulent," his "head and beard inclining to be grey," "About seven-and-fifty," Lowin's actual age when he took the part. Leon is a "goodly fellow," has a "giant's promise," is "made as strong as brass, is of brave years too," is a

---

[9] The physical description of Bartolus also confirms this assignment.

[10] The description of Palamon is much like that of Arcite in Edward's play at Oxford, 1566, of whom Queen Elizabeth said "he was a right Martiall Knight hauinge a swart countenance & a manly face" (Boas, F. S., *University Drama in the Tudor Age*, p. 103).

[201]

"strong fellow," of "portly presence." All of these allusions point to Lowin's known powerful physique.

Lowin's characters are also regularly middle-aged or old, only three—Palamon, Valentinian, and Piniero—being represented as definitely young. In the case of Palamon, tradition demanded youth. Piniero, the only character in the plot that could be treated in Lowin's style, is the nephew of Ruy Dias, who is himself a somewhat youthful lover. In these cases then time was obliged to turn back again in its flight and make Lowin a young man again just for that night, or rather afternoon. Since Lowin was well into his thirties when the first of these plays was produced, and all but fifty when the last, it appears that as in the case of Taylor, his theatrical age was regularly at least approximately his natural age. Indeed, in the only instance where a specific age is attributed to one of these characters, Aubrey, the age is exactly Lowin's. At least these two actors, Taylor and Lowin, "made up" their ages only when there was some real necessity.

Leading Lowin in the period 1610-19, was Richard Burbadge, Taylor's predecessor. As we have seen, Taylor would regularly have inherited practically all of Burbadge's rôles, giving us in this way some further clue to the latter's line. Since Taylor inherited Arbaces, we may be sure this part belonged originally to Burbadge, and may assign to the latter also those other "lily-livered heroes," Philaster and Amintor.[11] "They are all very loving, very noble, very generous," to which characterization Thierry and Arbaces add "ungovernable passion." However, since Thierry seems not to have been written originally for the company, but revamped in 1617, it is probable, as we shall see, that Burbadge in this play took Theodoret, and Field Thierry. But this type of character practically disappears with Beaumont, possibly the next nearest kinsmen being the somewhat stronger trio, Arcite who, as we shall see, has Burbadge's physical description impressed upon him, Antonio, and Philippo. Burbadge's natural genius was for a more vigorous type, as is shown for instance by his famous earlier creation of Richard III, and in this period of Ferdinand in *The Duchess of Malfi*. With these villainous, noble soldiers belong Crates and Mountferrat.

[11] Thorndike, *Influence*, p. 123.

This soldier, however, may be just as strongly loyal, as Aecius, Caratach, and Archas, with whom belongs Cardinal Wolsey, who we know with practical certainty belonged to Burbadge, since the only other big part, Henry VIII, was certainly Lowin's. This noble soldier is sometimes made the butt of the humor because of his high ideals, as in Memnon and Jacomo. Somewhat akin to these two is Don John, Burbadge's most broadly humorous character. It appears then that Burbadge as an actor was marked by dignity and strength. Of pure comedy he had almost none, his comic effects being procured by a half satiric contrast of high ideals turned loose to be laughed at in a practical world, somewhat after the manner of Cervantes.

From the description of his characters, we get an approximation of Burbadge's physical appearance. As Arcite, he is "lower" than Palamon-Lowin; but in wrestling he

> has a vengeance trick o' th' hip;
> Mark how his body's made for't,[12]

he being nearly as good a wrestler as Hercules. He is a "gently visaged," "black hair'd man," with an eye that has a "fiery sparkle and quick sweetness," and

> a brow broad and
> Arch'd like the great eyed Juno's.

This highly arched brow is a notable feature of Burbadge's portrait, and had already received attention from Shakespeare in Bertram of *All's Well*. Don John, too, has a "curl'd pate," a "well knit body," and is "Made up like Hercules." Memnon is also "A goodly-timber'd fellow"; and Jacomo is described satirically as having "Westphalia gammons" for legs, which promise "long strides"; and as being

> Of a left handed making, a lank thing
> As if his belly were ta'en up with straw,
> To hunt a match.

Seemingly then Burbadge was not so tall as giant-like Lowin; but was still of good physique, well fitted for the strong and dignified

---

[12] cf. Orlando in *As You Like It*, created by Burbadge some thirteen years before.

THE SHAKESPEAREAN COMPANY

parts he played. His characters are pretty well divided between comparative youth and age, as occasion might demand. Since Burbadge had not yet passed from his thirties when the earliest of these plays was performed, nor his forties when the latest, he would find no particular difficulty in presenting either age.

For a short period, 1616-19, Burbadge shared the lead with Field, giving us an old lead and a young lead. Up to 1616 the parts of Burbadge and Lowin, and after 1619 the parts of Taylor and Lowin, usually stand out from all others. But in the intervening period there is also a youthful lead, usually playing against Burbadge. Thus the plays of this period are usually "double-headers." Since Field was the only new actor at this period, suspicion at once attaches to him as the juvenile lead. This suspicion is made stronger when Jonson gives us Field's accustomed rôle before he came to the Shakespearean company.

> *Cokes.* Which is your Burbadge now?
> *Leath.* What mean you by that, sir?
> *Cokes.* Your best actor, your Field?
> *Lit.* Good, i' faith! you are even with me, sir.
> *Leath.* This is he that acts Leander, sir: he is extremely beloved of the womenkind, they do so affect his action.[13]

This gives us the young lover Leander as a typical part for Field, and also seems to give his actual part in this play as Littlewit, since it is hard to see how Cokes has produced a jest that balances a preceding one of Littlewit's, unless the jest lies in the fact that Cokes has given the name of the performer of that part.[14] Another of Field's lovers, though predominantly a soldier, was Bussy D'Ambois.[15] It appears then that Field was really a younger Burbadge, but more given to youthful love.

As has been said, Field usually plays with or against Burbadge; Polydore with Memnon, Euphanes to Crates, Thierry to

---

[13] *Bartholomew Fair* (1614), V. 3.
[14] It is supposed also that in this period Field played jealous Othello (Collier, *Memoirs*, p. 220); but the evidence is none too trustworthy.
[15] See prologue to that play. The question of the citizen's wife in *The Knight of the Burning Pestle* "were you never none of Master Moncaster's scholars?" (I. 1. 76a) was probably intended for Field, who had been. If so, he was either Venterwels or Humphrey, almost certainly the latter, another mock-heroic and mock-poetic lover.

Theodoret, Miranda to Mountferrat, in the first three of these cases being represented as Burbadge's younger brother, in the fourth a brother of the same order. In the fifth play, Burbadge-Archas is the father of Field-Young Archas. Thus did both poets and players seem to recognize a peculiar affinity between these two famous actors. In all these characters, Field is the noble young lover.

Naturally, Field's characters are all young men. Euphanes in the Queen of Corinth is:

> a young man
> Of an Herculean back,

also "a black man." Thierry in *Thierry and Theodoret* has "youth" and:

> a body may add to
> The famed night-labour of strong Hercules.

Young Archas in *The Loyal Subject*, disguised as Alinda, is described as having:

> a black eye,
> Which is of the least, too, and the dullest water;
> And when her mouth was made, for certain, madam,
> Nature intended her a right good stomach.

She has a good hand, but her color:

> If it be her own,
> 'Tis good black blood; right weather proof, I warrant it.

A strange pace she has:

> And what a manly body! methinks she looks
> As though she'd pitch the bar, or go to buffets.

Since Field was born October 1587, he was still naturally young; and the above allusions probably mean that he was of good physique, with small black eyes, a goodly mouth, and dark complexion, a description that very well fits the surviving portrait of Field preserved at Dulwich.[16] This portrait represents Field's eyes as very dark, seemingly coal black. They are certainly not large, and might well be jestingly termed "of the least, too." The lips are of sufficient prominence to give point to the jest concerning his

---

[16] *Shakespeare's England*, Vol. II, opp. p. 270; *Nero and Other Plays* (1888), in the Mermaid Series.

mouth. If we may judge from the shoulders, Field was also prob-ably of good physique. His hair is of raven blackness, and the gypsy appearance is heightened by earrings. He is smooth shaven except for an uncertain mustache, which looks like a complimentary addition of the painter. Surely he has excellent title to be called "a black man."[17] His hand is long fingered and slim, a very good hand indeed. The descriptions and the portrait tally exactly.[18]

Perhaps the assignment of Young Archas to Field calls for fur-ther comment because he disguises as a woman. It will be noticed, however, that the description quoted above shows that the performer was of quite manly build and not a mere boy. The part itself is thoroughly in keeping with the Field parts in other plays, while no other part in this play is. The Duke is nearest to it in age and prominence, but as we shall see, is much more evidently a rôle in Underwood's princely rascal line of libertines. The assignment of Young Archas to Field and of the Duke to Underwood gives each principal actor a characteristic part, and accounts for all principal parts. This cannot, I think, be done by any other assignment.

Further light is thrown on this problem by Jonson's *Devil is an Ass*, presented by the Shakespearean company in the latter part of 1616. This play has the typical construction of the 1616-19 plays, but its young lead Wittipol also disguises himself as a woman. Now in the play it had at first been planned that Robinson under his own name should be employed to dress as a woman and get into the presence of Mrs. Fitzdottrel; but Wittipol decides to take Robinson's place, since "Robinson might want audacity," which is precisely what Robinson did want if we may judge by the line taken by him both before and after. Gifford and Collier think[19] this is stage bluff and means that Robinson played the part of Wittipol; but in the light of the above facts it seems to me necessary to sup-pose that it is true and that Field was Wittipol. The suggested

[17] Field's bishop brother was also known as "black Dr. Field" (Birch, *Court of James First*, Vol. II, p. 244).
[18] It is likely that these rôles give us not only Field's physical but his moral portrait as well. We need only to remember the scandal in which Field was involved in 1619 (See above, p. 51, note 29), and various hints about Lady May (Collier, *Memoirs*, p. 217) to see that Jonson and Fletcher knew their man—and approved of him.
[19] Collier, *Memoirs*, p. 268.

exchange may have a basis of fact, since Field entered the company after April 1616, and this play was written sometime in the same year. Professor Kittredge very ingeniously shows that the setting of the play is in the autumn, probably in October.[20] Possibly it was intended originally that Robinson should have the part of Wittipol, which was enlarged for Field. Incidentally, the high praise of Dickey was thus likely in partial compensation for the loss of his part. Malone states that Field acted the parts of women with the Shakespearean company, in contradicting whom Collier takes particular pains in his biography of Field to state that he was too old to take such parts when he came to the company. It would seem therefore that Collier is right in that Field was too old to be a regular lady; but that Malone is right in that Field did on occasion disguise as a woman.

Possibly the next most notable line in the period 1610-14 is the rather dignified king and counsellor belonging to William Ostler. Though Antonio in *The Duchess of Malfi*, Ostler's one known part, is not of noble blood, yet he is of noble worth sufficient to be the husband of a Duchess. This character, as here, is regularly in this period third or fourth in importance for men. Ostler appears also as the lover, though not with the purity of Antonio, in the King of *The Maid's Tragedy*, again as Maximus, and as the Father in *The Captain*. A more dignified phase of this kingliness is presented in the King of Philaster, in *Theseus*, and, without the full rank, in Lord-Protector Gobrias, the Duke of Norfolk, and Roman General Suetonius. Evidently Ostler's ability was strongest in presenting characters of high rank and impressive position. His characters, however, are not mere figureheads, which shows that Ostler must have had considerable force as an actor. In keeping with their dignity, most of these characters are no longer young. There are no definite descriptions of physical appearance, but to present these parts Ostler must himself have been of good presence.

At Ostler's death in December 1614, he was succeeded both in membership and as an actor by Robert Benfield, who continued this line to the closing of the theaters. Benfield inherited Antonio,

[20] Kittredge, G. L., "King James I and The Devil is an Ass," *Modern Philology*, Vol. IX, pp. 195-209.

doubtless along with Ostler's other parts. It is instructive to note, however, that the line keeps its wonted third or fourth place for only one play with Benfield,[21] and then drops to the bottom of the list, whence it again very slowly works up. Evidently Benfield at entrance was a younger and much less powerful actor than Ostler, and had to begin at the bottom. A fair representative of Benfield's line is Father DeGard, fashioned to his needs in 1621. Though not usually very important, yet Benfield's line is perfectly clear. He is king, prince, governor, judge, and dignified old man. His characters were a few times too unimportant to give him mention among the principal actors, several of his parts having fewer than one hundred lines, and only half a dozen having as many as two hundred. With Benfield, the line becomes for the most part a mere figurehead, even the allusions to physical appearance being stereotyped.

The next most important line, 1610-19, is that of Henry Cundall, ranking usually fourth or fifth. In *The Duchess of Malfi* Cundall was the Cardinal, a plotting villain, lecherous, yet an excellent soldier. Close kin to the Cardinal is "King Antigonus, an old Man with young desires," the trio being completed by Frederick, who is still lecherous, though "time has blasted" him. Gomera is also an old beau, but represents more fully the soldier side of this line. Other typical manifestations of this "honest" soldier are the "old grey ruffian" Captain in *Philaster*; "honest Cashier'd" Pontius; Penius "A brave Roman Commander, but stubborn to the General"; Eumenes; and, with testily humorous turn, Bacurius; and "disbanded Officer" De Vitry. Buckingham, The Jailor, Sicily, and Alphonso have also more or less of this downright, honest soldier about them. Neanthes has some of the characteristics of the honest soldier, with humorous turn, but also appears for a time as pimping villain. This latter side is more fully developed in Boroskie, "a malicious seducing Councellor." A still further stretching of this characteristic gives cowardly gull Lodovico, possibly the least characteristic of Cundall's line at this period. It appears then that

---

[21] This situation shows either that *The Chances* had been plotted before Ostler's death, or that Benfield's part, he being a new actor, was built on the old model. In either case, it gives curious confirmation of our dating for the play.

Cundall's typical part was the honest old soldier, about midway between Burbadge's noble soldier and Lowin's gruff variety. Cundall's characters are nearly always old, and usually wrinkled. His line is thus easy to distinguish as the important old man not taken by Burbadge or Lowin.

Cundall was eventually succeeded in membership by George Birch,[22] who begins to be mentioned as a principal actor exactly when Cundall ceased acting. Unfortunately, we have no assigned part for Birch, and must arrive at his line by assigning him the residual line beginning about 1619, after other lines have been assigned. This line, however, is a more youthful continuation of Cundall's, and usually has a prominent representative wherever Birch is mentioned as a principal actor. Here we have the downright Senator Possene, forceful Captain Achillas, enamored Sea Captain Leopold, the roughly humorous Boatswain, the much more dignified Seberto, boasting King Bakam, dignified King Cosroe, hostile Bellides, fighting lover Lidian, honest Captain Castruccio, and aggressive Captain Grandpree. These parts do not give us the physical characteristics of Birch further than that he was occasionally represented as young.

Two other lines also have some affinity with this line of Cundall. The one is filled with princely libertines and rascals, marked by vigorous action; the other features the youthful, singing, roistering soldier, of comic turn. To the princely libertines belong "Prince of Spain" Pharamond, "vicious Prince" Theanor, "dishonourable pursuer" Clodio, "libidinous Tyrant" Ferrand, with whom belongs bullying Cardenes, "Spanish Count" Otrante, and without the princely dress, Marc-Antonio, and "Villain" Leon. Close kin to these are the villain lovers Roderigo and Ternata, the latter "An ill man." Julio also counterfeits this type, with whom the Duke of *The Loyal Subject* and he of *The Chances* both have considerable affinity. This princely lover occasionally has a fairly unsmirched love, as Tigranes, and Colonna. He is also once the gulled lover, Siphax. This princely actor may even be a good prince, general, or soldier, of a vigorous, preferably plotting type—Lysippus, Perithous, Decius, first Gentleman in *The Humorous Lieutenant*,

[22] cf. above, p. 58.

Vandort, Beaupre, "rough and confident," "blunt and bitter" Lugier, Milanes, the "honest merry" Master in *The Sea Voyage*, and Aper. He may, however, leave off the lover and be pure villain, as Septimius, with whom belong "Earwig" Latorch, and those other pretended noble, flattering panders, Chilax, Bawdber, "wicked instrument" Sorano, and gull Gonzalo. Possibly least characteristic of this princely villain line is Archbishop Cranmer, who by the process of elimination, seems to belong here. Truly, it looks as if this princely wolf had this time got him sheep's clothing. But Cranmer has a sarcastic tongue, and this princely actor was probably as good a godfather for Queen Bess as the company could then muster, unless it were Ostler, who seems already to have been supplied with a more important part.

This princely villain must have belonged to John Underwood. When Swanston succeeded to Underwood's membership, it was this villain line that he took up. Thus in the last Fletcher plays he must have taken Juan and Baptista. He must also have inherited at least Lugier, which he later played, giving us pretty certainly one character in Underwood's line. A known character for Underwood is Delio in *The Duchess of Malfi*. While Delio is not of the nobility, yet he carries the dignity and port of a noble. He is also a sarcastic soldier, and is made to tempt the Cardinal's mistress, Julia, for no other apparent reason than that he could play the rôle of tempter well. Another indication that this is Underwood's line is the fact that he is the only one of the remaining principal actors whose name appears on the lists where important representatives of this line occur. Thus Clodio, Ferrand, Roderigo, and Ternata are typical examples of this line, too important not to have the performer named in each case, and yet Underwood is the only one of the remaining principal actors whose name is mentioned in all four lists. Besides, at least two of the remaining three actors—Eccleston and Tooley—clearly took other lines, as we shall soon see. Thus it appears that this princely villain is certainly Underwood's.

Up to 1619, Underwood's characters are either young or of indeterminate age; but later a few old men appear. Other personal characteristics are rather meager. Pharamond is "a prince of wax," "growing to fatness," yet a "trim man." Marc-Antonio is "of a handsome body"; and Colonna is also "A handsome fellow." But Clodio is a "great blind fool," a "great booby"; Ferrand speaks of "the little blood is left me"; and Ternata has a "rugged face," upon which twenty years of priesthood have "stamp'd a meagreness." Seemingly Underwood was of rather large physique, and at least in his younger days was of handsome appearance, this physical appearance explaining in part why he was cast for this line. It is interesting to notice that Underwood in the earlier plays was somewhat overshadowed by Cundall; but when the latter ceased acting in 1619, Underwood had a free field.

Another somewhat humorous line belonged to William Eccleston, who had been with the company as apprentice before 1611, and returned as a member about March 1614, to succeed Alexander Cooke. Eccleston is the sprightly, sometimes petulant, young man, given to the foibles of youth, such as singing and seeking excitement in sword play or in love. A typical manifestation of this sprightly youth is the singing, roistering, usually young soldier, who is an expert swordsman. Typical of this phase are Junius; Stremon ,"a soldier that can sing"; the Corporal; the Ancient; and Duarte, who is an excellent swordsman. That this is Eccleston's type we know from the fact that he had been one of the teasing soldiers in *All's Well*. We shall see later that as an apprentice his regular rôle was the witty lady's-maid. Thus his line as a man is of a piece with his line as an apprentice, being merely clothed in breeches instead of dresses. The near-princely Duarte has as his close kindred the singing Agenor, Philander, Ptolemy, Ascanio, Ruy Dias, Raymond, and Leandro. Probably the sporting young soldier Modesbargen also belongs to this group, as does more distantly the Second Gentleman of *The Humorous Lieutenant*. Young Diphilus, of this type, was probably an Eccleston rôle just before he left the company at the end of apprenticeship. The comic phase of this soldier becomes also the cowardly Protaldye, whose close kinsman is the "roaring" gull Sampson. The singing Lopez, and probably Balbus and Diego are other manifestations of this gull. At the extreme of this comic phase, and probably least typical of Eccleston, is the comic servant Peter.

It appears that Eccleston was a good singer and a fair swordsman. In personal characteristics, Eccleston is regularly represented as youthful, handsome, soldierly, and strong. As Agenor, he seems to have had grey eyes.

As has been said, Eccleston succeeded Alexander Cooke, who had been mentioned as a principal actor in all lists 1603-14, and was presumably a comedian. In the period 1610-14, we find Bessus, twin brother of Protaldye. This clownish gull appears also as Piso, the Wooer, and Cuculo. To these comic characters is probably to be added the officious Chamberlain of *Henry VIII*. This then is presumably Cooke's line. It thus appears probable that Eccleston inherited the gull, uncharacteristic of his line, from Cooke. Of Cooke's personal characteristics, we get nothing definite.

In some respects, the line of Nicholas Tooley has kinship with those of Cooke and Eccleston. Tooley was Forobosco and one of the madmen in *The Duchess of Malfi*. Forobosco does not appear in the present form of the play, being merely mentioned (II. 2. 33); but from *The Fair Maid of the Inn* we learn he was an astrologer, and thus was probably the First Madman in *The Duchess*. Possibly, even, Forobosco has been enlarged and transplanted to *The Fair Maid*. At any rate, we get the astrologer as a characteristic rôle of Tooley's. Here then belong Vecchio, Paulo, and Lecure. Since astrologer was frequently only another name for pimp,[23] we may place Rocca, Menippus, and Zabulon along with Lecure in Tooley's line. An evident common characteristic of all these parts is that they employ some queer makeup. It is doubtless this art of makeup that gives Tooley "Achoreus, an honest Counsellor, Priest of Isis"; eunuch Aretus; disguised Briskie; and "lame old" Champernel. The actor lists seem to indicate that along with these rôles should go Gaspero, Nantolet, and Niger. While we have no direct indication that they appeared in queer makeup, they might very effectively have done so. Another of these makeups was the starved and unkempt castaway Sebastian. This character; Aretus the eunuch; Zabulon the Jew; etc., indicate that Tooley was small and lean, a characteristic that he turns to use in Judas, Incubo, Penurio, and Lopez of *The Spanish Curate*. To this crew of foolish gulls belong

[23] See Overbury trials and the case of Doctor Lamb (Gardiner, *History*, Vol. VI, p. 319.

also the Fool, the Tutor, and Castruccio. Gerrold the Schoolmaster, and the Master of the mad folk, managers of the show of fools, along with the Tutor, and probably Forobosco, have the humorous turn and probably the makeup as well. It seems then that Tooley's distinguishing characteristic was his ability at queer makeup. He seems to have been small and thin and to have capitalized his physical peculiarities for humorous purposes. We shall see later that his apprentice line was also comic.

One other of Tooley's probable makeup parts seems to deserve especial attention. From his parts 1614-23, we learn that he was small and, at least sometimes on the stage, of reddish complexion. We may get a full description of him as the little freckled knight of *The Two Noble Kinsmen*.

Mess. There's another,
A little man, but of a tough soul, seeming
As great as any; fairer promises
In such a body yet I never look'd on.
Per. Oh, he that's freckle-faced?
Mess. The same, my lord:
Are they not sweet ones?
Per. Yes, they are well.
Mess. Methinks,
Being so few, and well-disposed, they shew
Great, and fine art in Nature. He's white-hair'd,
Not wanton-white, but such a manly colour
Next to an auburn; tough, and nimble set,
Which shews an active soul; his arms are brawny,
Lined with strong sinews; to the shoulder-piece
Gently they swell, like women new-conceived,
Which speaks him prone to labour, never fainting
Under the weight of arms; stout-hearted, still,
But, when he stirs, a tiger; he's grey-eyed,
Which yields compassion where he conquers; sharp
To spy advantages, and where he finds 'em,
He's swift to make 'em his; he does no wrongs,
Nor takes none; he's round-faced, and when he smiles
He shews a lover, when he frowns, a soldier;
About his head he wears the winner's oak,
And in it stuck the favour of his lady;
His age, some six-and-thirty. In his hand
He bea1s a charging-staff, emboss'd with silver.

An important point is that the little red-headed freckle-faced knight is "some six-and-thirty" in 1613, indicating a date of birth about 1577. Tooley seems to have been born in February 1575.[24] Seemingly then the little knight bears Tooley's approximate age and description, indicating that he was probably small, muscular, round-faced, freckled, grey-eyed, and possibly red-headed. If so, how could he help having a sense of humor?

At Tooley's death, he was succeeded by William Rowley, who was more frankly a clown. Rowley's line we get from two of his definitely known parts. In his own play of *All's Lost by Lust* Rowley personated "Iaques, a simple clownish Gentleman." In Middleton's *Inner Temple Masque*, Rowley had been Plumporridge, and moved:

like one of the great porridge-tubs
Going to the Counter.[25]

Evidently then Rowley was a fat clown. This fat clown appears in the Beaumont and Fletcher plays as Bustopha in *The Maid in the Mill*, coincident with Rowley's appearance in the company; and waddles his foolish way through the last of the plays projected during his membership. It is thus very easy to get Rowley's rôles in all these plays except *The Lover's Progress*. His part there must have been Lancelot, who has probably been reduced by Massinger in revision, but still threatens to sweat as he goes about his duties. After Rowley disappeared in 1625, his rôles went to Pollard, as is shown by the Cook in *The Bloody Brother*. Pollard is thus the residuary legatee of both Rowley and, as we shall see, Eccleston. Also, at Rowley's withdrawal, William Penn entered to carry on the line of Tooley's caricatures, which in the interim had been partially supplied by Pollard. He would thus have presented Forobosco in *The Fair Maid of the Inn*.

As has just been pointed out, Pollard became the residuary legatee of Rowley and Eccleston. In the last three or four years of Eccleston's connection, Pollard was beginning to rival him, though usually taking more clownish parts. Pollard was the supposedly humorous Silvio in *The Duchess of Malfi* in 1623, and had been the comic Holderus in *Barnavelt*, 1619, originally a fairly long part,

24 Collier, *Memoirs*, p. 234.
25 Bullen, *Middleton*, Vol. VII, p. 203.

which seemingly fell under the censure of the Master of the Revels and was reduced to ten lines.[26] Whether he or Eccleston was the original Pinac in 1621 we do not know on direct evidence, but Pollard took the part in the revival of 1632. We seem to have fair evidence also that Pollard created the Humorous Lieutenant and La Writ. Certainly these two would belong to the same actor; certainly, also, Pollard was a principal actor in both these plays originally, and we know on contemporary evidence that he was at some time famous as the Lieutenant.[27] The parts seem themselves to indicate that they were fitted originally to the youthful Pollard. As Holderus, Pollard had been "little Sir Gregory." Now the Lieutenant is "a mad shaver," "boy"; and La Writ is "The Little French Lawyer." It would seem then that these parts belonged originally to Pollard, giving very strong probability that he also created Pinac.

We have already discussed Pollard's line after 1625. In the period 1619-25, his parts as a man gradually grow more prominent. His part in *The Spanish Curate* is found by elimination to be Diego. With this play, his part becomes a regular one, only one play after this failing to show his line. Most of the plays before this also have evident parts for him. He is mentioned in *The Humorous Lieutenant*, where, as we have seen, he must have been the Lieutenant, in *The Little French Lawyer*, where he must have been La Writ, in *The Laws of Candy*, where his part must have been Mochingo, and again in *The Island Princess*, where he probably doubled the Second Citizen and the Second Townsman. Later, he is mentioned as a principal actor in *The Maid in the Mill* and *Lover's Progress*, where his rôles appear to have been Franio and Malfort.

Pollard's earlier connections with the company are not quite so clear. He is mentioned as a principal actor in *The Queen of Corinth*, the winter 1616, where his part seems clearly the "exceeding meager" and "very foolish Traveller" Onos, "the youth/Of six and fifty." This physical description and those of his other early char-

---

[26] The first twelve lines of the scene between Holderus and the Widow were cancelled from 7 b; and the whole of sheet 8, about one hundred and six lines, was revised. These one hundred and eighteen lines were thus replaced by thirty-one. See Frijlinck, *Barnavelt*, pp. 21-2, 85.
[27] See above, p. 185.

acters indicate that Pollard began taking such parts before he was fully grown. This situation is further elucidated by John Shank, who claimed[28] in 1635 that he had furnished Pollard and Thompson, possibly Pollard's successor, to the company out of his own purse, which means that they were his articled apprentices. But Shank was not with the company earlier than December 1615, when, as we shall shortly see, Pollard must already have been some years an apprentice. It seems clear then that Pollard had been Shank's apprentice, and had not completed his time when Shank came to the company not earlier than December 1615. But he must have been very near the end of his time, and I find no certain trace of a female line for him.

There is, however, a female comedian just before 1616, showing the same general characteristics as does Pollard when he becomes a man. Here are the lecherous and drunken comic nurses, Gillian and Borachio, close kin to whom are Claudia and the Priestess. While this line is akin to certain phases of Thomas Holcomb's, it could not have belonged to him, since he too was Shank's apprentice, and consequently not with the company before December 1615. This line also has some kinship with an earlier one. As Dula in *The Maid's Tragedy* (winter 1610), the actor of this earlier line was "above fourteen," indicating a date of birth by or before the winter of 1596. Thus this person was born probably not long before the winter 1596, entered the company about 1606, was at least fourteen as Dula in the winter of 1610, and would have completed apprenticeship not later than the winter of 1617. It is probable then that this later clown line is the work of the earlier apprentice, who probably belonged to Armin. It seems likely then that Armin's apprentice had performed this general type of character at least till his master died, to be succeeded by Shank and his apprentices Pollard and Holcomb.

We are now able to check another statement concerning Pollard. Wright says[29] Pollard was superannuated at the outbreak of the war in 1642. The age of superannuation was then fifty.[30] If

[28] Halliwell, *Outlines*, Vol. I, p. 316.
[29] Wright, *Historia*, p. 426.
[30] Firth, C. H., *Cromwell's Army*, p. 21. In Queen Elizabeth's time, the age of service had been sixteen to sixty (*H.M.C.*, Fifteenth Report, Appen-

Wright's statement is technically correct, Pollard must have been born before 1592, have become an apprentice probably before 1602, and have been graduated at twenty-one before 1613. Thus if Wright's statement is correct, Pollard could have served no part of his apprenticeship in the Shakespearean company. But the evidence seems conclusive that he did. It seems then that Wright's statement is inaccurate, yet that Pollard was sufficiently old at the outbreak of the war to cause his nonparticipation to be attributed to superannuation as in the cases of Taylor and Lowin. It is to be remembered too that at best Wright is using hearsay a half century after the event. We may thus with some assurance fix the beginning of Pollard's apprenticeship with the Shakespearean company as about December 1615, and his time may not have been out for some two or three years later.

Throughout the period of the Beaumont and Fletcher plays there had been a regular clown in the company, first Robert Armin and then John Shank; but only Shank is mentioned in these lists of principal actors, and then just once. Even then the mention is in a revamped old play, *The Prophetess*. Shank's part here must have been Geta, the clown, as is shown by his physical description. Geta is "a man of a spare body," lacks "in growth and full proportion," and admits "My face was bad enough." The description and humor is much that of his known parts of Hilario and Cuculus in the later plays. Shank was also the waiting maid Petella, with no written part, but with the evident purpose of watching and coaching the apprentices, at least one of whom was his own, who were acting the stirring young ladies. It is likely too, then, that he was the Country Woman in *The Humorous Lieutenant*, breaking in a very young apprentice.

We have good reason to believe that this omission of the clown parts from the Beaumont and Fletcher plays was not accidental. Indeed, the contemporary eulogists of Beaumont and Fletcher take pride in the fact that these authors, in pleasing contrast to Shakespeare, found their humor elsewhere than in the clown. William Cartwright puts it boldly:

dix, Part X, p. 126; Wright, *Elizabeth*, Vol. II, p. 224); but had been changed to eighteen to fifty by 1617 (*H.M.C.*, Tenth Report, Appendix, Part IV, p. 365).

Shakspeare to thee was dull, whose best jest lies
I'th' ladies' questions, and the fools' replies,
Old-fashion'd wit, which walk'd from town to town
In trunk-hose, which our fathers call'd the clown;
Whose wit our nice times would obsceneness call,
And which made bawdry pass for comical,
Nature was all his art; thy vein was free
As his, but without his scurrility;
From whom mirth came unforced, no jest perplex'd,
But, without labour, clean, chaste, and unvex'd.[31]

J. Berkenhead is also a little apologetic for Shakespeare's humor as contrasted with that of Beaumont and Fletcher:

Shakspeare was early up, and went so drest
As for those dawning hours he knew was best;
But, when the sun shone forth, you two thought fit
To wear just robes, and leave off trunk-hose wit.[32]

The nearest regular approach to the clown in the Beaumont and Fletcher plays is to be found in the comic lines performed for the greater part of the period by Eccleston and Tooley. Such a situation is wholly fitting for scholars, and disciples of Ben.[33]

In 1610-11, there was one other principal actor, John Heminges, and there is one line left for him. Here we have a more or less comic, peppery old man of high rank—Cleremont, Calianax, Lygones,— who disappears at the same time Heminges stops acting. The nearest counterpart of this line in the plays 1612-23, seems to be Tooley's caricatures, which, however, are quite different in their rank and dignity. It is probably significant then that though Tooley had long been in the company, his line attained prominence only when Heminges ceased acting.

Besides these regularly appearing principal actors, a few others receive occasional mention, whose parts can be sometimes distinguished. Thus by the process of elimination, John Rice receives the part of Antony in *The False One*. Since Rice was a captain in

[31] Darley, *Beaumont and Fletcher*, Vol. I, p. lxii.
[32] *ibid.*, p. lxiii. The typical attitude of the scholars toward clownery is given by the Parnassus plays, acted at Cambridge, Fletcher's school, in which was given practical demonstration of how Kemp was hauled into the plays with a cart-rope.
[33] This situation raises the suspicion that in the later plays Rowley concocted his own clowns.

Barnavelt, the part fits him very well. This assignment is also in harmony with the fact, later to be established, that as an apprentice Rice performed strong parts. Again by the process of elimination, either Ronvere or the Boatswain is left in *The Double Marriage* for Richard Robinson. The Boatswain seems to be in the line of George Birch. Ronvere is not typical of Robinson's later line, though about this same time he was playing the Cardinal in *The Duchess of Malfi*. It is therefore probable that Ronvere belonged to him. Throughout the period 1619-25, Robinson and Rice performed such parts; but it is frequently impossible for me to feel any certainty as to which was which. Where I have felt fairly certain, I have inserted their parts, though the process is rather hazardous. In the latter part of this period, Sharp also had parts as a principal man actor; but since he had also been an apprentice, we may reserve the discussion for that phase of our study.

Having established the lines of the principal men actors in all the Beaumont and Fletcher plays with actor lists for the Shakespearean company, we may now turn to those of the principal apprentice actors, who usually played the parts of women, but sometimes those of boys. We have seen that in the period 1626-29 John Thompson was the lead, playing the part of the haughty and overweening beauty, the regal line; and that John Honyman played the second rôle, taking the part of the modest virtuous lady, while William Trigg was the witty waiting maid, the female comedian, and Alexander Goffe was the tender young lady. The most definite preceding clue is the actor list of *The Duchess of Malfi*, spring 1623, from which we find that Richard Sharp was then the regal lead, playing the Duchess, and John Thompson was being groomed as his successor, taking the part of the Cardinal's mistress Julia. Thus the question is when Sharp ceased acting as a woman to be replaced as lead by Thompson. Now Sharp became a member at some time 1623-24,[34] indicating that the change took place about 1623. For several years preceding 1623 the line of Sharp is strongly marked as leading lady. This leading lady is nearly always of royal blood or of the Amazonian type. She is very beautiful, proud, usually haughty, often overbearing. One of Sharp's qualifications

[34] See above, p. 58.

for this rôle was evidently a large physique. Hippolyta in *Custom of the Country* is "A building of so goodly a proportion," Quisara in *The Island Princess* is "of the strongest parts," Oriana in *The Wild Goose Chase* is "a tall woman," Violante in *The Spanish Curate* is a "giantess," and Marcelia in *The Duke of Milan* is "three foot too high for a woman," allusions which show that Sharp had finally become too large even for a "portly queen." *The Maid in the Mill* (August 29, 1623) no longer has this queenly lead. The corresponding lead in this play, Florimel, is but "fifteen and upwards," and would kiss Otrante if she were only tall enough. Evidently Thompson was now succeeding Sharp, as is also indicated by the fact that Florimel is given Thompson's known approximate age. Too, Thompson is evidently the chief apprentice, since he is the only one mentioned in the play. Also, Sharp now becomes a well marked juvenile lead, eventually succeeding to the more serious and dignified elements of Eccleston's line as Pollard succeeded to the comic. This line of Sharp is most clearly shown by *The Lover's Progress*. Since Sharp is among the principal actors of this play, since his female line has no representative, and since the only principal parts not accounted for are Lidian and Clarange, both young men, he must have taken the part of a young man. This conclusion is confirmed by the fact that he was juvenile lead 1626-29. It is hard at first sight to tell whether he was Lidian or Clarange, but the majestic appearance of the latter labels him as probably one of Sharp's characters.[35]

We have also a full set of allusions[36] to the age and appearance of Sharp, enabling us fairly to establish the dates of his connection with the company. As Martia in *The Double Marriage* (about May 1622) he was not yet "two and twenty." As Oriana in *The Wild*

[35] The later case of Edward Kynaston (See *D.N.B.*, Kynaston) forms an excellent parallel to that of Sharp. As an apprentice, he had performed the regal line, Evadne being one of his rôles; and ever after he "had something of a formal gravity in his mien, which was attributed to the stately step he had been so early confined to in a female decency" (Cibber, C., *An Apology for the Life of Mr. Colley Cibber* [1830], p. 75). Then as a man he continued these regal rôles, being Henry IV, etc.

[36] It is to be noticed in this and succeeding cases that the characters are first placed in lines, and that the ages attributed to these characters are then found to be consistent, showing that they are really based on the age of the apprentice.

Goose Chase (winter 1621), he was eighteen, indicating that he was born before the winter of 1603, and after that of 1602. Ordella in *Thierry and Theodoret* (winter 1617) was "some fifteen at the most," again indicating that Sharp was born hardly earlier than the winter of 1602 but not much later. It is indicated then that Sharp was born about the winter of 1602. He would thus have entered the company at ten about the winter of 1612 and have been about twenty-one at his graduation in the summer of 1623. We can trace his rôles in dwindling proportions back to his entrance in 1612, thus confirming the other facts.

The line of Thompson also adds a few more touches of personal description to his portrait. Since Florimel in *Maid in the Mill* (licensed August 29, 1623) is fifteen, Thompson must have been born at least by the summer of 1608; but he could hardly have been born earlier, since he was still acting the lady at least as late as Massinger's *Picture* (licensed June 8, 1629). Since Thompson was born about the summer of 1608, we should expect him to enter the company about the summer of 1618. We find the first trace of his line in 1619 when as Phoebe in *The Humorous Lieutenant* he is very small and young and has but a single line, indicating that he was just being broken in. Even nearly three years later when he had his second important part, that of Rosalura, it seems to have been thought wise to send his master Shank along as his waiting maid to coach and help him. Almost certainly then the country woman, Phoebe's mother, is also John Shank breaking his apprentice in. Doubtless then Thompson was born about 1608, entered at ten about 1618, and would have graduated about 1629, shortly after our last mention of him, which is either as Queen Honoria in Massinger's *Picture* (licensed June 8, 1629), or as Cleonarda in Carlell's *Deserving Favorite* (published 1629). We do not know whether he had further record with the company; but we do know that by 1635 he was dead, and I have shown above that his demise probably occurred in the plague of 1630.[37]

It is also easy enough to trace the backward projection of John Honyman's line, the very virtuous lady, still in 1626 of tender years. The reason for this tenderness is supplied by the information

[37] See above, pp. 60-1.

that as Bianca in *Fair Maid of the Inn* (written before September 1625) Honyman was thirteen. This age indicates that Honyman was born about 1612, the indication being confirmed by the fact that his line first appears in the plays of 1622. Thus the John Honyman, son of Richard Honyman, christened at St. Botolph's, Bishopsgate,[38] February 7, 1612, is doubtless our actor. No wonder Ismenia in *Maid in the Mill* (August 29, 1623) is "of the lowest stature," that of an eleven-year-old boy.

This leaves in the period 1623-25 a witty waiting-maid, who as Aminta in *Maid in the Mill* (August 29, 1623) says "I am a child," and as Margarita in *Rule a Wife* (October 16, 1624) is of "low stature," "but little," is wished to be a "size or two stronger," and is a "little piece of mischief." This is the general type of character that in the succeeding period was performed by William Trigg, most clearly and fully represented by Corisca in *The Picture* (June 8, 1629). But seemingly Trigg was only attaining prominence by 1629, whereas this line is prominent at least as early as 1623. We probably have the clue in *The Duchess of Malfi*, spring of 1623, where Cariola, the Duchess's waiting woman, was performed by Robert Pallant. Pallant is also mentioned in the protection of December 27, 1624,[39] among the musicians and necessary attendants, though there is no later mention of him. He seems then to have performed these parts at least 1623-24, though the fact that he was also the Doctor and various attendants in *The Duchess of Malfi*, as well as the listing among musicians and necessary attendants, may imply that he was not a regular apprentice.[40]

The very beginnings of the line of Alexander Goffe may possibly be seen in Clora of *Rule a Wife*, and Juliana of *Fair Maid*; but he had evidently not long been in the company. He must have replaced either Sharp, graduated about 1623, or Holcomb, graduated about 1623, or G. Lowin, who seems to have dropped out about 1623, since they are the only graduates at this time. Most likely then he came

[38] See printed Registers.
[39] Adams, *Herbert*, p. 74.
[40] This is evidently not the Robert Pallant who had belonged to the company in the nineties of the preceding century, but doubtless his son. Robert Pallant, senior, seems to have died in 1619 (Chambers, *Eliz. Stage*, Vol. II, p. 331).

to the company about 1624, when he was ten.[41] Another entrant at this time was probably Goffe's later running-mate Trigg. Pallant seems also to appear at this time. Since, as we shall see, Lowin seems to have been but seventeen at leaving about 1623, and Pallant is traceable only 1623-24, it may be that Lowin was the apprentice of one of the members who dropped out 1622-23, and that Pallant belonged to the man who replaced him.

In the period 1619-23, we find three actors of women's parts besides Sharp. Two of these in 1621 formed a small and mischievous pair—Juletta and Alinda, Rosalura and Bianca. One of these boys was certainly Thompson, since he is mentioned as a principal actor in *The Pilgrim*, where only this pair of actors takes part. His partner personates a slightly more modest young lady. This young lady as Anabell, about May 1621, is "A virgin of sixteen," as Alinda, about August 1621, is "fifteen, with the vantage," and in boy's dress as Ascanio, October 1622, was seemingly about seventeen. Thus Zenocia, winter 1619, is "very young," the actor being about fourteen; Bianca, winter 1621, is "Of a small body"; and Aminta, June 22, 1622, is "little," "young and tidy." This actor then was born about 1605, should have entered the company about 1615, and have graduated about 1626, being a little older than Thompson. He seems, however, as pointed out above, to have left the company about the end of 1622 or the beginning of 1623. This boy would seem pretty certainly to have been G. Lowin, who performed Barnavelt's Daughter in 1619. The third boy, Thomas Holcomb, is still more prominent than these two, receiving several mentions among the principal actors. He is first mentioned in *The Queen of Corinth*, winter 1616, and last in *The Prophetess*, May 14, 1623. He was buried at St. Giles, Cripplegate, in September 1625.[42] He had been married, leaving a widow, who soon consoled herself with another actor, as we learn from a note of licence by the Bishop of London. 1626, "Jan. 13 Ellis Worth, St. James, Clerkenwell, Middlesex, Gent., & Frances Holcombe, of St. Giles, Cripplegate, London, widow of Thomas Holcombe; at All Hallows the Less, Thames Street, London." The fact that Holcomb's parish records are at St. Giles, along

---

[41] cf. above, p. 35.
[42] Malcolm, *Londinium Redivivum* (1802-3), Vol. III, p. 304.

with those of Thompson, known to have been Shank's apprentice, shows that Holcomb was another of Shank's apprentices, since the latter was the only member to live in St. Giles. Since Shank did not come to the company before December 1615, Holcomb also would not have appeared in the company before that date.

To these facts Holcomb's line adds but little more. His one assigned part, the Provost's wife in *Barnavelt*, shows that he was the performer of the longing woman and the watery-mouthed maid frequently appearing in these plays.[43] This indicates that he would have begun as the witty waiting maid and have advanced regularly to leadership in his line.[44] The personal allusions seem to indicate that Holcomb was small. It appears then from his line that about 1616 Holcomb in reality succeeded the boy whom we have called Armin's apprentice.

Returning to the tracing of our apprentice lines, we find an apprentice of the virtuous line graduating about 1616-17. This virtuous lady as Lucina in *Valentinian* (summer 1614) is not yet eighteen, indicating a date of birth not earlier than the summer of 1596. In *The Tempest* (winter 1611) this lady as Miranda is not yet fifteen, indicating a date of birth not earlier than the winter of 1596. These two allusions indicate that this actor was born about the winter of 1596, entered the company about 1606, and graduated about 1617.[45] The line is found beginning in Shakespeare's plays about 1606, further confirming this conclusion. Who then was this lady, who would graduate about the winter of 1617? In a famous passage of *The Devil Is An Ass* (winter 1616), Ben Jonson sings the praise of that "ingenious youth" Dick Robinson, who makes such a fine lady and acts the part so well. Evidently Robinson was the chief apprentice in the winter of 1616, the actor of these

[43] Downes is labelling a characteristic figure in this line when he says "*Mosely* and *Floid* commonly Acted the Part of a Bawd and Whore" (*Roscius Anglicanus*, 1708 and Knight's reprint, p. 19).

[44] The age given for Leocadia in *Love's Pilgrimage*, seemingly sixteen, as those for other characters in this play, would seem to belong to the actor who took this part in a later revision of the play.

[45] The Jailor's Daughter in the original Fletcher work of *The Two Noble Kinsmen* (summer 1613) is at least fifteen, but in the revision, which I place after 1625, is eighteen (Brooke, *Apochrypha*, p. xli). We are also told that Theodosia in *Love's Pilgrimage* (winter 1615) is not above seventeen; but this, like other statements of age in this play, probably belongs to the revision.

fine ladies. A still more definite indication that Robinson was the actor is the fact that in *The Second Maiden's Tragedy* (licensed October 31, 1611) he was the Lady of Govianus,[46] who belongs to this line. Robinson's line as an apprentice appears to end with Beliza in *The Queen of Corinth* (winter 1616), though he was doubtless leading lady in the lost *Jeweler of Amsterdam* for the following summer, and probably acted the revised part of Brunhalt that winter. Thus Robinson's line and age seem clear. We have already seen that he later performed rather dignified and fatherly parts as a man.

We have also seen that Sharp entered the company to be trained for the regal line about 1612, indicating that the previous performer of this line was to be graduated about that time. The actor of a nearly related line as Euphrasia in *Philaster* (summer 1610) was "about eighteen," indicating a date of birth about the summer 1592. He would thus have entered the company about the summer of 1602, and have graduated about the summer of 1613. The fact that his last part seems to be for the summer of 1613 confirms this conclusion and indicates that our dates for him are not far wrong. What clue we have to the performer of this part may better be treated later under the Shakespearean plays.[47]

From the facts concerning apprentices, we are now able to deduce an important principle. We have seen that probably about the time Pollard graduated Shank brought in John Thompson to succeed him. When Thompson was approaching graduation about 1629, Shank brought in Nicholas Birch to succeed him.[48] I have not worked out the plays of the period in detail, but Birch would doubtless be found appearing as a ten-year old boy about 1630, and con-

[46] Greg's edition, ll. 1928-9.

[47] It should be noticed, however, that Dame Pliant in Jonson's *Alchemist* (1610), a nine-line rôle, was "But nineteen, at the most," and says of the Spaniards:

Never since eighty-eight could I abide them,
And that was some three year afore I was born, in truth.

This would indicate that the performer was born about the winter of 1591, and that he was about nineteen at the performance of *The Alchemist*, which thus must date the winter 1610. Apparently he was born about the winter of 1591, became an apprentice about the winter of 1601, and should have graduated about the winter of 1612.

[48] Wright, *Historia*, p. 423; see above, pp. 194-5.

tinuing till his master's death in 1636, when at the age of about sixteen he was secured by Beeston for the company of boys at his theater, where Birch would probably have continued the parts of women till about 1641. Incidentally, this transaction shows that an actor's apprentice did not belong to the company, but to the individual actor. Here then is one succession of Shank's apprentices. But he tells us in 1635 that he then had three apprentices.[49] Since Holcomb had been Shank's apprentice 1615-23, doubtless his successor, either Goffe or Trigg, pretty certainly the latter, who was a comedian, was also Shank's apprentice. We have seen[50] that Andrew Pennycuicke seems to have been another of Shank's apprentices, going with Birch to the Cockpit at Shank's death. It would appear then that Shank's three apprentices in 1635 were Nicholas Birch, Andrew Pennycuicke, and probably William Trigg. The predecessors of Birch and Trigg seem known back to the time of Shank's coming to the company, though I find no clue to the predecessor of Pennycuicke. But it is clear that at graduation usually one apprentice was succeeded by another.

We have now traced the main lines for apprentices through the Beaumont and Fletcher plays. There were other apprentices for various odd jobs and minor parts, but the representatives of these main lines were the regularly trained actors of rôles for women. It is evident then that there was a regular system of training for these apprentices. A boy was taken by the member whose duty it was to train a particular line, this line being usually in a general way the female counterpart of his own line as a man. He took the boy at ten and broke him in on minor parts supplied by the dramatist. As the boy grew older, his parts became more difficult till a few years before his graduation at the age of twenty-one he was playing the leading part in his line. About the time of his graduation his master brought in another boy to go through the same process. This system of training necessitated the closest cooperation on the part of the dramatist also. It was his business in cooperation with the master to supply proper parts for each youngster to begin with and develop in. He had also to be careful not to create any

[49] Halliwell, *Outlines*, Vol. I, p. 316.
[50] See above, pp. 195-6.

female part for which there was not a properly trained actor. How intimate this cooperation was may be seen from the fact that in nearly every one of the many specific allusions to the ages of the women, the ages given are not ideal ages but those of the boys who were to perform the parts. The only apparent exceptions I have noted in the Beaumont and Fletcher plays concern Rosellia in *The Sea Voyage*, whose age is the specific but round number of fifty, and the several ages given in *Love's Pilgrimage*, which belong to the revision. Some such approximate adjustment was necessary to avoid the Restoration predicament, when because of the long suppression these boys had all become mature men. Says Jordan:

> Our women are defective, and so siz'd
> You'd think they were some of the guard disguis'd:
> For to speak truth, men act, that are between
> Forty and fifty, wenches of fifteen;
> With bone so large, and nerve so incompliant,
> When you call Desdemona, enter Giant.[51]

The same situation holds good for the men. Specific allusions to age are not so frequent for them; but in all the cases that I have collected for principal actors the age given is that of the actor, unless Antonio in *The Chances* is allusively referring to his age in gaming terms when he says:

> If I lose mine own,
> Mine audit's cast, and farewell five and fifty!

Even so, the specific number is a round one, though the age might conceivably belong to a revived revision, which would thus date 1632. Physical allusions to height, color of eye, etc., are in some instances necessarily, in all instances usually, to the actor. Since the dramatist knew for whom he was constructing the part, and was thus fitting it to that actor as intimately as possible, it was the natural and necessary thing for him to describe that actor instead of his ideal. It would be his tendency to take the actor as he found him, without altering his age or physical appearance unless the story absolutely demanded it. Also, broad daylight and a closely surrounding audience neither demanded nor permitted the exaggerated bedaubing and refashioning of the present day. It is

[51] Furness, *Variorum Othello*, p. 397.

therefore natural that in general the age and physical characteristics should be those of the actor. We are not, however, for a
moment to suppose that the general allusions to age and physical
characteristics are always those of the actor, for upon real occasion these might be, and were, changed. It is evident then from this
discussion that the company had a regular system of training and
successions, and that the dramatist fitted his play to the company
as he found it, even in its most minute details.

We have now worked the lines of actors back to 1610. Since most
of the actors in the early Beaumont and Fletcher plays had also
been actors for many years in Shakespeare's plays, it ought to be
possible to continue the backward projection of these lines, as we
shall attempt to do in the next chapter.

CHAPTER IX

THE ACTORS IN SHAKESPEARE'S PLAYS

IT is somewhat more difficult to determine the assignment of
parts to actors in Shakespeare's plays than it was in the Beaumont and Fletcher, because we have no guiding lists to any of
the plays themselves, and but few assigned parts. We must thus
fall back on the lines represented, the known principal actors in the
company, and the allusions to some of the parts taken by the more
famous actors. Luckily, we have the assignment of parts for one
non-Shakespearean play of the company close to the very beginning
of Shakespeare's writing, *The Seven Deadly Sins* (1592).[1] Also,
the actor lists of Jonson's plays for the company, 1598-1611, serve
as a check to show who were the principal actors during the period
covered. Further, since the Shakespearean plays overlap the Beaumont and Fletcher plays for a few years, and since we have established the lines taken by the different leading actors in the latter
plays, it is a comparatively easy and safe matter to get the backward projection of their lines in the Shakespearean plays. Thus the
problem is not so hopeless as at first it might seem.[2]

[1] Chambers (*Eliz. Stage*, Vol. II, pp. 125-6) dates this plot 1590. It certainly does not date earlier than the junction with Alleyn in 1590. Our
only record of its performance is early in 1592 (Greg, *Diary*, Vol. II, p.
153), and does not indicate that this play was one of the old favorites kept
continuously on the boards, as it would be necessary to suppose if we date
the plot for 1590. Besides, Burbadge is the leading man, at the early age
of nineteen if we date the plot 1592, but at the very tender age of seventeen if we date it 1590. It is thus exceedingly improbable that the plot
antedates the known performance in 1592.

[2] It should be noticed that the problem of finding the lines in these
plays is by no means that of a modern manager who would cast them.
Because of the versatility of the individual actor, the modern manager
might have two or even more actors who could adapt themselves to a
given part. Likewise, in the Shakespearean company there were actors
whose characteristics were similar. Thus Shakespeare would need to decide
for which a given part was to be written. But when he had decided, if his
decision was based on a real difference, we ought to be able to discover
that difference and in consequence the actor of the part.
  This chapter represents my efforts to follow Shakespeare's mind in the
casting of his actors. It lays no claim to being the last word; it is only

Our best point of attack will be at the approximate time of our most definite record, the plot of *The Seven Deadly Sins*. It is a striking fact that all Shakespeare's plays before 1594, except the history plays and the revised *Love's Labor's Lost*, have only five major parts for men; and we shall soon give reason to believe that *Love's Labor's Lost* originally had but five. The history plays are the revamped *Henry VI* trilogy from another company, and its sequel, *Richard III*. Two of these plays contain six, as does the revised *Love's Labor's Lost*; and two, seven major parts for men. Evidently then the plays of the company, 1588-94, were constructed for five men, and, as we shall see, for their six chief apprentices. The reason is at once evident when we notice that there were but five members in the company 1588-94. Each member had his line. The first four comedies, constructed before the graduating apprentices began to claim places with their beginning lines as men, show clearly the five types involved. Each of these plays contains two comedians, two more or less young men, and one usually humorous old dignitary. We cannot do better than let Shakespeare himself introduce these five major actors of his company in the words of Hamlet, describing the tragedians of the city: "He that plays the king shall be welcome; his majesty shall have tribute of me; the adventurous knight shall use his foil and target; the lover shall not sigh gratis; the humorous man shall end his part in peace; the clown shall make those laugh whose lungs are tickle o' the sere; and the lady shall say her mind freely, or the blank verse shall halt for't."

Of the comedians, one is the pure blundering low-comedy clown, to whom Shakespeare refers under that name, the butt of all the pranks and practical jokes. Here belong evidently Costard, one of the Dromios, Launce, and the Clown of *Love's Labor's Won*, who was polished over into a jester for Armin in the later revision known

an attempt after careful sifting of the present evidence to say the first. As the evidence grows and others throw further light upon the problem, we may eventually arrive at a consensus of opinion. But even that will not be certainty, which can be given only by trustworthy contemporary statement. Thus my most positive inferences merely represent the present state of my own opinion, and should not be construed as meaning that I consider them beyond question. Because of this inevitable uncertainty, I have thought it best to attempt a complete casting of parts, even though the evidence for some of the minor actors is rather indefinite.

as *All's Well*. Since these are labelled and known of all men, it is
not necessary to consider them further. The other comedian, however, is much more of a high-comedy figure. He is the fantastic
Spaniard Armado, full of high words, regularly labelled "Brag."
in the folio; the braggart soldier Parolles, also given to word chop-
ping, the clownish Speed, who is the end man upon whom the
wit-chopping wordy jests are broken; and one of the Dromios,
though here the fundamental aim of the play to make the Dromios
alike has emphasized the likeness in the two lines, and minimized
the difference. It seems to me that Dromio of Syracuse shows more
of the fantastic wit-chopping, and certainly Dromio of Ephesus
receives the more blows. Thus it is apparent that our second comedian is more of the fantastic, braggart, *miles gloriosus* than he is
plain clown. To such a state is reduced our "adventurous knight"
in a realistic age, which usually prefers him as Don Quixote, the
Knight of the Burning Pestle, and Falstaff. It is easy to allocate
these two comic lines to their clown actors, since we know that contemporary opinion classed two of these early members as such.
The low comedian was William Kemp, as we know not only from
the general evidence of the time; but also from the specific fact that
shortly after this he was Peter in *Romeo and Juliet*, and toward
the end of his career with the Shakespearean company the immortal
Dogberry.

We have the witness of Samuel Rowland in 1600, and John Taylor a little later that Thomas Pope was also a famous comedian of
the company. Rowland in his *Letting of Humours Blood in the
Headvaine* (1600), asks:

Are Plough-men simple fellowes now adayes?
Not so, my Maisters: What meanes *Singer* then?
And *Pope* the Clowne, to speake so Boorish, when
They counterfaite the Clownes vpon the Stage?[3]

John Taylor[4] bears witness to the same effect:

O were my wit inspir'd with Scoggins vaine,
Or that *Will Summers ghost* had seaz'd my braine:
Or *Tarlton, Lanum, Singer, Kempe*, and *Pope*," etc.

[3] *The Complete Works of Samuel Rowlands* (Hunterian Club), Vol. I,
Satire 4; quoted in revised form by Collier, *Memoirs*. p. 121.
[4] *Taylor's Works* (1630, Spenser Soc., p. 220).

Here then is unimpeachable evidence that Pope was a famous comedian.

Further, we have one genuine assignment of a character to Pope, Arbactus in *The Seven Deadly Sins*. Now Arbactus is the general who fights and finally overcomes the slothful and effeminate young king Sardanopalus. It is evident then that Pope here represented the manly and gruff soldier. Thus we know by direct evidence that Pope as a principal actor was both a gruff soldier and a comedian. There were but two principal comic lines in the Shakespearean plays before 1600. The one was of broadly clownish type and, as we have just shown, belonged to Kemp and his successor Armin. The other started as Armado, Speed, and Quince; but, as we shall see, ended as Oldcastle and Toby. This is the line of the jolly roistering soldier, the *miles gloriosus*. Since then the comedian Pope was a principal actor, this is the only line he could have taken.

That the player of the Falstaff line was by some considered a fool or clown we know on the evidence both of Shakespeare and of Jonson. King Henry V calls Falstaff "a fool and jester." Also, in *The Poetaster*,[5] Tucca has extracted a promise from Histrio, manager of the Shakespearean company,[6] to make a supper, and is instructing him as to the guests who are to be invited from the company. Says Tucca "and your fat fool there, my mango, bring him too; but let him not beg rapiers nor scarfs, in his over-familiar playing face, nor roar out his barren bold jests with a tormenting laughter between drunk and dry.[7] Do you hear, stiff-toe? give him warning, admonition, to forsake his saucy glavering grace, and his goggle eye; it does not become him, sirrah: tell him so." The reference cannot be to Armin, and must be to the fat performer of Falstaff and Belch.[8] It is worth noticing too that this fool is of a

[5] *Poetaster*, III, 1, near end.

[6] See Penniman's edition, note to 78,320—79,346; and Adams, *Playhouses*, p. 226.

[7] Surely the part in which the fat fool was wont to "roar out his barren bold jests with a tormenting laughter between drunk and dry" is Sir Toby Belch in *Twelfth Night*, which is known to date before February 21, 1602; but since it contains a part for Armin, after the spring of 1600. If the reference is to Sir Toby, then *Twelfth Night* dates not later than January 1601, when *The Poetaster* was first performed. Since *As You Like It* occupies the summer 1600, this would place *Twelfth Night* the winter 1600-01, where other evidence also would fix it.

[8] It seems possible to identify most of the other actors alluded to in

military turn, being expected to beg rapiers and scarfs.[9] The description of the fat fool's manner in portraying such characters as Falstaff and Belch, even though in the mouth of his detracter, gives clear indication of how these parts were originally presented.

There seems also to be a point in Tucca's speaking of this fat

Poetaster. Jonson mentions seven, whereas there were nine members in 1601, so that he has evidently omitted two. The normal number of principal actors in any single play of the company at this time, however, was seven; and in *Satiromastix* there were eight. Thus Jonson is alluding to the principal actors rather than to the complete membership. We have already identified Pope as "your fat fool." Burbadge, as the greatest shareholder, is the only man who can qualify as "seven shares and a half," though even he owned only two shares and a half in the theater, and one as an actor, the next highest member having but one share in each group. Phillips would recognize his portrait as Histrio, manager of the company, who is promised that the poet will make him "a man of good parts" in the play. That Phillips had charge of arranging for the plays, as Histrio is represented as doing, we know from the fact that early in this very year 1601, he had scheduled the ill-fated performance of *Richard II* for the Essex faction (Halliwell, *Outlines*, Vol. I, pp. 192-3; Vol. II, p..360). The picture seems drawn even more intimately to the life when Tucca tells Histrio "we must have you turn fiddler again, slave, get a base viol at your back, and march in a tawny coat, with one sleeve, to Goose-fair," the base viol being the very one, we may believe, that Phillips willed in 1605 to his "late apprentice," Samuel Gilburne, his less masculine instruments going to the apprentice James Sands. A fourth character is "your Aesop, your politician," who is not to be brought to the supper "unless you can ram up his mouth with cloves; the slave smells ranker than some sixteen dunghills, and is seventeen times more rotten." This grave, aged, and decaying politician is the Polonius-Caesar type we attribute to John Heminges. There was also another duty of the politician player, which in this company fell to Heminges. "Good, good; and which is your politician amongst you? now i'faith, he that works out restraints, makes best legs at court, and has a suit made of purpose for the company's business" (Bullen, *Middleton*, Vol. III, p. 341). A fifth member of the company seems to meet with more favor from Tucca; "Frisker, my zany; he's a good skipping swaggerer." Here is the military swaggerer, who presumably was cast to zany Tucca in *Satiromastix.* This "skipping swaggerer" in the Shakespearean company seems to have been William Sly. The remaining two actors are not quite so clearly described, but probably we have some clue. One of these is "the villanous out-of-tune fiddler, Aenobarbus;" evidently a red-bearded musician-member of the Shakespearean company. Now Cowley had been a musician in *The Seven Deadly Sins* (Murray, Vol. I, p. 79). Further, as Aguecheek and Slender, he was endowed with flaxen hair and "a little yellow beard—a cane-coloured beard." Probably then Cowley was referred to as Aenobarbus. The last actor is "your eating player . . . the lean Poluphagus, his belly is like Barathrum; he looks like a midwife in man's apparel, the slave." The lean glutton ordinarily falls to the slap-stick, low comedian; in this case Armin. There seems to be no trace in these descriptions of the other two members at this period, Shakespeare and Cundall.

[9] Note Pope's bequest of arms in his will.

fool as "my mango." Tucca has already refused to hire the Pyrgi to Histrio; "you mangonising slave . . . you'll sell them for enghles, you," this charge and others of a similar nature seemingly being directed at the company as a whole. But of the company, the fat fool is singled out as the "mango" par excellence, a term which is defined in 1587 as: "*Mango* a baude that paynteth and pampereth up boyes, women, or servauntes to make them seeme the trimmer, thereby to sell them the deerer."[10] The chief point, then, of the epithet seems to lie in the fact that the actors took apprentices to dress them up as women, though this fact is used further to insinuate the charge of immorality. Now we know that Phillips, Pope, Heminges, and Burbadge all had apprentices at this time,[11] but Pope's household was most open to Jonson's insinuation. As appears from Pope's will in 1603,[12] this household was a queerly assorted aggregation. Good-wife Willingson kept house for the bachelor. Pope had reared Susan Gasquine from a child, and was then rearing Mary Clark and Thomas Bromley, the latter but eleven months old when the will was drawn,[13] and his mother still alive. Robert Goffe had not long before completed apprenticeship with him, and John Edmans was still in that capacity. Pope also remembered a sister of Mary Clark, Dorothea, in his will, though we have no other indication that she had belonged to Pope's orphanage. Certainly Pope's household was the fairest mark in the company for such descriptive insinuations.

Further evidence that Pope performed this line is to be found in the fact that Lowin, his successor in the company, is known to have acted the part of Falstaff,[14] presumably then having inherited it as Pope's successor in the line. Now Malone[15] says he remembers reading in some tract that Heminges was the original Falstaff; but Chalmers[16] says seven years later: "There is only a tradition, that he performed the arduous part of Falstaff," and Collier too doubts

[10] Penniman, *Poetaster*, p. 225.
[11] See Appendix VII.
[12] Collier, *Memoirs*, pp. 125-8.
[13] Chalmers, *Apology*, p. 388, note.
[14] Wright, *Historia*, p. 424.
[15] Malone, *Variorum*, Vol. III, p. 187; Malone does not record this in 1780, but does in 1790.
[16] Chalmers, *Apology*, p. 436.

that this was his part. I do not see how Heminges could have taken the part. It seems to me a striking confirmation that the Falstaff type, which had been given with variations for many years, does not extend beyond 1602, about the time of Pope's withdrawal, while Heminges continued to act till 1611. Therefore in view of the evidence to show that Pope must have taken the Falstaff line, and that Heminges could not have taken it,[17] I feel justified in rejecting Malone's undocumented memory.[18]

It appears then that Kemp was the low, and Pope the high comedian of the company. The line of the old dignitary, upon occasion merry or peppery, Shakespeare's "humorous man," is the line we saw fit in the Beaumont and Fletcher plays of 1610-11 to assign to John Heminges. Here belong the merry master of ceremonies Boyet, the equally merry old Lord Lafeu, the more serious old father Aegeon, and the somewhat peppery old father of Silvia, the Duke of Milan. Presumably this had been Heminges's line from the beginning.

This leaves the two more or less young men for Phillips and Bryane, the other two members of the company. Now these two young men from the hand of the youthful Shakespeare are none too clearly differentiated, but there is a real difference. The one is a king or other high dignitary of majestic port, sometimes old, never spoken of as young. Here is the King of Navarre, the older King

---

[17] It is to be remembered, however, that there are really two or three distinct Falstaffs, as is shown by the evolution of the character. First we have the coward in war, Sir John Falstolfe or Falstaff in *1 Henry VI*, winter of 1591-92. Then we have his complement, the coward in love, Falstaff in *The Merry Wives of Windsor*, winter of 1592-93. It was probably, then, the *Henry VI* Fastolfe, instead of the *Henry IV* Falstaff, that Queen Elizabeth wanted to see in love, if indeed there is any truth at all in the old tradition. Then in 1596 Shakespeare created the Falstaff of *Henry IV* under the name Oldcastle. When objection was raised to this name, he simply changed it to Falstaff, the preceding character of the same type. Thus Oldcastle of *Henry IV* is no more the same character as Falstaff of *The Merry Wives* than is Sir Toby Belch. They are all three close kinsmen in the line of one actor, but it was only by accident that two bear the same name. It is possible then that after Pope's death in 1603-04, the *Merry Wives* Falstaff was refurbished for Lowin, but that Heminges took the Oldcastle Falstaff as being better acquainted with and fitted for the part than Lowin.

[18] I have less hesitation because his Boswell informs us that Malone's "memory was far from tenacious" (*Variorum*, Vol. I, p. vii), "not remarkably retentive" (*Variorum*, Vol. I, p. xliv).

of France, and the noble Valentine. The other is a more volatile young man, much given to falling in love and quickly falling out again, best typified by Proteus, who is properly labelled. As with the clowns, so with the young men, it is difficult to be certain which is which in *The Comedy of Errors*; but Antipholus of Ephesus seems to me the more volatile, and later evidence will, I think, place him in this line. The one of these actors then is Shakespeare's "king," the other his "lover." The clue to allocation of these lines between Phillips and Bryane is furnished by *The Seven Deadly Sins*. There Bryane was the king-maker Warwick, and the old councilor Damasus, while Phillips was the effeminate but noble young king Sardanopalus. It is thus indicated that Phillips was the aggressive young lead, and Bryane the noble dignitary. The later development of the lines will confirm this conclusion. Thus the five lines for men before the winter of 1590 may be satisfactorily allocated to the five members. It appears then that each member in this period was a principal actor, and had his line.

But the problem from the winter of 1590, to the winter of 1594, is slightly more complicated. The first complicating fact is that Sly and Cundall had just graduated, and were beginning to carve out lines for themselves. The second is that young Richard Burbadge was in this period forcing himself to the front as lead. Thus there were eight actors upon whom the chief parts for men could be built, though, since the membership itself was as yet unchanged, the plays must still each be constructed for only five principal actors. It is interesting to see how the increased membership of 1594 was at once reflected in the plays by an increase of principal lines, these ranging now from seven to nine. Adjustment was then complete and again each principal actor was represented by his line. This situation is also shown by the actor lists of *Every Man in His Humor* (winter 1598) and *Every Man Out of His Humor* (summer 1599). The second of these names Burbadge, Heminges, Phillips, Cundall, Sly, and Pope. Since Kemp had just left the company, he does not appear in the second, though he does in the first, as does William Shakespeare also. As Bryane has by this time dropped out, he is not named. In addition, the exceptionally full first list also names Christopher Beeston, who was Phillips's "servant," and John Duke, who was also a hired man. It will be best then to consider the period after 1594 first, and then try to connect the lines 1590-94.

Burbadge had by this time established incontestably his inalienable right to the leading rôle, having already created Hamlet and Richard III by 1594,[19] others of his known later characters being Lear and Othello. These four are the only Shakespearean parts definitely assigned to Burbadge by contemporary evidence.[20] We also know, however, that he was Ferdinand in *The Duchess of Malfi*, Malevole in *The Malcontent*, Gorboduc and Tereus in *The Seven Deadly Sins*, and Jeronimo either in *The Spanish Tragedy* or the lost first part of that play.[21] Since Taylor succeeded Burbadge and in known cases inherited the latter's parts, it is also probable that most of the old parts known to have been performed by Taylor had originally belonged to Burbadge. This would add to Burbadge's rôles probably Mosca, Truewit, Face, and Arbaces. Too, since Lowin was Henry VIII, Wolsey seems the only possible part left in that play for Burbadge. There is thus no doubt that Burbadge was the lead in the company from about 1592. It is evident then that the youthful lead of the period 1594-1603 is Burbadge. Indeed, one of these characters, Prince Hal, bears Burbadge's age stamped upon him. To Richard III and Hal would be added the kings Henry V, Richard II, John, and the uncrowned Brutus. To Hamlet as lover and Tereus may be added the leading young lovers, Aurelius-Lucentio, Bassanio, Claudio, Orlando, and prob-

[19] *Shakspere All. Bk.*, Vol. I, pp. 272-3.
[20] For the tangled web surrounding *A Funeral Elegy* to Burbadge, from which most of these attributions come, see *Shakspere All. Bk.*, Vol. I, pp. 272-3; *Academy*, Vol. XV, pp. 32, 55, 77, 304, 345; Chambers, *Eliz. Stage*, Vol. II, pp. 308-9. If the spurious form of the *Elegy* represents Collier's opinion—and whose opinion else could it be?—he would attribute to Burbadge Romeo, Prince Hal, Henry V, Brutus, Shylock, Macbeth, Pericles, and Coriolanus. I do not know to whom he refers as Antonio. Wisely enough, he let the difficult assignments alone. Another alleged reference to Burbadge as Othello was published by Collier in his *New Particulars*, p. 56, on which see Ingleby, C. M., *Academy*, Vol. IX, p. 313. Malone, *Variorum*, Vol. III, p. 184, had already given as instances of Burbadge's line Richard III, John, Richard II, Henry V, Timon, Brutus, Coriolanus, Macbeth, Lear, and Othello. Thus I agree with Malone, and disagree with Collier only by not including Shylock.
[21] If Burbadge was Jeronimo in *The Spanish Tragedy*, the following passage probably describes him in a crucial scene: "hauing no apparell on but his shirt, a paire of slip-shooes on his feete, and a *Candle* burning in his hand like olde *Ieronimo*" (Grosart, *Dekker*, Vol. III, p. 298).

ably the revised Berowne. The hybrid lover-duke, Orsino, seems also to belong to this line. It is interesting to notice that one of these characters bears Burbadge's exact age, and that all the others of this period are specifically described as young, except John and Brutus, where no indication, so far as I find in the text, is given. In the source, however, Brutus is represented as a young man, and we may be certain he was not aged for Burbadge. Evidently then Burbadge played under his own age, except when the story absolutely demanded a change. Even in the plays after 1603, Lear is his only really old man, though Antony too has gray hairs, and some others are not youthful. It is apparent then that the age given is the age of Burbadge, unless the source absolutely demands another.

In the period from 1603, Burbadge's rôles would be Hamlet, Ford, Othello, Angelo, Timon, Lear, Macbeth, Antony, Bertram, Pericles, Coriolanus, Posthumus, Leontes, Prospero, Wolsey. There seems no very grave doubt about Burbadge's rôles in this period, except probably in the case of the play *Cymbeline*, where it may be doubted whether Posthumus or Cymbeline is the leading character. In all the other plays of the period, this line has contained all title rôles, which would indicate Cymbeline. Due chiefly to Lear, we may think of Burbadge as now too old to play Posthumus, who, if Shakespeare has harmonized his time references, is between thirty-five and forty. But previously to Lear, Burbadge has not been represented as old, and at least as Leontes, the year following *Cymbeline*, was represented at the beginning of the play as only thirty-four. Further, this leading rôle has in the majority of cases had the greatest number of lines of any man's part in the play. In three of the other four exceptions for this period, the character was a close second. This fact points to Posthumus but not to Cymbeline, who in point of lines is fourth for men. The mechanical importance of the two characters seems to me to correspond exactly to their real importance. Thus I think that the evidence favors Posthumus as the lead, and I have so marked him in the tables.

As has been pointed out, Burbadge was regularly represented on the stage as being his own age, except in a few plays where greater age for the lead was demanded by the story, as Lear, Antony, and possibly Prospero. Several of these characters bear Burbadge's age upon them, thus, with other evidence, enabling us to get the date of his birth pretty accurately. As Prince Hal in *1 Henry IV* (summer 1596) Burbadge is "two and twenty, or thereabouts"; and Hamlet (summer 1603) is thirty. These dates indicate that Burbadge was born about the summer of 1573, which is also indicated by the fact that he became a member about the summer of 1594.

This age external evidence confirms. James Burbage's children are enumerated in 1588, as "Cutbert Rychard Alce and Ellen Burbedge."[22] We also know that Cuthbert was about twenty-four years old February 16, 1591,[23] which means that he was born about 1566-67. Further, Richard was the youngest son,[24] and Alice was baptized March 11, 1576.[25] It appears then that the children are named in order, and that Richard was born between 1567 and 1575. Also, in 1635 Cuthbert Burbadge tells us that Richard was an actor for thirty-five years.[26] Since Richard died in March 1619, this statement would date the beginning of his theatrical connection as by or before March 1584. If he began at the usual age of ten, this would place the date of his birth as before March 1574. In view of this evidence then, we may be reasonably certain that these characters bear Burbadge's age, and that he was born about the summer of 1573.

It is in accord with this dating that Burbadge was playing leading parts before he was fully grown, since Talbot, winter 1591, is "a child, a silly dwarf," and there is considerable indication that Richard, afterward the third, a character known from contemporary allusion to have been created by Burbadge, was a hunch-backed dwarf.[27] Since Burbadge was but eighteen when he performed the first of these parts, there is no reason to suppose that he was small when he was fully grown. Even as Prince Hal, 1596, he was still thin, if we may believe Falstaff's blackguarding description, though

---

[22] Wallace, *First London Theatre*, p. 39.
[23] *ibid.*, p. 59.
[24] *ibid.*, p. 98.
[25] Collier, *Memoirs*, p. 12.
[26] Halliwell, *Outlines*, Vol. I, p. 317.
[27] Collier has also pointed out the allusions to the smallness of Jeronimo in *The First Part of Jeronimo* as probably having been dictated by Burbadge's youth at the time of performance (Collier, *Memoirs*, pp. 20-1), but the reference is probably to one of the Children of the Chapel. For evidence that Jeronimo and Richard III were Burbadge parts, see Macray, *Parnassus*, pp. 138-41.

[239]

probably of good height. However, a man who was thin by Falstaff's standard might be of very good size according to ordinary ideas. Certainly by the time he created Antony of *Antony and Cleopatra*, he was a "Herculean Roman," as Coriolanus, "What an arm he has," and later as Posthumus he had a "Martial thigh,/ The brawns of Hercules." Even as early as the final Hamlet, summer of 1603, the older texts would make him "fat, and scant of breath," though some modern editors would merely have him "faint, and scant of breath."[28] Neither was his cheek lean by the time he came to play Orlando, summer of 1600. Certainly then he lost his youthful trimness, and eventually became a man of good, if not "portly," size. I should consider that his portrait warrants the same inference, though its evidence is on this point by no means conclusive.

Various allusions give the color of Burbadge's hair and beard as brown or chestnut. Orlando's hair is "Something browner than Judas's," "An excellent colour: your chestnut was ever the only colour." Antony's white hairs reprove the brown. Burbadge's portrait, especially the chin of it, seems to confirm this coloring, though it shows that Burbadge might also be called a "black hair'd man," as he was in *The Two Noble Kinsmen*.[29] The beard was evidently not permitted to flourish in his younger days, since Orlando had but a little beard, and Falstaff pretends to despair that a barber would ever earn sixpence out of Prince Hal's allotment of that commodity. Claudio also is "Lord Lack-beard." But then this deficiency was probably in part atoned for by his "curls." We aren't told the color of his eyes further than that they were not blue and sunken; but he had "arched brows," and a "hawking eye," this broad brow "Arch'd like the great eyed Juno's" being again re-

---

[28] Professor M. P. Tilley (*The Journal of English and Germanic Philology*, Vol. XXIV, pp. 315-19) calls attention to the popular belief of Shakespeare's time that perspiration was oozing fat, and would interpret the statement as meaning merely that Hamlet is perspiring freely. But he does not give a single illustration where a lean man is said to perspire fat. Besides, the statement is unequivocal: "He's fat," not "He's oozing fat." This statement, taken with the others quoted, surely indicates that Burbadge had attained at least "portly" size.

[29] Of course, after all, Burbadge may have worn a wig; but the consistency of the allusions possibly indicates not. If so, at least we know what was his favorite color for a wig.

ferred to in *The Two Noble Kinsmen*. This arched brow is a noticeable feature of his portrait, and the eye is quite dark. Everything considered, he seems to have been reckoned a handsome man. Probably the Nurse's description of Romeo was not so exaggerated as to have been laughable when she said: "though his face be better than any man's yet his leg exceeds all men's; and for a hand, and a foot, and a body, though they be not talked on, yet they are past compare." Certainly he must have been a man of good physical as well as facial appearance to be able to personate characters of such handsome and heroic molds.

Nor is there likely to be grave difficulty in distinguishing the line of the clown. We know that Kemp was Dogberry and Peter. To them may be added Costard, Launcelot, Shallow, and Sander-Grumio. It is interesting to notice that this line is not written into the three plays beginning with the summer of 1595, and ending with that of 1596. It is possible that for this year and a half Kemp was away on one of his foreign jaunts; but it is just as likely that in these three plays he supplied his own applauded merriments, as he was sometimes accustomed to do. Kemp's successor, Armin, is also immediately reflected in the plays by the jesters Touchstone and Feste, to whom may be added the Fools of *Timon* and *Lear*, as well as Trinculo of *The Tempest*, all fully labelled. An unsavory variety of this fool and clown is represented by Pompey and Boult.[30] Near akin to the fool is the rustic or clown, so labelled in *Antony*, *All's Well*, and *Winter's Tale*. To this foolish, philosophical crew would belong the First Gravedigger, the Clown of Othello, the Porter, and the First Citizen of *Coriolanus*. Of more dignified position, but of equally comic characteristics, are the very Welsh parson Evans, and the clownish gull Cloten.

As has been said, we happen to know by direct evidence that Kemp was Peter in *Romeo and Juliet*, and Dogberry in *Much Ado*, these two parts showing accurately how Kemp was used as clownish servant or pompous official. Indeed, we have a contemporary account of Kemp's method of amusing, given in *The Pilgrimage to Parnassus*.[31]

---

[30] Douce, Francis, *Illustrations of Shakspeare* [1807], Vol. I, pp. 151-2.
[31] Macray, *Parnassus*, pp. 22-3.

Enter DROMO, *drawing a clowne in with a rope.*

Clowne. What now? thrust a man into the commonwealth whether hee will or noe? what the devill should I doe here?

Dromo. Why, what an ass art thou! dost thou not knowe a playe cannot be without a clowne? Clownes have bene thrust into playes by head and shoulders ever since Kempe could make a scurvey face; and therefore reason thou shouldst be drawne in with a cart-rope.

Clowne. But what must I doe nowe?

Dromo. Why, if thou canst but drawe thy mouth .awrye, laye thy legg over thy staffe, sawe a peece of cheese asunder with thy dagger, lape up drinke on the earth, I warrant thee theile laughe mightilie. Well, I'le turne thee loose to them; ether saie somwhat for thy selfe, or hang and be *non plus.*

Clowne. This is fine, y-faith! nowe, when they have noebodie to leave on the stage, they bringe mee up, and, which is worse, tell mee not what I shoulde saye! Gentles, I dare saie youe looke for a fitt of mirthe. I'le therfore present unto you a proper newe love-letter of mine to the tune of *Put on the smock o' Mundaye,* which in the heate of my charitie I pende; and thus it begins :—

'O my lovely Nigra, pittie the paine of my liver! That litell gallowes Cupid hath latelie prickt mee in the breech with his great pin, and almoste kilde mee thy woodcocke with his birdbolte. Thou hast a pretty furrowed forheade, a fine leacherous eye; methinks I see the bawde Venus keeping a bawdie house in thy lookes, Cupid standing like a pandar at the doore of thy lipps.'

How like you, maisters? has anie yonge man a desire to copie this, that he may have *formam epistolae conscribendae?* Now if I could but make a fine scurvey face, I were a kinge! O nature, why didest thou give mee soe good a looke?

Dromo. Give us a voyder here for the foole! Sirra, you muste begone; here are other men that will supplie the roome.

Clowne. Why, shall I not whistle out my whistle? Then farewell, gentle auditors, and the next time you see mee I'le make you better sporte.

Kemp probably revenged himself for being crowded almost out of the tragedies by using the little corner left him as a means for exercising this extemporal wit of his, "though in the mean time some necessary question of the play be to be considered." Of course such behavior is "villainous, and shows a most pitiful ambition in the fool that uses it," for the said fool is trying to star instead of to carry on his part in the teamwork, a foolish ambition of which Shakespeare himself was not guilty. Kemp as Bottom the weaver was probably unwittingly satirizing himself in his desire to be the whole show. Shakespeare's protest is evidently provoked by Kemp's type of comedy, and not by Pope's, though the quoted jests show that it is Tarleton's picture which is being drawn in *Hamlet*. To avoid subjecting Kemp to undue temptation, Shakespeare has usually incorporated him a sufficient part in the play. His most famous impersonations seem to have been "a foolish Mayre or a foolish iustice of peace," since he is represented as giving grave instructions in this type of performance to a prospective actor at the same time that Burbadge instructs another in the proper method of acting Jeronimo and Richard III.[32] We have only to remember Dogberry,[33] known to have been one of his parts, to see that the representation here is correct. Another sample of his foolery is given in *A Knack to Know a Knave* "With Kemp's applauded Merrimentes of the Men of Goteham, in receiving the King into Goteham." Kemp's written rôles in the Shakespearean plays are so evident, I think, as to need no further pointing out.

In physique, Kemp seems not to have been large. Robert Shallow, esquire, is a "starved justice," the "genius of famine," compared with whom Falstaff would "make four dozen such bearded hermit's staves." Grumio is "a little pot," a "three inch fool," Cade is much smaller than Iden. On the other hand, Costard "because of his great limb, or joint, shall pass Pompey the Great." It seems probable then that Kemp was not tall but of large joint. Perhaps the well-known woodcut of Kemp dancing the Morris represents a man of this type, but I for my part am not certain. However, Tarleton, whom Kemp succeeded in favor, is certainly represented as small; and the majority of allusions to clowns in the Shakespearean company, male and female, men and boys, represents the performers as small. Of course, when humor consists of practical jokes, it is the

[32] Macray, *Parnassus*, pp. 138-41.

[33] Indeed, the Parnassus reference to "a foolish iustice of peace" may have been aimed at Kemp's last Shakespearean rôle with the company, that of Dogberry, winter of 1598, though we must remember that this was the stock casting of the time: "they put all their fools to the constable's part still" (Bullen, *Middleton*, Vol. III, p. 349).

[243]

part of wisdom to have the victims small. We have no certain indications of Kemp's age; but he must have been above twenty-one when he appears in 1585, as Leicester's jesting player,[34] as we learn from the fact that he had a mature apprentice the next year. If this mature apprentice, Daniel Jones, was indeed the newly graduated predecessor of William Eccleston about 1587, as seems probable,[35] then Kemp was twenty-one probably not later than 1576, and was born probably about 1554-55, being thus about the age of Pope and Heminges, though possibly a year or so older. It is likely for this reason that Kemp's name is first in the list of 1593, followed by those of Pope and Heminges. He would thus probably be not much under thirty-five at the reorganization of 1588, not much under forty-five when he danced his famous Morris to Norwich, exceedingly strenuous exercise for a man that age. But these facts would harmonize well enough with the date of his burial November 2, 1603,[36] at the age presumably of nearly fifty.

As soon as Kemp leaves the company in 1599, the clown changes notably into the sly, roguish, jesting fool of the court. As Armin says of himself in his *Nest of Ninnies*, "I goe in Motly."[37] It is immediately evident that Touchstone, Feste, the Clown in the present form of *All's Well*, or the Fool in *Lear* are of another guess from the pompous, countrified, blundering clown of Kemp. Kemp's characters are what Cibber calls "still-life—I mean the stiff, the heavy, and the stupid."[38] But these comedians after 1599 are courtly fools, who may accompany their royal masters and mistresses into the best society, there to satirize and make a jest of the world in general. As it is put in *Wit Without Money*, II. 2; "There be three kinds of fools. . . . An innocent, a knave-fool, a fool politic." Armin was the "innocent" fool,[39] while Kemp was the knave-fool, and fool politic. This change in fools is not surprising when we

---

[34] *Modern Language Review*, Vol. IV, p. 88.
[35] See Appendix VII.
[36] Collier, *Memoirs*, p. 116.
[37] Grosart, A. B., *The Works of Robert Armin*, p. 46.
[38] Cibber, C., *An Apology for the Life of Mr. Colley Cibber* (1830), pp. 94-5.
[39] While these jesters were in actual life supposed to be more or less "innocents" or idiots, they frequently were not markedly so, some of them displaying considerable keenness. It is this type that Shakespeare has still further heightened for Armin.

remember that Armin had evidently made a special study of these naturals, publishing his information concerning the chief of them in his *Foole Vpon Foole or Six Sortes of Sottes*, 1600,[40] the very year he came to the Shakespearean company. The "life and simple maner of John in the Hospitall," one of these ninnies, he had already incorporated in his play of *The Two Maids of More-clacke*, first acted 1597-98, probably the autumn or winter of 1597.[41] Since the play was later revived by the "Children of the Kings Maiesties Revels," Armin regrets in his preface to the edition of 1609 that he was not able again to personate John, as he thus implies he had done about 1597. One of his allusions established the fact that he succeeded Kemp as Dogberry, as we should naturally expect.[42] It is evident, however, that this literary and jesting fool is of a different type from the bungling and blundering clown of Kemp.[43] It is interesting to note the frequent big parts for Kemp up to his withdrawal early in 1599, and then the lack of his part in *Henry V* and *Julius Caesar*, both known to belong to 1599, followed by the appearance of the court jester with Armin in 1600.

We have only a few references in the Shakespearean plays to Armin's physical appearance. Feste says when he is disguised as a priest: "I am not tall enough to become the function well, nor lean enough to be thought a good student," from which we may infer that Armin was short and probably plump, as seems also to have been true of Tarleton and Kemp before him. Aguecheek wishes "I had such a leg." Trinculo, who has "lesser legs" than Caliban (Lowin), is "made like a goose," and is "a jesting monkey," indi-

[40] Halliwell, *Outlines*, Vol. I, pp. 321-3.
[41] *Modern Language Notes*, Vol. XXXIX, pp. 447 ff.
[42] I suppose it is hardly necessary to do more than record Mr. Fleay's (*Drama*, Vol. I, p. 25) suggestion that the speech of the "Dutch Froe" to Mat. Flowerdale: "O here, God, so young an armine" (*The London Prodigall*, V. 1. 174) indicates that Armin was Flowerdale. Equally groundless, I think, is his supposition that Grumball or Lurchall in Dekker's *If it be not good the Devil is in it* is intended as a caricature of Armin (*Drama*, Vol. I, p. 26). Lurchall is a quite serious devil, and does not suggest the comic Armin. Armin evidently did play, however, the "philosophical fool," "good Robin" in *The Miseries of Enforced Marriage*.
[43] Incidentally, this distinction shows that *As You Like It*, *Twelfth Night*, and the present form of *All's Well* must date after the spring of 1600, when Armin entered the company, as they are already supposed to do; and that *Much Ado*, in which Kemp acted, must date before the summer of 1599 when he had withdrawn.

cating the same build; and Pompey seems also not to have been large. Armin appears thus to have been able to pass for a man much younger than he actually was, possibly even at times as a boy, a fact that explains why the Fool in *Lear* is a "lad," a "pretty knave," and "boy." The woodcut to Armin's *Two Maids of More-clacke*, probably intended as Armin's picture, represents such a man. Armin seems also, especially in his earlier connection with the company, to have displayed considerable ability as a singer.

For the line of the high-comedian Pope, the fantastic braggart Armado, and the *miles gloriosus* Parolles find their counterparts in bragging Falstaff and jolly Sir Toby Belch. The gruffly comic, genuine soldier Arbactus has as his counterparts Ferando-Petruchio, Philip the Bastard, the revised Mercutio,[44] Benedick, and Fluellen. Of still more serious type is the soldier Mowbray, but even he is an excellent scold, close kin to Philip. This scolding streak also finds vent in the bitter Casca and the scolding Jaques, who has been considered everything from a plain clown to the deepest philosopher. Since he was Pope, he was exactly that. It is not surprising then that this same man was hero-villain-clown Shylock. The Elizabethan Shylock is a characteristic part for Pope, and the process of elimination leaves him no other, but it must be admitted that Pope would not be much at home with the heroic figure Shylock has become. Pope's line has its most characteristic expression then as the bluff soldier, true or false, aimed at comic effect. Possibly the best composite representative of this line is the clownish Welsh soldier Fluellen, of whom as Pope's latest rôle Samuel Rowland[45] was probably thinking when he wrote about 1599-1600 the allusion quoted above to Pope as clown. Pope was thus the high comedian and gruff villain of the company.

Allusions to Pope show that he was a large man, as we should expect of his soldier type. His characters are never young, one of them, Mowbray, seeming to be represented as forty. The fact that this is a round number is a bit suspicious; but at that cannot be far wrong for Pope, who would thus probably be about the age of Heminges. This would give Pope a date of birth about 1555. Curiously enough, this age harmonizes with the age given for the two

[44] For the Mercutio tradition, see Halliwell, *Outlines*, Vol. I, p. 129.
[45] See above, p. 231.

sets of twins in *The Comedy of Errors*. The mother implies that the loss of the children occurred "Thirty-three years" before, shortly after their birth, which would carry us back not later than the winter of 1556.[46] Probably then Pope's age is given by these characters, he having been born about 1555. He would thus have been about thirty-two or three at the reorganization in 1588, approximately the same age as Heminges. Doubtless this is the reason that no one of his characters is represented as young. Pope's later characters show a tendency to excessive flesh, and Jonson calls him a fat fool, probably indicating that Pope had grown fat and forty; but of course we are to remember that padding must have been at least as cheap then as now. Yet almost certainly some physical difficulty had developed before March 1603, Pope having officially retired at that date, to die within the year. His last apparent rôle in Shakespeare's work is Sir Toby Belch, winter of 1600. It is also significant that while Pope had been Heminges's partner in receiving the court payments regularly after the withdrawal of Bryane, he appears in the records at court for the last time October 2, 1599.[47] It seems probable then that all of Sir Toby's flesh was not padding.

Pope's successor, Lowin, has also a line fairly well marked in its main characteristics. We are told that he created the part of "Bluff Harry" under the tutelage of Shakespeare himself,[48] in the gruff-soldier style as indicated by certain surviving allusions. A sonnet

[46] The age given for the twins in the source is "above thirty," which may have become to Shakespeare the definite thirty-three of Pope's age. It does not follow that all four of the actors for the twins were actually this age. Certainly these twins were not so much alike physically as to be indistinguishable by the audience. The personal allusions of the lines (See Appendix VI under Pope and Kemp) show that in size Pope and Kemp were very poor yokemates as the Dromios, and nearly as certainly indicate the same ill matching of Bryane and Phillips as the Antipholi. But what difference did it make? Indeed, the audience must in some way readily distinguish the difference in the actors in order to catch the fun in the errors; it is only necessary that the actors be unable to distinguish each other. In romantic Shakespeare's world of the imagination there was no difficulty. Of course this kind of solution disturbed the realist Jonson, and with him it would not down. He gave up the *Amphitruo* because "he could never find two so like others that he could persuade the spectators they were one" (*Jonson Allusion Book*, p. 116), indicating his superiority to friend Shakespeare in that respect.

[47] Murray, Vol. I, p. 107.
[48] Downes, *Roscius Anglicanus* (1708 and Knight's reprint), p. 24.

on the burning of the Globe alludes to "the rugged face of Henry the eight."[49] Some sixty years later (1672) Thomas Fuller tells us: "Indeed he was a Man of an Uncomptrolable spirit, carrying a Mandamus in his mouth, sufficiently sealed when he put his hand to his Hilt. He awed all into *Obedience*, which some impute to his skillfulnesse to Rule, others ascribe to his *Subjects* ignorance to resist."[50] Fuller then quotes an anecdote which shows that Henry was traditionally so represented on the stage. We have already seen that Lowin performed this line in the Beaumont and Fletcher plays, Melantius being one of his parts; and in the Jonson plays, where he performed Volpone and Mammon. We are also told that Lowin was Falstaff.[51] It thus appears, as we have seen before,[52] that Lowin took this line from the time of his entry in 1603. With Falstaff would go to Lowin the military braggarts Parolles, and Lucio. For the soldier and king as represented by Henry VIII, we have as counterparts the incestuous Kings Antiochus, and Claudius; the racy Earl of Gloucester, of whose pleasant vices the Gods did make instruments to plague him; but an honest, downright, outspoken noble nevertheless; the noble and impressive general Banquo; a second is treacherous Aufidius; another treacherous soldier is "strong Enobarb"; and ending the quartet, "honest" treacherous Iago,[53] of Lowin's own age. This is the "honest" soldier of the Beaumont and Fletcher plays; but usually less "merry," and more dignified. On the more bitter side, Bosola finds an own brother in Apemantus, and no distant relative in Caliban. Finding their places in this comico-villainous assemblage are also, "honest," jaundiced Iachimo, and possibly roguish Autolycus.[54] This then is Lowin's

---

[49] *Shakspere All. Bk.*, Vol. I, p. 240.

[50] Fuller, T., *The History of the Worthies of England* (1672), Part II, Kent, p. 66; quoted *Shakspere All. Bk.*, Vol. II, p. 183.

[51] Wright, *Historia*, p. 424. Since Lowin entered the company in 1603, the Falstaff of the revised *Merry Wives* would have fallen to his lot, this being in part the reason the original braggart but cowardly dupe Falstaff was not ennobled in revision by the sunny roguery of Oldcastle (See above, p. 235, note 17.)

[52] See above, pp. 179-80.

[53] Later, Rymer's hope (*A Short View of Tragedy*, p. 94) that Iago was not presented in a red coat shows both that Rymer had not seen the play, and that he would expect the actor of the part to use the regulation soldier's uniform, as quite likely Lowin did.

[54] Forman was impressed by "the rog that cam in all tottered like Coll

line of true or pretended military characters, bluff of bearing and plain of speech, this downrightness taking either an honest or villainous, serious or comic turn. Since the characteristics of Lowin have already been discussed in connection with the later plays, we need not repeat the information here.

We may also trace from early days the irascible and "humorous" old nobleman we have assigned to John Heminges.[55] This old gentleman is of fatherly, not to say grandfatherly, appearance. He is likely to be whimsically humorous or somewhat "peppery," though never intensely so. He is the faithful father, counsellor, servant, with all the privileges of oddity or whimsicality attaching to age. We may possibly sum up his line best by the commonplace phrase of "an old character," with the frequent addition of odd, queer, interesting, etc., by which we placard some venerable antique of the community. Whether as father, counsellor, or servant, he is usually giving advice, and laying down the law. As father, probably Capulet, Polonius, Leonato and Brabantio[56] are his most typical parts, to whom may be added Aegeon, the Duke of Milan in *The Two Gentlemen of Verona*, Marcus, Egeus, York, Glendower, and Duke Senior in *As You Like It*. His most typical part as counsellor-servant is probably honest old Kent, who seems even to have Heminges's age stamped upon him. To this category belong Boyet, Lafeu, Exeter, Gloucester, Hastings, Hubert, Chief Justice in *2 Henry IV*, Escalus, Flavius, Kent, Helicanus, Menenius, Pisanio, Camillo, and Gonzalo. Caesar, Pompey, and Ross also have the Heminges characteristics, but do not wear the customary livery of father-counsellor-servant. Also, the Host in *Merry Wives*, Salarino, and Fabian have the age and humor, lacking only the customary dress. When we remember Heminges's numerous family— Mr. Collier says Heminges had thirteen children, yet he enumerates at least fifteen,—and his successful guidance of the business af-

Pipci" (Halliwell, *Outlines*, Vol. II, p. 86; Lambert, D. H., *Shakespeare Documents*, p. 69), which was the typical dress of stage rogues (Grosart, *Dekker*, Vol. III, p. 261), referred to in our text.

[55] Roberts stated in 1729 that Heminges was a tragedian; but he blunders in so many particulars that his unconfirmed word is practically worthless, especially as he was writing so long after (Collier, *Memoirs*, p. 57).

[56] Booth calls Brabantio the "First Old Man," which is the technical description of this line of Heminges's (*Variorum Othello*, I. 3. 219, note).

fairs of the company, we must feel that in this line Heminges did not act; he was himself.

Naturally, in this line Heminges's stage make-up has all the outward insignia of age, such as gray hair, wrinkles, etc., meriting more times than one the description "reverend." More accurate description we do not get, so that our portrait of Heminges must remain somewhat indefinite in details. Perhaps much of the portrait was suggested by the fact that he was "old stuttering Heminges,"[57] as we are informed by a sonnet on the destruction of the Globe. The application of the adjective "stuttering" to Heminges is neither necessitated nor suggested, so far as I can see, by anything in the situation, and may well be an exaggeration of his usual stage manner, which in turn may have been based on some such real difficulty. Of course he himself was not always old. As Kent he was forty-eight, this age being altered from the source, where his counterpart is as old as Leir, the altered age thus being almost certainly that of the actor, as we have seen was regularly the case in the Beaumont and Fletcher plays. This would indicate that Heminges was born about 1556-57, Mr. Collier's estimate, based on other facts, being about 1556.[58] It is fairly certain then that Kent's age is that of Heminges, who must thus have been born not earlier than the winter of 1556, nor later than that of 1557. He must then have been about thirty-one when he married Rebecca Knell March 10, 1588, the same year he entered the reorganized Shakespearean company. In the early part of his line he himself was not old, but by the time of his retirement from acting he was about fifty-five.

Heminges's retirement seems to have occurred by the winter of 1611. He is last mentioned as an actor in Jonson's *Cataline*, summer of 1611. He is not mentioned in the lists of *Bonduca* and *Valentinian*, 1614. Since he is not named in *The Duchess of Malfi*, we may be sure Heminges had retired from acting before the summer of 1613.[59] Certainly, however, "old stuttering Heminges" was at

[57] Halliwell, *Outlines*, Vol. I, pp. 310-11.
[58] Collier, *Memoirs*, p. 58.
[59] Lawrence, W. J., *Athenaeum*, November 21, 1919; *Fortnightly Review*, Vol. CXIII, p. 942, note 1, shows that the play dates 1613, he believes for the autumn. That the play dates before December 1614, is indicated by the fact that Ostler had a part in it. That it dates before March 1614, is indicated by the fact that Eccleston had no part in it. Thus it certainly can-

the play that summer when *Henry VIII* burned the Globe, though not certainly as an actor.[60] Neither does Heminges appear in the list of *The Captain*, the winter of 1611. While the list is incomplete, there is hardly a possible representative of his line in this or later plays. It appears then that Heminges ceased acting about the summer of 1611. His line as such does not appear in the later Beaumont and Fletcher plays, and evidently died with his withdrawal from acting.

Possibly next clearest is the line that seems to belong to William Sly, for whom we have two non-Shakespearean parts. He was the would-be gallant of the Induction to Marston's *Malcontent*, and the young prince and king Porrex in *The Seven Deadly Sins* (1592).[61] He is mentioned as a principal actor in all the lists be-

not date later than the winter of 1613. That it is a summer play seems indicated by two allusions. We hear of:

some apricocks,
The first our spring yields (II. 1. 76-7, 137, 141) ;
and that "blackbirds fatten best in hard weather; why not I in these dog days ?" (I. 1. 39-40). The first of these allusions is all the more significant because these first apricots of spring were presented, mind you, according to the source about the ninth of December, 1504 (II. 3. 57). It appears then that *The Duchess* is for the spring and summer, not later than 1613.

That the year is 1613 is shown by various allusions. The French plot of the Switzer with a concealed pistol and button bullets (II. 2) ridicules a rumor current "that there was a ship of pocket-pistols came out of Spain, and that it was intended by the Papists to have made a massacre," whereupon it was proclaimed "that no man should carry a pistol in his pocket, nor any that should be less than a foot long in the barrel" (D' Ewes, *Autobiography* [1845], Vol. II, pp. 353, 354; Birch, *James First*, Vol. I, pp. 156, 158, 251; Winwood, *Memorials*, Vol. III, p. 429; *H. M. C., Report on the Manuscripts of the Duke of Buccleuch and Queensbury, K.G., K.T., preserved at Montagu House, Whitehall*, Vol. I, pp. 125, 239-40). This proclamation dates January 16, 1613, to take effect February 2 (*Tudor and Stuart Proclamations*, Vol. I, p. 132). Among the madmen is a farmer hindered in transportation (IV. 2). This refers to a proclamation against transportation of corn and grain January 19, 1613 (*Tudor and Stuart Proclamations*, Vol. I, p. 132). There is a reference to the slave-born Russian (III. 5), and to a Russian winter (IV. 1), while one of the madmen would drive snails to Moscow (V. 2). This interest in Russia and modes of transportation to Moscow was caused by a projected embassy to Moscow. It was being rumored May 6, 1613, that Overbury's notorious refusal to go abroad as an ambassador was to avoid going to Muscovy (Winwood, *Memorials*, Vol. III, p. 453). It seems that John Merrick and William Russel were sent at this time as commissioners to Russia, arriving by July 2, 1613 (*H.M.C.*, Buccleuch MSS., Vol. I, p. 136). There are other references to contemporary happenings, but these are sufficient to complete the evidence that *The Duchess* was written for the summer of 1613.

[60] Halliwell, *Outlines*, Vol. I, pp. 310-11.

[61] We have record in Henslowe's Papers of one other rôle: "Perowes sewt,

fore his death in 1608, and Heywood states in his *Apology for Actors* (1612) that Sly's "deserts yet live in the remembrance of many," the connection showing that Heywood regarded him as a prominent actor. His two known parts would indicate that he was a young gallant, either princely or comic. As Prince Porrex, he was probably represented as a stirring spirit, since he overthrows and kills his elder brother. There is such a line of vigorous young men, which seemingly ends just about the time of Sly's death. This is the expert and fiery young swordsman and lover, the duelling partner in love and war of Richard Burbadge. In war, he appears as Hotspur, Lewis, the Dauphin in *Henry V*, Octavius, Edmund, and Macduff opposing Burbadge; as Lancaster assisting him. In personal encounter, besides several of the preceding, he crosses swords with Burbadge as Tibalt and Laertes. Young Sebastian and the quat Roderigo are also swordsmen, though they do not duel with Burbadge. Evidently this actor is an expert with his weapon. But with Sly the duels end, for Burbadge too was now become "fat and scant of breath," and in consequence doubtless opposed to such vigorous exercise.[62] As Sebastian, Sly has also rivalled Burbadge in love, a situation recurring in the rôle of Valeria-Hortensio, and indirectly in that of Borachio. He is also the young lover, as Thurio, Lorenzo, Silvius, Fenton, Claudio, and Lysimachus.[63] He was probably too one of the young lovers in the revised *Love's Labor's Lost*, possibly Longaville, though the assignment is by no means certain. He is thus a mercurial and temperamental young man, in the early period appearing frequently as a stage Frenchman, so excellently described for us by Portia with Monsieur Le

which Wm Sley were" (Greg, *Papers*, p. 120). This part must have been performed 1590-94, while the Shakespearean company was connected with the Rose. But there is no character of this name in any known play of the period, unless Fleay (*Stage*, p. 115) is correct in supposing the reference is to Pyrhot in an earlier form of *Bussy D' Ambois*, which would thus date 1590-92. Pyrhot is just the type of character Sly would have taken at that time.

[62] These duels were not the creaky-kneed performances of the modern stage, but fencing exhibitions. For some idea of the contemporary interest in these martial contests, see Ordish, *Theatres*, pp. 46-9.

[63] About the time Sly was acting the parts of Claudio and Lysimachus, he was playing a similar rôle in real life. "Christened: John, sonne of William Sley (player), base-borne on the body of Margaret Chambers, 24 Sept., 1606;" buried October 4, 1606, at St. Giles, Cripplegate (Collier, *Memoirs*, p. 156).

Bon as the subject. "God made him, and therefore let him pass for a man. In truth, I know it is a sin to be a mocker; but, he! why, he hath a horse better than the Neapolitan's, a better bad habit of frowning than the Count Palatine; he is every man in no man; if a throstle sing, he falls straight a-capering; he will fence with his own shadow: if I should marry him, I should marry twenty husbands." In the last days, Sly's line was becoming somewhat older and gruffer, as in Menas, and Brutus in *Coriolanus*. Possibly the Poet of *Timon* also belongs with these.

We have no certain specific descriptions of Sly's appearance,[64] though Hotspur is said to have talked "thick" or fast, which might well be the accompaniment of this mercurial, nervous temperament. So far as I can find, there is no attribution of this characteristic to Hotspur in the source, it being thus probably suggested by Sly's own personal bearing.[65] For it seems true that Shakespeare's characters are regularly not only contemporary Englishmen but also the actors for whom he had written them.

At Sly's death, two young men, Ostler and Underwood, came to the company as actors, the one to succeed Sly, the other to succeed Laurence Fletcher, who seems never to have acted with the company. Neither of these men seems exactly to have carried on Sly's line, but both supplied some phases of it. Ostler took up the line of prominent and forceful but not impeccable kings, as we found in the Beaumont and Fletcher plays, taking presumably Cymbeline, Polixenes, and Alonso, besides the ones already assigned above. We have no definite description of any Shakespearean part for Ostler, but we probably have a punning allusion to his line. Davies in *The Scourge of Folly*[66] has lines "To the Roscius of these times, Mr. W. Ostler," in which he asks:

> Where was thine action when thy crowne was riu'n
> Sole king of actors?

Nearly all Ostler's parts in the Shakespearean plays are those of kings, and his line is the one to which mere kings as such would

[64] Dulwich College once had a picture of Sly; but it seems now to be missing (Collier, *Annals* [1879], Vol. III, p. 355).
[65] Tucca, possibly patterned to Sly, is also a stammerer.
[66] Licensed S. R. October 8, 1610. Grosart's edition in *Chertsey Worthies' Library*, p. 31.

fall, a conclusion we have already reached concerning Ostler's line in the Beaumont and Fletcher plays. In the same plays, we have also seen reason to ascribe to Underwood the gallant young prince— Guiderius, Florizel, Ferdinand,—who is so prominent in the Shakespearean plays after Underwood came to the company. In reality then, as will shortly appear, Ostler succeeded to the line of Sly's probable master, Phillips, while Underwood rejuvenated the line of Sly with adjustments.

Thus of the nine members in 1594, we still need to locate the lines of Bryane, Cundall, Phillips, and Shakespeare. Since Shakespeare's line, however, was never a major one, the real question is to discriminate the lines of the other three, which are not very far apart in type, and thus require careful examination. But the fact that Bryane was succeeded about 1597 by the comedian Cowley gives us a period 1598-1603, in which the question is only between Phillips and his probable former apprentice Sly. The line of Cowley is settled for us by the knowledge that he was Verges. To Verges must be added the frail old men, Silence and Gobbo. In younger guise, the line is evident as the thin-faced Robert, and the equally thin-faced Aguecheek, whose thinness is labelled with his name. To this crew must belong Aguecheek's companion as a disappointed lover, the country yokel William. Probably Sampson would also fall to Cowley's lot. Cowley then evidently belongs to the comic crew, and consequently does not appear in all the plays.

Cowley seems to have been decidedly thin, and to have capitalized this characteristic for comic effect. Thus half-faced Robert has legs that are:

two such riding-rods,
My arms such eel-skins stuff'd, my face so thin
That in mine ear I durst not stick a rose
Lest men should say, 'Look where three farthings goes!'

Aguecheek is a "thin-faced knave," named accordingly. Slender is also labelled with this characteristic, having but "a little whey face." Also Aguecheek's hair "hangs like flax on a distaff," and Slender has "a little yellow beard—a cane-coloured beard." As Slender walks, "does he not hold up his head, as it were, and strut in his gait?" In these youthful caricatures, Cowley was represented as approximately his own age, William in *As You Like It*, for instance, being twenty-five. But this slenderness was also used for aged comic caricatures. Here are Silence, Gobbo, and Verges, this last character being one that we know from contemporary evidence was Cowley's. As this comic old man, Cowley was usually paired with Kemp; but as the comic young man he was usually connected with Pope. He had succeeded to Bryane's membership in 1597; but the tide of educated public opinion was relegating the comedian to the sideshows, and in consequence Cowley's line never attained prominence in these succeeding tragedies and tragicomedies, though he remained a member till his death in 1619.

Thus for the period 1598-1603, the field is now narrowed to Phillips and Cundall for the two remaining principal lines. One of these lines is that of the dignified young man—Benvolio, Don Pedro, Antony, Oliver. To these the process of elimination would add Antonio of *Twelfth Night* and probably the Constable of *Henry V*. Here then we have a line of dignified and oratorical young men, advisers, and friends. The other of these lines is usually older, with a villainous cast, and has considerably more life as well as humor. Here are the lean Cassius, the usurping Duke Frederick, and the cross-gartered Puritan Malvolio. Younger than these is the plotting bastard Don John. Evidently this actor has dignity, but also force and some humor as well. Now we seem to have sufficient external evidence to discriminate between Cundall and Phillips as actors. In 1592, Cundall had taken the part of King Ferrex in *The Seven Deadly Sins*, with Sly as Porrex. In 1613, Cundall was the Cardinal in *The Duchess of Malfi*. Thus at the beginning of our period he was playing a young dignitary; at the end an old one. If the Ferrex of *Seven Deadly Sins* was presented as in the surviving *Gorboduc*, then he would fit exactly into this line of dignified young men for Cundall. This would leave the older, more forceful, more villainous, and more comic line to Phillips, this solution fitting quite well with his known part as the slothful, effeminate, even to dressing in woman's clothes, young king Sardanopalus, who nevertheless proved himself a hero in the end; and with the fickle young man we saw fit to assign him before 1590.

With the lines of Phillips and Cundall discriminated, it ought to be possible for us to project them backward from 1598 to 1594, and thereby untangle the line of Bryane. The *Henry IV* trilogy gives us the best point of attack. In these plays the three remaining lines, now in question, are, first, the forceful King Henry, still young in *Richard II* but old in both parts of *Henry IV*; second, the old Earl of Northumberland, father of Hotspur, at first the supporter but later the enemy of King Henry; third, a line composed of good old Gaunt; little less old Worcester, the brains of the rebellion against Henry; and silver-bearded Archbishop Scroop, still opposing Henry—statesmen all. This third line reminds one at once of plotting Warwick and the counsellor Damasus, played by Bryane in *The Seven Deadly Sins*. Also, King Henry fits the line of Phillips excellently, leaving Northumberland, the least important of the three, for the young actor Cundall. In *King John*, the parts to be decided for these actors are King Philip, Salisbury, and Pandulph. King Philip seems the natural companion of King Henry; the holy legate Pandulph fits Bryane's line of old counsellors and prelates; leaving the less important Salisbury for Cundall. In the two comedies, *The Taming of the Shrew* and *The Merchant of Venice*, these three lines seem to pair off as Antonio-Tranio, Gratiano-Gremio, and Morocco-Lord. Doddering old Gremio would belong with lean old Cassius and cross-gartered Malvolio to Phillips. His yokemate Gratiano has both the humorous tinge and the slight gruffness of this same line. Dignified Antonio fits well with Don Pedro and Antony into Cundall's line of noble young men. The equally dignified servant Tranio, who poses as his noble master, is also characteristic of this line. This leaves Morocco and the Lord for Bryane. They fit well enough with the incidental lordly characters belonging to Bryane in this period. In this time just preceding his withdrawal, Bryane is evidently losing to the younger Cundall, being supplied with a part by the padding of incidental characters into sufficient size.

This extent of Bryane's line coincides with the known facts concerning Bryane's leaving the company. He and Heminges had received the pay for court performances December 21, 1596;[67] but Bryane was out of the company before the Globe project of 1598, or the performance of *Every Man in His Humor*, the autumn of 1598.

[67] Murray, Vol. I, pp. 160-7; Greg, *Diary*, Vol. II, pp. 336-7.

It is thus significant that Bryane is replaced by Pope as Heminges's companion in receiving the pay at court November 27, 1597, and for some years thereafter. It is certain then that Bryane withdrew between December 21, 1596, and the autumn of 1598; almost certain that he withdrew before November 27, 1597, but after the production of *The Merchant of Venice* in the summer of 1597. If the next two plays had been original plays instead of revisions, we could have told accurately whether he had withdrawn before their production. But as it is, the fairly certain indication is that Bryane withdrew about the end of the summer 1597. The motive is supplied by the closing of all companies because of *The Isle of Dogs* in the latter part of July 1597 till about October of the same year.[68] Pretty certainly then Bryane dropped from the company during this temporary suppression, being succeeded by Richard Cowley, who was also attaining some prominence as an actor just at this period.

Therefore it would appear that in the revised plays of *Love's Labor's Lost*, and *Romeo and Juliet*, Bryane's former parts must be assumed by some one else. This person would naturally be Cundall, who was now a chief actor, but had been too young to be prominent in the original. Thus to the victor in this contest would go the spoils; the King, and Friar Laurence. But in *Love's Labor's Lost*, there was the further difficulty of supplying a part for Burbadge, who was only a boy of fifteen at the original performance in 1588, and probably was with another company at that; but was now undisputed lead. Almost certainly one character has been refurbished, since all other comedies before 1594 have only five principal parts for men, whereas the revised *Love's Labor's Lost* has six. Of course, Costard would still go to Kemp, Boyet to Heminges, Armado to Pope, and the King would fall to Cundall, leaving the claims of Phillips and Burbadge to be settled for Berowne. The solution seems to have been the natural one of giving young Burbadge the young lead Berowne, and furbishing up Holofernes for the older Phillips. This solution is further indicated by the fact that Holofernes appears only in the abnormally long fourth and fifth acts, which thus probably contain Shakespeare's

[68] Greg, *Diary*, Vol. II, pp. 87-8.

chief revision. It is also significant that, except for a few lines in the rustic play, Holofernes has no part in the rhyming verses of the earlier form of *Love's Labor's Lost*. Sir Sidney Lee,[69] following Capell and others, finds "an unmistakable resemblance between Holofernes . . . and Rombus, the pedantic schoolmaster in Sidney's masque," *The Lady of May*, first published in 1598, with the third edition of the *Arcadia*. While I see no way to prove conclusively that Shakespeare did borrow from this masque, and only in its printed form, yet the coincidence at least supports the other indications that Shakespeare vamped in or much enlarged the part of Holofernes for the 1598 revival. Pompous pedant Holofernes, with his no-face, chittern head fits well enough in physical and mental characteristics with "Pantelowne" Gremio, Cassius, and Malvolio into Phillips's line, and could be easily vamped into the play. An exactly analogous case is the old *Taming of a Shrew*, into which Gremio was vamped for Phillips, this solution probably pointing the way to that of *Love's Labor's Lost*. Since, as we shall see, all chief actors in the revised *Romeo and Juliet*, except Cundall, had principal parts in the original, the only adjustment necessary was for Cundall to take Bryane's former part, leaving his own minor part to be supplied by some one else.

Seemingly then we can safely discriminate between the lines of Bryane, Phillips, and Cundall. Bryane's typical part is that of the elderly statesman. Here are Warwick, Titus, Stanley, Gaunt, Worcester, and in priestly garb, Canterbury, Friar Laurence, Pandulph, and Scroop. Too, this statesman is usually plotting in the opposition, though not a Machiavellian. These characters are the twin brothers of king-making Warwick, and warning Damasus, both known to have been Bryane's in *The Seven Deadly Sins*. Such a serious character would be difficult to fit well into a rollicking comedy. In the first days, the problem was solved by making Bryane the noble and negatively good lover, with no special claims to youth—King in *Love's Labor's Lost*, Valentine, Antipholus of Syracuse. Even in those days he was cast as the elderly King of *Love's Labor's Won*, and a little later as the trusting husband and father Page; but as soon as younger men could qualify, Bryane

[69] *D.N.B.*, article Sidney, Sir Philip.

dropped all claim to the near-young lover, though even his last part was the princely and pompous Moorish suitor Morocco. Intermediate between these extremes of Bryane's dignified characters are the Player King of *Hamlet*, the Lord of *The Taming of The Shrew*, and Philostrate, Theseus's Master of the Revels (one wonders how Tilney reacted). With the passing of the history play of thronging statesmen Bryane passed, giving way to a younger man, Henry Cundall, more capable of bearing his part in the comedies then the fashion. We have no very accurate description of Bryane further than that he was of "able body," and "beautified with goodly shape," as he must have been to carry his impressive parts. To this impressive physique he added as statesman the appropriate dress of silver hair and beard. Too, the fact that no one of Bryane's characters is represented as young but most of them as old probably indicates that he himself was no longer young.

Augustine Phillips's favorite rôle may be described as the "luxurious" nobleman. In his earliest days, he was the fickle and naughty young lovers Bertram and Proteus, dominated by animal passion. The same leer is apparent in the Constable of France, Suffolk, Edward V, and King Claudius. All these show their kinship to Phillips's known rôle of the effeminate and slothful young king Sardanopalus of *The Seven Deadly Sins*, who even dresses "like a woman"; but is nevertheless a hero in the end. Phillips was thus in his younger days according to Elizabethan ideas, an excellent marrying man, Berowne, Saturninus, Theseus. But by 1594, being no longer so young, he could begin to qualify for the other side of the picture, with "an hoor heed and grene tayl"; and we find doddering old Gremio, and the lovesick puritan Malvolio. The revamped Holofernes also has the same caricature treatment as these two. Of course, Phillips is thus the jealous husband par excellence, Antipholus of Ephesus, Ford, Gratiano. This sinister slant to Phillips's characters enabled him also to be sometimes the noble villain or near-villain Don John, Cassius, Duke Frederick, as well as others already enumerated. But the same characteristic also enabled him to be the aggressive king, as Philip, Bolingbroke, afterward Henry IV; or noble, as Benvolio. When we remember Phillips's alleged fraudulent and flaunting acquisition of gentility, as also the actions of his wife directly after her husband's death, we must feel that this line of jealous, "luxurious" noblemen is not a bad biography for Phillips, written by the master's hand.[70]

The consistent descriptions of Phillips indicate that he was hazel-eyed, of "lean and hungry look," in his last days wrinkled and wither'd; but in his youth "complete in feature." We are not given his specific age; but the fact that his first characters are young, as well as the fact that he was married about 1592-93,[71] would indicate that he was not much above twenty-one when he became a member of the reorganized company of 1588. Thus when Cassius claims to be an "elder soldier" than Brutus-Burbadge, the claim is evidently biographical. So late as 1603, a sister of Phillips married young Robert Goffe, and even after Phillips's death in 1605, his wife lost little time in taking another husband. Thus Phillips could not have been younger than thirty-eight at his death; but could hardly have been much older, his wife being probably younger, possibly as much as ten years. In view of his early death, the rather frail physique attributed to him becomes significant, and explains such caricatures as Gremio and Holofernes, giving us still further clue as to Malvolio's probable appearance.

As we have seen, Cundall performed as a man the dignified princely rôle in characters of gradually increasing importance. As prince and king, he was young king Henry VI, Bassianus, Richmond, the King in the revision of *Love's Labor's Lost*, Don Pedro, the near princes Antony and Edgar, Malcolm, "young man" Caesar, Simonides, the Duke of *Measure for Measure*, and the King in *All's Well*, all doubtless closely akin to his known part of young prince and king Ferrex in *The Seven Deadly Sins*, where he was also a Lord. To these dignified young nobles would belong Eglamour, Paris, Lysander, the imitation noble Palidor-Tranio, the two Antonios, Oliver, Cassio, Horatio; and, of older days, Salisbury, Northumberland, Cominius, Belarius, Buckingham, and Antonio. Of similar acting quality, are the Shepherd and Jailor. The revisions

[70] If the letter of one A. P. to Henslowe, asking that the latter do not believe slanderous reports concerning him and his wife, is from Phillips as Greg, *Diary*, Vol. II, p. 11, plausibly suggests, the picture grows even more vivid.
[71] Collier, *Memoirs*, p. 80.

of Bryane's churchmen, Friar Laurence and Canterbury, doubtless fell to Cundall's lot, as also the elderly Page. Once he appears as a gentleman of military inclinations, "young" Alcibiades, to whom in that respect Belarius shows kinship. He began, of course, with small parts; but by 1597 had vanquished his predecessor, Bryane, who retired. On the stage he was usually represented as his own age, appearing but rarely before 1608 as old. His characters show that he was of good appearance; but give no specific details, unless indeed the "green" eyes of Paris are not merely a humorous blunder of the garrulous Nurse, rivalling those famous eyes of Pyramus-Bottom-Kemp, which were "green as leeks."

When Burbadge, Cundall, and Sly were admitted as members in 1594, William Shakespeare was also admitted, though he never, at least in his own plays, became one of the major actors. His line, however, is that of the constantly appearing old man who is of so high rank that the action of the play tends to center around him, but has less than one hundred lines to speak. There is very good evidence that it was William Shakespeare himself who took the part of the Ghost in *Hamlet*, a character in this line.[72] According to other evidence,[73] he also took the part of Adam in *As You Like It*, of the same acting type.[74] It is this line of Shakespeare's which gives whatever point may be admitted for Davies's effort:

To Our English Terence, Mr. Will: Shake-speare.
Some say, good Will, which I, in sport, do sing,
Hads't thou not plaid some kingly parts in sport,
Thou hadst bin a companion for a king,
And beene a King among the meaner sort.
Some others raile; but, raile as they think fit,
Thou hast no rayling, but a raigning wit;
And honesty thou sow'st, which they do reape,
So to increase their stocke which they do keepe.[75]

[72] Rowe, N., *The Works of Mr. William Shakespear*, Vol. I, p. VI. Possibly it was for this reason that the Ghost received so much jocular contemporary comment.

[73] *Variorum As You Like It*, p. 129, note.

[74] Fleay's suggestion (*Life of Shakespeare*, p. 14) that Shakespeare also performed the part of Edward I in Peele's play of that name is more ingenious than convincing.

[75] *Scourge of Folly*, entered S.R. October 8, 1610; quoted Halliwell, *Outlines*, Vol. II, p. 154. Possibly Davies's use of the past tense instead of the present in speaking of Shakespeare's acting implies that the latter had withdrawn before this epigram was written, presumably about 1610.

We may thus be certain that this line of characters is Shakespeare's own.

Shakespeare has practically always, because of rank or position, a prominent character in the play, but with comparatively little acting to do. Here is the august Ghost in *Hamlet*, who starts the action and serves as motive power, dominating our imaginations, if not the play; fatherly King Duncan, very similar in function and effect to the Ghost in *Hamlet*; the triumvir Lepidus, the peacemaker, who would always believe the best but was so lacking in common sense and humor as to be the easy butt of plots and practical jokes; the Duke in *All's Well*, merely a pivot upon which to swing Bertram's foreign exploits; the similar Duke in *Othello*; and Friar Peter, who helps justice to be done. This is the line of a great and important dignitary, whose weight comes usually from his position rather than from his vigor as a man, a part that calls for no hard acting. It will be noticed that there is a clear representative of this line in every one of the uncollaborated and unrevised plays 1603-07, except possibly in *Lear*. But in the tragicomedies, 1610-11, this line has no certain appearance. The only suggestion I can find is the physician Cornelius in *Cymbeline*. But he seems too utterly unimportant in position and influence to be a typical representative of this line. So far as I can see then, the line passes out of existence with the tragedies about 1607-08, and is not to be found in the tragicomedies.

This would probably indicate that Shakespeare did not again act after his long vacation following the reorganization in 1608. Confirmatory of this supposition is the fact that Shakespeare certainly did not act in *The Alchemist* (winter 1610), since the actor list names all performers of masculine rôles; and presumably did not act in *Cataline* (summer 1611), since he is not mentioned in the rather full list of actors, though he was back in London writing for the company when these plays were produced. He had been mentioned in two of the four preceding Jonson lists, the one dating 1598, the other 1603, which are the only actor lists for the company before 1611, except that of *The Seven Deadly Sins*. He is not mentioned in either of the two lists that contain six names; but is mentioned both in the list that contains eight, and the list that contains ten names. This fact suggests that as an actor he must have ranked between six and eight, which is precisely true of his line.[76] This is in keeping with Wright's statement[77] that Shakespeare "as I have heard, was a much better Poet than Player." Since then the actor list of *Cataline* contains ten names but does not mention Shakespeare, it is certain that he did not act in this play, as he had not in its predecessor, *The Alchemist*. It is thus certain, I think, that Shakespeare did not act after he returned from his long vacation 1608-10. His acting in *Sejanus* and in *Hamlet* makes it certain that he had continued acting through 1603. Thus he seems to have withdrawn from acting not earlier than 1604 nor probably later than 1608. The most logical time within these dates for him to bid farewell to the boards was while he was at Stratford 1608-10, during at least part of which time the company was performing without him. The evidence then gives fair indication that he ceased acting at the reorganization of 1608.

To the Ghost and King Duncan, in the period preceding 1603, may be added Charles VI, Lewis XI, and possibly Henry VI in *The Seven Deadly Sins*, though, if so, the fact that in this last play Henry was on the stage, obviating the necessity for the stage manager's keeping track of him, has robbed us of the reference. Shakespeare's Dukes are even more numerous than his Kings, including those of *Love's Labor's Won*, *Comedy of Errors*, *Romeo and Juliet*, *Merchant of Venice*, *Othello*, and *All's Well*. The line is then filled out chiefly with important fathers, both in the flesh and in the spirit, Antonio, Jerobel-Vincentio, Friar Francis, Peter. Close akin to these and to Adam is the Sea Captain of *Twelfth Night*. Since this line is found regularly appearing from the beginning till Shakespeare's long vacation about 1608-10, it is probable that a representative of

[76] Thus Fleay's supposition that Shakespeare did not act in *Every Man Out of His Humor* (1599) because he "disliked Jonson's personalities" (*Life of Shakespeare*, p. 36), and that in consequence "Jonson had to remove them from the Globe Theatre to the Blackfriars" is utterly without foundation, as are the personal reasons he assigns for Shakespeare's nonappearance in *Volpone* (*Life of Shakespeare*, pp. 50, 54). In this connection, we may note that Beeston, Duke, Pallant, etc., were not excluded from the list of the first folio on personal grounds (*Life of Shakespeare*, p. 38), but simply because they were never either members or chief apprentice actors, having been only servants.

[77] Wright, *Historia*, p. 424.

the line appears in every play, though in some I am not sufficiently certain of it to include the part.[78]

The fact is that this line is the box of the orchestra leader, from which he may guide and direct the performance. And therein lies his necessary contribution to the success of the whole, not in his individual musical skill as a performer. To minimize Shakespeare as an actor because of the few lines in his part is therefore analogous to condemning the orchestra leader because he doesn't take the biggest instrument in his band. Shakespeare chose or created his strategic position, and had the good sense to stay there. Surely also William Shakespeare the dramatist, writing the regular stint of two plays per annum, was kept sufficiently busy by even these small parts, without striving to rival Burbadge. There must surely be some limit to the physical endurance even of a genius. It is worthy of note that Shakespeare's line as such ceased with his withdrawal from acting, there being no longer need for it.

It is not therefore necessary to suppose that Shakespeare did not take greater parts and make greater name for himself as an actor merely because he did not have the qualifications. We know that actually he was judged to have been "a much better Poet than Player"; but yet we are also to remember that one of our very first references to him, dating before he had established himself as a poet and dramatist, informs us that he was "exelent in the qualitie he professes."[79] Further, Aubrey informs us that he "was an Actor at one of the Play-houses, and did act exceedingly well."[80] Certainly it required no mean ability as an actor to make the Ghost in *Hamlet* the height of his performance. It is at least as probable on the evidence given that Shakespeare could have been a prominent actor if he had so chosen as that he could not have been. That he did not choose to be is strongly indicated by the fact that when all other of the added members 1594-95 had major lines, Shakespeare continued to write the same minor lines for himself. The fact is

---

[78] We must of course distinguish Shakespeare's old man from those of Bryane and Heminges. Professor Matthews in trying to pick out characters probably taken by Shakespeare has chosen about equally from all three of these lines (*North American Review*, Vol. 195, p. 396), as is well nigh unavoidable without the check of definitely established lines.

[79] *Shakspere All. Bk.*, Vol. I, p. 4.

[80] *ibid.*, Vol. II, p. 260.

that under the evidence the only logical answer we can give as to why he did not occupy a more spectacular position as an actor is that he did not want to. But I think too the position he did occupy has been generally much underestimated. We especially underestimate it if we look at it from the modern point of view, in which the star is the thing, instead of looking at it from the Elizabethan point of view, in which teamwork was the thing. Certainly he considered his position the very best one for himself, since he created it for himself and kept it. In reality, what position in his company could have been better for the dramatist-director of his own productions?

Nor may we infer incompetence from Shakespeare's retirement at his first opportunity. Quite likely he would have agreed heartily with John Lyly, who at forty-three or forty-four, almost exactly Shakespeare's age in 1608, wrote: "I find it folly that on foot being in the grave, I shuld have the other on the stage."[81] We need also in this connection to remember the two-edged compliments of such friends as John Davies, who in print would refer to him by name:

Players, I love yee, and your Qualitie,
As ye are Men, that pass time not abus'd:
And some I love for painting, poesie,
And say fell Fortune cannot be excus'd,
That hath for better uses you refus'd:
Wit, Courage, good shape, good partes, and all good,
And long as al these goods are no worse us'd,
And though the stage doth staine pure gentle bloud,
Yet generous yee are in minde and moode.[82]

When we remember that but a few years before, Shakespeare had received a recognition of his gentle blood, which was being disputed at the time this "tribute" was published, we may suspect how deeply the last two lines must have cut. In such an atmosphere, doubtless Cibber gives us a pretty fair idea of Shakespeare's sentiments: "Had it never been my lot to have come on the stage, it is probable I might never have been inclined or reduced to have wrote for it: but having once exposed my person there, I thought it could be no additional dishonor to let my parts, whatever they were, take their fortune along with it."[83] Surely Shakespeare's deprecatory

81 Bond, R. W., The Complete Works of John Lyly, Vol. I, p. 69.
82 Microcosmos, 1603; quoted Shakspere All. Bk., Vol. I, p. 126.
83 Cibber, Apology (1830), p. 109.

sonnet references[84] to acting are autobiographical. If not, they at least represent the typical reaction of poets under such conditions, and thus amount to the same thing.

Naturally we do not have many physical peculiarities given for this line. Practically all references are to the marks of age and dress that lend dignity to the characters. Doubtless Shakespeare dressed his parts in the conventional way: "the King always is in a long beard and a red gown"; "he in the long beard and the red petticoat."[85] But to personate his parts he must have been "a handsome well shap't man."[86] In fact, dignity is the keynote of this character and there seems to be not a breath of humor about it, though of course we cannot know that Shakespeare did not take characters nearly allied in importance but of a slightly humorous turn. For instance, he may have been "the poet" Cinna as well as Cicero in *Julius Caesar*. If so, it would seem that the joke is decidedly on Shakespeare when he is torn for his bad verses and made to speak Greek, his share in both commodities having been but small. It would seem possible too that Shakespeare was the curate Nathaniel in *Love's Labor's Lost*. The chief objection to assigning Shakespeare the pedagogue or pedantic parson regularly is that the schoolmaster in Elizabethan drama is a comic pedant, while Shakespeare's known parts are thoroughly serious. But surely the man who could imagine such figures of pure fun as are found in Shakespeare's work could himself have created these parsons and schoolmasters, whose comic effect is secured chiefly by their pedantic seriousness. Therefore I assign this pedant to Shakespeare with a query till further light is to be obtained.[87]

With these lines established for major actors, we may now consider the remaining period, beginning with the winter of 1590, and ending with that of 1594, a period of very unsettled conditions. Luckily, we have the actor list of *The Seven Deadly Sins* just in the midst of our difficulties to serve as a guide. Also, the three plays of *Henry VI*, together with *Richard III*, form an interlocking series

[84] See especially Sonnets CX and CXI.
[85] *Edward IV, Sh. Soc.* ed., p. 89. For instructions as to how a Duke should be presented see the induction of Part I, *Antonio and Mellida*.
[86] *Shakspere All. Bk.*, Vol. II, p. 260.
[87] See below, p. 291, note 21 for a discussion of whether Shakespeare had himself been a teacher.

of four plays in which the lines prevalent at the time can be established, and, principally by the help of *The Seven Deadly Sins*, allocated to actors. These four historical plays have each six and seven principal parts for men, many of which run nearly through all four plays as the same character. Thus Warwick, York, and Henry VI run through all three of the Henry VI plays; and Richard, Suffolk, Gloucester, and Young Clifford appear in two each. Consequently, it is easy to match the Dauphin with Young Clifford, Hastings with Gloucester, Edward with Suffolk, and Talbot with Richard III to give the principal lines in these three plays. Of these, Richard III, Edward, and Hastings extend into *Richard III*, leaving Buckingham, Stanley, Richmond, and Clarence to be paired with the other four lines. Stanley had appeared in one brief scene of *3 Henry VI*, with not a single line to say, and Richmond had been a boy in the same play. There is thus no particular reason to suppose that either was impersonated as a principal character by the same actor nearly two years later. Clarence does not pair with either of the preceding lines, since he had also appeared as a principal actor in *3 Henry VI*, probably pairing with Cardinal Beaufort in the first two parts. Of the remaining three, Stanley seems to pair with Warwick, Buckingham with York, and young prince and king Richmond with young prince and king Henry VI. There is no evident running mate in *Richard III* for young Clifford, but the youthful actor of this line may have found a sufficiently important part in any one of several characters. Thus we find that all principal characters for men in these four plays are contained in eight lines.

Our next problem is to allocate these lines to actors. The known fact that Burbadge was Richard III would give him the Richard-Talbot line. Villain Richard would pair very well with villain Tereus of *The Seven Deadly Sins*, and so would the writhel'd old shrimp Talbot with equally old Gorboduc. This line, then, must have been young Burbadge's, just above eighteen in the first of these plays and twenty in the last, this fact accounting for Talbot's puny appearance, as well as in part for Richard's dwarfishness. Warwick we may certainly assign to Bryane, who had taken this character as well as the counsellor Damasus in *The Seven*

Deadly Sins. The ladies' men, King Edward and Suffolk, would pair with the effeminate young ladies' man, King Sardanopalus, for Augustine Phillips. Effeminate Sardanopalus and sickly Edward also fit the physical characteristics of Phillips as these later appear in Gremio, Holofernes, Cassius, etc. The young and dignified kings, Henry and Richmond, must belong to Cundall, who had been Ferrex; while the fiery young soldiers Clifford and the Dauphin must belong to Sly, who had been Porrex. The bluff generals, York and Buckingham, fit with Arbactus into Pope's line. The rather hasty and irascible old gentleman Gloucester, and Hastings, fit into the line of Heminges. We are thus left with Cardinal Beaufort and Clarence unassigned. This line was probably taken by one of the hired men, almost certainly by Robert Pallant, who appears to be the most prominent of this class in *The Seven Deadly Sins*, being the noble old counsellor Dordan, as well as other parts which would seem to call for the same general characteristics. It may be noticed that Cade would go to Kemp, of course, and that Lewis XI is characteristic of Shakespeare's line. Thus all lines are satisfactorily assigned in these four plays. All principal actors are accounted for, and the remaining hired men would find their places as minor characters and attendants, as they had done in *The Seven Deadly Sins*. We may also notice that in neither *The Seven Deadly Sins*, nor in the three parts of *Henry VI*, all dating the winter of 1591-92, is there any sign that any but the Shakespearean company took part, even though Edward Alleyn had some connection with the company 1590-94. *Richard III* may be taken as a little less certainly indicating the same situation for the winter of 1593.

We now have sufficient information to attack the plays for the winter of 1590 and the summer of 1591; *Henry V*, and *Romeo and Juliet*. For *Romeo and Juliet*, we know that Kemp was Peter. Shakespeare must have found a characteristic part in Prince Escalus, and the two young men Cundall and Sly would be lordly Paris and king of the cats Tibalt. Thus the five major parts must go to the four remaining members, and to Burbadge. The irascible old father Capulet is unmistakably Heminges's, as dignified Friar Laurence is Bryane's, leaving the young men, Romeo, Mercutio, and Benvolio to be distributed among Burbadge, Pope, and Phillips. The tender young lead Romeo is surely eighteen-year old Richard Burbadge, matching fourteen-year old Goffe as Juliet. The gruff humor of Mercutio is also that of Pope's line of gruff jesting soldiers, leaving the other young man, Benvolio, for Phillips, not a bad fit but less evidently characteristic than the parts for the other actors. The play of *Henry V* shows exactly the same structure, except that it has no evident part for Kemp, this last fact not surprising, of course. Young Henry pairs with Romeo, Archbishop Canterbury with Friar Laurence, and comic soldier Fluellen falls into Pope's line with Mercutio, as does the Constable probably into Phillips's line with Benvolio. Charles VI would pair with Escalus, and the French Dauphin with Tibalt. Probably either Gloucester or Bedford also pairs with Paris. Thus we have satisfactory allocation of all lines up to the summer of 1592.

It is important to notice that the line of Richard Burbadge does not extend visibly back of the winter 1590, when the Shakespearean company first came to his father's theater. If Burbadge is included as a principal actor, I can find no satisfactory assignment of parts either in the original form of *All's Well*, in *Comedy of Errors*, or *The Two Gentlemen*. Indeed, he was not quite eighteen when he performed *Henry V*, and could not have been a principal actor of men's parts long before. But neither can I find an adequate beginning line for him in these preceding plays; he simply springs up over night. Thus his line, as well as other facts already enumerated, indicates that Burbadge became attached to the Shakespearean company about 1590, when it came to his father's theater, remaining with that company ever after.

We may now attempt to bridge over the period beginning with the summer of 1592, and ending with that of 1594. The plays of the preceding two years show that we must expect to find Phillips, Burbadge, Bryane, Pope, and Heminges among the principal actors, with Kemp, Sly, Cundall, and Shakespeare probably to be distinguished. *Titus Andronicus* may be satisfactorily fitted to these actors by assigning the aged Titus to Bryane,[88] his son Lucius to Burbadge, Saturninus to Phillips, Marcus to Heminges, Aaron to

---

[88] Middleton had been impressed by some actor's "lamentable action of one arm, like old Titus Andronicus" (Bullen, *Middleton*, Vol. VIII, p. 94).

Pope, the clown to Kemp, and Bassianus to Cundall, all character-istic parts. Sly would also find a fitting rôle as one of the quarrelling sons of Tamora, probably the more aggressive Demetrius; and Shakespeare would have been one of the many dignitaries, though of which we can not be positive.

The Jealous Comedy has exactly the same structure as the four early comedies, a bit puzzling till we notice that even in the come-dies of 1594-1600, the part of Burbadge, the great tragedian, was frequently well down the list, just as in tragedy Kemp, at the other extreme, is likely to have small show. In this uproarious and farci-cal comedy then, it need not surprise us if Burbadge does not have one of the outstanding parts. Under the division of the earlier comedies, Phillips would be jealous Ford; Bryane would be the older and more dignified Page;[89] Heminges would be the jolly, badgered Host; Pope would be Falstaff; and Kemp Evans. Bur-badge would probably find his part as young Fenton; but the parts of Sly, Cundall, and Shakespeare are not certainly decipherable.

In Hamlet, of course, the tables are exactly turned; and we should expect Kemp and Pope to suffer most. We know that Ham-let was Burbadge's and the Ghost Shakespeare's. Also, Kemp must have been the First Gravedigger, Heminges worldly-wise old Co-rambis, and Sly the fiery young swordsman Laertes. It would seem that Bryane and Cundall must find their places as the Player King and Horatio. The young friend Horatio is too young for Bryane, but exactly of the type taken now and later by Cundall. The Player King is also a typical part for Bryane, except that it is rather small; but its incidental prominence would make up for its lack of lines. Of the evident major parts, we have left only the King to be settled between Phillips and Pope. The King hasn't suffi-cient gruff force as a villain to belong to Pope's line; but is char-acteristic of Phillips's line of lecherous nobles, especially in his desire for another man's wife. Almost certainly the king is Phil-lips's, this being the reason that the characters did not need any recasting in the revision of 1603, as they would have done had Pope been the King and Phillips jobless. Pope was probably the

[89] Probably the circumstance that Page begins as "Master Thomas Page" (I. 1. 46), but ends as "Good George" (V. 5. 223) is due to the fact that this was originally George Bryane's part.

ranting First Player, a part which he may have doubled with some other. It is also to be remembered that even in Shakespeare's first version, which I place in 1593, *Hamlet* was an old play formerly belonging to another company, but now being revised by Shakespeare.

The last play of the period is *Midsummer Night's Dream*, for the summer of 1594. While this play also is built on the five-man model, as were all preceding comedies, it shows a slight variation in lines. We have the two clowns, Bottom and Quince, for Kemp and Pope. We also have two young men, too young for the old combination of Bryane and Phillips. They must belong then to their young supplanters, Cundall and Burbadge, just being taken into the company as permanent members. Seemingly Demetrius is the more vigorous and would go to Burbadge, leaving Lysander for Cundall. But our irascible and humorous old gentleman doesn't seem to be the other principal character, Theseus, appearing instead as the vexed father Egeus. Theseus would thus be left for either Phillips or Bryane. The lover Duke Theseus fits into Phillips's line of lecherous potentates much better than into Bryane's line of old counsellors. The most likely character for the older and more staid Bryane seems to be Philostrate, Theseus's master of the revels, an important functionary with few lines, but of the incidental type which seems regularly to fall to Bryane's lot in the last five years of his membership, while he was being supplanted by the younger Cundall.[90] Sly would find his place in the rustic show, probably as Flute, the bellows mender, who objected to playing the part of Thisby because he had a beard coming, but finally compromised on a mask. Young Sly, just five years ceased from playing the merry madcap maid, would doubtless have a beard coming, and would make an excellent Thisby for this rustic show.

Thus we have at least a plausible assignment of parts in all the plays of the period, though the fact that most of the plays 1590-94 are revised from older ones originally for another company, as well as the fact that the company was itself in a transition stage, does not permit us to be dictatorial. In this connection, one other point

[90] It is probably because of this original assignment of Philostrate to Bryane that this character was stricken from the final version, found in the folio, all his lines going to Egeus except one speech of five lines to which his name is accidentally left attached.

had better come up for discussion. Did Edward Alleyn act with the company while he was furnishing it with plays 1590-94; and if so, what were his parts? The actor list of *The Seven Deadly Sins*, and the lines of the *Henry VI* trilogy are fairly conclusive that he was not acting with the company in the winter of 1591-92; and the sequel, *Richard III*, indicates the same thing for the winter of 1593. Neither do I find any evidence of a stray line such as Alleyn might have played, occurring in any of these plays. General principles would not demand that Alleyn act with the Shakespearean company rather than with any other of the companies he furnished about the same period at the Rose. But we have two suspicious facts in 1593, seeming to connect Alleyn with this company as an actor. The first of these circumstances is that Alleyn is mentioned, though designated as an Admiral's man, in the company's licence to travel; and the second is that he certainly did act on this trip.[91] But then, since the survivors of his own company were also along as the Admiral's men,[92] the natural inference is either that he acted with his own company, or that the two companies acted jointly, probably the latter. If the companies acted jointly, then the Shakespearean play or plays would have been constructed for the Shakespearean company; but would on this trip have been divided in some manner not now determinable, unless we could learn definitely what actors of each company took part, and what were the characteristics of the participating Admiral's men. Even then, because of the fact that the actors were supplying ready-made parts, not parts made to fit, our assignment would need to be classed among extrahazardous occupations. It seems probable that the two companies acted together on this tour of 1593; but I find no effect of this combination upon the cut of Shakespeare's plays, and see no reason why under the conditions it could or should have had any such effect. The arrangement was only a temporary makeshift enforced by the plague. The plays would not be affected by the temporary cooperation, which may not have been contemplated when the summer play of 1593 was being written, any more than they would be affected by the fact that they might possibly also be performed by

[91] Greg, *Diary*, Vol. II, pp. 74-5.
[92] See below, p. 329.

any other company that might come under Alleyn's management to be furnished. Certainly before and after this temporary amalgamation the company would perform the plays with its own personnel and it is upon this basis that we must allocate parts, as we have just attempted to do.

Since the remaining members had been apprentices in the company, we may now consider that class, tracing the line of each apprentice from the beginning of the Shakespearean company, and seeing what happened to that line at graduation.[93] The first graduates seem to have been William Sly and Henry Cundall, about 1589. Cundall, who was probably Heminges's apprentice, seems to have been the regal performer, taking the Princess in *Love's Labor's Lost*, the Countess in *Love's Labor's Won*, and Adriana in *The Comedy of Errors*, thus continuing as a man the line for which he had been trained as an apprentice, beginning about 1590 as a dignified young man and growing gradually in importance and age. William Sly, who had pretty certainly been the apprentice of Phillips, seems to have been the more vivacious and pertly witty lady. He had been Rosaline of the "merry, nimble, stirring spirit," and the aggressive Helena, who doesn't sit down and pine, but by her adventurous exertions forces love to be won. It is thus natural that Sly should have become a stirring, duelling young man, simply continuing his apprentice line in breeches. We have already examined the growth of Sly's line as a man.

About this same time Richard Cowley, possibly Kemp's apprentice, also completed apprenticeship as a female comedian. At graduation, as we have seen, he continued his comic caricatures of clownish importance, supplying the line of Verges and his counterparts.

The next graduates were probably Alexander Cooke and Nicholas Tooley, about 1594. Cooke, who had been Heminges's apprentice, was usually a strong-minded lady—Videna, Procne, Margaret, Tamora,—capable of anything to carry her point; but also shrewish Katharine of comic turn. As Julia, Cooke had a high forehead, eyes "grey as glass," hair a "perfect yellow," and a complexion said to be darkened by exposure. In next to his last part as a

[93] This summary is based on the detailed analysis in Appendix VI.

female, Helena, Cooke had come to be a "maypole," probably indicating very good height for him. In his last part, as Katherine in *The Taming of the Shrew*, he is said to be "straight and slender," and is "brown in hue as hazel nuts." By 1603, Cooke had attained a principal line as a man, being admitted a member, and appearing on all lists of principal actors thereafter. In this period then we should expect to find a predominantly villainous line for him, with some touches of comedy. Such a principal line we have. Here is the inquisitive young student Rosencranz; the amorous "Gallic" physician Caius; handsome Lodovico; the honest Provost of *Measure for Measure*; the villainous young Duke of Cornwall; the young noble Lennox; the worldly Painter, partner of the worldly Poet; the villainous tribune Sicinius, running-mate of the villainous tribune Brutus; the magician-physician Cerimon; the aggressive nobleman Antigonus; the fairly aggressive general Lucius; and finally Sebastian, who would make way with his brother for the kingdom. Thus we have a line predominantly, but not usually very aggressively, villainous, frequently of the gull variety. The characters in the early part of the line are young, but gradually lose that distinction.

Nicholas Tooley, who claimed Burbadge as his master, was much more broadly comic than his fellow Cooke, his favorite rôle being the garrulous nurse, best represented by Juliet's crone. He too became a member in 1603, with Cooke; but since he belonged to the comedians, had no part regularly written for him as a principal actor. It was not till nearly ten years later that fashions had sufficiently shifted, older comedians had sufficiently withdrawn, and Tooley had attained sufficient eminence to have a principal part regularly written for him. But by this time Shakespeare himself had practically withdrawn from theatrical affairs.

The next graduates were Robert Goffe and William Eccleston, about 1598. Goffe, seemingly Pope's apprentice, had evidently been an exceptionally good actor, first of the tender young heroine, and finally of the dignified queen, having been Juliet at fourteen, and Portia near the end of his apprenticeship, Portia's part being the largest in the play, the first time for a woman in Shakespeare's plays. As Luciana, he had "golden hairs." As Silvia, his forehead was lower than that of the older Cooke, but he was fairer; his eyes were "grey as glass"; and his hair was auburn. As Katherine in *Love's Labor's Lost* he had been "An amber-colour'd raven," and his "hairs were gold." Thus Portia's:

sunny locks
Hang on her temples like a golden fleece,

and her hair is a "golden mesh." Goffe should probably have made a fairly good young lover, though lacking in dash; but he fell upon the evil days of tragedy, nearly unlit with youthful love. Thus after his graduation we hear of him as a young lord in *All's Well*, an older lord in *The Second Maiden's Tragedy*, and probably as a lordly attendant of Leidenberch in *Barnavelt*;[94] but he never attained a principal line. Though a capable actor, he may have owed his membership at least in part to the fact that he was not only Pope's apprentice but also Phillips's brother-in-law, it being Phillips whom he succeeded.

Goffe's comic partner had been William Eccleston,[95] probably Kemp's apprentice, a pert page or a somewhat merry waiting-maid, comic, but not so clownish as Tooley's line had been. His women had been small, dark, with brown hair, smaller and darker than those of Goffe. Probably the scrubbed little boy of a lawyer's clerk Nerissa is the most characteristic expression of Eccleston's line. At graduation, as we have seen, he became the rollicking, singing soldier, a fair continuation of his line as an apprentice. Like Cowley and Tooley, and for much the same reasons, he did not receive a major line at graduation, and was late in attaining one, arriving at membership only in 1614, at least fifteen years after graduation. Cundall and Sly had waited about five years for admission, Cowley had waited probably a year or two longer, Cooke and Tooley had waited about nine years, Goffe about seven, Eccleston at least fifteen.

Even so, Eccleston was the next apprentice after Goffe to attain membership. When Fletcher and Sly died in 1608, they should have been succeeded by Eccleston, and either Samuel Gilburne or Ned

---

[94] See below, pp. 371-2.

[95] Fleay, *Stage*, p. 190, states that Eccleston came from the Children of the Chapel with Ostler and Underwood; but he had certainly been an apprentice in the Shakespearean company.

[Shakespeare?],[96] the two next graduates after Goffe and Eccleston. Besides these candidates, Jack Wilson and Samuel Crosse seem also to have been in the waiting line by 1608, but never attained membership. Instead of promoting some of these candidates, the company imported Ostler and Underwood from the Revels, probably as only a part of the company's attempt to break up the rival organization at this time, since taking their best actors would both weaken the rival and strengthen the Shakespearean company.

As has been said, Ned and Gilburne, the graduates about 1601, never became members, though both give evidence of having been capable actors. Gilburne, seemingly Phillips's apprentice, had been a golden-haired, grey-eyed serious lady, and Ned, probably Bryane's apprentice, a comic dark one, nearest akin probably to that of Sly. Phebe has been kind enough to give us a full picture of Ned as Rosalind, shortly before his graduation. She says:

> He'll make a proper man: the best thing in him
> Is his complexion; and faster than his tongue
> Did make offense his eye did heal it up.
> He is not very tall: yet for his years he's tall:
> His leg is but so so; and yet 'tis well:
> There was a pretty redness in his lip,
> A little riper and more lusty red,
> Than that mix'd in his cheek; 'twas just the difference
> Betwixt the constant red and mingled damask.

Doubtless he did make a proper man and a fair actor; but the fates were not kind.

Either Gilburne or Ned probably performed the part of a famous, usually young, warrior who appears about this time and has only from twenty-five to sixty lines. Here is the dignified young warrior Fortinbras; a replica of whom is the young King of France; possibly old Siward, general of the English forces; and probably Agrippa in *Antony and Cleopatra*. Remembering Shakespeare's line, we might follow analogy and offer the "pleasing suggestion" that as the older William was the performer of the important minor old man, so the younger Edmund Shakespeare (buried December 31,

[96] If Ned was Edmund Shakespeare, then he had died the Christmas of 1607-08, and there should have been no question about admitting Eccleston and Gilburne, provided the latter was still living.

1607, as "a player")[97] may have taken the much less important minor young man whom Underwood in a way replaced in 1608; but it is more probable, from the type of performance, that this was the line of Ned's running-mate, Samuel Gilburne.

The next graduates were Jack Wilson and Samuel Crosse, 1604-05. We probably know that at thirteen Jack Wilson, who may have been Burbadge's apprentice, was the singing Balthazar in *Much Ado*. His line also contains the plaintively singing Desdemona, and Ophelia. Since Wilson was of a family of musicians, he may have preferred to continue music rather than acting, especially in view of the waiting list between him and membership. His line is also notable for the fact that he was represented as having jet black hair and eyes, being in fact the best representative of Shakespeare's dark lady, so far as she is described in his plays. Crosse, possibly Heminges's apprentice, had been more of the comic and villainous type than Wilson; but his line is so broken by the gaps in 1601, and 1603, as not to give us characteristic detail, so that we have no description of his appearance.

Then John Edmans, Pope's apprentice, was graduated about 1609. Though he had probably boyed even Cleopatra's greatness, yet he never attained membership in the Shakespearean company, but became a member in the provincial company of Queen Anne, having no further connection with the company of his youth.

The next graduate was John Rice, Heminges's apprentice, about 1611. John Rice had been an excellent actor of the regal line, as we know from the fact that he had been "an angel of gladness" for the Merchant Taylors in 1607, and had played Corinea of Cornwall to Burbadge's Amphion in the city pageant of 1610, description of which is given elsewhere.[98] We have no accurate description of Rice in the Shakespearean plays, but Jonson seems to meet the need in his description of Dol Common in *The Alchemist*, who is posing as a Baron's daughter:

Mam. . . .   .
This lip, that chin! methinks you do resemble
One of the Austriac princes.

[97] Collier, *Memoirs*, p. xiv.
[98] See Appendix VII.

Face. Very like!
Her father was an Irish costarmonger. (*Aside*)

Mam. The house of Valois had such a nose,
And such a forehead yet the Medici
Of Florence boast.

This allusion pretty certainly gives us Rice's portrait, and may even hint truthfully at a humble pedigree for him as well.[99] After some eight years, at least part of which was spent with another company, Rice became a member of the Shakespearean company for a half dozen years, but his line was never regularly a major one. Rice, together with Eccleston, went to the Princess Elizabeth organization in August 1611, whence Eccleston was permitted to return, in 1614, to a membership in his old company, for which he had waited some fifteen years. Rice, being more fortunate, returned in 1619, after a wait of only eight years.

Rice was the last graduate in Shakespeare's day of writing; but three other apprentices took part in his plays: James Sands, Richard Robinson, and Armin's apprentice. Sands, Phillips's apprentice, was to graduate about 1613. We have a rather detailed description of him as Octavia (winter 1606), when he was about fourteen. At that time, he was "dwarfish" for a woman, as would be expected of a boy of his age, and not so tall as Cleopatra, taken by John Edmans, who was some years his senior. Octavia had brown hair, a low forehead, and round face. She was low voiced and about thirty. The age here, a round number guess, is of course that of the actual Octavia; and the low voice, like the dwarfish stature, may be due to the actor's tender years. The color of the hair may not be significant, since the boys likely wore wigs, yet the wig would probably be chosen in harmony with the boy's complexion. It is thus strongly probable that Sands was a blond rather than a brunet. The round face and low forehead perhaps also need slight discount for juvenile chubbiness, but are more permanent characteristics than the others. Probably we may fairly conclude that Sands was the common, round faced, rosy cheeked, Tom Tulliver type of English boy. As Helena in *All's Well*, he was still small, and as Marina in *Pericles*,

[99] At least, a John Rice of Allhallows in the Wall is described January 3, 1574, as a "burgonyan."

he was fourteen. Sand's age as Marina seems to be the last link in a chain of evidence that dates *Pericles* the summer of 1607. Other evidence shows that it was for either the summer or winter of 1607.[100] Now as Euphrasia in *Philaster* (summer 1610) Sands had been "about eighteen." He would thus have completed his fourteenth year about the summer of 1607, and consequently *Pericles* does not date later than the summer of 1607, hence it dates that summer. But while Sands was evidently a capable actor, yet at graduation about 1613 he drops from the record of the Shakespearean company, appearing with Queen Anne's, and the membership he might have expected to be his went to an outsider. Robinson, who seems to have been Burbadge's apprentice, and Armin's apprentice were just beginning to attain prominence in Shakespeare's last plays, and have received sufficient attention in our discussion of the Beaumont and Fletcher plays.

It is evident from this summary that an apprentice was trained by his master as the female counterpart of his own line, and that after graduation the candidate continued this line as a man. This does not mean, however, that the line of the apprentice at graduation would be identical with the master's. It would be of the same general type, but would of course reflect the younger actor's own personality. It is for this reason that the five types for men of the first of Shakespeare's plays had finally almost doubled. But long before the end of Shakespeare's writing the types had become standardized, and remained essentially the same in number and central quality till the closing of the theaters. By trial and error the company found the proper solution under the given mechanical conditions, and then stuck to it. By 1603, the period of experiment in organization for the Shakespearean company was practically ended. It is also evident from all this discussion of apprentices that the Shakespearean company maintained a regular school for actors, whose principal graduates would recruit the company. If the product was not to their minds, they had only themselves and nature to blame.

It is interesting too to notice the company's changed policy toward

[100] Graves, T. S., "On the Date and Significance of Pericles," *Modern Philology*, Vol. XIII, pp. 545-56; Lawrence, W. J., "The Mystery of Macbeth," *Fortnightly Review*, Vol. CXIV, pp. 778-9.

apprentices, first apparent in 1608, and the consequences of this changed policy. The company had absorbed most of its early graduates, chiefly by expanding from five to nine in 1594, and from nine to twelve in 1603; but thereafter the company only replaced lost members. In 1608, as we have seen, instead of admitting their own graduates to membership, the company had preferred to take two of the best actors from the Revels company, on the theory seemingly that these also had been trained in the king's service and hence had as good claim to promotion in the company as their own apprentices,[101] the real motive, however, being, as already indicated, probably a "purely business" one. As a result, all these late apprentices of theirs except Eccleston lost the opportunity to enter the mystery for which they had specially been trained. Even Eccleston was forced to wait some fifteen years, till Cooke's death early in 1614. In the natural course of events, another of these numerous waiting graduates should have succeeded Ostler at the end of 1614; but instead Robert Benfield, who was a rank outsider and had no claims at all on the organization, was brought in. Then at Shakespeare's death in 1616, still another graduate should have been admitted; and yet another should have received appointment at Cowley's death in 1618. But instead a Revels man, Nathan Field, was brought in to succeed Shakespeare; and a very recent apprentice, Richard Robinson, doubtless through his close connection with the Burbadge interests, succeeded Cowley. As a result, many of the graduates were never admitted, while Rice received tardy appointment only when Field withdrew in 1619. And so the story goes. Now under the conditions of the time, if an apprentice did not receive preferment in his own company, the main road of advancement was closed to him, and unless some other company happened to desire him, he could not practise the mystery for which he had spent his youth in training. This change in the company's policy was therefore vital to the apprentices of the company. Of course this change was adopted to "strengthen" the company. It is therefore very interesting to hear the chief of the Burbadge interests raise up his voice in 1635 and say :[102] "these new men, that were never bred from children in the Kings service, would take away[,]

101 Halliwell, *Outlines*, Vol. I, p. 317.
102 Halliwell, *Illustrations*, p. 91 a.

with oathes and menaces that wee shall bee forced and that they will not thanke us for it; soe that it seemes they would not pay us for what they would have, or wee can spare." But who had taken the attitude of "purely business," and had broken at least the spirit of old custom to bring "these new men" in?

The evolution of the early Shakespearean company is now readily evident. The original company was predominantly one of comedians. Of the five members, Kemp and Pope were almost entirely comic, and Heminges and Phillips were considerably so. Bryane was the only thoroughly serious principal actor, and seems not to have been a very strong one at that. The company, about 1590, began to supply this defect chiefly by the services of the brilliant young Richard Burbadge. It also used a recent graduate, Henry Cundall, as a dignified young man to help Burbadge and Bryane balance the overweight of comic and villain material. As soon as Burbadge became old enough, the company assured his permanent retention by making him a member, at the same time securing Cundall also. By the same means, they assured the retention of their promising young dramatist and actor William Shakespeare. Probably at the same time a fourth promising young actor, William Sly, who had graduated with Cundall about 1589, was taken into membership, and his part made at once regularly a major one. The company decided its future fate and to a considerable extent the future fate of William Shakespeare and the Elizabethan drama when at one reorganization it changed from a travelling company of musicians and tumblers to a settled and balanced company of serious and comic actors. Of course the development of the company in the preceding six years had been forced in this direction, and the company was but now officially recognizing the fact, and deciding on a continuation of the policy. The modified and enlarged organization was at once reflected in the modified and enlarged construction of the company's plays. It is a significant fact that of the four members admitted in 1594-95, only William Shakespeare does not have a major line already in existence or newly enlarged, this last fact being doubly significant when we remember that William Shakespeare was himself the playwright.

The personnel of the membership remained the same till Bryane the serious was succeeded in 1597 by Cowley the comic, who had graduated in the early nineties. But the comic tide receded a little when the dominating clown Kemp dropped out in 1599, to be succeeded by the docile jester Armin. Its recession received powerful impetus when the predominantly comic Pope was succeeded in 1603 by the predominantly villainous Lowin, and was slightly heightened when the "humorous" major actor Phillips was succeeded by the minor actor Goffe. The major personnel was now almost as predominantly tragic as it had originally been comic. In 1603, Cooke and Tooley, who had graduated about 1594, were promoted to membership, the predominantly comic Tooley remaining a minor actor, but the predominantly serious Cooke receiving a major line as a comico-villainous gull. It is interesting to note that of the apprentices promoted in 1603 and 1605, only Cooke was given a major line. The technique of plays had now hardened sufficiently to prevent very great changes, the company's policy being henceforth chiefly one of replacement.

Then in 1608 Sly died, and the honorary membership of Fletcher was vacated by death, while William Shakespeare was wishing to give up acting altogether. Also, the company was planning an enlarged program with an added theater. Ready to their needs was the breaking Revels company of children and young men, from whom they chose Ostler and Underwood, both rather serious actors. With the company so strengthened, Shakespeare seems to have been released from active duty on the boards. No further changes came before 1611, when Shakespeare seems to have stopped writing alone, discontinuing altogether about the time of the fire in 1613, before which time Heminges also ceased acting. Whether this evolution of the company is to be attributed to driving circumstance, to the judgment of the company as a whole, or to that of some leader or leaders, is a matter that the evidence so far given does not settle.

Thus are we able, at least in main outlines, to dissect out the lines running through Shakespeare's plays, and to determine the actor for each of those lines. Our dissection has made it apparent that Shakespeare cut his play to fit the actors of his company even in the details of age and physical appearance, fashioning for each principal actor a suitable principal part. This of course is the natural and well-nigh inevitable consequence of the type of organization in the company. It is further evident that only one who had been so intimately associated with these principal actors as Shakespeare is known to have been, could have presented, or would have been likely to present, such minutely realistic details. Not even royal blood, flowing in the veins of a Bacon as the alleged offspring of Leicester and Elizabeth, could have given an outsider such intimate knowledge as this.

CHAPTER X

FACING THE FACTS WITH SHAKESPEARE

NOW that we have studied in detail the organization and personnel of the Shakespearean company and the general organization of its contemporaries, we may finally attempt to evaluate the influence this system must have had on the drama and dramatists. It is at once evident that the system was radically different from that prevalent in the present day. Under the present system, the company is more or less temporary, and is assembled from the ends of the earth to present one play. The dramatist may thus deal with any character or subject within the bounds of reason, and hope to have it properly presented. But this the Elizabethan dramatist could not do. His company was rigidly fixed, and he could hope to get represented only such things as were within the ability of his particular company. Even if he was not attached to some particular company, he still usually had only five companies at most to choose from, or rather to be chosen by. For even here he rarely if ever had any real choice. It was he that was chosen by the company. He was not the master of the company but the servant. As a dramatist, he was a hired man, not a member. There is not a single recorded instance, so far as I can find, where an author became a member because of his services as a dramatist. He might become a member because of his services as an actor, as did Shakespeare. He might through royal favor or purchase become a master in the children's companies, just as any merchant or blacksmith might do the same if he had sufficient influence or money. But purely as a dramatist his place was that of a hireling. This does not preclude the probability, of course, that in actual practice the successful dramatist had considerable influence in shaping the dramatic ideas of his company. It simply means that as a dramatist, he was theoretically and actually a mere hireling.[1]

[1] This distinction should be borne in mind throughout this chapter. The

[284]

FACING THE FACTS

If then we would understand the problem the Elizabethan dramatist had to face, we must look at it with Elizabethan and not modern eyes. As has been shown in Chapter I, the acting company was really a monopoly under licence or patent, and the number of these monopolies was more and more narrowly limited until finally there were never more than five companies of men in London at one time. Thus the number of companies was limited. Not only so, but the number of members in each company was also limited by licence, and finally by patent.

Here then was a sufficiently limited and distinct class for the masters. It was not quite so limited as were the master-printers, for instance, but "'tis enough, 'twil serve." It follows that this class must provide for its perpetuation according to the best ideas of the time. This it would naturally do by the apprentice system. The acting apprentices received intensive education under the masters for about eleven years before they were graduated, to become masters themselves. Presumably therefore they had the best education available in their day for their type of work.

These members and apprentices were the two chief classes, but there grew up naturally a class corresponding to journeymen. The Shakespearean company absorbed most of its graduates, so that it did not create a large surplus of freemen who could not become members. But there was usually a company of children under royal patronage, whose graduates would have no assured membership to step into. The licensed country companies were also training up a surplus of material upon which the London companies might draw. Then finally the occasional dissolution of a London company set members adrift, who would gradually be absorbed by other companies as vacancies occurred in their memberships; but in the

purpose of the chapter demands that the influence of organization be emphasized, but it is to be remembered that there may always be modifying circumstances to alleviate the natural tendencies of the organization. It is the main purpose of the chapter to show the influence of the organization and personnel on the drama and dramatists, and not the influence of drama and dramatists on the organization and personnel, though there was certainly mutual influence. I do not wish to be understood by any means as arguing that the organization and personnel determined the development of the drama and dramatists. I do hold it a demonstrated fact, however, that these material circumstances conditioned the drama and dramatists.

meantime their only recourse was to become hired men wherever
they could get the best terms. There was thus this intermediate class
in the company corresponding to that of the journeyman. In organization then, the Elizabethan company was a limited monopoly,
organized on the gild system, with the regular gradations and system of perpetuation prevalent in such gilds.

Since William Shakespeare passed through every class in his
company, except possibly formal apprenticeship; and since after
all he is the objective of this work, we may proceed to face the
facts with him, and see what influence this type of organization
must have had upon him. It is at once evident that here is the school
in which Shakespeare was taught the technique of his acting and
writing. It is thus of importance to know exactly when Shakespeare entered this school. We know that he was an actor of some
standing by 1592, even though he never rose to the first rank, and
that he became a member of his company in 1594, this membership,
especially in this particular company, implying proficiency acquired
in many years of training. In the whole history of the company
1588-1642, all other members came from but two sources; its own
graduating apprentices, and recruits who had graduated from other
companies. Even if Richard Burbadge probably was not formally
apprenticed, still he had received the regular training, and had fulfilled the law concerning apprentices. Also, unless Shakespeare be
an exception, no member was drawn from another company before
1603. The presumption from this custom is thus strong that William Shakespeare had gone through the necessary period of training
in the company as an actor either as an apprentice or as a hired
man. Nor was this system confined to the Shakespearean company.
In the petition of the players in general December 3, 1581, they
state that they have been "only brought up from their youthe in
the practise and profession of musicke and playeng."[2] Since Gosson,
their opponent, admits this statement in his answering book of 1582,
we may accept it as true. "Most of the Players haue bene eyther
men of occupations, which they haue forsaken to lyue by playing,
or common minstrels, or trayned vp from theire childehood to this

[2] *Acts of the Privy Council* (December 3, 1581), quoted by Chalmers,
Apology, p. 381, note.

abhominable exercise & haue now no other way to get theire liuinge."[3] In any case, they had served an apprenticeship. This was not only the custom; it was the law.

Of course, Shakespeare must have been above the regular age for apprentices when he came to London; but in the trades at least it was so much a custom to take grown men as apprentices that regulations had to be made against doing so, especially if the man in question was married.[4] That there would be nothing peculiar in Shakespeare's becoming an apprentice in the company is shown by the early career of another dramatist, Anthony Munday, which in many respects furnishes a close parallel to that we have supposed for Shakespeare. Munday was apprenticed to John Allde, Stationer, August 24, 1576, for eight years, he being at the time twenty-two or twenty-three.[5] Under our supposition, Shakespeare would have become an apprentice at latest by May 1587, at the age of twenty-three, for at least the minimum period of seven years.

Since Shakespeare, on the testimony of Heminges and Cundall, seems certainly to have been with the company by the reorganization of 1588,[6] he had been with the company nearly six years at the very least when he became a member in 1594. Further, the fact that *Love's Labor's Lost* borrows from both *Endimion* and *Gallathea*,[7] Lyly's plays at court the Christmas season 1587-88, indicates pretty clearly that Shakespeare had reached London by the autumn of 1587-88, for plays seldom outlasted a season. The fact that Shakespeare thereafter echoes each one of Lyly's plays as it appears or is revived, but echoes no unrevived earlier play of Lyly's offers some probability that Shakespeare was not in London, or at least had not access to Lyly's plays before the season of 1587-88. The family records seem clearly to indicate that Shakespeare had not left Stratford by 1585. Both Halliwell[8] and Fleay[9] for once agree that Shakespeare's connection with the Lambert difficulties shows that

[3] Chambers, *Eliz. Stage*, Vol. IV, p. 218.
[4] Dunlop, *Apprenticeship*, pp. 34-5, 53-4, 135.
[5] Fleay, *Drama*, Vol. II, p. 108.
[6] See above, p. 82.
[7] Bond, *Lyly*, Vol. III, p. 13; Vol. II, pp. 276, note 2, 297. It should be noticed that this inference is independent of any dating we may assign to *Love's Labor's Lost*.
[8] Halliwell, *Outlines*, Vol. I, pp. 89-91.
[9] Fleay, *Life*, pp. 8, 95.

[287]

he was still in Stratford the spring of 1587; but in this agreement later writers[10] do not fully concur. Though certainly not conclusive, yet this circumstance offers some slight indication that Shakespeare did not leave Stratford before the spring of 1587. The supposition is made more probable by the fact that the English branch of Leicester's men, with whom we find Shakespeare the autumn of 1588, had been at Stratford in 1586-87. Since the year at Stratford was from Michaelmas to Michaelmas,[11] this visit was between September 29, 1586, and September 29, 1587. The company was at Dover March 4, 1587, at Canterbury and Southampton about March, at Bath before June 14, as far north as Latham House July 11, 12, 13, and back at Coventry by the end of July.[12] The company would thus have passed through Stratford either on its way north in April, May or June, 1587, or on its return a day or so before or after August 1, when it was at Coventry. Now on its northward swing in 1585, Leicester's company had required from June 12-16 to some time in August to go from Dover to Bath, and in 1564, from April 22 to July 1 to reach Leicester. It would thus take the company probably eight or nine weeks from Dover to Stratford. At this rate, Leicester's company would have passed near or through Stratford about May 1587. Thus the company was at Stratford either about May 1587, on its northward journey, or about August 1, 1587, on its return journey. I agree with Murray[13] that the stop was probably on the northward journey. It is thus at least a curious set of coincidences that but little more than a year before Leicester's men passed through Stratford William Shakespeare was certainly still abiding there, probably remaining till at least the spring of 1587; that a little more than a year after these men passed through Stratford, Shakespeare was with them in London, almost certainly having come as early as the autumn of 1587, and that seven years after the visit, probably to the month, the minimum time of apprenticeship, Shakespeare became a member of that company. The evidence then would strongly indicate that

[10] Lee, *Shakespeare* (1922), p. 33; Adams, *Shakespeare*, p. 94.
[11] Halliwell, *Outlines*, Vol. I, p. 39.
[12] Murray, Vol. I, p. 42. For a convenient map of these places, see frontispiece to Murray's first volume.
[13] Murray, Vol. I, p. 42.

Shakespeare was an apprentice.[14] If not formally apprenticed, he at least received apprentice training.

Tradition also has indicated that Shakespeare was either a hired man or apprentice in the company. Rowe says "he was received into the company then in being at first in a very mean rank." When Rowe speaks of "the company then in being," he is probably speaking in terms of the close monopoly of his own day; but we may also infer that so far as Rowe knew, Shakespeare's connection was continuous with one company. There is no direct evidence to indicate that he ever had connection with any other company. Malone records in 1780 a more specific form of this tradition, "that his first office in the theatre was that of prompter's attendant."[15] I know of no specific evidence that the prompter in the Shakespearean company ever had an attendant, but his duties were certainly sufficiently varied to make such an attendant useful.[16] This then may very well have been Shakespeare's first "office."

[14] If Shakespeare was an apprentice, to whom was he apprenticed? It must presumably have been to some member of the company of 1588, since practically all his term would have fallen in the time of that company. Since he must have been apprenticed to some member of the English branch of the company, only Phillips and Heminges are left as probable masters for him. Possibly Phillips's will, in which Shakespeare is not distinguished above his fellows, even though Phillips draws rather fine distinctions, may be taken to indicate that Phillips was not Shakespeare's master. Now Heminges, the residual member, was a member of the Grocers' Gild (Collier, *Memoirs*, p. 73). If therefore Shakespeare was his apprentice, the record was likely made at Grocers' Hall. The records of the company were still extant in 1891 (Heath, J. B., *Some Account of the Worshipful Company of Grocers*, p. 38; Stopes, Mrs. C. C., *Shakespeare's Environment*, p. 170). These records also offer considerable possibilities in other ways, since Heminges was chief business man of the Shakespearean company. They should inform us when and how Heminges became a grocer, throwing considerable light on his early life, where we need it. Cooke, who had seemingly been Heminges's apprentice, and thus should also be registered in Grocers' Hall, asked in 1614 (Collier, *Memoirs*, p. 187) that Heminges and others put certain sums of money for his children into Grocers' Hall. It is thus likely that this was Heminges's regular place of deposit, where some of his papers may yet remain. Another possibility is that Shakespeare was the prompter's apprentice, if tradition is to be trusted. Thus further light on the early prompter, Thomas Vincent, would be desirable.

[15] Lee, *Shakespeare*, p. 46; Malone, E., *Supplement to the edition of Shakespeare's plays published in 1778*, Vol. I, p. 67.

[16] See above, pp. 134-7. If with Simpson we could assign both hand C and hand D in *Sir Thomas More* to Shakespeare, which seems to be the one thing that experts now agree we cannot do, then we should have Shake-

THE SHAKESPEAREAN COMPANY

There is the further tradition that before Shakespeare was taken into the company he was employed at "the playhouse" to hold horses, almost certainly a myth.[17] Both of these traditions imply that Shakespeare was attached to the one company for a period before he began writing plays for it, as would appear, about the winter of 1588. They make it certain that Shakespeare was at first either a hired man or an apprentice in the company, and increase the probability that Shakespeare came to the company "in a very mean rank" when Leicester's men were at Stratford about May 1587.[18] All trails then so far as I can find lead to the conclusion that William Shakespeare worked from the beginning with just one single company, and that he became attached to this company, either as apprentice or as a hired man, when it passed through Stratford in 1587, probably about May.

Such a supposition explains most logically all of Shakespeare's known earlier connections. Under the survivals of the medieval system, Shakespeare would naturally turn to Leicester's players. Warwick was lord of the borough of Stratford, the reversion belonging to his brother Leicester.[19] Since Warwick seems to have had no players after 1580,[20] the proprietary players of Stratford and

speare doing the prompter's work in this play, since that is certainly the function of C, and should thus have clear confirmation of the tradition that he was the prompter's helper.

[17] Malone, *Variorum*, Vol. II, p. 158-67.

[18] If we could show that Shakespeare was formally apprenticed, we could be certain that he came to the company not later than the summer of 1587, and could make the inference practical certainty that Leicester's men picked him up at Stratford about that summer. Even as a hired man, there is no reason to believe that he was or could have been with another company. As we have seen, tradition implies his connection with only one company. Since he was with Strange's men in 1588, he could not regularly have come through the Admiral's men, as there was no contact with that company before 1590. He could hardly have belonged to Strange's tumblers, a company of boys, since he could no longer qualify as a boy when he left Stratford. He was not with Leicester's musicians and tumblers abroad. There were only five named and reiterated members of that expedition. They had no other members or apprentices with them at Elsinore, since they received pay for only five named members. But Kemp, who had his boy along, received the same pay for him as for himself. There is thus no probable opening for Shakespeare in this expedition even as a "boy." If then Shakespeare was an actor before 1588, the only organization through which he could regularly have come, either as apprentice or hired man, is that of Leicester's players.

[19] Malone, *Variorum*, Vol. II, pp. 44, 166.

[20] Murray, Vol. I, p. 286; Chambers, *Eliz. Stage*, Vol. II, p. 98.

[290]

Shakespeare were Leicester's. Thus attached to Leicester's household, Shakespeare would feel a family pride in Essex, Leicester's
brilliant and promising stepson—an enthusiastic pride that is to
be traced, it would seem, as early as the autumn of 1591, and has
about it something almost of obsession. From this point of vantage,
Shakespeare might also reach the bosom friend of Essex, young
Southampton. Thus Shakespeare's known connections are best explained by the supposition that he had become attached to Leicester's players.[21]

Of course, circumstantial evidence is notoriously tricky; but it
is hard to see how this chain of circumstances can mean anything
else than that Shakespeare became attached to Leicester's men
when they passed through Stratford the summer of 1587.[22] It isn't

[21] There is a plausible statement of how Shakespeare managed to secure
still another foothold in London, made, unfortunately, by one whose errors
are said to be as numerous as the lines he wrote. David Lloyd in *State
Worthies* (1670) wrote concerning Sir Fulke Greville: "One great argument for his worth was his respect for the work of others, desiring to be
known to posterity under no other notions than of Shakespear's and Ben
Johnson's master, Chancellor Egerton's patron, Bishop Overall's lord, and
Sir Phillip Sidney's friend" (London *Times*, Literary Supplement, March
23, 1922, p. 196). Now the Grevilles, father and son, were of considerable
local importance at Stratford. Fulke Greville, Sr., was recorder of Stratford (Stopes, Mrs. C. C., *Shakespeare's Industry*, p. 240), as was his son
later. They frequently sent venison to the Stratford corporation (Malone,
Variorum, Vol. II, p. 147), and in other ways kept up social, business, and
political relations (Malone, *Variorum*, Vol. II, p. 566). What is more to our
point, Sir Fulke, Sr., and Sir Thomas Lucy acted as arbitrators in a dispute
January 1584, between Shakespeare's very close friend, Hamnet Sadler, and
Ananias Nason (Malone, *Variorum*, Vol. II, p. 121; Halliwell, *Outlines*, Vol.
II, p. 386). It is hardly possible that the eldest son of one prominent
enough to be the chief official of Stratford would not be known to the
Grevilles. Indeed, there is some possibility that the families were related
(Adams, *Shakespeare*, p. 451). The statement that Sir Fulke Greville, Jr.,
himself a literary man but ten years older than the dramatist, gave Shakespeare a helping hand is inherently probable. Too, Greville is known to
have been a generous patron of literary men (Stopes, *Warwickshire Contemporaries*, pp. 170-2). He was also closely connected with Essex at least
from 1591 (Stopes, *Warwickshire Contemporaries*, pp. 168 ff.).

[22] If Shakespeare joined the company this summer of 1587, his first experience with Oxford was to be ordered to go along with his plays and not
bother the university (Boas, *Shakespeare & the Universities*, p. 17 and
facsimile opposite). It should probably be noted here that there is good
reason to believe that Shakespeare had been a country schoolmaster.
Aubrey records concerning Shakespeare on the authority of old Mr.
Beeston that "Though, as Ben: Johnson sayes of him, that he had little
Latine and lesse Greek, he understood Latine pretty well, for he had
been in his younger yeares a schoolmaster in the countrey." (See fac-

THE SHAKESPEAREAN COMPANY

quite so clear an inference that he was formally an apprentice; but it is certain that he received the approximate amount of training which was required of every apprentice before he became a master in his trade, and that practically all his training was in the same company. As an actor then, William Shakespeare received his "master's" degree from the school of Leicester's men, by far the oldest, and we may believe the best, school then in existence.[23]

simile of Aubrey's life in the *Catalogue of the Shakespeare Exhibition held in the Bodleian Library*, 1916, opp. p. 63). Now this informant was William Beeston, whose father, Christopher Beeston, had been Phillips's "servant" from at least 1592 till 1598, and therefore knew the early history of Shakespeare well (See Chambers, Malone Soc. *Coll.*, Vol. I, pp. 341-7). Further, William Beeston was himself born quite early in the seventeenth, or even in the latter part of the sixteenth century (Allardyce Nicoll, London *Times*, Literary Supplement, November 22, 1923). Since we have the records of births for Christopher Beeston's children from November 17, 1604 (Stopes, *Burbadge*, pp. 139-41; Registers of St. James, Clerkenwell), William Beeston must have been born by or before 1603. He may then have acquired this information concerning Shakespeare at first hand, especially since he was himself reared in theatrical affairs. Indeed, he may be another namesake or even godson of Shakespeare's. There is thus every reason to believe that Beeston had authentic information. At least one-half of his statement, the knowledge of Latin, finds confirmation in Shakespeare's demonstrated use of the *Menechmi* of Plautus (Malone, *Variorum*, Vol. II, p. 323; Sonnenschein, E. A., *Shakespeare's Knowledge of Latin*, quoting P. J. Enck, London *Times*, Literary Supplement, March 17, 1921, pp. 179-80. For an opposite opinion, based, however, on a theory I cannot regard as correct, see J. Dover Wilson's edition of the play), which argues that the reason given for this knowledge is also correct. It is probably also significant that among other crawfishings on the part of Rowe in his second edition, he changed the definite "that little Latin he was master of" to the much less invidious "what Latin he was master of" (Malone, *Variorum*, Vol. II, p. 69, and note 7). I am glad to find that so careful an investigator as Professor Adams (*Life of Shakespeare*, pp. 90-6) accepts Beeston's statement. Shakespeare's service as a schoolmaster would thus date before the summer of 1587, when as a young man of twenty-three he headed for London. It would most naturally fit into the vacancy 1585-87.

If he was a schoolmaster, some official record of the fact may still survive, since the law provided that the schoolmaster should be licensed by the Diocesan under his seal (23 *Eliz.* c. 1; see Ware, S.L., *The Elizabethan Parish*, p. 43). Professor Parrott suggests that if Shakespeare was a schoolmaster, it was possibly in this period that he picked up the intimate knowledge of Gloucestershire pointed out by Madden in *The Diary of Master William Silence*. Since Fulke Greville, said on very doubtful evidence to have been Shakespeare's patron, had received large grants in this locality March 16, 1585 (*H.M.C.*, Twelfth Report, Appendix, Part I, *Cowper Manuscripts*, Vol. I, pp. 40, 66-7), it is possible that through his patronage Shakespeare taught in Gloucestershire. But of course this is only one of thousands of possibilities.

[23] Recent theories of Shakespeare's connection with Pembroke's men are

Even his line of specialization in this school seems to have been of peculiar value to Shakespeare as a dramatist. We have seen that in the first three or four years of the course the students did odd jobs, such as placing chairs properly; and took small parts. Tradition assigns to Shakespeare as his first chore the place of prompter's attendant. We have seen elsewhere that at least Shakespeare knew and appreciated the problems and trials of this ubiquitous official. Indeed, since his picture of the prompter is given in *The Midsummer Night's Dream*, summer 1594, we are tempted to believe that he was there celebrating his graduation from the department of that instructor. I can think of no better place for a beginner to learn the strategy of a play, and a few things else besides. It was the business of the prompter to get everything in order for the play, and to marshal the actors through the performance. He secured licence for the new play, had any ordered reformations made, wrote out, or caused to be written, the part of each actor, assigned chores for the different hired men and apprentices, checking and changing the author's instructions in that regard if necessary, and when the performance finally arrived, kept an eye on everybody to see that no one bungled his duties or lines. As his assistant, William Shakespeare would be finely drilled in the importance of the strategy of a play. It is even possible that this instructor, like the rest of us, unduly magnified the importance of his own position, and was wont to insist that good strategy was all that was necessary for a good play; such things are not unheard of. On such occasions, William doubtless smiled after the fashion of wise students, and took due heed nevertheless.

But a feature of the position that would likely have more appeal to Shakespeare was the ready access to the playbooks of the company. It isn't beyond the bounds of possibility that he sometimes there neglected worldly ends for the bettering of his mind, possibly to the sore aggravation of a martinet instructor. In this position too, he would come in contact with the authors themselves as they

based fundamentally on the mistaken idea that plays recorded to several different companies in Henslowe's Diary and the Stationers' Registers had passed by sale successively from one company to another, whereas they merely belonged to Alleyn and were performed by the different companies he furnished at the Rose and elsewhere. (See below, pp. 327-9.)

turned in the fair form of their work, or sighed over the excision of some particularly excellent lines, demanded by a meticulous Master of the Revels, or by that same martinet of a prompter, for no better reason than that the said lines could not be properly acted on his stage. The prompter's attendant may even have been sent in breathless haste with peremptory orders to some dilatory dramatist without fail to have that new play in fair form at the playhouse by five of the clock on Tuesday next to be read to the company after the play for their approval and information. He may also have increased his own wonderful vocabulary, and have improved his knowledge of the world by hearing what the harassed author had to say about such cold-blooded demand on the muses in general, and upon his own peculiarly sensitive mistress in particular. If Shakespeare wasn't the prompter's attendant, in the poetic fitness of things he should have been. Certainly as apprentice, hired man, or master, Shakespeare was forced to come in close contact with that official's views, as a dramatist especially so.

As an actor, he would be coached both on and off stage by the more experienced members, especially by his master. One leaf from his diary he seems to have inserted in *Hamlet*. Doubtless he had been told that his speeches must be "well spoken; with good accent and good discretion." He must practise till he too:

> But in a fiction, in a dream of passion,
> Could force his soul so to his own conceit
> That from her working all his visage wann'd,
> Tears in his eyes, distraction in's aspect,
> A broken voice, and his whole function suiting
> With forms to his conceit.

In his first attempts at this suiting of forms to conceit he may have been guilty of "screwing his face like one of our country players, which must needs make him look like a fool,"[24] only to hear from the tiring room the rasping voice of the prompter: "pox, leave thy damnable faces, and begin." And then Sir Oracle his master just before the next performance would improve the occasion to First Player Shakespeare:

> *Ham.* Speak the speech, I pray you, as I pronounced it to you, trippingly on the tongue; but if you mouth it, as many of

[24] Bullen, *Middleton*, Vol. VIII, p. 73.

your players do, I had as lief the town-crier spoke my lines. Nor do not saw the air too much with your hand, thus; but use all gently: for in the very torrent, tempest, and—as I may say—whirlwind of passion, you must acquire and beget a temperance, that may give it smoothness. O! it offends me to the soul to hear a robustious periwigpated fellow tear a passion to tatters, to very rags, to split the ears of the groundlings, who for the most part are capable of nothing but inexplicable dumb-shows and noise: I would have such a fellow whipped for o'er-doing Termagant; it out-herods Herod; pray you, avoid it.

First Play. I warrant your honour.

Ham. Be not too tame neither, but let your own discretion be your tutor: suit the action to the word, the word to the action; with this special observance, that you o'erstep not the modesty of nature; for anything so overdone is from the purpose of playing, whose end, both at the first and now, was and is, to hold, as 'twere, the mirror up to nature; to show virtue her own feature, scorn her own image, and the very age and body of the time his form and pressure. Now, this overdone, or come tardy off, though it make the unskilful laugh, cannot but make the judicious grieve; the censure of which one must in your allowance o'erweigh a whole theatre of others. O! there be players that I have seen play, and heard others praise, and that highly, not to speak it profanely, that, neither having the accent of Christians nor the gait of Christian, pagan, nor man, have so strutted and bellowed that I have thought some of nature's journey-men had made men and not made them well, they imitated humanity so abominably.

First Play. I hope we have reformed that indifferently with us.

Ham. O! reform it altogether. And let those that play your clowns speak no more than is set down for them; for there be of them that will themselves laugh, to set on some quantity of barren spectators to laugh too, though in the meantime some necessary question of the play be then to be considered; that's villainous, and shows a most pitiful ambition in the fool that uses it. Go, make ready.

Exit William, this time to please his exacting master we hope. Thus Shakespeare would learn not only to speak his lines well, but also what kind of lines could be well spoken; not only to suit a passion with forms, but also what forms best suited what passions. Above all he would come to know the strength and weakness of all his fellows, and how to capitalize the strength and to minimize the weakness. From the most intimate and observant contact both on the stage and off in their clannish community life he would come to know and to capitalize even the characteristic peculiarities of appearance and tricks of expression of each of these fellow actors. Surely then his education as an actor was also excellent training for him as a dramatist.

Neither was his direct education as a dramatist neglected, even though it was not provided for in quite so formal a way. As has just been indicated, the young Shakespeare would necessarily become thoroughly acquainted as an actor with the work of the dramatists of the company. As an aspiring poet, he would read and be fired by the poetic beauties of their work; as prompter's attendant, he would be forced to study the strategy of their plays; as an actor, he would memorize many of their lines. Even as an ordinary hired man and actor, as we shall shortly see, he would come into contact with these dramatists themselves. As prompter's attendant, his contact would even in the earliest days have been still closer. As budding dramatist, he would have improved these opportunities we may be sure. It is natural then that when the connection with Edward Alleyn and the Admiral's men in 1590 brought the plays of Marlowe, Kyd, and Greene, as well as Marlowe and Greene themselves to the company, the influence is at once reflected in the work of the youthful Shakespeare. Here was the inspiration of emulation; and the record runs that William Shakespeare held his own even against his "superiors."[25] Indeed Greene seems to intimate just before his death that he had been superseded in the good graces of those "buckram gentlemen," those "rude grooms," "those puppets," "those antics," who had once sought like "burrs to cleave" to him, by this "upstart Crow, beautified with our feathers, that with his *Tiger's heart wrapped in a Player's hide*, supposes he is as well able to bombast out a blank verse as the best of you: and being

[25] I hope later to show that since the work of Marlowe, Greene, and Kyd before 1590 appears in both the English and German branches of the Admiral's men, the work must either have been written for the Admiral's men, or have come to them by sale before 1590. Thus the early work belonged to the Alleyns and appeared at the Rose. Since the later work of Marlowe and Green also appears at the Rose, these dramatists had continued to write for the Alleyns, and Shakespeare would be in contact with them from 1590.

an absolute *Johannes fac totum*, is in his own conceit the only Shake-scene in a country"; and to warn his companions to avoid a like fate.

As Greene here indicates, the company had permitted or caused Shakespeare to revise or rewrite several of their old plays, thus beautifying himself with the feathers of his predecessors, reaping not only the honor but also the reward that they considered should have been theirs. Greene alludes only to *3 Henry VI*, with which doubtless go the other two members of the trilogy; but we may probably include its seeming predecessor *Henry V*, and certainly *Romeo and Juliet*, and *Titus Andronicus*, both of which appear in the German branch of the Admiral's, thus dating in original form not later than 1590. Greene's case wasn't all spleen; but neither was Shakespeare especially to blame. This revision of old plays then was the custom, and formed part of Shakespeare's early exercise as a student dramatist.

There is thus nothing surprising about the fact that at th:s period Shakespeare shows so strongly the influence of Marlowe, Kyd, and Greene; it would have been very surprising if he hadn't. Not only is the work of these men pervasive of his writing at the period, but it is also specific in certain plays. Thus *Richard III* is his exercise in the style of Marlowe;[26] *Titus Andronicus* in the style of Marlowe and Kyd; etc. Indeed it may be only old plays of theirs that he is revising. Certainly then these three men—Marlowe, Kyd, and Greene—were instructors in Shakespeare's school of the dramatist. Where in all England or the world could Shakespeare have received better instruction in dramatic literature than under these three? The test of time declares that he could not have found it in either university, not a single member of either faculty being now enrolled among the great literary writers of the period. Neither did these instructors as a rule aspire to be so enrolled. Literature for

[26] If Professor Campbell is correct in his supposition that the Dutch play *De Roode en Witte Roos* is based on an English play, presumably antecedent to Shakespeare's *Richard III*, it would seem that this old play also belonged to the Admiral's men before 1590, and was carried abroad by the foreign branch, finally to become the basis of the Dutch play, and remained at home in the English branch to influence Shakespeare's play (Campbell, O. J., Jr., *The Position of the Roode En Witte Roos in the Saga of King Richard III*). Thus the likeness of Shakespeare's play to the work of Marlowe may have very solid foundation.

them was principally in Latin and Greek, certainly not in the vernacular. A glance at the university curriculum of those days should render somewhat less poignant our sorrow that Shakespeare was deprived of its benefits.

If Shakespeare had received the university training of his time, there is no particular reason to believe that he could have written his own language, or would have known its literature any better than actually he did. Even Sidney, with all his insistence on classical precedents, is forced in fairness to admit: "I have found in divers small-learned courtiers a more sound style than in some professors of learning." Ben Jonson well summed up what Shakespeare missed by not having had the formal education of his day when he accused him of having little Latin and less Greek. Shakespeare would doubtless have had a more accurate technical knowledge of these languages and their literatures than he actually had, but whether he would better have caught their spirit and inspiration is another question. He would doubtless have been a better "educated" man, but whether he would have been a more genuinely literary man is also an entirely different question. It is to be remembered too that the university "education" of the day was still for a special class, and hardly what we would now call liberal. It is fair to compare Shakespeare with Lyly, and Chapman, and Jonson, logical products of the technical training of the day in Greek and Latin, and to ask ourselves if the spirit of Shakespeare would have been improved or damaged by being cast in the same mold. After all, we read Shakespeare not for his technical learning, but because he is "sweetest Shakespeare, Fancy's child." It may be very seriously doubted whether the formal schooling of his day would have improved that fancy, whatever it might have done by way of furnishing that fancy material to work on. Possibly our best comparison here would be Spenser, whose matter Jonson praised but whose manner he reprobated.[27] It may be at least logically supposed that the fancy would be more stirred by the masters of fancy, who were certainly not among the professors in the famous schools at that time; and it is probably quite as well that Shakespeare's fancy fed on the mater-

---

[27] Carpenter, F. I., *A Reference Guide to Edmund Spenser*, p. 241; for Spenser's classics and reading in general, see p. 135.

ials of his own actual world rather than on ancient lore. Probably it was at least as well that Shakespeare's education was in the inspiring school of actual masters of literature and not in the school of dry commentators on dead producers of a dead literature, beautiful and noble though that literature is when the commentator gets out of the way and lets us see the actual literature itself. Nor does it appear that the influence of Shakespeare's instructors was any the less potent because it was not exerted in the formal courses of a school, and because these masters issued no signed statement of their endeavors, unless indeed we consider Greene's statement Shakespeare's diploma of proficiency. If then education be preparation for the work one is to do, surely Shakespeare could have found no better school in which to take his degrees both as actor and as dramatist, even though it had been his fortune to be apprenticed to learning instead of to acting, and to have become "Master of Arts in Both Universities." But after all is said and done, we must admit the genius of the man himself, for however much or little he may have been conditioned by his education or lack of it, he certainly was not created by these conditioning circumstances.

Before Marlowe, Kyd, and Greene came into Shakespeare's life, his master had been John Lyly, though in this case the influence seemingly was not mediated by personal contact in the service of the company. It is significant that of the major influences usually found in Shakespeare—Marlowe, Kyd, Greene, Jonson, Beaumont, Fletcher,—only that of Lyly and probably that of Kyd seem not to have been so mediated. Of course this situation is in part due to the fact that with his six-day acting schedule Shakespeare would have had little opportunity to observe the plays of other companies. But even so it also indicates the usual source of Shakespeare's inspiration—men rather than books. Even in the case of Lyly, all the influence could not have been through the printed play, since the influence of some of these plays is clearly apparent in Shakespeare's work before the former were printed.[28] Here then we have Shakespeare imitating, frequently burlesquing, the master dramatist of the rival organization even as in later days Beaumont and Fletcher imitated and burlesqued Shakespeare himself. Since Shake-

[28] Bond, *Lyly*, Vol. II, pp. 297-8.

speare's imitations of Lyly lie in general attitude and larger devices rather than in minute detail, he had doubtless only seen the imitated plays performed. He could not readily go to see the plays of other public companies, since they all acted at the same time he was himself on duty. But Paul's did not act till after prayers at four o'clock,[29] so that Shakespeare was doubtless able occasionally to see their plays. Probably this is one of the reasons why Shakespeare fell first under the influence of John Lyly. It appears then that Shakespeare had studied under nearly all of his famous predecessors, and doubtless took all they had to give. Both as actor and as dramatist he received the best that up to his time had been done. On that foundation, he reared the fabric of his genius to form the towering monument that has not yet been equalled. It took both the system and the man to make the product. The credit cannot be given wholly to the system, since it produced but one Shakespeare. Yet the system that produced such a one is not to be despised.

But the influence of the company upon Shakespeare and his work did not end with these early days of his special training. In the transmission of his dream of beauty and wisdom to the public, this company was as much a conditioning medium as the language in which the dream was embodied, even more truly in that day than in this. The modern author may, and usually does, produce his play with only general conditions in mind, sometimes but very general. His chief task is to clothe his idea in language; the rest is chiefly the task of the luckless manager. But Shakespeare faced a different problem. His play was to be produced, not by some company, but by the particular company to which he belonged. Each part was to be taken, not by some actor to be picked from the world's supply, but by a specific actor already in the company, Richard Burbadge, or John Heminges, etc. Nor was his problem lessened by the fact that in all this he was not the master but the servant. He did not pick the company either directly or indirectly, but the company picked him. The company was not fitted to the play, but the play to the company.

This situation had its effect on every stage of the play. We have no direct information concerning these stages in Shakespeare's

[29] Chambers, *Eliz. Stage*, Vol. III, p. 21.

company; but thanks to Henslowe and his impecunious crew we can trace all the stages in the Admiral's men and the amalgamations at the Hope, and from certain other facts show that the same system held good for Shakespeare. For the Admiral's men, we have a statement from Robert Shaa telling Henslowe "we haue heard their booke,"[30] and authorizing him to pay the poets. Another entry tells of "the Readynge of that boocke (*Henry I*) at the sonne in new fyshstreate,"[31] giving some indication of the company's method of "hearing" and approving the final form of a play. There are other direct references[32] to this final reading and approval of the play, and Henslowe's regular formula of entering payment for plays as authorized by some member indicates that the company each time passed decision on this final form. But the company was also accustomed to pass judgment upon the plot of the play before construction began. For one of his plays Ben Jonson "showed the plotte vnto the company" and received an advance upon the play he was to write.[33] John Day seems at one sitting to have had approved[34] both the completed form of one play and the plot of another. Also, this latter play was again checked and approved by at least one of the members, probably by all, for whom he merely certified, after the first five sheets had been written.[35] Certainly then plays for the Admiral's men were regularly checked and approved at various stages of the work, probably always by the whole company when the plays were plotted and when they were ready for the finishing touches.

From Daborne's correspondence with Henslowe 1613-14, we learn that the amalgamated company at the Hope followed the same system of checking and approving plays. Here we learn that the manager of the company sometimes furnished the "book" from which the story of the play was to be taken.[36] The manager or some member of the company might also check up the plot or prospectus of the play to get some idea of its value. The rough

---

[30] Greg, *Papers*, p. 49.
[31] Greg, *Diary*, Vol. I, p. 85.
[32] *ibid.*, pp. 85, 117, 150, 152, 166.
[33] *ibid.*, pp. 70, 82.
[34] Greg, *Papers*, p. 57.
[35] *ibid.*, p. 56.
[36] *ibid.*, pp. 65-85.

form of the first three acts seems usually to have been checked by these same officials, and then the first draft of the complete play was read to the whole company some afternoon after their regular performance. When the suggested revisions had been incorporated by the author, the play was copied in fair form, ready to be licensed. Thus at every stage the author's work was subject to direction and suggestion from the company. Since the company was paying good money to have the play constructed, it took proper precautions to see that the play was to its liking. This was of course the natural result of the author's position in the scheme of things. He had to please the company by the cut of his play just as much as did their tailors by the cut of the garments in which the play was to be performed.

Of course, Shakespeare probably had less surveillance even in his early days than did the poets under that heavy-handed taskmaster Henslowe; but the essential principle would be the same. While he would probably have been subjected to less surveillance, he would have been just as open to suggestion from the company at all stages of his work. The rustic rehearsal in *The Midsummer Night's Dream* shows that Shakespeare knew the joys of having the play read, and of hearing brilliant suggestions for the making of prologues and placatory speeches.

Indeed, we pretty certainly have one instance of such suggestions in *Much Ado*. It is now notorious that Kemp and Cowley have their names attached to the speeches of Dogberry and Verges (IV. 2).[37] The official manuscript of *The Second Maiden's Tragedy* shows how it happened. There a speech inserted after the manuscript was complete[38] is labelled by the bookkeeper with the name of the actor instead of that of the character, so that he would know into whose "part" the speech was to be inserted. These speeches of Kemp and Cowley are thus final insertions, in view of known customs, doubtless suggested if not phrased by the actors themselves. Certainly Shakespeare as much as another would need to suffer the agonies of "fitting" the play. To soothe that painful ordeal, let us hope his fellows could truthfully say:

[37] There are similar inserts in *3 Henry VI*, III. 1; and *2 Henry IV*(q), V. 4.
[38] Greg's edition, Malone Society Reprints, ll. 1723-4.

we're not factious,
Or envy one another for best parts,
Like quarrelling actors that have passionate fits;
We submit always to the writer's wits.[39]

It is also fairly to be inferred that the company occasionally supplied Shakespeare with "books." Indeed, the early revision of old play-books was likely done at the suggestion of the company rather than upon Shakespeare's own persistent begging for the privilege. At least it was so with Daborne and Henslowe, and it was stipulated in Brome's contract that he should do such revisions for Salisbury Court.[40] It is to be noticed too that in his distribution of epithets Greene is at least as generous with the company as with Shakespeare, implying that these antics were actively guilty in the matter. Thus we may be reasonably certain that any of the company who found a good story, or had a bright idea for a play was not slow to bestow it upon the dramatist of the company.

We have good indication that the company was also accustomed to give the dramatist the benefit of their advice in the plotting of the play. For instance, when Robert Armin came to the company in 1600, the clown at once became a jester or fool, of which type Armin had made a close study, as is indicated by his publication just previously of *Foole Vpon Foole or Six Sortes of Sottes*. Surely when William Shakespeare supplied Robert Armin with a part, he would have received the advice of that authority as to how the particular character ought to be presented. At least he had read Armin's work on the subject, as is shown soon after by an allusion to it.[41]

It is clear that this system at its worst might completely throttle both the dramatist and his art by ignorant dictation, though this dictation would eventually reap the reward of its own folly by loss of patronage. But where the dramatist and company worked in harmony together, as did Shakespeare and his company, dictation would be replaced by suggestion and consultation. Thus Shakespeare's plays represent not only his own individual invention but also the collective invention of his company. Just as he took the

[39] Bullen, *Middleton*, Vol. IV, p. 375.
[40] See above, p. 28.
[41] Halliwell, *Outlines*, Vol. I, pp. 321-3.

best he could find in story and used it regardless of its previous condition of servitude, so he doubtless made use of the best suggestions available in reshaping it, even though those suggestions emanated from Bottom the clown. Doubtless even Shakespeare's plays were the better for the suggestions of these the most expert actors of their age, whose lives had been spent in their profession, although the suggestions may at times have occasioned the dramatist a wry face. In view of the social standing of these men and the training through which they entered their profession, it is now high time that we ceased to brand them as only a source of contamination and pollution to the dramatist, labelling their contribution as only "the ill-conditioned interpolations and alterations of actors and theatrical managers."[42] Since their position rendered them and not the dramatist the dictators of the drama, that drama is their sufficient vindication. The criticism of their "educated" contemporaries, who honestly differed in artistic aims, is to be considered thoroughly legitimate and constructive. But it is a little hard that we who have espoused the actors' artistic aims rather than those of their critics, should yet join with those critics in regarding the actors as ignorant and inartistic. As editors, or technical scholars, or many other things, they were doubtless ignorant enough, even as you and I; but that fact should cast no more reflection upon them than it does upon us.

It is now evident that at every stage of his work the dramatist was forced to bear his company in mind. Consequently, that company must have been a very vital conditioning element of his work. However much or little the company actually detracted from or contributed to the plotting and writing of his play, the dramatist had still to fit his idea to the actors who were to perform that play. The first determinant of the form his story would take was the number and kind of principal actors in the company for which he was writing. Indeed, these factors must have had strong influence on his choice of the story itself. His story must contain, or be capable of having inserted, a major part for each major actor in the company; and this part must be in the "line" of that major actor. If one story would not serve, two must be in some way

[42] Craig, *Oxford Shakespeare*, Preface.

joined together, this necessity being a prime reason for double plot in Elizabethan drama. It was also regularly necessary for the dramatist to submit his plot to the company for their approval before he wrote his play. We may readily imagine how each principal actor tried to assure himself a suitable part, and to that end offered his suggestions for the dramatist to embody. It is this attitude that was partially responsible for Shakespeare's reproof in *Hamlet* of the clowns. If the clown did not find a part in the play suited to his needs, he proceeded to help the dramatist impromptu with his own petty devices, regardless of the effect upon the play as a whole.

When his story was finally safely selected and approved, the dramatist then proceeded to fit each character to the individual actor who was to bear the part. This fitting even extended to personal details, such as specific age and color of hair and eyes. Under the conditions, it is evident that the dramatist must to a certain degree give the personal characteristics of the person who is to perform the part, and not his own idealized character. For instance, I find it difficult to believe that Shakespeare would uninfluenced have conceived Hamlet as fat; but if Richard Burbadge had acquired undue weight, there was no use arguing the matter; Hamlet simply had to be fat.[43] Such a method had some especial advantages under the conditions of the day, since it obviated to a certain extent the necessity of makeup and permitted the actor to appear in his own person.

But the dramatist's task was not merely to fit the part to the actor in external characteristics. He must so shape the part as to bring out the capabilities of that particular person. Not only must he catch the characteristic tricks and gestures of that actor, he must also catch the inner spirit of the man. It is thus possible to take the characters belonging to the line of some actor and from them to deduce the general characteristics of that actor, though obviously this method does not apply to the particular details given for each character. The actor did not strive to be a fictitious person; he

---

[43] Even a century later (1710), Gildon records that the physical adaptation of the actor to his part, as short or tall, fat or lean, "is a thing . . . little regarded by our Managers or Audience" (Gildon, C., *Life of Betterton*, p. 139.

strove rather to be himself under fictitious circumstances. Neither he, his audience, nor his age was interested in psychological presentation, but in represented action. The story was the thing.

It is also obvious that under this system, not only must the dramatist include a part for each actor, but he must not include any part for which there was no actor. He could not develop along certain lines, however much he might desire to do so, unless there was proper material within his company for the presentation of his idea. He could, of course, take the chance of having his idea misrepresented, and probably often did. He might for instance be able to write excruciatingly funny comedies; but he wouldn't be permitted if his company was one predominantly of tragedians, and vice versa.

As a close corollary of this influence, it is also evident that the type of play must change as the type of actors in the company changed. It cannot therefore be wholly accidental that the four periods of Shakespeare's writing correspond to four major reorganizations in his company.[44] Since plays were thus intimately fitted to the actors of the company, the type of plays would necessarily change with the type of actors.

It is evident then that the successful dramatist had to be intimately acquainted with his company, the more intimately the better for all concerned. It is also evident that the modern dramatist does not have the same kind of condition to face. But whether the Elizabethan or the modern had the harder problem is an entirely different question, and one with which we are little concerned here.

The organization and personnel of the company had its influence on the drama not only directly through its conditioning influence on the dramatist himself but also through its establishment of many dramatic customs, which would in turn react on the dramatist and become further conditioning influences. One such important influence was the custom governing division of labor in the production of a play. The division of labor in a play was naturally evolved under the business organization of the company, which was the determining factor. Because of the permanent

[44] See above, Chapter II.

and rigid organization, the play had to be cut to the company and not the company to the play. The company engaged a playwright to cut a play to fit the company as one would engage a tailor to cut his clothes. When the suit got worn at some particular place, or when through growth or decay it ceased to fit the company, or when the company bought someone else's suit, the tailor-playwright was called in to remedy matters as best he could. The playwright was not master but servant. He was only a hired man. If wise, he accepted the limiting conditions of his trade and made the best use of them. If then he was permanently attached to one company as was Shakespeare, the only possible plan was to take the materials that chance and choice had assembled and by careful study to develop and bring out the best abilities and possibilities of each unit in that assemblage. If he refused to be so bound as did bull-headed Ben, he of necessity found no place of comfort in the scheme of things; he simply refused to fit and fared accordingly. By accident such a dramatist could occasionally find an opportune place to force his idea across, but Jonson had not the patience and tact to make the idea and the material for expressing that idea adapt themselves to each other. Of all Jonson's admirable qualities, adaptability certainly was not one, for lack of which he paid the natural penalty.

In constructing his play then, the dramatist would naturally fit it to the permanent elements of the company. Under the system of organization, the most permanent element was the membership, which in later days was usually broken only by death, seldom by withdrawal. In the formative days of the technique and customs of the drama this membership was not large. There were but five members in Leicester's company, and but five in the early Shakespearean. So far as we can find, other companies were organized with approximately the same numbers, as was true of the travelling companies all through the period under consideration. The fact that the plays of the time have also but five or six major parts for men is certainly no accidental coincidence. It is merely good business. In the present state of the evidence, we should hardly be justified in saying that the number of major parts in a play was originally determined by the traditional number of members

[307]

in an acting company, for theoretically it may just as well have been the number of actors required in a typical play that determined the number of members chosen. This is merely a variant of the old question as to whether the hen or the egg were first. As a matter of fact, the demands of the play, and the material at hand to satisfy those demands were probably interactive and equally potent in the evolution of the final form. But once the organization was crystallized by licence and finally by patent, the playwright had no recourse other than to accept the organization with its customs. He might indeed select that organization which could best express his idea, or adapt his idea to the ability of his particular organization. If he attached himself to a particular organization as did Shakespeare, it became a matter of mutual adaptation and growth for playwright and company. It was a fortunate circumstance in the Shakespearean company that playwright and company grew up together.

Thus a company would not want, and a playwright would not construct, a play with more major parts than the company by custom had permanent major actors. The company would want, and consequently their dramatist must write, a play that would use to advantage each of their major performers, or each member who thought himself so. But not only must the play use the present great actor; it must also provide opportunity for development to the great actor's future successor. This necessity, as well as artistic principles of harmony, balance, etc., had its weight in determining the number and kind of major parts in the play. The "lead" of the future must be given opportunity to develop as the "juvenile lead" of the present. If the "juvenile lead" does not develop sufficient dash and adaptability for a "lead," he may still serve a useful function as the important "old man" of the company. The "heavy" of the future must be developed from the "second villain" of the present, and so through the successions.

This principle applies not merely to successions among the major members, but also to the apprentices from whom the successors to members were to be recruited. These apprentices formed the second most permanent element in the company, since they were bound to members of the company for long terms, usually about eleven years. It would be natural but not necessary for an apprentice to be trained up in the line of his master as his possible successor. Thus Pollard, the apprentice of the clown Shank, became himself a comedian. It was with this apprentice element that the playwright would have some of his most serious problems. He was obliged by dramatic custom to use these apprentices to represent women, and he must have some principal women in his play, "For what's a play without a woman in it?" But these boys, like all others, had the disconcerting habit of growing up, changing in physical and mental characteristics and capabilities even from play to play. It was almost as if a sculptor had to express himself in perishable clay. Therefore the dramatist had to provide a simple part to begin with and gradually to increase that part in difficulty till the pupil was finally master in his art and quality. Then the apprentice graduated and the playwright-school teacher had the whole process to repeat with the next pupil. It is evident therefore that here, even more than with the members, the poet was at the mercy of circumstance, though as compensation he had a greater shaping influence. He could introduce only so many and so difficult parts for women as there were apprentices to take those parts. It is curious but natural that the plays of Shakespeare, and Beaumont and Fletcher should at regularly recurring intervals have a brilliant glow of women characters dominating them. When a class of apprentices was about to graduate and their successors were getting well able to take their places, the dramatist could come nearer to expressing his ideas in women. The natural rivalry of such a situation would stimulate both apprentices and playwright to do their best work. This custom was not an unmitigated evil; but in evaluating the woman the dramatist did create we must know something of the woman he could create with any hope of getting her tolerably represented. Since even each principal apprentice had his own individual strong points, it is natural that Shakespeare's heroines should appear in cycles,[45] not necessarily because Shakespeare was interested in that type of woman at that

---

[45] This phenomenon has already been observed by Professor H. D. Gray, *Journal of English and Germanic Philology*, Vol. XII, pp. 122 *ff*.

particular time but because he had the apprentice whose natural expression was that type of woman.

Even among the apprentices then the dramatist had to provide for the succession from entering to graduating apprentice. If the apprentice was finally graduated into membership, as was the usual custom, the dramatist would continue to fit parts to him as for other members.

But when the dramatist passed beyond these two permanent elements of the company, it would not be good policy to adapt particular parts to individuals, since there was nothing to hold the mere hired man with the company for any length of time. These parts then had to be cut rather on the principle of ready-made clothes, guaranteed to fit after a fashion any ordinary man. Still, such a part poorly or well done might contribute immensely to the failure or success of the play. It is not surprising therefore that the members not supplying major parts should be given the chief of these minor parts.

Again then it is evident that in order to do his work with any particular degree of success the dramatist would be obliged to know his company thoroughly from the "lead" himself to the youngest apprentice of them all, for it was his business to write his play, not for a star, but for a company whose component elements were rigidly fixed. The willingness and the ability to do this would distinguish the successful from the unsuccessful dramatist. It is evident that under such a system the type of play must reflect major changes in the personnel of the company. Therefore it cannot be accidental that Shakespeare's four periods corespond to four major reorganizations in the company. It is not to be supposed, however, that such changes in personnel were themselves cataclysmic nor that they caused startling and immediate differences in the type of play, although these differences are appreciable.

Shakespeare's first period is predominantly one of comedy. Of his fourteen plays that I place before the winter of 1594, six are comedies, three are tragedies, and five are histories. Also, there is good reason for believing that without exception the histories and tragedies are merely revisions of older plays, while the evidence seems just as good that most, if not all, the comedies are shaped by Shakespeare himself without the intermediary of an old play. This is not a surprising situation when we read the list of five members in 1593, and find that it was headed by the famous clown William Kemp. Further, three of the five—Kemp, Thomas Pope, and George Bryane—were abroad as Leicester's tumblers and musicians during 1585-87.[46] Also, the company supplanted Strange's tumblers. Besides, we have contemporary evidence that Pope, second on the list, was also a famous clown; and we have seen reason to believe that he was the creator of the *miles gloriosus* line, culminating in Falstaff. Besides these three, we have some indication that Augustine Phillips was a musician and took a line with some comic tendencies. We have seen that the remaining member, John Heminges, third on the list, probably performed a line of whimsically humorous characters. With such a membership, it ought to excite no surprise that Shakespeare wrote comedies in his first period, especially when we remember that he had not himself become a member, and throughout the period was merely a hired man or apprentice of the company. The natural tendency of the company would be to comedy, and Shakespeare was not in a sufficiently influential position to counteract that natural tendency, even if he had desired. The facts given in Professor Baker's book on *The Development of Shakespeare as a Dramatist* would strongly indicate that Shakespeare did not desire, and that his taste was at that time in harmony with that of his company.

During the greater part of the second period, 1595-1600, the former membership remained intact; but there were some significant additions in 1594. William Shakespeare himself entered at that time. If we may judge by his development as pointed out by Professor Baker, he was growing into a more serious view of life. Probably our strongest indication that this was Shakespeare's natural bent is his own line as an actor, technically that of an old man. Richard Burbadge also become a member at the same time as Shakespeare. Now Burbadge was famous as a tragedian, and not as a comedian. We have not a single comic character attributed on contemporary evidence to Burbadge, and his line grows steadily more serious. We shall expect then more serious work

[46] See above, p. 74.

when the one shall have become the chief dramatist and the other the chief actor of the company. Besides these two, William Sly and Henry Cundall probably became members at this time, certainly so by the third period. Now Henry Cundall performed a dignified line, being technically an "old man." William Sly's line was a rather fiery juvenile lead, with little touch of comedy. Thus the new blood was all serious, tragic, or high comedy, not low comedy

Besides, there are some notable developments in this period among the original performers. In the first period there are two comic lines, little distinguished, one belonging to Pope and one to Kemp. Kemp's line remained frankly the clown till he withdrew from the company in 1599; but Pope's was becoming higher comedy until it struck the rich vein of Falstaff, and continued to the end to work that vein. The lines of Heminges and Phillips do not change notably, but were not extremely comic in the beginning. Thus the natural tendency of the company in this period was to a more serious type of play, though still prevailingly comic, as we find is true of the plays in this second period. We have noticed elsewhere that the increased membership is also reflected in an increased number of principal parts in the plays of the second period.

Here we had best notice another potent influence for these first periods, probably tending in the same direction. "An objection being made against the acting of a tragedy in Christ<mas> before the Queen, it was answered that 'choice was made to put your Majesty in mind that since your reign, tragedies were from the State got upon the stage.' "[47] The direct address shows that it was the Queen who objected to the tragedy. It is just possible that her objection to the tragedy was only to its unfitness for the Christmas season, but the form of the answer implies a general objection to all tragedy. We need also to remember Elizabeth's fondness for Tarleton[48] and her traditional desire to see Falstaff in love. Nor should we forget that in her last days Queen Elizabeth did not call for her learned translations, with which she was accustomed to punish only her pious moments, but for the *Hun-*

[47] Smith, P., *The Life and Letters of Sir Henry Wotton*, Vol. II, p. 493.
[48] Halliwell, J. O., *Tarlton's Jests*, p. xxix.

dred Merry Tales.[49] It seems clear that good Queen Bess preferred comedy to tragedy, and that companies bidding for her favor would choose their plays accordingly. Here is another good reason for the predominance of comedy in the work of Shakespeare before the accession of James.[50]

But there were some quite important changes to inaugurate and accelerate the third period. In 1599, the famous clown William Kemp, who had headed the list in 1593, withdrew from the company. The praise of Meres in 1598 shows that Shakespeare was now a famous writer; and the business transactions connected with the building of the Globe early in 1599 show that Shakespeare and Burbadge are now dominant forces, if not the dominant forces, in the company.[51] Kemp was succeeded by Robert Armin, who as a newcomer would not be so influential in the company. Armin's specialty was imitating naturals, especially of the household jester type. Consequently, he is usually attached to some dignitary of the play, under whose patronage he launches his jests at the abuses of the world in true jester style. His humor would therefore have more of the sarcastic and satiric note than the pure slap-stick clownery of Kemp. The other comic line was occasionally also shot through with something of the same spirit, though its method was different. We have seen that it keeps playing variants on the *miles gloriosus*, a type with which we cannot always be kept in sympathy. In fact, we are predisposed to be out of sympathy with the type, even though we are captured by that jolly rogue Falstaff. Further, the natural inclination of the younger members has been toward tragedy, and the chief obstruction, William Kemp, has been removed. Therefore, in the period after 1600 we have tragedies and "bitter comedies."

The drift was still further accelerated by the withdrawal of Thomas Pope, the representative of the high comedy line, formally by 1603, but actually probably about 1601. His successor was John Lowin, who was famous as Morose, Mammon, Melan-

[49] Halliwell, J. O., *The Works of William Shakespeare* (1855), Vol. IV, p. 71.
[50] One would suspect that the Master of the Revels was chosen for his ability to satisfy "the Queen's taste," and that consequently his influence was in the same direction.
[51] Wallace, London *Times*, May 1, 1914, p. 4.

tius, and Henry VIII. This gruff soldier line is far removed from the oily humor of a Falstaff. Augustine Phillips was also soon to die and to be replaced by one of radically different line but never an important actor. Not only had the last bulwark of the old comedy days fallen; it had even been replaced by predominantly tragic material. Thus the remainder of the period is predominantly one of tragedy, with famous Dick Burbadge and his fellows illustrating the fancies of more famous William Shakespeare. The comedies that fit this tragic crew would naturally be "bitter."

But there was to be yet another change in direction, accompanying changing organization. In the summer of 1608, the company decided to take over Blackfriars also, where a company of children had been playing intermittently for many years. Not only did the company take over the theater; but it also took over two of the principal actors of the former company, William Ostler, and John Underwood, now become men. These were to replace William Sly and Laurence Fletcher, the latter of whom is not included in the folio list of principal actors in Shakespeare's plays. When we remember that there were usually only six or seven principal men actors in these plays, it will be seen that two new ones is a fairly weighty proportion. But there was a much heavier influence than this being brought to bear on the company and its dramatist. The manager of the former company at Blackfriars was still trying to hold his company together and even to retain Blackfriars as their acting place.[52] Even if he couldn't save his theater, he would strive to pull the former clientèle to whatever new place of business he might secure. It would therefore be necessary for the Shakespearean company to exert itself in order to retain the clientèle with the theater. It is evidently in line with this idea that it took over two of the chief actors of the former company. But the clientèle would be attached not only by the house and the former chief actors there; it would probably be more permanently attached by the type of play it found there. Evidently the situation also called for effective action on the part of the chief dramatist of the company, William Shakespeare himself. The situation evidently demanded that he exert himself to retain that clientele by

[52] Fleay, *Stage*, pp. 208-51; Wallace, *Associates*, pp. 80-100.

supplying material to its taste. The wailings and gnashings of teeth that ring through the lawsuits of the opponents for the succeeding four years show how effectively he must have performed his duty.[53] They complain that the clientèle not only stayed, but had even grown much better.

It has been repeatedly pointed out that the "little eyases" of Blackfriars emphasized certain features, and drew a select audience accordingly. In their performances, they originally emphasized music, both vocal and instrumental, dancing, and the masque element.[54] It is not without its significance that Jonson, the chief producer of court masques for many years, had been long connected with this company of children. Another chief dramatist for the children was Chapman, who besides Fletcher and himself was the only other man who in Jonson's opinion could make a masque. Of thirty surviving plays for this company, only six are tragedies— *Cupid's Revenge, Byron's Conspiracy and Tragedy, Revenge of Bussy, Sophonisba, Insatiate Countess, and Philotas,*—the rest some type of comedy.[55] It is true as Professor Thorndike says that "In addition to the personally satirical plays concerned with the 'War of the Theaters,' they produced some of the most revolting satire and gruesome tragedies to be found in the drama."[56] But the figures just quoted show that this was not a tragic audience, even if it did suffer a few gruesome tragedies. Indeed, this audience of itching ears would not have been content with any other type of tragedy but a sensational one. The children's company had been suppressed for its incorrigible penchant to satire. Therefore the only way open to hold the audience was a return to an emphasis on the earlier features of dance, music, and spectacle. It is still more significant that the first "full-fledged tragicomedy," Chapman's *Gentleman Usher,* was performed for this audience.[57]

Dr. Ristine's work makes it clearly apparent that the schools were the birthplace of tragicomedy. "It is significant that our first three English tragicomedies are all the work of scholars, men who

---

[53] Fleay, *Stage,* pp. 208-51 ; Wallace, *Associates,* pp. 80-100.
[54] Thorndike, *Theater,* p. 326.
[55] *ibid.,* p. 327.
[56] *ibid.,* p. 326.
[57] Lee, *Shakespeare,* p. 419; Ristine, F. H., *English Tragicomedy,* p. 100; Parrott, T. M., *The Comedies of George Chapman,* p. 757.

had every opportunity to be familiar with Renaissance dramatic activity, both at home and abroad, in humanistic circles and among vernacular imitators. Bower and Edwards had been in turn Masters of the Children of the Queen's Chapel, while Gascoigne had studied at Cambridge and fought in Holland."[58] Further, in summing up the development of the type to 1600, he says: "the main preparation for later tragicomedy has been found to identify itself thruout with the second great influence underlying the mixing of kinds—that contributed by romance. . . . In the period reviewed, this course of development properly begins with the plays of Edwards and Whetstone, is continued in the work of Lyly and the nonextant romantic plays of the seventies and eighties, reaches its highest expression in the "James IV" of Greene, and ends with the temporary cessation of the romantic note in the Shaksperian plays of the close of the century."[59] Edwards was at one time Master of the Children of the Queen's Chapel; Whetstone was an admirer and friend of Edwards and Gascoigne, and wrote to attract the attention of the court, his typical play seemingly having been a closet drama never acted; Lyly wrote for Paul's boys and the children of the Chapel, and was for a time "vice master" at Paul's. Greene was a Master of Arts, whose chief business was peddling romance. Only his work and that of Shakespeare was done for the popular stage, but by companies both of whom were seeking royal favor. It is evident then that the schools were the birthplace of tragicomedy, and that it was fostered by schools and court; hence was cultivated by the companies that catered to court patronage. Between 1600 and 1610, "the stamp of actual tragicomedy perhaps finds its closest aproximation during these years among socalled satiric or realistic comedies, due to the tragic admixture that necessarily finds its way into such plays."[60] Even in Jonson, *Volpone* has a touch of admixture. The best examples, however, are Marston's *Malcontent* and Chapman's *Gentleman Usher*. Marston's *Dutch Courtesan*, and Chapman's *Widow's Tears* also require mention here. Besides, Shakespeare's *Measure for Measure*,

[58] Ristine, *English Tragicomedy*, p. 64.
[59] *ibid.*, p. 95.
[60] *ibid.*, p. 98.

[316]

Middleton's *Phoenix*, and Sharpham's *Fleire* show some approximation to the comic-tragic mixture. But Daniel's *Queen's Arcadia* and Fletcher's *Faithful Shepherdess* are the two plays that did most to popularize the form. Of these plays, all but *Volpone* and *Measure for Measure* were performed by the children's companies, not in the public theaters by the companies for men. Further, *Volpone* belongs to the type merely by an accident of technique, but is far removed from it in spirit. It is thus evident that the type was fostered by the courtly, educated audience and not by the general public.

It is significant then that the first play that shows "all the features of a full-fledged tragicomedy,"[61] *The Gentleman Usher*, was performed at Blackfriars, having been written by George Chapman, one of the regular dramatists at that theater. Given then an author with the tragicomic germ latent in his veins, as is shown by some of Shakespeare's early plays, brought into contact with a tragicomic audience, as was the audience at Blackfriars, the result is likely to be tragicomedy. We need then find nothing strange about the fact that all of Shakespeare's uncollaborated plays after his company took over Blackfriars were tragicomedies. It would have shown that he had lost his characteristic adaptability if he hadn't written tragicomedy.

There was a further incentive, long ago pointed out by Professor Thorndike and now made certain I think by the facts of chronology,[62] that the company had retained with the Blackfriars temple the high priests of the new cult, Beaumont and Fletcher. They had already produced *Philaster* and probably *The Maid's Tragedy* when Shakespeare returned from his long vacation at Stratford 1608-10, and were about to produce *A King and No King* and *The Captain*, parallelling Shakespeare's last plays. It seems indicated then that Shakespeare's "spell" of tragicomedy was due to a natural predisposition, aggravated by direct exposure to the germ in the newly acquired Blackfriars, and most virulently in his newly acquired co-laborers, Beaumont and Fletcher.

It ought not therefore to be surprising that Shakespeare after

[61] Lee, *Shakespeare*, p. 419.
[62] See Preface, p. ii.

1608 emphasized the tragicomic elements in his plays. This does not necessarily imply that he imitated any preceding writers at Blackfriars or elsewhere. It is only a plain statement without implications that certain elements had been emphasized at Blackfriars; and that after the Shakespearean company took over the theater in 1608, the same elements are emphasized in Shakespeare's plays, showing that he aimed his plays at his audience, as any good playwright would have done. To what extent he had definite models in the shaping of these plays is another question, and one with which I do not here propose to deal.

It is interesting, however, to notice here one particularly difficult problem Shakespeare, as well as Beaumont and Fletcher, had to face in working out this type of play. This type seems necessarily to demand a prominent youthful lover. But Burbadge was getting old, and besides was rather serious. Therefore John Underwood was of necessity the juvenile lead. Shakespeare was thus under the double necessity of getting a principal serious part for Burbadge, and a juvenile character that would throw a proper glamor over the play. Probably his best solution of the problem is *The Tempest*, with Prospero-Burbadge directing the magic, music, and masque, and Ferdinand-Underwood, a central figure in that puppet show. Incidentally, Shakespeare may have received some hint at this solution from the city pageant May 31, 1610, when Burbadge represented "Amphion the Father of hermonie or Musick."[63] Also, if one remembers Underwood's princely-rascal characteristics, he will fully appreciate the reasons for the injunctions that father Burbadge-Prospero lays on lover Underwood-Ferdinand. Underwood's Ferdinand wasn't the modest, blushing hero that some expurgated minds have been able to conjure up.

Not only was there the difficulty of fitting the tragic Burbadge, now of dominating greatness, into this new scheme of things; but there was the further difficulty that Underwood himself was but a princely rascal. Consequently, the evolving tragicomic hero did not find ideal representation in the Shakespearean company till Field appeared in 1616, though there was still at that time the difficulty of supplying Burbadge an adequate part, causing the plays to be

---

[63] Wallace, London *Times*, March 28, 1913, p. 6.

"double-headers." But finally at Burbadge's death and Field's withdrawal, young Joseph Taylor came to the company, and the tragicomic hero of Fletcher found a clear field and adequate representation. Consequently, he is presented with infinite variations.

It is evident therefore from our studies that the organization and personnel of the company had an important influence on the drama and dramatists. The facts given indicate that under the system then existent the conditioning influence of these particular circumstances was considerably greater than at the present day. Yet it does not follow that these particular circumstances determined the development of either the drama or dramatists. It must be remembered that there were many interacting factors, of which the organization and personnel was only one, though a very important one. It is to be remembered also in the case of the Shakespearean company that the dramatist, the company, and the audience all grew up together, and each factor must have had its influence in the final result. This work has necessarily, but it is hoped not unduly, emphasized the influence exerted by the organization and personnel. It represents therefore but one angle, one-third of the story, yet a hitherto almost unexplored third. It pretends to be of value only in that it has given us a few further clues as to the influences that conditioned and helped to form the master dramatist of English literature.

THE ORGANIZATION AND PERSONNEL OF THE ADMIRAL'S MEN BEFORE 1595

BECAUSE of the entangling alliances between the Shakespearean company and the Admiral's men, it is necessary to reconstruct in some detail the history of the latter company to 1595. Between entries of December 14, 1594, and January 14, 1595,[1] Henslowe lists Edward Alleyn,[2] John Singer, Richard Jones, Thomas Towne, Martin Slaughter, Edward Juby, Thomas Downton, and James Donstall, these eight men being presumably the complete membership of the Admiral's company at that time. Our earliest knowledge of any one of these as a member of the Admiral's is 1589, when we have almost the complete membership. To begin with, John Alleyn, elder brother of Edward, is styled "servaunte to me the Lo. Admyrall" in a letter on his behalf from the Privy Council July 14, 1589.[3] John Alleyn had been with the Admiral's men at the Theater in 1590, probably as manager; but seems to have become involved in some of the disputes centering in that enterprise, this resulting in a final settlement November 24, 1590.[4] At this time, James Donstall also makes his appearance as a member.[5] Edward Alleyn seems certainly to have played Faustus at the Theater, presumably then before the severing of relations November 24, 1590.[6] Returning to January 3, 1589, we find John and Edward Alleyn buying Richard Jones's share of certain theatrical supplies that had belonged to the three and Robert Browne. All these men except John Alleyn are known formerly to have belonged to Worcester's men; but even John Alleyn must have been with the company for some time before this, as he was now one of the inner circle of financiers. Of these four, as we have just seen, John Alleyn appears July 14 in the same year as an Admiral's man; and all three of the others are soon afterward

---

[1] Greg, *Diary*, Vol. I, p. 5; Vol. II, pp. 99-100.
[2] I have used the orthography of Mr. Greg. Facts from the Diary for which references are not given may be easily found by referring to Vol. II, Chap. IV of Greg's edition, under the name of the person involved.
[3] Greg, *Diary*, Vol. II, p. 239.
[4] Wallace, *First London Theatre*, pp. 19, 101, 127; I doubt the deduction of Chambers, *Eliz. Stage*, Vol. II, p. 392, note 3.
[5] Wallace, *First London Theatre*, p. 19; Greg, *Diary*, Vol. II, p. 99.
[6] Adams, *Playhouses*, p. 73; Chambers, *Eliz. Stage*, Vol. II, p. 395, note 2; but see Vol. III, p. 423.

officially designated as Admiral's men.[7] It is at once evident that there had been simply a transfer of patronage from Worcester to the Lord Admiral. Certainly this was true of three of the four leaders.

It was also true of at least a majority of the members. Our only complete list of Worcester's men dates January 14, 1583.[8] This list names eight, the number we found in the Admiral's men 1594-95. These were Robert Browne, James Donstall, Edward Alleyn, William Harrison, Thomas Cook, Richard Jones, Edward Browne, and Richard Andrewes. Thus Donstall had also passed from Worcester's to the Admiral's, this being the reason of his appearance as an appraiser at the sale of January 3, 1589.[9] Moreover, Edward Browne also appears with the Admiral's men about 1599, though probably not as a member. Thus all but three—Harrison, Cook, and Andrewes—had passed to the Admiral's organization. One of these had been succeeded by John Alleyn. Since, therefore, at least five of the eight members, including three out of four leaders, had passed from Worcester to the Admiral, the lost three dropping entirely from acting records, it is evident that the transaction was simply a transfer of patronage. As we shall soon see, the other two men of Worcester's organization had been replaced before 1590, by John Bradstreet and Thomas Sacheville. The list of the company then about 1589, was Robert Browne, James Donstall, Edward Alleyn, Richard Jones, and John Alleyn certainly; E. Browne, Thomas Sacheville, and John Bradstreet probably.

When did this transfer take place? There is no trace of a company for Worcester either at court, in London, or in the provinces from March 1585 till his death February 21, 1589.[10] There is no trace of a company for the Admiral (under his previous title) either at court, in London, or in the provinces for some years preceding 1585; but a company appeared in his name June 1585, and has regular record thereafter.[11] It is evident that at the Admiral's appointment July 4, 1585, Worcester's company was transferred to his patronage, and henceforth was the Admiral's company.

This fact clears up several disputed points, and renders significant certain other events of the year 1585. On February 6, 1592, John Alleyn, manager of the Admiral's, made an estimate of receipts at the Theater, where the company had certainly been in

[7] Greg, *Papers.* p. 31, notes.
[8] Murray, Vol. I, p. 45.
[9] Warner, *Catalogue*, p. 126.
[10] Murray, Vol. I, pp. 57-8; Chambers, *Eliz. Stage*, Vol. II, p. 224.
[11] Murray, Vol. I, p. 112. I suppose the June entry is correct, but the Admiral received appointment July 4, 1585.

November 1590, for five years past, either from February 1592, when he bore witness, or from November 1590, when his connection ceased with the Theater,[12] this circumstance implying that he had been at the place regularly from 1585, or 1587. Alleyn also seems to claim knowledge of affairs at the Theater and Curtain before Brayne died in August 1586. We have no direct record, of course, that John Alleyn was an Admiral's man by 1585-86; but we do know that the company with which he seems to have been in 1580, passed out of existence about 1585.[13] Since we next find him with his brother Edward, fully established before 1589 in the inner circle of the Admiral's, it is at least probable that he had made the transfer by 1585. If so, the Admiral's were at the Theater by 1585-86.

Another straw shows the wind blowing in the same direction. In June 1584 James Burbage declared himself most emphatically a servant of Lord Hunsdon,[14] who became Lord Chamberlain July 4, 1585, succeeding his son-in-law, the Admiral. The companies of these two men are found cooperating in the provinces and at court this season of 1585-86.[15] In the case of the other well known actor-owner, Christopher Beeston, he was of whatever company regularly played at his theater. This had been true at least part of the time with James Burbage at the Theater. It is probable then that Hunsdon's men had been regularly playing at the Theater about 1584, and that their cooperation with the Admiral's the season 1585-86 may denote that the two companies were then both using the same building.

But the Queen's men were also certainly at the Theater and Curtain occasionally 1584-89.[16] They had received permission to perform at the Bell and Bull the winter of 1583-84, and petitioned for the same permission the winter of 1584-85. Since in our last record the city council was striving to dictate the conditions under which the petition might be granted, the matter was probably accommodated. It has been supposed that the Queen's men were acting at the Theater in June 1584; but the record, I believe, indicates the opposite. The record from which this inference is drawn is a letter, concerning which two things must be remembered. First, it is an exultant account of how both the players and playhouses are to be plucked up root and branch. Second, the writer of the letter was charged only with suppressing all playing. The storm centered around the Theater and Curtain, because of certain untoward

---

12 Wallace, *First London Theatre*, pp. 98, 99, 102, but see 126.
13 Murray, Vol. II, pp. 65-6.
14 Malone Soc. *Coll.*, Vol. I, pp. 39, 41.
15 Chambers, *Eliz. Stage*, Vol. II, p. 135.
16 *ibid.*, pp. 106-9.

occurrences in their neighborhood. This gave the Lord Mayor his chance to obtain an order not only against these hated houses but also "to suppresse theym all." Thus all acting was to be suppressed, and the two rebel buildings destroyed. The writer first gloats over this great victory. He then proceeds to relate his own privileged share in the matter, which was to notify the actors. He called in the Queen's, Lord Arundel's, and seemingly other players, since "they all well nighe obeyed the Lordes lettres." But the officer was warned by the Queen's men that the owner of the Theater would likely cause trouble. Accordingly, the owner was summoned, and did propose to resist, claiming certain immunities as Hunsdon's man. Now if either the Queen's or Arundel's controlled the building, why should James Burbage be sent for, and why should he claim to be Hunsdon's man? The binding of the companies should have been sufficient. Usually such a roundup would call for only the responsible leaders of each organization,[17] and accordingly we hear only of the "chiefest" of the Queen's men. It is probable then that Burbage was wanted in his capacity of "chiefest" of Hunsdon's men. It was none of this official's business to destroy these buildings; he was merely rounding up the players, and in doing so had a splendid incidental opportunity to lord it over the chief rebel. There was no more reason why Burbage as owner of the Theater should be summoned than Lanman as owner of the Curtain. It is thus doubtful that the Queen's men were occupying the Theater in or by June 1584. If not, they probably were not there before 1585.

But in this year 1585 a merger was formed of the Curtain and Theater.[18] Between 1585 and 1590, we have both the Queen's and the Admiral's connected with both these buildings, but no other companies certainly recorded there. The Queen's company of tumblers under Simons cooperated with the Admiral's at court the winter 1588. Now Simons's company had been the only one of tumblers for many years. Since the Admiral's are credited with these feats at court 1589-90, and 1590-91, this connection with Simons evidently continued till the Admiral's lost control of the Theater. For the last of these performances of feats of activity, George Ottewell or Atwell received pay. Our only other record of him dates June 1, 1595, when he witnessed a loan made by Philip Henslowe to the latter's nephew Francis,[19] then a Queen's man. Doubtless then Atwell had succeeded Simons as leader of the Queen's tumblers.

But not only had there been this cooperation between the Ad-

17 See for instance the procedure in 1615 (Malone Soc. *Coll.* Vol. I, p. 372).
18 Wallace, *First London Theatre*, pp. 126, 149.
19 Greg, *Diary*, Vol. I, p. 6.

miral's and the Queen's tumblers; there had also been some intimate connection with the Queen's actors before 1592, since, for
instance, we find in the Admiral's stock *The Seven Deadly Sins*,
which appears originally to have been put on by the Queen's in
the season 1585-86.[20] There are still other indications; but these
make it probable that the Admiral's and Queen's companies were
regularly at the Theater and Curtain 1585-90, and that the merger
was formed in 1585 with this purpose in view.

In 1590, however, the Admiral's company was split into exact
halves, by the withdrawal of a branch for foreign travel. We get
a complete list of this foreign company in February 1592, when
the Lord Admiral granted licence to Robert Browne, John Bradstreet, Thomas Sacheville, and Richard Jones, to travel in Germany, passing through Zealand, Holland, and Friesland.[21] They
were evidently following a previously travelled trail, for in 1590
we hear of Browne and "his fellows" in Holland,[22] and of Sacheville in Vienna.[23] We do not have either Bradstreet or Jones named
on this first trip abroad, but we do have some indication that before
the trip of 1592, Jones was separated from Alleyn and the English
branch of the company.[24] There is other evidence to the same effect;
but this is sufficient to show that the company split into a foreign

[20] It is practically certain that these companies were furnished in much
the same way as were the companies later at the Rose, the Alleyn stock
of plays thus representing the accumulations of both companies. Nor is it
improbable that other companies may have acted occasionally at these
theaters, as was later true at the Rose.

[21] Greg, *Diary*, Vol. II, p. 99; Murray, Vol. II, pp. 120-1.

[22] Murray, Vol. I, p. 49; Fleay's statement (*Life of Shakespeare*, pp.
287-8) that Jones was also at Leyden seems to be merely one of his usual
inferences stated as a fact.

[23] Price, L. M., *English>German Literary Influences*, p. 136.

[24] Murray, Vol. I, p. 50. It has been usual to date the letter from Jones to
Alleyn, on which this inference rests, February 1592, and have it refer to
the second expedition; but Mr. Chambers objects (*Eliz. Stage*, Vol. II, p.
287), on the ground that Jones mentions Mrs. Alleyn, while E. Alleyn's
first known marriage was October 1592, too late for the date of February
1592; and would date the letter "in or near 1615." Greg had previously
noted this seeming inconsistency, but offers as possible explanation the
Dulwich tradition that Alleyn was three times married (Greg, *Papers*, p.
33, note). It can also be shown, I believe, that Jones and Browne remained
with the management of the Revels company till it broke in 1617, only
then returning to Germany, which, on Chambers's assumption, would date
the letter February 1618. But Jones at the time of the letter was an acting
hired man at his shilling a day, while with the Revels he was a manager
and had ceased acting. Nor in this period is he likely to have been in so
reduced circumstances as the letter represents him. Pretty certainly, the
letter belongs to the early days of Jones's career, most likely where it is
usually placed, February 1592.

If this is the date, Jones and Browne were presumably not connected with

and a native branch at some time in 1590. As previously stated, the members of the foreign branch were Browne, Bradstreet, Sacheville, and Jones. The company had thus split into halves. Between 1590 and 1592, the foreign branch had been in England, with at least Browne and Jones connected with some company other than the English Admiral's or the Shakespearean. This foreign branch returned to Germany in 1592, and does not further concern us here.

The Alleyn brothers—who now owned the complete theatrical property of the English branch,—Donstall, and E. Browne were certainly not with the foreign branch. Further, this native branch made some arrangement that did not include the foreign branch at its temporary return 1591-92, though the members of this latter organization were still Admiral's men when they again went abroad in the early part of 1592, and possibly were still so considered by Heywood in 1612.[25] The key to this problem is to be found in the connection of the Admiral's men with the Shakespearean company and others. In the declared accounts for acting at court Christmas 1590-91, it is stated that payment was made to Strange's men for certain acting; but in the Acts the payment is supposed to have been to the Admiral's men. Further, if the companies acted together at court Christmas, they must have acted together for practice at least part of the preceding autumn. Yet, the Admiral's and the Shakespearean companies had certainly been separate organizations in November 1589.[26] The fact that the Admiral's and the Shakespearean companies were separate in November 1589, the fact that half of the Admiral's was abroad by the autumn of 1590, the fact that the remnant acted with the Shakespearean company at Christmas 1590-91, and the fact that Richard Burbadge, soon afterward a principal actor in the Shakespearean company, is connected with this remnant only a month before, all indicate that the two organizations formed some kind of association at least for the autumn of 1590. This connection was formed after November 1589; but at least several weeks before Christmas 1590.

There is some indication, also, of how the connection was formed. On November 5, 1589, the Shakespearean company disobeyed the

the Shakespearean company, since Alleyn, to whom the letter was written, was then furnishing that organization. They were seemingly not with the English branch of the Admiral's, because Jones was a hired man, as is shown by his wages and the general tenor of his letter. The treatment of Browne as given in the letter indicates the same relationship for him, though he had either been given a whole share originally, cut to one-half to prevent his going abroad, or had received the regular wage as a hired man originally and had been promoted to half a share in order to retain him, probably the latter, though Jones's statement rather implies the former.

[25] *Apology for Actors* (Shak. Soc., 1841), p. 40.
[26] Murray, Vol. I, p. 75.

APPENDIX I

Mayor's orders, with the result that they were ejected from the Cross Keys in London, and two of their number sent to the Counter. Seemingly they found refuge at the Curtain, out of the Mayor's jurisdiction. In *An Almond for a Parrot*, there is a reference to "the curtaine" of Kemp's countenance, seeming to indicate, as Fleay pointed out,[27] that Kemp was then acting at the Curtain. McKerrow dates the *Almond* February-March 1590,[28] this indicating that the Shakespearean company was by that date at the Curtain. Now in all known cases where a company used two theaters, one was used for summer, the other for winter. Since we find the Admiral's at the Theater the following winter season, presumably the Curtain was the summer house, possibly vacant then the winter of 1589-90, as a haven of refuge for the Shakespearean company. Then when the Admiral's split in 1590, it would be natural for the remnant Admiral's with its theaters, etc., to associate with the Shakespearean company with its actors.

It is fairly certain then that the associated companies were performing at the Theater by the autumn of 1590, but were forced to go elsewhere in November of that year.[29] By March 1592, the Shakespearean company was acting alone, as is shown by the plot of *The Seven Deadly Sins*, and by the fact that the Admiral's men appear with Derby's at Ipswich March 7,[30] while the Shakespearean company was certainly performing at the Rose. Facts connected with the lines for actors indicate that the acting connection had ceased almost certainly before the winter of 1591,[31] and probably before the summer of 1591. The association seems thus to have been confined to the single acting year 1590-91, and was likely wrecked by the loss of the Theater. It seems probable then that after the foreign branch of the Admiral's withdrew, the native branch formed an association with the Shakespearean company in order to hold the Theater and Curtain; but when they lost those buildings there was no longer particular reason for the association.

However, Edward Alleyn continued some relation with the Shakespearean company till 1594. That this relation was that of manager or furnisher of the company is shown by the evidence following, though here I have space to give only the sum of it, and must reserve detailed proof for publication elsewhere. The surviving facts make it clear that Alleyn was furnishing the Admiral's at the Rose for some time preceding 1597. He was already so engaged in 1589, when, as we have seen, he bought the share of

[27] Fleay, *Drama*, Vol. II, p. 126.
[28] McKerrow, *Nashe*, Vol. IV, p. 461.
[29] Wallace, *First London Theatre*, p. 19.
[30] Murray, Vol. II, p. 293.
[31] See above, pp. 271-3.

theatrical stock, including plays, that belonged to Richard Jones, the entire stock of the company thereafter belonging to the Alleyn brothers and Robert Browne. When Robert Browne withdrew in 1590, he and his companions seem to have taken abroad with them only the parts of plays they had in their heads, leaving the total stock of plays in the hands of the Alleyn brothers. This is indicated both by the fact that the players in England must have retained the licensed copies, without which they could not have acted these plays, and by the description Fynes Moryson gives of these plays and players in the German branch at Frankfort the autumn of 1592, "hauing nether a Complete number of Actours, nor any good Apparell, nor any ornament of the Stage," and "pro-nowncing peeces and Patches of English playes."[32] Thus by the autumn of 1590, the plays and stock in general had come into the hands of the Alleyn brothers.

Evidently then, plays that appear in both the foreign and the English branches of the Admiral's men and their associates must have belonged to the Admiral's men before the split in 1590, and must after that date have been the property of the Alleyn brothers. The known plays of this stock formed the bulk of the repertoire for each company that acted at the Rose 1592-94. Besides, we know directly that a few of these plays later belonged to Edward Alleyn. This explains why several plays were performed by more than one company; they belonged to no one of the companies but to the Alleyns. Evidently then one or both of the Alleyn brothers were furnishing the companies at the Rose, Edward being the one through whom arrangements were made.[33] That Alleyn was furnishing the Shakespearean company by the summer of 1591 is indicated by the fact that at that time Shakespeare used the old *Romeo and Juliet* of the Admiral's men as a basis for his

[32] Hughes, C., *Shakespeare's Europe*, p. 304; Chambers, *Eliz. Stage*, Vol. I, p. 343.
[33] That John Alleyn was at least a silent partner as late as 1591 is shown by a typical series of purchases. John Alleyn, "innholder," bought a cloak August 8, 1589; another November 23, 1590 (Warner, *Catalogue*, p. 3); he and Edward another May 6, 1591 (*ibid.*, p. 4); and the two acknowledge a debt to a tailor July 25, 1591 (*ibid.*, p. 127). John Alleyn's signing a bond with the actors Thomas Goodal and Robert Lee May 18, 1593 (*ibid.*, p. 127) looks as if he might have retained some kind of connection till that date. But he had ceased active participation before the reorganization of 1594, dying about May 1596, in the parish of St. Andrews, Holborn. He had been of St. Botolph's certainly from January 23, 1588, to February 6, 1592; but was "late" of that parish May 6 of the latter year (Warner, *Catalogue*, p. 252; Wallace, *First London Theatre*, pp. 98, 124). Whether there is any connection between John Alleyn's moving in the spring of 1592, and his withdrawal from acting I have not been able to determine.

APPENDIX I

Romeo and Juliet. The company was using the Alleyn plays at the Rose early in 1592, and continued to do so till it finally severed connections in 1594. That Alleyn was managing the company in the tour of 1593 is shown by various pieces of evidence. The travelling licence granted by the Privy Council May 6, 1593,[34] is for six men "being al one companie, servantes to our verie good the (*sic*) lord the Lord Strainge," though the list is headed by Edward Alleyn "servaunt to the right honorable the L. Highe Admiral."[35] That the company on tour was known as Strange's players is shown by the fact that Alleyn's wife directs a letter to "m^r edward allen one of my lord stranges players,"[36] as does Henslowe himself.[37] It appears then that the Alleyn brothers furnished, managed, and financed the company from at least the autumn and possibly the summer of 1590, till about the summer of 1594.

Also, the provincial records show that the Admiral's company was still in existence in the provinces throughout this period. Since its membership had been cut to at least four, and these four had lost their London theater, they again became a provincial company. During this period, at least eight and probably more provincial performances are attributed to the Admiral's men.[38] In at least one case, however, the attribution is to both the Admiral's company and the Shakespearean. At Shrewsbury for August 1593 we find "Itm pd and geven to my l. Stranges and my l. Admyralls players . . . xls."[39] This item and the fact that Alleyn was mentioned in the licence of 1593 both indicate that the two companies were again cooperating in this summer of 1593. That Alleyn acted on this tour we know from a letter stating that he was once too ill to perform,[40] and from the fact that *A Knack to Know a Knave* was published in 1594, as acted by "Ed. Allen and his Companie." Mr. Greg[41] is therefore evidently correct in supposing that Alleyn was acting in and managing the combined companies on this tour. The weakness of the English branch of the Admiral's company at this period is apparent from the fact that we find it cooperating with the Shakespearean company for the winter season 1590-91, probably with Pembroke's the summer of 1591, with Derby's the winter of 1591-92,[42] with Mordaunt's in April 1593,[43] and again with the Shake-

34 Murray, Vol. I, p. 88.
35 Greg, *Diary*, Vol. II, p. 74.
36 Greg, *Papers*, p. 41.
37 *ibid.*, p. 37.
38 Murray, Vol. I, p. 142; Boas, F. S., *Fortnightly Review*, Vol. C, p. 248.
39 Murray, Vol. II, p. 392.
40 Greg, *Diary*, Vol. II, p. 75.
41 *ibid.*
42 Murray, Vol. II, pp. 39, 293.
43 *ibid.*, pp. 90, 412.

[329]

spearean later in the summer of 1593, and for a few days in the summer of 1594. It is because of this weakened condition that the company did not make its accustomed appeareance at court from the Christmas of 1590 till that of 1594.[44]

Of the full membership for the English branch at this period we cannot be certain. As we have seen, the four members who were left in 1590 were Edward and John Alleyn, James Donstall, and possibly Edward Browne. All these, except possibly Browne, were certainly at the Theater in November of 1590; but neither John Alleyn nor Edward Browne was with the reorganized company in 1594-95. Also, it seems doubtful that Edward Alleyn travelled with the company before the summer of 1593, since he was presumably keeping his eye on the companies he was furnishing at the Rose. Of the reorganized company, Edward Alleyn and James Donstall had been members before 1590, and Richard Jones had returned from abroad between August 1593, and September 2, 1594;[45] but the remaining three of the foreign branch never returned to their allegiance. Besides these three former Admiral's men, Singer, Towne, Slaughter, Juby, and Downton had entered. Since Downton had been with the provincial company of 1593,[46] he had probably become a member of it by that time. In 1593, Downton and Jones were both living in Horseshoe Court in Southwark.[47] Since Jones had been in Germany as late as the latter part of August 1593,[48] this entry must date still later in that year, or else Jones must have been at home for Easter communion, as the law required. Singer had been with the Queen's men, and probably got attached to the Rose about May 8, 1594, since the Queen's men at that time "broke & went into the contrey."[49] Of Juby, Towne, and Slaughter we have no previous record of any kind.[50] Thus it appears that all the members of the latter part of 1594, except possibly these three, were almost certainly in the company when it began acting regularly at the Rose in June 1594. Presumably then the company was reorganized before the middle of June, when it began acting there; but after Singer left the broken Queen's men about May 8, of that year. The reorganization may thus have taken place either for

---

[44] Chambers, *Modern Language Review*, Vol. II, p. 10; Greg, *Diary*, Vol. II, p. 336.

[45] Murray, Vol. I, pp. 51-2.

[46] Greg, *Papers*, p. 41.

[47] Collier, *Memoirs*, p. 152.

[48] Murray, Vol. I, p. 51.

[49] Greg, *Diary*, Vol. I, p. 4; Vol. II, p. 80; Wallace, *First London Theatre*, p. 11.

[50] The fact that Slaughter's first mention in the Southwark token books is 1595 indicates that he had just come to the Rose (Chambers, *Eliz. Stage*, Vol. II, p. 340).

their three-day appearance there May 14-16, or when they returned June 15, after acting with the Shakespearean company at Newington Butts June 3-13. Presumably the reorganization and strengthening would have taken place before the company attempted to use the Rose May 14-16.

Probably but not certainly the number of members in the English branch from the split in 1590 till the reorganization in May or June 1594 had been four. If so, three of the four in the summer of 1593 were Edward Alleyn, James Donstall, and Thomas Downton. The other member would have been either Juby, Towne, or Slaughter, unless either John Alleyn[51] or possibly Edward Browne had remained in the company till this reorganization, one of whom Downton had succeeded before the summer of 1593. Further than this the evidence so far given does not enable us to go.

While there was an Admiral's company (under his former title) continuously from 1574 to 1581, it seems to have had no connection with the Alleyn company, and we know certainly the name of but a single member, John Adams,[52] who in 1583 became a Queen's man. This then completes our knowledge of the Admiral's men before 1595.

[51] A bond given May 18, 1593 (Warner, *Catalogue*, p. 127) by John Alleyn, Thomas Goodal, and Robert Lee may indicate that John was still active in some capacity. But since the company was now in effect a provincial one, its real organization was probably haphazard and temporary.

[52] Wallace, *Evolution*, p. 217; *First London Theatre*, p. 11.

FINANCE IN THE
SHAKESPEAREAN COMPANY

OUR first definite information concerning the financial affairs of the Shakespearean company comes from the Rose. Now the Shakespearean company calculated the full theatrical year as three hundred to three hundred and thirty-three days.[1] Their reason for this estimate may be seen by studying their early connection with Henslowe. From February 19, through June 23, 1592, there were one hundred and twenty-six days, but the Shakespearean company performed only one hundred and five times.[2] This would mean three hundred and five performances a year. From December 29, through February 1, is thirty-five days; but Strange's men performed only twenty-nine times.[3] This would mean three hundred and two performances a year. The reason for the approximate number of three hundred is indicated by the fact that the day missed was regularly Sunday, though any day might be missed, and sometimes Sunday is recorded as the day of acting. Mr. Greg, however, thinks that Sunday entries are usually errors.[4] It appears then that for uninterrupted acting a three-hundred-day year, and a five-and-three-quarter-day week is the norm.

The daily receipts of the Shakespearean company from its half galleries at the Rose 1592-93 had been in round numbers £1 15s. On the basis of a three-hundred-day acting year, this would mean a return of £525 per annum from half the galleries. Multiplying this by one and two-fifths, the ratio between door and gallery receipts,[5] we get £735 as the probable door receipts, the two items

---

[1] Halliwell, *Outlines*, Vol. I, p. 313.

[2] Greg, *Diary*, Vol. I, pp. 13-15.

[3] *ibid.*, pp. 15-16.

[4] *ibid.*, Vol. II, pp. 324. It was illegal to act on Sunday, and numerous references indicate that it was not usually done. For instance, see a statement of January 25, 1586, in Collier, *Annals* (1879), Vol. I, pp. 257-8; the agreement on daily expense at Whitefriars in 1608, which is figured on a six-day basis (N.S.S. *Transactions*, 1887-92, p. 276); and Fynes Moryson's statement about 1617 (Hughes, C., *Shakespeare's England*, pp. xli, 476).

[5] I have worked out in detail Henslowe's various financial dealings in an article "Posting Henslowe's Accounts," which is to be published in *The Journal of English and Germanic Philology*. Some of its results I have used in this appendix as illustrative material.

giving a total income of £1260 per annum for the actors. The expenses of the Admiral's and Worcester's men when they were first setting up at the same theater were about £400 per annum for all expenses except wages. The plot of *The Seven Deadly Sins* indicates that the Shakespearean company must have had at least twenty hired men and apprentices at this time, as was true a little later of the Admiral's men. These at the average wage of 6s per week would cost £300, making a total expense of £700. In the agreement with Herbert May 25, 1628,[6] the daily expense of the company was estimated at £2 5s, which would be £675 per annum for an uninterrupted year of three hundred acting days. In 1635, however, the expense per annum was estimated as over £1,000.[7] Our estimate of £700 therefore is probably not far wrong. This would leave a net profit to the company of £560 per annum. Since there were regularly five members of the company at this time, in an uninterrupted year each sharer should have cleared about £112 per annum.

But the company did not actually have an uninterrupted year. As a matter of fact, from February 19, 1592, to February 19, 1593, it acted at the Rose but slightly over two-fifths of the time. Thus its total income from the Rose in that period was probably about £525. In the interval between June 23, and December 29, 1592, the company was forced to travel for a while, but complained that it could not make expenses with so great a company.[8] For returns from acting in the provinces, the "rewards" given by city authorities are our most definite and significant source of information. Seventeen rewards between 1591 and 1597[9] netted the Shakespearean company about 17s each reward. The largest reward, in connection, however, with the Admiral's men, was 40s. Two of its rewards were as much as 30s and five were 20s. The other nine ranged as low as 2s 8d. The situation is well summed up in the story that when Ratsey had a certain company play before him he "gave them fortie shillings, with which they held themselves very richly satisfied, for they scarce had twentie shillings audience at any time for a play in the countrey."[10] Again, Sir Oliver Owlet's men, probably the Shakespearean company just about the period we are considering, were at first content with a reward of "forty pence," but later demanded £10, though that demand was regarded as the height of arrogance.[11] If then we consider the lessened number of performances possible under travelling conditions, and the smallness of

[6] Fleay, *Stage*, p. 333.
[7] Halliwell, *Outlines*, Vol. I, p. 313.
[8] Murray, Vol. II, p. 127; Greg, *Diary*, Vol. II. p. 53.
[9] Murray. Vol. I, pp. 108-9.
[10] Halliwell, *Outlines*. Vol. I, pp. 325-6.
[11] Simpson, R., *The School of Shakspere*, Vol. II, pp. 41, 52, 54.

returns for each performance, we will at once see why the country company had so small a number of mature actors, and conversely why a large company would have difficulty in making expenses in the country. It is probable, therefore, that the Shakespearean company actually lost money during the greater part of the year 1592-93. We must thus take two-fifths of our estimate for average clear profits per annum as the maximum profits possible for the company during this year. This would mean that each sharer could not have cleared more than £45. If we believe their own words, it is doubtful if the sharers cleared anything, since their £225 gain would be cancelled by a deficit of only £32 per month extending over the seven months they were not at the Rose. Since their ordinary monthly expense at a fixed house was upward of twice that amount, it is evident that they had no great margin of gain, and could not long hold together in idleness.

Possibly our best estimate as to the actual time a company usually lost from all causes is furnished by the Admiral's men, for whom we have consecutive daily records at the Rose from June 15, 1594, to shortly after the same date in 1597. In these three years, the company lost six intervals amounting to 261 days.[12] In the three-year period following, between July 19, 1597, and July 13, 1600, the company again missed six intervals amounting to 260 days. Even within the periods when it was acting between June 15, 1594, and July 19, 1597, the company lost all told 166 days, making a total loss of 427 days in three years, or 142 days per annum. Since the company lost the same time in intermissions for the next three years, 1597-1600, its total loss of time must have been almost exactly the same for this period as for the preceding three years. Consequently, 142 days per annum is about the average loss for the six years. This means 223 days to the actual acting year in the nineties for a company settled at a definite theater, instead of the three hundred days of an uninterrupted acting year.

We have fair indication that this was about the average time at the Swan 1610-13. Here we have the records of payment to the poor for a series of years, the total for each year being entered at Easter.[13]

---

[12] Greg, *Diary*, Vol. II, pp. 86, 94. Dr. Greg's statistics, through no fault of his, are not absolutely accurate, though sufficiently so for our present purpose.

[13] Wallace, *Englische Studien*, Vol. XLIII, p. 390, note 1; Chambers, *Eliz. Stage*, Vol. II, p. 413, gives the item for 1621 at £3 19s 4d, quoting P. Norman, *The Accounts of the Overseers of the Poor of Paris Garden*, 1608-71 (1901, *Surrey Arch. Colls.*, Vol. XVI, p. 55).

APPENDIX II

Apr. 5, 1611	4- 6- 8
Apr. 16, 1612	5- 3- 4
Apr. 16, 1613	5- 5- 0
Apr. 25, 1614	3- 0-10
Apr. 20, 1615	0-19- 2
Apr. 9, 1621	5- 3- 6

The amounts make it evident that the money unit of payment was expressed in pence. The only multiple of the amounts as they stand is two; but if the last one be omitted—and for some reason the authorities do not agree on this item,—we have two, five, or ten as the multiples. The time unit then cannot be either the month or the week, since the total sum is too large for that, and hence must be the day. Since accounting in the company which was occupying the Swan most of the time was by the day,[14] this conclusion is confirmed. The rate must be higher than 2d per diem, since that amount would not give the total; and less than 10d, since that amount would give too much. Thus we have 5d per diem as the probable rate. This would mean between Easter 1610 and Easter 1611 there were 208 days of acting; 1611-12, 248 days; 1612-13, 252 days; 1613-14, 146 days; 1614-15, 46 days; 1620-21, 248 (or 190) days. For the year 1613-14 we have a check on the time of acting in the fact that the company transferred to the Hope in the autumn, the contract calling for a completed building by November 30, 1613. Since the company acted at the Swan 146 days, or at least 24 weeks and two days, from Easter 1613, it went to the Hope not earlier than September 22, 1613, but probably a few weeks later. In the three full years at the Swan, there was acting 208, 248, and 252 days, an average of about 236 days per annum. If we had the average over as many years as we have at the Rose, it would probably be almost exactly the same. Thus the actual average acting year was about three-fourths of the uninterrupted year. On this basis, the Shakespearean company would have averaged about £945 per annum at the Rose, clearing £245, or £50 for each of the five members, in an average year.

We have no direct evidence as to the returns to the Shakespearean company at the Cross Keys, Theater, and Curtain 1594-99; but we have fair indication of the returns from the latter two theaters, 1586-92; and may be fairly certain that they were not greatly different in the later period.

We have several fairly definite statements that enable us to check returns at the Theater. The most authoritative is by Henry Lanman, who from September 29 (Michaelmas), 1585, to the

[14] Murray, Vol. I, p. 246.

same date in 1592, received half the combined profits of the Theater and Curtain, James Burbage and John Braynes receiving the other half. Certainly then Lanman knew exactly the profits arising. He says that Burbage received the full half of the profits from the two theaters after the death of John Braynes, August 1586, and that he "hath receyved & had for his parte of the proffittes of the said ij° playe howses one yere w^t another to this daye the some of one hundreth markes or fourscore poundes by the yere."[15] This estimate is reasonably confirmed by two others, both hostile to Burbage, and thus presumably not understating the case. The first of these is by John Alleyn, and is also expert, since he was financial manager for his company of actors at the Theater, and hence knew accurately the exact returns to the owners. For the five-year period ending either November 1590, when he left the Theater, or February 6, 1592, when he bears witness, exactly or approximately the same period Lanman covers, he estimates that James Burbage received "an hundreth poundes or CC markes by yere for his own share." His estimate is a gross estimate, not only for the theater but also for "other the premisses to the same belonging."[16] The rent received from the other buildings was a considerable item, a converted barn alone returning £11 per annum.[17] Also, if Lanman's estimate is a net one, as under the conditions it would likely have been, we must remember Burbage's annual rent of £14, and annual repairs. These items, together with the preceding, would cause a difference of at least £30 between a net estimate for the Theater alone as was Lanman's, and a gross estimate for the whole property as was Alleyn's. Thus these two estimates are consistent and supplementary. There is still a third estimate to confirm these two. Ralph Miles, who was trying to make the strongest possible case against Burbage, claimed February 10, 1592, that since the death of Braynes in August 1586, the said Burbage had received from the property £700 or £800, half of which belonged to the widow Braynes.[18] Miles admits that his evidence is based on hearsay, and not on direct knowledge. His estimate is thus a gross amount of £125 to £145 per annum, probably exaggerated from Alleyn's estimate of £100 to 200 marks. But Robert Miles, father of Ralph and much more prejudiced against Burbage, claimed July 30, 1592, that the Burbages had received at least 2000 marks in eight or nine years, £145 to £165 per annum, and that the Braynes faction should have received as much.[19] Some eight years later, however, October

[15] Wallace, *First London Theatre*, pp. 149, 150.
[16] *ibid.*, p. 102.
[17] *ibid.*, p. 13.
[18] *ibid.*, p. 106.
[19] *ibid.*, p. 147.

1, 1600, he estimates the total gain to the Burbages as only 1000 marks, an estimate in which his son Ralph also concurs.[20] Probably therefore Robert Miles meant to say in his first estimate that the Burbages had received 2000 marks, half of which belonged to Mrs. Braynes. His estimate for the Burbages would then be £75 to £85 per annum, and would harmonize quite well with those of Lanman and Alleyn. Our evidence then gives the total net profit to the Burbages as roughly £67 to £80 per annum, and the total gross profit from all sources as roughly £100 to £130. Gross profits from the theaters alone may be estimated, by adding rent and repairs to the net profit, as £75 to £100. It is fairly clear that the estimate is of the fourth of the owners' half which actually belonged to the Burbages, and not of the half that the Burbages actually received after the death of Braynes. If the estimate is of the eighth of total gallery receipts which legally belonged to the Burbages, the combined returns from the galleries of the two theaters were £600 to £800.

It is thus fairly apparent that the galleries of the Theater and Curtain returned about the same amount as those of the Rose, where in an average year the returns were about £750. We have no check on door receipts, but may feel fairly safe in estimating them as not greatly different. That these early theaters had a total return about as great as at the Rose is indicated by the statement in 1585 of Samuel Kiechel, an observant German merchant, that "the players take from fifty to sixty dollars, [£10 to £12,] at a time, particularly if they act anything new, when people have to pay double."[21] Since the average total return at the Rose was around £5 for a play, double rates would give the sum indicated by Kiechel. The same authority indicates that the actors "perform nearly every day in the week; notwithstanding plays are forbidden on Friday and Saturday, this prohibition is not observed."[22] Stockwood's sermon of 1578 indicates that the average receipt at that date had been about the same. He claims to know of eight playing places, and says that if each played but once a week returns would be £2000 per annum, an average of nearly £5 each performance.[23] It appears then that total returns at the Curtain and Theater were much the same as at the Rose. At the Rose, the net income for actors was not over £300 per annum in an uninterrupted year,[24] £225 in an average year. Thus each member of the Shakespearean company at the Theater and Curtain 1596-99, probably cleared not more than £33

[20] Wallace, *First London Theatre*, pp. 263, 266.
[21] Rye, W. B., *England as seen by Foreigners*, p. 88.
[22] *ibid.*
[23] Collier, *Annals* (1879), Vol. I, p. 328, note 1.
[24] Wallace, London *Times*, October 2 and 4, 1909.

per annum if the number of members was seven, not over £26 if the number was nine, as seems to have been true.

Most of the remaining evidence concerning the profits to actors and housekeepers in the Shakespearean company comes from law-suits in which it was to the advantage of somebody to overstate. Hence the evidence requires very careful sifting. These lawsuits are three in number: (1) Thomasina Ostler sued John Heminges 1615-16 for her husband's shares in Blackfriars and the Globe, and the accrued profits on them for a year;[25] (2) John Witter sued John Heminges for a share in the Globe, 1619-20;[26] (3) Robert Benfield, Eyllaerdt Swanston, and Thomas Pollard petitioned the Lord Chamberlain in 1635 for admission to the housekeepers both at the Globe and at Blackfriars.[27] Neither Thomasina Ostler nor John Witter was in position to know very much of the financial side of the company's affairs. We haven't the answer to Thomasina Ostler, and the answer to Witter is concerned chiefly with the legal divisions and transfers of shares, but not with their financial value. These two lawsuits then furnish but little information concerning the value of shares, and very little of that information can be accepted as authentic evidence. But the third disagreement centers around the relative value of actors' and housekeepers' shares. We had best therefore take this suit as a point of departure, and make use of information from the earlier lawsuits as supporting evidence.

Probably the best way to get the evidence is simply to review the case in so far as it applies to values of shares. It is important to bear in mind the order of the documents. The case follows the ordinary legal procedure of complaint, answer, and replication.[28] The Chamberlain is referring to this procedure when he says he has "considered this petition and the severall answeres and replyes of the parties."[29] Between May 18, and July 12, 1635, Benfield, Swanston, and Pollard make their petition, which involves John Shank, Cuthbert Burbadge, and Winifred Burbadge Robinson. Shank makes his answer alone; but Burbadge, Mrs. Robinson, and her son William, for sentimental effect, answer together. The petitioners then reply to all, after which the Chamberlain gives decision July 12, 1635, in favor of the petitioners.[30] The petitioners quote

25 Wallace, London *Times*, Oct. 2 and 4, 1909.
26 Wallace, *Associates*, pp. 48-76.
27 Halliwell, *Outlines*, Vol. I, pp. 312-19.
28 "The parties plaintiffe & defendant . . . proceed . . . by plaint or declaration, [barre or] answer, replication, reioinder, and so [by rebut, surrebut] to issue [and triall . . .]" (*Harrison's Description of England* (New Shak. Soc.), Part I, p. 202).
29 Halliwell, *Outlines*, Vol. I, p. 313.
30 Fleay, *Stage*, p. 324-5, gives the correct order for the documents except the further petition or replication of the actors, which he places immediately after the petition.

documentary evidence, or offer to produce it in each case; the .defendants do so in only a few instances. The petitioners were in position to know the details of financial arrangements for the whole company, since Swanston, one of their number, was associated with Lowin and Taylor in nearly all surviving purely business transactions of the company after the death of Heminges in 1630. Neither of the defendants was in position to know very much more about the financial affairs of the company than that which concerned him personally. Keeping these things in mind, we may proceed to weigh the evidence.

As to the basis for division of proceeds between the housekeepers and actors, the petitioners tell us: "That those few interested in the houses have, without any defalcation or abatement at all, a full moyety of the whole gaines ariseing therby, excepting the outer dores, and such of the sayd housekeepers as bee actors doe likewise equally share with all the rest of the actors both in th' other moiety and in the sayd outer dores also."[31] They more specifically represent in their reply that the housekeepers "have amongst them the full moyety of all the galleries and boxes in both houses, and of the tireing-house dore at the Globe.—That the actors have the other moyety, with the outer dores."[32] Cuthbert[33] Burbadge admits this arrangement; but shows how much better actors are now faring than in his father's time. He says, "The players that lived in those first times had onely the profitts arising from the dores, but now the players receave all the commings in at the dores to themselves and halfe the galleries from the houskepers."[34] Since, then, both parties admit the basis of division in 1635, we may consider it authentic. Restated, the housekeepers received half of all receipts from the two playhouses as such, except the admission fees at the outer doors; the actors received all admission fees at the outer doors and the remaining half of all other receipts connected with the theaters as such. The housekeepers bore all the expense of keeping the house itself in condition; the actors bore all the expense connected directly with acting. This had been the general basis of division at all public theaters from the beginning.

After this general statement of basis for division, the petitioners show that the housekeeping shares rest in the hands of a very few, the majority of whom are not actors nor His Majesty's servants, to the resulting disadvantage of the actors. The petitioners then out-

---

[31] Halliwell, *Outlines*, Vol. I, p. 312.
[32] *ibid.*, p. 313.
[33] I have regularly referred to Cuthbert Burbadge alone as the author of this answer, since the facts given are evidently from his experience, and not from that of Winifred or William.
[34] Halliwell, *Outlines*, Vol. I, p. 317.

line what they consider a fair readjustment. The Burbadges and Shank contend in their answers that the householders have heavy expenses and liabilities, with resultant small and uncertain profits, and that the petitioners are already receiving a fair wage. To establish the latter contention, Cuthbert Burbadge states, "it appeareth by their owne accomptes for one whole yeere last past, beginning from Whitson Munday, 1634, to Whitson Munday, 1635, each of these complainantes gained severally, as hee was a player and noe howskeeper, 180 *li*."[35] Shank mentions the same sum, but does not quote his source of knowledge.[36] Since Shank was himself an actor, he ought to know the definite amount of an actor's share. Burbadge probably secured his information from Shank, as in trying to prove that the petitioners are already receiving a fair wage, both make exactly the same points. Since the defendants quote documentary evidence which was readily accessible to all, and would of necessity be known to one or all, and since the petitioners enter no denial, we may again accept as certain that the share of each actor as such from Whitsun Monday 1634 to Whitsun Monday 1635—May 26, 1634, to May 18, 1635—was £180.

But the statement does not tell us whether this amount is gross or net. The petitioners do. Their reply is not categorical but general. After reciting again the basis of division between housekeepers and actors, they inform us that "out of those lesser shares the sayd actors defray all charges of the house whatsoever, vizt., wages to hired men and boyes, musicke, lightes, &c., amounting to 900 or 1000 *li*. per annum or theraboutes, beeing 3 *li*. a day one day with another; besides the extraordinary charge which the sayd actors are wholly at for apparell and poetes, &c."[37] In the agreement with Herbert May 25, 1628, concerning benefit plays, the daily expense was estimated at £2 5s 0d.[38] When one remembers that the company had twenty-one ordinary hired men in December 1624,[39] not including the apprentices, nor several of their best hired actors, the estimate seems fair enough. Allowing for the growth of the company during this period, we may consider that the estimate of the petitioners is fairly accurate but probably a maximum. Having deducted necessary expenses for both housekeepers and actors, the petitioners say: "Soe that upon a medium

[35] Halliwell, *Outlines*, Vol. I, p. 317.
[36] *ibid*., p. 314.
[37] *ibid*., p. 313. The actors at Salisbury Court had but a slightly better division 1637-38, but seem also to have forced much better terms in 1639. For a detailed summary of this adjustment, including an enumeration of nearly all items for which expense was incurred, see above, pp. 43 *ff*.
[38] Fleay, *Stage*, p. 333.
[39] Adams, *Herbert*, pp. 74-5.

APPENDIX II

made of the gaynes of the howskeepers and those of the actors one day with another throughout the yeere, the petitioners will make it apparent that when some of the housekepers share 12*s*. a day at the Globe, the actors share not above 3*s*."[40] At 3s per day, using their own estimate just given, each actor would have a net receipt of 900 or 1000 s; £45 or £50 per annum. This estimate, however, applies only to the Globe, where they acted but half the year.[41] Consequently, it must be cut in half for the receipts at that house, which means that each actor received a net income of £22 10s to £25 for his season at the Globe.

The second main point made by the defendants is that in view of the uncertain income, the expenses of the housekeepers are very high. Shank is the chief exponent of this idea, the Burbadges relying more upon the sentiment to be created by a recital of their past services. Shank says: "That your suppliant and other the lessees in the Globe and in the Blackfriers are chargeable with the payment of 100 *li*. yeerly rent, besides reparacions, which is dayly very chargeable unto them, all which they must pay and beare, whether

[40] Halliwell, *Outlines*, Vol. I, p. 313.
[41] The division of time is only approximate. Malone tells us on the authority of Herbert (*Variorum*, Vol. III, pp. 70-1; Adams *Herbert*, p. 67) that the Globe was usually opened in May each year. In the year 1610, the company was at the Globe by April 20, as we know from Forman, and a little later from Wurmsser (Halliwell, *Outlines*, Vol. II, p. 85-6); but this may have been unusually early, since the company was opening after the plague, and would prefer to open early at its summer theater rather than go to the trouble of making a transfer. Forman saw *The Winter's Tale* at the Globe May 15, 1611 (Halliwell, *Outlines*, Vol. II, p. 85). Sir Humphrey Mildmay went to the Globe May 16, 1633 (Collier, *Annals* (1879), Vol. I, p. 482). On the other hand, we have record of private performances at Blackfriars before the Queen, May 13, 1634; May 5, 1636; and April 23, 1638 (Adams, *Playhouses*, p. 232). Apparently then the Globe might be opened shortly after the middle of April and was regularly opened before the middle of May.

We have no direct statement of when the company ordinarily transferred to Blackfriars, but just as the bulk of its plays for the Globe season were licensed in May and June, so for the Blackfriars season they were licensed in October and November (Baldwin, *Duke of Milan*, p. 6; Herbert's Office Book). The two earliest records of licence specifically said to be for Blackfriars are dated October 24, and November 24 (Adams, *Herbert*, pp. 24, 32). Hunsdon had asked October 8, 1594, that the Shakespearean company might open at the Cross Keys for the winter season (Murray, Vol. I, p. 93), but in this case the opening was after a disturbed season, and may not have been at the regular time. The Council had asked the winter privilege for the Queen's men November 26, 1583, and about the same time in 1584 (Chambers, *Eliz. Stage*, Vol. IV, pp. 295, 298-9). We may thus accept Professor Adams's statement that "the evidence points to the first of November" as the time of opening Blackfriars (Adams, *Playhouses*, p. 225). It appears then that the Shakespearean company acted approximately half the year in each house.

they make any proffitt or nott."[42] The petitioners reply that "the sayd houskeepers out of all their gaines have not till our Lady Day last [March 25, 1635] payd above 65 *li.* per annum rent for both houses, towardes which they rayse between 20 and 30 *li.* per annum from the tap-howses and a tenement and a garden belonging to the premisses, &c., and are at noe other charges whatsoever, excepting the ordinary reparations of the houses."[43] There is thus a seeming disagreement about the amount of rent, an agreement that any further expense to the housekeepers came solely from the need of repairs to the buildings, but a disagreement as to whether these repairs cost much or little. In the case of repairs, no definite evidence is adduced by either side; but common sense would indicate that the expense for this item could hardly have been great. Henslowe seems to have spent about £125 for repairs at the Rose 1587-1603. Henry Evans paid a bill of £11 2d December 8, 1603, for repairs to Blackfriars, probably from April 20, 1602.[44] Cost of repairs could hardly average above £10 per annum. We have definite evidence, however, with regard to the rent paid, which shows that both were probably right, the petitioners certainly so. Under the original lease, which held good till 1629, and under its extension to 1644, as also under the pretended lease from Bodley to 1635, the rent at the Globe was £14 10s. This was certainly the amount till the confirmation of the new lease, dated March 25, 1635. The rent of Blackfriars was £40 till the expiration of the first lease June 24, 1629. Until 1629 then the rent at the two theaters had been £54 10s per annum. We have seen that the rent at Blackfriars was increased to £50 by the new lease. The total rent then yearly from 1629 to 1635 was £64 10s, or less than £65 as the petitioners claim. Shank is probably quoting the terms of the new lease, dated March 25, 1635, and it is probably for that reason that the petitioners limit their statement by that date. If so, the new lease called for £50 rent yearly as at Blackfriars. This is made more probable by the fact that Brend was trying to abrogate the old lease to secure a more profitable one. The result was probably a compromise, giving the company the term claimed, but giving Brend the building, and in consequence increasing the rent from £14 10s to £50 per annum, the same rent as at Blackfriars.

The statement of the petitioners concerning the receipts from sub-renting parts of the property is confirmed in part by Witter's offer in 1619 to take the rents from these sub-rented parts, pay Brend's total rent of £14 10s, and take the remainder in lieu of the profit on a share in the Globe. Since he also offers to pay all

[42] Halliwell, *Outlines*, Vol. I, p. 316.
[43] *ibid.*, p. 313.
[44] Wallace, *Children*, p. 89, note 7.

Brend's rent if the Globe housekeepers will give him a share, he evidently considers these sub-rents equal in value to a share in the Globe, which he himself estimates at £30 to £40 per annum.

One other regular item of expense, possibly two, are not specifically enumerated in these contentions by either side. At the Rose, Fortune, and Hope the owners of the building bore the expense of collecting gallery receipts, this being the logical outgrowth of the method of collecting. Cundall's bequest in his will to Elizabeth Wheaton of a "place or priviledge" in both the Globe and Blackfriars doubtless indicates that there were gatherers at both theaters.[45] Probably, therefore, the owners were at some £20 to £25 expense per annum for this item. Possibly because of its relatively small amount, this item does not receive specific mention. Another usual item of expense was licence from the Master of the Revels for the building. Previous to the closing of the theaters, Herbert had received a share from each of the four companies, excluding the Shakespearean, each share being estimated by Herbert at £100 per annum.[46] The share at Salisbury Court had in 1631 amounted to about £100 per annum,[47] but the share at the Cockpit seems to have been only £60. We have no check on the Bull or Fortune, but the two fairly certain cases indicate that Herbert in his estimate simply took his best returns as his average return from each. This is still more clearly indicated by Herbert's fee from the Shakespearean company. In 1662 he claims £100 from this company also, £50 from each of two benefits. But from Herbert's own account book we know that he at first received less than £10 a play on the average, and finally compounded for £10 each benefit, or £20 per annum.[48] It seems certain then that Herbert received only this £20 per annum, in the paying of which the whole company joined, and which consequently would not be mentioned in their contentions. It also seems certain that Herbert had put all companies on a share basis as a means of extracting greater pay. However, he had attempted to extract the fixed sum of £4 per week from each company in 1660,[49] and Tilney had extracted a fixed fee at the Rose amounting to £3 per month as early as 1599.[50] Buc seems to have secured £100 at the Hope 1614-15. Since the pay of the masters depended almost entirely on fees set by themselves, they of course took all they could get. A helpless company or theater-owner needing considerable countenance from the master would be unmercifully plucked, while one in less subservient circumstances would

[45] Collier, *Memoirs*, p. 148.
[46] Adams, *Herbert*, pp. 45, 101.
[47] See below, p. 348.
[48] Adams, *Herbert*, pp. 43-4.
[49] *ibid.*, p. 121.
[50] Greg, *Diary*, Vol. II, p. 118.

fare better. It appears then that no special deductions should be made for gathering or for licence of the theaters, neither of which items is mentioned by either side to the contention.

Now that the sources of income and expense are accurately apportioned and roughly estimated by the facts just given, we may proceed to calculate the receipts and expenses of the company from all sources during the year 1634-35. We have pretty good evidence for the average total income of the company for several years just preceding this period. The Shakespearean company agreed before May 25, 1628, to give Herbert the benefit of two days in the year, one in summer and one in winter, of the second day of a revived play, daily expenses of £2 5s to be deducted. Under this arrangement, the company regularly turned over the proceeds, which Herbert records, till June 1633, a period of more than five years. During this time, there were ten performances, the most profitable of which netted Herbert £17 10s at Blackfriars, the least profitable £1 5s at the Globe. Herbert's average net profit was £8 19s 4d, the average gross receipt being thus £11 4s 4d.[51] Herbert records October 30, 1633,[52] that he had agreed to accept £10 at Midsummer and at Christmas instead of these benefits. We have then an authentic daily average, extending over a period of five and one-half years, including both houses, and ending in the latter part of 1633, about six months before the year under discussion began. This daily average is in a way confirmed by the reward at court, which was regularly £6 13s 4d, but twice the amount if the actors missed their day at the theater. A gratuity was also given if the King was present, but this was of his pure bounty. Thus the actors' day was valued at £13 6s 4d, an amount that is supposed to represent a royal reward. The actual daily average as given by Herbert was £11 4s 4d. In the 1635 estimates, as we have seen, the actors use three hundred days as the acting year. Since this year 1634-35 was seemingly an uninterrupted acting year, we may be reasonably sure that three hundred was the approximate number of performances. This would give an average yearly income of £3,365. Of this, the actors received 12 × £180 = £2,160. Subtracting £2,160 from £3,365 gives the receipts of the housekeepers as £1,205 for the year 1634-35. Again £2,160 — 1,205 = £955, the receipts at the doors. The receipts from the galleries were £3,365 — £955 = £2,410. This makes the galleries return £2,410, while the doors return £955, or somewhat more than one-third as much.

We can check these conclusions by certain estimates given for the value of housekeeping and acting shares at the Globe. To begin with, Herbert's receipts again give us a fair check on the ratio

---

[51] Malone, *Variorum*, Vol. III, pp. 176-7; Adams, *Herbert*, pp. 43-4.
[52] Fleay, *Stage*, p. 337.

between receipts at the Globe and those at Blackfriars. For the five performances at the Globe, he received an average of £4 8s 8d. This, plus £2 5s for expenses, gives us a daily average of £6 13s 8d at the Globe. For the five performances at Blackfriars, he received an average of £13 10s. This, plus £2 5s for expenses, gives us a daily average of £15 5s at Blackfriars. Therefore, if the same number of performances was given in each house—and all indications are that such was approximately the case—the gross returns from Blackfriars would be more than twice as great as at the Globe.

Further, we know the approximate gross value of a housekeeping share in Blackfriars for 1634-35. Burbadge tells us that Swanston received "above 30 *li*." in the year 1634-35 from Blackfriars,[53] where he was a housekeeper. Shank says that Swanston "receaved this last yeere above 34 *li*. for the profitt of a third part of one part in the Blackfriers."[54] To begin with, Swanston was not legally a housekeeper in either of the houses at this time, and was suing for that very privilege at Blackfriars in exactly the amount specified; but we may suppose some makeshift arrangement by which he received the profits from one-third of a share at Blackfriars for the year 1634-35. Whatever the arrangement, it does not affect the truth of the statement concerning the returns from a share in Blackfriars for that year. Both Burbadge and Shank, as housekeepers, should know these returns accurately. Burbadge would place the value of a full share above £90; Shank says it was about £102. Since they gave gross amounts for the receipts of the actors, the presumption is that they are doing the same in this case. Probably Burbadge gives the approximate net returns, and Shank the gross. These estimates mean that the total returns on the eight shares in Blackfriars were £720 to £816 for the year 1634-35. Taking Shank's estimate as the more definite and probable gross one and dividing by two, the approximate ratio of returns between Blackfriars and the Globe, we get £408 as the returns to the housekeepers for the latter place. Adding the £816 from Blackfriars and the £408 from the Globe, we get £1,224 for the gross returns of the housekeepers in the two theaters for the year 1634-35, which checks accurately enough with the £1,205 we obtained previously as the estimate based on the total average returns, minus the known receipts of the actors. We may be certain then that the gross receipts for the actors were £2,160, and that those for the housekeepers were about £1,205, a total of about £3,365.

These figures cannot include the £250 that the actors received

[53] Halliwell, *Outlines*, Vol. I, p. 317.
[54] *ibid.*, p. 314.

May 24, 1635, for twenty performances at court during the year.[55] This is shown by the second of our independent estimates previously given, which balances accurately enough with the first if the rewards at court be omitted from the latter, but will not balance with it at all if they be included. Since the second estimate is based on the returns to housekeepers, and consequently is independent of the rewards at court, the first estimate must also omit such rewards. This conclusion is also clear from the dates given. The accounts were from Whitsun Monday 1634 to the same day 1635—May 26, 1634, to May 18, 1635. Since the rewards at court were paid April 27, 1634, and May 24, 1635, neither would be included in this year.[56] We do not know definitely, however, if these receipts include sub-rents to the housekeepers. If these sub-rents, amounting to £20 or £30 according to the petitioners,[57] are included in the receipts of the housekeepers, the total returns from the galleries may be as much as £60 less than the estimated £2,410, which would be £2,350. The minimum receipts possible for outer doors would be £2,160 — £1,205 = £955. The maximum would be £2,160 — £1,175 = £985. The doors at both houses thus returned about two-fifths as much as the galleries, one ratio being slightly above, the other slightly below that proportion. Later figures will enable us to see what the approximate ratio was in each house.

If the housekeepers received a total of £391 11s 3d, as previously estimated, for their part of the Globe, the share of each amounted to only £24 9s 5d. We have another estimate of a housekeeper's share at the Globe during this year. The petitioners say: "when some of the houskepers share 12 s. a day at the Globe, the actors share not above 3 s."[58] Since it was the purpose of the petitioners to make the contrast as strong as possible, they imply that they have selected the "some" with the most shares. We may be sure they have done so, because these "some" were the defendants. They tell us that Cuthbert Burbadge and Mrs. Robinson have three and one-half shares each, and that Shank has three. Using the actors' three-hundred-day year, and multiplying by twelve shillings, the receipts of "some" of the housekeepers each day, we get £180 for a year;

---

[55] Stopes, *Jahrbuch*, Vol. XLVI, p. 98.
[56] The fact that the warrant for 1635, as given by both Collier and Stopes, dates Sunday, May 24, does not indicate error, since the Privy Council regularly sat on Sunday afternoons, this being one of the things it was expected parliament in 1640 would remedy (See Winwood, *Memorials*, Vol. II, p. 46; Cheyney, *History*, Vol. I, p. 67; Acts of the Privy Council; and Thompson, E. N. S., *The Controversy between the Puritans and the Stage*, p. 183).
[57] Halliwell, *Outlines*, Vol. I, p. 313.
[58] *ibid.*

but this must be divided by two, since acting at the Globe covered but half a year, giving us £90 as the receipts of "some." Dividing this by three and one-half, the number of shares held by each of these two highest housekeepers, we get £25 14s 3d as the share of a housekeeper at the Globe, which is but slightly over a pound more than our previous estimate, and so confirms and checks it. We do not know whether either of these is a gross or a net estimate; but the amount cannot be affected much either way, since if it is net, the rent on each share was less than a pound, even this expense being almost entirely offset by sub-rents, while repairs could not have amounted to much. The two estimates show that the net share could hardly be under £22 nor the gross over £27 for the year. Therefore a housekeeping share in the Globe was worth roughly about one-fourth as much as one at Blackfriars.

This same estimate gives us a clue to the amount received by the actors at the Globe. They received 3s per diem each, which would be £22 10s for an actor in half of a three-hundred-day year. As we have seen, the connection shows that this is almost certainly a net estimate, the expenses of actors cutting their gross gains just about half. Since the gross receipt to each actor from both theaters was £180, this would give each in 1634-35 a net receipt of about £90. The actors' own estimate would give to each £22 10s of this from the Globe, thus leaving £67 10s for his net proceeds at Blackfriars. Thus the actors received approximately three times as much at Blackfriars as at the Globe, an estimate that agrees well enough with the housekeepers' four times as much, when we consider that the more fashionable and wealthy audience at Blackfriars would expect to pay more for the mere physical conveniences of the house. They would pay not merely to see the play, but also to be comfortable as they saw the play.

From these estimates, we can get a fair guess as to the comparative returns from doors and galleries in the two houses. The housekeepers at the Globe received approximately £25 × 16 = £400; those at Blackfriars £816. The actors at the Globe received £22 10s × 12 + £525 for a half-year's expenses = £795. Total receipts were £400 + £795 = £1,195. Since the receipts from the galleries were £400 × 2 = £800, the receipts at the door were £1,195 — £800 = £395. The receipts at the outer door for the Globe were thus about one-half of those from the galleries. Since the total receipts at the Globe were £1,195, the total receipts at Blackfriars would be £3,365 — £1,195 = £2,170. Also, £2,170 — 2 × £816 = £538, the total receipts at the outer door of Blackfriars. At Blackfriars then, the receipts at the door were about one-third those of the galleries. The ratio at Blackfriars, 1/3, + the ratio at the Globe, 1/2, ÷ 2 = 5/12, the average ratio at both houses, which is but 1/60 greater than our previously deduced approximate ratio of 2/5. It is evident therefore that our results check with a sufficient degree of accuracy for our method of approximation. Since a connected summary of these results is given in the text, it will not be repeated here.[59]

To check against this estimate of receipts for the Shakespearean company, we have some indication of returns to another company at this period. We have seen how the Shakespearean company had given Sir Henry Herbert a benefit performance at the Globe and one at Blackfriars, "for his good will," or any other euphemistic term we care to use. The Salisbury Court theater ransomed itself by giving Herbert a ninth share as a housekeeper. He records his receipts on this ninth share for six performances of *Holland's Leaguer* in December 1631, as £1 19s.[60] This would be 6s 6d for each performance. Since there were nine shares, the return for half the galleries would be 9 × 6s 6d = £2 18s 6d[61] on each performance, or £877 10s for an uninterrupted, three-hundred-day year, an annual return of £97 10s for Herbert, an amount that he remembered at the Restoration as an even £100. Very good "business" for Herbert. Incidentally, this was seemingly Herbert's best paying place, and he conveniently remembered the same sum for other places, though he actually received only £60 per annum at the Cockpit, and £20 for the Globe and Blackfriars. It is evident that the rate of gallery receipts at Salisbury Court in 1631 was not very different from the rate at the Globe in 1634, since half the galleries at Salisbury Court should have returned £877 for the whole year, while the whole galleries at the Globe probably returned about £800 for half the year. Since there was the same number of actors at the time in the company at Salisbury Court (Prince Charles's company, the lineal descendant of the Admiral's men) as in the Shakespearean company, we may get a very rough guess at returns to individual members of the company by doubling the half-year returns at the Globe, which would give £45. Thus the indication of returns at Salisbury Court checks and confirms our estimates for the Shakespearean company. Perhaps we may also get a little complacent comfort out of the fact that, thanks in part to Blackfriars, the Shakespearean company had now outdistanced in the race of money-getting its old friend and rival, the Admiral's company.

These figures for the Shakespearean company enable us to check

---

[59] See above, Chapter VI.

[60] Adams, *Playhouses*, pp. 375-6; Malone, *Variorum*, Vol. III, p. 178, note.

[61] To this almost certainly should be added the gatherers' fee, which in recorded instances was one-eighteenth to one-twenty-fifth of the whole galleries, which would be two-seventeenths to one-twelfth of the half galleries.

a number of statements concerning values in the company. For one thing, it becomes evident that the report of the special committee, dated November 20, 1633, is not so exaggerated after all.[62] The first item is for rent at £50 per annum, which, as we have already seen, was the sum being paid at the time. For all rent items, the committee allows "14 years' purchase, as an indifferent recompense to the said Burbidges"; it is allowed as recompense, and not because the Burbadges had leased the property that long.[63] The next item is £75 per annum rent for four adjoining tenements, and £6 for a void piece of ground to turn coaches in, again at fourteen years' purchase. We have no check on this item; but Henslowe's rents[64] show that the amount is quite reasonable, and the committee could readily have ascertained the facts. This leaves the claim of each sharer, both among the housekeepers and actors, sixteen in all, for £150 each, though the committee thought they would accept 100 marks each or £66 13s 4d. The lower figure would be only the net receipt of an actor there for one uninterrupted season, and considerably less than that of a housekeeper for the same time. The upper figure would hardly cover two seasons. It is evident then that Blackfriars was the goose that laid the golden egg, and that the company consequently had great respect for her neck.

Seemingly Blackfriars had proved a profitable house from the beginning of occupancy by the Shakespearean company. On this point we have the testimony of two experts, who had themselves been long connected with the house, and should have known what they were talking about; but since both are claiming damages, we may regard their estimates as probably maxima. Edward Kirkham claimed in November 1612 that he and his partners had received a net sum of £150 per annum from Keysar and the children when the latter were masters in the theater (1605-08).[65] The expression means that Keysar and the children simply rented the building from the owners, and would consequently follow the regular custom of paying half the receipts of the galleries for the building. Now Kirkham and his partners controlled half the building,[66] bearing half expenses and receiving half profits. The annual returns from the owners' half of the galleries would thus be 2 × £150 + £40 + repairs = £340, + annual repairs. Kirkham again estimates in another suit July 1612, that the half belonging to himself and his two partners would have returned for the four

---

[62] Collier, *Annals* (1879), Vol. I, p. 478.

[63] This was the usual business custom of the time (Lodge, *Illustrations*, Vol. II, p. 454, and note; Birch, *James First*, Vol. II, pp. 213-14, 222).

[64] Greg, *Diary*, Vol. I, pp. 208-11.

[65] Fleay, *Stage*, p. 249.

[66] *ibid.*, pp. 211-12.

years 1608-12, £160 per annum besides the rent.[67] This estimates total returns from half the galleries as 2 × £160 + £40 = £360. In still another suit, June 1612, he estimated that he had lost £60 per annum for four years on a sixth part in the building. He is thus again representing the returns for the owners' half galleries as £360. It is apparent therefore that in three instances Kirkham, whose connection began ten years before, estimates the total returns to the housekeepers as £340 to £360 per annum, such profits being evidently the returns of half the galleries. We have seen that the returns from the whole galleries in 1634-35 were three times those from the door. Since seemingly the prices of admission had long been the same, we may assume that the same ratio held in 1612. This would give an annual return of £906 12s 4d to £960 per annum. That this was about the annual return we find from two other statements. Keysar claims February 8, 1610, that the Shakespearean company had gained at least £1500 at Blackfriars since taking it over in August, or September, 1608.[68] Since this is about a year and a half, he is estimating yearly receipts as about £1000. Then Kirkham claims in November 1612 that the Shakespearean company "gott & as yet dothe, more in one Winter in the said great Hall by a thousand powndes then they were vsed to gett in the Banckside."[69] Since the winter represents the acting year for the Shakespearean company at Blackfriars, this is Kirkham's very loose way of stating that the returns from Blackfriars are about £1000 per annum. Since both these men, especially Kirkham, had been long associated with this theater, and since both concur in their estimates of returns, we must accept their statements as approximately correct, especially since these statements are not at all unreasonable. Briefly, they say that the returns for a year at Blackfriars, 1608-12, should be about £1000, since this is the amount that had been earned regularly just before 1608. The returns to housekeepers they estimate at £320 clear. Since at Blackfriars the half galleries were about equal to door receipts, the actors should receive about £640 per annum. It follows also that each of the seven housekeepers would clear in a regular season, 1608-12, about £45 14s 3d per annum. We may better estimate the amount for each of the actors when we have examined returns at the Globe.

We have pretty good evidence that the returns from the Globe

[67] Fleay, *Stage*, p. 225. Kirkham seems to speak of the whole rent, but he may mean only the half for which he and his partners were responsible. In the latter case, the estimate would be reduced to £340.

[68] Wallace, *Associates*, p. 83. Since Keysar is suing for damages, it is of course immaterial to him that the building had been closed practically the whole time by the plague, and that he was now moved to sue because of prospects of reopening.

[69] Fleay, *Stage*, p. 248.

were probably much the same about this period of 1608-12 as in 1634-35. Witter claimed in 1619 that he had regularly received before the burning of the Globe a net profit of £30 to £40 per annum on his seventh share of the actors' half of the galleries.[70] He confirms this estimate by making the sub-rents, which the actors say in 1635 amount to £30 or £40 per annum, equal to the returns of a share. If Witter is accurate, his statement must be for the year 1612-13, since the actors' half was divided into sevenths by the admission of Ostler February 21, 1612, and the Globe was burned June 29, 1613. I suspect, however, from the qualifying "regularly" that Witter is speaking of sixth shares, which had obtained during most of his connection with the company. If he refers to sevenths, the housekeepers for 1612-13 received £420 to £560 + £14 10s rent, and charges for repairs, a rough estimate of £450 to £590. It is more probable, however, that he is referring to sixths, in which case the housekeepers received regularly 1608-12, £360 to £480 + £14 10s rent + charges for repairs, a rough estimate of £390 to £510. Either estimate would, because of the point Witter was trying to make, probably be a maximum. We get thus an estimate of either about £390 or about £590, probably the former, as the maximum receipts for housekeepers at the first Globe 1608-13. The receipts for housekeepers at the Globe for the uninterrupted year 1634-35 were about £400. The receipts then at the first Globe were probably about the same as at the second.

We have also seen that the returns at the second Globe about 1634, for an average interrupted year were around £900, of which £600 came from the galleries, and £300 from the doors. Thus the actors received 1608-12, probably about £600 per annum at the Globe, and £640 at Blackfriars, a total of £1240. Incidentally, this estimate receives some confirmation from the fact that the annual returns to the actors at the Fortune about this time were estimated as £1100 to £1200. The annual expense of the company in the latter part of the sixteenth century was probably £700, but had increased to over £1000 by 1634. We may estimate it as some £800 in the period under consideration. This would leave the actors a net gain of £440 per annum, or about £35 each. We have seen that at this period the housekeepers are supposed to have received about £45 14s 3d each at Blackfriars. At the Globe, they would receive £300, from which must be taken rent and repairs, leaving about £275 net. This would be a net return of £22 18s 4d on each of the twelve shares in the Globe for an average year. It is thus apparent that it was at Blackfriars the company began to make its increased profits, and that its increased earnings came from the development

[70] Wallace, *Associates*, pp. 69-70.

of this theater, and not primarily from a general rise in prices, or necessarily from a general increase of interest in the drama, and consequent increase in attendance.

Our knowledge of receipts for the Shakespearean company between 1599 and 1608, is not very definite, but we may get a general idea from our knowledge of what was the approximate rate in other theaters at the same time. We have seen that the returns at the Theater and Curtain 1587-92 were approximately the same as at the Rose 1592-1600, and that the same approximate returns prevailed at the Fortune 1600-08 and at the Hope 1614-15. Further, the Swan must have returned approximately the same in 1597, as the other theaters.[71] We have seen that at the Rose 1592-93, the actors would have received in an uninterrupted year a total of about £1260 or £945 for an average year. We have also seen that in an average year around 1634 the actors' receipts at the Globe for half a year had been about £600, and that this had been the rate as early as 1608-13. This would mean £1200 per annum if they received the same amount in winter as in summer. But what information we have indicates that the winter receipts were often really less, especially in the early days. "In the *Poetaster* (1601), Jonson makes Histrio, representing the Globe Players, say: 'O, it will get us a huge deal of money, and we have need on't, for this winter has made us all poorer than so many starved snakes; nobody comes at us.' "[72] It seems, therefore, that our estimate for the early part of the period is probably large rather than small, and should consequently be reduced to about £1000 for an average year. This means that the rate of returns to the Shakespearean company probably remained approximately the same at the Rose 1592-94, at the Theater and Curtain 1594-99, and at the Globe 1599-1608, although the savings had been regularly increasing as tenancy and acting conditions had grown more settled. The companies for men were no longer a political football, subject to the kicking of struggling partisans; but were business organizations with assured and stable position. If the company received an average of £1000 per annum 1599-1608, and its expense was £700 as usual, its net profits would be £300, or £25 per annum for each member when the number was twelve, £33 6s 4d when the number was nine.

This comparative estimate of returns at the various theaters throws light on the relative income and size of the Red Bull, probably the only other not hitherto discussed theater for men's com-

---

[71] See above, p. 166.

[72] Adams, *Playhouses*, p. 226; the fact that the company was persuaded by a subsidy of only £2 to put on the old *Richard II* in 1601 (Halliwell, *Outlines*, Vol. I, p. 191) indicates that their receipts were not exceedingly heavy.

panies 1602-08, there being then but three men's companies all told. We shall see later that the building seems to have cost less than the first Globe, presumably indicating either that it was smaller or that it was more poorly finished.[73] Thomas Woodford claimed in 1613, that the return from a one-seventh housekeeping share was about £30 per annum.[74] Unless Woodford is giving gross receipts, this would mean that half the galleries returned about £210 per annum + £17 10s rent + repairs. If Woodford is giving net receipts, the total receipts from the galleries were £420 to probably £475 per annum; if he is giving gross, they were about £420. It is not apparent, however, whether the Red Bull was used the whole year, or only half. At least 1607-09, the Curtain had been the summer and the Red Bull the winter house,[75] both houses being patented to the company April 15, 1609.[76] There is thus good reason to believe that the Red Bull was occupied but half the year. If so, the £420 of Woodford's estimate shows good returns, since total receipts at the Fortune were but around £565 per annum in average years, while at the Globe before 1608, the rate was probably about the same as at the Fortune. Still we must remember that this estimate at the Red Bull is only for the winter season, and that the average for the full year may have been somewhat lower. But another piece of evidence also indicates that the Red Bull paid well. Alleyn records that October 3, 1617, at the Bull he received "but £3 6s 4d" for *The Younger Brother*.[77] This sum had been the average for new plays at the Rose, and Alleyn's disappointment indicates that returns at the Bull should have been somewhat higher. It would seem likely therefore that the Red Bull returned somewhat more from the galleries than the Rose, the Globe, or the Fortune. We have no clue to the receipts at the doors for the Red Bull, but they would likely have been in proportion to those from the galleries. Probably then the Red Bull was about the size of the other theaters, its heavier receipts being due to the fact that it was a winter house. This conclusion as to size finds fair confirmation in Wright's[78] statement that "The 'Globe,' 'Fortune,' and 'Bull' were large houses." It is probably worth adding that the same authority says [79] the Fortune and the Bull "were mostly frequented by citizens, and the meaner sort of people."

It would seem then from our previous discussion that the Shakespearean company received little if any more for an uninterrupted

---

[73] cf. below, p. 357.
[74] Wallace, *Three London Theatres*, pp. 8-9.
[75] Adams, *Playhouses*, p. 297.
[76] Malone, Soc. *Coll.*, Vol. I, pp. 270-1.
[77] Warner, *Catalogue*, p. 166.
[78] Wright, *Historia*, p. 426.
[79] *ibid.*, p. 425.

year at the Globe 1599-1642, than it would have received at the Rose in 1592-93. It seems true also that average receipts at any given theater remained practically the same throughout its existence, and that the Theater, Curtain, Rose, first Globe, Fortune, Red Bull, second Globe, and presumably the second Fortune were of the same approximate size. The Swan is said to have been larger than the Theater, Curtain, and Rose; and the Hope was modelled on it.[80] The larger size of the Swan and the Hope was due to the fact that these theaters were also used for bear and bull baitings. It would appear, therefore, that the Theater had established the type for the public theaters.

But besides the direct returns from their theaters, the actors had as a further source of income the plays performed at court. The return from this source of income was not usually very great for any particular company under the frugal Elizabeth, but gradually grew greater under James and Charles, till it finally amounted frequently to upward of £300 per annum. Before Shakespeare's death, the amount was rarely over £100. Occasionally, also, the Shakespearean company received special gifts from its royal patrons to tide it over difficult places; but these were only occasional and not to be included in average receipts. Presumably the housekeepers would have no share in either of these sources of income, since these sources were not connected with the theaters themselves. A housekeeper would not be affected by the acting at court unless in so doing the actors lost their day at his theater. In our only two recorded instances, which occurred at the Rose and the Hope, Henslowe seems not to have received any share. In the first instance, he received nineteen-twentieths of the reward as part payment on a debt from the actors.[81] The other one-twentieth doutbless went for fees to secure the warrant and to get it cashed. In the second case, Henslowe forced the actors at the Hope, 1613-15, to give him bond on a reward of £10 at court to cover a debt of £6.[82] It is thus fairly certain that the housekeepers did not share in the rewards at court.

In the Shakespearean company, rewards at court would on the average add £10 to £15 per annum to the actor's income, and might in an exceptional year add as much as £25. From Whitsun Monday 1608, to Whitsun Monday 1625, the Shakespearean company performed at court two hundred and eleven times, receiving £1946 7s as reward, an average of about £114 10s per annum, or

[80] Adams, *Playhouses*, pp. 164, 167-8.
[81] Greg, *Diary*, Vol. I, p. 140.
[82] Greg, *Papers*, p. 89. This must have been the reward for *Bartholomew Fair* November 1, 1614, since this was the only £10 warrant to the company during the period.

slightly less than £10 for each actor.[83] Since we have regular lump payment at the end of each fiscal year, there is no likelihood that more than two or three irregular payments for single plays might be missing; and consequently our average of £10 for each member per annum can not be many shillings wrong either way. The largest amount was £180 in 1617-18, or £15 for each actor. The smallest amount was £60 in 1624-25, or £5 for each actor.[84] From Whitsun Monday 1625 to the same date in 1641, the record of only one year, 1626-27, is missing. In the fifteen recorded years, the actors received £2880, or £192 per annum, this being £16 per member. The smallest amount shared was £100, in 1625-26; the largest £300, in 1638-39. Thus the annual share per member in this period varied from £8 to £25, the average being £16. Consequently, the average gains of £35 to £50 per annum, plus the average court reward of £10 to £16 per member, gives a total average annual net income of £45 to £66 for 1608-42.

Between 1594 and 1599, our indications point to an annual net receipt of about £26 to £33 per member. From 1599 to 1608, we have seen that average returns were probably £25 to £34 per annum for each member in an average year. Thus the net earnings of each actor 1594-1608, remained about £25 to £34 per annum in an average year, the gradual increase in total net earnings being absorbed by increasing the number of sharers from five to twelve. This income would be increased some £3 to £8 by the performances at court. In the nine years 1599-1608, the Shakespearean company had received £673 for sixty-seven performances at court, a rough average of £75 per annum. However, the first three years they received but £30 per annum, and in the latter six an average of approximately £95 per annum. Consequently, before 1603 the gain from this source was slightly over £3 per member per annum. From 1603 to 1608, it was nearly £8 per member per annum. Thus (in an average year 1594-1608) a member probably received from £28 to £42 clear per annum.

Before 1594, our knowledge is practically a guess, since the company seems to have shifted around quite a bit. We have seen that the company acted at the Rose 1592-93, and that each of the five sharers would probably have cleared about £112 in an uninter-

---

[83] Murray, Vol. I, pp. 177 ff.; Stopes, *Jahrbuch*, Vol. XLVI, pp. 92 ff.; Chambers, *Modern Language Review*, Vol. II, pp. 1 ff.; Vol. IV, pp. 153 ff. The company would doubtless expend a pound or so on each warrant in fees.

[84] It seems that the entry of May 24, 1635, quoted by Collier, *Annals* (1879), Vol. II, p. 5, for £250 in payment for twenty plays acted between May 13, 1624, and May 30, 1626, should have been for plays between May 13, 1634, and March 30, 1635, being the regular payment for 1634-35 (Stopes, *Jahrbuch*, Vol. XLVI, p. 98).

rupted year; but that as a matter of fact the company probably did well to clear expenses. We may sum up our indications then by saying that from 1594 to 1608, each member probably cleared on the average £28 to £42 per annum. This was somewhat increased by the acquisition of Blackfriars, the income from 1608 to 1642 being probably £45 to £66 clear, but might be as much as £110 at the latter part of the period in an uninterrupted year. There was thus a steady increase of the average income in the Shakespearean company from about £25 in 1594, to about £60 in 1635. Net incomes much more than doubled.

We have also fairly good indications of the value put on housekeeping shares in several of the prominent theaters. Such a share may be looked at in two ways, from the point of view of cost, or from that of returns and consequent value as a financial bargain. The former seems to have been the usual view, though this seems strange to the modern mind with its attitude of exacting "all the traffic will bear." The actual cost of such a share would be the price paid for the building, the annual rent for the ground upon which the building stood, and the annual cost of repairs. Our most definite knowledge of the valuation put on housekeeping shares, as well as the reasons for that valuation, comes from the second Fortune. The price paid for the shares there was to be the cost of the building. Each sharer was then to pay a certain ground rent per annum and his part of necessary repairs on the building.[85] Incidentally, the second Fortune was to cost £1000. The shares in the first Fortune had evidently been estimated in the same way. An unexecuted lease for an eighth of a fourth share in this building, dated 1608, provides that Thomas Downton should pay £27 10s for the share, 10s per annum rent, and his share of necessary repairs, the share to be non-transferable, and Downton to remain with the company during the term of the lease.[86] The first Fortune was thus valued at £880. We happen to have Alleyn's own statement about this time of what the property had cost him, which, up to June 1610, was exactly £880.[87] It seems, however, that £120 of this amount was for private buildings in which the lease does not specifically give Downton a share, though these buildings were included in the lease to the company in October 1618, and in the various leases of the second Fortune. It appears therefore that a housekeeper simply paid for his share of the building, which he thus became bound to keep in repair; and paid a certain yearly rent for the ground on which the building stood. In such an arrangement, the owner simply sold the building as a whole or in

[85] Greg, *Papers*, pp. 28-30.
[86] *ibid*., pp. 13-14.
[87] *ibid*., p. 108.

APPENDIX II

part, and continued to receive a certain rent for the ground on
which it stood.

The same custom was evidently practised at the Red Bull. In
each of three transfers 1605-12, a one-seventh share in the building sold for £50.[88] The fixed price in all transfers must be due to
the original cost of the building, as had been true at the first and
second Fortune. This means that the building was valued at £350.
The first Fortune was to have cost £440, and the first Globe is
supposed to have cost about £400. The Globe, however, was built
in part from old material, and the Fortune actually cost £520. It
seems therefore that the Red Bull was probably either a much
smaller or a much more poorly furnished building than either the
Globe or the slightly larger Fortune.

This method of valuing shares explains several statements concerning shares in the Shakespearean company. It is difficult to get
the actual cost of the first Globe, since it was built in part from the
old materials of the Theater. Since the first Fortune, built after a
slightly modified and enlarged plan of the Globe, was to have cost
£440, it is probable that the actual cost of the Globe was estimated
as about £400. However, the Fortune actually cost £520. It is not
surprising therefore that the Globe was valued at £600, though
actually it cost its builders somewhat less.[89] The shares were valued
accordingly. Heminges considered an eighth share as worth at
least £50 in 1606, since he loaned that amount under mortgage
upon one.[90] This would put a value of at least £400 on the building.
Heminges also stated, in 1619, that a sixth share of the actor-
housekeepers' half in the first Globe had sold for less than half of
£120.[91] This must have been either Sly's or Cundall's share, since
theirs were the only sixth shares to change hands; and the transaction must have taken place 1606-12. Since Heminges refers to a
single share, one-twelfth of the whole, it seems fairly conclusive
that,he is referring to the price paid by himself and Cundall for
Sly's share 1608-11. This would place a valuation of less than
£720 on the building, our two estimates fixing the limits as £400
to £720, within which the £600 estimate falls. It is evident therefore that at the Globe also it was the custom for each sharer to
buy his part of the building, this being the cost of his share. Presumably, each actor paid for his housekeeping share on being
admitted to the body, though we have no definite record in a single
case.

But housekeeping was a different matter at Blackfriars. There

[88] Wallace, *Three London Theatres*, pp. 8-9.
[89] Wallace, London *Times*, October 2, 1909, p. 9.
[90] Wallace, *Associates*, p. 56.
[91] *ibid.*, p. 61.

the Burbadges owned both land and building. The company rented both the building, and the land upon which it stood. Since the Burbadges took all risks in connection with the building, such as fire, etc., they naturally charged the housekeepers a higher rent than they would have done for merely the land upon which the building stood. Their charge was at first £40 per annum, but later £50. The rent for the land itself at the Globe was £14 10s; at the Theater it was £14;[92] at the Red Bull it was £17 10s;[93] at the first Fortune it was £16.[94] Thus, as was natural, housekeepers paid more rent on the perishable building than on the imperishable land.

Our knowledge of other rent transactions shows that the Burbadges were quite reasonable. The rent at Whitefriars had been £50,[95] at Salisbury Court £100; at the Hope £100. Alleyn rented the first Fortune to the Palsgrave's men October 31, 1618,[96] together with all other property connected, for £200 per annum, and two rundlets of wine, worth 10s each, for Christmas. The lessees were to receive 24s per annum for a two-room tenement that had been already assigned to a former gatherer of the company. In case of Alleyn's death, the rent was to be reduced to £120 per annum, and the rebate on the tenement to 4s per annum. We may get Alleyn's approximate valuation of the rent for the building from the leases May 20, 1622, on the second Fortune, which included practically the same property except the theater building, which in this case was to be furnished by the lessees.[97] In the latter case, the rent was to be £128 6s, leaving a difference of £71 14s for the building. Thus the provision in the lease of October 1618, that reduced the rent to £120 in case of Alleyn's death, means that in such event he gave the company the building. The provision was doubtless made because this was Alleyn's own company, in which he had played for many years. Under this interpretation, Alleyn valued the Fortune theater, in 1618, at £80 per annum rent, and the remainder of the property at £120. This increase of £8 6s rent on the property in 1622, over 1618, probably means that Alleyn had erected other buildings, the rent from which he valued at the sum mentioned. Thus the rent at Blackfriars was just half the rent at the Fortune. This is in part accounted for by the fact that the Fortune probably accommodated about twice as many spectators as Blackfriars.[98] A further contributing factor was likely the

[92] Wallace, *First London Theatre*, pp. 173, 271, etc.
[93] Wallace, *Three London Theatres*, pp. 8-9.
[94] Greg, *Papers*, pp. 13, 26; Wallace, *Three London Theatres*, p. 52.
[95] Adams, *Playhouses*, p. 314; Collier, J. P., *Memoirs of Edward Alleyn*, p. 160.
[96] Greg, *Papers*, pp. 27-8.
[97] *ibid.*, pp. 29-30.
[98] Wallace, *Children*, p. 49.

greater risk from fire at the Fortune than at Blackfriars. At any rate, the rent at Blackfriars seems to have been a reasonable one. Incidentally, if the Shakespearean company had to pay £50 rent per annum at the Globe after 1635, as seems likely, the change means that the theater was now considered as having reverted to Brend at the expiration of his lease. The amount of rent charged at the Globe under this condition would be naturally suggested by the rent at Blackfriars.

When the building was rented, as well as the land upon which it stood, the cost of a share to the housekeeper was confined to rent and repairs. This was the cost of housekeeping shares at Blackfriars, and was probably the cost at the Globe after 1635. Before that date, the cost of a share in the Globe was its proportionate part of the cost of the building, plus repairs and yearly rent; at Blackfriars, only rent and repairs.

Thus Thomasina Ostler and John Shank in their contentions introduce a different and not generally accepted attitude. They consider, not the cost of the share, but its returns and consequent value as a bargain. This was a particularly obnoxious view in the Shakespearean company, whose tradition insisted that only actors of the company who had rendered long and brilliant service might be admitted as housekeeping actors, this being a mark of promotion and not merely a commercial bargain. Thomasina Ostler does not tell us definitely what a share considered as a bargain was worth, but John Shank does. He says that in 1633 he paid £156 for a share in Blackfriars and one in the Globe.[99] In 1634, he paid £350 for a share in Blackfriars, and two in the Globe. A simple algebraic calculation shows that Shank could not have paid the same rate for shares in the two years.[100] I have no doubt that the transaction

[99] Halliwell, *Outlines*, Vol. I, p. 314.

[100] In 1635, Shank asserts that Swanston bought a third of a share in Blackfriars two or three years before for £20, and that he himself paid £60 for the same amount at the same time. This would mean that Swanston paid at the rate of £60 per share, and Shank at the rate of £180 (Halliwell, *Outlines*, Vol. I, pp. 314-15). But Swanston owned no share or part of a share legally, though he may have subrented in some way. The evidence of price in his case is thus worth comparatively little. Shank seems plainly to state that he himself paid £180 for the 1633 share in Blackfriars. He says that for a third of a share Swanston paid "20 *li.*, and yet hath injoyed the same two or three yeeres allready, and hath still as long time in the same as your suppliant hath in his, who for soe much as Mr. Swanston bought for 20 *li.* your suppliant payd 60 *li.*" This seems to be a plain statement that Swanston bought his part in 1633, at the rate of £60 per share, while Shank paid at the rate of £180 per share at the same time. But elsewhere he tells us he paid only £156 in 1633, for both the share in Blackfriars and one in the Globe. He cannot therefore be referring to the transaction of 1633. If he refers to that of 1634, since he paid £350 for one share in Blackfriars and two in the Globe, he must have paid £85 for each of the shares in the

of 1633 was at least semi-official, since it gave Shank one share in the Globe and one in Blackfriars, to which his age, prominence, and length of service entitled him, just as it did Taylor and Lowin about the same time. If so, he would have paid for his share at the Globe on the basis of its reputed cost, about £87 10s. Since he paid £156 for the two, he probably paid £86 for the Globe share and £70 for the the Blackfriars share. We have just seen that he probably paid £85 for each of two shares in the Globe in 1634. It seems certain then that the Globe in 1633-35 was estimated at £1400, and that a share cost its pro rata proportion of that amount, £85-88. When we remember that the committee of November 1633,[101] stated that the sharers at Blackfriars valued their shares at £150 each, but would probably take £66 13s 4d, it seems reasonable that Shank should have paid £70 a few months before for a share as a member, and £180 a few months later for a share acquired "surreptitiously." In the case of the Blackfriars share of 1634, the transaction then was almost a pure bargain, with William Heminges wanting to sell because of financial and other difficulties, and John Shank wanting to buy because he considered the commodity a good bargain.

It will be noticed that it was the Blackfriars shares that caused the bargain attitude. There was no original cost to base the value of shares upon. The only principles possible were either gift or bargain. With the close connection between the Globe and Blackfriars, it was almost impossible to keep a custom that applied to one from getting attached to both, as the Burbadges found in the matter of shares. Therefore, in view of the general customs of the Shakespearean company, it is not surprising that the Lord Chamberlain decided against Shank's bargain view in the matter of the extra shares. Probably the same thing happened in the case of Thomasina Ostler, though we have no record of results. It appears therefore that the value of a share in the Globe or Blackfriars as a bargain depended not on cost or returns, but on how badly one person wanted to sell and the other to buy, as supposedly in the present day. However, the custom of the company was against such a transaction. So far as we know, Shank was the only man who tried to break the custom, and he eventually failed.

We are now in position to estimate the profit to housekeepers in the Shakespearean company. We have seen that the cost of the first

Globe. Further, £1400, the alleged cost of the Globe, divided by sixteen, the number of shares, gives £87 10s as the value of a share in the Globe. It is probable then that Shank is referring to the transaction of 1634, and that he paid £85 for each share in the Globe, and £180 for a share in Blackfriars.

[101] Collier, *Annals* (1879), Vol. I, p. 478.

Globe was probably estimated at £600. Thus each of the original ten shares would be valued at £60, and would bear an annual expense of 29s for rent, as also its part of necessary repairs. When Sly and Cundall were admitted to sixth shares of the actor's half, each share would be valued at £50, and would bear 24s 2d annually for rent, as well as its part of necessary repairs. When Ostler was admitted to a seventh of the actors' half, each share would be valued at £42 17s 2d, and would bear annually 20s 9d for rent, also its part of necessary repairs.

It would seem that the second Globe was estimated to cost £700 to £840, since Heminges tells us that one sharer was asked to put up £50 or £60.[102] He states, however, that each share bore an expense of about £120, which would be £1680 for the building.[103] Shank claimed in 1635 that it had cost £1400.[104] Professor Wallace says: "I have other contemporary documents showing the cost was far less than £1,400."[105] Shank's statement almost certainly represents the valuation that was put on the building when he paid for his shares. This would be an even £100 to each of the original fourteen shares. It may be that Heminges was putting this valuation on each of the sixteenth shares, and dividing by the original fourteen when he arrived at £120 as the approximate cost of a share. Since the shares remained thereafter as sixteenths, it is probable that each was valued at £85 to £100, and certain that each bore 18s 2d per annum rent, besides its part of repairs. If Brend was awarded £50 per annum rent after 1635, he was evidently awarded the building. Sixteenth shares after that would cost £3 2s 6d per annum rent, and would bear one-sixteenth of repairs. The expense at Blackfriars was only for rent and repairs. The original seventh shares paid £5 14s 3d rent; the eighth shares paid £5 rent per annum till 1629, after which date it was £6 5s.

As a return on the investment, from 1599 to 1608, the housekeepers at the Globe, according to previous estimates, would receive in an average year about £500 gross. At this rate, when there were ten shares, the annual returns would be £50 gross each; when there were eight, the returns would be £62 10s gross each; when there were twelve, the returns would be about £42 gross each. It is to be remembered, however, that returns had been gradually increasing throughout this period, so that our estimate per share is probably too large at the beginning, and too small at the end of the period. It seems likely that the shares remained about £50 each throughout the period, extra shares absorbing the surplus as created. The ex-

[102] Wallace, *Associates*, p. 60.
[103] *ibid.*, p. 61.
[104] Halliwell, *Outlines*, Vol. I, p. 316.
[105] Wallace, London *Times*, October 2, 1909, p. 9.

pense for rent and repairs probably did not amount to more than £5 per annum. Thus net returns were probably not more than £45 per annum for each share in the Globe till 1608. After 1608, the total returns to housekeepers at the Globe were cut about in half; but according to Witter's testimony were now about the same amount as in 1634, which was about £300 per annum. Thus the twelfth shares would return about £25 gross, the fourteenth £21 8s 7d, the sixteenths £18 15s. Net returns would thus probably be £15 to £25 per annum for an average year. When Witter stated that he regularly received £30 to £40 net per annum, he was probably giving the largest amount he had ever received in any year, which in an uninterrupted year would be one-third larger than the estimate given above. His estimate seems to have been on twelfths, which probably returned about £25 each. The addition of one-third would give £33 6s 8d gross for an uninterrupted year. If the returns were exceptionally good, this amount might be increased a few pounds.

Blackfriars was a much better paying proposition. Here the gross returns by 1635 were about £600 per annum for an average year, but had been estimated at only £360, 1608-12. Thus the net returns to a housekeeper on a seventh share for an average year, 1608-12, were about £45, and on an eighth around 1634, about £75.

ANALYSIS OF PLAYS
WITH ASSIGNED PARTS

IN *The Roman Actor*, eight members take part, two taking minor parts, however (eleven and twelve according to number of lines). The other five members take no assigned parts (two of them are superannuated). Three named parts are not assigned (19, 9, 16), besides various attendants, etc. All named members take the parts of men. Four men's parts are also taken by hired men, two of them livery servants. There are four women's parts by apprentices (4, 6, 12, 14), two chief parts and two minor. There are thus sixteen assigned parts. Taking the eight highest, the principal parts, as was done in the second Beaumont and Fletcher folio, we get six members and two apprentices, six men and two women, precisely as in one form of the Beaumont and Fletcher lists.

In *The Picture*, again eight members are named, two taking minor parts as before (10, 11). The other four members take no assigned parts (one of them is superannuated). All named parts are assigned, but there are various supernumeraries unassigned. No assigned men's parts are by apprentices or hired men. There are four assigned women's parts by apprentices (2, 3, 9, 12), two major and two minor. There are thus twelve assigned parts. Taking the eight highest, we get six members and two apprentices, six men and two women as before.

Analyzing *The Deserving Favorite*, we find that seven members perform, one taking a minor part (11). The other five members take no assigned parts (one of them is superannuated). Three minor named parts are unassigned (10, 12, 13). No assigned men's parts are by apprentices or hired men. There are three assigned women's parts (4, 3, 8), all by boys. There are thus ten assigned parts. Taking the eight highest, we get five members and three apprentices, five men and three women, precisely as in one typical form of the Beaumont and Fletcher lists; but taking the nine highest, we get six members and three apprentices, six men and three women.

Continuing with *The Wild Goose Chase*, we find that eight known members perform, two taking minor parts (11, 13). The other four members take no assigned parts. All named parts are assigned, but there are various attendants, etc. There are five women's parts, three by apprentices, one by a member, and one unassigned. There are thus twelve assigned parts. Taking the eight highest parts, we get five members and three apprentices, five men and three women; but taking the nine highest, we get six members and three apprentices, six men and three women, as in the preceding play.

Returning now to *The Duchess of Malfi*, list for revival, we find seven known members taking part, two taking minor parts. Also, one assigned and named man's part is given to Pollard, who was probably a member. If so, eight members took part, four not (two of them are superannuated). Four named parts are not assigned, and there are various attendants, etc. There are four women's parts, three of them assigned, by apprentices. There are thus eleven assigned parts. The eight highest include six members and two apprentices, six men and two women.

A few plays furnish interesting illustration of how the personnel was distributed.

THE DESERVING FAVORITE

In *The Deserving Favorite*, the characters are not very well distinguished, or rather the types emphasized are different from the ordinary, bringing some actors into more prominence than usual. The name part, the Duke, goes to Taylor. The only villain of the play must go to Lowin, though Jacomo is not much in Lowin's ordinary style. Still it was that or nothing. As a consequence of the heroics, the hero actors have heavy parts thrust on them. Benfield must be the King of course. Then Sharp gets his opportunity, for here is a character in his line, Lysander, with more lines than any other in the play. On the other hand, Swanston had occasion fervently to quote, "Othello's occupation's gone," for there was nothing more villainous left for him than Utrante, a father who tries to persuade his daughter to marry that he himself may be saved. Since there is no comedy, Pollard fares even worse, getting no part at all. But the part of Orsinio is still to be supplied. So first handyman, Richard Robinson, fills the part. Thus practically all the actors have had their parts juggled. Possibly Sharp was the only man who had special reason to feel proud of himself. There is still one other man's part, the deer-keeper Gerard, a minor "old man," which falls to the lot of Smith, exactly why we do not know, since we cannot tell from his sixteen lines what manner of man this was. We have the names of three other very unimportant characters that could be taken by almost any of the men. For the apprentices, there is the masculine, athletic girl Cleonarda in the style of Thompson, and the feminine Clarinda in that of Honyman. There are no support parts, the only other female, the middle-aged

APPENDIX III

Mariana, being assigned to Edward Horton. Quite evidently, this
play was not cut to fit the company; but the company had to adapt
itself to the play. For that reason, it is the more valuable in this
study.

BELIEVE AS YE LIST

Believe As Ye List is difficult to work out because of its rambling
structure. Only a few major characters run through the story, the
others shifting as the scene shifts from court to court. The wandering and oppressed Antiochus goes naturally to Taylor. His
persecutor, the villain Flaminius, goes as naturally to Lowin. The
jesting Berecinthius goes to Pollard of course, made up for the
occasion as a very fat man. These are the only parts that run entirely through the play. But in some cases there are certain corresponding parts at each stage of the journey. For instance, we
have Amilcar, Prusias, possibly Metellus, and certainly Marcellus,
all of the dignified type affected by Benfield. His name is connected
with the last, and he may have doubled one or more of the other
three. These four parts would about give Benfield his proper
place. The deep-dyed villain Chrysalus would fall to Swanston.
No other of the unassigned characters would seem to be distinc-
tively his, but then neither is any of them of any importance.
Robinson finds a part to supply as Lentulus, successor to Flaminius, a serious messenger with a short message. The remaining
small parts are then apportioned to the other actors. Hobbs takes
Calistus, Patrick a captain, and Baxter Titus; Penn, Greville, and
Honyman are merchants. "Mr. Balls," William Mago and Nicholas
Underhill were attendants. This play furnishes splendid illustrations of how the less prominent members and hired men were
used. There are two important women: the noble, sympathetic Cor-
nelia; and the pert Courtezan. These ought to fall to the leading
ladies, Goffe and Trigg; but we have no assignment given.

THE DUCHESS OF MALFI

The Duchess of Malfi gives us the principal actors at two periods
in the Shakespearean company. It was first acted in 1613.[1] In this
play, the nearest approach to a hero is Antonio, who is quite evidently of the dignified type. As such, he fell to Ostler and passed
to Benfield. The two big parts for men were evidently intended to
be Ferdinand and Bosola. Now Bosola is the grumpy villain of
the Lowin type, and as such falls to him. Ferdinand, a very passionate part, calling for emotional acting, goes to Burbadge and
passes to Taylor. Since Ferdinand is the leading rôle, and since
Burbadge played that rôle regularly, villain or hero, the assign-

[1] See above, pp. 250-1, note 59.

ment is not peculiar. The Cardinal then fell to Cundall and passed to Robinson. The noble friend Delio goes to the then "juvenile lead" Underwood. The blunt Pescara fell to a person unknown, not one of the six main male actors, since the others were still surviving at the revival and did not have this part. Besides, there are but seven main parts in the play, five men and two women, Pescara being notably a minor part. The part must thus have been taken by one of the minor "old men." We have no guess as to the original Silvio, the nearest approach to light comedy, taken by Pollard at the revival. Tooley found his part as a comic madman. Besides these, R. Pallant supplied some minor parts at the revival.

In view of these facts, certain things connected with the revival of this play for the spring and summer of 1623 are put in their true light. Of the big six in the company at this period, Lowin, Underwood, and Tooley retained their parts; Taylor took Burbadge's part, and Benfield took Ostler's. This leaves Cundall's part to be supplied by roistering soldier Eccleston. But since Eccleston had just withdrawn from the company, first handyman Robinson supplied the place. Thus Robinson is not Cundall's successor among the big six, as the other lists of the period also show. As we have seen, it was necessary for Rice to supply the minor "old man's" place, for Pollard to take the only approach to light comedy, and for the apprentice parts to be reassigned, Sharp taking the majestic Duchess, and Thompson the bewitching Julia. This curiously illustrates a principle of assignment. Of the apprentices, Sharp is evidently best fitted for the majestic Duchess because of his size; he would be regularly the haughty villainess also. Since he can't be both at the same time, his support Thompson, not his comic running mate, Holcomb, must take the second part. We have exactly the same situation in *The Duke of Milan*, of about the same date as the revival of *The Duchess of Malfi*.

LOVER'S MELANCHOLY

With the business of the various actors and the method of part assignment determined, we ought to be able to assign parts in a period where the actors are known, especially if we have the further aid of knowing what actors had parts. Fortunately for experiment, we have a good illustration in Ford's *Lover's Melancholy* (1628), just in the midst of the period. There are sixteen name parts and seventeen named performers. Unfortunately, this particular play is not clear cut, all the chief actors having about the same number of lines, there being but one hundred and eight lines difference between the first character and the eighth. The comic insertion also about equals the half-serious main thread, so that structurally the play is a botch. However, the eight main characters and the clown stand out from the others, since there is a difference of about one hundred lines between the clown and the next man below him, who has a part of only seventy-four lines. These principal parts in the order of Dyce's dramatis personae, are, for the men, Palador, Amethus, Meleander, Menaphon, Corax, Cuculus (the clown), Rhetias; and for the boys, Thamasta and Eroclea. All six of the leading men and the clown are in the list of principal actors. Robinson, who sometimes took a principal part, is out, so that the problem is not complicated in this way. As we have seen, the six leading actors are Taylor, Lowin, Benfield, Swanston, Pollard, and Sharp. Shank is the clown. Thus our problem is merely a matter of determining which is which. The two leading ladies are also named, so that again our problem is only one of which is which. The name part is Palador, the noble but melancholy young prince, mourning for a lost love. He is supposedly the chief character, but is not much distinguished from the other lovers of the play. This part would of course go to Taylor, as the Duke in *The Deserving Favorite* had gone in similar circumstances. At first glance, Palador's youth might seem to interfere; but Taylor was still playing the young Mirabel some four years later. When we look for Lowin's part, we find it must have been either Corax, the bluff, blunt physician, who scolds the king and the court in general, still wishing to return to his university for fear he may go mad with the whimsies of the court, or the almost equally bluff, blunt old councilor Rhetias, who at times speaks his mind quite plainly concerning the court and fools in general. Since this is the bluff, honest side of Lowin, his support would have been Pollard, who would have taken the other character. Corax has thirty more lines, and is probably more consistently bluff. He is also the leader in curing Palador, employing Rhetias among the rest for a device to that end. It is thus probable that Lowin was Corax, supported by Pollard as Rhetias. It may be noticed that when Corax has a set-to with Rhetias at their first meeting, a commenter is sure that the ban-dog Rhetias will get the worst of it. Benfield's part is very easy to find. He would naturally have been the dignified and serious but distracted Meleander, who has lost his property and daughter rather than submit to the king's lust. His fortune is restored, the lost daughter becomes queen, another daughter marries royalty, and virtue is mightily rewarded. This leaves only Sharp and Swanston to be the lovers Amethus and Menaphon. Now Menaphon is at first the very modest lover of Thamasta; but after he has played the eavesdropper and witnessed a meeting between Thamasta and Parthenophil, he becomes ragingly jealous, rather a mild Othello, a part which, as we have seen, Wright says Swanston played. Amethus, the suitor of Cleophila, is not a very strongly marked lover.

[367]

As cousin of Palador, his chief requisite would be a princely bearing, which Sharp, as we have seen, seems to have had. It is probable then that Swanston was Menaphon, and Sharp Palador. The clown Cuculus would of course be taken by Shank. Not only would his position demand it, but also the personal allusions are his. Cuculus is a "young old gull" (I. 2. 18), "an old youth" (III. 1. 48), a "trim old youth" (IV. 1. 73). Shank was a gull by profession, now old by course of nature, and exceedingly trim by condition, if we are to trust the description of Hilario, given but a little over six months later.

Perhaps we had best assign the parts of the women characters next. First is Thamasta, who "is abominably proud, a lady of a damnable high, turbulent, and generous spirit" (III. 1, 50). This is Thompson's favorite rôle, and must have been taken by him. In contrast is the gentle Parthenophil-Eroclea, the beautiful, feminine type, beloved of Honyman. Supporting these are two other female characters with more than one hundred lines each, who would fall of course to Trigg and Goffe. Thamasta's erotic waiting maid Kala would go to Trigg. Cleophila, the very dutiful daughter of Meleander, and modest mistress of Amethus, would go to Goffe. Returning to the minor men, we find that Aretus and Sophronos are two old lords, the former Palador's tutor, the latter an adviser of Palador, being Meleander's brother. These parts must have been taken by Smith and Penn, who regularly performed such parts, they being the only other two members on the list. But again the parts are so little distinguished that I have no very good guess as to which is which. Penn may have been the (portly?) counsellor Sophronus, and Smith the (wizend?) scholar Aretus.[2] Also the schoolmaster is usually a comic part in Elizabethan drama, again indicating Smith as the actor. This leaves the parts of Pelias, Trollio, and Grilla to be assigned. Grilla is played by one who passes for a boy, but no other boy is on the list. We have seen, however, that Horn[3] seems to have played the Fool in *The Pilgrim* (1621), a part exactly corresponding to Grilla. Since none of the other actors of this list has ever been connected with such a part, it seems fairly safe to assign it to Horn. This assignment is made practically certain by the fact that the list of actors sets off from the rest at the foot of the list the four apprentice actors of women's parts, with Horn in the center. This leaves Greville, Vernon, and Baxter for the other two named places. Both Pelias and Trollio are comic. Greville is comic. Of the other two, we haven't sufficient record to know, so that we have no means of determining further assignment.

[2] The lean schoolmaster is depicted in the frontispiece to *Pedantius*, 1631. See facsimile in *Shakespeare's England*, Vol. I, p. 227.
[3] cf. above, p. 192.

APPENDIX III

THE BLOODY BROTHER

We have also the cast of *The Bloody Brother or Rollo, Duke of Normandy*, as performed in 1648.[4] Rollo, the petulant and somewhat self-worshipping young man, who becomes in the hands of Latorch the "bloody brother," falls to Taylor. The "huffing" old lord Aubrey goes as naturally to Lowin. The jolly, jesting, half-villainous Cook is the property of Pollard. The other two chief men characters are taken by actors newly risen in the organization. In the period 1625-31, the part of the villainous Latorch would have fallen to Swanston, who had now turned Presbyterian and become a jeweller in Aldermanbury.[5] Therefore, a less godly man, Nicholas Birch, had to supply his place. This is the same Nicholas Birch who had been Shank's apprentice; had gone after Shank's death in 1636, to Beeston's Boys at the Cockpit, where he became famous as an actor of women's parts; and had now returned to the old organization, being at the time of this play probably about thirty years of age. He later was a leading actor on the Restoration stage. The part of Otto was taken by a young man who was also destined later to acquire fame on the Restoration stage, Charles Hart, the grandson of Shakespeare's sister, an actor who had been trained in the company from a boy as Robinson's apprentice,[6] and was now probably about twenty-four. We have no assignment of women's parts for this performance. All the actors mentioned in the 1648 performance of the play were in the company in 1624, except the performers of Latorch and Otto, parts which would be thoroughly in the lines of Underwood and Sharp. However, Rowley must originally have been the fat Cook, and have been succeeded by Pollard. Thus there is no difficulty in the assignment of parts for this play.

BARNAVELT

In working out the parts taken in *Barnavelt*, it is necessary for us to remember that there is no formal list of actors; but that our knowledge of the actors who took parts comes from jottings of names on the manuscript. The first noticeable thing is that no principal actor is named in these jottings; at least not as they are given by Mr. Bullen in his reprint,[7] and later by Miss Frijlinck in her accurate transcription. Murray[8] does assign Lowin and Benfield parts, and refers to Bullen and Fleay as authority. He has in nearly

---

[4] Wright, *Historia*, p. 427.
[5] *ibid.*
[6] *ibid.*, p. 423.
[7] Bullen, A. H., *A Collection of Old English Plays*, Vol. II, pp. 201 ff.; Frijlinck, Wilhelmina P., *The Tragedy of Sir John Van Olden Barnavelt*.
[8] Murray, Vol. I, opp. p. 172.

all the other Beaumont and Fletcher lists followed Fleay without checking the originals. Since Fleay interpreted "Mr. Rob." as referring to Robert Benfield, in which error he is followed by Miss Frijlinck, Murray has retained Benfield as given by Fleay, and inserted Robinson from some other source. The actor referred to is, of course, Mr. Robinson; and not Mr. Robert anybody, either Benfield or Goffe. Common usage alone of the time would determine this, but the lines for actors also make it certain. I do not know where Fleay, followed by Murray, got Lowin, as Bullen doesn't mention him, though he does suggest (p. 206) that G. Lowin may really be J. Lowin, a suggestion that is wholly untenable, since the part concerned is that of a female. The only Lowin given in either Bullen or Frijlinck is G. Lowin, an actor of female parts. Fleay, followed by Frijlinck, has also supposed that Nicholas Tooley appears as Barnavelt's wife; but Bullen (p. 278) demurs in favor of a younger actor. Bullen transcribes the abbreviated form of the name as "Nich," which Fleay interprets as Nicholas and applies to Tooley, as supposedly the only known actor bearing that name in the company at that time. Miss Frijlinck (p. 55) transcribes as "nich," and follows Fleay in ascribing the part to Tooley. Now the apprentice who was at this time taking the line to which Barnavelt's wife belongs was Richard Sharp. It seems quite probable then that an r has been interpreted as an n, and that the manuscript will show "rich" instead of "nich." The small r and small n of this scribe appear from the facsimiles to be very much alike when carelessly made. But if the entry is "nich," then the person referred to is more likely Nicholas Underhill, certified December 27, 1624, among the musicians and necessary attendants of the company.[9]

Thus the jottings on the manuscript do not deal with the major actors. These jottings are merely guides for the prompter through the maze of minor characters. For instance, Robinson, Rice, and "Migh" are all captains, with no further distinction in titles, making necessary a jotting of the actor's name opposite the appearance of each captain. For this reason, we must be careful, since usually the name is in the margin, unattached to any particular character. For instance, in III. 3, two captains enter, "mr. Rob." and "mighell"; but there is no clue as to which is which. An instance of the kind has led to a fairly serious mistake in the assignment of parts. In V. 1, there is at the right of the page a direction that chairs be brought in, which Miss Frijlinck (p. 72) gives thus

"—2. Chaires

S^{tr}: $[m]^r$ Bir."

To the left of the lower line of this direction begins a speech by Vandort. Bullen thus supposed that Birch took the part of Vandort.

9 Adams, *Herbert*, pp. 74-5.

[370]

APPENDIX III

Miss Frijlinck (p. clx) prefers Morier, just why is hard to say. In view of the bookkeeper's customs, the entry is perfectly clear, and should never have caused the least stumbling. As the handwriting shows, the scribe had written "—2. Chaires," under which the bookkeeper added "S^{tr}: [m]^r Bir." to be responsible for wagging those chairs in. But two chairs of the style required would be rather an unwieldy load for one person. Miss Frijlinck's puzzled note relieves Birch a bit. She writes "the S^{tr} is doubtful; it is possible that g^{tr} (i.e. *gatherer*) may be meant." Not only so, but her brackets show that the second element is not clearly "Mr." Plainly there were two people for those two chairs, Birch being one. Probably also the second element is not "Mr.," since Birch was not yet officially a member; but is part of the first name, whatever that may be. In fact, there is this element of slight uncertainty in many of these minor assignments. Rice was the English captain (II. 4), the captain of the guard (III. 2; IV. 1) which was sent for Modesbargen, and the more prominent of Barnavelt's servants (V. 1). He was also one of the two captains of V. 3, probably the second if we may judge from characteristics. On the other hand, it is impossible in many cases to know what captains were taken by Robinson and what by Michael, though it seems certain that Robinson was Boisise, one of the ambassadors, and the Captain of Orange's guard (II. 4; III. 3; IV. 2; IV. 3). He was probably the first captain (III. 3), and "mighell" the second.[10] R. T.'s unimportant parts seem correctly catalogued by Miss Frijlinck (p. clx), except that it is not certain whether he was the Provost or the Servant with him (p. 47). Since he was certainly one of Barnavelt's servants later, he was probably so here.

Two other assignments look suspicious: Bredero to Pollard, and Leidenberch to Goffe. Miss Frijlinck's transcript by its "Ser. T : p:" (p. 52) shows that Pollard was the servant, as I had already demonstrated on other grounds, but now cut the demonstration as useless. As to the case of Leidenberch, I had originally objected to Goffe as the performer of the character, but did not see how to prove my case against seemingly unshakable evidence in the manuscript itself. Miss Frijlinck shakes the evidence for me. She transcribes (p. 24)

> "—Enter
> Leidenberge
> [& m^r Gough.]"

noting that Gough is "added in a different hand: the & is doubtful." While the writing may not be absolutely clear, the other evidence makes it clear that the bookkeeper wrote "and," meaning that Goffe came in as some kind of attendant with Leidenberch.

[10] See Frijlinck's transcription.

For Goffe has no other principal part in these lists, either before or after. The only other parts known to have been taken by him were one of the counsellors in *The Second Maiden's Tragedy* (1611),[11] a minor part; and a comic part concocted of various lords and gentlemen in *All's Well*. The man who was at this time performing the type of character to which Leidenberch belongs was Henry Cundall. It is clear then, I think, that Miss Frijlinck's transcription is correct, and that Goffe was some kind of attendant to Leidenberch, perhaps a lord.

The assignment of Barnavelt's daughter to G. Lowin seems correct, as also that of the Provost's wife to Thomas Holcomb. This is the only assignment that we have for G. Lowin. Though Holcomb's part has but four lines, as we have seen, it is quite characteristic of his line of longing women. Thus all assignments have been of minor parts. For the major parts, we must rely upon characteristic lines as usual; but without any list of principal actors to serve as a check.

The principal characters are Barnavelt, Orange, Leidenberch, Vandort, Bredero, and Modesbargen. The rather gruff old soldier Barnavelt would fall to Lowin. The younger Orange, the princely type, would go to Taylor. Leidenberch has most kinship with Cundall's line, which disappears about this period. Of the other three characters, Vandort seems to be nearest Underwood's line, as is shown especially by his vengeful treatment of the victims. The dignified counsellor Bredero probably belonged to Benfield, while the sporting Modesbargen probably went to young Eccleston. No principal part seems especially adapted to Tooley, who probably took the part of the "humorous" successful executioner. This seems to be the best assignment of parts for the play, but the characters are so roughly drawn that in many cases we cannot feel certain. The play bears in it the marks of having been flung together in haste, as we know it was.

[11] Greg's *edition*, ll. 1723-4.

PERSONAL ALLUSIONS TO CHARACTERS IN THE BEAUMONT AND FLETCHER PLAYS FOR THE SHAKESPEAREAN COMPANY

THE aim has been to list all personal allusions to characters, except insignificant repetitions, under the name in each case of the actor who probably took the part. Where there is considerable doubt as to the actor, the allusion has been placed at the end under the heading "Unclassified." It must not be supposed that in every case the personal allusion is an accurate description of the real appearance of the actor taking the part, for or course allowance must be made for makeup. Still, with the author cutting the play to fit the actors, there was much less need for makeup than in a modern play with the author's idealized picture to which the actor must conform. Unless then some good reason can be shown to the contrary, specific allusions to personal characteristics probably are to be attributed to the actor who took the part, rather than to the author's idealized picture. For instance, color of eye, stature, and to a less extent, specific, not general, references to age not in the source are necessarily or naturally, under the conditions, attributed to the actor. While the aim has been to include all personal allusions in this appendix, yet these allusions have been thoroughly sifted to yield the few significant allusions to actors used in the text. A few significant descriptions of character are also included because the editor in his list of dramatis personae has certain stereotyped phrases to describe similar characters. Since this first editor knew the actors of the parts, his phrases frequently indicate a series of characters as belonging to the same actor. The references are to page and column of Darley's edition of Beaumont and Fletcher, except for *Barnavelt*, where the references are to Bullen's edition of that play. Items from the tables of dramatis personae are marked D. P. These items for the plays with actor lists conform with the copy of the second folio owned by the University of Chicago, checked by that of the University of Illinois. The names of actors are arranged alphabetically, and the separate items under these names are given the order that the plays from which they are quoted occupy in the tables of parts.

Armin's Apprentice

Dula in *Maid's Tragedy* is above "fourteen" (5b).

Clora in *Captain* sings (626a); is "a witty companion" (D.P.).

Gillian in *Chances* is old (505a, 506a, 507a, etc.); "not above fifteen" (sarcastically) (505b); "like a miller's mare" (505b).

Benfield, Robert

Fernando in *Laws of Candy* is a "young lord" (377b).

Caesar in *False One* is "An old blind fool" (403a); "At these years" (396b).

Duke in *Women Pleased* tenders "youth" (187a).

Vertaigne in *Little French Lawyer* is "An old man" (413a, 423b); "old" (415a).

De Gard in *Wild Goose Chase* is "A Noble stay'd Gentleman" (D.P.); "He carries a fair port, is a handsome man too" (554b).

Pandulpho in *Double Marriage* is an "old man" (102b).

Don Henrique in *Spanish Curate* is "twelve months elder" than Jamie (158a, 157b); "We are young" (158b); has been married "sixteen years" (158a); is "an uxorious Lord" (D.P.).

Alphonso in *Wife for a Month* is the "eldest" of the brothers (569a).

Birch, George

Bakam in *Island Princess* is youth (235b).

Lidian in *Lover's Progress* is a "youth" (638a, 657b).

Burbadge, Richard

Amintor in *Maid's Tragedy* is "young" (1b, 2b, etc.); "boy" (9b).

Arbaces in *King and no King* is "youth" (75b).

Jacomo in *Captain* is still classified as a young man (632a, 634b); but has been a soldier "Above these fourteen years" (624a); seems to have lacked teeth, and to have had a small lower leg (623a); he is of a "rusty, swarth complexion" (625a); and seems to have had a long nose (625a); his legs are "Westphalia gammons" (626b); and promise "long strides" (629a); he is "Of a left-handed making, a lank thing/As if his belly were ta'en up with straw,/To hunt a match" (633b); "an angry Captain, a Woman-hater" (D.P.).

Arcite in *Two Noble Kinsmen* is "lower" than Palamon (559a); also not so tall as the Doctor (577a); but he "has a vengeance trick o' th' hip;/Mark how this body's made for't" (wrestling) (562a); nearly as good wrestler as Hercules (562b); "gently visaged" (577b); "black hair'd man" (565b); eye

APPENDIX IV

has "fiery sparkle, and quick sweetness" (572a); has a brow broad and "Arch'd like the great-eyed Juno's" (572b).

Aecius in *Valentinian* is "too coarse for ladies" (441b); "old" (442b, 457b, 459a); and has "wither'd arm" (459a).

Don John in *Chances* has "curl'd pate" (496b); is "in mine old days" (496b); but still "wanton boy" (509b); younger than Frederick (507a); has "well-knit body" (502b); "Made up like Hercules" (503a).

Philippo in *Love's Pilgrimage* is "young" (616a); "boy" (632a & b).

Memnon in *Mad Lover* is "An old man now" (289a); "Soldier and soldier's mate these twenty-five years" (289a); "old" (290b, 303a); "old dried timber" (292b); "old rude soldier" (299b); "A goodly-timber'd fellow" (289a).

Crates in *Queen of Corinth* has not wept for "thirty years" (42b); is "a malicious beautefeu" (D.P.).

Theodoret in *Thierry and Theodoret* is "young courser" (406b); "unlick'd lump" (406b); year older than Thierry (417b); yet has a marriageable daughter (409b, etc.).

Mountferrat in *Knight of Malta* has been a recognized champion for "full sixteen years" (126a); is in his "heat of summer" (133b); and is "a villain" (D.P.).

Archas in *Loyal Subject* is "old" (315a); has "aged locks" (315a); "wasted body" (316b); and is "dried up" (316b).

Cooke, Alexander

Piso in *Captain* is "abler" than Lodovico (639b); and "young" (644b).

Cundall, Henry

Captain in *Philaster* is "old grey ruffian" (46b).

Frederick in *Chances* "time has blasted" (507a).

Alphonso in *Love's Pilgrimage* is "strange old man" (614a).

Gomera in *Knight of Malta* has served "ten years" (129a); is "old and stiff" (133b); "old man" (134a, 147b); says "Time hath set/Some wrinkles in this face" (129b-130a).

Boroskie in *Loyal Subject* is a "good old courtier" (321b); "old Erra Pater" (330b); "wither'd" (331b).

Antigonus in *Humorous Lieutenant* is "old" (244b, 250b); and hears of "your age" (234a).

Leidenberch in *Barnavelt* is "An old man" (266); "a plaguy, heavy Lubber" (307).

Eccleston, William

Junius in *Bonduca* is "boy" (53b); he would "Leap at sixteen" (53b); sings (53b, 68b); is called "Tom Puppy" (69a); "young man" (69a).

[375]

Peter in *Chances* speaks of "my elders" (504b).

Stremon in *Mad Lover* is "boy" (309b).

Agenor in *Queen of Corinth* is "young" (23a); might complain "his eyes looked too grey" (29a); ?sings (36b, 37a).

Protaldye in *Thierry and Theodoret* is "strong" (406a, 426b); "dry stockfish" (416b).

The Ancient in *Loyal Subject* is "old True-penny" (318a); "a stout merry Souldier" (D.P.); sings (322b, etc.).

Duarte in *Custom of the Country* is "vain glorious" (D.P.); a swordsman (114a).

Ptolemy in *False One* is "young" (388a, 391a, 393b); "a boy" (394a).

Ruy Dias in *Island Princess* is a "youth" (233a, 234a).

Lopez in *Women Pleased* is "old" (188a); "hairy" (183b); sings (190b); "this youth" (191b).

Raymond in *Sea Voyage* is a "young able" man (326b).

Leandro in *Spanish Curate* is "Like a young clerk" (160a); "a young man, and a handsome gentleman" (160a, etc.); "young, high, and buxom" (160b); "a young man, a man able" (165a); "young fool" (164b); ?sings (165b); "He is made most handsomely" (165b); "a young factor" (168a).

Field, Nathan

Polydore in *Mad Lover* is "young" (300a, 301b, 305b, 309b, 311a).

Euphanes in *Queen of Corinth* is: "a young man,/Of an Herculean back" (26b); "young" (34a); "a black man" (35a); "A noble young Gentleman" (D.P.).

Thierry in *Thierry and Theodoret* "hath a body may add to/The famed night-labour of strong Hercules" (408b); has "youth" (426a).

Miranda in *Knight of Malta* is "young" (127a, 131b, 133a, 134b, 137a, 138a); had served ten years (129a); is a "boy" (135a); speaks of "My youth" (133a).

Young Archas in *Loyal Subject*, disguised as Alinda, is described as having:

> "a black eye,
> Which is of the least too, and the dullest water:
> And when her mouth was made, for certain, madam,
> Nature intended her a right good stomach."

She has a good hand but her color:

> "If it be her own,
> 'Tis good black blood; right weather-proof, I warrant it."

She has a strange pace:
"And what a manly body! methinks she looks
As though she'd pitch the bar, or go to buffets" (314b).
Same age as Olympia (315a); "boy" to old Archas (343a).

Heminges, John
Calianax in *Maid's Tragedy* is old (3a, 3b, 12b, etc.); has "poor sickly week" to live (3b); Melantius wishes "threescore years" plucked from him (3b); is "heap of age" (3b); a "weak old man" (12b).
Lygones in *King and no King* is "old" (73a, 73b); his legs are wither'd kexes" (73b).

Holcomb, Thomas
Leocadia in *Love's Pilgrimage* is "little boy" (616b); "sixteen years" (622a); not so tall as Theodosia (622a); at least as young (622a).
Merione in *Queen of Corinth* is "A virtuous Lady" (D.P.).
Honora in *Loyal Subject* is more "strongly built" than Viola (330a).
Leucippe in *Humorous Lieutenant* is "the fat woman" (256b); "a fat lady" (257b); "This is three bawds beaten into one" (246a); "your'e fat" (246a).
Guiomar in *Custom of the Country* is "set in years" (130a); and speaks of "my age" (130b); is "a vertuous Lady" (D.P.).
Isabella in *Women Pleased* is "little one" (186a); "little rascal" (196a).
Nurse in *Little French Lawyer* is an "old fairy" (420a); "Like a miller's mare" (430a); speaks of twenty years (436b).
Rosellia in *Sea Voyage* says "I am old" (319b); is "one that's fifty" (319b); is told "you are old" (321a).
Delphia in *Prophetess* is "A small one" (3b); is included among "old women" (3b); "Their age" (3b).

Honyman, John
Ismenia in *Maid in the Mill* is "of the lowest stature" (583a, etc.).
Olinda in *Lover's Progress* is "a noble Maid" (D.P.).
Maria in *Wife for a Month* hears of "Your age" (568b); "a vertuous Lady" (D.P.).
Bianca in *Fair Maid* is thirteen (365a, 379b); is young (366a, 367a).

Lowin, G.
Lucinda in *Knight of Malta* is "A virgin of fourteen" (140a).
Viola in *Loyal Subject* is "not so strongly built" as Honora (330a); is "little one" (331b, 332a, 335b).

Zenocia in *Custom of the Country* is "very young" (106a) "a chaste Wife" (D.P.).

Arsinoe in *False One* is "young" (409b).

Belvidere in *Women Pleased* is "A virtuous Princess" (D.P.); "young smug wench" (192b).

Alinda in *Pilgrim* is above "fifteen" (591b); "The boy is young" (597a); "thou stripling" (601b); "a young boy" (603a); "little one" (605a); "small hobgoblin" (606b); sings (607a).

Lillia-Bianca in *Wild Goose Chase* is "Of a small body" (547b); speaks of "these ten years" (544b); sings (543a); dances (548b).

Juliana in *Double Marriage* is a "matchlesess (*sic*) Wife" (D.P.); young (114a).

Aminta in *Sea Voyage* is "young and tidy" (317b); "a little lean" (317b); "This little gentlewoman" (324b); "a noble French Virgin" (D.P.).

Ascanio in *Spanish Curate* is a "young lad" (157a); "raw untutor'd youth" (157a); "boy" (157b, 166a, 169a); "little steward" (160a); is at least sixteen or seventeen years old, since Don Henrique has been married to Violante "sixteen years" (158a); and his intrigue with Jacinta was before his marriage.

Lowin, John

Melantius in *Maid's Tragedy* was a conquering general when Amintor was a boy (1b); "a trim cheating soldier" (9b); "He's stout and able" (12b); "bears more years" than Amintor (14a); is a "sturdy fellow" (20a).

Mardonius in *King and no King* is "old and rough" (54b); "old" (68b).

Fabritio in *Captain* is "young and handsome yet" (623a); but he has been a soldier "Above these fourteen years" (624a); is "a merry Souldier" (D.P.).

Palamon in *Two Noble Kinsmen* is "tall young man" (571b); is "swarth and meagre," has heavy eye, still temper, "bold gravity," "brown manly face" (572b); "menacing aspect" (578a).

Valentinian in *Valentinian* is "young" (441a); "young and handsome" (451b); and speaks of "my youth" (454a).

Petilius in *Bonduca* is "A merry Captain, but somewhat wanton" (D.P.).

Antonio in *Chances* says "Mine audit's cast, and farewell five and fifty" (497b).

Sanchio in *Love's Pilgrimage* is "good old man" (621a).

Chilax in *Mad Lover* has served twenty-five years (290b); is "my old tough soldier" (298a); says "I am old" (300b); ironically "we young men" (308a); in disguise was "a tall stallion-nun" (309b); is "an old merry Souldier" (D.P.).

Norandine in *Knight of Malta* is "A valiant merry Dane" (D.P.); has "too much flesh" to be a knight of Malta (151a).

Theodore in *Loyal Subject* is a "boy" to his father Archas (324a); "valorous, but impatient" (D.P.).

Leontius in *Humorous Lieutenant* is "old" (235b); and has an "old body" (240b); he is "a brave old merry Souldier" (D.P.).

Barnavelt in *Barnavelt* is "old" (211, 246, 277, 282, 285, 292, 302, 311); and grey (211, 241); has had the power of a King "thirtie yeeres" (212); and speaks of "forty yeares endeavoures" (242).

Rutilio in *Custom of the Country* is "A merry Gentleman" (D.P.), who says "I have lived this thirty years" (105a); but speaks of "my years" (130a); and is older than Arnoldo, who is thirty (106a, 116b); has beard (113b); is "wondrous able" (118b); "of a goodly person" (125b); has "manly set" (130a); "Strong and goodly" (131a).

Cassilane in *Laws of Candy* is "old" (369a); has fought fifty years (369b); "forty years a drudge, a pack-horse" (372a); "I that some seven apprenticeships commanded" (377a).

Sceva in *False One* is "a free Speaker"; "Captain" (D.P.); he is "old" (396b, 398b); says "I am a porter,/A strong one too" (396a).

Piniero in *Island Princess* is "A merry Captain" (D.P.); and speaks of "my able youth" (245a).

Bartello in *Women Pleased* is "old" (185b, 195b); "fat" (196b); a dry neat's tongue (188b); "Captain of the Citadel" (D.P.).

Cleremont in *Little French Lawyer* was a soldier "At fifteen" (412a); and has been one "five-and twenty years" (412a); yet he is grouped with Dinant as "young" (427a, 433a); he is "a merry Gentleman" (D.P.).

Alphonso in *Pilgrim* is "an old angry Gentleman" (D.P.); "old" (610b, 611b, 615b); "He has flesh, and hide enough" (611b).

Belleur in *Wild Goose Chase* is "a great fellow" (542b); "The tall fat fellow" (551b); "a maypole! A great dry pudding" (558a); a "mighty dairy-maid in man's clothes" (558a); "of a stout blunt humour" (D.P.).

Duke of Sesse in *Double Marriage* is "old" (108a); "his age" (103a); "so young again" (110a); "A goodly personage" (115b).

Tibalt in *Sea Voyage* "was born quarreling" (311a); is "a merry Gentleman" (D.P.); "gross" (323b).

Bartolus in *Spanish Curate* is a "churl" (159a); and has "that fat of thine" (169a).

Dioclesian in *Prophetess* is "cut with an axe out" (13b).

Dorilaus in *Lover's Progress* hears of "age" (656a); is "kill-cow Dorilaus" (647a); a "merry old man" (D.P.).

Frederick in *Wife for a Month* is "younger" of the brothers, but his wife Maria hears of "Your age" (568b); "unnatural and libidinous Brother" (D.P.).

Aubrey in *Bloody Brother* is "somewhat high of stature," "About seven-and-fifty," "fat," "somewhat corpulent," "His head and beard inclining to be grey" (535a).

Leon in *Rule a Wife* is a "goodly fellow" (345a); has a "giant's promise" (345a); "He's made as strong as brass, is of brave years too" (350a); "good presence," "lusty body" (350b); "strong fellow" (351a); "portly presence" (353b); "lean" (353b).

Alberto in *Fair Maid of the Inn* is old (359a, 362a, 370b); friend to Baptista fifty years (362a).

Ostler, William

The Father in *Captain* is "old" (620a, 630b); a soldier "twenty winters" (624a).

Maximus in *Valentinian* speaks of "my youth" (463b).

Pallant, Robert

Aminta in *Maid in the Mill* says "I am a child, sir" (590b).

Clarinda in *Lover's Progress* is "a lustful Wench" (D.P.).

Cassandra in *Wife for a Month* is "old" (570a, 570b, 573b, 580b, 582a, 585b); is called "good antiquity" (570b); and "Time" (580b); hears of "age" (582b); and is "all one crookedness" (570a); "an old Bawd" (D.P.).

Margarita in *Rule a Wife* is constantly described as young, is of "low stature" (356a); "but little" (356a); is wished to be a "size or two stronger" (356b); a "little piece of mischief" (357a); has a "greedy eye" (347a).

Clarissa in *Fair Maid* is year younger than Cesario (368a); "young" (369a); has "youth" (378a).

Pollard, Thomas

Onos in *Queen of Corinth* is "the youth/Of six and fifty" (26b); "exceeding meagre" (27a); described in detail (34a); "he is fifty" (34a); has been a ward forty years (38b); "A very foolish Traveller" (D.P.); sold tobacco to the gentlemen at the theater (34a).

[380]

The Lieutenant in *Humorous Lieutenant* is "A goodly man" (254a); "a mad shaver" (241a); "boy" (253b); "I do believe a horse begot this fellow;/He never knew his strength yet" (248b).

Holderus in *Barnavelt* is "little Sir Gregory" (241).

Mochingo in *Laws of Candy* is "an ignorant Servant" (D.P.).

Soto in *Women Pleased* is "A merry servant" (D.P.).

La-Writ in *Little French Lawyer* is "A rare youth" (417b); "little" (418a, 423a, 424a, 431a); "What an alphabet of faces he puts on!" (419a); his sword "has not seen sun these ten years" (418a); sings (419b).

Pinac in *Wild Goose Chase* is "young Pinac" (541a); "a young man" (548b); sings (548a).

Villio in *Double Marriage* is "A Court fool" (D.P.).

Diego in *Spanish Curate* has been "old honest sexton" for twenty years (162a); "loved to feed well" (174b); "grew fat by the brewis of an egg-shell" (174b); wishes "some forty pound of lovely beef" (180b); has "lenten-chaps" (180b).

Franio in *Maid in the Mill* had known Gillian "forty summers" (605a); and hears of "age" (605a).

Malfort in *Lover's Progress* has a "reverend beard and shape" (635a); but is a "walking skeleton" (635b); "renew'd his youth" (636b); a "piece of motley" (636b); "a foolish Steward" (D.P.).

Norbrett in *Bloody Brother* has been a magician twenty-one years (532b).

Alonzo in *Rule a Wife* pulls his legs after him (347a); and is an "old seducer" (350a).

Rice, John

Arethusa in *Philaster* is "young and tall" (41b).

Evadne in *Maid's Tragedy* speaks of "my years" (7a); has "black eye" and "red cheek" (11a); is told "Thy body is too little for the story" (15b).

Robinson, Richard

Aspatia of *Maid's Tragedy* in disguise is "Gentle youth" (23b); above "twelve years old" (24a), "but young" (24a).

Spaconia in *King and no King* is "That little one" (61a).

Frank in *Captain* sings (626a); is "a Lady passionately in love" (D.P.).

Jailor's Daughter in *Two Noble Kinsmen* says "when fifteen once has found us" (562b); "She's eighteen" (576b, revision); sings frequently.

Lucina in *Valentinian* is "yet not eighteen" (438a); and could be managed "If she were fat" (439a) ; a "chast abused Wife" (D.P.).

Constantia in *Chances* is "young as the Morning" (501a) ; has "a handsome body" (502a) ; ?sings (501b, 502a).

Theodosia in *Love's Pilgrimage* is "yet in growing" (608b) ; "can not be/Above seventeen" (609a) ; "young" (616a) ; "little,/A demy dame" (622a) ; "taller" than Leocadia (622a).

Brunhalt in *Thierry and Theodoret* is old (405b, 406a, 406b, 407b).

Charino in *Custom of the Country* is "old" (107b, 109b) ; and hears of "your age" (106b).

La Castre in *Wild Goose Chase* is an "Indulgent Father" (D.P.).

Marco (and Rugio) in *Wife for a Month* are "Old and experienced men" (579a).

Baldwin in *Bloody Brother* is old (528a & b).

Rowley, William

Bustopha in *Maid in the Mill* is "a child" (585a) ; "With all that flesh about him" (586a) ; "at these years" (586b) ; "hopeful youth" (588a) ; "taken him for Hector" (588a) ; "his flesh" (590b, 591a) ; "mountain" (598b) ; "boy" (605b) ; "a Clown" (D.P.).

Tony in *Wife for a Month* calls himself "the old fool" (577b) as compared with Evanthe ; " 'Twould pose a fellow that had twice my body" (573a) ; sings (578a) ; a "Knavish fool" (D.P.).

The Cook in *Bloody Brother* is heavy (523b).

Cacafogo in *Rule a Wife* is frequently referred to as very fat (348a, 348b, 355a, 355b, 356a, 357a, 360a, 362a, 363b, 365b) ; needs a ladder to beat Leon, blows fall too low by a foot (348b).

Clown in *Fair Maid of the Inn* is very fat (374a, 374b, 377b, 380a, 380b).

Sands, James

Euphrasia of *Philaster* in disguise is "boy" (31a, 31b, etc.) ; "tender youth" (32a) ; "about eighteen" (35b, 39a) ; "A little boy" (37a).

Panthea in *King and no King* was only nine when Arbaces went to war (52a).

Lelia in *Captain* is "brown" (627a) ; "neither a bud, nor blown" (627a) ; "a cunning wanton Widow" (D.P.).

Emilia in *Two Noble Kinsmen* is "young virgin" (563a) ; "fair-eyed" (570a) ; her friend died "when our count/Was each eleven" (557a).

[382]

APPENDIX IV

Shank, John
  Geta in *Prophetess* is "a pretty youth" (10b); "of a spare body" (11a); "My face was bad enough" (17b); "what you want in growth and full proportion" (11a); "A Jester," "a merry Knave" (D.P.).

Sharp, Richard
  Patience in *Henry VIII* ?sings (III. 1. 3-14).
  Hengo in *Bonduca* is "A brave boy" (D.P.); "little vermin" (55b); "A dwarf devil in a doublet" (63a).
  Ordella in *Thierry and Theodoret* is "Some fifteen at the most" (410b).
  Celia-Enanthe in *Humorous Lieutenant* (? revision) has a "little tongue" (233b); and "She is very young, sure" (245b).
  Erota in *Laws of Candy* is "a Princess, imperious, and of an overweaning Beauty" (D.P.).
  Hippolyta in *Custom of the Country* is "A building of so goodly a proportion" (117a); "wantonly in Love" (D.P.).
  Cleopatra in *False One* is "Young" (388b).
  Quisara in *Island Princess* is "of the strongest parts" (236b).
  Martia in *Double Marriage* is "a goodly woman" (113a); large (119a); under "two-and-twenty" (116a); was with Nurse when father took her away to sea fourteen years before (104a).
  Oriana in *Wild Goose Chase* is "eighteen now" (546b); "She's a tall woman" (562b); "Of a fair size" (562b); "witty follower of the Chase" (D.P.).
  Clarinda in *Sea Voyage* is "improved/In height and large proportion" (314a).
  Violante in *Spanish Curate* hears "In stature you're a giantess" (178b).
  Clarange in *Lover's Progress* speaks of "our youths" (641b); and is about the same age as Lidian, who is a "youth" (638a, 641a);
                    "in his face appears
  A kind of majesty which should command,
  Not sue for favour" (638b).
  Otto in *Bloody Brother* is "youth" (522a); "young traitor" (528b).
  Duke in *Rule a Wife* is "youth" (366a).
  Mentivole in *Fair Maid of the Inn* is "young" (360a, 362a, 380a); "youth" (362a).

Swanston, Eyllaerdt
  Baptista in *Fair Maid of the Inn* is "old" (357b, 359a); has known Alberto fifty years (362a).

THE SHAKESPEAREAN COMPANY

Taylor, Joseph

Demetrius in *Humorous Lieutenant* is "young" (234a, 238b);
"youth" (235b, 236b, 251b); a "sweet young man" (234b).

The Prince of Orange in *Barnavelt* seems to be "younger still
and fresher" than Barnavelt (248); he seems not to be old,
since it is hoped that in the future "though old and bruizd"
he may be happy (220); and that he may die "an old and
good Prince" (313).

Arnoldo in *Custom of the Country* is the "younger brother" of
Rutilio (106a); has no beard (113b); is "a handsome young
fellow" (107a); hears of "your youth" (107b); finds that
he has been poor "these thirty years" (116a); but is finally
rich.

Antinous in *Laws of Candy* is "young" (369a); "youth" (379a);
"boy" (369b, 370a); "stripling" (370a); his father was a soldier fifty years, "more than half of this" before the birth of
Antinous (369b). He is thus under twenty-five years old.

Armusia in *Island Princess* is "a handsome gentleman" (241b);
"a noble daring Portugueze" (D.P.).

Silvio in *Women Pleased* is "youth" (178b, 198b); "young"
(178a, 184b, 189b, 193a); has been "twenty years" a friend
of Claudio (179a).

Dinant in *Little French Lawyer* is "boy" (415a); "boyish"
(419b); "youth" (420a); a "young lord" (424b).

Pedro in *Pilgrim* is "handsome" (592a); "A handsome well-built
person" (593b); "Both young and handsome;/Only the sun
has been too saucy with him" (593b); "handsome youth"
(594a); "How young" (594a); "You are young and fair"
(594a); "a noble Gentleman" (D.P.).

Mirabel in *Wild Goose Chase* is "A young and handsome man"
(541b); a "pretty-timber'd man" (544a); and sings (555b).

Albert in *Sea Voyage* has known the seas "these twenty years"
(308b); he is "A strong young man" (310a); "youth, and
heat of blood" (313a); "A middle stature, and of brown complexion" (320b); "my youth and strength" (323a); "young
able man" (326b).

Jamie in *Spanish Curate* is a "young lord" (157a); a year
younger than Henrique (157b, 158a); "We are young"
(158b).

Maximinian in *Prophetess* is "young" (4a); "This rare and
sweet young man" (13a); "a little younger" than Dioclesian
(13b).

Lisander in *Lover's Progress* is a "brave youth" (639b); a
"curl'd-hair gentleman" (639b); "A handsome-timber'd man"
(640b); "youth" (645b).

[384]

APPENDIX IV

Valerio in *Wife for a Month* is a "youth" (571a, 576a, 577a, 577b, 580a); "young" (577b, 583a, 588b); "smug boy" (577b); "a noble young Lord" (D.P.).

Perez in *Rule a Wife* is "young" (349b); "mighty Mars" (352a); "proper man" (352b).

Cesario in *Fair Maid of the Inn* is constantly alluded to as young, but was "thirty and odd winters" (376a).

Thompson, John

Phoebe in *Humorous Lieutenant* is very small and young (240a).

Eros in *False One* is "a young plump villain" (399b).

Juletta in *Pilgrim* is "A little foot-boy" (603a); "little gentleman" (606a); "I am a little foot-boy" (615b); "little devil" (613b); "a witty Lass" (D.P.).

Rosalura in *Wild Goose Chase* is "that grasshopper" (561b).

Florimel in *Maid in the Mill* is "fifteen, and upwards" (586b); would kiss Otrante if tall enough (601a); had been with Franio "fourteen years" (605b); sings (601a).

Calista in *Lover's Progress* is "a vertuous Lady" (D.P.).

Evanthe in *Wife for a Month* is a "chaste Wife" (D.P.).

Estifiana in *Rule a Wife* is "young" (350b, 352a, 355b, 358a).

Mariana in *Fair Maid of the Inn* is "a virtuous Lady" (D.P.); has "too many years" to marry (371a).

Tooley, Nicholas

Detailed description in *Two Noble Kinsmen* as little freckled knight of thirty-six (573a & b).

Judas in *Bonduca* has "Nothing but flesh and bones left" (49b); is "corporal Curry-comb" (50a); "He looks like Hunger's self" (55a); "Thou skin of man" (55b); "That hungry fellow/With the red beard there" (55b); "the thin starved rascal" (63a); "A Corporal, a merry hungry knave" (D.P.).

Incubo in *Love's Pilgrimage* is "six-and-thirty" (609a).

The Fool in *Mad Lover* is "boy" (296b); "The fins grow out of thy face" (296a).

Tutor in *Queen of Corinth*, Onos, and his uncle are spoken of as "lean famine" (27a); "thin cubs" (33a).

Briskie, disguised as Putskie, in *Loyal Subject* is "old" (322b).

Penurio in *Women Pleased* is a "Lean-gut" (188a); "thin" (188b;) "lean rogue" (196b); fallen "to a spindle" (195a); "shotten friend" (183b); and advised to "Be fat" (183b); "A hungry servant" (D.P.); also a "bow-case" (188b); and "Shadow" (188b).

Champernel in *Little French Lawyer* is "old" (413a); "a lame old Gentleman" (D.P.).

Nantolet in *Wild Goose Chase* is noticeably fat or lean (561a).

Castruccio in *Double Marriage* is "a sweet youth" (110b); "A court Parasite" (D.P.).

Sebastian in *Sea Voyage* seems to have a lean and hungry look (311a & b); "good old man" (312b); says "I feel nor age, nor weakness" (327a).

Lopez in *Spanish Curate* is "poor thin thief" (161a); has a "pig belly" (161a); is "old vicar" (167b); "these twenty years" (166b).

Trigg, William

Pipeau in *Bloody Brother* is "infant" (533a).

Old Woman in *Rule a Wife* is "great-grandmother" (356a).

Underwood, John

Pharamond in *Philaster* is "large speaker" (28b); "a prince of wax" (29a); "growing to fatness" (32b); "young" (34b, 41a); "trim man" (47b).

Lysippus in *Maid's Tragedy* is "Royal young man" (23a).

Julio in *Captain* is "young," "sober" (621b).

Marc-Antonio in *Love's Pilgrimage* is young (612b, 614b, 618a, 618b); and is "of a handsome body" (612b).

Siphax in *Mad Lover* is a "boy" (295b); a "foolish young man" (297b).

Colonna in *Knight of Malta* is "A handsome fellow" (133b).

The Duke in *Loyal Subject* is "young" (313b, 314a); "Boy" (337b); speaks of "my youth" (319b).

Clodio in *Custom of the Country* is a "great blind fool" (110a); a "great booby" (110a).

Gonzalo in *Laws of Candy* is "An ambitious Politick Lord" (D.P.).

Septimius in *False One* is "old" (389b, 405b); "a revolted Roman Villain" (D.P.).

Ternata in *Island Princess* has a "rugged face" (235a); "dangerous eyes" (235a); is "no such boy" (236a); has been "these twenty years" a priest (248a); which has "stamp'd a meagreness" (248a).

Claudio in *Women Pleased* is "young" (185a, 195b); "boy" (186b); and speaks of "My youth" (185b).

Roderigo in *Pilgrim* is "young" (591a); "handsome" (591a); has beard (607b).

Lugier in *Wild Goose Chase* is "youth" (553b).

Ferrand in *Double Marriage* speaks of "the little blood is left me" (101b).

The Master in *Sea Voyage* is "A poor old man" (319a);

[386]

"though he be old, he's tough" (319a) ; "old lad" (326a) ; "You are old" (319a).

Milanes in Spanish Curate is "young" (158b).

Leon in *Lover's Progress* is "young as Lisander" (649b) ; who is "youth."

Unclassified

The Host in *Captain* is a "fat man" (634a).

The Woman in *Captain* is a "little varlet" (630b).

Two Noble Kinsmen has full description of two unidentified actors (573a & b).

Proculus in *Valentinian* has been at his job "two-and-thirty years" (439a).

Slave Girl in *Very Woman* is "nine year old" (III. 1).

Bonvica in *Bonduca* is Bonduca's "little daughter" (55b) ; "Her youngest " (51b).

Courtezan in *Mad Lover* is "a good round virgin" (306a).

Timon in *Humorous Lieutenant* has served Antigonus twenty or twenty-five years (237b).

Arcanes in *Laws of Candy* is "old" (377a).

Decius in *Laws of Candy* is a "Rash young man" (378a).

Syana, and Governor in *Island Princess* are "youths" (235b) ; Syana is "Young man" (235a).

Lamure in *Sea Voyage* has been "twenty years" making his money (309b).

Sulpitia in *Custom of the Country* speaks of "mine age" (118a) ; and is an "old cat" (118b).

THE LISTS OF ACTORS
IN THE SECOND BEAUMONT AND
FLETCHER FOLIO

THESE lists are taken from the copy of the second folio owned by the University of Chicago, checked by that of the University of Illinois, and are given in the same order as the plays in the tables, except *The Wild Goose Chase*. The second folio is numbered for two volumes, the second beginning with *The Queen of Corinth*. The arrangement of the title pages, ornamental initial letters, and the arrangement and punctuation of the actor lists are all different for the two volumes. For the lists, the first volume uses periods and brackets as below, the second uses commas.

The Captain.

Richard Burbadge.
Henry Condel.

William Ostler.
Alexander Cooke.

Valentinian.

Richard Burbadge.
Henry Condel.
John Lowin.

William Ostler.
John Vnderwood.

Bonduca.

Richard Burbadge,
Henry Condel,
William Eglestone,
Nich. Toolie,

William Ostler,
John Lowin,
John Vnderwood,
Richard Robinson.

The Mad Lover.

Richard Burbadge.
Robert Benfeild.
Nathanael Feild.
Henry Condel.

John Lowin.
William Eglestone.
Richard Sharpe.

The Queen of Corinth.

Richard Burbadge,
Henry Condel,
John Vnderwood,
Thomas Polard,

Nathan Feild,
John Lowin,
Nich` Toolie,
Tho. Holcomb,

The Knight of Malta.

Rich: Burbadge,	Henry Condel,
Nathan Field,	Robert Benfeild,
John Vnderwood,	John Lowin,
Rich. Sharpe,	Thomas Holcome.

The Loyal Subject.

Richard Burbadge.	Nathanael Feild.
Henry Condel.	John Vnderwood.
John Lowin.	Nicholas Toolie.
Richard Sharpe.	William Eglestone.

The Humorous Lieutenant.

Henry Condel.	Joseph Taylor.
John Lowin.	William Eglestone.
Richard Sharpe.	John Vnderwood.
Robert Benfeild.	Thomas Polard.

The Custom of the Country.

Joseph Taylor.	Robert Benfeild.
John Lowin.	William Eglestone.
Nicholas Toolie.	Richard Sharpe.
John Vnderwood.	Thomas Holcomb.

The Laws of Candy.

Joseph Taylor.	John Lowin.
William Eglestone.	John Vnderwood.
Nicholas Toolie.	George Birch.
Richard Sharpe.	Thomas Pollard.

The False One.

John Lowin.	Joseph Taylor.
John Vnderwood.	Nicholas Toolie.
Robert Benfield.	John Rice.
Richard Sharpe.	George Birch.

The Island Princess.

John Lowin,	Joseph Tailor,
John Vnderwood,	Robert Benfield,
William Eglestone,	George Birch,
Rich. Sharpe,	Tho. Polard.

Women Pleas'd.

Joseph Taylor,	John Lowin,
John Vnderwood,	Will. Eglestone,
Rob. Benfield,	Nicholas Toolie,
Rich. Sharpe,	Thomas Holcombe.

The Little French Lawyer.

Joseph Taylor.
John Lowin.
John Vnderwood.
Robert Benfield.

Nicholas Toolie.
William Egleston.
Richard Sharpe.
Thomas Holcomb.

The Pilgrim.

Joseph Taylor.
Nicholas Toolie.
Robert Benfield.
John Thompson.

John Lowin.
John Vnderwood.
George Birch.
James Horn.

The Double Marriage.

Joseph Tailor,
Robert Benfield,
John Vnderwood,
George Birch,

John Lowin,
Rich. Robinson,
Nich. Tooly,
Rich. Sharp.

The Sea Voyage.

Joseph Taylor,
William Eglestone,
Nich. Toolie.

Joh Lowin.
John Vnderwood.

The Spanish Curate.

Joseph Taylor.
John Lowin.
Nicholas Toolie.

William Eglestone.
Thomas Polard.
Robert Benfeild.

The Prophetess.

John Lowin.
Robert Benfield.
John Shanke.
Richard Sharpe.

Joseph Taylor.
Nicholas Toolie.
George Birch.
Thomas Holcombe.

The Maid in the Mill.

Joseph Tailor,
John Lowin,
John Vnderwood,
William Rowly,

John Thompson.
Robert Benfield,
Tho. Polard.

The Lover's Progress.

Joseph Taylor.
Robert Benfield.
Thomas Polard.
George Birch.

John Lowin.
John Vnderwood.
Richard Sharpe.
John Thomson.

[390]

A Wife for a Month.

Joseph Taylor.   Robert Benfield.
Richard Robinson.   John Vnderwood.
Nicholas Toolie.   George Birch.

The Wild Goose Chase.

Robert Benfield.   John Lowin.   William Trigg.
Richard Robinson.   William Penn.   Sander Gough.
Joseph Taylor   Hilliard Swanston.   Mr. Shank.
Thomas Pollard.   Stephen Hammerton.   John Honyman.

Now that we have worked out the parts taken by each principal actor in the Beaumont and Fletcher plays, it may be well to ascertain what method the editor followed in formulating his lists of principal actors. Why did he select eight for his typical number? The plays 1611-19, have six to nine men, and one to three women with one hundred lines and over. The plays after 1619, have from four to eight men, usually five, and one to four women with one hundred lines and over. It is interesting to note in this connection that Jonson names six, eight, or ten in his lists of principal actors. The Beaumont and Fletcher editor would also probably prefer to have an even number, because the names were to be arranged in parallel columns, and the above figures show that eight was nearer the average number of principal actors than six or ten.

How did the editor supply this information as to actors? A few suggestive facts point clearly to memory rather than to complete manuscript records. Indeed it is very doubtful that any complete manuscript record was ever made. It will be noticed that all lists name eight principal actors except *The Captain*, 1611; *Valentinian*, 1614; *The Mad Lover*, 1616-19; *The Sea Voyage*, *The Spanish Curate*, and *The Maid in the Mill*, 1622-23; and the bungled list of *A Wife for a Month*, 1624. Leaving the bungled list and *The Mad Lover* out of consideration for the time, the irregular lists belong to two periods, 1611-14, and 1622-23. In both of these periods, it is chiefly the apprentices who are omitted. Now as we have seen, a set of apprentices was graduating and new apprentices were taking their places precisely at each of these dates. This would seem to indicate that the editor did not remember exactly whether the parts were taken by the graduating or by the entering apprentices. Indeed in *The Captain* there is not even a full list of men. The same trusting to memory probably accounts for the blunder of listing Tooley as a principal actor in *A Wife for a Month*, when he had been some months dead before the play was produced.[1] In *The Mad Lover* the editor omits the second appren-

[1] Not only does *A Wife for a Month* contain Tooley's name, though he

tice, who according to the line represented would have been Robinson.

Who supplied the publishers with this information concerning the principal actors in these plays? They do not make direct statement in this matter, but we may infer that they received it from the "ingenious and worthy Gentleman" who is credited with having corrected many of the errors of the first folio. "His corrections were the more to be valued, because he had an intimacy with both our Authors, and had been a Spectator of most of them when they were Acted in their life-time." To have possession of all the things credited to him, this "ingenious" person must have been more than a mere spectator; he must have been intimately connected with the company, since only one so connected could have supplied the lists of principal actors. As we have seen, there were almost certainly no such lists in manuscript, the lists being supplied only from memory, as we have already seen cause to believe these were.

We may get a clue to the compiler's identity by seeing over what period his memory extends. It is to be noticed first that the statement made by the publishers that the corrections were made on the first folio is confirmed by the fact that no one of the plays added to the second folio from quarto has an actor list except *The Wild Goose Chase*, which was separately published from manuscript in 1652, with a complete assigned list of actors. But not even every play of the first folio is given a list. Of the thirty-four plays in this folio, the compiler gives lists for only twenty-four. These twenty-four are divided, twenty-two for the Shakespearean company dating 1611-24, and two for the amalgamated Rossiter-Princess Elizabeth's company of 1613-14. The ten plays of the first folio for which principal actors are not given are: *Beggars' Bush*, *Chances*, *Fair Maid of the Inn*, *Four Plays in One*, *Love's Cure or the Martial Maid*, *Love's Pilgrimage*, *Nice Valour or The Passionate Mad Man*, *Noble Gentleman*, *Wit at Several Weapons*, and *Woman's Prize*. For the period 1610-23, only *The Chances*, summer 1615, and *Love's Pilgrimage*, winter 1615, were not supplied with lists. One of these plays had been sufficiently revised to be re-

had been dead more than a year when the play was licensed; but also it is the only play with a fairly complete list that omits Lowin's name. It has been suggested that the two names were interchanged, but our troubles will not be relieved by this supposition. According to the lines represented, the six chief men actors in the play must have been Joseph Taylor, John Lowin, Robert Benfield, John Underwood, William Rowley, and Richard Robinson; and this should have been the list. Thus Lowin and Rowley have been omitted from the list as it now appears, and Tooley inserted. Possibly some accident happened to the list, as seems indicated also by the fact that it contains six instead of the usual eight names. But more probably the compiler of the list mistook the date of the play, found a tangle, and left his list incomplete.

licensed, and the other had also probably received the same treatment, this fact constituting them new plays to the informant, and
accounting for his not being able to supply the lists. It must be
significant therefore that in giving actor lists all unrevised Beaumont and Fletcher plays from 1611 to 1624 are included, and all
plays before and after those dates excluded.

Who was connected with the Princess Elizabeth and Shakespearean companies at the periods mentioned? The connection of
one man, and only one, covers these periods exactly. This man was
William Eccleston, who went from the Shakespearean company in
1611, seemingly just after *The Captain* had been produced, to the
Princess Elizabeth organization, from which he returned in 1614
to the Shakespearean company, to remain till about the spring of
1623, when he withdrew from the company. He alone could have
known the intimate details attributed to the "ingenious" gentleman who was intimate with both Beaumont and Fletcher.

Collier noticed that W. E. signed some lines to the 1652 quarto
of *The Wild Goose Chase*, and queried if the initials could be those
of William Eccleston.[2] If one remembers the roistering, singing
soldier Eccleston as he reads:

> "In this late dearth of wit, when *Jose* and *Jack*
> Were hunger-bit for want of fowl and Sack,
> His nobleness found out this happy meanes
> To mend their dyet with these WILD-GOOSE scenes,
> By which he hath revived in a day
> Two Poets, and two Actors with one Play"

the conviction becomes strong that W.E. is William Eccleston still
alive as a merry old gentleman of some seventy-five years, and in
touch with his old fellows, though his active connection with the
company had long since ceased. It seems quite probable that the
actor list of *The Wild Goose Chase* suggested a similar plan to
him for the plays of the first folio. He had thus probably amused
his old age, and instructed the younger generation by reliving
the good old days before "this late dearth of wit." If so, his copy
of the first folio, which the publishers bought, almost certainly
had the parts assigned to the principal characters as in *The Wild
Goose Chase*. The publishers then detached them in lists, precisely
as they did for the quarto of that play. Would that the ingenious
gentleman's corrected and annotated copy of the first folio might
yet be found, or rather would that it had been found in time to
save me from all this drudgery.

[2] Collier, *Memoirs*, p. 248. Perhaps the record of burial at St. Michael,
Cornhill, 1672, "Aug. 11 William Egleston; in the churchyd; a stranger" is
too late for the actor. A William Eaglestone and Susan his wife had a
daughter Susan baptized November 10, 1633; buried October 8, 1638, at
Allhallows in the Wall, where Taylor for a time resided.

PERSONAL ALLUSIONS
IN SHAKESPEARE'S PLAYS

R EFERENCES are to the Oxford edition of Shakespeare by
W. J. Craig. For the principles of selection, see Appendix
IV, heading.

Armin, Robert

Touchstone in *As You Like It* is "The clownish fool" (I. 3. 133);
"roynish clown" (II. 2. 8); "A motley fool" (II. 7. 13); sings
a snatch of a ballad (III. 3).

Feste, the fool in *Twelfth Night*, "has an excellent breast" (II.
3. 20-21); sings (II. 3; IV. 2; V. 1); says as priest "I am
not tall enough to become the function well, nor lean enough
to be thought a good student" (IV. 2. 7-8); Aguecheek wishes
"I had such a leg, and so sweet a breath to sing" (II. 3. 22).

Evans in *Merry Wives* sings (III. 1. 17-21, 23-26).

Pompey in *Measure for Measure* is told "your bum is the greatest thing about you" (II. 1. 234-5).

Fool in *Lear* is "pretty knave" (I. 4.108); "lad" (I.4.154);
"boy" (I. 4. 119, 146; I. 5. 18, 55; III. 2. 68; III. 4. 26);
sings frequently.

Cloten in *Cymbeline* does "reek as a sacrifice" (I. 2. 2-3); "fool"
(I. 2. 26; II. 1. 52, etc.); "no less young, more strong" than
Posthumus (IV. 1. 11); "Being scarce made up,/I mean, to
man" (IV. 2. 109-10); "then but young" (IV. 4. 23) when
Belarius knew him twenty years before. He must thus have
been at least thirty-five, probably about forty; but this would
make his mother quite old. He wears the clothes of Posthumus
(IV. 1. 2-3), and his dead body is mistaken for that of Posthumus (IV. 2. 310-11).

The Clown in *Winter's Tale* is a "young man" (IV. 3. 842); and
is regularly addressed as boy by his father; he and father
"rough and hairy" (IV. 3. 747).

Trinculo in *The Tempest* has "lesser legs" than Caliban (II. 2.
112); is "made like a goose" (II. 2. 141); is a "jesting
monkey" (III. 2. 53); "a pied ninny" (III. 2. 73).

Armin's Apprentice

Mamillius in *Winter's Tale* is a "child" (I. 1. 42).

Bryane, George

King in *All's Well* is "old" (V. 3. 40; I. 2. 29); but "of as able body as when he numbered thirty" (IV. 5. 87).

Antipholus of Syracuse in *Comedy of Errors* is the twin brother of the other Antipholus, whose description see under Phillips.

Valentine in *Two Gentlemen of Verona* is "youthful" (1. 3. 26, etc.); told: "you are beautified/With goodly shape" (IV. 1. 55-6); "a proper man" (IV. 1. 11).

Friar Laurence in *Romeo and Juliet* is old (II. 3. 74; V. 3. 122, 229, 267).

Warwick in *3 Henry VI* has "coal-black hair" (V. 1. 54).

Titus Andronicus is old (I. 1. 166, etc.); he has "silver hair" (III. 1. 260); his head "shakes for age and feebleness" (I. 1. 188); and he says "Rome, I have been thy soldier forty years" (I. 1. 193); arms are "wither'd herbs" (III. 1. 178); says "Marcus, we are but shrubs, no cedars we;/No big-bon'd men fram'd of the Cyclops' size;/But metal, Marcus, steel to the very back" (IV. 3. 45-7).

John of Gaunt in *Richard II* is old (I. 1. 1, 160, etc.).

Archbishop Scroop in *2 Henry IV* is a man "Whose beard the silver hand of peace hath touch'd" (IV. 1. 43); in "white investments" (IV. 1. 45).

Morocco in *Merchant of Venice* has "complexion of a devil" (I. 2. 141).

Burbadge, Richard

Romeo in *Romeo and Juliet* is young (I. 5. 72; II. 3. 89; II. 4. 128; III. 1. 71, 136, 150, etc.); "He bears him like a portly gentleman" (I. 5. 70); "though his face be better than any man's, yet his leg excels all men's; and for a hand, and a foot, and a body, though they be not to be talked on, yet they are past compare" (II. 5. 40-3); wears "French slop" (II. 4.48-9).

Talbot in *1 Henry VI* "is a child, a silly dwarf," "this weak and writhled shrimp" (II. 3. 23-4); "grey-beard" (III. 2. 50); speaks of "My age" (IV. 5. 46; III. 2. 54, etc.).

Richard in *2 Henry VI* is a : "heap of wrath, foul indigested lump,/As crooked in thy manners as thy shape" (V. 1. 157-8).

Richard in *3 Henry VI* is younger than Edward (Phillips) (I. 2. 1); "crook-back prodigy" (I. 4. 75); "foul misshapen stigmatic" (II. 2. 136); has withered arm, hunch back, legs of unequal size, general deformity (III. 2. 156-62); cf. V. 5. 30, 35; V. 6. 51; V. 7. 23; called Roscius (V. 6. 10).

Lucius in *Titus Andronicus* is "boy" (III. 1. 283) to his father, and speaks of "My youth" (III. 1. 166).

Fenton in *Merry Wives* is "young" (III. 2. 70), and has "eyes of youth" (III. 2. 71), and "Have not your worship a wart above your eye " (I. 4. 152-3).

Richard in *Richard III* is "rudely stamp'd" (I. 1. 16); is "halt and am misshapen thus" (I. 2. 252); "bunch-back'd toad" (I. 3. 246; IV. 4. 81); withered arm (III. 4. 68).

Hamlet in *Hamlet* is consistently "young" in the quarto of 1603 (II. 1. 78; II. 2. c92; III. 3. c4; V. 1. c190); but these references are omitted in the final edition, though elsewhere we hear of "young Hamlet" (I. 1. 170; I. 2. 124; I. 5. 16, 38, etc.); wears "inky cloak . . . customary suits of solemn black" (I. 2. 77-8); has "too too solid flesh" (I. 2. 129); full description of appearance (II. 1. 78-84); has "beard" (II. 2. 608); "unmatch'd form and feature of blown youth" (III. 1. 168); "thou noble youth" (I. 5. 38); Claudius is no more like Hamlet's father "Than I to Hercules" (Q₁ I. 2. 153); "He's fat, and scant of breath" (V. 2. 301).

Demetrius in *Midsummer Night's Dream* is "disdainful youth" (II. 1. 261).

Lucentio in *Taming of the Shrew* is "young" (I. 2. 172; II. 1. 79).

Richard in *Richard II* is young (II. 1. 2. 20, 69; III. 3. 204).

Prince Harry does not appear in *Richard II*, but we hear of him as a "young wanton and effeminate boy" (V. 3. 10).

Prince Hal in *I Henry IV* is young (I. 1. 86; I. 2. 1, 91; III. 2. 26; IV. 1. 104); and is "you starveling, you elf-skin, you dried neat's-tongue, you bull's-pizzle, you stock-fish! O! for breath to utter what is like thee; you tailor's yard, you sheath, you bow-case, you vile standing-tuck" (II. 4. 274-8); "a fine thief of the age of two and twenty, or thereabouts" (III. 3. 210-12); has "a villanous trick of thine eye and a foolish hanging of thy nether lip" (II. 4. 50-2).

Harry in *2 Henry IV* is young (I. 2. 165, 166, 224; V. 2. 9; V. 3. 119); and has no beard (I. 2. 22-30); is same size and weight as Poins (II. 4. 265, 276-7).

Bassanio in *Merchant of Venice* is young (I. 1. 130, 147; II. 5. 19; II. 9. 87).

Claudio in *Much Ado* is "young" (I. 1. 11; I. 3. 68; V. 4. 9, 16); "doing in the figure of a lamb the feats of a lion" (I. 1. 14-15); in "His May of youth and bloom of lustihood" (V. 1. 76); "boy" (V. 1. 79, 83, 84, 91, 94, 192); "Lord Lackbeard" (V. 1. 200).

Henry V is a vain "youth" (I. 2. 250; II. 4. 28, 130); "frail and worthless trunk" (III. 6. 166); athletic (V. 2. 141-4); "stubborn outside, with an aspect of iron" (V. 2. 242-3).

Brutus in *Julius Caesar* was actually young enough to be

claimed by Caesar as his son according to Shakespeare's *Plutarch*, Vol. I, p. 114.

Orlando in *As You Like It* is young (I. 1. 56, 137, 150-1, 182; I. 2. 159, 164, 172, 180, 184, 185, 193, 215, 246, etc.); "he hath but a little beard" (III. 2. 220); he hasn't "A lean cheek" (II. 2. 397); "a blue eye and sunken" (III. 2. 398); "a beard neglected" (III. 2. 400); his hair is "Something browner than Judas's" (III. 4. 8); "An excellent colour: your chestnut was ever the only colour" (III. 4. 11-12).

Orsino in *Twelfth Night* is "of fresh and stainless youth" (I. 5. 280); "in dimension and the shape of nature/A gracious person" (I. 5. 282-3).

Othello in *Othello* has "thick-lips" (I. 1. 66); "black ram" (I. 1.88); "Barbary horse" (I. 1. 142); "the devil" (I. 1. 91); says "the young affects/In me defunct" (I. 3. 265-6); "black" (I. 3. 292, etc.); "She must change for youth" (I. 3. 356); "this little arm" (probably not literal; V. 2. 261); "I am declin'd/Into the vale of years" (III. 3. 265-6).

Angelo in *Measure for Measure* broke with Mariana five years before the story opens (V. 1. 211, 216).

Lear in *King Lear* is "Fourscore and upward" (IV. 7. 61); has "bald crown" (I. 4. 179); "beard" (II. 4. 196); "white hair" (III. 1. 7; III. 2. 6, 24, etc.); many references to "age" and "old."

Macbeth in *Macbeth* says "my way of life/Is fall'n into the sear, the yellow leaf," etc. (V. 3. 22-3).

Antony in *Antony and Cleopatra* has "goodly eyes" (I. 1. 2); "beard" (II. 2. 7); is "Herculean Roman" (I. 3. 84); his white hairs reprove the brown (III. 9. 13-14; IV. 8. 19-20); has "grizzled head" (III. 11. 17); is "old ruffian" (IV. 1. 4).

Bertram in *All's Well* has "His arched brows, his hawking eye, his curls" (I. 1. 106); is young (I. 2. 19; II. 1. 29; II. 3. 112, etc.); "Too young" for wars (II. 1. 28); "handsome gentleman" (III. 5. 79-80).

Pericles in *Pericles* is at beginning "Young Prince" (I. 1. 1, 110); "fair" (I. 1. 114, 115); "a handsome fellow" (II. 1. 85); lets hair grow (III. 3. 29; V. 3. 75); "goodly person" (V. 1. 36); but at end has mourned his wife "this fourteen years" (V. 3. 75).

Coriolanus in *Coriolanus* has "grim appearance" (III. 5. 66); "What an arm he has," etc. (IV. 5. 160-1).

Posthumus in *Cymbeline* has "So fair an outward and such stuff within" (I. 1. 23); "His foot Mercurial, his Martial thigh,/The brawns of Hercules" (IV. 2. 310-11); is "no less young" than Cloten (IV. 1. 11), who is probably between thirty-five and forty if Shakespeare has harmonized his time references; wears "silly habit" (V. 3. 86; V. 5. 3-4).

Leontes in *Winter's Tale* was like Mamillius twenty-three years before the story opens (I. 2. 156). His counterpart in the source is about fifty at the end of the story, hence about thirty-four at the beginning.

Prospero in *The Tempest* has "old brain" (IV. 1. 159); dresses in "hat and rapier" (V. 1. 84).

Wolsey in *Henry VIII* wears "long coat," "piece of scarlet," "cap" (III. 2. 277, 281, 283); has "age" (IV. 2. 67).

Cooke, Alexander

Julia in *Two Gentlemen of Verona* is "but a swarthy Ethiope" to Silvia (II. 6. 26); tells Silvia that Julia was once as fair as Silvia herself, but now "she is become as black as I" from exposure (IV. 4. 163); again she says of Silvia: "Her hair is auburn, mine is perfect yellow" (IV. 4. 196); also "Her eyes are grey as glass, and so are mine:/Ay, but her forehead's low, and mine's as high" (IV. 4. 199-200).

Lady Capulet in *Romeo and Juliet* says to Juliet "I was your mother much upon these years" (I. 3. 72); she was thus about twenty-eight, but we hear of her "old age" (V. 3. 207).

Margaret in *3 Henry VI* has little beauty (I. 4. 128-9; cf. II. 2. 146).

Tamora in *Titus Andronicus* says of Saturninus that she will be "a mother to his youth" (I. 1. 332).

Mrs. Page in *Merry Wives* is told "You are not young" (II. 1. 6).

Helena in *Midsummer Night's Dream* hears of "her height" (III. 2. 291, 293); and "her tall personage" (III. 2. 292); she is called "maypole" (III. 2. 296); and says "My legs are longer" than Hermia's (III. 2. 343). See Eccleston for comparison.

Katharine in *Taming of the Shrew* is "young and beauteous" (I. 2. 87); but is asked:

"Why does the world report that Kate doth limp?
A slanderous world! Kate, like the hazel twig,
Is straight and slender, and as brown in hue
As hazel nuts, and sweeter than the kernels.
O! let me see thee walk: thou dost not halt" (II. 1. 247-51).

Lodovico in *Othello* "is a proper man./A very handsome man" (IV. 3. 35-6).

Lennox in *Macbeth* has "young remembrance" (II. 3. 68).

Sicinius (and Brutus) in *Coriolanus* are "old men" (II. 1. 15); "reverend grave men" (II. 1. 68); do not "have good faces" (II. 1. 69); have "beards" (IV. 1. 98); "bald" (III. 1. 164); "old goat" (III. 1. 176); "Aged sir" (III. 1. 177).

Antigonus in *Winter's Tale* is "ignorant by age" (II. 1. 172);
and hears "thy beard's grey" (II. 3. 161); speaks of "little
blood" (II. 3. 165); and is an "old man" (III. 3. 111).

Cowley, Richard

Courtezan in *Comedy of Errors* is "Pretty and witty, wild and
yet, too, gentle" (II. 1. 110).

Robert in *King John* "hath a half face" (I. 1. 92);

"And if my legs were two such riding rods,
My arms such eel-skins stuff'd, my face so thin
That in mine ear I durst not stick a rose
Lest men should say, 'Look, where three-farthings goes'"
(I. 1. 140-3); sarcastically "Colbrand the giant, that same
mighty man" (I. 1. 225).

Silence in *2 Henry IV* remembers the doings of Falstaff and
Shallow "fifty-five year ago" (III. 2. 227); and is an "old
man" (V. 3. 80); sings (V. 3).

Gobbo in *Merchant of Venice* is "old man" (II. 2. 84, 146, 153,
154).

Sampson in *Romeo and Juliet* says "I am a pretty piece of flesh"
(I. 1. 33-4).

Dull in *Love's Labor's Lost* plays tabor for Worthies (V. 1.
164-5).

Verges in *Much Ado* is "old man" (III. 5. 11, 16, 36).

William in *As You Like It* is "a youth" (V. 1. 6); he is "Five-
and twenty" (V. 1. 21).

Aguecheek in *Twelfth Night* is "a foolish knight" (I. 3. 17); "a
great quarreler" (I. 3. 32); his hair "hangs like flax on a
distaff" (I. 3. 110-11); "Nothing of that wonderful promise,
to read him by his form" (III. 4. 293-4); "a thin-faced
knave" (V. 1. 215); sings catch (II. 3); proud of his leg "in
a flame-coloured stock" (I. 3. 146); "manakin" (III. 2. 59).

Osric in *Hamlet* is "young" (V. 2. 204, 273).

Slender in *Merry Wives* is young (I. 1. 78; III. 4. 36); is "a
world of vile ill-favour'd faults" (III. 4. 32); a "Banbury
cheese" (I. 1. 133); "he hath but a little wheyface, with a
little yellow beard—a cane-coloured beard" (I. 4. 22-4);
"does he not hold up his head, as it were, and strut in his
gait?" (I. 4. 30-1); "yond fool" (III. 4. 87).

Elbow in *Measure for Measure* has been constable "Seven year
and a half, sir" (II. 2. 281).

Oswald in *Lear* has "epileptic visage" (II. 2. 86).

Stephanos in *Tempest* sings (II. 2. 45-6, 49-57; III. 2. 133-4).

Crosse, Samuel

Maria in *Twelfth Night* is "your giant" (I. 5. 218); "the little villain" (II. 5. 16); "the youngest wren of nine" (III. 2. 73-4).

Mrs. Quickly in *Merry Wives* sings (1. 4. 44).

Overdone in *Measure for Measure* is "A bawd of eleven years' continuance" (III. 2. 212).

Cundall, Henry

Sir Eglamour in *Two Gentlemen* is "fair" (I. 2. 9); "well-spoken, neat and fine" (I. 2. 10).

Paris in *Romeo and Juliet* is "young" (I. 2. 26, etc.); "boy" (V. 3. 70); "The gallant, young, and noble gentleman" (III. 5. 114); "Proportion'd as one's thought would wish a man" (III. 5. 184); "a lovely gentleman" (III. 5. 220);

> "an eagle, madam,
> Hath not so green, so quick, so fair an eye
> As Paris hath" (III. 5. 221-3).

King Henry in *1 Henry VI* is "young" (I. 1. 170, etc.); speaks of "tender years" (III. 1. 71; IV. 1. 149); is "a child" (III. 1. 133); is "not old" (III. 4. 17); his "years are young" (V. 1. 21); and we hear of the scepter "in children's hands" (IV. 1. 192); but he is old enough to be married at the end of the first part.

King Henry in *2 Henry VI* is "of age to govern of himself" (I. 1. 167); has "childish fist" (I. 1. 246); "a king of years" (II. 3. 28).

Lysander in *Midsummer Night's Dream* is "young" (II. 2. 118, 125).

Tranio in *Taming of the Shrew* is young (II. 1. 331, 334, etc.).

Northumberland in *1 Henry IV* is "old" (II. 4. 381).

Antonio in *Merchant of Venice* looks like "fawning publican" (I. 3. 42).

Don Pedro in *Much Ado* is called a boy (V. 1. 91, 94).

Antony in *Julius Caesar* is of such age as to be spoken of as a hypothetical son to Caesar (III. 1. 225); yet has "seen more days" than Octavius (IV. 1. 18).

Oliver in *As You Like It* is "eldest brother" (I. 1. 47); but is "too young in this" (I. 1. 57-8.)

Cassio in *Othello* is "handsome, young" (II. 1. 251-2); "He hath a person and a smooth dispose" (I. 3. 403); "a proper man" (I. 3. 398).

Duke in *Measure for Measure* has let certain laws sleep nineteen years (I. 3. 31; I. 2. 178); is "old fantastical duke" (IV. 3. 167-8); "goodman bald-pate" (V. 1. 324-5); "bald pated" (V. 1. 352); but I. 3. 5-6, 9-10 seem to imply that he is young.

Edgar in *Lear* is one year older (I. 1. 20) than Edmund, who is "goodman boy" (II. 2. 49); ?sings (III. 4; III. 6); "outside looks so fair and war-like" (V. 3. 144).

Alcibiades in *Timon of Athens* is "young" (V. 3. 8; V. 4. 13).

Malcolm says in *Macbeth* "I am young" (IV. 3. 14); is "the boy Malcolm" (V. 3. 3); "young Malcolm" (V. 7. 57); "Our eldest" (I. 4. 38).

Caesar in *Antony and Cleopatra* is "scarce-bearded" (I. 1. 21); "rose/Of youth" (III. 11. 20-1); "young Roman Boy" (IV. 10. 61); "boy" (IV. 1. 1); "the young man" (III. 9. 62); "the boy Caesar" (III. 11. 17); "novice" (IV. 10. 27).

King in *All's Well* is "old" (V. 3. 40; I. 2. 29); but "of as able body as when he numbered thirty" (IV. 5. 87); wears beard (V. 3. 76).

Cominius in Coriolanus is told "Thou hast years upon thee" (IV. 1. 45).

Belarius in *Cymbeline* is "an ancient soldier" (V. 3. 15); has "white beard" (V. 3. 17); is in "stiff age" (III. 3. 32); and is repeatedly called "old."

Shepherd in *Winter's Tale* is "old man" (III. 3. 124); "fourscoure three" (IV. 3. 466); and is called "old" many times.

Buckingham in *Henry VIII* "a most rare speaker" (I. 2. 111).

Eccleston, William

Young Lucius in *Titus Andronicus* is "tender boy" (III. 2. 48); "tender sapling" (III. 2. 50); "thine infancy" (V. 3. 165).

Anne Page in *Merry Wives* "has brown hair, and speaks small like a woman" (I. 1. 48-9); she will inherit money "when she is able to overtake seventeen years old" (I. 1. 54-5); probably small (IV. 4. 49-50).

The Duchess of York in *Richard III* says "Eighty odd years of sorrow have I seen" (IV. 1. 95).

Hermia in *Midsummer Night's Dream* is an "Ethiop" (III. 2. 257); a "tawny Tartar"; says "I am so dwarfish and so low" (III. 2. 295); is "something lower" than Helena (III. 2. 304); is "little" (III. 2. 325); and a "dwarf" (III. 2. 328).

Biondello in *Taming of the Shrew* is "boy" (I. 1. 242; IV. 4. 8, 59).

Mrs. Quickly in *2 Henry IV* has known Falstaff twenty-nine years (II. 4. 419-20).

Nerissa in *Merchant of Venice* is "a little scrubbed boy" (V. 1. 162, 261).

Moth in *Love's Labor's Lost* is "Boy" (I. 2. 1); "my tender juvenal" (1. 2. 8); "thy young days" (I. 2. 15); "Thou pretty, because little" (I. 2. 22); "infant" (I. 2. 100); "A man, if I live" (III. 1. 43); sings (III. 1. 3).

Beatrice in *Much Ado* says "I am sun burnt" (II. 1. 333).

Lords in *All's Well* are "young" (II. 1. 1, 10).

Arviragus in *Cymbeline* was stolen "Some twenty years" (I. 1. 62), having been "two years" old when stolen (III. 3. 101). He is thus about twenty-two. Sings (IV. 2); is a stripling (V. 3. 19).

Edmans, John

Mrs. Ford in *Merry Wives* "is not young" (II. 1. 114); has "right arched beauty of the brow" (III. 3. 59-60).

Regan in *Lear* is "our second daughter" (I. 1. 69).

Lady Macbeth in *Macbeth* has "little hand" (V. 1. 57).

Cleopatra has a "twany front" (I. 1. 6); "a gipsy's lust" (I. 1. 10); says to Antony "I would I had thy inches" (I. 3. 40); "That am with Phoebus' amorous pinches black,/And Wrinkled deep in time" (I. 5. 28-9, cf. I. 3. 57); "half blasted" before Antony knew her (III. 11. 105).

Countess in *All's Well* is old (I. 3. 218, etc.).

Thaisa in *Pericles* has "square brows" (V. 1. 109); is same size as Marina (V. 1. 110).

Queen in *Cymbeline* "was beautiful" (V. 5. 63).

Gilburne, Samuel

Richmond in *3 Henry VI* is "pretty lad" (IV. 6. 70, etc.).

Prince Edward in *Richard III* is "young" (I. 3. 11, etc.).

Arthur in *King John* is "boy" (II. 1. 8, 18, etc.); "little abstract" (II. 1. 101); "child" (II. 1. 159, 160, etc.); "little kinsman" (III. 3. 18); "fair" (III. 1. 51); "little prince" (IV. 1. 9); requires "Three foot" of ground (IV. 2. 100).

Jessica in *Merchant of Venice* has "a fair hand;/And whiter than the paper it writ on/Is the fair hand that writ" (II. 4. 12-14); she is also "like a little shrew" (V. 1. 21).

Katharine in *Love's Labor's Lost* has "amber hairs" (IV. 3. 87); is "An amber-colour'd raven" (IV. 3. 88); and "her hairs were gold" (IV. 3. 142).

Hero in *Much Ado* is "too low for a high praise, too brown for a fair praise, and too little for a great praise" (I. 1. 179-81); she is "Leonato's short daughter" (V. 1. 224).

Celia in *As You Like It* is "smaller" than Rosalind (I. 2. 289); after she smirches her face with umber, she is "low,/And browner" than Rosalind (I. 3. 115; IV. 3. 89-90); she is "pretty little coz" (IV. 1. 217).

Olivia in *Twelfth Night* has "grey eyes" (I. 5. 268).

Fortinbras in *Hamlet* is "young" (I. 1. 95; I. 2. 17, 28, etc.); "delicate and tender prince" (IV. 4. 48).

Siward in *Macbeth* is "Old" (IV. 3. 134); "An older and a better soldier none" (IV. 3. 191).

Goffe, Robert

Katharine in *Love's Labor's Lost* has "amber hairs" (IV. 3. 87); is "An amber-colour'd raven" (IV. 3. 88); and "her hairs were gold" (IV. 3. 142).

Luciana in *Comedy of Errors* has "golden hairs" (III. 2. 48); is "Possess'd with such a gentle sovereign grace" (III. 2. 166).

Silvia in *Two Gentlemen of Verona* is "Not so fair . . . as well-favoured" (II. 1. 56); fairer than Julia (II. 6. 26; IV. 4. 163); "Her hair is auburn" (IV. 4. 196); "her eyes as grey as glass" (IV. 4. 199); "her forehead's low" (IV. 4. 200); "Too low a mistress for so high a servant" as Proteus (II. 4. 107).

Juliet in *Romeo and Juliet* "hath not seen the change of fourteen years" (I. 2. 9); "Come Lammas-eve at night shall she be fourteen" (I. 3. 17, 21); her father speaks satirically of her "one little body" (III. 5. 131).

John Talbot in *1 Henry VI* is "young" (IV. 3. 35, 40, etc.); has not seen father "This seven years" (IV. 3. 37).

Eleanor of *2 Henry VI* is "a woman of invincible spirit" (I. 4. 9); "in her youngest days" (II. 3. 46).

Prince Edward in *3 Henry VI* is a "goodly boy" (II. 2. 34, 39); "young prince" (II. 3. 241; IV. 1. 117; V. 5. 13, 31, 32, 51, 56, 57, 67, etc.).

Young Lucius in *Titus Andronicus* is "a Boy" (III. 2); "tender boy" (III. 2. 48, 50, etc.).

Mrs. Ford in *Merry Wives* "is not young" (II. 1. 114); "right arched beauty of the brow" (III. 3. 59-60).

Portia in *Merchant of Venice* has "her sunny locks/Hang on her temples like a golden fleece" (I. 1. 170-1); and "her hairs . . ./A golden mesh" (III. 2. 120-2); speaks jestingly of "my little body" (I. 2. 1).

Princess in *Love's Labor's Lost* is "maid of grace and complete majesty" (I. 1. 135).

Albany in *Lear* says "we that are young" (V. 3. 327).

Lords in *All's Well* are "young" (II. 1. 1, 10).

Heminges, John

Boyet in *Love's Labor's Lost* has "beard" (II. 1. 201); hears "Thou art an old love-monger . . ./He is Cupid's grandfather . . ./. . . her father is but grim" (II. 1. 252-4). cf. description (V. 2. 316-35).

Aegon in *Comedy of Errors* is an "old man" (I. 1. 96; cf. V. 1. 312 *ff*.).

Duke in *Two Gentlemen of Verona* speaks of "mine age" (III. 1. 74) ; "my aged eloquence" (III. 1. 83).

Capulet in *Romeo and Juliet* is "old" (I. 1. 96; I. 2. 3) ; when he wants a sword, his wife advises "A crutch, a crutch" (I. 1. 82) ; his last masque was "thirty years" before (I. 5. 37, 43).

Gloucester in *2 Henry VI* is "surly" (I. 3. 50) ; "the haught protector" (I. 3. 71) ; hears of "thine age" (II. 3. 18) ; has "well-proportion'd beard" (III. 2. 175).

Marcus in *Titus Andronicus* is "reverend" (V. 3. 137) ; and has "frosty signs and chaps of age" (V. 3. 77) ; Titus says "Marcus, we are but shrubs, no cedars we ;/No big-bon'd men fram'd of the Cyclops' size" (IV. 3. 45-7).

Hubert in *King John* has "abhorr'd aspect . . . fit for bloody villany" (IV. 2. 224-5, 264-6).

York in *Richard II* is "aged" (II. 2. 74) ; "old" (I. 2. 67; II. 3.52) ; "weak with age" (II. 2. 83) ; arm "prisoner to the palsy" (II. 3. 104).

Chief Justice in *2 Henry IV* is "old" (I. 2. 199) ; "Your lordship, though not clean past your youth, hath yet some smack of age in you, some relish of the saltness of time" (I. 2. 111-13).

Leonato in *Much Ado* is old (III. 2. 73; IV. 1. 195; etc.) ; is "the white-bearded fellow" (II. 3. 133) ; and has "grey hairs and bruise of many days" (V. 1. 65).

Caesar in *Caesar* is "of such a feeble temper" (I. 2. 129) ; says he is deaf in left ear (I. 2. 212) ; "hath the falling-sickness" (I. 2. 255) ; in *Antony and Cleopatra* he is said to have grown "fat" in Egypt (II. 6. 65) ; and to have been "Broad-fronted" (I. 5. 29) ; in Shakespeare's *Plutarch*, Vol. I, p. 26, we read "For concerning the constitution of his body, he was lean, white, and soft skinned, and often subject to headache, and otherwhile to the falling sickness." cf. Polonius below.

Duke Senior in *As You Like It* is older than Frederick (I. 1. 107) ; who is "old" (I. 2. 88).

Polonius in *Hamlet* is spoken of several times as "old" (II. 1. 114, etc.) ; "I did enact Julius Caesar: I was killed i' the Capitol: Brutus killed me (III. 2. 109-10) ; "Hunts . . . the trail of policy" (II. 2. 47) ; has "beard" (II. 2. 530) ; "His beard was as white as snow/All flaxen was his poll" (IV. 5. 194-5).

Brabantio in *Othello* is "old man" (I. 3. 78) ; "old thread" (V. 2. 204) ; is told "you shall more command with years" (I. 2. 60).

Escalus in *Measure for Measure* is "Old" (I. 1. 45; V. 1. 2).

Kent in *Lear* is "forty-eight" (I. 4. 42) ; "ancient ruffian" (II.

APPENDIX VI

2. 66, 133); "grey beard" (II. 2. 67, 72); "reverend braggart" (II. 2. 133); "old fellow" (II. 2. 90, etc.).

Ross in *Macbeth* calls the Old Man who can remember seventy years well "father" (II. 4. 4, 39).

Pompey in *Antony and Cleopatra* has two sons (III. 6. 13, 15).

Lafeu in *All's Well* says "I'd give bay Curtal, and his furniture,/My mouth no more were broken than these boys/And writ as little beard" (II. 3. 65-7); is old (II. 3. 205, 206, etc.); has a "beard" (V. 3. 76).

Helicanus in *Pericles* is "ancient" (V. 3. 51); "Old" (IV. 4. 13); "aged patience" (II. 4. 48); speaks of "the age I am" (V. 1. 15).

Menenius in *Coriolanus* is "humorous patrician" (II. 1. 52); "old" (III. 1. 250; III. 3. 7; IV. 1. 21; etc.); has "half pint of blood" (V. 2. 59-60); "decayed dotant" (V. 2. 47).

Pisanio in *Cymbeline* is "old servant" (III. 5. 54); is asked to "speak thick" (III. 2. 57).

Camillo in *Winter's Tale* is looked on by King Polixenes as a father (I. 2. 461).

Gonzalo in *Tempest* is "ancient morsel" (II. 1. 294); "Old lord" (III. 3. 4; V. 1. 15); speaks of "old bones" (III. 3. 2); hears of "thine age" (V. 1. 121); has "beard" (V. 1. 16).

Kemp, William

Costard in *Love's Labor's Lost* "because of his great limb, or joint, shall pass Pompey the Great" (V. 1. 138-40).

Dromio of Ephesus in *Comedy of Errors* is "a sweet-fac'd youth" (V. 1. 421); the same age as the Antipholi, whose description see under Phillips.

Launce in *Two Gentlemen* is "but a fool" (III. 1. 262).

Cade in *2 Henry VI* is much smaller than Iden (IV. 10. 45-57), who, however, seems to have been exceptionally large (IV. 10. 59 ff.).

Clown in *Titus Andronicus* is in his "young days" (IV. 3. 90).

Evans in *Merry Wives* sings (III. 1. 17-21, 23-6).

Pyramus in *Midsummer Night's Dream* has: "These lily lips,/This cherry nose,/These yellow cowslip cheeks,/. . . His eyes were green as leeks" (V. 1. 338-43).

Grumio in *Taming of the Shrew* is "a little pot" (IV. 1. 6); a "three-inch-fool" (IV. 1. 27, 29); and says "a taller man than I will take cold" (IV. 1. 11-12).

Shallow in *2 Henry IV* is a "starved justice" (III. 2. 330); "genius of famine" (III. 2. 341); played "Sir Dagonet," Arthur's fool (III. 2. 303); he and Falstaff played pranks as youngsters "fifty-five year ago" (III. 2. 227); is compared to

[405]

a bearded hermit's staff (V. 1. 69-71); of which Falstaff would make four dozen.

Launcelot in *Merchant of Venice* is "young" (II. 2. 34, 40, etc.); "boy" (II. 2. 71).

Dogberry in *Much Ado* speaks of "My years" (IV. 2. 80).

Lowin, John

Claudius in *Hamlet* is "bloat king" (III. 4. 180); has "beard" (IV. 7. 32).

Iago in *Othello* says "I have looked upon the world for four times seven years" (I. 3. 313-14); sings (II. 3).

Apemantus in *Timon of Athens* says "If I were a huge man" (1. 2. 52); seems past his "youth" (IV. 3. 257).

Gloucester in *Lear* is "old," and his beard is "white" (III. 7. 36, 37, etc.).

Enobarbus in *Antony and Cleopatra* is "strong Enobarb" (II. 7. 129); and is told of "thy plainness" (II. 6. 78).

Parolles in *All's Well* is a "snipt-taffeta fellow" (IV. 5. 2); "the soul of this man is his clothes" (II. 5. 49); a "red-tailed humble-bee" (IV. 5. 7); wears scarf (III. 5. 85); has beard (IV. 1. 54).

Autolycus in *Winter's Tale* sings (IV. 2; IV. 3); is dressed in "rags" (IV. 2. 57); is notably different in size from Florizel (IV. 3. 664-5), since after exchange of clothes "His garments are rich, but he wears them not handsomely" (IV. 3. 778-9).

Caliban in *Tempest* has larger legs than Trinculo (II. 2. 112); "long nails" (II. 2. 181); sings (II. 2. 193-8); is "dispro-portion'd . . . in his shape" (V. 1. 290-1).

Ostler, William

Polixenes in *Winter's Tale* is "of middle age" (IV. 3. 108); "Old sir" (IV. 3. 368); has "white beard" (IV. 3. 417, 729).

Pallant, Robert

Winchester in *1 Henry VI* wears a "broad cardinal's hat" (I. 3. 36, 49); and "scarlet robes" (I. 3. 42); has "beard" (I. 3. 47).

Cardinal Beaufort in *2 Henry VI* is "The imperious churchman" (I. 3. 72).

Phillips, Augustine

Berowne in *Love's Labor's Lost* is "the merry madcap lord:/Not a word with him but a jest" (II. 1. 213-14).

Antipholus of Ephesus in *Comedy of Errors* was restless to go in search of his brother "At eighteen years" (I. 1. 125); and his father has been searching for him "Five summers" (I. 1. 132); so that he is at least twenty-three. The father says "seven years since" they parted (V. 1. 322); thus Antipholus

is at least twenty-five, as is his twin, and the two Dromios.
But the mother implies that she lost her sons "Thirty-three
years" before (V. 1. 403). The dates may be reconciled by
supposing that Antipholus became restless at eighteen, but did
not start till twenty-six. That this is the correct solution is
pretty clearly indicated by the fact that in the *Menechmi*
Peniculus is "Plus triginta annis" (III. 1. 1). His jealous
wife says: "He is deformed, crooked, old and sere, Ill-fac'd,
worse bodied, shapeless every where;/Vicious, ungentle, foolish, blunt, unkind,/ Stigmatical in making, worse in mind"
(IV. 2. 19-22).

Proteus in *Two Gentlemen* is of "tender days" (I. 1. 3);
"youth" (I. 1. 8, etc.); "but young" (II. 4. 70); and is
"complete in feature" (II. 4. 74); Silvia is "Too low a mistress
for so high a servant" as he (II. 4. 107).

Benvolio in *Romeo and Juliet* has a beard (III. 1. 19); and
"hazel eyes" (III. 1. 22).

Suffolk in *2 Henry VI* is of good proportions and appearance
(1. 3. 57).

Edward in *3 Henry VI* is "wanton" (I. 4. 74); "proud insulting
boy" (II. 2. 84); has "youth" (III. 2. 35).

Saturninus in *Titus Andronicus* is "eldest son" (I. 1. 224; I. 1.
5); but is a "youth" (I. 1. 332).

King Edward in *Richard III* is "sickly, weak, and melancholy"
(I. 1. 136).

Gremio in *Taming of the Shrew* is "A proper stripling" (I. 2.
147); old (II. 1. 333, etc.); a "Greybeard" (II. 1. 332; III.
2. 148); and has a "wither'd hide" (II. 1. 398); "dotard"
(V. 1. 109).

Bolingbroke in *Richard II* is young (I. 3. 66, 83, etc.).

King in *1 Henry IV* has "old limbs" (V. 1. 13).

King in *2 Henry IV* is "bare wither'd trunk" (IV. 5. 228).

Gratiano in *Merchant of Venice* wishes to "play the fool" (I.
1. 79); is "too wild, too rude and bold of voice" (II. 2. 196);
"good youth" (IV. 1. 141).

Holofernes in *Love's Labor's Lost* has "no face," "A cittern-
head," "The head of a bodkin," "A death's face in a ring,"
"The face of an old Roman coin, scarce seen," "The pommel of
Caesar's falchion," "The carved-bone face on a flask," "Saint
George's half-cheek in a brooch," "in a brooch of lead"
(V. 2. 609-18).

Don John in *Much Ado* looks "tartly" (II. 1. 3).

Cassius in *Julius Caesar* "has a lean and hungry look" (I. 2.
193); "Would he were fatter" (I. 2. 197); is "spare Cassius"
(I. 2. 200); an "elder soldier" than Brutus (IV. 3. 56); ac-

cording to *Antony and Cleopatra* he was "lean and wrinkled Cassius" (III. 9. 37).

Frederick in *As You Like It* is the "younger brother" of Duke Senior (I. 1. 107); but is "old" (I. 2. 88).

Malvolio in *Twelfth Night* has beard (II. 3. 173); "yellow stockings . . . cross-gartered" (II. 5. 182-3).

Pope, Thomas

Armado in *Love's Labor's Lost* is "tough senior" (I. 2. 11); has "that face" (I. 2. 147); hears of "your thin belly-doublet" (III. 1. 20); when he comes in as Hector, we hear: "I think Hector was not so clean-timbered./*Long.* His calf is to big for Hector./*Dum.* More calf, certain./*Boyet.* No; he is best indued in the small" (V. 2. 640-3); "his humour is lofty, his discourse peremptory, his tongue filed, his eye ambitious, his gait majestical, and his general behaviour vain, ridiculous, and thrasonical. He is too picked, too spruce, too affected, too odd, as it were, too peregrinate, as I may call it" (V. 1. 10-16).

Dromio of Syracuse in *Comedy of Errors* is the same age as the Antipholi, whom see under Phillips.

Speed in *Two Gentlemen* is to undergo "the boy's correction" (III. 1. 398); "sweet youth" (II. 5. 3); "my boy" (III. 1. 258).

York in *1 Henry VI* speaks of "my young years" (II. 5. 107); but has sons that are grown by *2 Henry VI*, Act V; and is "grumbling York" (I. 3. 73).

Aaron the Moor in *Titus Andronicus* is "wall-ey'd slave" (V. 1. 44); has "fiend-like face" (V. 1. 45).

Falstaff in *Merry Wives* is "Two yards and more" about the waist (I. 3. 42, 43-4); "well-nigh worn to pieces with age" (II. 1. 21-2); "old" (II. 2. 146, 147; IV. 4. 15); "has a great peard" (IV. 2. 207-8).

Petruchio in *Taming of the Shrew* is "young" (I. 2. 50, 141; II. 1. 232, 233); yet he is "wither'd" (II. 1. 234); and his face is like a crabapple (II. 1. 228-32); he is "old lad" (V. 2. 182); sings (IV. 1).

Philip in *King John* is of "large composition" (I. 1. 88); "A good blunt fellow" (I. 1. 71); is "Knight, knight, good mother, Basilisco-like" (I. 1. 244), the latter being of same line of characters.

Mowbray in *Richard II* has spoken English "these forty years" (I. 3. 159); and is accused of doing all the plotting "these eighteen years" (I. 1. 95).

Falstaff in *1 Henry IV* is "old" (I. 2. 47; II. 1. 75); "huge hill of flesh" (II. 4. 273); has a "bald crown" (II. 4. 425); "grey iniquity" (II. 4. 506); "old white-bearded Satan" (II. 4. 516);

"Some fifty, or by'r lady, inclining to threescore" (II. 4. 473);
"withered like an old apple-john" (II. 3. 4-5); has known
Bardolph thirty-two years (III. 3. 54); has associated with
Poins twenty-two years (II. 2. 18).

Falstaff in *2 Henry IV* requires "two and twenty yards of satin"
for a suit (I. 2. 48-9); is "written down old with all the
characters of age: Have you not a moist eye, a dry hand, a
yellow cheek, a white beard, a decreasing leg, an increasing
belly? Is not your voice broken, your wind short, your chin
double, your wit single, and every part about you blasted
with antiquity, and will you yet call yourself young?" (I.
2. 205-12); Mrs. Quickly has known him twenty-nine years
(II. 4. 419-20); Silence remembers his doings "fifty-five year
ago" (III. 2. 227); he would make four dozen of the size of
Shallow (V. 1. 69-71); cf. V. 5. 50 *ff*.; has foolish affected
manners (II. 1. 206-7); is "dry, round, old, withered knight"
(V. 4. 8-9); "a fool and jester" (V. 5. 53).

Shylock in *Merchant of Venice* is "old" (III. 1. 38; IV. 1. 175);
"at these years" (III. 1. 38-9).

Benedick in *Much Ado* was "a child" when Hero was born
(I. 1. 112-13); "looks younger than he did, by the loss of a
beard" (III. 2. 48-9); and is then "the sweet youth" (III.
2. 52-3); sings (V. 2. 26-9); "He is a very proper man" (II.
3. 200); "He hath indeed a good outward happiness" (II. 3.
201-2); "the prince's jester" (II. 1. 144); sings (V. 2. 26-9);
"For shape, for bearing, argument and valour,/Goes fore-
most in report through Italy" (III. 1. 96-7).

Casca in *Julius Caesar* is "sour" (I. 2. 179).

The melancholy Jaques in *As You Like It* is "old" (V. 1. 4).

Toby in *Twelfth Night* sings a catch (II. 3).

Rice, John

William Page in *Merry Wives* is "young man" (IV. 1. 8); "boy"
(IV. 1. 88); "little son" (IV. 4. 49).

Widow in *All's Well* has "age and honour" (V. 3. 163).

Bawd in *Pericles* is "old" (IV. 2. 32).

Paulina in *Winter's Tale* is "old turtle" (V. 3. 132).

Robinson, Richard

Perdita in *Winter's Tale* must be sixteen, since that is the time
between the beginning and the end of the story (V. 3. 31, 50).
This is the age of her counterpart in the source.

Miranda in *Tempest* was "not/Out three years old" (I. 2. 40-1)
when she came to the island, which was "twelve years since"
(I. 2. 53). She is thus "not out" fifteen.

[409]

Sands, James

Anne Page in *Merry Wives* "has brown hair, and speaks small like a woman" (I. 1. 48-9); she will inherit money "when she is able to overtake seventeen years old" (I. 1. 54-5); probably small (IV. 4. 49-50).

Mariana in *Measure for Measure* was forsaken by Angelo five years before (V. 1. 211, 216).

Cordelia in *Lear* is "youngest daughter" (I. 1. 48); "So young" (I. 1. 85, 108); "little-seeming" (I. 1. 201).

Octavia in *Antony and Cleopatra* is "of a holy, cold, and still conversation" (II. 6. 130); not so tall as Cleopatra (III. 3. 11); "dull of tongue, and dwarfish" (III. 3. 15); "low-voic'd" (III. 3. 13); hair brown, forehead low (III. 3. 33-4); face "Round even to faultiness" (III. 3. 30); "I do think she's thirty" (III. 3. 28).

Helena in *All's Well* is "Little Helen" (I. 1. 205).

Marina in *Pericles* has "fingers, long, small, white as milk" (IV, prologue, 22); "excellent complexion" (IV. 1. 40); is "fourteen" (V. 3. 8, 75); a "gosling" (IV. 2. 91); "young foolish sapling" (IV. 2. 93); "young one" (IV. 2. 147); is asked "Were you a gamester at five or at seven" (IV. 6. 82-3); sings (V. 1. 80-1); has mother's "square brows;/Her stature to an inch; as wand like straight" (V. 1. 109-10).

Imogen in *Cymbeline* is "No elder than a boy" (III. 6. 44); etc.

Hermione in *Winter's Tale* is "a goodly lady" (II. 1. 65); has "full eye" (V. 1. 53); was "not so much wrinkled, nothing/So aged as this seems" (V. 3. 27-8); "in age" (V. 3. 108).

Ariel in *Tempest* was imprisoned by Sycorax "A dozen years" (I. 2. 279, 295) before Prospero came, "twelve year since" (I. 2. 53); sings frequently (I. 2. 375-84, 394-401; II. 1. 308-13; V. 1, 88-94); plays 'on a Tabor and Pipe" (III. 2, 135/6).

Ceres in *Tempest* sings (IV. 1. 110-17).

[Shakespeare], Edmund

York in *Richard III* is nearly as large as Prince Edward (II. 4. 7); "young" (II. 4. 26).

Francis in *1 Henry IV* must serve "five years and as much as to—" (II. 4. 46, 49); birthday "about Michaelmas next" (II. 4. 59).

Rosalind in *As You Like It* is "more than common tall" for a woman (I. 3. 118); "slender" (III. 2. 113); Orlando says she is "as high as my heart" (III. 2. 287); Phoebe says of the disguised Rosalind:

"He'll make a proper man: the best thing in him
Is his complexion; and faster than his tongue

Did make offence his eye did heal it up.
He is not very tall: yet for his years he's tall:
His leg is but so so; and yet 'tis well:
There was a pretty redness in his lip,
A little riper and more lusty red
Than that mix'd in his cheek; 'twas just the difference
Betwixt the constant red and mingled damask"

(III. 5. 115-23). See Gilburne for comparison with Celia.

Viola in *Twelfth Night* is "Not yet old enough for a man, nor young enough for a boy" (I. 5. 166-7); "between boy and man" (I. 5. 169-70); "Diana's lip/Is not more smooth and rubious" (I. 4. 32); her father died the day she was thirteen (V. 1. 255, 258); and she and her brother Sebastian were "both born in an hour" (II. 1. 20-1).

Shakespeare, William

Bedford in *1 Henry VI* is "old" (III. 2. 100); of "crazy age" (III. 2. 89).

Vincentio in *Taming of the Shrew* is "old, wrinkled, faded, wither'd" (IV. 5. 43, 45, 50).

Friar Francis in *Much Ado* speaks of "my age" (IV. 1. 169).

Cicero in *Julius Caesar* has "silver hairs" (II. 1. 144).

Adam in *As You Like It* is "old" (I. 1. 87, 88, etc.); is "almost four-score" (II. 3. 71, 74).

Ghost in *Hamlet* has "fair and war-like form" (I. 1. 47); is in "armour" (I. 1. 60); "majestical" (I. 1. 143); "a goodly king" (I. 2. 186); fully armed (I. 2. 200, 226-7; I. 4. 52); beaver up (I. 2. 229); pale countenance (I. 2. 233); beard "A sable silver'd" (I. 2. 241).

Duncan in *Macbeth* has "silver skin" (II. 3. 119); is "old man" (V. 1. 43).

Lepidus in *Antony and Cleopatra* "is high-coloured" from drinking (II. 7. 4).

Sly, William

Rosaline in *Love's Labor's Lost* is: "A wightly wanton with a velvet brow,/With two pitch balls stuck in her face for eyes" (III. 1. 206-7); "O! but her eye" (IV. 3. 10); "Of such a merry, nimble, stirring spirit" (V. 2. 16). The physical description is probably of Wilson at the revision.

Thurio in *Two Gentlemen* says "my face is black" (V. 2. 10); "What! that my leg is too long?/No, that it is too little" (V. 2. 4-5); is "foolish rival" (II. 4. 175); "blunt Thurio's dull proceeding" (II. 6. 41).

Tibalt in *Romeo and Juliet* is young (I. 5. 81, etc.).

The Dauphin in *1 Henry VI* "is a proper man" (V. 3. 37).

Demetrius in *Titus Andronicus* is "a year or two" older than Chiron (II. 1. 31); and he and Chiron are "brave boys" (I. 1. 129); "Young lords" (II. 1. 69; IV. 2. 94, etc.).

Flute in *Midsummer Night's Dream* has "a beard coming" (I. 2.51).

Hortensio in *Taming of the Shrew* is classed among "young folks" (I. 2. 141); is handsome (II. 1. 11-17).

Dauphin Lewis in *King John* is "boy" (II. 1. 495); "young" (II. 1. 521, 533); "a beardless boy" (V. 1. 69); "unhair'd sauciness" (V. 2. 133); "youth" (V. 2. 128).

Harry Percy in *Richard II* is "young" (II. 3. 21, 36, 42).

Hotspur in *1 Henry IV* is young (I. 1. 92, 99; III. 2. 145, etc.); "no more in debt to years" than Prince Hal (III. 2. 103); "governed by humours" (III. 1. 237-8).

Prince John (Lancaster) in *2 Henry IV* is "young" (I. 1. 17, 134; IV. 3. 94).

Hotspur does not take part in *2 Henry IV*, but is referred to as "young" (I. 3. 26); and seems to have had the habit of "speaking thick" (II. 3. 24).

Lorenzo in *Merchant of Venice* is "young" (V. 1. 18).

Of Longaville, a "merry mocking lord" (II. 1. 52), in *Love's Labor's Lost* we hear "few taller are so young" (V. 2. 844).

Octavius in *Julius Caesar* is "young" (III. 1. 296; IV. 3. 92, 152, 167; V. 1. 60); "A peevish schoolboy" (V. 1. 61); younger than Antony (IV. 1. 18); Shakespeare's *Plutarch*, Vol. I, p. 148, says he was "a stripling or springal of twenty years old."

Silvius in *As You Like It* is "young" (II. 4. 20, 90).

Sebastian in *Twelfth Night* and Viola were "both born in an hour" (II. 1. 20-1); "boy" (V. 1. 81).

Laertes in *Hamlet* is wild (II. 1. 19-24); "young" (IV. 5. 101, etc.).

Fenton in *Merry Wives* is "young" (III. 2. 70); has "eyes of youth" (III. 2. 71); and "Have not your worship a wart above your eye?" (I. 4. 152-3).

Roderigo in *Othello* is "young quat" (V. 1. 11; V. 2. 110).

Claudio in *Measure for Measure* is "a young man" (II. 3. 13); "riotous youth" (IV. 4. 32).

Edmund in *Lear* has been away from home for nine years (I. 1. 34); is "young fellow" (I. 1. 13, etc.); "goodman boy" (II. 2. 49); a year younger than Edgar (I. 1. 20; I. 2. 5-6); "rough and lecherous" (I. 2. 146-7).

Brutus (and Sicinius) in *Coriolanus* are "old men" (II. 1. 15);

"reverend grave men" (II. 1. 68); do not "have good faces" (II. 1. 69); have "beards" (II. 1. 98); "bald" (III. 1. 164).

Tooley, Nicholas

Nurse in *Romeo and Juliet* is "ancient lady" (II. 4. 151); "Ancient damnation" (II. 5. 235); "she is lame" (II. 5. 4); etc.

Joan in *1 Henry VI* "was black and swart before" visitation, but now has "beauty" (I. 2. 84, 86).

Mrs. Quickley in *Merry Wives* sings (I. 4. 44).

Queen Elizabeth in *Richard III* is "Well struck in years, fair, and not jealous" (I. 1. 92); "beauty-waning . . . in the afternoon of her last days" (III. 7. 184-5).

Underwood, John

Guiderius in *Cymbeline* is twenty-three (I. 1. 58, 62; cf. III. 3. 69, 101); has "An arm as big as Cloten's" (IV. 1. 77); sings (IV. 2); a stripling (V. 3. 19).

Florizel in *Winter's Tale* is "youth" (IV. 3. 147); "young swain" (IV. 3. 379); "fond boy" (IV. 3. 439, etc.); and if Leontes were twenty-one, he would call him brother. His counterpart in the source is twenty; he is notably different in size from Autolycus, whom see, under Lowin, John.

Ferdinand in *Tempest* is "Young" (III. 3. 92; IV. 1. 40).

Wilson, John

Rosaline in *Love's Labor's Lost* is: "A wightly wanton with a velvet brow,/With two pitch balls stuck in her face for eyes" (III. 1. 206-7); "O! but her eye" (IV. 3. 10); "Of such a merry, nimble stirring spirit" (V. 2. 16).

Lucius in *Caesar* is "boy" (II. 1. 40, etc.); sings (IV. 3. 265).

Balthazar in *Much Ado* sings (II. 3).

Phebe in *As You Like It* hears of "your inky brows, your black silk hair,/Your bugle eyeballs, . . . your cheek of cream" (III. 5. 46-7); and says "He said mine eyes were black and my hair black" (III. 5. 130); also "she has a leathern hand,/A freestone-colour'd hand; I verily did think/That her old gloves were on, but 'twas her hands:/She has a housewife's hand" (IV. 3. 25-8).

Ophelia in *Hamlet* sings (IV. 5).

Desdemona in *Othello* has "An inviting eye; and yet methinks right modest" (II. 3. 24-5); sings (IV. 3); has "a good hand" (III. 4. 44); "whiter skin . . . than snow" (V. 2. 4).

Goneril in *Lear* is "Our eldest-born" (I. 1. 56); has "young bones" [with child] (II. 4. 165); "brow of youth" (I. 4. 308).

Unclassified

Dumaine in *Love's Labor's Lost* is "young" (II. 1. 56); is

wished "A beard" (V. 2. 832); and called "smooth-fac'd" (V. 2. 836).

Pinch in *Comedy of Errors* has "saffron face" (IV. 4. 63); had "beard" (V. 1. 171); is "a hungry lean-fac'd villain,/A mere anatomy . . . /A needy, hollow-ey'd, sharp-looking wretch,/A living-dead man" (V. 1. 238-42).

Montague in *Romeo and Juliet* is "Old" (I. 1. 83, etc.); and speaks of "mine age" (V. 3. 212).

Salisbury in *1 Henry VI* is "old" (II. 2. 4).

Mortimer in *1 Henry VI* speaks of "weak decaying age" (II. 5. 1); "gray locks" (II. 5. 5); "weak shoulders . . . pithless arms" (II. 5. 10-11).

Somerset in *1 Henry VI* is "young Somerset" (II. 4. 37); and "peevish boy" (II. 4. 76).

Salisbury in *2 Henry VI* speaks of "my age" (I. 1. 191); has "silver hair" (V. 1. 162); "frosty head" (V. 1. 167); etc.

Iden in *2 Henry VI* is much larger than Cade (IV. 10. 50-5); "burly-boned clown" (IV. 10. 60).

Old Clifford in *2 Henry VI* has "the silver livery of advised age" (V. 2. 47).

Rutland in *3 Henry VI* is "child" (I. 3. 8, etc.).

Mayor of York in *3 Henry VI* is "good old man" (IV. 7. 31).

Mutius in *Titus Andronicus* is "boy" (I. 1. 290); "young" (I. 1. 382); "youngest son" (I. 1. 418).

Chiron in *Titus Andronicus* hears that his "years want wit" (II. 1. 26); is "a year or two" younger than Demetrius (II. 1. 31); "boy" (II. 1. 38, 45); "Youngling" (II. 1. 73); "youth" (III. 1. 166); and he and Demetrius are "Young lords" (II. 1. 69).

Fitzwater in *Richard II* is "boy" (IV. 1. 65).

Aumerle in *Richard II* is "boy" (V. 2. 69, 85).

Bardolph in *1 Henry IV* has been acquainted with Falstaff thirty-two years (III. 3. 54); stole a cup of sack eighteen years before (II. 4. 350); "was shaved" (III. 3. 68).

Poins in *1 Henry IV* is "straight enough in the shoulders" (II. 4. 167).

Bracy in *1 Henry IV* is "old" (II. 4. 327).

Lancaster in *1 Henry IV* is "this boy" (V. 4. 23).

Robin in *2 Henry IV* is "giant" (I. 2. 1); a "little tiny thief" (V. 3. 58).

Mouldy in *2 Henry IV* is "a good-limbed fellow; young, strong" (III. 2. 113-14).

Shadow in *2 Henry IV* is "half-faced fellow" (III. 2. 286).

Bardolph in *2 Henry IV* has a "red lattice" (II. 2. 88).

Poins in *2 Henry IV* is same size and weight as Prince Harry (II. 4. 265, 276-7).

APPENDIX VI

First Beadle in *2 Henry IV* is a "thin man in a censer" (V. 4. 20-1, etc.).

Antonio in *Much Ado* has a "dry hand" (II. 1. 125); is known "by the waggling of your head" (II. 1. 121); is an old man "without teeth" (V. 1. 116-17).

Boy in *Henry V* says "As young as I am" (III. 2. 30).

Erpingham in *Henry V* is "old" (IV. 1. 13, 34, 98, 306).

Suffolk in *Henry V* has beard (IV. 6. 13).

Pistol in *Henry V* says "Old I do wax" (V. 1. 89).

Metellus in *Julius Caesar* speaks of "Our youths" (II. 1. 148).

Caius Ligarius in *Julius Caesar* is "lean" (II. 2. 113).

Soothsayer in *Julius Caesar* is "a feeble man" (II. 4. 36).

Publius in *Julius Caesar* hears of "your age" (III. 1. 93).

Lepidus in *Julius Caesar* is "a tried and valiant soldier" (IV. 1. 28).

Cato in *Julius Caesar* is "young" (V. 3. 107; V. 4. 9).

Corin in *As You Like It* is "old" (II. 4. 20, 25).

Amiens in *As You Like It* sings (II. 5).

Montano in *Othello* hears of "The gravity and stillness of your youth" (II. 3. 193).

Bardolph in *Merry Wives* is "he in the red face" (I. 1. 175).

Robin in *Merry Wives* is "skirted page" (I. 3. 91); "little" (II. 2. 119, 120-1, etc.).

Simple in *Merry Wives* is "young" (I. 4. 39, 51, 68, 75).

Shallow in *Merry Wives* is old (II. 3. 47; I. 1. 40, 270); "fourscore years and upward" (III. 1. 56-7).

Old Man in *Lear* is more than "fourscore years" (IV. 1. 14).

Witches in *Macbeth* are "So wither'd and so wild in their attire" (I. 3. 40); have "choppy finger" (I. 3. 44); "skinny lips" (I. 3. 45); "beards" (I. 3. 46).

Old Man in *Macbeth* says "Threescore and ten I can remember well" (II. 4. 1).

Fleance in *Macbeth* is "boy" (II. 1. 1).

Murderer in *Macbeth* is "shag-hair'd villain" (IV. 2. 81).

Gower in *Pericles* is "ancient" (I, prologue, 2, etc.).

Escanes in *Pericles* is old (IV. 4. 15).

Young Marcius in *Coriolanus* is "little" (I. 3, 57).

Second Lady in *Winter's Tale* has blacker brows than first (II. 1. 8).

Sir Harry Guilford in *Henry VIII* is "young" (I. 3. 9); "pretty" (I. 3. 63).

THE CHIEF APPRENTICES AND
THEIR LINES IN SHAKESPEARE'S PLAYS

OUR information concerning apprentices in Shakespeare's plays seems fairly definite, though less so than for members. Our best point of attack for apprentices in the Shakespearean company before 1600 is furnished by the plot of *The Seven Deadly Sins*, March 1592, which gives us the names of the chief apprentices at that time, and furnishes good evidence as to the type of character each performed. We find six such performers named, though some evidently had very small parts. Now if we examine Shakespeare's plays, 1592-94, we find that each requires about that number of apprentices. Further, beginning with the summer of 1590, for upward of two years the company can muster but four apprentices. There is a similar period beginning the winter of 1595, another beginning the summer 1599, and so on. Also, just before these slumps the women have unusually prominent parts. Evidently at these periods certain apprentices reached their zenith as actors of women, graduated to become men, and were succeeded by new material which had to receive considerable training before it was capable of filling even minor parts.

Thanks to the plot of *The Seven Deadly Sins*, we can be reasonably certain of the lines taken by most of the apprentices around 1592. Alexander Cooke is evidently the strong-minded regal lady. He is Queen Videna, who to avenge one son kills the other; and Procne, who also sacrifices her son to secure vengeance. To this actor must belong the line of forceful queens, which includes Queen Margaret the virago, tigress Tamora, and Hamlet's luxurious, but less colorful mother.

As a foil to Cooke we have Robert Goffe with his gentle Philomela. Evidently Goffe was the tender sentimental lady; Luciana, Juliet, Ophelia. There is a third prominent type with characteristic appearance as Juliet's Nurse and Mrs. Quickly. Here is the female comedian, frequently attached to one of the prominent ladies in some capacity as servant. Now there were two other prominent ladies at this time, Nicholas Tooley and T. Belt. Since Belt, however, was a Servant as well as a lady, it is pretty certain that he was already fairly grown, and likely that he was only filling in as a female. Besides, there is other evidence to indicate that this comic line is Tooley's. It is to be noticed that the actor of this line is Cooke's running mate, since their lines both drop out 1594-95. Now we find "Nick"[1] Tooley appearing as a messenger in *The Taming of the Shrew*, winter of 1594, showing that he was by that time just budding into manhood. Further, Cooke and Tooley were admitted members of the company at the same time, showing that they were running mates. It is also to be noticed that Tooley's rôle of the Lady in *Gorboduc*, evidently "Marcella, a Lady of the Queen's privy-chamber," who reports the tragedy of the queen, might in her garrulous grief very well be presented after the fashion of Juliet's Nurse. All these facts together make it reasonably certain that Tooley was the comic running mate of the more serious Cooke.[2] It is probable then that Collier[3] was right in supposing that the entry at St. Anne's, Blackfriars, "Nicholas Wilkinson, sonne to Charles Wilkinson, baptized 3 Feb., 1574" refers to this Nicholas Tooley, alias Wilkinson.[4] If so, Tooley should have become an apprentice about February 1585, and have been graduated about February 1596, which is approximately true of this line we have assigned him.

It is also plain that William Eccleston is the comic running mate of the tender Goffe. He appears in *The Seven Deadly Sins* as the youthful Itys, just twelve years old in the original story. Chance jottings of the bookkeeper preserve for us two of Eccleston's parts in the Shakespearean plays. Just before Mrs. Quickly and Doll enter in *2 Henry IV*, the first quarto (1600) has "Enter Will" (II. 4. 20), showing that Eccleston took one of these parts, presumably the former, since, as frequently, the prompter notes only the leader of a procession, and expects the others to follow the leader. Again, the folio version of *All's Well*, summer of 1607, has

---

1 Halliwell, *Outlines*, Vol. II, p. 281; Fleay, *Life*, p. 226.

2 It must be remembered, however, that Ned, the actor of Rhodope, evidently performs a similar line; and that Joan, acted in the same season, is likened to Rhodope, Tooley appears to have been the older apprentice and entitled to the major line at this period, but Ned may have been. Fleay, F. G., *The Life and Work of Shakespeare*, p. 266, would identify some half-dozen names in *More*, including Ned Butler, with apprentices of the company. If we knew that *More* was performed by the company 1588-92, then it would be possible that the apprentice Harry is Henry Cundall, Robin is Robert Goffe, and Kit is Christopher Beeston. Robin also appears as an apprentice in *2 Henry VI* (II. 3), and as Falstaff's diminutive page in *Merry Wives*. In the latter, we should have Pope as Falstaff and his apprentice Goffe as his page. It is possible that in each case Robin is Robert Goffe, the only known boy Robert in the company at the time.

3 Collier, *Memoirs*, p. 234.

4 If so, the Nicholas Tooley who was naturalized 1600-01 by 43 Eliz., Private Acts, c 3 was hardly our Tooley. The curious circumstance, however, that Tooley mentions no kinsmen in his will would argue that he probably had no kindred in England.

preserved the initials of Goffe and Eccleston to several pairs of jesting lords and soldiers, who were thus fused together to supply the manly needs of these young actors. Eccleston's composite part in *All's Well* is that of a roistering young soldier, more comic than Goffe's. Evidently these two are also running mates, Goffe being in 1592 the tender heroine, who will blossom with time into a dignified and important line, and Eccleston being the female comedian. Since these two are next in rank to Cooke and Tooley, they should be the graduates of about 1598. Now the line to which Mrs. Quickly belongs, Eccleston's line, drops out as a major line about this time. So does the regal line which must have been Goffe's. Further, Goffe as Juliet in the spring of 1591 would be fourteen "Come Lammas-eve at night." It must be significant that Goffe's line concludes the summer of 1598, almost exactly when Juliet should have been twenty-one, the end of legal apprenticeship. As in the plays of Beaumont and Fletcher, so in those of Shakespeare, it appears that the age of the heroine when specifically given is that of the actor. This age for Goffe finds further confirmation in the fact that he was married February 13, 1603,[5] showing that he had completed apprenticeship before that date, but was still probably young. Not to be outdone, one week later, or February 20, 1603, his running mate Eccleston also took himself a wife, as we find recorded at the same church.[6] One character that I have assigned to Goffe's line seems especially significant. As Lady Mortimer, Goffe sings in Welsh. The reason would seem to appear in Camden's comment[7] on this name: "Goff, *id est*, Smith in Welsh." It would seem that Shakespeare capitalized this youth's nationality by having him sing some of his native songs.[8]

It is evident now that there must have been a couple of graduates about the winter of 1589, succeeded by two other hopeful youths, who would be just beginning to take very small parts in 1592. As to these earlier graduates, we have only inferential evidence, which may be more clearly presented after we have established the later apprentices in these plays. The successors of these graduates, however, should graduate about 1601, where we find evidence that two apprentices, one comic and one more serious, did graduate. The names of these apprentices we can probably establish. One of these seems to have been Samuel Gilburne, who is listed as a principal actor in the folio but was never a member, indicating that he must have been a principal apprentice actor of

[5] Collier, *Memoirs*, p. 265.
[6] *ibid.*, p. 245.
[7] Camden, W., *Remains Concerning Britain* (1870), p. 133.
[8] Quite likely Goffe was also expected to speak considerable Welsh impromptu.

women's parts. Confirmatory of this supposition is the fact that
Phillips in his will, May 1605,[9] speaks of Gilburne as his "late
apprentice." Thus Gilburne had been a chief apprentice actor before 1605, though we have not a single assigned part for him. We
may reasonably infer, however, from known practice that Gilburne would be a regal lead, reflecting the line of his master.
Before 1605, there seems to be but one of these lines unattached,
that ending about 1601. There is another ending about 1605, but it
seems, as we shall see, assignable on direct evidence to Jack Wilson.
It is probable then that Gilburne was the graduating regal lead
of about 1601. That he does not appear in the plot of *The Seven
Deadly Sins* is not peculiar, since he could at that time have been
with the company but barely two years, and could not have taken
an important part.

Yet his running mate was probably the only other female actor
in that plot, one Ned by name, who performed the part of
Rhodope.[10] We do not know certainly who this Ned was. Two
Edwards appear years later (1624) as servants of the company:
Edward Knight, and Edward Ashborn.[11] If Ned was either of these,
the chances are in favor of Ashborn, since Edward Knight came
to the Shakespearean company seemingly from the Prince Charles
company not earlier than 1623.[12]

But there is much greater likelihood that this actor was Edmund
Shakespeare, younger brother of William, baptized May 3, 1580.[13]
It is true that we have no other record that Edmund was ever
connected with the Shakespearean company, and yet it is practically
certain that he was so connected at his death, since he was buried in
St. Saviour's as a "player" December 31, 1607.[14] This player-
brother of Shakespeare, buried at the parish church in which the
Globe was situated, must surely have been attached to the Shakespearean company. Further, the age of Edmund was almost
exactly that which belonged to this line. Baptized May 3, 1580, he
would have entered the company at ten about the summer of 1590,

[9] Collier, *Memoirs*, p. 87.
[10] John Taylor gives us the Elizabethan interpretation of Rhodope:
> There was a famous Whore *Rhodope* nam'd,
> Who for her gaine at such high price she gam'd,
> That she (most liberall) did the charges beare,
> A stately high Piramides to reare.

(*Taylor's Works* [1630, Spenser Soc., p. 271 a]). This Rhodope is mentioned
in *1 Henry VI*, I. 6. 22, produced in the same season as *The Seven Deadly
Sins*, and in the former play connected with Joan of Arc.
[11] Adams, *Herbert*, p. 74.
[12] See above, p. 88.
[13] Halliwell, *Outlines*, Vol. II, p. 51. Fleay, *Stage*, p. 85 has already made
this suggestion.
[14] Collier, *Memoirs*, p. xiv.

would have been not quite twelve as Rhodope in *The Seven Deadly Sins*, and would have graduated at twenty-one about the summer of 1601. Now one character in this line seems to give fairly definite indication concerning the age of the actor. Francis, the drawer, in *1 Henry IV*, summer of 1596, has five years to serve, and seemingly as much more as till Michaelmas. He is thus ending his apprenticeship about Michaelmas 1601, the approximate time when this line ends. Thus Edmund Shakespeare was almost exactly of the age demanded by this line. There is strong probability then, though no certainty, that Ned was Edmund Shakespeare.

As our next graduates, we should expect to find two who entered 1593-94 to succeed Cooke and Tooley, and should graduate 1604-05. There seems to be two such lines, a fairly serious one ending with Goneril of *King Lear*, and a comic one ending with Overdone, "a bawd of eleven years continuance," the length of the actor's service in such characters being the point of the joke. The chance information that Jack Wilson as Balthazar sang "Sigh no more ladies" in *Much Ado* (winter season of 1598) seems to indicate that he was the performer of the serious line of sentimental singing ladies—Desdemona, Ophelia—which ends about 1605. At least Balthazar seems clearly a rudimentary character in this line, whether Wilson was the original performer or not. Unfortunately, at least two John Wilsons seem to have gotten themselves inextricably entangled. One of these is the eminent Doctor John Wilson, an excellent composer of music, born, according to his tombstone, April 5, 1595.[15] Evidently this John Wilson could not have been the original Balthazar in 1598. But, unfortunately, we cannot be quite certain that the jotting does belong to the original performance, since this actor's name does not occur in the quarto of 1600, but is added in the folio. However, this very fact shows that the folio was using the official stage version of the play, as the quarto had done. It repeats the names of other actors mentioned in the quarto, adding only Wilson. Now if Wilson's name had been inserted for a later revival, at the same time the name of Kemp, who left the company in 1599, should have been stricken out. But as no change of this kind has been made in the folio version except the insertion of Wilson's name, it is almost certain that the quarto merely took the author's original jotting "Enter prince Leonato, Claudio, Musicke," while the folio took the prompter's annotation of Jack Wilson, inserted for "Musicke," which the prompter would simply have scored through, writing the name above. Further, there is a Wilson who would exactly fit into this line. Collier[16] proposed to identify this Jack Wilson with John, the son of Nicholas Wilson, baptized

[15] *Grove's Dictionary of Music and Musicians*, Article John Wilson.
[16] Collier, *Memoirs*, pp. xvii-xix.

April 24, 1585. This John would thus have entered the company about April 1595, at ten, and have graduated about April 1606, at twenty-one. His last rôle would have been about the winter of 1605, where the line to which Balthazar belongs seems to end. While then the evidence is not absolutely conclusive, yet I think it quite strong that John, the son of Nicholas Wilson was the Jack Wilson who performed Balthazar in *Much Ado*.[17]

The evidence for allocating Wilson's comic partner, who seems to have graduated in 1604, is purely inferential and not very strong. Most indications point to Samuel Crosse, who is mentioned by the folio as a principal actor, but like Gilburne, was seemingly never a member, indicating that he had at some time been a chief apprentice actor. All lines seem accounted for up to this one of 1593-1604. The succeeding lines seem also accounted for, as we shall see, leaving only this one for Crosse. Possibly the fact that Crosse is mentioned shortly before Gilburne in the roughly chronological first folio list also indicates that he served about the time here assigned him.

After these two apprentices of 1593-94-1604-05, we should expect the next entrants to appear in 1598, to succeed the two graduates of that year. These successors should then have become the principal actors in 1604-05. The serious line does so appear; but not so, I think, the comic. There seems to be a plausible reason for this situation. One master of comic apprentices, we may infer, was William Kemp, who left the company early in 1599. Now Kemp abroad in 1586 had as boy Daniel Jones, who must have been practically or entirely free, since he received pay at the same rate as the six men.[18] His successor could not have graduated as a principal actor in the Shakespearean company before 1598. Nor, if our inference concerning the approximate majority of Daniel Jones in 1586 be correct, would his successor likely have completed ap-

---

[17] It is, of course, possible that April 5, 1595, on Doctor Wilson's tomb is an error for April 5, 1585; and that the two Wilsons are one, though even then we should have the unusually long period April 5-24 from birth to baptism. The fact that "Doctor" Wilson wrote the music for a very important masque by January 6, 1614, would also indicate that he was probably older than his tombstone indicates. Too, he seems at some time to have written music for two of Shakespeare's songs, "Take oh take those lips away" in *Measure for Measure* (IV. 1, winter 1604), and the lawn song in *Winter's Tale* (IV. 3, summer 1611; see Grove). Since the second of these was sung by one of the major actors as Autolycus, Wilson could not have sung the song, even if he may have composed the music to it. The same conclusion is probable in *Measure for Measure*. Still, if Wilson was born in April 1585, he may have composed the music of the first of these songs in 1604 at nineteen, the second in 1611 at twenty-six, and the masque for January 6, 1614, at twenty-eight.

[18] See above, p. 74.

prenticeship later than these graduates of 1598. It is thus probable that the comedian William Eccleston was William Kemp's apprentice, and that there was no successor to Eccleston because of Kemp's leaving the company.

There was, however, a successor to Robert Goffe. By his will of July 22, 1603, Pope divides his theatrical equipment between Robert Goffe and John Edmans, the latter of whom was dwelling with him, as is shown by his signing[19] Pope's will. Evidently Goffe had been Pope's apprentice from the summer of 1587, to the summer of 1598, and had been succeeded by Edmans, who should thus have served the summer of 1598 to the summer of 1609. But since Pope had retired by March 1603, it is not certain that Edmans continued his training in the company. There is never a hint in Pope's will of any continued connection with his former fellows. Bequests there are galore, but never a one for them. A good imagination could readily conjure up from the circumstances of his withdrawal and his silence in his last will a disagreement with his fellows and a consequent severing of diplomatic relations, ending speedily in death from a broken heart; but it is at least as plausible that accumulating flesh had finally rendered this "fat fool" incapable even of Falstaff, and necessitated a retirement of ease, soon ended by a fatty heart instead of a broken one. But to return to Edmans, there are some indications that he continued with the Shakespearean company. He would already have served nearly five years at the time of Pope's withdrawal, and would be just budding into usefulness, so that the company would probably have desired to retain him. He certainly did not give up acting, his first recorded connection as a man being with Queen Anne's company.[20] Also, he had married Marie Clark and half of Pope's share in the Globe by February 20, 1611,[21] indicating that he had completed apprenticeship before that date, as we saw reason to believe he should have done about the summer of 1609. Now the lines of apprentices show that there was a graduate about this time. Probably then, but not quite certainly, Edmans continued with the company, and was this graduate.

Our next graduates should be the successors of the graduates of 1600-01. One of these was John Rice, who seems to have been completing apprenticeship about the summer of 1611. As "A very

[19] Does this fact indicate anything concerning Edman's age? I do not know what the age qualification then was; but some three-quarters of a century earlier William Rastell had acted as witness at the age of sixteen or seventeen, probably the approximate age of Edmans (*The Library*, series 4, Vol. IV, p. 27).

[20] See above, p. 277.

[21] Wallace, London *Times*, October 4, 1909. Since there was no wife or daughter extant, the model apprentice had married his master's heiress.

proper Child, well spoken, being clothed like an angell of gladness with a Taper of Ffrankincense burning in his hand," Rice had delivered July 16, 1607, an eighteen-verse speech by Ben Jonson to King James for the Merchant Taylors.[22] In the city pageant of May 31, 1610, at the creating of Henry the Prince of Wales,[23] Mr. Burbadge and John Rice "two absolute Actors, euen the verie best our instant time can yeeld," "rode vpon the two fishes and made the speeches." Burbadge was "Amphion the Father of her-monie or Musick," "a graue and iudicious Prophet-like personage, attyred in his apte habits, euery way answerable to his state and profession, with his wreathe of Sea-shelles on his head, and his harpe hanging in fayre twine before him." Rice was Corinea of Cornwall, "a very fayre and beautifull Nimphe, representing the Genius of olde Corineus Queene, and the Prouince of Cornewall, suited in her watrie habit yet riche and costly, with a Coronet of Pearles and Cockle Shelles on her head." Evidently then Rice was a chief apprentice actor in the Shakespearean company 1607-10. But Rice had gone to Princess Elizabeth's company by August 1611,[24] presumably being now graduated. Further, there is a comico-villainous line ending the summer of 1611, the two last characters in it being the Queen in *Cymbeline*, and Paulina. This line then is probably that of Rice.

The other entrant of 1600-01 seems to have been James Sands. From the will of Phillips in 1605 we learn that Gilburne had been his "late" apprentice, succeeded by James Sands. Since Gilburne was graduated about 1601, Sands should have succeeded him 1601-02, and have completed his indenture 1612-13. That Sands was also an actor is indicated by the nature of the heritage he divided with Gilburne, they receiving Phillips's equipment as an actor. Thus Sands succeeded Gilburne 1601-02, and should have graduated as the regal apprentice of 1612-13. But then there is the possibility that the death of his master in 1605 may have altered the prospects of Sands. That this misfortune did not take Sands from the company is indicated by the fact that William Sly in his will August 4, 1608,[25] leaves Sands £40. The explanation is that John Heminges, Richard Burbadge, and William Sly as executors of Phillips's will would continue the training of the boy in the company, the actual training doubtless having fallen to Sly. At Sly's death, Heminges, who had become officially executor of the will, would

---

[22] Clode, C. M., *The Early History of the Guild of Merchant Taylors*, Vol. I, p. 290, and note; Chambers, *Eliz. Stage*. Vol. II, p. 213, and note.
[23] *Athenaeum*, May 19, 1888, p. 641; Wallace, London *Times*, March 28, 1913, p. 6.
[24] Greg, *Papers*, pp. 18, 111.
[25] Collier, *Memoirs*, p. 157.

probably either himself continue Sands's much checkered education, or would have some one else in the company do so. It is thus probable that Sands was the performer of the regal line ending in 1613.

Sands seems to have gone to Queen Anne's company, appearing with Ellis Worth in a scene direction of Daborne's *Poor Man's Comfort*.[26] Since this was a Cockpit play in which Worth performed, the production dates before the middle of 1619, when Worth's connection ceased with that theater. If these jottings refer to the original production of the play, they cannot date later than 1617, since Daborne had become a preacher by 1618. The play has a fairly clear allusion that helps further in dating it. The distracted father in seeking justice falls among the promoters, who demand his cause.

Gisb. Tis a particular grief Sir.

Jasp. Of some particular corporation.

Gisb. That lies as heavie on the bearers shoulders.

Licus. Some suit from porters hall, belike not worth begging.[27]

Now Daborne had for many years been writing for a "particular corporation," which attempted from about June 3, 1615, till January 27, 1617, to set up a playhouse in "porter's hall," finding it necessary to present various petitions, which eventually did them no good. I take it that this is the point to an otherwise forced and pointless joke. Since the petition is not worth begging, the reference denotes a closed issue, probably after January 27, 1617. Since Daborne had been regularly connected with the Revels as a manager from 1610, and as a poet in all other of his known plays except this, the most logical date for it is after the breaking of the coalition in 1617, which would set Daborne adrift. Doubtless then he placed this play with Queen Anne's in 1617 before turning amphibion by the ministry. A perhaps unwarrantably strict interpretation of the statement that the play was a Cockpit play would also indicate a time not earlier than 1617, when that house was opened. It seems fairly clear, however, that the play was produced about 1617. If then the reference to Sands in this play is to James Sands,[28] and there is no other known actor of the name at this period, it shows

[26] *Anglia*, Vol. XXI, p. 382.

[27] *ibid.*, p. 402.

[28] A James Sands is recorded in the token books of St. Saviour's 1596-1612 (Chambers, *Eliz. Stage*, Vol. II, p. 337). Now these token books contain "all people of age to take the Sacrament" (Rendle, *Antiquarian Magazine*, Vol. VII, p. 211), provided they were in good standing (*Notes and Queries*, 5th ser., Vol. XI, p. 51). Also, "All persons over fourteen had to receive communion at Easter, and at least on two other occasions during the year" (Ware, *Elizabethan Parish*, p. 36). It would appear then that this James Sands was at least fourteen by Easter 1596, and would have been at least

that he was with Queen Anne's men by 1617, with which organization another former dependent of the Shakespearean company,
John Edmans, was also associated.

There should next be a comic apprentice to enter about the summer of 1604, graduating about the summer of 1615; and a serious
apprentice to enter about the spring of 1606, graduating about
1617. There is very good evidence that the serious apprentice
was Dickey Robinson himself. In *The Second Maiden's Tragedy*,
autumn 1611, a chance jotting by the prompter has given us
the information that Robinson performed the Lady of Govianus.
Now this play, Fletcher's *Captain*, and Shakespeare's *Tempest*,
all for the same season, show that there were three apprentices
for major rôles at the time. There is the leading lady—Wife
(236 lines), Lelia (438 lines), Ariel (191 lines),—with the greatest number of lines and presenting the most difficult rôles. Next
is the virtuous lady—Lady of Govianus (151 lines), Frank
(274 lines), Miranda (142 lines). Then comes the witty, erotic
waiting maid—Leonella (148 lines), Clara (257 lines), not definitely represented in *The Tempest*. We are thus certain of Robinson's line, which has already been checked up in the Beaumont
and Fletcher plays. The leading lady we have seen occasion to
assign to James Sands, leaving only the witty waiting maid for
allocation. Since this line attains importance along with Robinson's, the inference is that here is Robinson's running mate, who
should have entered 1604-05, though who he was we have no clue.
Since he seems, however, to have been replaced by Shank's comic
apprentices, Holcomb and Pollard, 1616, he may have been Armin's
apprentice; and we have, for convenience, so labelled him.

Now it is apparent that while we do not have complete details
concerning these apprentices, yet we do know the general principles of their government and training. It appears that throughout
the period of Shakespeare's writing these apprentices worked in
pairs, a serious one being yoked with a comic. There were usually
three of these pairs in the company at the same time, with different
degrees of training, a new pair being introduced when an old was
graduated. Thus the work of an apprentice was divided into three
stages of three or four years each. For the first three or four years,
or till about fourteen, the apprentice usually supplied only small
and unimportant parts. Then for the second three or four years, or

twenty-three at the time of Phillips's will May 4, 1605. Since the actor
James Sands was still Phillip's apprentice at the time of the will, it seems
clear that he could not have been the James Sands of the token books, who
may have been his father. It is also uncertain whether the James Sands
who married Alice Chipps, July 25, 1624, at St. Saviour's (*Genealogist*, n.s.,
Vol. IX, p. 234) was the actor.

till about seventeen, his parts were secondary. In the final period, or till twenty-one, he was leading lady in his line.

This number and order of apprentices was established in the early days of the company, and was probably as much the result of chance as plan. For it seems to rest originally chiefly upon the fact that the apprentices of all members were used in the acting, as we are now in position to see. We have seen that Goffe, and then probably Edmans, were the apprentices of Pope; and that Gilburne, succeeded by Sands, were the apprentices of Phillips. We have also seen good reason to believe that Eccleston was the apprentice of Kemp. By the reference in his will to "my master Hemings," Cooke gives us to understand that he had been the apprentice of John Heminges. Similarly Tooley by reference in his will to "my late Mr. Burbadge" would claim connection with Richard Burbadge. Since Tooley and Burbadge were of almost the same age, Tooley could not formally have been the latter's apprentice. But it may well be that Tooley was officially James Burbage's apprentice, and in consequence the inseparable companion of Richard. Tooley seems to have been residing with Richard at the latter's death, signing his nuncupative will. He then went to Cuthbert, dying in the latter's home a few years later and leaving the bulk of his property to the various members of the Burbadge clan. It seems certain then that Tooley was in some way connected with Richard Burbadge, who was not himself a member before the summer of 1594. Thus we are left with one member, Bryane, and one other apprentice, seemingly Ned, to belong to him. Since neither Bryane nor Pope had an apprentice abroad in 1586-87, it is probable that neither took an apprentice before the return to England in 1587. Pope seems, however, to have taken Goffe immediately on return, since the latter completed apprenticeship about the summer of 1598. It is likely that Bryane would in no long time have followed suit. It is thus probable that Bryane also had his apprentice, and plausible that this apprentice was the left over Ned [?Shakespeare], who probably entered about 1590.[29] It seems probable then that the number of six for apprentices is due to the simple fact that there were originally five members in the company, each with his apprentice; and that the non-member Richard Burbadge, who was even then acting a member's rôle, had his apprentice also.

This number seems for various reasons not to have increased with the increased membership of 1594. For one thing, more apprentices could not be profitably used, so that there was no necessity for increase. For another, the new members probably did not have

[29] If Ned was Shakespeare's brother Edmund, then he may have been under the dramatist's care, and Bryane may have had no apprentice.

households, making the keeping of an apprentice somewhat difficult. Shakespeare was seemingly rooming around as a "grass
bachelor."[30] Sly was never married, and had no household. Cundall
was hardly married before 1598. Though Richard Burbadge was
still a bachelor, he was in his father's home, and might well have
taken a successor to Tooley.

There is some indication that Burbadge did take a successor to
Tooley. We have fair evidence that at least Richard Robinson was
Burbadge's apprentice. Together with Tooley he had signed Richard's nuncupative will in 1619, indicating that he at that time
belonged to the family, the presumption being that he too was
Richard's apprentice. It would seem then that when Robinson married Richard's widow he was but acting the model apprentice. Now
Robinson had succeeded Jack Wilson about 1606, who was one of
the entrants of 1594-95. Besides, the lines of Wilson and Robinson
were quite similar. Surely Burbadge, who could be "Amphion the
Father of hermonie or Musick," would have been a good tutor for
young Jack Wilson, and to his care in the present state of the evidence we must leave him. Presumably then Crosse, the other
entrant of 1594, was Heminges's apprentice, succeeding Cooke.

When Kemp dropped out in 1599, just after Eccleston's graduation, there seems to have been no attempt to bring in another youthful broad comedian. Just as the clowns were being crowded from
the plays at this period, so were their apprentices. Shortly before
this, Bryane had also dropped out; but probably had left his
apprentice, Ned, with the company. At the graduation of this apprentice, Heminges seems to have supplied his place by taking
John Rice[31] as a second apprentice in addition to Crosse. Heminges
the grocer, a substantial citizen with a large family, might well
have considered another apprentice no notable addition to his
responsibilities. By this time the number of apprentices had become
fixed, and the custom had been established of having them trained
by only a few members of the company instead of one by each as

[30] It is highly improbable that Shakespeare ever had his family in London. All the family records are in Stratford. Certainly the family was in
Stratford at the death of Hamnet in August 1596; and the evidence seems
clear thereafter. Thus it is fairly clear that Shakespeare did not buy New
Place in 1597 for the purpose of moving his family from London. It
would have been folly for hireling Shakespeare to have brought his family
from cheap and healthy Stratford to costly and unsanitary London in those
early days. Besides, his name would then have been recorded each year at
Easter in the token books of the parish where he resided. The fact that
no such record has survived during all his London connection indicates
that he remained a "stranger" in London, keeping his church membership
at Stratford. Too, he always describes himself as of Stratford, never of
London.

[31] Chambers, *Eliz. Stage*, Vol. II, p. 213, and note.

originally. Seemingly this process continued, since by 1635 Kemp could claim to be furnishing three apprentices to the company;[32] but of the later details we know too little to make further discussion worth while.

An understanding of these principles enables us a little better to guess at the situation before 1594. We have seen that there were two graduates 1589-90, not yet determined. The next preceding graduates, on our principles of succession, should have been about 1587-88, to be succeeded by Goffe and Eccleston. We have seen that Eccleston seems to have been preceded as Kemp's apprentice by Daniel Jones; but that Goffe seems not to have had a predecessor as Pope's apprentice. The yoking of these apprentices together then was probably accidental. There seems to have been more reason for the yoking of Tooley and Cooke. They must have become apprentices about 1583, when the old Leicester acting company was completely reorganized. If these apprentices came through either branch of the Leicester organization, they must have come through the acting branch, since there were no apprentices with the musicians abroad. So far as Cooke is concerned, this indication is consistent with known facts, since his master Heminges was pretty certainly a member of Leicester's actors and not of the musicians. The case of Tooley is bound up with that of Richard Burbadge, and may best be considered in connection with him.

It seems fairly certain that Richard Burbadge did not come to the Shakespearean company through the Leicester organization. Burbadge became a member at the age of twenty-one in 1594, implying that he had begun acting probably at ten in 1583. That he did begin about this time we have the word of his brother Cuthbert, who fixes the term of Richard's acting as thirty-five years,[33] which would launch Richard between March 1583, and March 1584. Notwithstanding his tender years, Richard had been principal actor of male rôles in The Seven Deadly Sins early in 1592. He seems certainly to have been with the amalgamated Shakespearean-Admiral's company at the Theater in the autumn of 1590. There our first definite record finds him just before a performance November 16, 1590, manfully repelling the invader.[34] Presumably he was connected with the Shakespearean company at least from that time, since we find him as a principal actor with this organization less than a year and a half later. This presumption the lines of characters seem clearly to support, giving Burbadge a leading rôle from the winter of 1590.

But it also seems clear that before the amalgamation in 1590

[32] Halliwell, Outlines, Vol. I, p. 316.
[33] ibid., p. 317.
[34] Wallace, First London Theatre, pp. 17-18, 100-2, 114-15.

Burbadge had been associated with the Admiral's men. In the plot of *The Dead Man's Fortune*, probably one of Edward Alleyn's plays, Burbadge appears seemingly as a messenger.[35] So unimportant a part could have fallen to Burbadge's lot only some years before 1592, almost certainly before 1590. Further, Darlowe and Lee appear as his fellow actors. Now of Darlowe we know nothing, but all of Lee's connections are with the Admiral's men, the connection being pretty certainly at least as early as 1593.[36] Neither of these two appears in the very full plot of 1592 for the Shakespearean company. Almost certainly then *The Dead Man's Fortune* was performed by the Admiral's men before 1590, with whom Richard Burbadge was at the time acting. Nor is this surprising, since Alleyn's organization had been acting at the Theater, the property of Richard's father, probably from 1585, certainly from 1587.[37] We need not suppose, however, that Burbadge was formally apprenticed at all. As his father's son, Richard would be entitled to enter that father's mystery without formal apprenticeship. It is likely therefore that he acted under his father's tutelage with the companies performing at the Theater, thus becoming attached to Alleyn's company for the formative part of his apprentice days. So attached did he become to this company, and such brilliant opportunity did the amalgamated company offer him that he drifted away with it from the Theater, soon to become the principal actor of the Shakespearean company alone. Thus Richard would have had the advantage not only of the mature experience of his father, who for many years had led Leicester's men themselves, but also would have had the advantage of acting in his formative years with and against his only rival to fame, the great Ned Alleyn, not quite seven years Richard's senior. Apparently then Burbadge, and with him Tooley, came through the Admiral's men; but the taking of Tooley as an apprentice by James Burbadge about 1583 may have been occasioned by the reorganization of Leicester's men, to whom Burbadge had previously belonged. Presumably then neither Burbadge nor Tooley had any part in the Shakespearean plays before 1590.

We are thus to look not only for two chief apprentices who graduated in 1589, but also for a comic actor of considerable prominence before the appearance of Tooley. We have several clues to these probable graduates. Members regularly came to the company only through apprenticeship either in the company or elsewhere. Now after the reorganization of 1588, Shakespeare,

[35] See Greg, W. W., "Elizabethan Theatrical Plots," *Review of English Studies*, Vol. I, p. 263 and note.
[36] Warner, *Catalogue*, p. 127.
[37] See above, p. 323.

Burbadge, Cundall, and Sly became members in 1594, and Cowley about 1597, these being the only entrants through the company before the admission of Cooke and Tooley in 1603. Presumably these represent the majority of graduates up to 1594. Burbadge we have already discussed, and Shakespeare we may omit for our present purpose as too old to have been a regular apprentice-actor of female parts. We seem now to have three probable candidates left, Cundall, Sly, and Cowley, all of whom were prominent young actors by 1592, and later became members. Now if these came through Leicester's actors, they must have been controlled by Heminges, Phillips, or Kemp. Curiously enough Cundall tends to pair off with Heminges in later affairs, as does also Sly with Phillips. We have seen that Sly was an executor of Phillips's will and took over the training of the latter's apprentice. Before this we find both living in Horseshoe Court during the year 1593.[38] Since Sly must have been quite young and was not a householder, he was probably living with Phillips. Further, Phillips took a new apprentice about 1590, implying that his previous apprentice had graduated about 1589; and we find Sly taking youthful parts as a man soon thereafter. It seems probable, therefore, that Sly had been Phillips's apprentice, graduating about 1589. If so, we may infer from his later line that he had been the witty waiting-maid.

In the same way, Heminges and Cundall tend to pull together. So famous is the connection that we need not give illustration of it here. Most significant probably from our present point of view is the fact that the two men lived in the same community, inconveniently separated from their work and the rest of the clan. And yet Heminges must have been several years older than Cundall. By 1594, Heminges must have been nearing forty,[39] while Cundall as a youthful bachelor not yet to be married for some years[40] was just being admitted a member. It is thus quite probable that Cundall had been the apprentice of John Heminges. It may be significant then that Heminges took John Rice as apprentice seemingly in 1600, just an acting apprenticeship away from 1589, when Cundall probably was graduated, though we have no definite trace of such an intermediate apprentice.

This allocation would leave Cowley as an understudy to Kemp, this being the well known pairing in *Much Ado*—Verges and Dogberry. It is true that Cowley could hardly have been Kemp's apprentice originally, since we know that the latter had another apprentice in 1586, and Cowley was already acting the man by March 1592. He was also old enough by August 1593, to be the

[38] Collier, *Memoirs*, p. 152.
[39] cf. above, p. 250.
[40] Collier, *Memoirs*, p. 134.

bearer of a letter, presumably alone, from London to Edward Alleyn, acting with the Shakespearean company in the provinces.[41] He was old enough to be married by 1595, since his first child was born March 1596.[42] He must thus have completed apprenticeship by or about 1592. But we need not suppose that Cundall, Sly, or Cowley belonged to these masters originally. It is only necessary to suppose that these three apprentices had belonged originally to Leicester's actors, and had eventually fallen to the lot of the three residuary members, who passed to the Shakespearean company.

There is thus every indication that these three had been apprentices in the organization, and some reason to believe that Cundall and Sly had been the graduates of 1589, slightly preceding Cowley, this being the order of their admission to membership. If so, then, as has been pointed out, Sly would have been the witty waiting maid. Cowley would of course have been the comedian, leaving the regal lead for Cundall, a type of character which fits quite well with his later line.

We have then at least a possible allocation of parts to apprentices, and of apprentices to masters. We do not have quite sufficient evidence to be sure who were the masters of all the apprentices after Shakespeare's connection ceased. The number of lines was reduced by the graduation of Rice and Edmans to four, and training was provided by bringing in the successor a year or two before the graduation of his predecessor. Since Edmans had been the apprentice of Pope, who had died some years before, and Rice the apprentice of Heminges, who retired at the time of Rice's graduation, it seems that these lines were simply permitted to drop with their masters. We saw in the Beaumont and Fletcher plays that John Shank succeeded Robert Armin as master of at least one of these lines, continuing it till his death in 1636. Wright tells us that Hart was Robinson's apprentice, indicating that when Robinson married his master Burbadge's wife he came into control of his apprentices also, and continued the training of them. We do not know who were the masters of the other two lines.

Besides these apprentices, however, certain of the masters had hired men controlled by them individually. Thus Phillips, in his will of May 1605, calls Christopher Beeston "my servaunte." Beeston appeared with the company 1592-98, but had gone to Worcester's by 1602.[43] It was in this period then 1592-98 that Beeston had been Phillips's servant. In the same period, William Toyer seems to have been the servant of John Heminges. Toyer was the trumpeter ushering in the rustic show of *Midsummer Night's*

41 Young, W., *The History of Dulwich College*, Vol. II, p. 9.
42 Collier, *Memoirs*, p. 161.
43 Murray, Vol. I, pp. 80, 101, 52.

Dream (summer, 1594), was licensed as a musician and necessary attendant of the company December 27, 1624,[44] and died in 1625, being buried as "Mr. Heminge's man."[45] Thus Toyer was Heminges's servant, serving as a musician and necessary attendant. The case of Toyer suggests that if Ned was either Edward Ashborn or Edward Knight, both of whom appear with Toyer as musicians and necessary attendants in 1624,[46] then he and the singing Jack Wilson, member of a family of musicians, probably also belonged to this class of servants, this being the reason they are not mentioned in the folio list of 1623. This would leave only John Edmans of the chief apprentice actors in Shakespeare's time not so included, and there may be a similar reason in his case. It appears then that before 1594, at least Heminges and Phillips had other servants besides apprentices. Whether Kemp, Pope, and Bryane also had servants we do not know.

[44] Adams, *Herbert*, p. 74.
[45] Collier, *Memoirs*, p. 65.
[46] Adams, *Herbert*, p. 74.

JONSON'S PLAYS FOR THE
SHAKESPEAREAN COMPANY, 1598-1616

SINCE most of our actor lists for the term of Shakespeare's service are from Jonson's plays, and since Jonson himself is the only other known poet of the period, besides Beaumont and Fletcher, who wrote with any degree of regularity for the company, it will be well to examine his plays also. But first we must establish the dates of Jonson's plays for the company, and the nature of his connection with the organization.

(A) DATES

Jonson tells us that he wrote *Cataline* in 1611. Since Eccleston was a principal actor in the play, it must have been produced well before August 29, of that year, when he appears as a member of another company.[1] Hence *Cataline* was for the summer season 1611. Also, Doctor Hathaway has shown that *The Alchemist* was certainly for the autumn and winter of 1610,[2] though I do not feel sure that all the details of dating are correctly interpreted. It appears then that Jonson wrote *The Alchemist* for the winter season 1610, and *Cataline* for the summer 1611, supplying one play for winter, and one for summer, as was the regular custom of dramatists for the Shakespearean company.

In the same way, he participated in *The Bloody Brother* for the company the summer of 1616, and wrote *Devil Is An Ass* for the winter of the same year.[3] His only other certain period of connected service with the Shakespearean company before this was for *Every Man in His Humor*, 1598; and *Every Man Out of His Humor*, 1599. Hence the first of these was presumably for the winter of 1598, and the second for the summer of 1599. That the first of these could not have been produced before the winter of 1598 is indicated by the fact that Jonson had been with the Admiral's men as playwright and actor till about the time he killed Gabriel Spencer in a duel September 1598.[4] In fact, it seems reasonably certain that this is "A new play called, Every mans humour," referred to under

---

[1] Greg, *Papers*, pp. 18, 111.
[2] Hathaway, C. M., *The Alchemist* (Yale Studies), pp. 12-15.
[3] Kittredge, *Modern Philology*, Vol. IX, pp. 195 *ff*.
[4] Greg, *Diary*, Vol. II, p. 289.

date of September 20, 1598.[5] That the second of these plays was produced for the summer 1599 is indicated by the fact that by August 1599 Jonson was again writing for Henslowe. It is evident then that although Jonson was "so slow an Inuentor"[6] that "You and your Itchy Poetry breake out like Christmas but once a yeare,"[7] yet when he was with the Romans he did as the Romans did; when he was with the Shakespearean company, he wrote two plays a year. Possibly this rigid necessity was in part the reason that Jonson never remained longer than a year at the time with the Shakespearean company.

Further, *Volpone* was Jonson's winter play of 1605,[8] produced for the Shakespearean company after he was forced from the Revels company for his share of *Eastward Ho*. The evidence is also rather strong that Jonson revised *Every Man in his Humor*, presumably for the Shakespearean company, about April 24, 1605.[9] Pretty certainly Jonson did this work for the summer, immediately after his expulsion from the Revels, and continued with *Volpone* for the winter.

Sejanus was presented in 1603, as Jonson informs us. Since Lowin was a principal actor, the play was not performed earlier than the company patent of May 17, 1603,[10] in which Lowin is not named. All public acting was prohibited by the plague May 26, 1603, till about April 9, 1604.[11] There is no certain record that the Shakespearean company went to the provinces this summer, but it did appear there in the autumn by way of preparation for the court season.[12] It seems clear then that *Sejanus* was presented the winter of 1603.

These dates also make it clear that the Shakespearean company was Jonson's regular haven of refuge in time of storm. When he killed Spencer in 1598, and was forced from the Admiral's men, he found refuge in the Shakespearean company. After he had returned in 1599 for a short time to the Admiral's, he became attached in 1600 to the Revels, remaining with the various reorganizations of this company till its approaching final dissolution about 1616. Throughout 1603, this organization seemingly was closed down.

---

[5] *Jonson Allusion Book.*, p. 451; misdated 1588.

[6] Macray, *Parnassus*, p. 87.

[7] Dekker's *Satiromastix*, (Penniman), p. XVIII; cf. *Jonson Allusion Book*, pp. 226, 235.

[8] Fleay, *Drama*, Vol. I, pp. 372-4; Rea, John D., *Volpone*, (Yale Studies), pp. VIII-IX.

[9] III. 1.; Carter, H. H., *Every Man in his Humor* (Yale Studies), pp. lxiii-lxiv.

[10] Murray, Vol. I, opp. p. 172.

[11] *ibid.*, pp. 147, 149.

[12] *ibid.*, p. 183.

	1598, WINTER (10+0) 11+0	1599, SUMMER (6+0) 12+1	1603, WINTER (8+0) 9+0	1605, WINTER (6+0) 8+1	1610, WINTER (10+0) 7+1	1611, SUMMER (9+1) 8+2
	Every Man in Humor	*Every Man out of Humor*	*Sejanus*	*Volpone*	*Alchemist*	*Cataline*
Augustine Phillips	*1 Thorello 411	*7 Deliro 194	*2 Tiberius 430	*1 Mosca 971	*1 Face 1215	*1 Cicero 1050
Richard Burbadge	*2 Musco 295	*3 Brisk 412	*1 Sejanus 741	*2 Volpone 851		*2 Cataline 751
Thomas Pope	*3 Bobadilla 269	*1 Buffone 610				
John Lowin				*4 Politick 329	*3 Memnon 509	*4 Cethegus 194
Henry Cundall	*7 Prospero 200	*5 Cordatus 274	*4 Silius 285	*5 Voltore 224	*5 Surly 222	*5 Caesar 177
William Ostler			*6 Sabinus 209		*6 Lovewit 175	*6 Cato 176
John Heminges	*6 Dr.Clement 221	*4 Puntarvolo 344	*3 Arruntius 424	*3 Corvino 340	*2 Subtle 1066	
William Sly	*11 Giuliano 116	*9 Fungoso 189	*5 Macro 242			
John Underwood						*8 Lentulus 146
William Shakespeare	*4 Lorenzo,Sr. 263	12 Mitis 127	*8 Lepidus 119			
William Kemp	*8 Cob 189				* Dapper 95	
Robert Armin				9 Nano 116	* Drugger 84	
Richard Cowley	10 Stephano 158	6 Sogliardo 259	*7 Terentius 142	8 Corbaccio 147	*8 Ananias 122	*7 Curius 153
Alexander Cooke				*6 Peregrine 215		
John Duke	*9 Matheo 159	8 Asper 191				
Christopher Beeston	*5 Lorenzo,Jr. 234	2 Macilente 585				
Benjamin Jonson						
Nicholas Tooley					* Wholesome 61	* Sylla's Ghost 72
William Eccleston	Tib 28				*7 Kastril 132	*9 Petreius 130
Samuel Gilburne	Hesperida 29	Saviolina 60				
Ned (Shakespeare)	Bianca 66	11 Fallace 174				
Jack Wilson						
Samuel Crosse			Aggripina 76	Castrone 2		
John Edmans			Livia 38			
John Rice				7 L.Would-be 206	4 Dol 223	3 Fulvia 253
James Sands				Celia 70		*10 Sempronia 124
Richard Robinson						Galla 71
Armin's Apprentice						

NOTE. For details of arrangement, see note to Beaumont and Fletcher tabulation, Chap. VIII.

All companies were closed March 19, 1603, seemingly for Lent, by order of the Privy Council.[13] Before the end of Lent, Queen Elizabeth had died, leaving the company patronless, a condition in which it remained till the patent of February 4, 1604. There had been no need for hurry in securing a new patron, since the plague, as we have just seen, stopped all public acting from May 26, 1603, till about April 9, 1604. There is no record of the company's having acted at this period either in public or in private till after the patent of February 4, 1604.[14] With his own company closed down, again Jonson turned to the Shakespearean company, to place *Sejanus* the autumn of 1603. When his company was again closed over *Eastward Ho*, Jonson seemingly revised *Every Man in his Humor* and placed *Volpone* with the Shakespearean company. When Jonson's company was almost shipwrecked by dissensions and adverse circumstances about 1610, he again turned to the Shakespearean company till better days. At the final catastrophe, about 1616, Jonson turned to the Shakespearean company for a time before he finally bade goodbye for some years to the loathed stage. Even when many years later he decided to give the stage another trial, it was to the Shakespearean company that he turned.

It appears then that this supposed arch-drifter,[15] Jonson, drifted only when he was wrecked. He was regularly attached to one organization, and did not write for another except when forced to do so by personal or company difficulties. It is also abundantly clear that whatever may have been the attitude of Jonson toward Shakespeare and the company, at least the company and Shakespeare were always ready to lend Jonson a hand. On Jonson's side, we need to remember that if Jonson made a joke of the actors' heraldric pretensions, he did it with their consent, and that even Shakespeare in the best of humor had bestowed a red-nosed ancestor upon his fellow Phillips. If Jonson is disrespectful to *Titus Andronicus*, patched by Shakespeare, still he couples it with *The Spanish Tragedy*, upon which he himself had done his endeavors.

(B) LINES OF ACTORS

Jonson's plays for the Shakespearean company are rather difficult to assign to principal actors, notwithstanding the fact that we have full actor lists for nearly all of them. As a matter of fact, the chief value of these lists lies in the circumstance that they show us who were the chief actors of the company at the time, rather than in any direct indication they give us as to what actor took what part in any particular play.

[13] *Acts of the Privy Council*, 1601-04, p. 492.
[14] Murray, Vol. I, p. 354; Malone Soc. *Coll.*, Vol. I, p. 267.
[15] Thorndike, *Influence*, pp. 11-12.

The reasons for our difficulty in assigning parts are chiefly two. In the first place, Jonson constructed his play primarily to suit himself rather than to suit the company. He seems to have written his plays to express his own ideas, and then to have placed his plays where he could best get them produced. The result was something like the fit of ready-made clothes, which may fit a number of people after a fashion, but rarely fit anybody well. While the suit may fit many, there is no way of telling to what particular individual of the many it did actually belong. There is very little about a Jonson play to indicate the company by which it was performed. Even when we know the company, it is still difficult to apportion parts. There is naturally almost nothing of that intimate adaptation of parts to the individual actor which was the rule in Shakespeare or Fletcher. Rarely are there any individualizing or personal references. Thus for the most part we must fall back on the type characters or lines running through the plays.

But here we meet the second great difficulty, which is that Jonson did not produce characters but essentially caricatures. Whatever Jonson's own insistence that a "humor" was not merely an outward fashion, still these inner humors had to dramatize themselves in outward form. The whole point of such an outward dramatization might lie in some physical peculiarity real or assumed in the actor, not known to us and not described in the play except incidentally, since it is visible to the audience. Of these outward individualizing traits we know too little to be very certain in conclusions based on them. Jonson's parts, being caricatures, depended to a considerable extent upon those external peculiarities which have so well nigh completely perished. Therefore our material for classifying these caricatures into lines is rather scanty.

Nevertheless Jonson as well as Shakespeare tended to have a type structure for his comedies, whereby one play can be compared with another. In three of the four comedies for the Shakespearean company, there are two conspirators to catch the gulls, and in the fourth there is only one. To trace this feature chronologically, we have Musco-Brainworm alone to catch the gulls and direct events in *Every Man in his Humor*. Then we have Macilente and Carlo Buffone in *Every Man out of his Humor* going gulling with only slight cooperation. Finally in *Volpone* and *The Alchemist* the conspirators work together, in the first as master and man, in the second as co-conspirators. On the other side, we have the grist that comes to the conspirators' mill in the form of gulls. This idea is but loosely developed in the first of the comedies, but has taken very definite shape by the time *Volpone* was written. There are a few evidently repeated or imitated gulls or humor characters in some of the plays, the first two and second two comedies having several caricatures in common, especially the second two.

The two Roman plays show a slight modification of the same structure. In *Sejanus*, everything centers around Sejanus and Tiberius; in *Cataline*, around Cicero and Cataline. Yet parts that serve the same mechanical function in different plays, comedies or tragedies, may not be of the same type, though they frequently are. Therefore, in the last analysis we must fall back on our knowledge of the type of character taken by each principal actor named in the actor lists.

We receive some help in settling the problem of parts taken, from the fact that *The Alchemist* shows signs of having been actually constructed with the purpose of fitting the Shakespearean company, even in personal allusions. For this play, Jonson has named ten actors, while the play has ten parts for men and two for women. That the actors were all for the masculine rôles is indicated by the fact that only Eccleston was not a member, though even he had graduated several years before. Thus Jonson has named all the actors for masculine parts. Incidentally, the only apprentice actor of female rôles who receives mention from Jonson is Richard Robinson in *Cataline*, who is also given high praise in *The Devil is an Ass* (II. 3). For an apprentice actor of female rôles to win even a mention from the realist Jonson was no mean accomplishment. But to return to *The Alchemist*, our problem is to allocate one actor for each of the masculine rôles. Since Taylor was later Face, this part was originally Burbadge's. Also, we know that Mammon was Lowin's rôle.[16] Subtle, the other important man, thin, old, and decrepit must be the rôle of John Heminges. Surly is a characteristic member of Cundall's old soldier-villain line. Lovewit, with his "old man's gravity," is the only part that can fit kingly William Ostler. The angry boy Kastril, not yet cold in his one and twenty, seems an unmistakable rôle for Eccleston. Drugger is kind enough to inform us that he plays the Fool. This, his small size, and general clownishness assign him to Armin. The puritan preacher Tribulation Wholesome would furnish Nicholas Tooley an excellent opportunity for one of his caricature parts. We thus have Dapper and Ananias to be allocated between Cooke and Underwood. The lawyer's youthful clerk Dapper would probably go to young Underwood, and the older Deacon Ananias to the older Cooke.

It is also possible to allocate the parts in *Cataline* with some confidence. Since Jonson has named nine performers of rôles for men, and since there are but nine parts of any importance for men, it is evident that, as in *The Alchemist*, Jonson has named all male

16 Wright, *Historia*, p. 424.

actors of any importance, our problem in this play being also simply one of allocation. Cicero would certainly go to Burbadge, and gruff villain Cataline to Lowin. Potentate Caesar would go to Ostler, and noble old patriot Cato to Heminges. Stirring soldier Cethegus would go to Cundall. Lentulus, third to Cinna and Sylla, who:

> looks already
> As if he shook a sceptre o'er the senate (I. 1),

he and Cethegus being "heirs of Mars" (I. 1), would belong to the princely rascals of Underwood. We thus have Petreius, Curius, and the Ghost of Sylla left for Cooke, Eccleston, and Tooley. Probably roistering soldier Eccleston found his part in this dignified play as soldier Petreius, leaving the gulled lover Curius for Cooke. This would give the Ghost of Sylla to Tooley, probably because of his ability in impressive makeup. Thus *Cataline* also may be assigned with fair definiteness.

The female rôles in these plays are not numerous, but may be fairly distributed in lines. Galla is a typical waiting-maid for Armin's apprentice. Dol and Fulvia seem to be yokemates for comico-villainous John Rice, leaving Sempronia for Richard Robinson, who is mentioned as a principal actor in *Cataline*. One would have expected Jonson to use Sands; instead of his junior, Robinson; but then Jonson had a partiality for "Dickey."

The next earlier play is *Volpone* (winter 1605). We know that Volpone was Lowin's rôle.[17] Since Mosca later belonged to Taylor,[18] he must originally have been a Burbadge rôle, being also the prototype of Face. The "mummia" Voltore was probably the part of old Heminges, corresponding in description with Subtle. Young Peregrine would seemingly be the part of young Cooke, not long since made a member. The knight, Sir Politick Would-be, would go to the actor of noble rôles, Henry Cundall. Of the other important parts for men, Nano, the dwarfish singing fool, belonged certainly to Robert Armin, who is not mentioned, however, in the actor list. Incidentally, his singing companion, the eunuch Castrone, is probably young Jack Wilson, whose voice doubtless would no longer pass for a woman's, and not yet for an ordinary man's; but voice, size, and appearance would do excellently for "an Eunuch." Thus only Corvino and Corbaccio are left for Sly to pick from. Deaf old Corbaccio seems a characteristic part for Richard Cowley, not mentioned in the list of actors, leaving Corvino for Sly. Blustering Corvino is also a characteristic part for soldier Sly. For the women, Lady Politick Would-be seems to belong in the line of John

[17] Wright, *Historia*, p. 424.
[18] Collier, *Memoirs*, p. 261.

Edmans. Celia would seem to belong with Cordelia and Anne Page in the line of James Sands. Thus *Volpone* seems also fairly assignable.

In *Sejanus*, the leading rôle, Sejanus, goes of course to Burbadge; and the lustful Tiberius belongs, it would seem, to Phillips's line of "luxurious" noblemen. The noble Lepidus is pretty certainly Shakespeare's. Probably young Terentius was Cooke's, and plotting villain-soldier Macro, Sly's. It seems hardly possible to distinguish with certainty between the three virtuous nobles Arruntius, Silius, and Sabinius for Heminges, Lowin, and Cundall, the assignment given in the tables representing my best guess for the present. For the women, noble Aggripina seems to belong to Jack Wilson, and lecherous Livia to Samuel Crosse.

Every Man out of his Humor also permits a fairly certain allocation of parts to the six principal actors. The play itself assigns Asper and Macilente to Jonson;[19] Sogliardo, "a kinsman to justice Silence" (V. 2), must belong with that character to Cowley. This assignment is rather important as showing the spirit underlying many of Jonson's jokes, by some considered merely malicious. Sogliardo is "an essential clown . . . yet so enamoured of the name of gentleman, that he will have it, though he buys it." He purchases for £30 arms "of as many colours as e'er you saw any fool's coat in your life" (III. 1), receives his parchment from the "harrots," and can write himself gentleman. Now a little later Cowley and Shakespeare were both quoted as illustrations of improper dealings on the part of the Heralds' Office.[20] I haven't been able to find exactly when Cowley's grant was made, but Shakespeare's was given in 1599. Doubtless Cowley had actually just been to the "harrots," this being well known, and adding tremendously to the joke.[21] Obviously, Jonson could not have perpetrated this joke without the consent both of the victim and of the company as a whole. As a clown, Cowley was "in his kingdom when in company where he may be well laughed at," even if the laugh was at his pretensions to gentility. Besides, if the facts show anything, it is that not even the heralds any longer took seriously this matter of gentility. An age that produced and so hugely enjoyed Falstaff

---

[19] Aubrey says Jonson in his early days acted at the Curtain, doubtless alluding to 1598-99, when he was there with the Shakespearean company.

[20] Lee, *Shakespeare* (1922), pp. 286-7.

[21] It would be interesting to compare Cowley's arms with Jonson's description. Jonson later holds up to ridicule in *Poetaster* the general desire of the Shakespearean company for arms. It is quite likely then that Sogliardo's arms are a composite of all these. It will be hard for Cowley's arms to show better right than Shakespeare's to the motto, "Not without mustard."

and Don Quixote could hardly have set an extraordinary value on the mere trappings of nobility.

Of the remaining characters in this play, jesting, bragging Buffone goes to Pope, jealous Deliro to Phillips, young gallant Brisk to Burbadge, "humorous" old knight Puntarvolo to Heminges, dignified moderator Cordatus to Cundall, and probably would-be courtier Fungoso to Sly, to match his known part in *The Malcontent*. It seems likely that Shakespeare was Mitis, the peacemaker, probably his real rôle in the Jonson controversies. Other minor characters for men we have no means of assigning. For the women, "proud mincing peat" Fallace, more than common tall, would seem to belong with Rosalind in Ned's line, while "court lady" Saviolina would seem to fit the line of Samuel Gilburne.

Jonson has also furnished us a complete list of the actors in *Every Man in his Humor*, naming ten, whereas there are eleven principal parts for men. Of these eleven, the country gull Stephano-Master Stephen is close kin to Sogliardo, belonging to the line of Cowley, who is not named. Thus the other ten are left for the ten named actors. Jealous Thorello-Kitely goes to Phillips, and blustering Bobadilla to Pope. Musco-Brainworm would belong with his machinating brethren Mosca and Face in the line of Burbadge. Cob the clown would of course go to Kemp. Of the older men, the "old merry Magistrate" Clement is characteristic for Heminges, and dignified Lorenzo-Knowell, Sr., for Shakespeare. Duelling young Giuliano-Downright seems characteristic for Sly, as is Prospero-Wellbred, labelled with his name, for Cundall. This leaves Lorenzo-Knowell, Jr., and Mateo-Mathew for Christopher Beeston and John Duke. It would seem that Duke, who had been "Will Fool" in *The Seven Deadly Sins* must have been the town gull Mathew, leaving Knowell, Jr., for Beeston, whose parts in *The Seven Deadly Sins* are not of a type to show certainly his line, but are not out of harmony with the assignment given above. For the apprentices, Biancha-Dame Kitely would seem to match with Fallace in Ned's line, and Hesperida-Bridget with Saviolina in Gilburne's. Also, Tib would seem to belong to William Eccleston. It must be confessed, however, that Jonson's women are but roughly and crudely done, being thus even more difficult and uncertain of assignment than the men. Nevertheless, in spite of difficulties we have now a tenable assignment of parts in all the Jonson plays for the Shakespearean company.

Since the line of each of these actors has been described in detail under the Shakespearean plays, it is not necessary to repeat that analysis here. We do get, however, some slight additional information concerning one or two actors in the company, the most detailed coming from *The Alchemist*. Perhaps the most minute information is that given concerning Robert Armin. As Nano, he is a dwarf, corresponding well with the descriptions of Armin's line in the Shakespearean plays. But further, Drugger in *The Alchemist* has little beard and "Your chestnut or your olive-colour'd face ... and your long ear." It appears then that Armin was small, probably with olive complexion, and possibly with noticeably long ears, though this latter may well be merely a reference to Drugger's general asininity. We also learn that Sly as Giuliano is "A tall, big man"; and that Cundall as Surly was "too fat to be a Spaniard," and yet was "the lean gentleman." This description corresponds very well with the references to Cundall in other plays. We get in the Jonson plays what appears at first sight to be our most minute description of John Heminges, but a close examination shows that these characteristics are merely the make-up of a supposedly decrepit old man, so that we are not justified in supposing that they throw any light on the actual physical appearance of Heminges. We learn also that Henry Cundall as Cordatus is "a well-timber'd fellow, he would have made a good column, an he had been thought on, when the house was a building." William Eccleston as Kastril was "Scarce cold in his one and twenty." We have already considered elsewhere the minute description of John Rice given in *The Alchemist*.

Perhaps we should also note that Macilente, presumably Jonson himself, was a lean and raw-boned individual. If Jonson actually doubled Asper and Macilente, as seems plainly stated in the text itself, we get an interesting and enlightening contrast between Shakespeare and Jonson. Jonson would thus have taken the greatest number of lines, and performed the most prominent parts in his own plays. Presumably he constructed his play with this idea in view. Now we have seen that Shakespeare followed a radically different method when he constructed a part for himself in one of his plays. Jonson put both himself and his play first; Shakespeare put the success of his company first. Jonson demanded that the company adapt itself to his idea; Shakespeare adapted his idea to his company, and then educated his company to his idea.

(C) PERSONAL ALLUSIONS TO ACTORS

References are to Professor F. E. Schelling's edition of Jonson in the Everyman series.

Armin, Robert
  Nano in *Fox* is "a Dwarf" (D.P.).
  Drugger in *Alchemist* is a "young beginner" (I. 1, p. 14); he is about to be called to the highest rank among the grocers: "What, and so little beard?"; also:

"Your chestnut or your olive-colour'd face
Does never fail: and your long ear doth promise"
(I. 1, p. 15); "little" (II. 1, p. 37); he inquires "did you
never see me play the Fool?" (IV. 1, p. 72).

Beeston, Christopher

Lorenzo, Jr., in *Every Man in his Humor* is "young" (II. 1, p.
16; II. 2, p. 19); "a fair young gentleman" (III. 4, p. 37).

Cooke, Alexander

Peregrine in *Fox* is a "young gentleman" (IV. 1, pp. 456, 458);
also "He seems a youth" (IV. 1, p. 456).

Cowley, Richard

Sogliardo in *Every Man out of his Humor* is a "simple youth"
(IV. 4, p. 123); "a kinsman to Justice Silence" (V. 2, p. 131).
Corbaccio in *Fox* says "This makes me young again, a score of
years" (I. 1, p. 413).

Cundall, Henry

Prospero in *Every Man in his Humor* is called "boy" (III. 4,
p. 36).
Cordatus in *Every Man out of his Humor* is "a well-timber'd
fellow, he would have made a good column, an he had been
thought on, when the house was a building" (Induction, p. 66).
Surly in *Alchemist* "does look too fat to be a Spaniard" (IV. 1,
p. 60); but is "the lean gentleman" (V. 1, p. 79).

Eccleston, William

Kastril in *Alchemist* is "Scarce cold in his one and twenty" (II.
1, p. 37).
Petreius in *Cataline* has been a soldier "these thirty years" (IV.
6, p. 158).

Gilburne, Samuel

Fallace in *Every Man out of his Humor* is rather tall (IV. 4,
p. 118).

Heminges, John

Of Puntarvolo in *Every Man out of his Humor* we hear: "Heart,
can any man walk more upright than he does? Look, look;
as if he went in a frame, or had a suit of wainscot on" (II. 1,
p. 81); is the "stiff-necked gentleman" (III. 1, p. 104).
Concerning Voltore in *Fox* it is advised "Sell him for mummia;
he's half dust already" (IV. 2, p. 459).
Subtle in *Alchemist* is told of "your pinch'd-horn-nose" and
"your no buttocks" (I. 1, p. 4); he is also old (II. 1, p. 22;
IV. 1, p. 59; V. 1, p. 61).

Jonson, Ben
Macilente in *Every Man out of his Humor* is "lean" (I. 1, p.
71; IV. 2, p. 114; V. 4, p. 136; V. 7, p. 148); "raw-boned"
(IV. 4, p. 117; V. 4, p. 138).

Lowin, John
Volpone in *Fox* has:
"those same hanging cheeks,
Cover'd with hide instead of skin—Nay, help, sir—
That look like frozen dish-clouts set on end"
(I, 1, p. 418); and is:
"An old decrepit wretch,
That has no sense, no sinew . . . a voice, a shadow"
(III. 5, p. 444); but remembers when:
"For entertainment of the great Valois,
I acted young Antinous"
(III. 5, p. 447);
"Do you not think
These limbs should affect venery? or these eyes
Covet a concubine? pray you mark these hands"
(IV. 2, p. 464).
Mammon in *Alchemist* is "the fat knight" (V. 1, p. 79).

Ostler, William
Lovewit in *Alchemist* has "An old man's gravity" (V. 3, p. 90).

Phillips, Augustine
Deliro in *Every Man out of his Humor* "looks like one of the
patricians of Sparta" (IV, 4, p. 117).

Pope, Thomas
Buffone in *Every Man out of his Humor* is "a public, scurrilous,
and profane jester. . . . A good feasthound, or banquet-
beagle . . . will swill up more sack at a sitting than would
make all the guard a posset" (p. 59); cf. Falstaff.

Rice, John
Dol Common in *Alchemist* hears of:
"This lip, that chin! methinks you do resemble
One of the Austriac princes.
Face.   Very like!
Her father was an Irish costarmonger," etc.
(IV. 1, p. 53).
Fulvia.in *Cataline* has "youth and freshness" (II. 1, p. 111).

Robinson, Richard
Sempronia in *Cataline* "is in years" but "hides/Her decays very
well" (II. 1, p. 108).

THE SHAKESPEAREAN COMPANY

Shakespeare, William

Lorenzo, Sr., in *Every Man in his Humor* is "a fox in years" (II. 2, p. 19).

Lepidus in *Sejanus* has:

> "preserved thy hairs to this white dye,
> And kept so reverend and so dear a head
> Safe on his comely shoulders"

(IV. 5, p. 367).

Sly, William

Giuliano in *Every Man in his Humor* is "A tall, big man" (V. 1, p. 47).

Underwood, John

Dapper in *Alchemist* is "A fine young quodling" (I. 1, p. 8); a "lawyer's clerk" (I. 1, p. 8).

Unclassified

Shift in *Every Man out of his Humor* is "a young, straight, and upright gentleman, of the age of five or six and twenty at the most . . . and hath little legs" (III. 1, pp. 98, 104).

Bonario in *Fox* is young (IV. 2, pp. 459, 460, 461); and a "fine well-timber'd gallant" (IV. 2, p. 463).

Dame Pliant in *Alchemist* is "But nineteen, at the most" (II. 1, p. 36); and says of the Spaniards:

> "Never since eighty-eight could I abide them,
> And that was some three year afore I was born, in truth"

(IV. 2, p. 63).

Longinus in *Cataline* is fat (III. 3, pp. 134, 136).

INDEX OF ACTORS IN THE
SHAKESPEAREAN
COMPANY

I have grouped together here all the actors and attendants of the Shakespearean company mentioned in this volume. I have also included a few not mentioned, chiefly from the ticket of privilege in 1636, and *The Seven Deadly Sins*. Those who were dramatists also, as Shakespeare and Jonson, have those activities covered in the General Index.

GENERAL INDEX

For actors of the Shakespearean company, see preceding index. I have not included rôles, since they can generally be located through the tabulations and actors. I have included the first reference for each work cited in the volume.

accounting, 38 *ff.*
acrobats, 75
acting year, 165
actor lists, 46n
actor's part, 123 and n, 124n, 132, 138
Actor's Remonstrance, 29, 121
Acts of the Privy Council, 77n
Adams, John, 331
Adams, J. Q., 66n, 74n, 91n, 150n, 151n, 292n, 341n
  The Dramatic Records of Sir Henry Herbert, 8n
  The Housekeepers of the Globe, 92n
  A Life of William Shakespeare, 6n
  Shakespearean Playhouses, 12n
Adams, J. Q., and J. F. Bradley,
  The Jonson Allusion Book, 29n
Admiral—Prince Henry—1 Palsgrave—3 Prince Charles, 6n, 7n, 9, 10, 21, 22, 23, 24, 26n, 27, 36, 37, 71, 72, 77, 80, 86, 90, 95, 133, 138n, 143, 144, 145, 151, 156n, 173, 272, 290n, 296 and n, 297 and n, 301, 321-31, 333, 334, 348, 358, 428, 429, 433, 434
admission charges, 18, 172
Agusten, William, 36
Alchemist, 225n, 262, 263, 277, 433, 436, 437, 440, 441
Aldermanbury, 71n, 148, 149, 152, 153, 158, 159, 161, 369
Aldgate, 47n, 133n, 151, 153n, 158n, 161
Allde, John, 287
Alleyn, Edward, 21, 22, 23, 27, 38, 61, 70, 72, 88, 93, 123, 134, 144 and n, 145, 159 and n, 160, 168, 229n, 272, 273, 293n, 296 and n, 321, 322, 323, 325 and n, 326 and n, 327, 328 and n, 329, 330, 331, 353, 358, 429, 431
Alleyn, Gyles, 91

Alleyn, Joan Woodward, 159n, 329
Alleyn, John, 16n, 18n, 132, 144, 321, 322, 323, 326, 328 and n, 329, 330, 331 and n, 336, 337
Allhallows, Honey Lane, 34, 64n
Allhallows in the Wall, 157, 393n
All Hallows the Less, Thames Street, 223
All Saints, Lombardstreet, 70
All's Lost by Lust, 214
All's Well, 52, 137, 138, 203, 211, 231, 241, 244, 245n, 260, 262, 263, 269, 275, 278, 372, 417, 418
Almond for a Parrot, 327
America, 173
Amphitruo, 247n
Andrewes, Richard, 322
Andrews, C. E., *Richard Brome*, 11n
Andrews, George, 23
Anne, Queen of England, 7n, 277, 279
Antonio and Mellida, 143, 144, 266n
Antony and Cleopatra, 198n, 240, 241, 276
apprentices, 3, 25, 26, 32 *ff.*, 38, 65, 68, 72, 73, 79, 86, 87, 88, 89, 100n, 106n, 117, 118, 125, 128, 148, 149, 150, 152n, 159, 167, 175, 176, 184, 189-97, 211, 217, 219-28, 273-81, 285-90, 292, 293, 294, 299, 308-10, 311, 333, 340, 363, 364, 365, 391, 416-32
  act women, 36
  age qualifications, 33 *ff.*
  belonged to individuals, 36, 37, 40, 226
  company paid for, 37, 38, 40
  controlled by owners, 63, 79
  law on, 32 *ff.*, 37n
  length of service, 33 *ff.*
  might be sold, 38
  price paid for, 36
Arber, E. A., *A Transcript of the Stationers Registers*, 37n

172, 183-4, 193n, 333, 340, 341, 343, 344, 348
Herz, E., *Englische Schauspieler*, 74n
Heton, Richard, 28, 42 *ff*., 45
Hewitt, Mr., 61
Heywood, Thomas, 4, 62, 71, 76, 81, 82n, 252, 326
  An Apology for Actors, 4n, 69, 252
High Commission Court, 66n
hired men, 3, 25, 26 and n, 27, 37, 38, 40, 42, 63, 80, 87, 88, 117, 118-47, 156, 167, 175, 176, 193n, 196, 197, 284, 286, 289, 290n, 293, 294, 296, 307, 310, 311, 326n, 333, 340, 363, 364, 365, 431-2
Historical Manuscripts Commission, 5n, etc.
Histrio-Mastix, 23
Hog Lane, 157
Holborn, 328n
Holcomb, Frances, 223
Holland, 316, 325
Holland, Aaron, 95
Holland's Leaguer, 348
The Hollander or Love's Trial, 63n
Holloway, T., 180
Honest Man's Fortune, 127, 130
Honest Whore, 143
Honey Lane, 34, 64n
Honyman, Richard, 222
Hope, 17n, 19, 21, 88, 136n, 146, 147, 166, 167, 301, 335, 343, 352, 354, 358
Horseshoe Court, 153, 330, 430
housekeeping, 15, 17n, 18, 32, 39-40, 42, 43, 44, 47, 65, 83, 84n, 90-117, 121n, 163-70, 338-61
Howard, Charles, Lord Admiral, 4, 321, 325
Howell, James, *Dictionary*, 199n
Howes, Edmund, 103
Hughes, C., *Shakespeare's Europe*, 328n
Humorous Lieutenant, 129, 185, 200, 209, 211, 215, 217, 221, 389
Hundred Merry Tales, 313
Hunsdon, 73, 74, 90, 91, 323, 324, 341n
Hunt, Thomas, 26n
Hunt's Rents, 160
If it be not good the Devil is in it, 31 and n, 245n
impressment of boys, 34, 41, 42
Index of Wills proved in the Prerogative Court of Canterbury, 70n

Inner Temple Masque, 214
inns, 17, 18, 45
Inns of Court, 121
Insatiate Countess, 315
Ipswich, 327
Island Princess, 215, 220, 389
Isle of Dogs, 257
Jack, 143
James, King of England, 3, 6, 11, 12, 13, 45, 46, 47n, 83n, 84, 119, 134n, 181, 313, 354, 423
James IV, 316
Jealous Comedy, 270
Jeffes, Humphrey, 137, 152, 159
Jeweler of Amsterdam, 225
Johnson, A. H., *The History of the Worshipful Company of Drapers*, 128
Johnson, George, 9n
Johnson, William, 73
joint tenancy, 93, 94, 95 *ff*., 96, 98, 101, 104, 106, 107, 108, 115, 116, 163
Jones, Daniel, 74, 244, 421, 428
Jones, Richard, 22, 23, 26n, 321, 322, 325 and n, 326 and n, 328, 330
Jonson, Benjamin, 1, 11, 33, 51n, 153, 157, 167, 177, 204, 206n, 218, 224, 229, 232, 233n, 234, 247 and n, 248, 263n, 291n, 298, 299, 301, 307, 315, 391, 423, 433-44
Jonson folio, 167
Jordan, Thomas, 190, 191, 227
  Poeticall Varieties, 60
journey-men, 3, 26, 27, 285, 286
Juby, Edward, 321, 330, 331
Julius Caesar, 245, 266
juvenile lead, 60, 61, 184, 186, 192, 193, 204, 308, 312, 366
Kendall, Thomas, 23
Kendall, William, 26n
Keysar, Robert, 112, 349, 350 and n
Kiechel, Samuel, 337
Killigrew, Thomas, 66, 67
King and No King, 65n, 142, 317
King John, 256
King John and Matilda, 196
Kinge, Thomas, 46n, 74, 80
King's company, provincial, 69, 71, 72
King's Musicians, 61, 134n
King's porter, 181
2 King's Revels, 24
4 King's Revels, 63, 66n, 67, 194
6 King's Revels, 88

GENERAL INDEX

Spanish Curate, 57, 212, 215, 220, 390, 391
Spanish Infanta, 53n
Spanish Tragedy, 124n, 237 and n, 435
Spanish Viceroy, 52, 57
Spedding, J., *An Account of the Life and Times of Francis Bacon*, 169n
Spencer, Gabriel, 69, 71, 137, 157, 433, 434
Spenser, Edmund, 168, 298
Spittle, 157
stagekeeper, see bookkeeper
Stephens, John, 37n
Stevenes, Thomas, 46n, 74, 75, 80
The Stage-Players' Complaint, 65n
stage seats, 17n, 43
Stanley's boys, see Strange
Star Chamber, 66n
Stationers' Company, 37n
Stockwood, John, 337
Stone, Philip, 95
stools on stage, 17n, 43
Stopes, Mrs. C. C., 6n, 346n
    Burbage and Shakespeare's Stage, 39n
    Shakespeare's Environment, 289n
    Shakespeare's Industry, 291n
    Shakespeare's Warwickshire Contemporaries, 168n
Stow, John, *Annals*, 6n
    A Survey, 9n, 168
Strange's boys, 25n, 72, 73, 78, 79, 80, 81, 290n, 311, 326
Stratford-on-Avon, 150, 168, 170, 263, 288, 290n, 291n, 317, 427n
strowings on stage, 43
Stubbs, William, *Constitutional History of England*, 8n
subsidies, players in, 6n, 71, 74
Sullivan, Mary, *Court Masques of James I*, 6n, 53
Summer, Will, 231
    Summer's Last Will, 124, 143
Sumner, John, 63
Sun in New Fishstreet, 301
Sun's Darling, 196
Sunday acting, 332 and n
superannuation, 216 and n
suppression of theaters, 91
surreptitious performances, 66
Sutton, Thomas, 158, 159
Swan, 17n, 18n, 19, 20, 154, 166, 167, 334, 335, 352, 354
sweepers, 43
Swinnerton, Thomas, 14, 95

sworn servants, 6n, 55, 62, 64, 65
Tamburlaine, 31n, 70
Taming of a Shrew, 137n, 258
Taming of the Shrew, 137, 138, 256, 259, 274, 417
Tannenbaum, S. A., *Reclaiming one of Shakspere's Signatures*, 47n
Tarleton, Richard, 69, 70, 71, 157, 231, 243, 245, 312
Tarlton's Jests, 50, 70
Taylor, Anne, 157
Taylor, Elizabeth, 157
Taylor, Hester, 157
Taylor, John, 103, 124, 129, 231, 419n
    Taylor's Feast, 124 and n
Taylor, Samuel, 157
Tempest, 224, 241, 318, 425
Terence, 261
Thaler, Alwin, 41n, 45n
    Shakspere to Sheridan, 67
Thames, 92, 173
Thames Street, 223
Theater, 16n, 17n, 18n, 19, 73, 74, 90, 91 and n, 92 and n, 93, 94, 155, 156, 162, 166, 167, 321, 322, 323, 324, 325, 327, 330, 335, 336, 337, 352, 354, 357, 428, 429
Thierry and Theodoret, 205, 221
Thompson, E. M., *Shakespeare's Handwriting*, 141n
Thompson, E. N. S., *The Controversy between the Puritans and the Stage*, 346n
Thorndike, A. H., 2, 315, 317
    The Influence of Beaumont and Fletcher on Shakspere, 200n
    Shakespeare's Theater, 2n
Thrane, C., *Fra Hofviolonernes Tid*, 75n
Three Lords and Three Ladies· of London, 71n
Tilley, M. P., 240n
Tilney, Edmund, 8, 132 and n, 134n, 141n, 259, 343
Timon of Athens, 241, 253
tireman, 17n, 125
Titus Andronicus, 139, 140, 269, 297, 435
Topping, Richard, 7
town house, 42
Towne, Thomas, 321, 330, 331
tragicomedy, 315 ff.
travelling companies, 45, 307
Troilus and Cressida, 140

GENERAL INDEX